当代国外语言学与应用语言学文库

Intercultural Communication in Contexts

社会、历史背景下的跨文化交际

[第四版]

Judith N. Martin

Thomas K. Nakayama

U0115123

外语教学与研究出版社
FOREIGN LANGUAGE TEACHING AND RESEARCH PRESS

麦格劳-希尔公司
THE MCGRAW-HILL COMPANIES, INC.

北京 BEIJING

京权图字: 01-2008-3146

图书在版编目(CIP)数据

社会、历史背景下的跨文化交际: 第 4 版 = Intercultural Communication in Contexts, Fourth Edition: 英文 / (美) 马丁 (Martin, J. N.), (美) 中山 (Nakayama, T. K.) 著. — 北京: 外语教学与研究出版社, 2009.10
(当代国外语言学与应用语言学文库)
ISBN 978-7-5600-9075-7

Ⅰ. 社⋯ Ⅱ. ①马⋯ ②中⋯ Ⅲ. 文化交流—研究—英文
Ⅳ. G115

中国版本图书馆 CIP 数据核字 (2009) 第 182792 号

你有你"优"——点击你的外语学习方案
www.2u4u.com.cn
阅读、视听、测试、交流
购书享积分,积分换好书

出 版 人: 于春迟
责任编辑: 杨书旗
封面设计: 牛茜茜
出版发行: 外语教学与研究出版社
社　　址: 北京市西三环北路 19 号 (100089)
网　　址: http://www.fltrp.com
印　　刷: 北京市鑫霸印务有限公司
开　　本: 650×980　1/16
印　　张: 32.25
版　　次: 2009 年 10 月第 1 版　2009 年 10 月第 1 次印刷
书　　号: ISBN 978-7-5600-9075-7
定　　价: 65.00 元
＊　　＊　　＊
如有印刷、装订质量问题出版社负责调换
制售盗版必究　举报查实奖励
版权保护办公室举报电话: (010)88817519
物料号: 190750001

当代国外语言学与
应用语言学文库

专家委员会
（按姓氏笔画排列）

当代国外语言学与应用语言学文库 第三辑*

Psychology of Language *(Fifth Edition)* / D. W. Carroll
《语言心理学》（第五版）

A Course in Phonetics *(Fifth Edition)* / P. Ladefoged
《语音学教程》（第五版）

Linguistics: An Introduction to Language and Communication *(Fifth Edition)* / A. Akmajian, R. A. Demers, A. K. Farmer & R. M. Harnish
《语言学：语言与交际导论》（第五版）

The Minimalist Program / N. Chomsky
《乔姆斯基的最简方案》

Speaking: From Intention to Articulation / W. J. M. Levelt
《说话的认知心理过程》

Introducing Second Language Acquisition / M. Saville-Troike
《二语习得引论》

Minimalist Syntax: Exploring the Structure of English / A. Radford
《最简句法入门：探究英语的结构》

Analyzing Discourse: A Manual of Basic Concepts / R. A. Dooley & S. H. Levinsohn
《话语分析中的基本概念》

Curriculum Development in Language Teaching / J. C. Richards
《语言教学中的课程设计》

Fossilization in Adult Second Language Acquisition / ZhaoHong Han
《成人二语习得中的僵化现象》

A Student's Introduction to English Grammar / R. Huddleston & G. K. Pullum
《剑桥学生英语语法》

Introducing Phonology / D. Odden
《音系学导论》

---

* 本文库采用开放式结构，今后还将陆续出版其他有影响的语言学著作

Introducing Function Grammar *(Second Edition)* / G. Thompson
《功能语法入门》（第二版）

An Introduction to Functional Grammar *(Third Edition)* / M. A. K.
Halliday & C. Matthiessen
《功能语法导论》（第三版）

An Introduction to Cognitive Linguistics *(Second Edition)* / F. Ungerer &
H. -J. Schmid
《认知语言学入门》（第二版）

Typology and Universals *(Second Edition)* / W. Croft
《语言类型学与普通语法特征》（第二版）

English Phonetics and Phonology: A Practical Course *(Third Edition)* / P.
Roach
《英语语音学与音系学实用教程》（第三版）

Approaches and Methods in Language Teaching *(Second Edition)* / J. C.
Richards & T. S. Rodgers
《语言教学的流派》（第二版）

Understanding Phonology *(Second Edition)* / C. Gussenhoven & H. Jacobs
《音系学通解》（第二版）

Metadiscourse / K. Hyland
《元话语》

The Language of Evaluation: Appraisal in English / J. R. Martin & P. R. R.
White
《评估语言：英语评价系统》

Language in Literature: An Introduction to Stylistics / M. Toolan
《文学中的语言：文体学导论》

Pragmatics / Yan Huang
《语用学》

The Oxford Handbook of Computational Linguistics / R. Mitkov 编
《牛津计算语言学手册》

Intercultural Communication in Contexts / J. N. Martin & T. K. Nakayama
《社会、历史背景下的跨文化交际》

导读

⊙ 贾玉新　宋　莉

一、关于跨文化交际的理论研究

21世纪是全球经济一体化的时代，伴随经济一体化而来的是文化的多元化。这种经济一体、文化多元，或多元文化并存的时代向我们提出了新的挑战：不同文化之间应尊重差异，努力发掘不同文化资源，究其源流，择善而从；做到东方与西方、传统与现代的互动，达到不同文化间的"和而不同"的和平相处，共存共荣的融合。费孝通先生非常精辟地把当今文化并存和互动的时代比喻为一个"各美其美，美人之美，美美与共，天下大同"的时代（2002）。

21世纪是不同文化共存和互动的时代，跨文化交流空前频繁，深入发展，成为人们日常社会生活中的必须，是地球村每一个居民在生活中回避不了的现实。不同文化间能否有效进行交往、对话，不仅影响我们能否完成某项跨文化交际任务和开展具体的交往，还会直接决定我们能否相互容纳，求同存异，共存共荣，和平相处。从这个角度看，我们所生活的时代不仅为跨文化交际研究提出了新的任务和课题，而且已经把此领域研究推向了一个与实现全球和平共处直接相关的具有战略意义的高度。

近二三十年来，跨文化交际研究在国内外都取得了飞跃性的进步，其中一个很重要的标志是本学科在理论上的成熟和突破（Gudykunst, W. B., 2005；贾玉新，2007）。正是理论上的巨大进步为跨文化交际研究的发展指出了方向，提供了广阔的空间。实际上，20和21世纪跨文化交际的理论研究具有划时代的历史意义，起到了里程碑的作用。

跨文化交际的著名理论学家 William B. Gudykunst 在其重要著作《跨文化交际之理论》（*Theorizing about Intercultural Communication*, 2005)中把现存的有关理论概括为17种之多，可见此领域研究的繁荣与昌盛。尽管学者们研究的视角不同，对文化和交际的界定各异，但他们的研究无论在研究理论框架、内容，还是研究方法等方面，都颇有异曲同工、殊途同归之妙。概括地讲，跨文化交际研究的理论研究有以下几个特点：

1) 在研究中，把文化和交际相融合，并把文化当作理论变量，用其对跨文化交际进行描绘、解释和预测。

2) 跨文化交际研究一般分为两个层面：文化层面（intercultural communication at cultural level）研究和个体层面(intercultural communication at individual level) 研究。前者是指文化之间的交际，后者是指人际间（群体和个人之间）的交际。文化层面的研究通常以Geert Hofstede 提出的集体主义–个体主义这对截然不同的价值观作为不同文化对比的参照系，进行跨文化研究。而个体层面的研究则克服了这种黑白相分的整齐划一的做法，把个体元素（自我建构、个人价值观和人格）作为个人主义和集体主义对交际产生影响的媒介，从而研究人际之间的跨文化交际。据笔者观察，迄今为止，多数学者的研究都囊括了这两个层面，但是在个体层面的深入研究，尤其理论研究，近年则刚刚起步。尽管如此，全球范围内跨文化交际研究方兴未艾，在我国也已开始，并已取得可喜进步。

3) 文化层面和个体层面对文化影响的因素在理论上都可用来对跨文化交际进行预测，但产生的效果是有所区别的。在文化层面上的预测结果与文化规范和规则（cultural norms and rules）相关。换言之，在预测某一行为的时候，把有关行为与其文化规范或规则相联系，即该行为与文化规范和规则是因果关系。比如，有的学者认为群体主义取向的文化对圈内的人（in-group members）大多采用平等（equality）的分配规范。而个体主义取向的文化则无论对圈内或圈外的人都倾向采用公平(equity）的分配规范。在交际规范方面，中国文化中的"客气"和"含蓄"规范，显然与中国式的间接交际风格相关，而西方的"真实"或"不强加于人"规范则与其直接交际风格相关。但是，不同文化在规范上的差异，显然是不同文化层面上的价值观的差异所造成的。

二、关于跨文化交际的研究方法

目前跨文化交际研究通常采用的研究方法有两种：一种是以局外人或旁观者的身份对不同文化间交际所存在的共性或差异性的研究，这种方法叫做客位研究（etic approach）；另一种是以某一具体文化为中心，是圈内人对自身文化的交际的研究，叫做主位研究（emic approach）。两个术语渊源于 K. Pike 的音系学和语音学的研究。etic是指不同文化所共有的发音，而emic则是指某一文化所特有的音位（phoneme）。J. Berry（1980）曾对这两种方法进行对比分析：etic approach 是局外人的客观研究，而emic approach则是圈内人对自己的文化或自己的群体文化的主观研究。etic通常是对两种或两种以上的不同文化的对比研究，而且采用的标准被认为具有绝对性或普世性。这种方法常以现实主义、实证主义、决定主义等形式出现。而emic则立足于本体文化，很少涉及其他文化，常以经验主义、相对主义和反实证主义等形式出现。etic主要采用量化的研究方法，而emic则常进行定性研究或近来被哲学界称之为"体证"性的研究方法。

W. B. Gudykunst 认为，极端的主观主义和极端的客观主义的做法都是不可取的，而单独采用etic 或emic途径也有很大问题，理性的做法是对二者取长补短，科学地融合。关键是内容决定方法，即被研究的问题和内容决定研究方法，而不是相反。

在跨文化研究中，研究者经常有意无意地把不同文化中的概念相互等同，在翻译时仅注重语言而忽略哲学和文化内涵的传递，这会产生把自己文化中的哲学和文化概念强加于其他文化的趋向，这种跨文化概念迁移现象被学者称之为"强加客位"（imposed etic），其后果自然是对一方文化的哲学思想的曲解。比如，在把儒家的哲学概念译成英文时，我们必须兼顾它们的哲学和文化内涵，即语言翻译与哲学和文化内涵传递并重。而有些中国传统的哲学概念几乎是不可直译的，我们必须寻求一种适合的办法。实际上"强加客位"的做法是十分普遍的，但其后果往往难以估量。从古至今，东西方的相互误解，尤其西方对东方文化的理解失误恐怕与这种"强加客位"不无关系。

在探讨跨文化交际中的共性的研究中，学者们普遍认为较为理想的做法是emic与etic相结合，把在emic基础上所收集到的文化特有概念在从不同文化所收集的数据中加以验证，总结出不同文化的共性概念。这包括对有关概念仔细推敲并反复翻译，对各种不同的文化进行初始数据收集，以及在此基础上，比较参详，发现不同文化共享的概念。这是由etic研究方法衍生而成的研究方法，被称之为衍生客位(derived etic)。实际上，这种方法也是用emic方法来检验etic方法的一种做法，即用主位检验客位的一种方法。

三、本书作者的贡献

本书作者以批评的态度审视目前跨文化交际研究的众多方法，在综合和批判的基础上，提出一个新的研究视角——辩证法（dialectic approach）。这一视角博采众长，使辩证方法成为一个独立、系统的体系。

首先，作者对各家理论进行客观审视、梳理、分析、对比和批判，指出各家之长及其局限性。在此基础上，综合各家所长，构建了辩证法理论。

1）综合较为普遍流行的三种研究方法

在把交际与文化相融合的研究中，无论是文化层面还是个人层面上的跨文化交际研究，学者们都把文化作为一种理论变量对交际或进行描绘、解释，或进行预测。学者们由于受各自世界观和文化观的影响，对跨文化交际研究采用不同的方法，但总体上采用三种具体的研究方法：(1) 社会科学研究方法或功能主义法（social science/functionalist approach）；(2) 解释法（interpretive approach）；(3) 批判主义方法（critical approach）。三种方法各异，反映出学者们对文化、文化与交际的关系、人类行为以及知识论或认识论、本体论等基本问题在观点上的差异。然而，每一种方法对我们对文化、交际以及二者之间关系等方面的理解都有独特的贡献。同时，它们也都存在各自的局限性。本书作者对以上三种方法进行较客观的对比分析：

	社科/功能法	解释法	批判法
学科基础	（社会）心理学	人类/社会语言学	综合不同的方法
研究目标	描绘/预测行为	描绘行为	行为的动态变化
现实观	外在/客观，可以描绘	主观存在	主观/物质世界
人类行为观念	可以预测	创造/任意性	动态及可变性
研究方法	纵览/观察	实地考察/现场观察	媒体语篇分析
交际与文化关系	文化影响交际	交际创造和传承文化	文化是权势斗争之战场/交际差异直接与权势差异相关
主要贡献	指出交际之多方面差异，但对环境因素考虑不够	强调交际与文化以及文化差异研究应与环境密切结合	强调文化和交际中要充分考虑政治和经济因素，权势关系是所有跨文化交际研究中的关键因素

　　本书作者对以上三种方法进行了分析，在指出它们的优点的同时，也指出了它们的局限性。社会学（科学）方法是基于社会心理学的研究，流行于20世纪80年代，代表人物是知名学者G. Hofstede，W. B. Gudykunst, Ting-Toomey，Young Yun Kim等。这一方法突出群体（group-related）文化的研究，尤其注重不同文化群体间的文化差异研究；在对影响交际的社会、文化以及心理因素的对比研究的基础上，提出跨文化交际的可预测性，为此学科研究作出了独特的贡献。然而，本书作者认为跨文化交际过程中的创造性往往多于可预测性，就像我们不能对所有的交际进行准确的预测一样，我们不可能确认所有的影响交际的内在和外在因素。如何认识和发展交际创造性能力就迫在眉睫。另外，由于研究者往往远离他们所研究的目标文化和文化群体，他们缺乏对目标文化的敏感性，也缺乏对目标文化和群体的理解，其结果是，研究者常常自觉或不自觉地把不同文化的文化/语言概念等值对待（conceptual equivalence），并进行跨文化概念迁移，造成强加客位。

　　解释法流行于80年代末，代表人物是Clifford Geertz（1973）等。这一方法是基于民族交际学（ethnography of communication）的研究。其最大的特点是由于它突出交际与环境（历史、宗教、民族、权势等）的关系，因此强调研究应把交际置身于环境之中。比如在宗教背景下了解非洲裔美国人，在脱口秀（talk show）环境中研究美国流行的交际风格。作者认为脱离环境的一般的问卷形式等不足以了解交际的特点。然而，解释法的局限性也是很明显的：（1）在采用这种方法的研究者中，真正了解不同文化群体的人们在交往时会发生什么情形的学者为数不多；（2）采用这种方法的研究者常常是局外人，他们很难准确地展示所研究的文化群体的交际模式。

批判主义方法的代表人物有Richard Delgado (2002)、Linda Putnam 和 Michael Pacanowsky (1983) 等学者。批判主义方法与社会学和解释法的视角不同，它的最大特点是把文化看作是多样化和动态多变的，而且，文化之间很难有固定的界限。这一点显然区别于社会学和解释法。批判法主要侧重于权势和交际的研究，特别重视在社会和历史的大环境中研究交际的来龙去脉。这也意味着这种方法忽视了特定情景中的面对面交流（face-to-face interaction）的研究，因此在很大程度上缺乏实用性。

2）作者的视角：辩证法理论框架

在客观地审视和综合以上三种方法的基础上，作者提出了辩证的方法。辩证法对以上三种方法进行客观的审视，扬长避短，择善而从，并且吸收了其他各家的真知灼见，有机组合成为一个独立的综合性的辩证法框架（dialectical framework）。

跨文化交际研究中的辩证法凸显交际的过程（processual）、重视交际中各种变量之间的关系（relational）、强调对传统的一切二分或黑白截然相分的传统哲学思想的超越，同时又突出既辩证又统一的理念。辩证法重视过程的特点主要表现在它强调交际中的文化适应和认同，以及交际模式不是整齐划一和一成不变而是动态多变的过程的理念。这种方法重视关系，表现在它提倡要以综合性思想来对待影响交际的各种变量，一定要改变把它们当作各自孤立的存在的思维定势。比如，在研究某一现象时应把价值观、信仰、历史等因素综合对待。从哲学的角度看，辩证统一的思想是作者对西方一切二分的传统哲学思想的挑战。作者认为交际是十分复杂的过程，应把各种相互矛盾的因素和现象统筹考虑，克服简单的文化群体之间黑白相分或截然对立的研究方法。

实际上，作者所采用的是东方，尤其中国文化的思维传统，是以既对立又统一的辩证思想为基础。而这种辩证统一主要体现在：文化与个体、个人与环境、差异与相似、静态与动态、过去/历史/现在和将来、社会受利者与社会非受利者等方面的既统一又辩证的关系。作者认为所谓辩证法在某种意义上讲,不是跨文化交际研究的一种理论,而是一个观察跨文化交际中所出现的各种现象或问题的透视镜。

3) 本书研究特点

作者把三种研究方法有机组合的辩证法视角首先继承并突出了解释法的环境因素,即交际必须与环境相结合,突出环境对交际的影响。但是,作者尤其强调在社会、政治、历史、宗教等大环境中对交际加以研究,这一点与解释法,比如,社会语言学方法所突出的重点是有区别的。后者似乎更突出社会情境因素对交际的影响。

其次,作者非常重视权势与交际的关系,并突出权势是如何影响交际研究的。作者认为,绝对平等的交际几乎不存在,这种历史造成的交际双方的不平等现象影响我们如何给对方以及自己定位,而且直接影响交际。交际中的交往双方地位"永远不平等"的观点,是本书两位作者的独特见解。

再之,多数跨文化交际研究是在国际层面上的研究,即对不同国家或民族的跨文化交际研究,而本书作者则把重点放在美国国内不同亚文化或不同共存文化(co-cultures)之间的交际方面,这对我们了解和认识美国不同群体文化的交际大有助益。

在批判继承各家思想的基础上,作者集三种方法之大成,提出辩证的研究框架,有其独到之处,使其在跨文化交际研究领域独树一帜。

但是,我们必须清醒地认识到,任何研究方法都有其长,也有其短,面对跨文化交际的严重挑战和极为复杂的交际现实,恐怕不存在什么能解决所有问题的灵丹妙药,我们所能提供的答案与所面临的问题相比,可谓杯水车薪,因为我们所生活的多元文化的时代无时无刻不在变化,跨文化交往日益频繁,冲突和合作屡见不鲜。不仅跨文化交际的研究不断推陈出新,文化与交际的关系也是异常复杂多变。在这个意义上讲,跨文化交际研究是永无止境的。

各章导读

第一部分 跨文化交际学基础。 这部分包括四章，主要追溯了跨文化交际研究的发展历程，并介绍了该领域研究的不同视角和方法。值得注意的是，作者在综述他人研究的基础上对跨文化交际研究的理论方法提出了独特的辩证法思想， 这一思想是全书的精髓所在。

第一章：为什么研究跨文化交际。 作者从科技、人口、经济、和平、自我意识、伦理等七个方面，以鲜活和丰富的事例说明了跨文化交际研究的必然性和必要性。 作者认为科学技术的进步，特别是通讯技术的大量应用，使不同群体间的交往日益频繁，同时也引发了现代通讯技术使用者对文化身份和权利的思考。而世界人口格局的变化，特别是国内与国际范围的人口流动也加速了区域性民族、种族、社会阶层、宗教和语言等的多元化，无论个人还是社会都面临由多元化所带来的种种冲突的挑战。这一多元化的挑战随着全球经济一体化的飞速发展而变得更加严峻，如何跨越文化障碍、在全球化市场经济中抢占更多的阵地、寻求理解和发展已成为亟待解决的问题。作者以历史和发展的眼光审视了殖民主义和全球经济多极化发展对人类社会的深远影响，指出在多元化与一体化、挑战与发展并存的形势之下，跨文化理解对于化解由种族、民族和宗教差异而导致的冲突的重要性。作者强调为使地球村的居民实现和平共处，不同性别、年龄、民族和种族，以及不同的语言、社会经济地位和文化背景的人们必须首先实现相互间的理解和认同。而对其他文化和群体的发现之旅也往往是我们对于自身的了解和对于自我身份的认识的过程。换言之，跨文化交际是自我觉醒和自我意识提高的重要途径，而自我觉醒和自我意识的提高则是跨文化交际的结果。作者在本章最后讨论了跨文化交际中的伦理问题。指出了极端普世论和相对论的局限性，主张在跨文化交际中应该秉承对话原则 （dialogical appraoch），即在协调个人与群体的关系、权衡正确的行为准则时，要注重通过对话寻求符合特定社会文化环境的交际行为和策略。对于学习跨文化交际的学生而言，伦理问题体现在其任务不仅是要学习自我反思、了解他人，还应该在获得跨文化交际知识的基础上培养建立和维护社会公正的责任感与能力；唯如此，方能成为有伦理修养的跨文化交际研究者和实践者。

第二章：跨文化交际研究的历史。本章追溯了跨文化交际研究的发展史，并在综合以往研究范式的基础上提出了辩证法研究框架。作者首先介绍了跨文化交际研究早期人类学家E. T. Hall的研究，尤其他的非言语交际行为理论对不同文化模式的揭示和对跨文化交际的影响等。作者指出，美国跨文化交际研究初期对于国际背景中发生的实际问题的关注和早期学者研究背景的多学科性决定了现今跨文化交际研究实用主义和跨学科的特点。随后作者将跨文化交际研究的范式概括为三大学派：社会学派、解释学派和批判学派，三种理论方法的区别渊源于研究者对于人类行为、文化和交际理解的不同和其研究目的与具体方法的不同。社会科学法又叫做功能法，盛行于20世纪80年代，是基于心理学和社会学的理论方法，主张人类行为是可以预知的，其研究目的是描述和预测行为，特别是预测文化对交际行为的影响，通常以定量研究为主要方法。代表性研究有Gudykunst的焦虑与不确定性管理理论，Min-Sun Kim的会话约束理论和C. Gallois等人的交际顺应理论。作者指出，该理论方法有利于发现影响交际过程的心理和社会变量，但又受制于所能发现变量的有限性，而研究者和被研究者的文化意识也会影响研究的结果。上世纪80年代后期，出现了解释法，就是D. Hymes（1974）提出的民族交际学的理论方法。这一理论认为人类的行为是主观的而非预先设定的，因而也是不可预测的。文化的创造和维系是通过人类的行为交际而实现的，研究者的目的就是理解和描述交际行为如何发生并创造和维系交际者的所属文化，而非依据某些文化模式和变量对交际行为作出预测。此类研究多采用定性研究的方法，研究的侧重点是描述特定文化环境中的交际行为而非交际行为的跨文化对比。作者指出，虽然这一理论方法对交际情境和文化背景的强调有助于深入研究某一特定文化群体的交际模式，但是以往此类研究很少是真正意义上的跨文化研究，而且研究者对所观察的交际行为的描述与解释因其局外人的身份而往往不够准确全面。作者继而介绍了跨文化交际研究中与解释法关联密切的另一重要理论方法：批判法。此派学者同样强调对客观世界的主观性和交际情境的研究，但是他们更关注宏观社会文化和历史背景，如社会结构和权势、后殖民主义现象等对交际行为和过程的影响。其研究目的不仅仅是理解人类行为，而且还通过研究的发现去改变人们的生活，如抵抗权贵势力的影响。其研究方法以文本分析为主，将对电视等多媒体文本的分析作为跨文化交际研究的重要内容和手段。但是，对大众媒体语篇文本分析的偏好使其常常忽略了面对面人际交流的研究，从而削弱了其研究成果的实用价值。另外，缺乏实证研究也使得批判法的跨文化交际研究停留于研究者主观的论述。最后，作者提出跨文化交际研究应该在综合上述三种传统理论方法的基础上采用辩证的理论方法。这是作者对跨文化交际理论研究的重要贡献，也是贯穿于此书的中心思想和方法。辩证法跨文化交际研究强调跨文化交际的过程性、关联性和矛盾性。首先，作者认为任何行为模式、文化和个人都是发展变化的，应该以动态的眼光研究跨文化交际，不应该只关注交际的结果而忽略交际的过程。另外，作者还认为跨文化交际的各个方面都是互相联系的，应该以联系的和整体的、而不是孤立的眼光研究跨文化交际中的问题。最后，作者指出跨文化交际是一个充满了矛盾和对立的辩证过程，例如差异与相同、静态与动态、历史（过去–现在）与未来、优势与劣势都并存于跨文化交际的各个阶段。因此，作者要求本书的读者坚持辩证的思维，并透过辩证的视角，以发展的、联系的和整体的眼光，多角度、多方面地审视跨文化交际的问题。这一思想是本书的精髓，是对传统跨文化交际理论局限性的突破，也是对跨文化交际过程认识的重要飞跃。了解这一辩证思想对本书的学习和跨文化交际研究意义重大。

第三章：文化、交际、环境/背景和权势。本章是对跨文化交际研究中文化、交际、环境/背景和权势四个核心概念的界定和论述，也是对作者倡导的辩证法思想的进一步阐述。作者首先梳理了三个传统范式对文化和交际概念的解读及其对文化与交际关系的不同认识，进而指出辩证法理论承认传统理论方法关于文化的不同观点及其相互之间的联系。作者认为文化既是群体共享的认知和信仰模式，也是不同意义争相较量的战场。辩证地看待和研究文化将有助于人们认识对立的文化理念，从而全方位地认识客观世界。对于交际作者采用了L. A. Samova、R. E. Porter 和 J. W. Carey等多数学者的看法，认为意义赋予了交际最本质的特性。但是作者似乎更强调交际的能动性，指出交际过程是动态的，意义的协商过程即是人们创造、维护、修复或者改变客观世界的过程。由此看来，作者对跨文化交际研究的态度也应该是动态的和发展的。作者还详细介绍了人类学家F. Kluckhohn、F. Strodtbeck和社会心理学家G. Hofstede的价值取向理论框架，说明辨别和研究交际的跨文化差异，并从辩证的角度指出其理论框架在揭示价值取向个体差异方面的局限性。作者的辩证思想还体现在对文化与交际关系的认识上。正如书中指出的，文化与交际互为影响：文化既直接作用于交际行为，又通过交际得以实现和加强；同时交际亦可以是非主流文化与主流文化抗衡的手段。作者对影响跨文化交际的另外两个要素，即环境和权势也作了简要的说明。交际发生的客观环境和社会环境，包括物理场景和社会、历史及政治背景，交际者之间的权势关系和斗争始终伴随着交际，环境和权势都深刻影响着交际的过程和结果。环境与权势对交际的影响又因文化而异，这就加剧了跨文化交际活动的复杂性，也使得跨文化交际研究更加富于挑战性。作者在本章最后再次强调了辩证思维对于跨文化交际研究的重要意义，鼓励读者辩证地、多方位地思考制约交际的各项要素，在具体环境和背景中研究和探索跨文化交际。

第四章：历史与跨文化交际。本章重点论述了各种历史因素对跨文化交际实践与研究的重要作用，再次体现了两位作者对跨文化交际研究的独到见解。作者以独特的视角透视了历史的多面性，指出历史可以从多方面影响文化和文化身份的建构。历史按其性质和范围的不同可以进一步划分为政治历史、思想历史、社会历史、家庭历史、国家历史和文化群体历史；这些历史相互渗透、相互影响的结果造就了我们和我们的世界。对于我们自身历史和他人历史的无知将严重阻碍双方的跨文化交际。作者认为历史是通过叙事建构的，而对叙事文本的创建和解读则取决于权力的操纵者。换言之，权力的拥有者决定了历史如何描写和发展，也就决定了人们在社会中的地位和彼此间的权势关系。根据作者的观点，文化身份的建构与历史密不可分。而了解有别于显性的主流文化叙事的隐性历史，即基于性别、性取向、种族与民族、殖民和社会经济诸因素的历史，可以帮助人们了解现实是他人对历史的文化态度协商的产物。作者在此深入讨论了殖民史是如何影响当今政治经济结构并进而影响跨文化关系的。作者在本章中讨论的历史问题通常在跨文化交际研究中被人们所忽视。作者还列举了促使"接触假设"（即不同文化的人只要相互接触就可达成理解和沟通）成立的八个基本条件，凸显了历史的复杂性和多面性对跨文化交际的影响。最后，作者重申了过去与现在、现在与未来的辩证关系和协调这种对立统一对于在跨文化交际中理解自我及他人的重要性。

第二部分 跨文化交际过程。包括第五章、第六章和第七章，主要说明影响跨文化交际动态过程的身份、语言和非言语因素。

第五章：身份与跨文化交际。本章以美国社会中不同的阶层和人群为例，用辩证的观点阐述了身份与跨文化交际的关系。作者在本章的开篇明确指出了身份的重要性和交际与身份的关系：身份是交际与文化之间的桥梁；交际是身份构建和表达的手段。根据传统的跨文化交际研究范式，学者们对于身份的理解各有不同。社会科学派的身份观是静态的，认为身份是个体对其所属不同群体的文化归属。解释学派的身份观是动态的，认为身份是在与人的社会交往中建构的。而批判学派的身份观更进一步，认为环境因素是身份形成的动因。而本书作者主张以辩证的观点认识身份，强调身份既是静止的也是变化的，既产生于人际间的交往中，也发生在环境的相互作用中。作者指出身份是通过语言符号传达的；表示身份的语言标签的变化映射着文化的变迁。身份的认同以文化而异，恰当的语言表达直接关系着跨文化交际中双方对彼此身份的界定是否得到认同，也关系着交际的成败。作者还指出人们普遍拥有多重身份，人们既分属于主流文化或非主流文化群体，同时也属于不同性别、年龄、宗教、民族、阶级、区域和国家等文化群体。作者详细列举了这些不同身份的特点和表现。人们的多重身份是同时并存的，这就意味着他人对我们的认识以及我们对他人的认识也应该是多方面的。对于跨文化交际而言，辩证的身份观就是要认识到交际者同时具有多重身份，而且这些身份彼此联系，其共同作用的结果构成了交际者的身份。作者随后指出由于个人和社会环境的原因，各种身份特征经常是形成刻板印象、偏见和歧视的基础。而随着全球化和多元化的发展，越来越多的人生活在两种或多种文化边缘，他们具有多重文化身份，并经常处于不同文化价值和生活方式的抉择中。作者最后进一步阐明了身份与交际的关系以及辩证的身份观对跨文化交际的积极意义。身份问题是目前跨文化交际研究关注的热点之一，而本章内容充分体现和诠释了作者在前面几章提出的辩证思想和历史观，为研究跨文化交际中复杂多变的文化身份提供了理论框架和科学方法。

第六章：语言与跨文化交际。本章综合了社会科学派、解释学派和批判学派对语言的研究，包括语言的跨文化变异、语言与权势、语言与身份、语言与全球化、双语和多语问题、跨文化翻译和语言政治与政策等。作者首先讨论了静态的语言系统与动态的语言使用之间的关系，指出对语言符号意义的解读必须与具体的社会文化背景相结合。同时语言符号的使用或意义的解读依赖于经济、历史、政治和宗教等其他符号系统。作者随后说明了语言与感知的关系，介绍了三种不同的立场和最近的相关研究发现对Sapir-Whorf假说的挑战。作者接着详述了不同文化背景的人的交际风格（如强语境和弱语境、直接和间接、明确和含蓄等）和特定情境中的交际风格的选择，进一步说明了意义的建构离不开具体的文化环境和情境；作者以亚文化群体与主流文化群体间的交际为例，强调权势关系对交际行为和交际方略会产生重大影响。作者详细讨论了跨文化交际与双语和多语的关系，指出人们通过语码转换应对不同交际情境和文化环境。作者还把笔译和口译看作跨文化的交际，并指出译者面临的一大挑战是如何妥善处理文化非对等程度的问题。两种语言的差异实质上就是文化上的差异，其文化意义的解读应是文化协商的结果，因为意义的对等是建立在限定意义的文化对等之上，如何处理文化的非对等是翻译成败的关键。从这个意义上讲，跨文化交际研究是翻译研究的助推器。作者在本章还论及身份、语言政治、语言政策等方面。在讨论英语国际化时指出全球化的发展改变了国际社会或地区原有的语言格局，其突出的变化就是英语作为国际语所产生的英语与民族身份的协调问题。本章反映出作者对跨文化交际中语言问题的辩证思考和后殖民主义的语言观。

第七章：非言语语码与文化空间。本章集中讨论了非言语语码与跨文化交际的关系，其内容延续着前一章"人际–环境"、"静态–动态"的辩证思路。作者以非言语语码与语言语码的对比为基础，说明了非言语语码的概念、特征和范畴，并结合新近的研究发现分析了非言语语码的普世性和相对性，指出非言语交际普遍存在但更多时候是隐性的、不被人们觉察的，非言语行为传递人们对彼此的感觉和交际者之间的社会及权势关系。作者认为非言语语码同语言语码一样都是符号系统，其所指代的意义总是受到符号运用的具体社会文化等环境因素的影响。本章的贡献突出地体现在两位作者提出的文化空间的概念及后现代文化空间在跨文化交际中的作用。文化空间指的是身份和意义建构所依赖的社会和文化环境，是建构意义的交际活动之组合；它不仅仅包括家庭、周边环境、地区和国家这些物理场所，也包括这些场所中所创造的文化意义。文化空间因此可以是实体的场所，也可以是隐喻的社会场所。作者借用"社会地图"一词说明不同的社会地位和角色营造了影响人际交往或意义协商的文化空间。作者强调理解文化空间与文化、权势、人和文化之间的关系关键在于辩证的思维。作者指出文化空间是变化的，旅行和流动是改变文化空间的两大方式，而文化空间格局的变化将带来意义和身份建构的变化。后现代文化空间是本章的另一重要概念，也是作者辩证的和动态的研究思想的又一体现。后现代文化空间指的是由诸如被使用的语言、扮演的身份、以及相关的仪式等文化实践所限定的动态多变场所或空间。作者以网络空间或虚拟空间为例，说明了后现代文化空间同物理空间一样充盈着文化意义，同时简要介绍了相关的研究发现。在作者的眼中，现代文化空间的特点是它的流动性和易变性，它只存在于建构意义和身份的需要和过程中。文化空间和后现代文化空间也是不同文化相互协商和抗衡的空间。本章的辩证思想、符号学的视角、对新研究发现的介绍，特别是对文化空间和后现代文化空间的论述都为读者学习和研究跨文化交际中的非言语交际提供了新的思路和启示。

第三部分 跨文化交际的实践。这部分包括四章，其目的是要帮助学生将前面两部分的理论知识应用于具体的跨文化交际之中。

第八章：大众/通俗文化与跨文化交际。本章重点是说明大众/通俗文化和民间文化对于建构、维系和体验文化，特别是跨文化交际的重要性。通俗文化与精英文化或高雅文化相对，指的是为大多数人所共享和熟知的，包括电视、音乐、录像和流行杂志在内的体制或物质。但它又有别于传统的和非主流的民间文化，是文化产业的产物，并因其普遍存在于人们的日常生活而对大众行为乃至其所生活其中的文化产生影响。作者引用了近年发生在美国的抵制大众文化和英语语言的垄断以及国际上大众传媒的事例，说明人们与通俗文化的关系协商是一个复杂的过程。通俗文化媒介对意义的建构、受众对通俗文化意义的解读经常受到社会、历史和文化等环境因素的影响。作者指出文化文本同文化空间一样，受众在对通俗文化产物的消费中或者接受或者抵制，不断地协商他们与文化身份之间的关系。文化群体通常是依照流行的文化定型而被大众文化塑造或表现的。通俗文化或大众媒体也是再现文化群体的手段，是我们了解其他文化的渠道。主流文化群体和非主流文化群体，比如移民和少数族裔之间的相互了解（或者误解）和沟通往往是通过通俗文化媒介达成的。人类社会中的权势关系也无不例外地融入到这些大众文化产物中，各媒体所用语言的选择就足以说明权力抗衡与通俗文化的密切关系。作者在本章最后讨论了通俗文化传播中的文化帝国主义现象及相关研究。作者的结论是通俗文化对于解读全球社会林林总总的关系起着重要作用，对于理解其他文化和民族的社会力量和动态变化、对于跨文化交际研究与实践都有着不容忽视的积极意义。

第九章：文化、交际和跨文化关系。本章全面地探究了跨文化交际中的各种人际关系，包括殖民历史和当今社会制度对来自不同性别、年龄、身体条件、种族、民族、信仰、阶层、地区和国家的不同文化的人们之间的同事关系、友谊、家庭和爱情等关系的影响。作者首先描述了六种辩证的跨文化关系：个人–环境、不同(求新)–相同(求同)、文化–个人、优势–劣势、不变–变化、历史/过去–现在/将来这六对因素互相区别又互为影响，同时存在并平衡协调着交际者之间的跨文化关系。随后作者概括了人们从跨文化关系中可以获得的利益和面临的挑战，指出跨文化关系是一种学习方式(关系式学习)，可以增强我们对世界的了解、打破文化定式、从中获得新的技能等等。但同时跨文化关系中固有的价值观、世界观、交际风格以及交际者特有的文化背景等方面的差异则为人们的交际设置了障碍。作者以丰富的实例介绍了不同学派的学者如何看待和研究跨文化关系，并为指导人们冲破文化障碍、建立和谐的跨文化关系而付出努力。社会科学派学者致力于发现不同文化如何界定、建立和发展诸如友情等人际关系。解释学派则更专注于对跨文化关系深层次的探索，特别是交际在跨文化关系中发挥的作用。作者在这一部分的讨论涉及当今多元化与全球化、信息化和数字化与现实世界中特殊的跨文化关系等。批判学派强调的是社会制度、政治和历史等环境因素对跨文化关系的作用。作者着重从家庭与社区、教育与宗教制度、历史和政治背景三大方面说明环境如何左右跨文化关系。本章对跨文化关系的探索和分析全面透彻，同时也传达了作者一贯主张的辩证法思想。作者认为，跨文化人际关系的建构和协调机制是研究跨文化关系的着眼点，而求同存异、和谐共处是跨文化关系发展的关键。

第十章：文化、交际和冲突。本章从辩证的角度讨论了跨文化冲突。作者重点分析了全球化和经济发展不平衡所带来的跨文化冲突，以及社会制度在加剧或缓解跨文化冲突中所发挥的作用。作者首先从辩证的角度说明了跨文化冲突是经济、社会、政治、宗教、语言等多方力量对抗的结果。作者将有关跨文化冲突的观点归结为两大类："机遇观"和"破坏观"。前者认为冲突是互不相容的两种目标、价值观、期望、过程和结果所造成的，同时认为应该直面冲突，通过协商、调节去寻找化解冲突、建立新型关系的机会。后者则将冲突视为对已有关系和社会制度的破坏，主张应该尽力避免冲突，并惩戒制造冲突的人；借助第三者的调停是解决冲突常用的手段。作者指出社会学派主要关注不同文化在冲突问题上的差异，如不同文化的人在情感、偏好、价值、认知和目标五个方面的冲突和解决冲突的策略方面的差异。而解释学派和批判学派则更注重研究社会冲突和群体间的冲突，以及冲突的社会情境、经济环境、历史环境和政治环境等背景因素，认为跨文化对冲突的理解和调和不能脱离冲突发生发展的背景和当事人的背景。本章最后讨论了东西方不同的跨文化冲突管理策略。作者在本章依旧强调应该以辩证的观点看待和处理复杂多面的跨文化冲突，跨文化冲突既可以是有价值的，也可以是破坏性的，其结果如何很大程度上取决于研究者或当事人是否能辩证地、全方位地把握跨文化冲突。

第十一章：跨文化交际前景展望。在本书最后一章，两位作者针对提高跨文化交际能力从而成功地与不同文化背景的人交流阐明了观点，并提出了建议。作者首先介绍了社会科学法将交际能力解构为个人层面的动机、知识、态度、行为和技能，然后重点说明了解释学派和批判学派在背景和环境层面对交际能力的理解，即交际能力来自对影响交际的文化、历史、社会结构、政治、经济等各种背景和环境因素的理解。作者劝诫读者在应用跨文化交际知识时，应该辩证地认识个人交际技能和环境因素对改善跨文化人际关系的重要性，并建议读者开展真诚对话，在相互承认、尊敬、欣赏和平等的基础上建立跨文化同盟（友谊），在不同的跨文化关系中协调自己的多重身份，学会谅解，以成为一个有责任和有道德修养的跨文化人。作者在最后描述了全球化政治、军事和经济等方面多变且多样的复杂形势对跨文化交际研究与实践的挑战，同时重申了以辩证的思维面对这一挑战的重要性，因为这是成功跨文化交际之旅的第一步。

参考文献

Berry, J. (1980). Introduction to Methodology. In Hellen Spencer-Otey (eds.), *Culturally Speaking: Managing Rapport Through Talk Across Cultures*. Shanghai: Shanghai Foreign Language Education Press. pp. 293-294.

Delgado, F. (2002). Mass-Mediated Communication and Intercultural Conflict. In J. N. Martin, T. K. Nakayama & L. A. Flores (eds.), *Reading in Intercultural Communication: Experiences and Contexts*. Boston: The McGraw-Hill Companies. pp. 351-359.

Geertz, C. (1973). *Interpretation of Culture*. New York: Basic Books.

Gudykunst, W. B. (ed.) (2003). *Cross-Cultural and Intercultural Communication*. CA: Sage Publications. pp. 1-3.

Gudykunst, W. B. (ed.) (2005). *Theorizing about Intercultural Communication*. CA: Sage Publications.

Gudykunst, W. B. (2000). Methodological Issues in Conducting Theory-Based Cross-Cultural Research. In Helen Spencer-Oatey (ed.), *Culturally Speaking: Managing Rapport Through Talk Across Cultures*. London: Continnuum International Publishing. pp. 293-315.

Gudykunst, W. B. & Nashida, T. (1989). Theoretical Perspectives for Studying Intercultural Communication. In M. K. Asante & W. B. Gudykunst (eds.), *Handbook of International and Intercultural Communication*. CA: Sage Publications. pp.17-46.

Hymes, D. (1974). *Foundations in Sociolinguistics: An Ethnographic Approach*. Philadelphia: University of Pennsylvania Press.

Jia, Y. X. (贾玉新) (2008). Sociolinguistic Approach to the Study of Intercultural Communication. In Steve J. Kulich (ed.), *Intercultural Perspectives on*

Chinese Communication. Shanghai: Shanghai Foreign Language Education Press. pp. 125-179.

Putnam, L. & Pacanowsky, M. (eds.) (1983). *Communication and Organizations: An Interpretive Approach.* CA: Sage Publications.

费孝通，2002，论文化与文化自觉，北京：科学出版社，第302页。

贾玉新，2007，导读（Cross-Cultural and Intercultural Communication），上海：上海外语教育出版社，第XV-XVIII页。

贾玉新，2007，跨文化交际学，上海：上海外语教育出版社。

About the Authors

The two authors of this book come to intercultural communication from very different backgrounds and very different research traditions. Yet we believe that these differences offer a unique approach to thinking about intercultural communication. We briefly introduce ourselves here, but we hope that by the end of the book you will have a much more complete understanding of who we are.

Judith Martin grew up in Mennonite communities, primarily in Delaware and Pennsylvania. She has studied at the Université de Grenoble in France and has taught in Algeria. She received her doctorate at the Pennsylvania State University. By background and training, she is a social scientist who has focused on intercultural communication on an interpersonal level and has studied how people's communication is affected as they move or sojourn between international locations.

She has taught at the State University of New York at Oswego, the University of Minnesota, the University of New Mexico, and Arizona State University. She enjoys gardening, going to Mexico, and hosting annual Academy Awards parties, and she does not miss the harsh Midwestern winters.

Tom Nakayama grew up mainly in Georgia, at a time when the Asian American presence was much less than it is now. He has studied at the Université de Paris and various universities in the United States. He received his doctorate from the University of Iowa. By background and training, he is a critical rhetorician who views intercultural communication in a social context. He has taught at the California State University at San Bernardino and Arizona State University. He is a voracious reader and owns more books than any other faculty member in his department. He watches TV—especially baseball games—and lifts weights. Living in the West now, he misses springtime in the South.

The authors' very different life stories and research programs came together at Arizona State University. We have each learned much about intercultural communication through our own experiences, as well as through our intellectual pursuits. Judith has a well-established record of social science approaches to intercultural communication. Tom, in contrast, has taken a nontraditional approach to understanding intercultural communication by emphasizing critical perspectives. We believe that these differences in our lives and in our research offer complementary ways of understanding intercultural communication.

Since the early 1990s, we have engaged in many different dialogues about intercultural communication—focusing on our experiences, thoughts, ideas, and analyses—which led us to think about writing this textbook. But our interest was not primarily sparked by these dialogues; rather, it was our overall interest in improving intercultural relations that motivated us. We believe that communication is an important arena for improving those relations. By helping people become more aware as intercultural communicators, we hope to make this a better world for all of us.

Contents

PART III   INTERCULTURAL COMMUNICATION APPLICATIONS   311

THE INCREASING IMPORTANCE OF INTERCULTURAL COMMUNICATION IN THE RAPIDLY CHANGING WORLD

When we look back upon the international and intercultural situation at the time we first began writing this book, we recognize how rapidly the world has changed, with even more pressing issues for intercultural communication scholars and practitioners. In the third edition of this book, we were writing in the shadow of the events of September 11. Since then, human events such as the invasion of Iraq and bombings in London, Russia, and Spain have focused more attention on interethnic and religious conflicts. Natural disasters such as the tsunami in Indonesia and hurricanes Katrina and Rita that hit the Gulf Coast summoned a variety of positive responses, including tremendous caring and compassion across intercultural and international divides, but these tragedies also exacerbated enduring social-group inequities. In addition, the increasing use of the Internet and cell phones has made intercultural interactions that may once have seemed distant or peripheral to our lives now far more immediate.

In this climate, the study of intercultural communication takes on special significance, offering tools to help us as we grapple with questions about religious and ethnic differences, hate crimes, and many other related issues. Those who study, teach, and conduct research in intercultural communication are faced with an increasing number of challenges and difficult questions to address: Is it enough to identify differences among people? Are we actually reinforcing stereotypes in emphasizing differences? Is there a way to understand the dynamics of intercultural communication without resorting to lists of instructions? Don't we have to talk about the broader social, political, and historical contexts when we teach intercultural communication? How can we use our intercultural communication skills to help enrich our lives and the lives of those around us? Can intercultural communication scholars promote a better world for all?

Such questions are driven by rapidly changing cultural dynamics—both within the United States and abroad. On one hand, attempts to establish peace between Israel and Palestine by withdrawal of Israeli settlements in Gaza, as well as the continued expansion of the European Union, CAFTA (Central American Free Trade Agreement), and the African Union (formerly the Organization of African States), reflect some global movement toward unity. On the other hand, the increase in nuclear armaments, continuing conflicts between India and Pakistan over Kashmir, and the conflict with and within Iraq illustrate continuing intergroup conflict. These extremes demonstrate the dynamic nature of culture and communication.

We initially wrote this book in part to address questions and issues such as these. Although the foundation of intercultural communication theory and research has always been interdisciplinary, the field is now informed by three identifiable and competing *paradigms*, or "ways of thinking." In this book, we attempt to integrate three different research approaches: (1) the traditional social-psychological approach that emphasizes cultural differences and how these differences influence communication, (2) the interpretive approach that emphasizes understanding communication in context, and (3) the more recent critical approach that underscores the importance of power and historical context in understanding intercultural communication. In this edition, we extend the critical paradigm to include recent scholarship in postcolonial approaches.

We believe that each of these approaches has important contributions to make to the understanding of intercultural communication, and that they operate in interconnected and sometimes contradictory ways. In this fourth edition, we have further strengthened our *dialectical* approach that encourages students to think critically about intercultural phenomena as seen from these various perspectives.

Throughout this book, we acknowledge that there are no easy solutions to the difficult challenges of intercultural communication. Sometimes our discussions raise more questions than they answer. We believe that this is perfectly reasonable. Not only is the field of intercultural communication changing, but also the relationship between culture and communication is—and probably always will be—complex and dynamic. We live in a rapidly changing world where intercultural contact will continue to increase, creating an increased potential for both conflict and cooperation. We hope that this book provides the tools needed to think about intercultural communication, as a way of understanding the challenges and recognizing the advantages of living in a multicultural world.

SIGNATURE FEATURES OF THE BOOK

Students usually come to the field of intercultural communication with some knowledge about many different cultural groups, including their own. Their understanding often is based on observations from television, movies, the Internet, books, personal experiences, news media, and more. But many students have a difficult time assimilating information that does not readily fit into their pre-existing knowledge base. In this book, we hope to move students gradually to the notion of a *dialectical framework* for thinking about cultural issues. That is, we show that knowledge can be acquired in many different ways—through social scientific studies, experience, media reports, and so on—but these differing forms of knowledge need to be seen dynamically and in relation to each other. We offer students a number of ways to begin thinking critically about intercultural communication in a dialectical manner. These include:

- An explicit discussion of differing research approaches to intercultural communication, focusing on both strengths and limitations of each
- Ongoing attention to history, popular culture, and identity as important factors in understanding intercultural communication
- "Point of View" boxes in which diverse viewpoints from news media, research studies, and other public forums are presented
- Incorporation of the authors' own personal experiences to highlight particular aspects of intercultural communication

NEW FEATURES IN THE FOURTH EDITION

- Running glossary that gives students immediate definitions for terms used in the chapter
- Chapter objectives which guide students reading through each chapter

NEW CONTENT IN THE FOURTH EDITION:

- To reflect the increasing influence of globalization, we have expanded our discussion of globalization and its importance to intercultural communication. For example, in Chapter 1, we discuss how globalization and related economic disparities influence intercultural communication.

• The continuing and expanding influence of communication technology in our daily lives is addressed by new material in Chapter 7 on virtual spaces (e.g., blogs) and expanded coverage of online intercultural relationships in Chapter 9.

• Our expanded discussion of the implications of religious identity in Chapters 5 and 10 is prompted by continued awareness of the important role religion plays in intercultural communication.

• We have also incorporated new sections on the important roles that institutions play in intercultural contact. In Chapter 9, we address the role of institutions in supporting or discouraging intercultural relationships; in Chapter 10, we examine how institutions can exacerbate or ameliorate intercultural conflict.

CHAPTER-BY-CHAPTER OVERVIEW OF THE BOOK

Intercultural Communication in Contexts is organized into three parts: Part I, "Foundations of Intercultural Communication"; Part II, "Intercultural Communication Processes"; and Part III, "Intercultural Communication Applications."

Part I, "Foundations of Intercultural Communication," explores the history of the field and presents various approaches to this area of study, including our own.

We begin **Chapter 1** with a focus on the dynamics of social life and global conditions as a rationale for the study of intercultural communication. We introduce ethics in this chapter to illustrate its centrality to any discussion of intercultural interaction. **In this edition, we have expanded our discussion of the impact of globalization and global economic disparities, as well as the increasing role of technology in intercultural encounters.**

In **Chapter 2**, we introduce the history of intercultural communication as an area of study, as well as the three paradigms that inform our knowledge about intercultural interactions. We establish the notion of a dialectical approach, so that students can begin to make connections and form relationships among the paradigms. We utilize the example of Hurricane Katrina to help explicate the three paradigms. **In this edition, we have extended the critical approach to include recent scholarship on postcolonial approaches**—helping students learn how past colonization impacts contemporary intercultural relations.

In **Chapter 3**, we focus on four basic intercultural communication components—culture, communication, context, and power. In this edition we have strengthened **the discussion of culture**—to more clearly reflect our dialectical approach.

Chapter 4 focuses on the importance of historical forces in shaping contemporary intercultural interaction. We have expanded our discussion of the ways in which **colonial histories are related to current economic and political structures that influence intercultural relations.**

Part II, "Intercultural Communication Processes," establishes the factors that contribute to the dynamics of intercultural communication: identity, language, and nonverbal codes.

Chapter 5 on identity has extended coverage of religious identity, multicultural identity, as well as **the new concept of cultural hybridity.**

Chapter 6 addresses language issues, including sections on code-switching and globalization, and expanded coverage of interlanguage. We also emphasize the **postcolonial views on language.**

Chapter 7 focuses on nonverbal codes and cultural spaces and **includes new material on postmodern virtual spaces.**

Part III, "Intercultural Communication Applications," helps students apply the knowledge of intercultural communication presented in the first two parts.

In **Chapter 8**, we focus on popular and folk culture and their impact on intercultural communication. We have also added **recent examples of popular-culture resistance and English-language dominance** as well as **international examples of popular culture.**

Chapter 9 explores intercultural relationships. We have added new material on **the effect of colonial histories and contemporary institutions on intercultural relationships.** Another new section addresses **online intercultural relationships.**

In **Chapter 10**, we focus on intercultural conflicts. We have strengthened the discussion of a dialectical approach to conflict and incorporated new material on the **effects of globalization and economic disparities in intercultural conflict; there is new material on the role of institutions in exacerbating or ameliorating intercultural conflicts.**

Finally, in **Chapter 11**, we turn to the outlook for intercultural communication. We have expanded our discussion on motivation and the difficulty in achieving effective intercultural communication and provided **contemporary examples of groups working together to promote better intercultural relations.**

ACKNOWLEDGMENTS

The random convergence of the two authors in time and place led to the creation of this textbook. We both found ourselves at Arizona State University in the early 1990s. Over the course of several years, we discussed and analyzed the multiple approaches to intercultural communication. Much of this discussion was facilitated by the ASU Department of Communication's "culture and communication" theme. Department faculty met to discuss research and pedagogical issues relevant to the study of communication and culture; we also reflected on our own notions of what constituted intercultural communication. This often meant reliving many of our intercultural experiences and sharing them with our colleagues.

Above all, we must recognize sponsoring editor Suzanne Earth, developmental editor Josh Hawkins, media producer Nancy Garcia, marketing manager Leslie Oberhuber, project manager Melissa Williams, designer Violeta Diaz, and media project manager Stacy Bentz. In addition, we want to thank all the reviewers of this and previous editions of *Intercultural Communication in Contexts*, whose comments and careful readings were enormously helpful. They are:

First Edition Reviewers

Rosita D. Albert, *University of Minnesota*
Carlos G. Aleman, *University of Illinois, Chicago*
Deborah Cai, *University of Maryland*
Gail Campbell, *University of Colorado, Denver*
Ling Chen, *University of Oklahoma*
Alberto Gonzalez, *Bowling Green State University*
Bradford "J" Hall, *University of New Mexico*
Mark Lawrence McPhail, *University of Utah*
Richard Morris, *Northern Illinois University*
Catherine T. Motoyama, *College of San Mateo*
Gordon Nakagawa, *California State University, Northridge*
Joyce M. Ngoh, *Marist College*
Nancy L. Street, *Bridgewater State College*
Erika Vora, *St. Cloud State University*
Lee B. Winet, *State University of New York, Oswego*
Gust A. Yep, *San Francisco State University*

Second Edition Reviewers

Eric Akoi, *Colorado State University*
Jeanne Barone, *Indiana/Purdue University at Fort Wayne*
Wendy Chung, *Rider University*
Ellen Shide Crannell, *West Valley College*
Patricia Holmes, *University of Missouri*
Madeline Keaveney, *California State University, Chico*
Mark Neumann, *University of South Florida*
Margaret Pryately, *St. Cloud State University*
Kara Shultz, *Bloomsburg University*

Third Edition Reviewers

Marguerite Arai, *University of Colorado at Colorado Springs*
Rona Halualani, *San José State University*
Piper McNulty, *De Anza College*
Karla Scott, *St. Louis University*
Candace Thomas-Maddox, *Ohio University, Lancaster*
Susan Walsh, *Southern Oregon University*
Jennifer Willis-Rivera, *Southern Illinois State University*

Fourth Edition Reviewers

Sara DeTurk, *University of Texas, San Antonio*
Christopher Hajek, *University of Texas, San Antonio*
Mary M. Meares, *Washington State University*
Kimberly Moffitt, *DePaul University*
James Sauceda, *California State University, Long Beach*
Kathryn Sorrells, *California State University, Northridge*
David Zuckerman, *Sacramento State University*

Our colleagues and students provided invaluable assistance. Thanks to our colleagues for their ongoing moral support and intellectual challenges to our thinking. Thanks to graduate student Tsai-Shan (Sam) Shen for his consistent and productive searching for interesting examples to make our writing come alive; for collecting material for the "Student Voices"; and for his excellent work revising the glossary. And of course, we owe thanks to our undergraduate students who continue to challenge us to think about intercultural communication in ways that make sense to their lives.

We thank our families and friends for allowing us long absences and silences as we directed our energies toward the completion of this book. We want to acknowledge both Ronald Chaldu and David

L. Karbonski, who continue to be supportive of our academic writing projects.

Our international experiences have enriched our understanding of intercultural communication theories and concepts. We thank all of the following people for helping us with these experiences: Tommy and Kazuko Nakayama; Michel Dion and Eliana Sampaïo of Strasbourg, France; Jean-Louis Sauvage and Pol Thiry of the Université de Mons-Hainaut, Belgium; Christina Kalinowska and the Café "Le Ropieur" in Mons, Belgium; Scott and the others at Le BXL in Brussels, Belgium; Emilio, Vince, Jimmy, Gene and the others at the Westbury Bar in Philadelphia; Jerzy, Alicja, Marek, and Jolanta Drzewieccy of Bedzin, Poland; as well as Margaret Nicholson of the Commission for Educational Exchange between Belgium, Luxembourg, and the United States. Some research in this book was made possible by a scholarship from the Fulbright Commission and the Fonds National de la Recherche Scientifique in Brussels. In addition, we thank the countless others we have met in cafés, train stations, bars, and conferences, if only for a moment of international intercultural interaction.

Other people helped us understand intercultural communication closer to home, especially the staff and students at the Guadalupe Learning Center at South Mountain Community College, and also Dr. Amalia Villegas, Laura Laguna, Felipa Montiel, Cruzita Mori, and Lucia Madril.

In spirit and conceptualization, our book spans the centuries and crosses many continents. It has been shaped by the many people we have read about and encountered. It is to these guiding and inspiring individuals—some of whom we had the good fortune to meet and some of whom we will never encounter—that we dedicate this book. It is our hope that their spirit of curiosity, openness, and understanding will be reflected in the pages that follow.

Many textbooks emphasize in their introductions how you should use the text. In contrast, we begin this book by introducing ourselves and our interests in intercultural communication. There are many ways to think about intercultural interactions. One way to learn more about intercultural experiences is to engage in dialogue with others on this topic. Ideally, we would like to begin a dialogue with you about some of the ways to think about intercultural communication. Learning about intercultural communication is not about learning a finite set of skills, terms, and theories. It is about learning to think about cultural realities in multiple ways. Unfortunately, it is not possible for us to engage in dialogues with our readers.

Instead, we strive to lay out a number of issues to think about regarding intercultural communication. In reflecting on these issues in your own interactions and talking about them with others, you will be well on your way to becoming both a better intercultural communicator and a better analyst of intercultural interactions. There is no endpoint from which we can say that we have learned all there is to know. Learning about communication is a lifelong process that involves experiences and analysis. We hope this book will generate many dialogues that will help you come to a greater understanding of different cultures and peoples and a greater appreciation for the complexity of intercultural communication.

COMMUNICATING IN A DYNAMIC, MULTICULTURAL WORLD

We live in rapidly changing times. Although no one can foresee the future, we believe that changes are increasing the imperative for intercultural learning. In Chapter 1, you will learn more about some of these changes and their influence on intercultural communication.

You stand at the beginning of a textbook journey into intercultural communication. At this point, you might take stock of who you are, what your intercultural communication experiences have been, how you responded in those situations, and how you tend to think about those experiences. Some people respond to intercultural situations with amusement, curiosity, or interest; others may respond with hostility, anger, or fear. It is important to reflect on your experiences and to identify how you respond and what those reactions mean.

We also think it is helpful to recognize that in many instances people do not want to communicate interculturally. Sometimes people see those who are culturally different as threatening, as forcing them to change. They may believe that such people require more assistance and patience, or they may simply think of them as "different." People bring to intercultural interactions a variety of emotional states and attitudes; further, not everyone wants to communicate interculturally. Because of this dynamic, many people have had negative intercultural experiences that influence subsequent intercultural interactions. Negative experiences can range from simple misunderstandings to physical violence. Although it may be unpleasant to discuss such situations, we believe that it is necessary to do so if we are to understand and improve intercultural interaction.

Intercultural conflict can occur even when the participants do not intentionally provoke it. When we use our own cultural frames in intercultural settings, those hidden assumptions can cause trouble. For example, when renting a small apartment in a private home in Grenoble, France, coauthor Judith Martin invited a number of her U.S. friends who were traveling in Europe to stop by and stay with her. The angry and frustrated response that this drew from her landlady came as a surprise. She told Judith that she would have to pay extra for all of the water they were using, that the apartment was not a motel, and that Judith would have to move out if the practice of having overnight guests continued. Differing notions of privacy and appropriate renter behavior contributed to the conflict. Intercultural experiences are not always fun. Sometimes they are frustrating, confusing, and distressing.

On a more serious level, we might look at "Operation Iraqi Freedom" in the spring of 2003 as yet another example of intercultural communication. The subsequent interpretations of and reactions to that televised event by different communities of people reflect important differences in our society and in the world at large. Although some people in the United States and abroad saw this effort as an attempt to liberate an oppressed people, others viewed it as imperialist aggression on the part of the United States. These differing views highlight the complexity of intercultural communication. We do not come to intercultural interactions as blank slates; instead, we bring our identities and our cultures.

IMPROVING YOUR INTERCULTURAL COMMUNICATION

Although the journey to developing awareness in intercultural communication is an individual one, it is important to recognize the connections we all have to many different aspects of social life. You are, of course, an individual. But you have been influenced by culture. The ways that others regard you and communicate with you are influenced largely by whom they perceive you to be. By enacting cultural characteristics of masculinity or femininity, for example, you may elicit particular reactions from others. Reflect on your social and individual characteristics; consider how these characteristics communicate something about you.

Finally, there is no list of things to do in an intercultural setting. Although prescribed reactions might help you avoid serious faux pas in one setting or culture, such lists are generally too simplistic to get you very far in any culture and may cause serious problems in other cultures. The study of communication is both a science and an art. In this book, we attempt to pull the best of both kinds of knowledge together for you. Because communication does not happen in a vacuum but is integral to the many dynamics that make it possible—economics, politics, technology—the ever-changing character of our world means that it is essential to develop sensitivity and flexibility to change. It also means that you can never stop learning about intercultural communication.

PART I

Foundations of Intercultural Communication

CHAPTER 1
Why Study Intercultural Communication?

CHAPTER 2
The History of the Study of Intercultural Communication

CHAPTER 3
Culture, Communication, Context, and Power

CHAPTER 4
History and Intercultural Communication

WHY STUDY INTERCULTURAL COMMUNICATION?

CHAPTER OBJECTIVES

After reading this chapter, you should be able to:

1. Identify six imperatives for studying intercultural communication.

2. Describe how technology can impact intercultural interaction.

3. Describe how global and domestic economic conditions influence intercultural relations.

4. Explain how understanding intercultural communication can facilitate resolution of intercultural conflict.

5. Explain how studying intercultural communication can lead to increased self-understanding.

6. Understand the difference among a universalistic, a relativist, and a dialogic approach to the study of ethics and intercultural communication.

7. Identify and describe three characteristics of an ethical student of culture.

When I was back home [Kuwait], before I came to the United States to go to college, I knew all about my culture and about my religion. However, I did not really know what other people from the other world [United States] think of Middle Eastern people or Muslims in general. So, what I have witnessed is a lot of discrimination in this country, not only against my race but against other groups. . . . Yet I understand that not all Americans hate us, I met a lot of Americans who are cooperative with me and show me love and are interested to know about my country and culture.

—Mohamad

The major experience that has affected me is seeing the celebration of Hanukkah on campus as a major holiday celebration. At school here the diversity has caused me to change from "Merry Christmas" to "Happy Holidays," which might not seem that significant but is an extreme change in my perceptions of people and their views! Similarly, the Easter holiday is also a great change. During my first year I remember telling a girl in my class—Happy Easter—and she simply and gently replied— "Thanks, but I don't celebrate Easter, I'm Jewish." That is something that I had never ever thought about at home! She and I talked a lot about that after class. This shows that the learning process is a continuous state outside the classroom because of the diversity inside the classroom.

—Maureen (from http://www.diversityweb. org/Digest/Sp.Sm00/development.html)

Both Mohamad's and Maureen's experiences point to the benefits and challenges of intercultural communication. Through intercultural relationships, we can learn a tremendous amount about other people and their cultures, and about ourselves and our own cultural background. At the same time, there are many challenges. Intercultural communication can also involve barriers like stereotyping and discrimination. And these relationships take place in complex historical and political contexts. Mohamad's experience in the United States is probably more challenging today than it would have been several years ago because of recent political events. An important goal in this book is how to increase your understanding of the dynamics at work in intercultural interaction.

This book will expose you to the variety of approaches we use to study intercultural communication. We also weave into the text our personal stories to make theory come alive. By linking theory and practice, we hope to give a fuller picture of intercultural communication than either one alone could offer.

We bring many intercultural communication experiences to the text. As you read, you will learn not only about both of us as individuals but also about our views of intercultural communication. Don't be overwhelmed by the seeming complexity of intercultural communication. Not knowing everything that you would like to know is very much a part of this process.

Why is it important to focus on intercultural communication and to strive to become better at this complex pattern of interaction? We can think of at least six reasons; perhaps you can add more.

THE TECHNOLOGICAL IMPERATIVE

Today, with the explosion of computers and other communication technologies, we truly live in the **global village** envisioned by media expert Marshall McLuhan (1967). Communication technology links us to events from the most remote parts of the world and connects us to persons we may never meet face-to-face from around the world. Perhaps the most revolutionary advancement has been the Internet.

Technology and Human Communication

The impact of technology on our everyday communication is staggering. Think of how often you use technology to communicate in any given day: You may text-message friends about evening plans, e-mail your family to tell them the latest news, participate in a discussion board for one of your courses, and check your cell phone Web site to see how many more minutes you can use this month without getting charged. And you are not alone. The number of hours U.S. Americans spent online continues to increase, and young people are the most frequent users of the Internet (Pew Internet and American Life Project, 2005) and cell phones (Progue, 2004; http://www.clickz.com/stats/sectors/wireless/print.php/ 3530886).

More and more people around the world are using technology to communicate with each other.

Consider these statistics:

- Sweden has the highest percentage of population online—73%, followed closely by Japan, Denmark, the United States, the Netherlands, and Iceland—with approximately 70% of population online (Progue, 2004; http://www.clickz.com/stats/sectors/wireless/print.php/3530886).

---

global village A term coined by Marshall McLuhan in the 1960s that refers to a world in which communication technology unites people in remote parts of the world.

- The rate of Internet usage in Africa jumped 258% from 2000 to 2005 (http://www.internetworldst ats.com/stats.htm).
- The rate of Internet use in South America jumped 230% in the same time period, with Uruguay leading other countries with 37% of its population online (http://www.internetworldstats.com/stats. htm).
- Internet usage in Caribbean and Latin American countries in creased almost 500%, with Barbados and Costa Rica having the highest percentage, about 35%, of their respective populations on line (http://www.internetworldstats.com/ stats.htm).

The advent of the Internet and other communication technologies has tremendous implications for intercultural communication. We will focus on five aspects of culture and technology: (1) increased information about peoples and cultures, (2) increased contact with people who are different from us, (3) increased contact with people who are similar to us who can provide communities of support, (4) identity, culture, and technology, and (5) differential access to communication technology.

Increase in Information You may have found that the Internet provides access to information about other cultures and other peoples. We can now instantaneously find out almost anything about any group in the world simply by searching the Internet. This *should* give us a better understanding of our global neighbors and perhaps some motivation to coexist peacefully in our global village; however, the evidence seems to be to the contrary. According to the Center for Systemic Peace, of the approximately 75 armed conflicts in the world between 1990 and 2004, only 10 have been traditional international conflicts. The rest have arisen between ethnic or political groups within a country—for example, in Cyprus, Russia, Turkey, Kashmir, Ethiopia, Bosnia, and Sudan (http://members.aol.com/cspmgm/warlist.htm). Apparently, knowledge about others does not necessarily lead to better communication or heightened understanding. We will tackle issues like this in later chapters.

Through communication technologies like the World Wide Web, people also have access to increasing amounts of information about what is happening in their own and other countries. This is especially important in countries where media are government controlled. For example, people in Pakistan and Afghanistan learn more about military actions in their countries by accessing CNN.com than through their local newspapers. In some ways, the Internet has democratized information, in that more people control and disseminate information than ever before.

In spite of some governments' attempts to limit their citizens' access to computer-mediated communication (CMC), the Internet is providing information, world news, and possibilities for interpersonal communication that were not available previously (Scanlon, 2003; Wheeler, 2001).

Increased Contact With People Who Differ   Communication technology brings us in contact with people we might never have the opportunity to know otherwise. And many of these people are from different cultural backgrounds. The Internet/e-mail allows us to have "pen pals" from different cultures and to carry on discussions with these people in virtual chat rooms and on discussion boards.

However, such mediated communication across cultures does present unique challenges. Unlike face-to-face communication, mediated communication filters out important nonverbal cues. One of our students, Val, described the challenges of intercultural e-mails:

> *I met a girl from Korea my junior year of college, and we became good friends. When it came time for her to go back to Korea we decided we would stay friends and become pen pals via e-mail. I found it much more difficult to communicate with her because she didn't always understand what I was writing and I couldn't repeat my sentences like I could if I were speaking to her, and the same applied to her. It definitely puts a strain on our relationship.*

When we are talking to individuals face to face, we use nonverbal information to help us interpret what they are *really* saying—tone of voice, facial expressions, gestures, and so on. The absence of these cues in mediated contexts (e.g., e-mail, chat rooms) makes communication more difficult and can lead to misunderstandings. And these misunderstandings can be compounded when communicating across cultures. For example, a U.S. colleague reports that she was offended when the e-mails she received from colleagues overseas seemed too brief and to the point. She has since discovered that her colleagues overseas are charged computer time by the minute and so have learned to be very concise in their e-mail messages. What she interpreted as rudeness had more to do with the economic context in which the interaction took place than with the communicators themselves. If she had been able to observe their nonverbal cues while communicating, she probably would have known that they were not being rude.

Also, language may be a factor. The people we talk to on e-mail networks may speak languages different from our own. An interesting situation arose recently for one of the authors of this book. Tom was using an electronic bulletin board when someone posted a message in Dutch. It was met with a flurry of hostile responses from people protesting the use of an exclusionary language, one most people couldn't read. A discussion ensued about which languages might be acceptable on the network.

The decision reached was that subscribers could post messages in any language as long as there was an English translation. In a subsequent posting, someone from a university in South Africa recommended a book "for those of you who can read Dutch (heh-heh, all four of us)"—an apparent reaction to the exclusionary sentiments of other subscribers. Machine translations are one way also to facilitate online intercultural communication, as seen in the "Point of View" box (Aaronson, 2005). The use of some languages is given even more privilege in the high-tech communication world, where we are likely to encounter many more people. Although many experts think that the Internet is dominated by English, there are indications that Chinese is becoming a formidable linguistic player in the Internet world. According to one source, the first day that registration opened for Chinese language domain names, 360,000 applications were filed (english1.e21times.com/asp/sacd.asp?r=880&p=0). Surprisingly, the most recent research suggests that the move is actually toward more multilingualism on the Net—rather than toward a global English Internet (Dor, 2004). Some speculate that this is because global businesses need to adapt to local languages to sell their products, and also that learning a language is an awesome task and it is not feasible to think of the entire world learning a second language to accommodate.

Increased Contact With People Who Are Similar Communication technology also allows us to have more contact with people who are very similar to ourselves. Perhaps you participate in chat rooms or discussion boards with people who share your interests and opinions. Perhaps you turn to Internet groups for support and community. For example, international students can stay in touch with their local communities, keep up with what's going on at home, and receive emotional support during difficult times of cultural adaptation.

The Internet can also be used to strengthen a sense of identity, as is the case for some **diasporic groups**—ethnic and/or national groups that are geographically dispersed throughout the world, sometimes as refugees fleeing from war, sometimes as voluntary emigrants. A recent study of children of South Asian immigrants found that the Internet plays a major role in creating a sense of community and ethnic identity for these young people. Whereas earlier generations of immigrants were expected to assimilate as quickly as possible into the host culture, the Internet now allows these children of immigrants to connect with other Indian adolescents, discussing religion and issues concerning Indian and immigrant identity. Similar diasporic discussions are held in the *Kava Bowl* and the *Kamehameha Roundtable*, online meeting places for the Polynesian diaspora and other people from the Pacific Islands who live in the United States, Australia, and New Zealand (Franklin, 2003). Similarly, discussion boards can provide virtual communities of support for cultural minorities (e.g., Planetout.com, a discussion board for gays and lesbians). However, the Internet can also provide a venue for like-minded people to promote prejudice and hatred. According to a recent report from a British e-mail filtering company, the number of hate and violence Web sites has grown by nearly 300% since 2000. In 2000, this company was monitoring about 2,756 Web sites that were categorized as hate and violence sites. By April 2004, that figure had risen to 10,926. Even more worrying, however, is that since January 2004, the number of sites that promote hatred against Americans, Muslims, Jews, homosexuals, and people of non-European ancestry, as well as graphic violence, have risen by, more than 25% (http://www.theregister.co.uk/2004/05/10/hate_websites_flourish/).

Identity, Culture, and Technology   Advances in communication technology lead us to think differently about ourselves and our **identity management**. In *The Saturated Self*, psychologist Kenneth Gergen describes the changes that occur as technology alters our patterns of communication. Gergen suggests that with the removal of traditional barriers to forming relationships—time and space—these technological advancements lead to **multiphrenia**, a splitting of the individual into many different selves. We are available for communication, via answering machine, fax, and e-mail, even when we're not physically present. Gergen (1991) writes:

---

diasporic groups Ethnic and/or national groups that are geographically dispersed throughout the world.

identity management The way individuals make sense of their multiple images concerning the sense of self in different social contexts.

multiphrenia The splitting of the individual psychologically into multiple selves.

In this essay, journalist Lauren Aaronson describes the growing use of machine translation in blogging, pointing out both the increased opportunity for communicating across cultures and the limitations of such translation.

Tens of thousands of people around the Middle East read Ali Abdulemam's online discussion forum every day. Yet few Westerners knew that authorities in Bahrain detained Abdulemam over his Web site for two weeks in earlyMarch; although his detention sparked local protests, the story didn't grab much attention beyond the Arab world. Westerners who don't understand Arabic can't read the controversial posts (which criticized the government's treatment of the Shiite majority), nor can they read Abdulemam's personal blog, a firsthand look at life in the Middle East.

Current technology lets bloggers around the world make their voices heard, but only to a degree. If a blogger speaks Arabic and a reader speaks English, or vice versa, it doesn't matter how fast or how global the Internet is. A blogger and reader who can't understand each other might as well be living in the days of the Pony Express.

To push the frontier of cross-cultural communication and bridge the gap in understanding between citizens of the United States and the Middle East, some pioneers have called for an enhancement of blogging technology, suggesting that machine translation software might be able to crack the language barrier. . . .

A growing number plug Arabic characters into the English interfaces of popular blog-publishing tools, like the nonprofit Spirit of America's Arabic-language publishing tool that has made blogging accessible to a wider swath of the population. While the disparate nature of the Web makes it hard to determine exactly how many Arabic blogs exist, the total is clearly mounting; for instance, more than 250 users have created blogs with the Spirit of America tool since its launch in December 2004.

The relatively coherent and unified sense of self inherent in a traditional culture gives way to manifold and competing potentials. A multiphrenic condition emerges in which one swims in ever-shifting, concatenating, and contentious currents of being. One bears the burden of an increasing array of oughts, of self-doubts and irrationalities. (p. 80)

Identity on the Internet not only is potentially fragmented but also involves more choice and management issues than in face-to-face

Like the blogs in Farsi that have swept Iran, Arabic blogs have sneaked what substitutes for a free press into some countries that lack one. What's more, the Comment button on most blogs encourages discussion among people who would otherwise never meet, whether they live in the Middle East or the United States. Many people in the international blogging community see their vocation as a route to cross-cultural understanding, and some view machine translation as a vehicle for speeding down that route.

[However], many Arabic blogs include cultural references that don't resonate with non-Arabs. Moreover, machine-translated prose may not capture the real punch of Arabic, says fellow Iraqi "Riverbend," whose blog Baghdad Burning portrays the severity of war in expressive English. "Arabic is sort of a dramatic, flowery language," she e-mails, "and a literal translation—as most automatic translations tend to be—makes things seem very strange and overdramatized.". . .

[And], the output from machine translation software doesn't necessarily make for pleasant, or even accurate, reading. Users can scan the output to get the gist of a document, or they can search for keywords to locate a relevant piece of text, but the translations don't approach human quality. . . .

So the software might not spit out an ideal translation of the blog that landed Ali Abdulemam in jail. But the translation might be good enough for citizens of other countries to recognize that they share interests with Bahrainis, and Arabic and non-Arabic speakers alike could then cobble together a meaningful interaction. "That's the real goal, to get people to talk to each other," Oren continues. "And if the technology facilitates that either directly or just by attracting the right audience, then that's cool."

interaction. As noted previously, many of the identity cues individuals use to figure out how to communicate with others—such as age, gender, and ethnicity—are filtered out on the Internet. For instance, when you send an e-mail, you can choose whether to reveal certain aspects of your identity. The recipients won't know if you are male or female, young or old, and so on—unless you tell them. The same is true for chat room participation. You can choose which aspects, if any, of your identity you want to reveal. In fact, you can even give false information about your identity.

This capability has resulted in the opportunity for **identity tourism**—taking on the identities of other races, gender, classes, or sexual orientations for recreational purposes. And some online contexts (e.g., virtual games like Dungeons and Dragons) *require* users to take on new identities. How is this related to intercultural communication? One of the oft-touted skills of intercultural communication is empathy, the ability to understand what it's like to "walk in someone's shoes." Communication technology now affords an opportunity to do this— virtually. Thus, for instance, by taking on the virtual identity of a male, by participating in male-only online discussions, females might come to understand better what it feels like to be a male (Danet, 1999). The same might be true for other identities as well.

Although identity tourism provides intriguing possibilities for improving intercultural understanding, it also raises some important ethical questions. In one celebrated example, a male psychiatrist participated in online discussions as a disabled female. Ostensibly, he did so because he wanted to understand something of what it felt like to be a woman and to be disabled. The project backfired, however, as other chat room participants responded to him as a woman and, over time, even fell in love with him. Ultimately, many of the women suffered severe psychological problems as a result of their experiences with him (Turkle, 1995).

The idea of identity tourism may seem somewhat scary, but the same lack of nonverbal cues can result in less prejudice and stereotyping in mediated intercultural interaction. Some of these same nonverbal cues that are filtered out (indicators of age, gender, ethnicity, race) are often the basis for stereotyping and prejudice in initial interactions. When these cues are absent, communication may be more open because people cannot use the information to form impressions that often negatively impact communication (Carter, 2004).

Access to Communication Technology

As we've seen, technology plays a huge role in our everyday lives and often has a lot to do with our success as students and professionals. What would you do if you had no access to communication technology? If you were not able to text-message your friends or could not use your cell phone? Could not e-mail your family? How might you feel in our technology-dominated world? Although communication technolo-

identity tourism A concept that refers to people taking on the identities of other races, genders, classes, or sexual orientations for recreational purposes.

gies are a fact of life for millions of people around the world, lack of access to these technologies is a reality for many people. Consider that

- About a quarter of Americans live unconnected to the Internet, meaning that they have never been online and don't know many others who use the Internet (Lenhart et al., 2003).
- Of those who do not use the Internet, 41% live in households earning less than $30,000; only 6% come from households earning more than $75,000 (Lenhart et al., 2003).
- Even when education and income are the same, blacks and Latinos are less likely to go online than whites (Hacker & Steiner, 2002; Jackson, Barbatsis, Biocca, von Eye, Zhao, & Fitzgerald, 2004).

Even larger inequities exist outside the United States:

- There are more telephones in New York City than in all of rural Asia, more Internet accounts in London than all of Africa. As much as 80% of the world's population has never made a phone call.
- Finland alone has more Internet users than the whole of Latin America.
- The estimated number of personal computers in Australia is 10 million, in New Zealand is 1.5 million, in the United States is 178 million, and in all of Africa 7.55 million.
- The United States, Canada, France, Germany, Italy, Japan, Russia, and the United Kingdom account for less than 20% of the world's population but "own" 80% of Internet hosts and most traffic.

Source: From http://www.caslon.com.au/dividesprofile.htm.

These inequities are called the "digital divide" and have enormous implications for intercultural communication. In the global information society, information is an important commodity. Everybody needs it to function. This ability is especially important in an increasingly "networked" society. It is easy to see how without these skills and knowledge one can feel marginalized and disconnected from the center of society (Rojas, Straubhaar, Roychowdhury, & Okur, 2004; van Dijk, 2004).

The implications for intercultural communication are enormous. How do people relate to each other when one is information technology rich and the other is not? When there is increasing use of English on the Internet, what happens to those who don't speak English? Can this lead to resentment? Will the increase in communication technology lead to increasing gaps between haves and have-nots? To more misunderstandings?

Recent communication technology has impacted our lives in ways our grandparents could not have imagined and requires that we re-examine even our most basic conceptions of self, others, and culture. As Sherry Turkle (1995) observes, once we take virtuality seriously as a way of life, we need a new language for talking about the simplest things. Each individual must ask: What is the nature of my relationships? What are the limits of my responsibilities? And even more importantly: Who and what am I? What is the connection between my physical and virtual bodies? And is it different in different cyberspaces? . . . What kind of society or societies are we creating, "both on and off the screen" (p. 231)? We might also examine our own technological use: Who are we in contact with? People who are like ourselves? People who are different? Do we use technology to increase our contact with and understanding of other cultures or merely to hang out with people who are like us? What does this say about us and our identities?

THE DEMOGRAPHIC IMPERATIVE

You have probably observed that your world is increasingly diverse. You may have classes with students who differ from you in ethnicity, race, religion, and/or nationality. College and university student bodies are becoming increasingly more diverse. According to a recent report, minority student enrollment will rise both in absolute number of students—up about 2 million—and in percentage terms, growing from 29.4% of overall undergraduate enrollment in 1995 to 37.2% in 2015. The share of white students on campuses nationwide will decline to 62.8% in 2015, a drop of 7.8% over 1995 levels (Carnevale & Fry, 2000).

You may have also noticed that sports are increasingly diverse. When Jack Nicklaus made his first trip to the Augusta National 46 years ago, there were 8 international players. In 2005, there were 45—the top ranked is Fijan Vijay Singh (Shepard, 2005). And every year more non-Americans are in the NBA; starting with 1 player in 1992, and last year there were 20; about 20% of NBA players are now foreign born (Hochman, 2004) (http://www.diversityweb.org/Digest/Sp.Sm00/geny.html). This increasing diversity in the United States comes from two sources: (1) changing U.S. demographics, and (2) changing immigration patterns.

Changing U.S. Demographics

U.S. demographics are projected to change dramatically during your lifetime—the next 50 years. According to the U.S. Population Reference Bureau, the nation's Hispanic and Asian populations are expected to triple by 2050; non-Hispanic whites are expected to grow more slowly to represent about half of the nation's population (Figure 1.1). Hispanic origin (who may be of any race) will increase from 36 million to 103 million. The Asian population is projected to triple, from 11 million to 33 million. The black population is projected to grow from 36 million to 61 million in 2050, an increase of 71%. That change will increase blacks' share of the nation's population from 13% in 2000 to 15% in 2050.

The population representing "all other races"—a category that includes American Indians, Alaska Natives, Hawaiian and other Pacific Islanders, as well as those who indicated two or more races on census forms—is also expected to triple between 2000 and 2050, growing from 7 million to about 22 million (Scommegna, 2003).

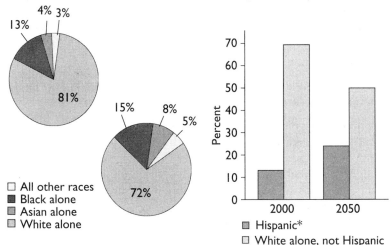

FIGURE 1.1   Estimated and projected U.S. population, by race and Hispanic origin, 2000 and 2050. Source: U.S. Census Bureau, "U.S. Interim Projections by Age, Sex, Race, and Hispanic Origin" (http://www.census.gov/lpc.www/ usinterimproj; accessed March 29, 2006).
Note: Totals may not equal 100 because of rounding.
*Hispanic origin and race are treated as distinct concepts. For more information, see the U.S. Census Bureau Web site (http://www.census.gov/population/www/ socdemo/ compraceho.html; accessed March 29, 2006).

demographics The characteristics of a population, especially as classified by race, ethnicity, age, sex, and income.

What is also interesting is the racial distribution in the various geographical regions. The Population Reference Bureau (PRB) computed a "diversity index" showing that the highest ethnic diversity is concentrated in the southeastern and southwestern regions of the United States. Minority concentrations are projected to increase especially in the South, Southwest, and West. The PRB estimates that, by 2025, minority groups will account for over 50% of the population in four states (Hawaii, California, New Mexico, Texas) (www.prb.org/ Ameristat Template.cfm?Section=Estimates).

There is increasing diversity in the U.S. workforce as well. The workforce is expected to continue to get older, and there will also be proportionately more women working. What accounts for these changes? The workforce will be older because the baby boomers are aging. More women are in the workforce for several reasons. First, economic pressures have come to bear; more women are single parents, and even in two-parent families, it often takes two incomes to meet family expenses. Second, the women's movement of the 1960s and 1970s resulted in more women seeking careers and jobs outside the home. In addition, the workforce is more ethnically and racially diverse—in part, simply because there are more minorities now than before, but also because of civil rights efforts, which led to more opportunities for minorities in business and industry.

Changing Immigration Patterns

The second source of demographic change is different immigration patterns. Although the United States has often been thought of as a nation of immigrants, it is also a nation that established itself by subjugating the original inhabitants and that prospered to some extent as a result of slave labor. These aspects of national identity are important in understanding contemporary society.

Today, immigration has changed the social landscape significantly. One in five Americans either was born abroad or born of parents who were born abroad ("Now a Nation," 2002). Prior to the 1970s, most of the immigrants to the United States came from Europe, but this changed in the 1980s and 1990s. As of 1999, over half (51%) the foreign-born population came from Latin America, 27% from Asia, and only 16% from Europe. Of the one million immigrants who now enter the United States every year, 90% are from Latin America or Asia. These shifts in patterns of immigration have resulted in a much more racially and ethnically diverse population. In 1890, only 1.4% of the foreign-born population was nonwhite; by 1970, 27% were nonwhite, and by 1999, 75% were non-white (www. prb.org/AmeristatTemplate.

cfm?Section=Migration1&template=ContentManage). It's not hard to see that the United States is becoming more heterogeneous. We address the issue of whites losing majority status in Chapter 5.

This **heterogeneity** presents many opportunities and challenges for students of intercultural communication. The tensions among heterogeneous groups, as well as fears on the part of the politically dominant groups, must be acknowledged. California's Proposition 187, which passed in the November 1994 election, excludes nondocumented immigrants from receiving public health and social services. This proposition has remained highly controversial and has led to protests and court challenges. The subsequent California Civil Rights Initiative (Proposition 209), which passed in November 1996, further extended the challenges to diversity by eliminating many affirmative action programs. And in 1997, Californians passed Proposition 227, which will eliminate bilingual education in schools, pending court rulings. Yet in October 2003, Californians voted to defeat Proposition 54, the Racial Privacy Initiative, that would have prohibited much of the racial information collected and used by the state and local governments in California. Fearful that the loss of this information would further erode protections against racial discrimination, as well as other concerns, led to the defeat of this proposition, but its proponent, Ward Connerly, had indicated his interest in bringing it forward again (Flores, Moon, & Nakayama, 2006).

We should also note the potential opportunities in a culturally diverse society. **Diversity** can expand our conceptions of what is possible—linguistically, politically, socially—as various lifestyles and ways of thinking converge. However, increased opportunity does not always lead to increased interaction. The annual "freshman survey" conducted by a research institute at UCLA reported that in 2004 "a growing number of students appeared unlikely to have a diverse set of friends in college." Apparently, only about 60% of students surveyed said they expected to socialize with people other than their own racial or ethnic group—the lowest level since the question was first added to the survey (Farrell, 2005). This may be because these students are graduating from high schools that are becoming increasingly more segregated (see Point of View).

To get a better sense of the situation in the United States today, let's take a look at our history. As mentioned previously, the United States has often been referred to as a nation of **immigrants**, but this

---

heterogeneity Consisting of different or dissimilar elements.
diversity The quality of being different.
immigrants People who come to a new country, region, or environment to settle more or less permanently. (Compare with **sojourners**.)

In this essay Scott Jaschik explores the reasons for continuing inter-racial problems at some colleges and universities.

Monday is Halloween, a holiday that has in recent years sparked controversies at numerous campuses after white students attend parties dressed as illegal immigrants, in blackface, or in various other ways that offend.

However sincere the apologies are from those responsible for these and many other incidents, they raise the question of why—year after year—students are so hurtful about race, and are then surprised when someone is hurt. Experts on student life and race relations offer a variety of explanations and views.

Many say that the students who offend today aren't just younger versions of those who were doing racist things on campuses a decade ago or as some campuses first integrated. Rather, they say that today's students—and the ignorance many of them display—are the products of an unusual time in which minority culture is omnipresent, but more and more white high school students have no significant interaction with anyone of another race.

"We all assume that more progress has been made than has really been made," says Beverly Tatum, president of Spelman College. A psychologist and the author of Why Are All the Black Kids Sitting Together in the Cafeteria and Other Conversations About Race, *Tatum says: "While colleges and universities are more diverse today than they were 20 or 30 years ago, that isn't true for public schools, many of which are more segregated. So you have a lot of young people growing up in racially segregated schools and their only exposure to other groups comes from stereotypes in the media."*

is only partly true. When Europeans began arriving on the shores of the New World, an estimated 8 to 10 million Native Americans were already living here. Their ancestors probably began to arrive via the Bering Strait at least 40,000 years earlier. The outcome of the encounters between these groups—the colonizing Europeans and the native peoples—is well known. By 1940, the Native American population of the United States had been reduced to an estimated 250,000. Today, about 1.9 million Native Americans (from 542 recognized tribes) live in the United States (Brewer & Suchan, 2001).

African American Immigrants   African Americans represent a spe-

Popular culture gives these students—many of whom are clueless about those who are different from themselves—a false sense of race relations, says Charles A. Gallagher, an associate professor of sociology at Georgia State University who studies white attitudes about race.

"People who are 18 to 20 have been raised in a cultural environment with 'Cosby Show' re-runs, hip hop, identifying with black characters, they have gone through the multicultural training—for whatever it's worth—in school," he says. 'They have the perception that they are not only not racist, but they share a kind of social space with nonwhites through the media, so they think race doesn't matter anymore, which just isn't the case."

"These pranks reflect the students' idea that we are in a post-race society and we can make fun of everyone, and make fun of everything," Gallagher says. "So they don't see the difference between a 'ghetto' party and a toga party."

Not only are students unaware of the feelings of minority students, many have so little sense of history that they don't know instinctively that images like lynching aren't going to be looked at casually by black people. And for all the talk about how colleges these days focus on multiculturalism, experts points out that most white students never study minority history in a sophisticated way or have any sustained focus on race relations.

Source: From S. Jaschik, "Dumb and Dumber." *Inside Higher Ed*. Retrieved October 27, 2005, from http://insidehighered.com/news/2005/10/27/race.

cial case in the history of U.S. immigration. African Americans did not choose to emigrate but were brought here involuntarily, mainly as slave labor. Many Europeans also emigrated as indentured servants. However, the system of contract servitude was gradually replaced by perpetual servitude, or slavery, almost wholly of Africans. Many landowners wanted captive workers who could not escape and who could not become competitors. They turned to slave labor.

The slave trade, developed by European and African merchants, lasted about 350 years, although slavery was outlawed in Europe long before it was outlawed in the United States. Roughly 10 million Africans reached the Americas, although most died in the brutal overseas passage (Curtin, 1969). Slavery is an important aspect of U.S. immigration history. As James Baldwin (1955) suggested, the legacy of slavery makes contemporary interracial relations in the United States very different from interracial relations in Europe and other regions of the world.

Slavery presents a moral dilemma for many whites even today. A common response is simply to ignore history. Many people assert that because not all whites owned slaves we should forget the past and move on. For others, forgetting the past is not acceptable. In fact, some historians, like James Loewen, maintain that acknowledging and understanding the past is the only viable alternative in moving forward. In his book *Lies My Teacher Told Me*, Loewen (1995) analyzes the content in contemporary high school history books and acknowledges that they do present the horrors of slavery. What is missing, however, is the connection of slavery to the current racial tensions in the United States:

> *Perhaps telling realistically what slavery was like for slaves is the easy part. After all, slavery as an institution is dead. We have progressed beyond it, so we can acknowledge its evils.... Without explaining its relevance to the present, however, extensive coverage of slavery is like extensive coverage of the Hawley-Smoot Tariff—just more facts for hapless eleventh graders to memorize. Slavery's twin legacies to the present are the social and economic inferiority it conferred upon blacks and the cultural racism it instilled in whites. Both continue to haunt our society. Therefore, treating slavery's enduring legacy is necessarily controversial. Unlike slavery, racism is not over yet. To function adequately in civic life in our troubled times, students must learn what causes racism.* (p. 143)

Scholar and theologian Cornel West (1993) agrees that we should begin by acknowledging the historical flaws of U.S. society and recognizing the historical consequences of slavery. For instance, the United States has several Holocaust museums but no organized, official recognition of the horrors of slavery. Perhaps it is easier for us to focus on the negative events of another nation's history than on those of our own. In Chapter 4, we explore the importance of history in understanding the dynamics of intercultural communication.

Relationships With New Immigrants   Relationships between residents and immigrants—between oldtimers and newcomers—have often been filled with tension and conflict. In the 19th century, Native Americans sometimes were caught in the middle of European rivalries.

During the War of 1812, for example, Indian allies of the British were severely punished by the United States when the war ended. In 1832, the U.S. Congress recognized the Indian nations' right to self-government, but in 1871, a congressional act prohibited treaties between the U.S. government and Indian tribes. In 1887, Congress passed the Dawes Severalty Act, terminating Native Americans' special relationship with the U.S. government and paving the way for their removal from their homelands.

As waves of immigrants continued to roll in from Europe, the more firmly established European—mainly British—immigrants tried to protect their way of life, language, and culture. As one citizen lamented in 1856,

> *Four-fifths of the beggary and three-fifths of the crime spring from our foreign population; more than half the public charities, more than half the prisons and almshouses, more than half the police and the cost of administering criminal justice are for foreigners. (quoted in Cole, 1998, p. 126)*

The foreigners to which this citizen was referring were mostly from Ireland, devastated by the potato famines, and from Germany, which had fallen on hard economic and political times. Historian James Banks (1991) identifies other anti-immigrant events throughout the nation's history. As early as 1729, an English mob prevented a group of Irish immigrants from landing in Boston. A few years later, another mob destroyed a new Scots-Irish Presbyterian church in Worcester, Massachusetts. In these acts, we can see the **Anglocentrism** that characterized early U.S. history. Later, northern and western European (e.g., German and Dutch) characteristics were added to this model of American culture. Immigrants from southern, central, and eastern Europe (e.g., Italy and Poland) were expected to assimilate into the so-called mainstream culture—to jump into the "**melting pot**" and come out "American."

In the late 19th and early 20th centuries, a **nativistic** (anti-immigrant) movement propagated violence against newer immigrants. In 1885, 28 Chinese were killed in an anti-Chinese riot in Wyoming; in 1891, a white mob attacked a Chinese community in Los Angeles and killed 19 people; also in 1891, 11 Italian Americans were lynched in New Orleans.

Anglocentrism Using Anglo or white cultural standards as the criteria for interpretations and judgments of behaviors and attitudes.
melting pot A metaphor that assumes that immigrants and cultural minorities will be assimilated into the U.S. majority culture, losing their original cultures.
nativistic Extremely patriotic to the point of being anti-immigrant.

Nativistic sentiment was well supported at the government level. In 1882, Congress passed the Chinese Exclusion Act, officially prohibiting anyone who lived in China from immigrating to this country. In 1924, the Johnson-Read Act and the Oriental Exclusion Act established extreme quotas on immigration, virtually precluding the legal immigration of Asians. According to Ronald Takaki (1989), these two laws "provided for immigration based on nationality quotas: the number of immigrants to be admitted annually was limited to 2 percent of the foreign-born individuals of each nationality residing in the United States in 1890" (p. 209). The nativistic sentiment increasingly was manifested in arguments that economic and political opportunities should be reserved solely for whites, and not just for native-born Americans.

By the 1930s, southern and eastern European groups were considered "assimilatable," and the concept of race assumed new meaning. All of the so-called white races were now considered one, so racial hostilities could focus on ethnic (nonwhite) groups, such as Asian Americans, Native Americans, and Mexican Americans (Banks, 1991). Sociologist David Roediger (1991) traces how devastating this racialization was, particularly for African Americans. In the growing, but sometimes fragile, economy of the first half of the 20th century, white workers had an advantage. Although white immigrants received low wages, they had access to better schools and to public facilities, and they were accorded greater public acceptance. People of color often were considered less fit to receive economic benefits and, to some extent, to be not truly American (Foner, 1998).

Economic conditions make a big difference in attitudes toward foreign workers and immigration policies. During the Depression of the 1930s, Mexicans and Mexican Americans were forced to return to Mexico to free up jobs for white Americans. When prosperity returned in the 1940s, Mexicans were welcomed back as a source of cheap labor. This type of situation is not limited to the United States but occurs all over the world. For example, Algerian workers are alternately welcomed and rejected in France, depending on the state of the French economy and the demand for imported labor. Guest workers from Turkey have been subjected to similar uncertainties in Germany. Indian workers in Kenya, Chinese immigrants in Malaysia, and many other workers toiling outside their native lands have suffered the vagaries of fluctuating economies and immigration policies.

The tradition of tension and conflict between cultures continues to this day. The conflicts that arise in Southern California exemplify many aspects of the demographic changes in the United States. We can examine on a variety of levels the tensions in Los Angeles among Latinos/as, African Americans, Korean Americans, and European Americans. Some of the conflict is related to different languages, values, and lifestyles. Some African Americans resent the economic success of recent Korean immigrants—a reaction that reflects a typical historical pattern. The conflict may also be due to the pattern of settlement that results in cultural **enclaves.**

Immigration and Economic Classes   Some of the conflict may be related to the economic disparity that exists among these different groups. To understand this disparity, we need to look at issues of economic class. Most Americans are reluctant to admit that a class structure exists and even more reluctant to admit how difficult it is to move up in this structure. Indeed, most people live their lives in the same economic class into which they were born. And there are distinct class differences in clothing, housing, recreation, conversation, and other aspects of everyday life (Fussell, 1992). For example, the driveways to the homes of the very rich are usually obscured, whereas those of upper-class homes usually are long and curved and quite visible. Driveways leading to middle-class homes, in contrast, tend to go straight into garages.

The myth of a classless society is hardly benign. It not only reinforces middle- and upper-class beliefs in their own superior abilities but also promotes a false hope among the working class and the poor that they can get ahead. Whereas real-life success stories of upward mobility are rare, fictitious ones abound in literature, film, and television. But all such accounts perpetuate the myth. The reality is that the income gap between rich and poor in the United States is more extreme than in most industrialized countries. The ratio between rich and poor (measured as the percentage of total income held by the wealthiest 20% versus the poorest 20%) is approximately 11:1, one of the highest ratios in the indus-trialized world. The ratio in Germany and Japan, in contrast, is 4:1 (Mantsios, 2001). As Katrina was making its devastating landfall, the U.S. Census Bureau released new figures that show that since 1999, the income of the poorest fifth of Americans has dropped 8.7% in inflation-adjusted dollars. In 2004 alone, 1.1 million were added to the 36 million already on the poverty rolls (Scheer, 2005).

It may be common knowledge that the gap between the wealthy and everyone else is growing wider, but the extent of the current gap is staggering. In a series investigating class in the United States, *New York Times* writer David Caty Johnston (2005) reported that between 1950 and 1970, for every additional dollar earned by the bottom 90% of

---

enclaves (1) The territories that are surrounded by another country's territory; (2) cultural minority groups that live within a larger cultural group's territory.

In this article, Craig Ray, an entrepreneur, describes the advantages of integrating immigrants into the U.S. workforce and gives some suggestions for businesses that have immigrant employees.

When my partner and I purchased Tommaso's Fresh Pasta *three years ago, our idea of a melting pot was what you use to make sauce.*

Today, however, it is our company's workplace that is a melting pot of cultures and languages, thanks to a core work force of immigrants.

[We] didn't set out to hire immigrants, just good employees. When a dramatic sales increase created an immediate need for workers and our state Employment Commission's matching system began identifying people who met our needs, many potential candidates were immigrants. Our employee diversity increased as we grew. Today, just 12 of our 33 employees are native-born Americans.

Hiring immigrant workers can create challenges but also can have rewards, such as employee loyalty and dedication. Here are some suggestions to consider in integrating such workers into your company:

- *Know the law. Familiarize yourself with Immigration and Naturalization Service regulations and make sure proper employment forms are completed and filed. The INS will help you learn the law.*

- *Recognize, too, that you may want to get involved as an employee's advocate if you believe his or her work status or eligibility to stay in the U.S. has been questioned wrongly.*

- *Limit the number of languages spoken. Each language you bring into the workplace carries with it communication barriers. While your firm ultimately might resemble the United Nations, don't go in that direction too fast. Adding workers who speak the same language as your current workers allows you to limit the number of employee interpreters needed and the amount of miscommunication.*

- *Create a culturally tolerant and supportive environment. You and your workers must be as tolerant of the ways of immigrants as you are of the ways of Americans. We had one employee, for example, who kept her country's custom of fasting, wearing black, and not cutting her hair for more than a month after the death of her father. Largely because our company promotes tolerance, this behavior elicited no negative comment from her co-workers.*

- *Offer classes in English as a second language. Encourage employees to take English classes. If possible, offer classes on-site and at no cost before shifts or during lunch, for example. For us, these classes are a win-win proposition. Our employees learn skills that make communication easier, and we get a venue for covering training and procedures. Also, the opportunity for education helps attract workers.*

- *Don't have separate staff meetings. Initially, we organized employee meetings according to the linguistic backgrounds of our workers. We quickly found that employees wanted to meet as a group so that issues raised by one person could be discussed by everyone. Now that we have switched to general meetings, everyone hears the same information and moves forward together.*

- *Look at the potential beyond the language. Don't bypass an immigrant employee's capabilities simply because he or she hasn't mastered English. For instance, we have a Vietnamese employee with little mastery of English but great learning retention and math abilities. We have taught him to handle all of our computerized production planning, and we expect him to handle additional responsibilities as his English skills improve. He, in turn, knows how we see his future, and that has made him work harder toward achieving his potential.*

A good worker is a good worker—if given the chance to do the job. Don't let someone's origin or language limit their potential, or your company's.

Source: From C. Ray, "The Potential of Immigrants," *Nation's Business*, August 1998, www.findarticles.com/cf_dls/m1154/n8_v86/20934415/print.jhtml.

the population, the top 0.01% earned an additional $162. Since then, that gap has skyrocketed. Between 1990 and 2002, for every additional dollar earned by the bottom 90%, each taxpayer in that top bracket earned an extra $18,000. The widening gap is due partly to the loss of stable industrial jobs as companies move to cheaper labor markets within the United States and abroad. Class and demographic issues also play a role, with racial and ethnic minorities typically hardest hit by economic downturns.

Religious Diversity   Immigration also contributes to religious diversity, bringing increasing numbers of Muslims, Buddhists, Confucians, Catholics, and others to the United States. Religious beliefs and practices often play an important role in everyday cultural life. One example is the very different views on abortion, described by our student Tanya:

> Pro-choice and pro-lifers have incredibly different worldview lenses. These different lenses they see through are most of the time influenced by religion and social upbringing. The values are different, yet no side is wrong and cannot see through the same worldview lens as their opponents.

These different worldviews can sometimes lead to prejudices and stereotypes. For example, stereotypes about Islam are widespread in U.S. popular culture. Political scientist Ali Muzrui (2001) describes Islam as the "ultimate negative 'Other' to the Christian tradition" and laments the rising tide of "Islamophobia" (fear of Islam and the hostility toward it). He lists the contrasting stereotypes:

> Whereas Christianity is supposed to be peace loving, Islam is portrayed as fostering holy war (Jihad). Whereas Christianity liberates women, Islam enslaves them. Whereas Christianity is modern, Islam is medieval. Whereas Christianity is forward looking, Islam is backward looking. Whereas Christians prefer nonviolence, Muslims easily resort to terrorism. (p. 110)

Muzrui goes on to present evidence to debunk each of these stereotypes. Religious diversity is part of the demographic imperative that challenges us to learn more about intercultural communication.

These increasingly diverse ethnic, racial, economic, and religious groups come into contact mostly during the day in schools, businesses, and other settings, bringing to the encounters different languages, histories, and economic statuses. This presents great challenges for us as a society and as individuals. The main challenge is to look beyond the stereotypes and biases, to recognize the disparities and differences, and to try to apply what we know about intercultural communication. Perhaps the first step is to realize that the melting pot metaphor probably was never viable, that it was not realistic to expect everyone to assimilate into the United States in the same way. Today we need a different metaphor, one that reflects the racial, ethnic, and cultural diversity that truly exists in our country. Perhaps we should think of the United States as a "salad," in which each group retains its own flavor and yet contributes to the whole. Or we might think of it as a "tapestry," with many different strands contributing to a unified pattern.

In any case, the United States is hardly a model of diversity; many countries are far more diverse ethnically. For example, Nigeria has some 200 ethnic groups, and Indonesia has a similar number. Nigeria was colonized by the British, and artificially drawn boundaries forced many different groups into one nation-state, which caused many conflicts. The diverse groups in Indonesia, in contrast, have largely coexisted amiably for many years. Diversity, therefore, does not necessarily lead to intercultural conflicts.

Fortunately, most individuals are able to negotiate day-to-day activities in spite of cultural differences. Diversity can even be a positive force. Demographic diversity in the United States has given us tremendous linguistic richness and culinary variety, varied resources to meet new social challenges, as well as domestic and international business opportunities.

THE ECONOMIC IMPERATIVE

The recent trend toward globalization—the creation of a world market in goods, services, labor, capital, and technology—is shown dramatically in the account of a journalist who asks a Dell computer manager where his laptop is made. The answer? It was codesigned by engineers in Texas and Taiwan; the microprocessor was made in one of Intel's factories in the Philippines, Costa Rica, Malaysia, or China; the memory came from factories in Korea, Germany, or Japan. Other components (keyboard, hard drive, batteries, etc.) were made by Japanese, Irish, Israeli, or British firms with factories mainly in Asia, and finally, the laptop was assembled in Taiwan Province of China (Friedman, 2005).

What is the ultimate impact of globalization on the average person? Some economists defend it, saying the losses are always offset by the gains in cheaper consumer prices. However, many working people, seeing their jobs outsourced to cheap labor in India, China, and

Malaysia, feel threatened. An increasing number of economists agree. As one of the world's leading economists, Paul Samuelson (2005), argues, consumer gains are offset by income losses—if globalization causes enough Americans to suffer lower wages, America as a whole loses. The answer is not to resign from the world trading system, but rather to understand how and why the big winners from globalization, the Asian nations, are gaining and to learn from them, just as in the past, they learned from us (Maital, 2005).

The point is that, to compete effectively in this new global market, Americans must understand how business is conducted in other countries. U.S. businesspeople should be able to negotiate deals that are advantageous to the U.S. economy. However, they are not always willing to take the time and effort to do this. For example, most U.S. automobile manufacturers do not produce automobiles that have right-hand drive, which prevents them from penetrating markets in nations like Japan. Stories abound of U.S. marketing slogans that were inaccurately translated, like Pepsi's "Come alive with the Pepsi Generation," which was translated into Chinese as "Pepsi brings your ancestors back from the grave" ("Ten Great Global Marketing Mistakes," 1998).

Cross-cultural trainers in the United States report that Japanese and other business personnel often spend years in the United States studying English and learning about the country before they decide to establish operations here or invest money. In contrast, many American companies provide little or no training before sending their workers overseas and expect to close business deals quickly, with little regard for cultural idiosyncrasies.

Many management experts have examined other countries' practices for ways to increase U.S. productivity. One such idea was "quality circles," borrowed from the Japanese and now popular in the United States. Another Japanese strength is the belief in effort for its own sake. Japanese employees work longer hours and sometimes produce better products simply as a result of persistence. This trait also pays off in schools: Japanese students score higher on standardized exams than do American students (Fallows, 1989).

It will also behoove Americans to research how to do business in the huge emerging market that is 21st-century China. As shown in the Point of View box, (see page 32), arecent gaffe by Nike reflects the general lack of cultural understanding about the Chinese.

Why do so many businesspeople have difficulty succeeding in Chinese and other Asian markets? The reasons involve both differences in business practices and cultural differences between East and West. Ambler and Witzel (2000) explain that business dealings in China, as in many Eastern countries, are relationship oriented, that businesses cannot succeed without respect and harmony. Specifically, in China, three concepts are crucial:

- *Qingmian* (human feelings), which involves respect for the feelings of others

- *He* (harmony), which emphasizes the smooth functioning of a group or society

- *Guanxi* (relationship or connection), which underscores the importance of relationships in Chinese business

The high value placed on these concepts highlights other differences as well. For example, contract law is practiced very differently in China. Whereas in the West the law is the essential set of rules of conduct, the "rules of conduct" in China are the ethics and standards of behavior required in a Confucian society. This means that sometimes social pressures rather than legal instruments are used to ensure compliance. Thus, what we might conceptualize as a legal issue may be seen in China as a relationship issue.

Sometimes there are cultural differences in work ethics. One of our students, Vincent, describes a difference he observed while working as an intern in a manufacturing company:

When looking back at this internship I can easily see that Mexican workers were more loyal to the company. I constantly noticed that American workers at this company would be walking around talking or smoking while they were supposed to be at their work stations, but the Mexican workers would never leave their stations until it was time for break. This sometimes created problems between Mexicans and other employees because of the differences in work ethics.

We discuss the implications of these types of cultural differences for relationships (Chapter 9) and conflicts (Chapter 10).

Cultural differences in business practices have implications not only when people from different companies do business with each other but also when people from different cultures work on the same team. One effect of globalization is increasing numbers of international teams—sometimes working as vir-tual teams and rarely meeting face-to-face. These teams present large challenges in intercultural communication. A recent Hewlett-Packard project involved a 16-country multilingual virtual team that operated on both sides of the international dateline. The leaders describe the challenges: "Relatively routine tasks, such as scheduling a meeting, become complex and fraught with interpersonal friction when one person's work day begins as another is sitting down to dinner or sound asleep. A simple e-mail exchange frazzles nerves because of cultural misunderstandings" (Snyder, 2003).

Even when employees have good language skills, they naturally interpret written and verbal communication through the filter of their own culture. For example, Israeli workers in the project just described wondered why their U.S. counterparts would sometimes seem upset by e-mail exchanges. It turned out that Israelis, who tend to be rather direct and sometimes blunt, were sending e-mails that seemed rude to their American counterparts. And Americans' e-mails seemed "wishy-washy" to the Israelis. The Americans' requests, with phrases like "Thanks in advance for sending me . . . ," mystified the Israelis who would say, "Thanks for what? I haven't done anything yet." After some cultural training, both sides adapted to the other (Snyder, 2003). In later chapters, we explore the implications of these and other cultural differences in communication practices.

Globalization presents many new issues. Increasingly, **multinational corporations** are moving operations to new locations, often overseas, because of lower labor costs. These business moves have far-reaching implications, including the loss of jobs at closed facilities. Many U.S.-owned companies have established production facilities, known as *maquiladoras,* along the U.S.-Mexican border, where workers produce goods bound mainly for U.S. markets. These companies benefit from lower labor costs, tax breaks, and relaxed environmental regulations. Although Mexican laborers profit from the jobs, there is a cost in terms of environmental hazards. *Maquiladoras* thus present intercultural challenges for Mexicans and U.S. Americans.

Domestic diversity also requires businesses to be attentive to cultural differences. As the workforce becomes more diverse, many businesses are interested in capitalizing on these differences for economic gain. As trainers Bernardo M. Ferdman and Sara Einy Brody (1996) suggest, "Once organizations learn to adopt an inclusive orientation in dealing with their members, this will also have a positive impact on how they look at their customer base, how they develop products and assess business opportunities, and how they relate to their communities" (p. 289).

Understanding cultural differences involves not only working with diverse employees but also recognizing new business markets, developing new products, and so on. From this perspective, diversity is a potentially powerful economic resource if organizations view the chal-

multinational corporations Companies that have operations in two or more nations.
maquiladoras Assembly plants or factories (mainly of U.S. companies) established on the U.S.-Mexican border and using mainly Mexican labor.

lenge as an opportunity. In this sense, then, business can capitalize on diversity.

THE PEACE IMPERATIVE

The bottom line seems to be this: Can individuals of different genders, ages, ethnicities, races, languages, socioeconomic statuses, and cultural backgrounds coexist on this planet? Both the history of humankind and recent world events lead us not to be very optimistic on this point. And this imperative is even more evident after the events of September 11, 2001. Contact among different cultural groups—from the earliest civilizations until today—often has led to disharmony. For example, consider the ethnic/religious strife between Muslims and the Western world; the ethnic struggles in Bosnia and the former Soviet Union; the war between Hutus and Tutsis in Rwanda (Africa); the continued unrest in the Middle East; and the racial and ethnic struggles and tensions in neighborhoods in Boston, Los Angeles, and other U.S. cities.

Some of these conflicts are tied to histories of **colonialism** around the world, whereby European powers lumped diverse groups—differing in language, culture, religion, or identity—together as one state. For example, the division of Pakistan and India was imposed by the British; eventually, East Pakistan declared its independence to become Bangladesh. Nevertheless, ethnic and religious differences in some areas of India and Pakistan continue to cause unrest. And the acquisition of nuclear weapons by both India and Pakistan makes these antagonisms of increasing concern. The tremendous diversity—and accompanying antagonisms—within many former colonies must be understood in the context of histories of colonialism.

Some of the conflicts are also tied to economic disparities and influenced by U.S. technology and media. Many people in the United States see these influences as beneficial, but they also stimulate resistance. Communication scholar Fernando Delgado (2002) explains:

Such cultural dominance, though celebrated at home, can spark intercultural conflicts because it inhibits the development of other nations' indigenous popular culture products, stunts their economic development and foists U.S. values and perspectives on other cultures. These effects, in turn, often lead to resentment and conflict. (p. 353)

---

colonialism   (1) The system by which groups with diverse languages, cultures, religions, and identities were united to form one state, usually by a European power; (2) the system by which a country maintains power over other countries or groups of people to exploit them economically, politically, and culturally.

CHINA CHOPS NIKE AD

The U.S. sportswear firm Nike has apologized for running a commercial in China which has been banned by popular demand for offending the country's national dignity.

The 90-second advertisement was meant to combine Kill Bill–style martial arts with sassy basketball bravado. U.S. National Basketball Association star LeBron James is shown running rings around the animated figure of a wizened and bearded kung fu master, who resembles the martial arts teacher from Quentin Tarantino's latest movie.

In the commercial, the American athlete also gets the better of two women in traditional Chinese attire, and a pair of dragons—considered to be a symbol of China.

In a sign of the growing influence of internet opinion, the government has pulled the "Chamber of Fear" advertisement off the airwaves, after protests in online chat rooms overturned the initial approval by state censors.

According to the U.S. company, the commercial was designed by its advertising agent, Wieden and Kennedy, to encourage teenagers to overcome temptation, envy, complacency and self-doubt. But it has only managed to stir up irritation in China.

The state administration for radio, television and film posted a statement saying that Nike had violated the condition that all advertisements in China should uphold national dignity.

"This ad shows Chinese characters losing again and again. It makes our country look helpless against America," said one chat room contributor.

Faced with the loss of business from a market in which its sales have nearly doubled in the past year, Nike meekly accepted the government's decision.

"We had no intention of hurting the emotions of Chinese consumers," the company said in a statement.

"We place much attention on the Chinese market and there was a lot of careful consideration before launching the advertisement," they said.

Source: From J. Watts, "China Chops Nike Ad; Multinational Apologizes After Outcry," *The Guardian* (London), December 8, 2004, p. 15.

For example, according to many Canadians, a Canadian cultural identity is almost impossible because of the dominance of U.S. media. This type of cultural domination is very complex. Delgado recalls that he noticed anti-American sentiments in graffiti, newspapers, and TV programs during a recent trip to Europe, but that he also saw U.S. influence everywhere—in music, television, film, cars, fast food, and fashion. He notes that "resentment, frustration, and disdain among the locals coexisted with an amazement at the penetration of U.S. popular culture" (p. 355).

Some of the conflicts have roots in past foreign policies. For example, the attacks in September 2001 were partly related to the confusing and shifting alliances among the United States, Afghanistan, and Arab and Islamic countries. In Afghanistan in the early 1990s, the Taliban seized power in response to the destructive rule of the Northern Alliance, a loose coalition of warlords. The United States had supported the Taliban in the fight against Soviet aggression in the late 1980s and had promised aid in rebuilding their country after the hostilities were over. However, with the withdrawal of Soviet forces and the fall of the Soviet Union, the United States wasn't as concerned about fulfilling its promises to the Afghan nation, leaving the Afghan people at the mercy of the Taliban. In addition, U.S. foreign policies toward many Arab countries in the last half century, coupled with open support for Israel, have caused widespread resentment (Friedman, 2002). Although there is no simple explanation for why terrorists attacked the United States, the attacks clearly did not happen in a vacuum. They need to be understood in historical, political, religious, and economic contexts.

It would be naive to assume that simply understanding the issues of intercultural communication would end war and intercultural conflict, but these problems do underscore the need for individuals to learn more about social groups other than their own. Ultimately, people, and not countries, negotiate and sign peace treaties. An example of how individual communication styles may influence political outcomes can be seen in the negotiations between Iraqi president Saddam Hussein and representatives of the United States and the United Nations. For example, just prior to the Gulf War, in 1990, many Middle East experts assumed that Hussein was not ready to fight, that he was merely bluffing, using an Arabic style of communication. This style emphasizes the importance of animation, exaggeration, and conversational form over content (Feghali, 1997). Communication specialists note that in conflict situations Arab speakers may threaten the life and property of their opponents but have no intention of actually carrying out the threats. Rather, Arab speakers use threats to buy time and intimidate their opponents. Thus, declaratory statements by U.S. leaders, such as "We will find the cancer and cut it out," seemed mundane and unintimidating to Arab listeners. Verbal exchanges, regardless of the different speech styles, often take the place of physical violence (Griefat & Katriel, 1989).

However, we always need to consider the relationship between individual and societal forces in studying intercultural communication. Although communication on the interpersonal level is important, we must remember that individuals often are born into and are caught up in conflicts that they neither started nor chose.

THE SELF-AWARENESS IMPERATIVE

One of the most important reasons for studying intercultural communication is the awareness it raises of our own cultural identity and background. This is also one of the least obvious reasons. Peter Adler (1975), a noted social psychologist, observes that the study of intercultural communication begins as a journey into another culture and reality and ends as a journey into one's own culture.

We gain insights in intercultural experiences overseas. When Judith was teaching high school in Algeria, an Islamic country in North Africa, she realized something about her religious identity as a Protestant. December 25 came and went, and she taught classes with no mention of Christmas. Judith had never thought about how special the celebration of Christmas was or how important the holiday was to her. She then recognized on a personal level the uniqueness of this particular cultural practice. Erla, a graduate student from Iceland, notes the increased knowledge and appreciation she's gained concerning her home country:

> *Living in another country widens your horizon. It makes you appreciate the things you have, and it strengthens the family unit. You look at your country from a different point of view. We have learned not to expect everything to be the same as "at home," but if we happen to find something that reminds us of home, we really appreciate it and it makes us very happy. Ultimately we are all very thankful that we had the opportunity to live in another country.*

However, it is important to recognize that intercultural learning is not always easy or comfortable. And what you learn depends on your social and economic position in society. Self-awareness through intercultural contact for someone from a racial or minority group may mean learning to be wary and not surprised at subtle slights by members of the dominant majority—and reminders of their place in society. For example, a Chinese American colleague is sometimes approached at professional meetings by white communication professors who ask her to take their drink order.

If you are white and middle class, intercultural learning may mean an enhanced awareness of your privilege. A white colleague tells of feeling uncomfortable staying in a Jamaican resort, being served by blacks whose ancestors were brought there as slaves by European colonizers. On the one hand, it is privilege that allows travelers like our colleague to experience new cultures and places. On the other hand, one might wonder if we, through this type of travel, are reproducing those same historical postcolonial economic patterns.

Self-awareness, then, that comes through intercultural learning may involve an increased awareness of being caught up in political, economic, and historical systems—not of our own making.

THE ETHICAL IMPERATIVE

Living in an intercultural world presents ethical challenges as well. **Ethics** may be thought of as principles of conduct that help govern the behavior of individuals and groups. These principles often arise from communities' consensus on what is good and bad behavior. Cultural values tell us what is "good" and what "ought" to be good. Ethical judgments focus more on the degrees of rightness and wrongness in human behavior than do cultural values (Johannesen, 1990).

Some judgments are stated very explicitly. For example, the Ten Commandments teach that it is wrong to steal, tell a lie, commit murder, and so on. Many other identifiable principles of conduct that arise from our cultural experience may be less explicit—for instance, that people should be treated equally and should work hard. Several issues come to mind in a discussion of ethics in intercultural communication. For example, what happens when two ethical systems collide? Although an individual may want to "do the right thing" to contribute to a better society, it is not always easy to know what is "right" in specific situations. Ethical principles are often culture bound, and intercultural conflicts arise from various notions of what is ethical behavior.

One common cross-cultural ethical dilemma involves standards of

---

ethics Principles of conduct that help govern behaviors of individuals and groups.

POINT OF VIEW

This writer decries a certain kind of intercultural learning—the learning that some study-abroad students pursue—whereby people in other countries are objectified and viewed as exotic and strange. The real problem arises when these students are hired to write television commercials and to present ideas about other cultures.

One type of commercial model shows us exotic humans in all their tribal finery, but, in a multicultural twist, they—Masai warriors, Sicilian matrons, Tibetan monks, Irish fishermen—are revealed as strangely prescient consumers with a quirky knowledge of luxury cars or Internet stock trading. In one commercial, we witness an Inuit elder teaching his grandson about tracking by identifying marks in the snow. "That," he says, "is a caribou." Then, after a pause, during which the wise man stares at the snow, he reverentially intones the single word "Audi." From ads like those, astute students learn that foreigners are obsessed with us—our commodities and displays. What we may learn from them pales in comparison with the glories that they see in our consumer lifestyle.

Other commercials reduce distant lands to images of animals or nature and imply that nature can be thoroughly dominated by SUV's or swaggering, extreme-sports youths. Athletes and Nissan Pathfinders fight bulls in a ring, giant outdoorsmen tap the miniaturized Rockies, a hiker butts heads with a bighorn sheep. And, of course, sophisticated viewers know that all those animals are the creation of technology.

In one commercial, a driver—insulated in his fully self-sufficient cocoon—is able to program both the road and the various beautiful and exotic settings it passes through. Not only is the technologically empowered American greater than nature, we create nature to suit our whims. There is no outside world anymore, no dark places of mystery, yet to be seen. Our SUV's do not travel to an unknown world so much as create different options from a well-known list. Television's emphasis is on how the actor—whether a contestant on a reality-TV show or the driver in a car ad—is seen and manipulates how she is seen. Even when outsiders exist, everyone is looking at us.

When a promotional piece for the reality-TV show The Amazing Race *shows an American woman in a clearly foreign space—perhaps India—she is not troubled, confused or interested in her environment. Instead she strips down to a bikini emblazoned with a U.S. flag to get directions to the next challenge from a bug-*

*eyed and eager native. "Will I wear this if it helps me get home?"
she says. "Hell, yeah!" The young woman clearly did not travel to
broaden her horizons. For her, India becomes, as much as Salt Lake
City or Kandahar, a place for aggressive performance of her American
identity—unwrapping herself in the flag, so to speak.*

*We now are the world, to be looked at, admired, or despised; what
is important about the activity of others is their response to our display.
. . . [Study-abroad students] talk about interactions with outsiders
only in vague abstractions, while expostulating brilliantly about the
nuances of American students' interactions with one another. The few
individuals who left their peers to engage the outside world explained
that move as an individual rejection of the group and still found it
easier to discuss their fellow students than the generically defined
"friends" they met at bars.*

*One young American who traveled to Guatemala bragged that "I
have a surprising ability to relate to almost everyone," but "everyone"
turned out to mean members of preconceived categories of human-
rights workers, Indians, and children, whom she described as objects of
more first-person sentences. She specifically excluded less exotic, fast-
talking city folk who were "just different" and not worth mentioning.*

*Students return from study-abroad programs having seen the
world, but the world they return to tell tales about is more often than
not the world they already knew, the imaginary world of globalized,
postmodern capitalism where everything is already known, everyone
speaks the same language, and the outside world keeps its eyes on those
of us who come from the center.*

*. . . we should avoid pre- and post-travel orientation sessions
that focus on group dynamics and individual growth. Instead, those
sessions could be used as opportunities for students to learn how to
question the way that we tell stories about our travels, and to discover
for themselves how those stories share features with commercials about
men who play football with lions and reality shows where contestants
dare each other to swallow centipedes.*

Source: From B. Feinberg, "What Students Don't Learn Abroad," *The Chronicle Review*, May 2, 2000, p. B20.

conducting business in multinational corporations. The U.S. Congress and the Securities and Exchange Commission consider it unethical to make payments to government officials of other countries to promote trade. (Essentially, such payments smack of bribery.) However, in many countries, like China, government officials are paid in this informal way instead of being supported by taxes (Ambler & Witzel, 2000). What, then, is ethical behavior for personnel in multinational subsidiaries?

Relativity Versus Universality

In this book, we stress the relativity of cultural behvavior—that no cultural pattern is inherently right or wrong. So, is there any universality in ethics? Are any cultural behaviors always right or always wrong? The answers depend on one's perspective. A universalist might try, for example, to identify acts and conditions that most societies think of as wrong, such as murder, theft, or treason. Someone who takes an extreme universalist position would insist that cultural differences are only superficial, that fundamental notions of right and wrong are universal. Some religions take universal positions—for example, that the Ten Commandments are a universal code of behavior. But Christian groups often disagree about the universality of the Bible. For example, are the teachings of the New Testament mainly guidelines for the Christians of Jesus' time, or can they be applied to Christians in the 21st century? These are difficult issues for many people searching for ethical guidelines (Johannesen, 1990). The philosopher Immanuel Kant (1949) believed in the universality of moral laws. His well-known "categorical imperative" states that people should act only on maxims that apply universally, to *all* individuals.

The extreme relativist position holds that any cultural behavior can be judged only within the cultural context in which it occurs. This means that only those members of a community can truly judge the ethics of their own members. According to communication scholar William S. Howell (1982),

> *The environment, the situation, the timing of an interaction, human relationships all affect the way ethical standards are applied. . . . The concept of universal ethics, standards of goodness that apply to everyone, everywhere, and at all times, is the sort of myth people struggle to hold onto. (pp. 182, 187)*

And yet, to accept a completely relativistic position seems to tacitly accept the horrors of Nazi Germany, South African apartheid, or

U.S. slavery. In each case, the larger community developed cultural beliefs that supported persecution and discrimination in such extreme forms that worldwide condemnation ultimately resulted (Hall, 1997, p. 23).

Philosophers and anthropologists have struggled to develop ethical guidelines that seem universally applicable but that also recognize the tremendous cultural variability in the world. And many ethical relativists appeal to more natural, humanitarian principles. This more moderate position assumes that people can evaluate cultures without succumbing to **ethnocentrism**, that all individuals and cultural groups share a fundamental humanistic belief in the sanctity of the human spirit and the goodness of peace, and that people should respect the well-being of others (Kale, 1994).

Communication scholar Bradford J. Hall (1997) reminds us that relativistic and universalistic approaches to ethics should be viewed not as a dichotomy but rather as a compound of universalism and relativism. All ethics systems involve a tension between the universal and the relative. So, although we recognize some universal will toward ethical principles, we may have to live with the tension of not being able to impose our "universal" ethic on others.

A recent suggestion for meeting the ethical imperative is to employ a **dialogical approach** (Evanoff, 2004). The dialogical approach emphasizes the importance of relationships and dialogues between individuals and communities in wrestling with ethical dilemmas. Communication scholars Stanley Deetz, Deborah Cohen, and Paige P. Edley (1997) suggest that, even in international business contexts, a dialogical approach can work. As an example, they cite the ethical challenges that arise when a corporation relocates its operations overseas. Although this relocation may make good business sense, the move often has difficult personal and social (and therefore ethical) ramifications. The move may cause a wave of unemployment in the old location and raise issues of exploitation of the workforce and harm to the environment in the new location (especially where poverty is a problem).

Deetz and colleagues (1997) suggest that moving from an owner/manager model to a dialogical stakeholder model can help clarify some of the ethical issues. The dialogical approach emphasizes the importance of the relationship and dialogue between the company and the various communities and stakeholders. They propose forums for discussion even while acknowledging that sometimes discussions and

ethnocentrism (1) An orientation toward one's own ethnic group; (2) a tendency to elevate one's own culture above others.
dialogical approach Focuses on the importance of dialogue in developing and maintaining relationships between individuals and communities.

forums are used by management to suppress or diffuse conflict rather than to promote genuine debate for the sake of company improvement. In this case, a dialogical approach

> *does not rest in agreement or consensus but in the avoidance of the sup-pression of alternative conceptions and possibilities . . . the heterogeneity of the international community and the creative possibilities residing in intercultural communication provide possibilities that may have been overlooked in national cultures. (Deetz, et al., 1997, pp. 222–223)*

The study of intercultural communication not only provides insights into cultural patterns but also helps us address the ethical issues involved in intercultural interaction. Specifically we should be able to (1) judge what is ethical and unethical behavior given variations in cultural priorities, and (2) identify guidelines for ethical behavior in intercultural contexts in which ethics clash.

Being Ethical Students of Culture

Related to the issue of judging cultural patterns as ethical or unethical are the issues surrounding the study of culture. Part of learning about intercultural communication is learning about cultural patterns and cultural identities—our own and others. There are three issues to address here: developing self-reflexivity, learning about others, and acquiring a sense of social justice.

Developing Self-Reflexivity   In studying intercultural communication, it is vital to develop **self-reflexivity**—to understand ourselves and our position in society. In learning about other cultures and cultural practices, we often learn much about ourselves. Immigrants often comment that they never felt so much like someone of their own nationality until they left their homeland.

Think about it: Many cultural attitudes and ideas are instilled in you, but these can be difficult to unravel and identify. Knowing who you are is never simple; rather, it is an ongoing process that can never fully capture the ever-emerging person. Not only will you grow older, but your intercultural experiences change who you are and who you think you are. It is also important to reflect on your place in society. By recognizing the social categories to which you belong, and the implications of those categories, you will be in a better position to understand how to communicate. For example, being an undergraduate student positions you to communicate your ideas on specific subjects

self-reflexivity A process of learning to understand oneself and one's position in society.

and in particular ways to various members of the faculty or staff at your school. You might want to communicate to the registrar your desire to change majors—this would be an appropriate topic to address to that person. But you would not be well positioned during an exam to communicate to your chemistry professor your problems with your girl- or boyfriend.

Learning About Others   It is important to remember that the study of cultures is actually the study of other people. Never lose sight of the humanity at the core of the topic. Try not to observe people as if they are zoo animals. Communication scholar Bradford Hall (1997) cautions against using the "zoo approach" to studying culture:

> *When using such an approach we view the study of culture as if we were walking through a zoo admiring, gasping and chuckling at the various exotic animals we observe. One may discover amazing, interesting and valuable information by using such a perspective and even develop a real fondness for these exotic people, but miss the point that we are as culturally "caged" as others and that they are culturally as "free" as we are. (p. 14)*

Remember that you are studying real people who have real lives, and your conclusions about them may have very real consequences for them and for you. Cultural studies scholar Linda Alcoff (1991/1992) acknowledges the ethical issues involved when students of culture try to describe the cultural patterns of others; she recognizes the difficulty of speaking "for" and "about" others who have different lives. Instead, she suggests, students of culture should try to speak "with" and "to" others. Rather than merely describe others from a distance, it's better to engage others in a dialogue about their cultural realities.

Learn to listen to the voices of others, to cultivate experiential knowledge. Hearing about the experiences of people who are different from you can broaden your ways of viewing the world. Many differences—based on race, gender, sexual orientation, nationality, ethnicity, age, and so on—deeply affect people's everyday lives. Listening carefully as people relate their experiences and their ways of knowing will help you learn about the many aspects of intercultural communication.

Developing a Sense of Social Justice   A final ethical issue involves the responsibility that comes with the acquisition of intercultural knowledge and insights—that this educational experience is not just transformative for the individual but should also benefit the larger society and other cultural groups in the increasingly interdependent world.

Everett Kleinjans (1975), an international educator, stresses that intercultural education differs from some other kinds of education: Although all education may be potentially transformative, learning as a result of intercultural contact is particularly so in that it deals with fundamental aspects of human behavior. Learning about intercultural communication sometimes calls into question the core of our basic assumptions about ourselves, our culture, and our worldviews, and challenges existing and preferred beliefs, values, and patterns of behavior. Liliana, a Colombian student, describes such a transformation:

> *When I first came to the States to study and live I was surprised with all the diversity and different cultures I encountered. I realized I came from a country, society, school and group of friends with little diversity. During all the years I lived in Colombia I did not meet more than five people from other countries. Even at my school, there was little diversity — only two students of color among three thousand students. I realized that big difference when I was suddenly sharing a college classroom with students from all over the world, people of all colors and cultures. At the beginning it was difficult getting used to it because of the wide diversity, but I like and enjoy it now and I wish my family and friends could experience and learn as much as I have.*

As you learn about your self and others as cultural beings, as you come to understand the larger economic, political, and historical contexts in which interaction occurs, is there an ethical obligation to continue learning? We believe that as members of an increasingly interdependent global community, intercultural communication students have a responsibility to educate themselves, not just about interesting cultural differences, but also about intercultural conflicts, the impacts of stereotyping and prejudice, and the larger systems that can oppress and deny basic human rights—and to apply this knowledge to the communities in which they live and interact.

What constitutes ethical and unethical applications of intercultural communication knowledge? One questionable practice involves people who study intercultural communication in order to proselytize others without their consent. (Some religious organizations conduct Bible study on college campuses for international students under the guise of English language lessons.) Another questionable practice is the behavior of cross-cultural consultants who misrepresent or exaggerate their ability to deal with complex issues of prejudice and racism in brief, one-shot training sessions (Paige & Martin, 1996).

A final questionable practice concerns research on the intercultural communication of U.S. minority groups. A common approach in the United States is for a white tenured faculty member to conduct such research employing graduate and undergraduate students from the minority groups being studied:

> *Minority students are sometimes used as a way to gain immediate access to the community of interest. These students go into communities and the (usually white) professors are spared the intense, time-consuming work of establishing relationships in the community. (Martin & Butler, 2001, p. 291)*

These students are then asked to report their findings to and interpret their community for the faculty member. Unfortunately, doing so can jeopardize their relationship to their community, which may be suspicious of the academic community. The faculty member publishes articles and reaps the tangible rewards of others' hard work—promotions, pay raises, and professional visibility. Meanwhile, the community and the students may receive little for their valuable contributions to this academic work.

We feel there is a concomitant responsibility that goes along with this intercultural knowledge: to work toward a more equitable and fair society and world. We want you to keep in mind this ethical issue as you study the various topics covered in this book. In the final chapter, we'll address this issue again with practical suggestions for meeting this ethical challenge.

DISCUSSION QUESTIONS

1. How do electronic means of communication (e-mail, the Internet, fax, and so on) differ from face-to-face interactions?
2. How do these communication technologies change intercultural communication interaction?
3. What are some of the potential challenges organizations face as they become more diverse?
4. Why is it important to think beyond ourselves as individuals in intercultural interaction?
5. How do economic situations affect intergroup relations?

ACTIVITIES

1. *Family Tree.* Interview the oldest member of an American family you can contact. Then answer the following questions:

   a. When did their ancestors come to the United States?

   b. Where did they come from?

   c. What were the reasons for their move? Did they come voluntarily?

   d. What language(s) did they speak?

   e. What difficulties did they encounter?

   f. Did they change their names? For what reasons?

   g. What were their occupations before they came, and what jobs did they take on their arrival?

   h. How has their family status changed through the generations?

   Compare your family experience with those of your classmates. Did most immigrants come for the same reasons? What are the differences in the various stories?

2. *Intercultural Encounter.* Describe and analyze a recent intercultural encounter. This may mean talking with someone of a different age, ethnicity, race, religion, and so on.

   a. Describe the encounter. What made it "intercultural"?

   b. Explain how you initially felt about the communication.

   c. Describe how you felt after the encounter, and explain why you think you felt as you did.

   d. Describe any challenges in trying to communicate. If there were no challenges, explain why you think it was so easy.

   e. Based on this experience, identify some characteristics that may be important for successful intercultural communication.

REFERENCES

Adler, P. S. (1975). The transition experience: An alternative view of culture shock. *Journal of Humanistic Psychology, 15*, 13–23.

Alcoff, L. (1991/1992). The problem of speaking for others. *Cultural Critique, 20*, 5–32.

Ambler, T., & Witzel, M. (2000). *Doing business in China.* New York: Routledge.

Baldwin, J. (1955). *Notes of a native son.* Boston: Beacon Press.

Banks, J. (1991). *Teaching strategies for ethnic studies.* Needham, MA: Allyn & Bacon.

Brewer, C. A., & Suchan, T. A. (2001). *Mapping Census 2000: The geography of U.S. diversity.* (U.S. Census Bureau, Census Special Reports, Series CENSR/01–1.) Washington, DC: U.S. Government Printing Office.

Carnevale, A. P., & Fry, R. A. (2000). *Crossing the great divide: Can we achieve equity when generation Y goes to college?* Princeton, NJ: Educational Testing Service. (ERIC Document Reproduction Service No. ED443907)

Carter, D. M. (2004). Living in virtual communities: Making friends online. *Journal of Urban Technology, 11,* 109–136.

Cole, D. (1998). Five myths about immigration. In P. S. Rothenberg (Ed.), *Race, class, and gender in the United States: An integrated study* (4th ed., pp. 125–129). New York: St. Martin's Press.

Curtin, P. D. (1969). *The Atlantic slave trade: A census.* Madison: University of Wisconsin Press.

Danet, B. (1999). Text as mask: Gender, play and performance on the Internet. In S. G. Jones (Ed.), *Cybersociety 2.0: Revisiting computer-mediated communication and community* (pp. 129–159). Thousand Oaks, CA: Sage.

Deetz, S., Cohen, D., & Edley, P. P. (1997). Toward a dialogic ethic in the context of international business organization. In F. L. Casmir (Ed.), *Ethics in intercultural and international communication* (pp. 183–226). Mahwah, NJ: Lawrence Erlbaum.

Delgado, F. (2002). Mass-mediated communication and intercultural conflict. In J. N. Martin, T. K. Nakayama, & L. A. Flores (Eds.), *Readings in intercultural communication* (pp. 351–359). Boston: McGraw-Hill.

Dor, D. (2004). From Englishization to imposed multilingualism: Globalization, the Internet, and the political economy of the linguistic code. *Public Culture, 16,* 97–118.

Evanoff, R. J. (2004). Universalist, relativist, and constructivist approaches to intercultural ethics. *International Journal of Intercultural Relations, 28,* 439–458.

Fallows, J. (1989). *More like us: Putting America's native strengths and traditional values to work to overcome the Asian challenge.* Boston: Houghton Mifflin.

Farrell, E. (2005, February 4). More students plan to work to help pay for college. *The Chronicle of Higher Education,* pp. A1, A34.

Feghali, E. (1997). Arab cultural communication patterns. *International Journal of Intercultural Relations, 21,* 345–379.

Ferdman, B. M., & Brody, S. E. (1996). Models of diversity training. In D. Landis & R. Bhagat (Eds.), *Handbook of intercultural training* (2nd ed., pp. 282–303). Thousand Oaks, CA: Sage.

Flores, L. A., Moon, D. G., & Nakayama, T. K. (2006). Dynamic rhetorics of race: California's Racial Privacy Initiative and the shifting grounds of racial politics. *Communication and Critical/Cultural Studies.*

Foner, E. (1998). Who is an American? In P. S. Rothenberg (Ed.), *Race, class, and gender in the United States: An integrated study* (4th ed., pp. 84–92). New York: St. Martin's Press.

Franklin, M. I. (2003). I define my own identity: Pacific articulations of 'race' and 'culture' on the Internet. *Ethnicities, 3,* 465–490.

Friedman, T. L. (2002, March 6). The core of Muslim rage. *The New York Times,* www.nytimes.com/2002/03/06/opinion/06FRIE.htm l?ei=1&en=%20bd6293bb96564.

Friedman, T. L. (2005). *The world is flat: A brief history of the twenty-first century.* New York: Farrar, Straus & Giroux.

Fussell, P. (1992). *Class: A guide through the American status system.* New York: Touchstone Books.

Gergen, K. (1991). *The saturated self: Dilemmas of identity in contemporary life.* New York: Harper Collins/Basic Books.

Griefat, Y., & Katriel, T. (1989). Life demands *musayara*: Communication and culture among Arabs in Israel. In S. Ting-Toomey & F. Korzenny (Eds.), *Language, communication and culture: International and intercultural communication annual* (Vol. 13, pp. 121–138). Newbury Park, CA: Sage.

Hacker, K. L., & Steiner, R. (2002). The digital divide for Hispanic Americans. *Howard Journal of Communications, 13,* 267–283.

Hall, B. J. (1997). Culture, ethics and communication. In F. L. Casmir (Ed.), *Ethics in intercultural and international communication* (pp. 11–41). Mahwah, NJ: Lawrence Erlbaum.

Hochman, (2004, June 21). NBA teams continue to look outside U.S. *Times-Picayune* (New Orleans), p. 2.

Howell, W. S. (1982). *The empathic communicator.* Belmont, CA: Wadsworth.

Jackson, L. A., Barbatsis, G., Biocca, F. A., von Eye, A., Zhao, Y., & Fitzgerald, H. E. (2004). Home Internet use in low-income families: Is access enough to eliminate the digital divide? In E. P. Bucy & J. E. Newhagen (Eds.), *Media access: Social and psychological dimensions of new technology use* (pp. 155–186). Mahwah, NJ: Lawrence Erlbaum.

Johannesen, R. L. (1990). *Ethics in human communication* (3rd ed.). Prospect Heights, IL: Waveland Press.

Johnston, D. C. (2005, June 5). Richest are leaving even the rich far behind. *New York Times,* p. 1.

Kale, D. W. (1994). Peace as an ethic for intercultural communication. In L. Samovar & R. E. Porter (Eds.), *Intercultural communication: A reader* (7th ed., pp. 435–441). Belmont, CA: Wadsworth.

Kant, I. (1949). *Fundamental principles of the metaphysics of morals* (T. Abbott, Trans.). Indianapolis, IN: Library of Liberal Arts/Bobbs-Merrill.

Kleinjans, E. (1975). A question of ethics. *International Education and Cultural Exchange, 10,* 20–25.

Lenhart, A., Horrigan, J., Rainie, L., Allen, K., Boyce, A., Madden, M., & O'Grady, E. (2003, April 16). *The ever-shifting Internet population: A new look at Internet access and the digital divide.* Washington, DC: Pew Internet & American Life Project (http://www.pewinternet.org).

Loewen, J. W. (1995). *Lies my teacher told me.* New York: Simon & Schuster.

Maital, S. (2005, May 26). Globalization is a two-way street: It's time we started taking ideas from China and India. Global Newswire.

Mantsios, G. (2001). Class in America: Myths and realities. In P. S. Rothenberg (Ed.), *Race, class, and gender in the United States: An integrated study* (5th ed., pp. 168–182). New York: Worth.

Martin, J. N., & Butler, R. L. W. (2001). Toward an ethic of intercultural communication research. In V. H. Milhouse, M. K. Asante, & P. O. Nwosu (Eds.), *Transcultural realities: Interdisciplinary perspectives on cross-cultural relations* (pp. 283–298). Thousand Oaks, CA: Sage.

McLuhan, M. (1967). *The medium is the message.* New York: Bantam Books.

Muzrui, A. (2001). Historical struggles between Islamic and Christian worldviews: An interpretation. In V. H. Milhouse, M. K. Asante, & P. O. Nwosu (Eds.), *Transcultural realities: Interdisciplinary perspectives* on cross-cultural relations (pp. 109–120). Thousand Oaks, CA: Sage.

Now a nation of more immigrants than ever. (2002, February 7). *Christian Science Monitor*, p. 1.

Paige, R. M., & Martin, J. N. (1996). Ethics in intercultural training. In D. Landis & R. Bhagat (Eds.), *Handbook of intercultural training* (pp. 35–60). Newbury Park, CA: Sage.

Pew Internet and American Life Project. (May–June 2005). Tracking. http://www.pewinternet.org/trends/User_Demo_08.09.05.htm

Progue, D. (2004, August 19). RUOK? A tutorial for parents. *New York Times*, p. E1.

Roediger, D. (1991). *The wages of whiteness: Race and the making of the American working class*. New York: Verso.

Rojas, V., Straubhaar, J., Roychowdhury, D., & Okur, O. (2004). Communities, cultural capital, and the digital divide. In E. P. Bucy & J. E. Newhagen (Eds.), *Media access: Social and psychological dimensions of new technology use* (pp. 107–130). Mahwah, NJ: Lawrence Erlbaum.

Samuelson, P. J. (2005). Think locally, act globally [Editorial and opinion]. *New York Sun*, p. 9.

Scanlon, J. (2003, August). 7 ways to squelch the Net. *Wired*, p. 31.

Scheer, R. (2005, September 6). The real costs of a culture of greed. *Los Angeles Times*, p. B11.

Schmitt, E. (2001, April 3). Analysis of census finds segregation along with diversity www.nytimes. com /2001/04/04/national/04CENS. html? ex=987410510&ei=1&en=a 2cf77e31f7952.

Scommegna, P. (2003). U. S. growing bigger, older and more diverse. Population Reference Bureau Web site. http://www.prb.org/Template. cfm? Section=PRB&template=/Content-Management/ ContentDisplay. cfm&ContentID=10201

Shepard, B. (2005, April 7). International numbers grow. *Chattanooga Times Free Press*, p. D6.

Snyder, B. (2003, May). Teams that span time zones face new work rules. Stanford Graduate School of Business Web site: http://www. gsb.stanford.edu/ news/bmag/ sbsm0305/feature_virtual_teams. shtml

Takaki, R. (1989). *Strangers from a different shore*. New York: Penguin Books.

Ten great global marketing mistakes. (1998, January 19). *Sarasota Herald-Tribune*.

Turkle, S. (1995). *Life on the screen: Identity in the age of the Internet*. New York: Simon & Schuster.

van Dijk, J. (2004). Divides in succession: Possession, skills, and use of new media for societal participation. In E. P. Bucy & J. E. Newhagen (Eds.), *Media access: Social and psychological dimensions of new technology use* (pp. 233–254). Mahwah, NJ: Lawrence Erlbaum.

West, C. (1993). *Race matters*. Boston: Beacon Press.

Wheeler, D. (2001). New technologies, old culture: A look at women, gender and the Internet in Kuwait. In C. Ess (Ed.), *Culture, technology, communication: Towards an intercultural global village* (pp. 187–212). Albany: State University of New York Press.

THE HISTORY OF THE STUDY OF INTERCULTURAL COMMUNICATION

CHAPTER OBJECTIVES

After reading this chapter, you should be able to:

1. Identify four early foci in the development of intercultural communication.

2. Describe three approaches to the study of intercultural communication.

3. Identify the methods used within each of the three approaches.

4. Explain the strengths and weaknesses of each approach.

5. Identify three characteristics of the dialectical approach.

6. Explain the strengths of a dialectical approach.

7. Identify six intercultural communication dialectics.

Now that we've described a rationale for studying intercultural communication, we turn to ways in which the study of intercultural communication is conducted. To understand the contemporary approaches to this discipline, it's important to examine its historical and philosophical foundations. Why should you study how the field of intercultural communication got started? Before answering this question, let us pose a few others: Whom do you think should be regarded as an expert in intercultural communication? Someone who has actually lived in a variety of cultures? Or someone who has conducted scientific studies on how cultural groups differ in values and attitudes? Or someone who analyzes what popular culture (movies, television, magazines, and so on) has to say about a particular group of people?

Consider a related question: What is the best way to study intercultural communication behavior? By observing how people communicate in various cultures? By asking people to describe their own communication patterns? By distributing questionnaires to various cultural groups? Or by analyzing books, videos, movies, and other cultural performances of various groups?

The answers to these questions help determine what kind of material goes into a textbook on intercultural communication. And intercultural communication scholars do not agree on what are the "right" answers to these questions. Thus, these questions and answers have implications for what you will be exposed to in this book and this course. By choosing some types of research (questionnaire, observation data), we may neglect other types (interviews, travel journal, media analysis).

To help you understand why we chose to include the material we did, we describe the origins of the discipline in the United States and the philosophical worldviews that inform the current study and practices of intercultural communication. We then outline three contemporary perspectives that recognize contributions from other disciplines. Finally, we outline our dialectical approach, which integrates the strengths from all three contemporary perspectives.

THE EARLY DEVELOPMENT OF THE DISCIPLINE

The current study of intercultural communication is influenced in part by how it developed in the United States and in part by the **worldviews**, or researchphilosophies, of the scholars who pursue it. The roots of the study of intercultural communication can be traced to the

---

worldview Underlying assumptions about the nature of reality and human behavior.

post–World War II era, when the United States increasingly came to dominate the world stage. However, government and business personnel working overseas often found that they were ill equipped to work among people from different cultures. The language training they received, for example, did little to prepare them for the complex challenges of working abroad.

In response, the U.S. government in 1946 passed the Foreign Service Act and established the Foreign Service Institute (FSI). The FSI, in turn, hired Edward T. Hall and other prominent anthropologists and linguists (including Ray Birdwhistell and George Trager) to develop "predeparture" courses for overseas workers. Because intercultural training materials were scarce, they developed their own. In so doing, FSI theorists formed new ways of looking at culture and communication. Thus, the field of intercultural communication was born.

Nonverbal Communication

The FSI emphasized the importance of nonverbal communication and applied linguistic frameworks to investigate nonverbal aspects of communication. These researchers concluded that, just like language, nonverbal communication varies from culture to culture. E. T. Hall pioneered this systematic study of culture and communication with *The Silent Language* (1959) and *The Hidden Dimension* (1966), which influenced the new discipline. In *The Silent Language*, for example, Hall introduced the notion of **proxemics**, the study of how people use personal space to communicate. In *The Hidden Dimension*, in elaborating on the concept of proxemics, he identified four **distance zones**— intimate, personal, social, and public—at which people interact and suggested that people know which distance to use depending on the situation. He noted that each cultural group has its own set of rules for personal space and that respecting these cultural differences is critical to smooth communication.

Application of Theory

The staff at the FSI found that government workers were not interested in theories of culture and communication; rather, they wanted specific guidelines for getting along in the countries they were visiting. Hall's initial strategy in developing materials for these predeparture

---

proxemics The study of how people use personal space.
distance zones The area, defined by physical space, within which people interact, according to Edward Hall's theory of proxemics. The four distance zones for individuals are intimate, personal, social, and public. (See also **proxemics**.)

training sessions was to observe variations in cultural behavior. At the FSI, he was surrounded by people who spoke many languages and who were from many cultures, so it was a great place to observe and test his theories about cultural differences. For example, he might have observed that Italians tend to stand close to each other when conversing, or that Greeks use lots of hand gestures when interacting, or that Chinese use few hand gestures in conversations. He could then have confirmed his observations by consulting members of different cultural groups. Today, most textbooks in the discipline retain this focus on practical guidelines and barriers to communication.

This emphasis on the application of theory spawned a parallel "discipline" of **cross-cultural training**, which began with the FSI staff and was expanded in the 1960s to include training for students and business personnel. More recently, it has come to include **diversity training**, which facilitates intercultural communication among members of various gender, ethnic, and racial groups, mostly in the corporate or government workplace (Landis & Bhagat, 1996).

An Emphasis on International Settings

Early scholars and trainers in intercultural communication defined *culture* narrowly, primarily in terms of "nationality." Usually, scholars mistakenly compared middle-class U.S. citizens with all residents of other nations, and trainers tended to focus on helping middle-class professionals become successful overseas.

One might ask why so few scholars focused on domestic contexts, particularly in the 1960s and 1970s when the United States was fraught with civil unrest. One reason may be the early emphasis of the FSI on helping overseas personnel. Another reason may be that most scholars who studied intercultural communication gained their intercultural experience in international contexts such as the Peace Corps, the military, or the transnational corporation.

An Interdisciplinary Focus

The scholars at the FSI came from various disciplines, including linguistics, anthropology, and psychology. Not surprisingly, in their work related to communication, they drew from theories pertinent to their

---

cross-cultural training Training people to become familiar with other cultural norms and to improve their interactions with people of different domestic and international cultures.
diversity training The training meant to facilitate intercultural communication among various gender, ethnic, and racial groups in the United States.

specific disciplines. Contributions from these fields of study blended to form an integrated approach that remains useful to this day.

Linguists help us understand the importance of language and its role in intercultural interaction. They describe how languages vary in "surface" structure and are similar in "deep" structure. They also shed light on the relationship between language and reality. For example, the **Sapir-Whorf hypothesis**, developed by linguists Edward Sapir and Benjamin Whorf, explores phenomena such as the use of formal and informal pronouns. French and Spanish, for instance, have both formal and informal forms of the pronoun *you*. (In French, the formal is *vous* and the informal is *tu*; in Spanish, the formal is *usted* and the informal is *tu*.) In contrast, English makes no distinction between formal and informal usage; one word, *you*, suffices in both situations. Such language distinctions affect our culture's notion of formality. In Chapter 6, we'll look at some more recent studies that problematize this hypothesis. Linguists also point out that learning a second or third language can enhance our **intercultural competence** by providing insights into other cultures and expanding our communication repertoire.

Anthropologists help us understand the role that culture plays in our lives and the importance of nonverbal communication. Anthropologist Renate Rosaldo (1989) encouraged scholars to consider the appropriateness of cultural study methods, and other anthropologists have followed Rosaldo's lead. They point out that many U.S. and European studies reveal more about the researchers than about their subjects. Further, many anthropological studies of the past, particularly of non-Europeans, concluded that the people studied were inferior. To understand this phenomenon, science writer Stephen Jay Gould (1993) argues that "we must first recognize the cultural milieu of a society whose leaders and intellectuals did not doubt the propriety of racial thinking, with Indians below whites, and blacks below everyone else" (p. 85).

The so-called scientific study of other peoples is never entirely separate from the culture in which the researchers are immersed. In his study of the Victorian era, for example, Patrick Brantlinger (1986) notes that "evolutionary anthropology often suggested that Africans, if not nonhuman or a different species, were such an inferior 'breed' that they might be impervious to 'higher influences'" (p. 201). Consider this famous case, which dates back to the early 19th century:

Sapir-Whorf hypothesis The assumption that language shapes our ideas and guides our view of social reality. This hypothesis was proposed by Edward Sapir, a linguist, and his student, Benjamin Whorf, and represents the relativist view of language and perception.
intercultural competence The ability to behave effectively and appropriately in interacting across cultures.

The young African woman was lured to Europe with false promises of fame and fortune. She was paraded naked before jeering mobs. She was exhibited in a metal cage and sold to an animal trainer. When she died in Paris in 1816, she was penniless and friendless among people who derided her as a circus freak.

White scientists intent on proving the inferiority of blacks dissected her body, bottled her brain and genitals, wired her skeleton and displayed them in a French museum. That might have been the end of Saartjie Baartman, the young African woman derisively labeled the "Hottentot Venus."

[However,] 192 years after she last looked on these rugged cliffs and roaring sea [of South Africa], her remains returned to the land of her birth. In an agreement negotiated after years of wrangling between South Africa and France, her remains were finally removed from the Musée de l'Homme in Paris and flown back home. (Swarns, 2002, p. A28)

This return of Baartman's remains is part of a larger movement away from a scientific "era when indigenous people were deemed worthy of scientific study, but unworthy of the consideration commonly accorded to whites" (Swarns, 2002, p. A28). Indeed, the conclusions from such studies reveal more about the cultural attitudes of the researchers (e.g., ethnocentrism, racism, sexism) than they do about the people studied. An **interdisciplinary** focus can help us acquire and interpret information in a more comprehensive manner—in ways relevant to bettering the intercultural communication process, as well as producing knowledge.

Psychologists such as Gordon Allport help us understand notions of stereotyping and the ways in which prejudice functions in our lives and in intercultural interaction. In his classic study *The Nature of Prejudice* (1979), he describes how prejudice can develop from "normal" human cognitive activities such as categorization and generalization. Other psychologists, such as Richard Brislin (1999) and Dan Landis (Landis & Wasilewski, 1999), reveal how variables like nationality, ethnicity, personality, and gender influence our communication.

Whereas the early study of intercultural communication was characterized as interdisciplinary, over time, it became increasingly centered in the discipline of communication. Nevertheless, the field continues to be influenced by interdisciplinary contributions, including ideas from cultural studies, critical theory, and the more traditional disciplines of psychology and anthropology (Hart, 1999).

interdisciplinary Integrating knowledge from different disciplines in conducting research and constructing theory.

PERCEPTION AND WORLDVIEW OF THE RESEARCHER

A second influence on the current study of intercultural communication is the research **paradigm**, or worldview, of the scholars involved. People understand and learn about the world through filtering lenses; they select, evaluate, and organize information (stimuli) from the external environment through **perception**. As Marshal Singer (1987) explains:

> *We experience everything in the world not "as it is"—because there is no way that we can know the world "as it is"—but only as the world comes to us through our sensory receptors. From there, these stimuli go instantly into the "data-storage banks" of our brains, where they have to pass through the filters of our censor screen, our decoding mechanism, and the collectivity of everything we have learned from the day we were born.* (p. 9)

In this sense, all of the information we have already stored in our brains (learning) affects how we interpret new information. Some of our learning and perception is group related. That is, we see the world in particular ways because of the cultural groups (based on ethnicity, age, gender, and so on) to which we belong. These group-related perceptions (worldviews or value orientations) are so fundamental that we rarely question them (Singer, 1998). They involve our assumptions about human nature, the physical and spiritual world, and the ways in which humans should relate to one another. For example, most U.S. Americans perceive human beings as separate from nature and believe that there is a fundamental difference between, say, a human and a rock. However, other cultural groups (Japanese, Chinese, traditional Native Americans) see humans and human reality as part of a larger physical reality. For them, the difference between a human and a rock is not so pronounced.

The key point here is that academic research is also cultural behavior because research traditions require particular worldviews about the nature of reality and knowledge and particular beliefs about how research should be conducted. And these research paradigms are often held as strongly as cultural or spiritual beliefs (Burrell & Morgan, 1988; Kuhn, 1970). There are even examples of intercultural conflicts

---

paradigm A framework that serves as the worldview of researchers. Different paradigms assume different interpretations of reality, human behavior, culture, and communication.
perception The process by which individuals select, organize, and interpret external and internal stimuli to create their view of the world.

in which scholars strongly disagree. For example, Galileo was excommunicated from the Catholic Church in the 17th century because he took issue with theologians' belief that the earth was the center of the universe.

More recent examples of the relation between academic research and cultural behavior can be seen in the social sciences. Some communication scholars believe there is an external reality that can be measured and studied, whereas others believe that reality can be understood only as lived and experienced by individuals (Casmir, 1994). In short, beliefs and assumptions about reality influence research methods and findings, and so also influence what we currently know about intercultural communication.

At present, we can identify three broad approaches, or worldviews, that characterize the study of culture and communication (Gudykunst, 2002a, 2002b; Gudykunst & Nishida, 1989; Hall, 1992). All three approaches involve a blend of disciplines and reflect different worldviews and assumptions about reality, human behavior, and ways to study culture and communication.

THREE APPROACHES TO STUDYING
INTERCULTURAL COMMUNICATION

Three contemporary approaches to studying intercultural communication are (1) the social science (or functionalist) approach, (2) the interpretive approach, and (3) the critical approach. (See Table 2.1.) These approaches are based on different fundamental assumptions about human nature, human behavior, and the nature of knowledge (Burrell & Morgan, 1988). Each one contributes in a unique way to our understanding of the relationship between culture and communication, but each also has limitations. These approaches vary in their assumptions about human behavior, their research goals, their conceptualization of culture and communication, and their preferred methodologies.

To examine these three approaches, let us start with a situation that illustrates a communication dilemma. You may remember when you first heard about Hurricane Katrina. Perhaps it was when it was in the Atlantic, maybe when it hit Florida, maybe when it strengthened over the Gulf of Mexico or when it hit Louisiana, Mississippi, and Alabama. A second hurricane, Rita, shortly followed, bringing more devastation to the Gulf Coast. Four years after September 11, 2001, the *Los Angeles Times* noted,

If 9/11 showed how much the world had changed, then 8/29 showed how much it hadn't. Four years ago, when terrorists crashed jets into the World Trade Center and the Pentagon, history was cleaved in half—the era before 9/11 and after. Will 8/29, the day Hurricane Katrina made landfall along the Gulf Coast, prove to be a similar demarcation line? The answer is complicated by the slow realization, with each anniversary, that 9/11 did not change the world (or America) as much as we thought. The response to Katrina, from both the government and the public, is the best illustration. ("9/11 and 8/29," 2005)

TABLE 2.1 THREE APPROACHES TO INTERCULTURAL COMMUNICATION

	Social science (or functionalist)	Interpretive	Critical
Discipline on which approach is founded	Psychology	Anthropology, sociolinguistics	Various
Research goal	Describe and predict behavior	Describe behavior	Change behavior
Assumption of reality	External and describable	Subjective	Subjective and material
Assumptions of human behavior	Predictable	Creative and voluntary	Changeable
Method of study	Survey, observation	Participant observation, field study	Textual analsis of media
Relationship of culture and communication	Communication influenced by culture	Culture created and maintained through communication	Culture a site of power struggles
Contribution of the approach	Identifies cultural variations; recognizes cultural differences in many aspects of communication but often does not consider context	Emphasizes that communication and culture and cultural differences should be studied in context	Recognizes the economic and political forces in culture and communication; asserts that all intercultural interactions are characterized by power

The federal, state, and local government response to the needs of those affected by the hurricanes was highlighted by communication about these events on television, the Internet, and blogs. Communication played a key role in shaping our understanding of these events. Howard Kurtz of the *Washington Post* noted, "Journalism seems to have recovered its reason for being. As in the weeks after 9/11, news organizations have plunged into the calamity in New Orleans, with reporters chronicling heartbreaking stories under harrowing conditions in a submerged city" (2005, p. C1). Similarly, the British Broadcasting Corporation reported that "good reporting lies at the heart of what is changing. But unlike Watergate, 'Katrinagate' was public service journalism ruthlessly exposing the truth on a live and continuous basis. [. . .] Amidst the horror, American broadcast journalism just might have grown its spine back, thanks to Katrina" (Wells, 2005). The kind of journalism that emerged in the wake of Katrina recentered the importance of communication in our national discussions, along with "bloggers who have organized aid drives for Katrina's victims" (Kurtz, 2005, p. C1). Many people watched television news; read magazines and newspapers, as well as Internet blogs and e-mails; listened to the radio; and talked with family and friends to get a better understanding of what was going on. We read e-mails from colleagues at universities in the New Orleans area and read their reports. Many of those in New Orleans turned to WWL-AM as it turned to serving New Orleans with reports of lost people, trapped people who called into the radio station, and generally people who "needed to communicate with one another: to seek or offer help, to criticize this agency or praise that one, to vent, cry, reassure or just find comfort in the soothing radio voice of someone who has shared their loss" (Barry, 2005).

The events surrounding the hurricanes are another example of intercultural communication interaction that offers useful insights into how we might think about intercultural communication and the ways that different cultural groups understood what happened and why. In analyzing Hurricane Katrina, we will also outline the characteristics of the three approaches to studying intercultural communication—both contributions and limitations.

The Social Science Approach

The **social science approach** (also called the **functionalist approach**), popular in the 1980s, is based on research in psychology and sociology. This approach assumes a describable external reality. It also assumes that human behavior is predictable and that the researcher's goal is to describe and predict behavior. Researchers who take this ap-

---

social science approach See **functionalist approach**.
functionalist approach A study of intercultural communication, also called the *social science approach*, based on the assumptions that (1) there is a describable, external reality, (2) human behaviors are predictable, and (3) culture is a variable that can be measured. This approach aims to identify and explain cultural variations in communication and to predict future communication. (Compare with **critical approach** and **interpretive approach**.)

proach often use **quantitative methods**, gathering data by administering questionnaires or observing subjects firsthand.

Social science researchers assume that culture is a **variable** that can be measured. This suggests that culture influences communication in much the same way that personality traits do. The goal of this research, then, is to predict specifically how culture influences communication.

Applications   Other social scientists might investigate some of the perceived reasons for the response of local, state, and federal officials to the hurricane and then try to frame appropriate action based on these findings. For instance, they might measure differences in perception among various cultural groups to try to understand how different cultures experienced Katrina and what they view as appropriate and inappropriate responses by the government. In this type of study, social scientists would be using culture as a variable to measure these differences while focusing on the perceptions that are widely held in a particular culture. To understand the aftermath of Hurricane Katrina, social scientists might try to measure how African Americans and whites viewed the government response. One study done on September 6–7, 2005, about a week after the hurricane, found that 70% of African Americans felt angry, whereas only 46% of whites felt angry (Kohut et al., 2005). In this same study, 66% of African Americans felt the government response would have been faster if the victims had been white, whereas only 17% of whites shared this view. Based on these differences, social scientists might then try to predict how these different views may influence future differences in political views and conflicts between these groups.

Or social scientists might study what kinds of communication media people used after the hurricane and how they used them. In this same study, the researchers found that "Television, and cable news channels in particular, are the main sources of news for most Americans during a crisis, and that was again the case for Hurricane Katrina" (Kohut et al., 2005, p. 7). CNN was most cited as the main source of their news at 31%, whereas newspapers, radio, and the Internet all fell in the ratings compared to their use in more normal circumstances. Two thirds gave favorable ratings of the media coverage that "is considerably more favorable than the public's ratings a year ago for press coverage of the presidential election campaign" (p. 7). This kind of

quantitative methods Research methods that use numerical indicators to capture and ascertain the relationships among variables. These methods use survey and observation.
variable A concept that varies by existing in different types or different amounts and that can be operationalized and measured.

study tries to see trends in communication usage and can then predict that people will again turn to cable television, particularly CNN, for news when a similar crisis situation emerges.

Other contemporary research programs illustrate the social science approach. One such program was headed by William Gudykunst, a leading communication researcher. Gudykunst was interested in whether people from different cultures varied in their strategies for reducing uncertainty on first encounter. He found that strategies varied depending on whether people were from **individualistic** or **collectivistic** cultures (Gudykunst, 1985, 1988). For example, many people in the United States, which has an individualistic orientation, ask direct questions when interacting with acquaintances. In cultures with a more collectivistic orientation, such as Japan and China, people are more likely to use an indirect approach.

Gudykunst (1998, 2005) later extended this theory to include the element of anxiety and mindfulness in the **anxiety uncertainty management** (AUM) **theory**, which explains the role of anxiety and uncertainty in individuals' communicating with host culture members when they enter a new culture. The theory suggests certain optimal levels of uncertainty and anxiety motivate individuals to engage in successful interaction.

A related social science program is Stella Ting-Toomey's (1985, 2005) face negotiation theory. *Face is* the sense of favorable self-worth, and in all cultures people are concerned about saving face. Ting-Toomey suggests that conflict is a face negotiation process in which people often have their face threatened or questioned. She and her colleagues have conducted a number of studies in which they try to identify how cultures differ in conflict style and face concerns. For example, they found that members of individualistic societies like the United States are concerned with saving their own face in conflict situations and so use more dominating conflict resolution styles. In contrast, members of collectivistic cultures, like China, South Korea, and Japan, are more concerned with saving the other person's face in conflict situations and use more avoiding, obliging, or integrating conflict resolution style (collectivistic cultures use other-oriented face-saving strategies more than members (Ting-Toomey et al., 1991). More recent research shows that Latino and Asian Americans in the United

---

individualistic The tendency to emphasize individual identities, beliefs, needs, goals, and views rather than those of the group. (Compare with **collectivistic**.)

collectivistic The tendency to focus on the goals, needs, and views of the ingroup rather than individuals' own goals, needs, and views. (Compare with **individualistic**.)

anxiety uncertainty management theory The view that the reduction of anxiety and uncertainty plays an important role in successful intercultural communication, particularly when experiencing new cultures.

States use more avoiding and third-party conflict styles than African Americans and more than European Americans (Ting-Toomey, Yee-Jung, Shapiro, Garcia, Wright, & Oetzel, 2000).

Another social science research program focuses on cultural differences conversational strategies. The **conversational constraints theory**, developed by Min-Sun Kim (2005), attempts to explain how and why people make particular conversational choices. It suggests five universal conversational constraints, or concerns: (1) clarity, (2) minimizing imposition, (3) consideration for the other's feelings, (4) risking negative evaluation by the hearer, and (5) effectiveness.

Kim and her colleagues have discovered that people from individualistic and collectivistic cultures place varying importance on these various conversational concerns. Individualists seem to be most concerned with clarity; collectivists, with concerns about hurting the other's feelings and minimizing imposition. Concerns for effectiveness and avoidance of negative evaluation by others seem to be universally important (Kim, 1994, 2005).

The **communication accommodation theory** is the result of another social science program in which researchers attempted to identify how and when individuals accommodate their speech and nonverbal behavior to others during an interaction. The researchers posited that in some situations individuals change their communication patterns to accommodate others (Gallois, Giles, Jones, Cargile, & Ota, 1995). Specifically, individuals are likely to adapt during low-threat interactions or situations in which they see little difference between themselves and others. The underlying assumption is that we accommodate when we feel positive toward the other person. For example, when we talk to international students, we may speak more slowly, enunciate more clearly, use less jargon, and mirror their communication. We also may adapt to regional speech. For example, when Tom talks with someone from the South, he sometimes starts to drawl and use words like "y'all." Of course, it is possible to overaccommodate. For example, if a white American speaks black English to an African American, this may be perceived as overaccommodation.

Many social science studies explain how communication styles vary from culture to culture. Dean Barnlund (Barnlund & Yoshioka, 1990), a well-known intercultural communication scholar, compared Japanese and U.S. communication styles. He identified many differences, including how members of the two groups give compliments and offer

---

conversational constraints theory The view that cultural groups vary in their fundamental concerns regarding how conversational messages should be constructed.
communication accommodation theory The view that individuals adjust their verbal communication to facilitate understanding.

apologies. Although people in both countries seem to prefer a simple apology, U.S. Americans tend to apologize (and compliment) more often; further, Japanese prefer to *do* something, whereas Americans tend to *explain* as a way to apologize.

Another group of social science studies investigated how travelers adapted overseas. In trying to predict which travelers would be the most successful, the researchers found that a variety of factors—including age, gender, language, preparation level, and personality characteristics—played a role (Kim, 2001).

Strengths and Limitations   Many of these social science studies have been useful in identifying variations in communication from group to group and specifying psychological and sociological variables in the communication process. However, this approach is limited. Many scholars now realize that human communication is often more creative than predictable and that reality is not just external but also internally constructed. We cannot identify all of the variables that affect our communication. Nor can we predict exactly why one intercultural interaction seems to succeed and another does not.

Scholars also recognize that some methods in this approach are not culturally sensitive and that researchers may be too distant from the phenomena or people they are researching. In other words, researchers may not really understand the cultural groups they are studying. For example, suppose we conducted a study that compared self-disclosure in the United States and Algeria using the social science perspective. We might distribute Jourard's self-disclosure measure (a common instrument used in U.S. research) to students in both countries. However, we might not realize that the concept of self-disclosure does not translate exactly between the United States and Algeria, and that Algerians and U.S. Americans have different notions of this concept.

To overcome these kinds of problems, social scientists have developed strategies for achieving equivalence of measures. A leading cross-cultural psychologist, Richard Brislin (1999), has written extensively on guidelines for cross-cultural researchers. He has identified several types of equivalencies that researchers should establish, including **translation equivalence** and **conceptual equivalence**. For example, in cross-cultural studies, literal translations are inadequate. To establish

---

translation equivalence The linguistic sameness that is gained after translating and back-translating research materials several times using different translators. (See also **conceptual equivalence**.)
conceptual equivalence The similarity of linguistic terms and meanings across cultures. (See also **translation equivalence**.)

POINT OF VIEW

Especially in times of tragedy, people use humor to cope with overwhelming events. Communication of this kind helps to create bounds and coping strategies among people.

washingtonpost.com
HUMOR HELPS HURRICANE KATRINA VICTIMS COPE

By MATT SEDENSKY
The Associated Press
Saturday, October 22, 2005; 2:43 PM

ARABI, La. — The grimy residue of receded floodwater covered the blue Chevrolet pickup parked outside a shattered two-story house, but the offer spray-painted on the vehicle in white overflowed with enthusiams: "For Sale. Like New. Runs Great."

The tongue-in-cheek sale pitch in this New Orleans suburb is evidence that Hurricanes Katrina and Rita didn't necessarily destroy victims' sense of humor, which is surfacing in signs painted on wrecked homes and on bumper stickers and inevitable T-shirts.

It jumps out from an Arabi auto glass shop: "Katrina was bad. The old lady and the dogs were more trouble."

And from a refrigerator left on a French Quarter street: "Loot this!!!!"

The drink offerings at popular eatery Bacco's now include "Katrina Rita," "Cat 5 Hurricane," and "Curfew & Coke."

translation equivalence, research materials should be translated several times, using different translators. Materials that proceed smoothly through these multiple steps are considered translation equivalent.

Researchers can establish conceptual equivalence by ensuring that the notions they are investigating are similar at various levels. For example, problem solving is one aspect of intelligence that may be conceptually equivalent in many cultures. Once this equivalence is established, researchers can identify culture-specific ways in which problem solving is achieved. In the United States and western Europe, good problem solving might mean quick cognitive reasoning; in other cultures, it might involve slow and careful thought (Serpell, 1982).

Elsewhere, bumper stickers and T-shirts are available with the saying "Make levees not war."

Another T-shirt picks on a popular target: "Where is FEMA? Federal Employees Missing Again."

"It's been known for a long time one of the best coping mechanisms we have is humor," said Kathryn Kirkhart, a clinical psychologist who has been working with evacuees in New Orleans. "It's best used in situations where we have no control."

Some anonymous jokesters have chosen subtlety: "Garage Sale. Shoes. Games. Toys," says a sign posted along a driveway that leads to a foundation where only the barest traces of the garage are still attached.

A house that floated off its foundation came to rest at the side of 38-year-old Philip Troxclair's house. Another house is at the end of the driveway, decorated with the phrase "Wicked witch of the East was here."

"Thank you Katrina," deadpans a sign painted in blue on a hard-hit, one-level brick house.

Friday night in the French Quarter, a musician taking a break between songs at a restaurant blurted out: "We're all trying here in New Orleans to get back to abnormal."

Note: Associated Press Writers Ross Sneyd and John Christoffersen contributed to this report. © 2005 The Associated Press

Source: From http://www.washingtonpost.com/wpdyn/content/article/2005/10/22/AR2005102200690_pf.html.

Establishing these equivalencies allows researchers to isolate and describe what distinguishes one culture from another.

The Interpretive Approach

The **interpretive approach** gained prominence in the late 1980s among communication scholars. One interpretive approach, rooted

---

interpretive approach An approach to intercultural communication that aims to understand and describe human behavior within specific cultural groups based on the assumptions that (1) human experience is subjective, (2) human behavior is creative rather than determined or easily predicted, and (3) culture is created and maintained through communication. (Compare with **critical approach** and **functionalist approach**.)

in sociolinguistics, is the **ethnography** of communication (Hymes, 1974). Ethnographers of communication are devoted to descriptive studies of communication patterns within specific cultural groups. Interpretive researchers assume not only that reality is external to humans but also that humans construct reality. They believe that human experience, including communication, is subjective and human behavior is neither predetermined nor easily predicted.

The goal of interpretive research is to understand and describe human behavior. (Predicting behavior is not a goal.) Whereas the social scientist tends to see communication as influenced by culture, the interpretivist sees culture as created and maintained through communication (Carbaugh, 1996). This type of research uses **qualitative methods** derived from anthropology and linguistics such as field studies, observations, and participant observations. (A researcher engaging in **participant observation** contributes actively to the communication processes being observed and studied. The researcher thus is intimately involved in the research and may become good friends with members of the communities he or she is studying.)

Another example of interpretive research is the **rhetorical approach**, perhaps the oldest communication scholarship, dating back to the ancient Greeks. Rhetoricians typically examine and analyze texts or public speeches in the contexts in which they occur.

Cross-cultural psychologists use the terms **etic** and **emic** to distinguish the social science and interpretive approaches (Berry, 1997). These terms were borrowed from linguistics—*etic* from *phonetic* and *emic* from *phonemic*. Social science research usually searches for universal generalizations and studies cultures objectively, with an "outsider's" view; in this way, it is "etic." In contrast, interpretive research usually focuses on understanding phenomena subjectively, from within a particular cultural community or context; in this way, it is "emic."

---

ethnography A discipline that examines the patterned interactions and significant symbols of specific cultural groups to identify the cultural norms that guide their behaviors, usually based on field studies.

qualitative methods Research methods that attempt to capture people's own meanings for their everyday behavior in specific contexts. These methods use participant observation and field studies.

participant observation A research method where investigators interact extensively with the cultural group being studied.

rhetorical approach A research method, dating back to ancient Greece, in which scholars try to interpret the meanings or persuasion used in texts or oral discourses in the contexts in which they occur.

etic A term stemming from *phonetic*. The etic inquiry searches for universal generalizations across cultures from a distance. (Compare with **emic**.)

emic A term stemming from *phonemic*. The emic way of inquiry focuses on understanding communication patterns from inside a particular cultural community or context. (Compare with **etic**.)

These researchers try to describe patterns or rules that individuals follow in specific contexts. They tend to be more interested in describing cultural behavior in one community than in making cross-cultural comparisons.

Applications How might an interpretive researcher investigate the various meanings given to the hurricane events? One possible approach would be to interview people who were in the Gulf Coast and experienced the hurricane, as well as those people who watched the media coverage but did not live in the affected areas. From these interviews, as well as conversations with others, the researcher might gain insight into a variety of potential responses. For example, in the weeks after Katrina, many of the people from the Gulf Coast were evacuated across the nation. An interpretive researcher might interview them about their experiences and their adaptation to their new environment. One reporter noted, "'The people are so nice, but this place is really strange to me,' said Desiree Thompson, who arrived in Albuquerque last Sunday with six of her children and two grandchildren, along with about 100 other evacuees. 'The air is different. My nose feels all dry. The only thing I've seen that looks familiar is the McDonald's'" (Egan, 2005, pp. A1, A32). Many will have to decide if they wish to stay or move on, but the adaptation issues they face can be explored by an interpretive researcher to see how they make sense of their new environments, environmental differences as well as demographic differences.

Other interpretive researchers may want to focus on the rich oral culture of Louisiana and interview many who experienced Hurricane Katrina and/or Rita. One reporter after talking to survivors writes, "The disaster was incremental rather than cataclysmic. Instead of a crystalline moment of memory, there are infinite numbers, each with its own marker: a long journey, a recurring noise, the last words of a dear relative. Depending on where people were, what decisions they made in the blur of the crisis and how the authorities responded, every portrait of the storm is different, like a jigsaw puzzle in which no two pieces are alike" (Johnson, 2005, p. A25).

Some interpretive studies investigate the language patterns in many different groups—from the Burundi in Africa, to the Athabascan in northern Canada, to various groups within the United States, such as urban blacks or Cajuns. Other interpretive studies investigate the different communication patterns of one cultural group. For example, communication scholar Gerry Philipsen (1990) studied communication patterns in a white working-class neighborhood of Chicago called Teamsterville. Philipsen discovered that men in this community con-

POINT OF VIEW

Michael Brown, former director of the Federal Emergency Management Agency (FEMA), came under tremendous fire for the response
of his agency to the aftermath of Hurricane Katrina. Later, a series
of e-mails sent to Brown from his FEMA agent in New Orleans
and Brown's responses were posted on the Web site of Louisiana
representative Charles Melancon at http://www.melancon.house.
gov/SupportingFiles/documents/Brown_Emails.pdf.
These e-mails point to the importance of communication, especially e-mail and the Internet, in helping better understand how
communication shaped the federal response. Think about how a
social scientist, an interpretivist, and a critical scholar might study
these e-mails.
For example, on August 31, 2005, Marty Bahamonde, the
FEMA agent in New Orleans, wrote this e-mail:

From:	Brown, Michael D
Sent:	Wednesday, August 31, 2005 12:24 PM
To:	'Marty.Bahamonde@dhs.gov'
Subject:	Re: New orleans

Thanks for update. Anything specific I need to do or tweak?

-----Original Message-----
From: Bahamonde, Marty <Marty.Bahamonde@dhs.gov>
To: 'michael.d.brown@dhs.gov' <Michael.D.Brown@dhs.gov>
Sent: Wed Aug 31 12:20:20 2005
Subject: New orleans

Sir, I know that you know the situation is past critical. Here some things you might not
know.
Hotels are kicking people out, thousands gathering in the streets with no food or water.
Hundreds still being rescued from homes.

The dying patients at the DMAT tent being medivac. Estimates are many will die within
hours. Evacuation in process. Plans developing for dome evacuation but hotel situation
adding to problem. We are out of food and running out of water at the dome, plans in works
to address the critical need.

FEMA staff is OK and holding own. DMAT staff working in deplorable conditions. The sooner
we can get the medical patients out, the sooner wecan get them out.

Phone connectivity impossible

More later

Sent from my BlackBerry Wireless Handheld

sider speaking to be important only in some situations. For example,
Teamsterville men speak when expressing male solidarity but not
when asserting power and influence in interpersonal situations. That
is, they are more likely to talk when they are with their equals—their
buddies—than when they are with their children or with authority
figures. With superiors or subordinates, other forms of communication are appropriate. With children, for example, they are more likely

to use gestures or disciplinary action than speech. When they are with someone of higher status, such as a school principal, they may seek out a mediator (e.g., the neighborhood priest) rather than speak directly to the principal.

In more recent ethnography of communication studies, Donal Carbaugh (1999) describes the important role of silence and listening in Blackfeet (American Indian) communication; Carbaugh and Berry (2001) describe th   e tendency of Finns to be rather reserved in communication. More importantly, they show how these communication patterns are inextricably tied to cultural identities in these communities (Carbaugh, 1996).

A number of interpretive scholars have emphasized that descriptions of the communication rules of a given people must be grounded in their beliefs and values. Most scholarly studies of communication are rooted in a European American perspective, and this frame of references is not necessarily applicable to communication of all cultural groups. For example, Molefi Asante (1987, 2001) developed the framework of **Afrocentricity** to apply to studies about African or African American communication. He identifies five cultural themes shared by peoples of African descent:

- A common origin and experience of struggle
- An element of resistance to European legal procedures, medical practices, and political processes
- Traditional values of humaneness and harmony with nature
- A fundamentally African way of knowing and interpreting the world
- An orientation toward communalism

Communication scholars have used this framework to understand various aspects of contemporary African American communication. For example, Thurmon Garner (1994) stresses the strong oral tradition of African Americans and identifies rhetorical patterns such as indirection, improvisation and inventiveness, and playfully toned behavior. These patterns underlay communication in many African American contexts, including rapping, playing the dozens (an aggressive verbal contest, often involving obscene language), and signifying (the verbal art of insult, in which a speaker jokingly talks about, needles, and puts down the listener).

Similarly, Asian scholars have developed Asiacentric frameworks to study communication of people from Asian cultures. Communication

---

Afrocentricity An orientation toward African or African American cultural standards, including beliefs and values, as the criteria for interpreting behaviors and attitudes.

scholar Yoshitake Miike (2003, 2004) has identified five Asiacentric themes (circularity, harmony, other-directedness, reciprocity, and relationality). Based on these themes, he developed five propositions on human communication.

Communication is a process in which

- We remind ourselves of the interdependence and interrelatedness of the universe.

- We reduce our selfishness and egocentrism.

- We feel the joy and suffering of all beings.

- We receive and return our debts to all beings.

- We moralize and harmonize the universe.

From this Asiacentric framework, other scholars are developing specific communication theories, for example, a Chinese model of human relationship development (Chen, 1998) and a Buddhist consciousness-only model of intrapersonal communication (Ishii, 2004).

It is important to remember that scholars like Asante and Miike are not suggesting that these culture-specific frameworks are superior or should replace the traditional Eurocentric models, only that that they are not inferior.

Another important interpretive theory, a communication theory of identity, was developed by Michael Hecht (1993). He argues that communication is a communicative process and our identities emerge in relationships with others and are expressed in core symbols, meaning, and labels. He also contends there are four identity frames: personal, enacted, relational, and communal. These frames help us interpret reality and understand the social world. We discuss this theory further in Chapter 5.

Several scholars have used this framework to understand the identities of various cultural groups. For example, Mark Orbe (2004) conducted a recent study investigating how first-generation college students negotiated this identity—using the four frames in Hecht's identity theory. Through interviewing the students, he discovered that their identities as first-generation college students clearly emerged as personal (in the pressure to succeed and in the economic hardships they experienced), enacted, and relational (in their experiences with friends and families who often give them special attention). However, they did not seem to develop a communal identity—they did not really know or interact with other groups of first-generation college students.

In a related study, Saskia Witteborn (2004) used this theory to understand how some Arab women changed the expression of their identity after 9/11. Through extensive interviews, she found that before September 11, the women referred to themselves mainly with their communal identities as Arab, Palestinian, or Arab American. And one of the core symbols related to this communal label was family. After September 11, the women emphasized their national identities, and the core symbol of family was expanded to include social relationships in a community organization.

Strengths and Limitations   The utility of the interpretivist approach is that it provides an in-depth understanding of communication patterns in particular communities because it emphasizes investigating communication in context. Thus, for example, we learn more about African American communication in religious contexts and more about popular U.S. communication in talk show contexts than we would by distributing questionnaires with general questions on African American or European American communication.

The main limitation of this approach is that there are few interpretivist studies of *intercultural* communication. Interpretive scholars typically have not studied what happens when two groups come in contact with each other. However, there are some comparative studies, including Charles Braithwaite's (1990), which compares rules for silence in 15 different communities, and Hammer and Rogan's (2002) study comparing how Latino and Indochinese view and negotiate conflict with law enforcement officers.

A second limitation is that the researchers often are outsiders to the communities under investigation, which means they may not represent accurately the communication patterns of members of that community. For example, Fred Jandt and Dolores Tanno (2001) recount the dilemma of many marginalized cultural groups who have been studied by outsiders who characterize the group rather erroneously and negatively. A number of scholars, members of these groups, are now trying to rewrite these cultural descriptions. One of these is Tuhiwai Smith (1999), a Maori scholar, who lists the words used to describe her people in anthropological accounts: not civilized, not literate, incapable of inventing, creating, or imagining, and not fully human. After analyzing the impact of these negative labels, she makes arguments for insider research and develops an indigenous research agenda and process—part of a movement by peoples throughout the world who have too long been explained by outsiders and have been offered no opportunity to explain themselves. One of her contributions is a Maori-based code of conduct for ethnographic researchers:

- A respect for people
- Presenting yourself face-to-face
- Look, listen . . . speak
- Share and host people, be generous
- Do not flaunt your knowledge

Jandt and Tanno conclude that this ethical code should apply to all those who study groups of people who traditionally have been the object of study rather than participants in research.

The Critical Approach

A third approach to the study of intercultural communication includes many assumptions of the interpretive approach. For instance, researchers who use the **critical approach** believe in subjective (as opposed to objective) and material reality. They also emphasize the importance of studying the context in which communication occurs—that is, the situation, background, or environment. However, critical researchers usually focus on **macrocontexts**, such as the political and social structures that influence communication. Critical scholars, unlike most social scientists and interpretivists, are interested in the historical context of communication (Delgado, 2002; Putnam & Pacanowsky, 1983).

Critical scholars are interested in the power relations in communication. For them, identifying cultural differences in communication is important only in relation to power differentials. In this perspective, culture is, in essence, a battleground—a plan where multiple interpretations come together but a dominant force always prevails. The goal of critical researchers is not only to understand human behavior but also to change the lives of everyday communicators. Researchers assume that, by examining and reporting how power functions in cultural situations, they can help the average person learn how to resist forces of power and oppression.

The methods preferred by critical scholars are usually **textual analyses**, which sometimes occur within the economic contexts of the culture industries that produce these texts. That is, the scholars generally analyze cultural "products," such as media (television, movies,

---

critical approach A metatheoretical approach that includes many assumptions of the interpretive approach but that focuses more on macrocontexts, such as the political and social structures that influence communication. (Compare with **interpretive approach** and **functionalist approach**.)

macrocontexts The political, social, and historical situations, backgrounds, and environments that influence communication.

textual analysis Examination of cultural texts such as media—television, movies, journalistic essays, and so on.

journals, and so on), as powerful voices in shaping contemporary culture, rather than observing or participating in face-to-face interactions or conducting surveys.

Applications In analyzing the aftermath of the hurricanes that swept the Gulf Coast, a critical scholar might try to situate the attacks within a larger cultural struggle that has much longer history than simply the hurricanes that roared through the Gulf. *Newsweek* noted that Katrina put the image of the United States on the world stage again: "It takes a hurricane, it takes a catastrophe like Katrina to strip away the old evasions, hypocrisies and not-so-benign neglect. It takes the sight of the United States with a big black eye—visible around the world—to help the rest of us begin to see again [see Figure 2.3]. For the moment, at least, Americans are ready to fix their restless gaze on enduring problems of poverty, race and class that have escaped their attention" (Alter, 2005, p. 42).

Communication scholar Marita Sturken (2005) looked at the Department of Homeland Security (DHS) public service ad campaign and concludes,

> *Government campaigns that sell the idea of individual preparedness operate to reassure citizens that the government is doing everything it can to keep the country safe. Thus, the emphasis in the DHS campaigns on how individuals should respond to a crisis elides the fact that individuals and families can do little to affect the most important security decisions of the country. [. . .] The disaster of Katrina has dramatically exposed the way that resources have been drained away from the "homeland" by the war in Iraq. The homeland, we learned from Katrina, is primarily at risk not from the weather or from foreign terrorists, but from its own failed infrastructure and its callous disregard for the rights of all citizens to the most basic of human needs.*

Thrust on to the world stage, the international image of the United States was up for discussion. The British Broadcasting Corporation wondered why, in this time of need, did the food donations from Britain, France, Germany, Russia, and Spain get turned down because of U.S. legalities ("Why Was UK's Katrina Aid Rejected by the US?," 2005). One French magazine, *L'Express,* played off the Steinbeck novel *The Grapes of Wrath* and pointed to the "grapes of poverty" and underscored the tremendous poverty and neglect in New Orleans before the hurricanes (Coste, 2005). Similarly, the French newspaper *Le Monde* reported on "The Third World in Louisiana," noting that "After Katrina, America interrogates the weaknesses of its model"

(Dhombres, 2005). Another commentator for *Le Monde* asks, "Four years after the attacks of September 11, 2001 which disrupted American foreign policy, has Hurricane Katrina also had such a profound effect, but in the opposite sense?" (Vernet, 2005).

At the same time, however, the *New York Times* offered a different view from Paris: "The French news media were captivated by Hurricane Katrina, pointing out how the American government's faltering response brought into plain view the sad lot of black Americans. But this time the French, who have long criticized America's racism, could not overlook the parallels at home" (Tagliabue, 2005, p. A4). In light of the riots that broke out in the fall of 2005, a *New York Times* writer noted: "Just two months ago, the French watched in horrified fascination at the anarchy of New Orleans, where members of America's underclass were seen looting stores and defying the police in the wake of Hurricane Katrina. Last week, as rioters torched cards and trashed businesses in the immigrant-concentrated suburbs of Paris, the images of wild gangs of young men silhouetted against the yellow flames of burning cars came as an unwelcome reminder for France that it has its own growing underclass" (C. S. Smith, 2005, sec. 4, p. 3). Thus, the struggle over the image of each nation is, in part, fought out in the press.

A critical scholar might also look at the struggle over the maintenance of Creole culture that has lost its geographical base: "The Creoles have been more distinctly connected to a place—New Orleans—than perhaps any other American ethnic group but their rural Louisiana neighbors, the Cajuns. But unlike the Cajuns, who settled in Louisiana after being expelled from Canada by the British, the Creoles lived in the birthplace of their culture" (Saulny, 2005). Some people fear the loss of this cultural identity after the hurricane dispersed them across the nation. Others predict that this dispersal will make them stronger. By watching how they rebuild their cultural community, what communication media they use, and what resources and barriers they encounter, a critical scholar can situate the rebirth of this cultural community within the larger social structure of the United States. A critical scholar might ask if the pressure from other U.S. Americans and institutions to assimilate will overwhelm their attempts to hang on to their unique culture.

Similarly, a critical scholar might focus on how different cultural groups are responding to Hurricanes Katrina and Rita by looking at the ways that different media are covering Katrina. The anger in the African American news is very clear in the editorial pages. For example, *Amsterdam News*, an African American newspaper in New York City, wrote, "We will be told again that this has noth-ing to do with race or economic circumstance, but by an accident of history. Black Americans, white Americans who have a vision about what America is to become, should not allow this big lie to sit there like a 'Raisin in the Sun.' Black people know that there is little regard for them and for their lives here in America" (Tatum, 2005). Another African American newspaper, the *Chicago Defender*, in a guest editorial, noted, "Bush's poll free-fall or dip is chalked up to his comatose response to Katrina disaster relief, the horrific scenes of poor Blacks fleeing for their lives in New Orleans, and his walk on eggshell reaction to William Bennett' s foot-in-the mouth racial slur. Whether Bush actually skidded to rock bottom, or simply skidded in the ratings, it mattered little" (Hutchinson, 2005).

Asian Week, an Asian American newspaper, focused on the "tens of thousands [of Vietnamese Americans who] lived along the Louisiana and Mississippi coasts. Most of them worked in shrimping, shipbuilding and operating convenience stores" (Tang, 2005). This newspaper focused on the stories of these Asian Americans: "Kim Vu was a member of the Queen Mary of Vietnam church in Versailles, Louisiana. About 300 members of the church were stranded in the church for days in neck-deep floodwater. For days, rescue helicopters flew missions around New Orleans, but did not rescue the church-full of Vietnamese Americans" (Tang, 2005), which may not have been covered by the mainstream media. Yet the newspaper notes their plans to rebuild: "Their community is now scattered across the American South due to Hurricane Katrina. Those who have returned are laying a foundation for the rest to rejoin them. The church and the nonprofit Vietnamese American Community in Louisiana are calling on community members to join work crews to rehabilitate and reconstruct homes and businesses" (Joe, 2005).

Likewise, *The Advocate*, a gay and lesbian newsmagazine, noted, "Thousands of other gay men and lesbians say they owe it to the city to return. It's not an easy choice. Many New Orleans residents, especially those in lower income brackets, will likely never come back. [...] For more than a century this has been their town. Since the early 1800s New Orleans welcomes those with same-sex attractions into a sea of fabulous architecture, boozy decadent affairs, outrageous parades, fabulous costumes, and gender-bending" (Hernandez, 2005, p. 43). The emphasis on returning and rebuilding is emphasized in this report because of the importance of New Orleans' gay history, its community, and the commitment of the people.

Taken together, these various viewpoints emphasize how different cultural groups are dealing with Hurricane Katrina, what different experiences they had, and how they look to the future. A critical perspective would emphasize the economic, political, and cultural differences between these groups, in understanding what happens to these cultural groups in the rebuilding phase and how they do or do not recover.

An important recent critical perspective is **postcolonialism**, an intellectual, political, and cultural movement that calls for the independence of colonized states and liberation from colonialist *mentalité* or ways of thinking. The legacy of this cultural invasion often lasts much longer than the political relationship. "It theorizes not just colonial conditions but why those conditions are what they are, and how they can be undone and redone" (Shome & Hegde, 2002, p. 250).

Postcolonialism is not simply the study of colonialism but the study of how we might deal with that past and its aftermath, which may include the ongoing use of the colonial language, culture, and religion. For example, a study by Marwan Kraidy (2005) explores how youth in Lebanon negotiate their postcolonial identity though their media consumption. Lebanon was colonized at various times by Arabs, Ottomans, and the French, and partly because of this colonial past, Lebanese have access to a wide range of television channels (all Arab satellite channels, some Indian, and the major U.S. and European cable and satellite channels). Kraidy shows how the young people pick and choose specific shows to watch, and then he analyzes how they interpret those shows. He concludes that, because of their colonialist legacy, they gravitate toward Western shows in addition to the Arabic shows, and this media consumption ultimately contributes to their having a **hybrid identity**—an identity comprised of both Western and Arabic elements.

Another example of critical scholarship is Fabienne Darling-Wolf's (2004) study of Westernized images of feminine beauty and how Japanese women in one small community are influenced by them. She interviewed 29 women at least twice, and 6 of these became key informants. Through interviews with these women, Darling-Wolf examined their negotiation of beauty in the context of Western media images. She found that the young women tended "to condemn the high incidence of white model and Western celebrities in the Japanese media and express a preference for Japanese models" (p. 339).

Darling-Wolf emphasizes that these women "negotiated global and local influences on a daily basis as they engaged in the media-saturated life of their small community" (2004, p. 340). But this negotiation is complex because of "Japan's relationship to the rest of the world—

---

postcolonialism An intellectual, political, and cultural movement that calls for the independence of colonialized states and also liberation from colonialist ways of thinking.
hybrid identity An identity that is consciously a mixture of different cultural identities and cultural traditions.

POINT OF VIEW

Alive in Truth is a group of New Orleans residents who got together to collect oral histories of those who survived Hurricane Katrina. Go to their Web page and read some of these oral histories. Think about how this might help you better understand their experiences from an interpretivist perspective. The URL is http://www.alivein-truth.org/. Note the interviewing guidelines they suggest, and keep in mind the larger context for these interviews. How is this information different from what a social scientist or critical theorist might find?

governed by its position as both colonizer and quasi-colonized, non-Western but economically dominating" (2004, p. 340), which underscores the importance of understanding the media images in the context of living in a world where media images circulate from the West to the rest, where some countries have tried to colonize others, and where there is resistance to domination. Darling-Wolf complicates this struggle over culture by noting that the "fact that the women I interviewed enjoyed, resisted, and even reinterpreted the popular culture texts they avidly consumed does not make Westernized media imagery less problematic. On the contrary, the very pleasure provided by acts of resistance may make dominant representations more powerful as it encourages continued media consumption" (p. 341). Hence, critical scholars should be attentive to these larger relationships between nations and power in order to situate the ways that struggles over culture play out.

Another example of a critical study is Davin Grindstaff and Kevin DeLuca's (2004) analysis of the media coverage of the kidnapping and execution of Daniel Pearl, a journalist for the *Wall Street Journal* who was pursuing terrorism leads in Pakistan and was later captured and decapitated, which was videotaped. This videotape becomes a contested site where it "takes on starkly different meanings in the construction of both claims to 'terrorism' and to national identities in both Pakistan and the United States" (p. 306). The struggle between these readings must be contextualized within the larger power relations between Pakistan and the United States.

Grindstaff and DeLuca note that the same week Daniel Pearl was murdered, two Pakistani children were murdered in the United States. The outcry over Pearl and the deafening silence over these children's murders underscores the way that bodies represent national identities and "exacerbates Pakistani anti-Americanism and complicates Pakistani national identity" (2004, p. 316). In contrast, U.S. American discourses about Pearl's murder focus on Pearl as both a hero in the "war on terrorism" *and* an innocent victim. This paradox points to the way that multiple ideological needs are serviced and empowered by this video and its meanings.

A final example of a critical study is Dreama Moon's (1997) investigation of gender and social class communication. In her study, Moon analyzed interviews of white women from working-class backgrounds. She discovered that social class is a "marked feature" in the communication practices in academia that restricts upward mobility. Subtle communication practices that reinforce social class differences are not so invisible to women from working-class backgrounds. Moon shows how culture, social class, and communication work together to reproduce the contemporary social structure. She also identifies some strategies used by these women to resist this process of **social reproduction**.

Strengths and Limitations   The critical approach emphasizes the power relations in intercultural interactions and the importance of social and historical contexts. However, one limitation is that most critical studies do not focus on face-to-face intercultural interaction. Rather, they focus on popular media forms of communication—TV shows, music videos, magazine advertisements, and so on. Such studies, with their lack of attention to face-to-face interactions, may yield less practical results. Thus, for example, although understanding different discourses about racism may give us insights into U.S. race relations, it may not provide individuals with specific guidelines on how to communicate better across racial lines. However, one exception is cocultural theory, presented in Chapter 6, which is used to understand how people's location in a social hierarchy influences their perceptions of reality regarding, among other things, relational issues or problems (Orbe, 1998).

Also, this approach does not allow for much empirical data. For example, Davin Grindstaff and Kevin DeLuca did not measure Pakistani or U.S. American reactions to the decapitation of Daniel Pearl; instead, their essay analyzed the media discourses. Grindstaff and DeLuca's argument rests on the discussions about the videotape of the murder, how it was used, and its influence on these international audiences.

---

social reproduction The process of perpetuating cultural patterns.

A DIALECTICAL APPROACH TO UNDERSTANDING CULTURE AND COMMUNICATION

Combining the Three Traditional Paradigms: The Dialectical Approach

The social science, interpretive, and critical approaches operate in interconnected and sometimes contradictory ways. Rather than advocating any one approach, we propose a **dialectical approach** to intercultural communication research and practice (see also Martin, Nakayama, & Flores, 2002). The dialectical approach emphasizes the processual, relational, and contradictory nature of intercul-tural communication, which encompasses many different kinds of intercultural knowledge.

First, with regard to the **processual** nature of intercultural communication, it is important to remember that cultures change, as do individuals. For example, the many cultures that constituted New Orleans and the Gulf Coast included Cajuns, Creoles, African Americans, white Americans, Vietnamese Americans, Chinese Americans, gay and lesbian Americans, and many other cultural groups. Intercultural communication studies provide a static but fleeting picture of these cultural groups. It is important to remember that the adaptation, communication, and other patterns identified are dynamic and ever changing, even if the research studies only provide a snapshot in time.

Second, a dialectical perspective emphasizes the relational aspect of intercultural communication study. It highlights the relationship among various aspects of intercultural communication and the importance of viewing these holistically rather than in isolation. The key question becomes, Can we really understand culture without understanding communication, and vice versa? Specifically, can we understand the ways that different cultural groups responded to the hurricanes and how they survived without looking at the values, beliefs, and histories of the various cultural groups there, the cultural institutions that different groups had in place, the relative wealth available to different cultural groups, and so on?

A third characteristic of the dialectical perspective involves holding contradictory ideas simultaneously. This notion may be difficult to comprehend because it goes against most formal education in the

---

dialectical approach An approach to intercultural communication that integrates three approaches—functionalist (or social science), interpretive, and critical—in understanding culture and communication. It recognizes and accepts that the three approaches are interconnected and sometimes contradictory.
processual Refers to how interaction happens rather than to the outcome.

United States, which emphasizes dichotomous thinking. Dichotomies such as "good and evil," "arteries and veins," and "air and water" form the core of our philosophical and scientific beliefs. The fact that dichotomies such as "far and near," "high and low," and "long and short" sound complete, as if the two parts belong together, reveals our tendency to form dichotomies (Stewart & Bennett, 1991). One such dichotomy that emerged after Hurricane Katrina was that government officials were callous and uncaring and many victims of the hurricane were further victimized by the nonresponse of these officials. However, a dialectical approach requires that we transcend dichotomous thinking in studying and practicing intercultural communication.

Certainly, we can learn something from each of the three traditional approaches, and our understanding of intercultural communication has been enriched by all three. One of our students described how the three perspectives can be useful in everyday communication:

> *The three paradigms help me understand intercultural communication by giving me insight into how we can work with people. Understanding how to predict communication behavior will make it easier for us to deal with those of other cultures—the social science approach. By changing unfair notions we have [about people from other cultures], we can gain more equality, as in the critical approach. We try to change things. Finally, the interpretive perspective is important so we can see face-to-face how our culture is.*

Combining these approaches, as our discussion of the aftermath of Hurricane Katrina shows, provides us with extensive insight into the problems and challenges of this and other intercultural ventures. Clearly, if we limit ourselves to a specific research orientation, we may fail to see the complexities of contemporary intercultural interaction in contexts. Although this kind of paradoxical thinking is rather foreign to Western minds, it is quite accepted in many Asian cultures. For example, people doing business in China are advised to recognize this dialectical thinking: "It is not possible to overstate the importance of 'and' versus 'or' thinking. It recurs, in various forms, throughout business in China and the Orient as a whole" (Ambler & Witzel, 2000, p. 197).

In fact, research findings can make a difference in the everyday world. From the social science perspective, we can see how specific communication and cultural differences might create differing worldviews, which can help us to predict intercultural conflicts. An interpretive investigation gives us an opportunity to confirm what we predicted in a hypothetical social science study. In the case of Hurricane Katrina, a social science study might show large differences in responses between various cultural groups affected by this storm. An interpretive study might show how these different cultural groups interpreted these experiences and why they believe they had different experiences. These interpretations may help explain different responses and why some cultural groups feel differently from others and how some cultural groups adapted to new environments. The critical approach might focus on the different access to financial, political, and material resources among the cultural groups, such as the state of poverty before and after the storm, which groups were and were not relocated, and how these power differentials influenced their intercultural experiences.

Employing these different perspectives is similar to photographing something from different angles. No single angle or snapshot gives us the truth, but taking pictures from various angles gives a more comprehensive view of the subject. The content of the photos, of course, to some extent depends on the interests of the photographer. And the photos may contradict one another, especially if they are taken at different times. But the knowledge we gain from any of these "angles" or approaches is enhanced by the knowledge gained from the others.

However, a dialectical approach requires that we move beyond simply acknowledging the contributions of the three perspectives and accept simultaneously the assumptions of all three. That is, we need to imagine that reality can be at once external *and* internal, that human behavior is predictable *and* creative *and* changeable. These assumptions may seem contradictory, but that's the point. Thinking dialectically forces us to move beyond our familiar categories and opens us up to new possibilities for studying and understanding intercultural communication.

Six Dialectics of Intercultural Communication

We have identified six **dialectics** that characterize intercultural communication and have woven them throughout this book. Perhaps you can think of other dialectics as you learn more about intercultural communication.

Cultural–Individual Dialectic   Intercultural communication is both

---

dialectic (1) A method of logic based on the principle that an idea generates its opposite, leading to a reconciliation of the opposites; (2) the complex and paradoxical relationship between two opposite qualities or entities, each of which may also be referred to as a dialectic.

cultural and individual, or idiosyncratic. That communication is *cultural* means we share communication patterns with members of the groups to which we belong. For example, Sandra, a fifth-generation Italian American, tends to be expressive, like other members of her family. However, some of her communication patterns—such as the way she gestures when she talks—are completely idiosyncratic (that is, particular to her and no one else). Consider another example, that of Angela, who tends to be relationally oriented. Although her role as a woman and the relationships she cultivates in that role are important, being a woman does not completely define her behaviors. In this book, we often describe communication patterns that seem to be related to membership in particular cultural groups. However, it is important to remember that communication for all of us is both cultural and individual. We need to keep this dialectic in mind as we try to understand and develop relationships across cultural differences.

Personal–Contextual Dialectic   This dialectic involves the role of context in intercultural relationships and focuses simultaneously on the person and the context. Although we communicate as individuals on a personal level, the context of this communication is important as well. In some contexts, we enact specific social roles that give meaning to our messages. For example, when Tom was teaching at a Belgian university, he often spoke from the social role of professor. But this role did not correspond exactly to the same role in the United States because Belgian students accord their professors far more respect and distance than do U.S. students. In Belgium, this social role was more important than his communication with the students. In contrast, his communication with students in the United States is moreinformal.

Differences–Similarities Dialectic   Intercultural communication is characterized by both similarities and differences, in that people are simultaneously similar to and different from each other. In this book, we identify and describe real and important differences between groups of people—differences in values, language, nonverbal behavior, conflict resolution, and so on. For example, Japanese and U.S. Americans communicate differently, just as do men and women. However, there also are many similarities in human experiences and ways of communicating. Emphasizing only differences can lead to stereotyping and prejudice (e.g., that women are emotional or that men are rational); emphasizing only similarities can lead us to ignore the important cultural variations that exist. Therefore, we try to emphasize both similarities and differences and ask you to keep this dialectic in mind.

POINT OF VIEW

This excerpt demonstrates a dialectical tension between dealing honestly with racial difference and misinterpreting or misusing racial information.

For a long time, African Americans experienced discrimination not just for being the only race to pass on the genetic disease [sickle cell anemia], but because of the mistaken impression that even those with a single recessive gene—the sickle cell carriers—were somehow physically impaired. In the 1970s, for example, the U.S. Navy and the Air Force Academy restricted training opportunities for blacks with sickle cell trait, policies that were later criticized as discriminatory.

Subsequent research revealed that the carriers actually were more healthy in one important respect than people with no sickle cell anemia [gene] at all. In the malaria-infested parts of Africa from which most American blacks' ancestors came, sickle cell carriers were more resistant to malaria than non-carriers. This theory explained why such a devastating disease could perpetuate itself through the generations.... Other observations about different racial or ethnic groups' susceptibility to disease have similar explanations.... Scientists must regularly confront these racial or ethnic differences, and must deal with them honestly in order to ferret out their origins and implications. . . . While genetic researchers forge ahead in their population-based research, they know from experience that many of their findings may be misinterpreted or possibly even abused. The real burden of care belongs not only to scientists, but to the rest of us.

Source: From R. M. Henig, "Genetic Misunderstandings: The Linking of Jews with Cancer Is an Accident of Science and How Ethnic Groups Are Studied," *The Washington Post National Weekly Edition*, October 13, 1997, p. 23.

Static–Dynamic Dialectic This dialectic suggests that intercultural communication tends to be at once static and dynamic. Some cultural and communication patterns remain relatively constant, whereas other aspects of cultures (or personal traits of individuals) shift over time—that is, they are dynamic. For example, as we learned in Chapter 1, anti-immigrant sentiment traditionally has been a cultural constant in the United States, although the groups and conditions of discrimination have changed. Thus, the antagonism against Irish and Italian immigrants that existed at the turn of the 20th century has largely disappeared but may linger in the minds of some people. To understand interethnic communication in the United States today, we must recognize both the static and dynamic aspects of these relations.

History/Past–Present/Future Dialectic   Another dialectic emphasizes the need to focus simultaneously on the past and the present in
understanding intercultural communication. On the one hand, we need
to be aware of contemporary forces and realities that shape interactions of people from different cultural groups. On the other hand, we
need to realize that history has a significant impact on contemporary
events. One of our students described how this dialectic was illustrated
in a televised panel discussion on race relations:

> *The panelists frequently referred to and talked about the history of dif-
> ferent cultural groups in the United States and the present. They also
> touched on racial conflicts of the past and future possible improvement for
> certain groups. They were, therefore, communicating in a history/past–
> present/future dialectical manner. The discussion of past and present
> were critical to the overall goal of understanding current cultural iden-
> tity. Without understanding the history of, for example, the slave trade
> or the Jim Crow laws, can we truly comprehend the African American
> experience in the United States today? The history of each cultural group
> plays a major role in the present role of that group.*

Privilege–Disadvantage Dialectic   A dialectical perspective recognizes that people may be simultaneously privileged and disadvantaged,
or privileged in some contexts and disadvantaged in others. For example, many tourists are in the position of economic privilege because
they can afford to travel, but in their travels, they also may be disadvantaged if they do not speak the local language. We can also be simultaneously privileged and disadvantaged because of gender, age, race,
socioeconomic status, and other identities. One of our Asian American
colleagues relates how he is simultaneously privileged because he is
educated, middle class, and male, and disadvantaged because he experiences subtle and overt mistreatment based on his race and accent
(Collier, Hegde, Lee, Nakayama, & Yep, 2002, p. 247).

Keeping a Dialectical Perspective

We ask that you keep a dialectical perspective in mind as you read
the rest of this book. The dialectics relate in various ways to the topics discussed in the following chapters and are interwoven throughout
the text. Keep in mind, though, that the dialectical approach is not a
specific theory to apply to all aspects of intercultural communication.
Rather, it is a lens through which to view the complexities of the topic.
Instead of offering easy answers to dilemmas, we ask you to look at the
issues and ideas from various angles, sometimes holding contradictory

notions, but always seeing things in processual, relational, and holistic ways.

The dialectical approach that we take in this book combines the three traditional approaches (social science, interpretive, and critical) and suggests four components to consider in understanding intercultural communication: culture, communication, context, and power. Culture and communication are the foreground, and context and power are the backdrop against which we can understand intercultural communication. We discuss these four components in the next chapter.

DISCUSSION QUESTIONS

1. How have the origins of the study of intercultural communication in the United States affected its present focus?

2. How did business and political interests influence what early intercultural communication researchers studied and learned?

3. How have the worldviews of researchers influenced how they studied intercultural communication?

4. How have other fields contributed to the study of intercultural communication?

5. What are the advantages of a dialectical approach to intercultural communication?

ACTIVITIES

1. *Becoming Culturally Conscious.* One way to understand your cultural position within the United States and your own cultural values, norms, and beliefs is to examine your upbringing. Answer the following questions:

   a. What values did your parents or guardians attempt to instill in you?

   b. Why were these values considered important?

   c. What were you expected to do when you grew up?

   d. How were you expected to contribute to family life?

   e. What do you know about your ethnic background?

   f. What was your neighborhood like?

   Discuss your answers with classmates. Analyze how your own cultural position is unique and how it is similar to that of others.

2. *Analyzing Cultural Patterns.* Find a text or speech that discusses

some intercultural or cultural issues, and analyze the cultural patterns present in the text. Consider, for example, the "I Have a Dream" speech by Martin Luther King, Jr. (Andrews & Zarefsky, 1992), or Chief Seattle's 1854 speech (Low, 1995).

3. *Analyzing a Video*. View a feature film or video (e.g., *Crash* or *Brokeback Mountain*) and assume the position of a researcher. Analyze the cultural meanings in the film from each of the three perspectives: social science, interpretive, and critical. What cultural patterns (related to nationality, ethnicity, gender, and class) do you see? What does each perspective reveal? What does each one fail to reveal?

REFERENCES

9/11 and 8/29. (2005, September 11). *Los Angeles Times*, p. M4.

Allport, G. W. (1979). *The nature of prejudice*. Reading, MA: Addison-Wesley.

Alter, J. (2005, September 19). The other America. *Newsweek*, pp. 42–48.

Ambler, T., & Witzel, M. (2000). *Doing business in China*. New York: Routledge.

Andrews, J. R., & Zarefsky, D. (1992). *Contemporary American voices: Significant speeches in American history, 1945–present* (pp. 78–81). New York: Longman.

Après Katrina, l'Amérique s'interroge sur les failles de son modèle. (2005, September 7). *Le Monde*. http://www.lemonde.fr/web/imprimer_element/0,40-0@2-3222,50-6864 07,0.html

Asante, M. K. (1987). *The Afrocentric idea*. Philadelphia: Temple University Press.

Asante, M. K. (2001). Transcultural realities and different ways of knowing. In V. H. Milhouse, M. K. Asante, & P. O. Nwosu (Eds.), *Transcultural realities: Interdisciplinary perspectives on cross cultural relations* (pp. 71–82). Thousand Oaks, CA: Sage.

Barnlund, D. C., & Yoshioka, M. (1990). Apologies: Japanese and American styles. *International Journal of Intercultural Relations*, 14, 193–205.

Barry, D. (2005, September 9). The radio station that could, and did, and still does, help. *New York Times*, p. A15.

Berry, J. W. (1997). Preface. In P. R. Dasen, T. S. Saraswathi, & J. W. Berry (Eds.), *Handbook of cross cultural psychology: Vol. 2. Basic processes and human development* (pp. xi–xvi). Boston: Allyn & Bacon.

Braithwaite, C. (1990). Communicative silence: A cross cultural study of Basso's hypothesis. In D. Carbaugh (Ed.), *Cultural communication and intercul-tural contact* (pp. 321–328). Hillsdale, NJ: Lawrence Erlbaum.

Brantlinger, P. (1986). Victorians and Africans: The genealogy of the myth of the dark continent. In H. L. Gates Jr. (Ed.), *"Race," writing and difference* (pp. 185–222). Chicago: University of Chicago Press. (Original work published 1985)

Brislin, R. (1999). *Understanding culture's influence on behavior* (2nd ed.). Belmont, CA: Wadsworth.

Burrell, G., & Morgan, G. (1988). *Sociological paradigms and organizational analysis*. Portsmouth, NH: Heinemann.

Carbaugh, D. (1996). *Situating selves: The communication of social identities in American scenes.* Albany: State University of New York Press.

Carbaugh, D. (1999). "Just listen": "Listening" and landscape among the Blackfeet. *Western Journal of Communication, 63,* 250–270.

Carbaugh, D., & Berry, M. (2001). Communicating history, Finnish and American discourses: An eth-nographic contribution to intercultural com-munication inquiry. *Communication Theory, 11,* 352–366.

Casmir, F. L. (1994). The role of theory and theory building. In F. L. Casmir (Ed.), *Building communication theories* (pp. 7–41). Hillsdale, NJ: Lawrence Erlbaum.

Chen, G.-M. (1998). A Chinese model of human relationship development. In B. L. Hoffer & J. H. Koo (Eds.), *Cross-cultural communication East and West in the 90's* (pp. 45–53). San Antonio, TX: Institute for Cross-Cultural Research, Trinity University.

Chomsky, N. (2001). 9–11. New York: Seven Stories Press.

Collier, M. J., Hegde, R. S., Lee, W., Nakayama, T. K., & Yep, G. A. (2002). Dialogue on the edges: Ferment in communication and culture. In M. J. Collier (Ed.), *Transforming communication about culture (International and Intercultural Communication Annual,* Vol. 24, pp. 219–280). Thousand Oaks, CA: Sage.

Coste, P. (2005, September 15). Les raisons de la misère. *L'Express,* p. 33.

Darling-Wolf, F. (2004). Site of attractiveness: Japanese women and westernized representations of feminine beauty. *Critical Studies in Media Communication, 21,* 325–345.

Delgado, F. (2002). Mass-mediated communication and intercultural conflict. In J. N. Martin, T. K. Nakayama, & L. A. Flores (Eds.), *Readings in intercultural commu-nication: Experiences and contexts* (2nd ed., pp. 351–359). Boston: McGraw-Hill.

Dhombres, D. (2005, September 6). Le tiers-monde en Louisiane. *Le Monde.* http://www.lemonde.fr/ web/ imprimer_element/0,40-0@ 2-3232,50-686223,0.html

Egan, T. (2005, September 11). Up-rooted and scattered far from the familiar. *New York Times,* pp. A1, A32.

Gallois, C., Giles, H., Jones, E., Cargile, A. C., & Ota, H. (1995). Accommodating intercultural encounters: Elaborations and extensions. In R. L. Wiseman (Ed.), *Intercultural communication theory* (pp. 115–147). Newbury Park, CA: Sage.

Garner, T. (1994). Oral rhetorical practice in African American culture. In A. González, M. Houston, & V. Chen (Eds.), *Our voices: Essays in culture, ethnicity and communication* (pp. 81–91). Los Angeles: Roxbury.

Gould, S. J. (1993). American polygeny and craniometry before Darwin: Blacks and Indians as separate, inferior species. In S. Harding (Ed.), *The "racial" economy of science: Toward a democratic future* (pp. 84–115). Bloomington: Indiana University Press. (Original work published 1981)

Grindstaff, D. A., & DeLuca, K. M. (2004). The corpus of Daniel Pearl. *Critical Studies in Media Communication, 21,* 305–324.

Gudykunst, W. B. (1985). A model of uncertainty reduction in inter-group encounters. *Journal of Language and Social Psychology, 4,* 79–98.

Gudykunst, W. B. (1998). Individual-istic and collectivistic perspectives on communication: An introduction. *International Journal of Inter-cultural Relations, 22,* 107–134.

Gudykunst, W. B. (2002a). Intercultural communication theories.

In W. B. Gudykunst & B. Mody (Eds.), *Handbook of international and intercultural communication* (2nd ed., pp. 183–205). Thousand Oaks, CA: Sage.

Gudykunst, W. B. (2002b). Cross-cultural communication theories. In W. B. Gudykunst & B. Mody (Eds.), *Handbook of international and intercultural communication* (2nd ed., pp. 25–50). Thousand Oaks, CA: Sage.

Gudykunst, W. B. (2005). An anxiety/uncertainty management (AUM) theory of effective communication: Making the mesh of the net finer. In W. B. Gudykunst (Ed.), *Theorizing about intercultural communication* (pp. 281–323). Thousand Oaks, CA: Sage.

Gudykunst, W. B., & Nishida, T. (1989). Theoretical perspectives for studying intercultural communication. In M. K. Asante & W. B. Gudykunst (Eds.), *Handbook of international and intercultural communication* (pp. 17–46). Newbury Park, CA: Sage.

Hall, B. J. (1992). Theories of culture and communication. *Communication Theory, 1,* 50–70.

Hall, E. T. (1959). *The silent language.* Garden City, NY: Doubleday.

Hall, E. T. (1966). *The hidden dimension.* Garden City, NY: Doubleday.

Hammer, M. R., & Rogan, R. G. (2002). Latino and Indochinese interpretive frames in negotiating conflict with law enforcement: A focus group analysis. *International Journal of Intercultural Relations, 26,* 551–576.

Hart, W. B. (1999). Interdisciplinary influences in the study of intercultural relations: A citation analysis of the *International Journal of Intercultural Relations. International Journal of Intercultural Relations, 23,* 575–590.

Hecht, M. L. (1993). A research odyssey: Towards the development of a communication theory of identity. *Communication Monographs, 60,* 76–82.

Hernandez, G. (2005, October 11). Rebuilding our city. *The Advocate,* pp. 42–44, 49–50, 52.

Hutchinson, E. O. (2005, September 19). *Guest editorial:* How can Bush go? Chicago Defender. http://www.chicagodefender.com/page/local.cfm?ArticleID=2642

Hymes, D. (1974). *Foundations in sociolinguistics: An ethnographic approach.* Philadelphia: University of Pennsylvania Press.

Ishii, S. (2004). Proposing a Buddhist consciousness-only epistemological model for intrapersonal communication research. *Journal of Intercultural Communication Research, 33,* 63–76.

Jandt, F. E., & Tanno, D. V. (2001). Decoding domination, encoding self-determination: Intercultural communication research processes. *Howard Journal of Communications, 12,* 119–135.

Joe, M. (2005, October 28). Resurrecting the church after Katrina. *Asian Week.* http://news.asianweek.com/news/view_article.html?article_id=387bf08b8c87729a3144164b9850fb4c

Johnson, K. (2005, September 11). For storm survivors, a mosaic of impressions rather than a crystalline moment. *New York Times,* pp. A25, A32.

Kim, M. S. (1994). Cross-cultural comparisons of the perceived importance of conversational constraints. *Human Communication Research, 21,* 128–151.

Kim, M.-S. (2005). Culture-based conversational constraints theory: Individual and culture-level analyses. In W. B. Gudykunst (Ed.), *Theorizing about intercultural communication* (pp. 93–117). Thousand Oaks, CA: Sage.

Kim, Y. Y. (2001). *Becoming intercul-*

tural: An integrative theory of communication and cross-cultural adaptation. Thousand Oaks, CA: Sage.

Kohut, A., Allen, J., Keeter, S., Doherty, C., Dimock, M., Funk, C., et al. (2005). *Two-in-three critical of Bush's relief efforts: Huge racial divide over Katrina and its consequences.* The Pew Center for the People & the Press. Available at http://people-press.org/reports/pdf/255.pdf. Accessed November 1, 2005.

Kraidy, M. M. (2005). *Hybridity, or the cultural logic of globalization.* Philadelphia: Temple University Press.

Kuhn, T. (1970). *The structure of scientific revolutions* (Rev. ed.). Chicago: University of Chicago Press.

Kurtz, H. (2005, September 5). At last, reporters' feelings rise to the surface. *Washington Post,* p. C1.

Landis, D., & Bhagat, R. (1996). *Handbook of intercultural training* (2nd ed.). Thousand Oaks, CA: Sage.

Landis, D., & Wasilewski, J. H. (1999). Reflections on 22 years of the International Journal of *Intercultural Relations* and 23 years in other areas of intercultural practice. *International Journal of Intercultural Relations, 23,* 535–574.

Low, D. (1995). Contemporary reinvention of Chief Seattle's 1854 speech. *American Indian Quarterly, 19*(3), 407.

Martin, J. N., Nakayama, T. K., & Flores, L. A. (2002). A dialectical approach to intercultural communication. In J. N. Martin, T. K. Nakayama, & L. A. Flores (Eds.), *Readings in intercultural communication: Experiences and contexts* (2nd ed., pp. 3–13). Boston: McGraw-Hill.

Miike, Y. (2004). Rethinking humanity, culture and communication: Asiacentric critiques and contributions. *Human Communication, 7,* 69–82.

Miike, Y. (2003). Beyond Eurocentrism in the intercultural field: Searching for an Asiacentric paradigm. In W.

J. Storosta & G. M. Chen (Eds.), *Ferment in the intercultural field (International and Intercultural Communication Annual,* Vol. 26). Thousand Oaks, CA: Sage.

Moon, D. (1997). *Deconstructing the 'intra'/'inter' divide: Toward a critical inter/cultural practice.* Unpublished Ph.D. disssertation. Tempe: Arizona State University.

Orbe, M. (1998). *Constructing co-cultural theory: An explication of culture, power and communication.* Thousand Oaks, CA: Sage.

Orbe, M. P. (2004). Negotiating multiple identities with multiple frames: An analysis of first-generation college students. *Communication Education, 53,* 131–149.

Philipsen, G. (1990). Speaking "like a man" in Teamsterville. In D. Carbaugh (Ed.), *Cultural communication and intercultural contact* (pp. 11–20). Hillsdale, NJ: Lawrence Erlbaum.

Putnam, L., & Pacanowsky, M. (Eds.). (1983). *Communication and organizations: An interpretive approach.* Newbury Park, CA: Sage.

Rosaldo, R. (1989). *Culture and truth: The remaking of social analysis.* Boston: Beacon Press.

Saulny, S. (2005, October 11). Cast from their ancestral home, Creoles worry about culture's future. *New York Times,* p. A13.

Serpell, R. (1982). Measures of perception, skills and intelligence: The growth of a new perspective on children in a third world country. In W. Hartrup (Ed.), *Review of child development research* (Vol. 6). Chicago: University of Chicago Press.

Shome, R., & Hegde, R. (2002). Postcolonial approaches to communication: Charting the terrain, engaging the intersections. *Communication Theory, 12,* 249–270.

Singer, M. R. (1987). *Intercultural communication: A perceptual approach.* Englewood Cliffs, NJ: Prentice-Hall.

Singer, M. R. (1998). Culture: A perceptual approach. In M. J. Bennett (Ed.), *Basic concepts of intercultural communication* (pp. 97–110). Yarmouth, ME: Intercultural Press.

Smith, C. S. (2005, November 6). France has an underclass, but its roots are still shallow. *New York Times*, sec. 4, p. 3.

Smith, L. T. (1999). *Decolonizing methodologies: Research and indigenous peoples.* New York: St. Martin's Press.

Stewart, E. C., & Bennett, M. J. (1991). *American cultural patterns: A cross-cultural perspective* (Rev. ed.). Yarmouth, ME: Intercultural Press.

Sturken, M. (2005, October 5). Weather media and homeland security: Selling preparedness in a volatile world. *Understanding Katrina: Perspectives from the social sciences.* http://understandingkatrina. ssrc.org/Sturken/

Swarns, R. (2002, May 5). France returns old remains to homeland. *The Arizona Republic*, p. A28.

Tagliabue, J. (2005, September 21). A French lesson: Taunts about race can boomerang. *New York Times*, p. A4.

Tang, I. (2005, September 16). Hurricane Katrina victims recover from 'tragic shock.' *Asian Week.* http://news.asianweek.com/news/ view_article.html?article_id=736d a18dle494642b993e854400c7f30

Tatum, W. A. (2005, September 21). Proof positive of a racist president, misleading a racist America. *Amsterdam News.*http://www.am sterdamnews.org/ News/search/ Article_Search.asp? NewsID=617-23&sID=16

Ting-Toomey, S. (1985). Toward a theory of conflict and culture. In W. Gudykunst, L. Stewart, & S. Ting-Toomey (Eds.), *Communication, culture and organizational processes* (pp. 71–86). Beverly Hills, CA: Sage.

Ting-Toomey, S. (2005). The matrix of face: An updated face-negotiation theory. In W. B. Gudykunst (Ed.), *Theorizing about intercultural communication* (pp. 71–92). Thousand Oaks, CA: Sage.

Ting-Toomey, S., Gao, G., Trubisky, P., Yang, Z., Kim, H. S., Lin, S.-L., et al. (1991). Culture, face maintenance, and styles of handling interpersonal conflict: A study in five cultures. *International Journal of Conflict Management, 2,* 275–296.

Ting-Toomey, S., Yee-Jung, K. K., Shapiro, R. B., Garcia, W., Wright, T. J., & Oetzel, J. G. (2000). Ethnic/cultural identity salience and conflict styles in four US ethnic groups. *International Journal of Intercultural Relations, 24,* 47–81.

Vernet, D. (2005, September 8). Katrina bouscule la diplomatie américaine. *Le Monde.* http://www.lemonde.fr/web/ imprimer_element/0,40-0@2-3232,5 0-686932,0.html

Wells, M. (2005, September 5). Viewpoint: Has Katrina saved US media? *British Broadcasting Corporation News.* http://news. bbc.co.uk/1/hi/ world/americas/4214516.stm Accessed November 1, 2005.

Witteborn, S. (2004). Of being an Arab woman before and after September 11: The enactment of communal identities in talk. *Howard Journal of Communications, 15,* 83–98.

Why was UK's Katrina aid rejected by US? (2005, September 18). *British Broadcasting Corporation News.* http://news.bbc.co.uk/1/hi/ magazine/ 4349916.stm

CULTURE, COMMUNICATION, CONTEXT, AND POWER

CHAPTER OBJECTIVES

After you read this chapter, you should be able to:

1. Identify three approaches to culture.

2. Define communication.

3. Identify and describe nine cultural value orientations.

4. Describe how cultural values influence communication.

5. Understand how cultural values influence conflict behavior.

6. Describe how communication can reinforce cultural beliefs and behavior.

7. Explain how culture can function as resistance to dominant value systems.

8. Explain the relationship between communication and context.

9. Describe the characteristics of power.

10. Describe the relationship between communication and power.

In Chapter 2, we touched on the history of intercultural communication studies, examined three theoretical approaches, and outlined an integrated dialectical approach to intercultural communication. In this chapter, we continue our discussion of the dialectical approach and identify four interrelated components or building blocks in understanding intercultural communication: culture, communication, context, and power. As noted previously, culture and communication are the foreground, and context and power form the backdrop against which we can understand intercultural communication. First, we define and describe culture and communication. Then we examine how these two components interact with issues of context and power to enhance our understanding of intercultural communication.

WHAT IS CULTURE?

Culture is often considered the core concept in intercultural communication. Intercultural communication studies often focus on how cultural groups differ from one another: Muslims differ from Christians; Japanese differ from U.S. Americans; men differ from women; environmentalists differ from conserva-tionists; pro-lifers differ from pro-choicers; old differ from young, and on and on (Gudykunst, 2002).

Perhaps it is more helpful here to think of the similarities–differences dialectic in trying to understand intercultural communication. That is, we are all similar to *and* different from each other simultaneously. Humans, regardless of cultural backgrounds, engage in many of the same daily activities and have many of the same wants and desires. We all eat, sleep, love, pursue friendships and romantic relationships, and want to be respected and loved by those who are important to us.

And yet some real differences exist between cultural groups. How we pursue these activities varies from culture to culture. Men and women often do not see the world in the same way. Old and young have different goals and dreams. Muslims and Christians have different beliefs, and the old adage "When in Rome do as the Romans do" implies that it is easy simply to adapt to different ways of thinking and behaving, yet anyone who has struggled to adapt to a new cultural situation knows that only the Romans are Romans and only they know how to be truly Romans. The challenge is to negotiate these differences and similarities with insight and skill. First, we need to examine what we mean by the term *culture*.

Culture has been defined in many ways—from a pattern of perceptions that influence communication to a site of contestation and conflict. Because there are many acceptable definitions of culture, and because it is a complex concept, it is important to reflect on the centrality of culture in our own interactions. The late British writer Raymond Williams (1983) wrote that culture "is one of the two or three most complicated words in the English language" (p. 89). And this very complexity indicates the many ways in which it influences intercultural communication (Williams, 1981). Culture is more than merely one aspect of the practice of intercultural communication. How we think about culture frames our ideas and perceptions. For example, if we think that culture is defined by nation-states, then communication between a Japanese and an Italian would be intercultural communication because Japan and Italy are different nation-states. However, according to this definition, an encounter between an Asian American from North Carolina and an African American from California would not be intercultural because North Carolina and California are not different nation-states.

We do not advocate a singular definition of culture because any one definition is too restrictive (Baldwin & Lindsley, 1994). A dialectical approach suggests that different definitions offer more flexibility in approaching the topic. We believe that the best approach to understanding the complexities of intercultural communication is to view the concept of culture from different perspectives (see Table 3.1).

TABLE 3.1 THREE PERSPECTIVES ON DEFINING CULTURE		
Social Science	**Interpretive**	**Critical**
Culture is:		
Learned and shared	Learned and	Heterogeneous,
Patterns of	sharedContextual	dynamic Site of
perception	symbolic meanings	contested meanings
The relationship between culture and communication:		
Culture influences	Culture influences	Communication
communication	communication.	reshapes cult
	Communication	
	reinforces culture.	

Source: Adapted from J. N. Martin and T. K. Nakayama, "Thinking Dialectically About Culture and Communication," Communication Theory, 9 (1999): p. 5.

By and large, social science researchers focus not on culture per se but on the *influence* of culture on communication. In other words, such

---

Culture Learned patterns of behavior and attitudes shared by a group of people.

In this essay, communication scholar Wen Shu Lee identifies different common uses of the term *culture* and then describes how each definition serves particular interests. She also defends her preferred choice, the sixth definition.

1. Culture=unique human efforts (as different from nature and biology). For example, "*Culture* is the bulwark against the ravages of nature."

2. Culture=refinement, mannerism (as different from things that are crude, vulgar, and unrefined). For example, "Look at the way in which he chows down his food. He has no *culture* at all."

3. Culture=civilization (as different from backward barbaric people). For example, "In countries where darkness reigns and people are wanting in *culture*, it is our mandate to civilize and Christianize those poor souls."

4. Culture=shared language, beliefs, values (as different from language beliefs and values that are not shared; dissenting voices; and voices of the "other"). For example, "We come from the same *culture*, we speak the same language, and we share the same tradition."

5. Culture=dominant or hegemonic culture (as different from marginal cultures). For example, "It is the *culture* of the ruling class that determines what is moral and what is deviant." [This definition is a more charged version of definitions 2, 3, and 4 through the addition of power consciousness.]

researchers concern themselves with communication differences that result from culture. They pay little attention to how we conceptualize culture or how we see its functions. In contrast, interpretive researchers focus more on how cultural contexts influence communication. Critical researchers, for their part, often view com-munication—and the power to communicate—as instrumental in reshaping culture. They see culture as the way that people participate in or resist society's structure.

Although research studies help us understand different aspects of intercultural communication, it is important to investigate how we think about culture, not simply as researchers but as practitioners as well. We therefore broaden our scope to consider different views of

6. Culture=the shifting tensions between the shared and the unshared (as different from shared or unshared things). For example, "American *culture* has changed from master/slave, to white only/black only, to antiwar and black power, to affirmative action/multiculturalism and political correctness, to transnational capital and anti-sweatshop campaigns."

Each of these definitions privileges certain interests. Definition 2 privileges high culture and leaves out popular culture. . . . Definition 3 privileges nations that are/were imperialistic, colonizing. . . . Definition 4 privileges a "universal and representative" view of a society, but such a view often represents only a specific powerful group and silences other groups that do not readily share this view. Definition 5 privileges the interaction of the culture authorized by the dominant group/sector/nation—more politically explicit than definitions 2, 3, and 4. Definition 6 is the one I like the most. It is more of a meta view of cultures. It focuses on the "links" between "the shared" and the "little shared." But the sharedness, the unsharedness, and their links remain not only situated but also unstable, shifting, and contested.

Source: From Collier, Hegde, Lee, Nakayama, & Yep, "Dialogue on the Edges: Ferment in Communication and Culture." In M. J. Collier et al. (Eds.), *Transforming Communication About Culture* (Thousand Oaks, CA: Sage, 2002), pp. 229–230.

culture, especially in terms of how they influence intercultural communication.

Social Science Definitions: Culture as Learned, Group-Related Perceptions

Communication scholars from the social science paradigm, influenced by research in psychology, view culture as a set of learned, group-related perceptions (B. Hall, 1992). Geert Hofstede (1984), a noted social psychologist, defines culture as "the programming of the mind" and explains his notion of culture in terms of a computer program:

Every person carries within him or herself patterns of thinking, feeling, and potential acting which were learned throughout [his or her] lifetime. Much of [these patterns are] acquired in early childhood, because at that time a person is most susceptible to learning and assimilating. (p. 4)

Hofstede goes on to describe how these patterns are developed through interactions in the social environment and with various groups of individuals—first in the family and neighborhood, then at school and in youth groups, then at college, and so on. Culture becomes a collective experience because it is shared with people who live in and experience the same social environments.

To understand this notion of the collective programming of the mind, Hofstede and other scholars studied organizational behavior at various locations of a multinational corporation; this study is discussed in detail later in the chapter. Social scientists also have emphasized the role of perception in cultural patterns. They contend that cultural patterns of thought and meaning influence our perceptual processes, which, in turn, influence our behavior:

Culture is defined as a pattern of learned, group-related perception—including both verbal and nonverbal language attitudes, values, belief system, disbelief systems, and behavior. (Singer, 1987, p. 34)

Interpretive Definitions: Culture as Contextual Symbolic Patterns of Meaning

Interpretive scholars, influenced by anthropological studies, also view culture as shared and learned; however, they tend to focus on contextual patterns of communication behavior, rather than on group-related perceptions. Many interpretive scholars borrow anthropologist Clifford Geertz's definition of culture. According to Geertz (1973), culture denotes

an historically transmitted pattern of meaning embodied in symbols, a system of inherited conceptions expressed in symbolic forms by means of which men (sic) communicate, perpetuate and develop their knowledge about and attitudes toward life. (p. 89)

One of the most common examples of interpretive scholarship is

ethnography of communication; these scholars look for symbolic meaning of verbal and nonverbal activities in an attempt to understand patterns and rules of communication. This area of study defines cultural groups rather broadly—for example, as talk show participants or Vietnam War veterans.

Ethnography of communication scholar Donal Carbaugh (1988) suggests that it is best to reserve the concept of culture for patterns of symbolic action and meaning that are deeply felt, commonly intelligible, and widely accessible. Patterns that are deeply felt are sensed collectively by members of the cultural group. Gathering around the coffee machine at work every morning, for example, could be a cultural pattern, but only if the activity holds **symbolic significance** or evokes feelings that extend beyond itself. Then the activity more completely exemplifies a cultural pattern. Suppose that gathering around the coffee machine each morning symbolizes teamwork or the desire to interact with colleagues. To qualify as a cultural pattern, the activity must have the same symbolic significance for all members of the group; they must all find the activity meaningful in more or less the same way. Further, all participants must have access to the pattern of action. This does not mean that they must all use the pattern; it only means the pattern is available to them.

Communication theorist Gerry Philipsen extends Carbaugh's notion of culture by emphasizing that these patterns must endure over time, passed along from person to person. Philipsen (1992) writes,

Culture . . . refers to a socially constructed and historically transmitted pattern of symbols, meaning, premises, and rules. . . . A cultural code of speaking, then, consists of a socially constructed and historically transmitted system of symbols and meanings pertaining to communication—for instance, symbols "Lithuanian" or "communication" and their attendant definitions; beliefs about spoken actions (that a man who uses speech to discipline boys is not a real man); and rules for using speech (that a father should not interrupt his daughter at the dinner table). (pp. 7–8)

These definitions of culture suggested by Philipsen are influenced by communication ethnographer Dell Hymes's (1972) framework for studying naturally occurring speech in depth and in context. The framework comprises eight elements: scene, participant, end, act

---

ethnography of communication A specialized area of study within communication. Taking an interpretive perspective, scholars analyze verbal and nonverbal activities that have symbolic significance for the members of cultural groups to understand the rules and patterns followed by the groups. (See **interpretive approach**.)
symbolic significance The importance or meaning that most members of a cultural group attach to a communication activity.

sequence, key, instrumentality, norm, and genre. In this sequence, the terms form the acronym *SPEAKING*. The *S*cene is the setting of the communication event. The *P*articipants are the people who perform or enact the event. The *E*nd is the goal of the participants in conversation. The *A*ct sequence is the order of phrases during the enactment. The *K*ey is the tone of the conversation. The channel of communication is the *I*nstrumentality. The *N*orms, as you know, are the rules that people follow. And *G*enre is the type or category of talk. By analyzing speech using this descriptive framework, we can gain a comprehensive understanding of the rules and patterns followed in any given speech community. Later in this chapter, we'll provide an example of how the framework can be used to explore cultural communication in context.

Although the notion of culture as shared, learned group patterns of perception or symbolic behavior has long been the standard in a variety of disciplines, more and more people are beginning to question its utility. They question how much of "culture" is truly shared. For example, one colleague reports that in a class discussion about the definition of culture in which most students were giving the usual definitions, "one student almost indignantly jumped into our discussion and said, 'Do we really have a common culture?'" She then followed with the question "Whose version of a shared and common culture are we talking about?" (Collier, Hegde, Lee, Nakayama, & Yep, 2002, p. 269). Indeed, these are important questions, and so the next section describes an alternative approach to defining culture. (For a challenge to common notions of a "shared" U.S. culture, take the "Test of U.S. Cultural Knowledge" on page 98.)

Critical Definitions: Culture as Heterogeneous, Dynamic, and a Contested Zone

A more recent approach to culture, influenced by cultural studies scholarship, emphasizes the heterogeneity of cultural groups and the often conflictual nature of cultural boundaries. For example, what is the "U.S. American culture"? Is there *an* American culture? How many perceptions, attitudes, and beliefs and behaviors are actually shared among the many diverse people living in the United States? Critical scholars suggest that in emphasizing only the shared aspects of culture, we gloss over the many interesting differences among U.S. Americans. Further, they emphasize that cultural boundaries are often contested and not easily agreed upon. For example, increasing numbers of people like Tiger Woods have multicultural identities. He considers himself Cablinasian—Caucasian, black, Indian, and Asian—because of his racially

POINT OF VIEW

Tiger Woods media statement on his race/ethnicity:

The purpose of this statement is to explain my heritage for the benefit of members of the media who may be seeing me play for the first time. It is the final and only comment I will make regarding the issue.

My parents have taught me to always be proud of my ethnic background. Please rest assured that is, and always will be, the case — past, present, and future.

The media has portrayed me as African-American; sometimes, Asian. In fact, I am both. Yes, I am the product of two great cultures, one African-American and the other Asian. On my father's side, I am African-American. On my mother's side, I am Thai. Truthfully, I feel very fortunate, and EQUALLY PROUD, to be both African-American and Asian! The critical and fundamental point is that ethnic background and/or composition should NOT make a difference. It does NOT make a difference to me. The bottom line is that I am an American . . . and proud of it!

That is who I am and what I am. Now, with your cooperation, I hope I can just be a golfer and a human being.

Signed,
TIGER WOODS

http://www.geocities.com/Colosseum/2396/tigerrace.html

diverse background. He resists the many efforts by some to pigeonhole his race/ethnicity or to focus more on his cultural background than his achievements as a golfer, as shown in the Point of View Box.

This notion of culture as heterogeneous and often conflictual originated with British cultural studies scholars in the 1960s. Cultural studies scholars were fiercely interdisciplinary and dedicated to understanding the richness, complexity, and relevance of cultural phenomena in the lives of ordinary people.

This desire to make academic work relevant to everyday life resonated in other fields. Most people, in fact, want to find the connections between what they learn in the classroom and what is occurring in contemporary society. In any case, this movement led to the reconfiguration of the role of the university in society.

Cultural studies soon spread from Britain to Australia, Latin America, and other parts of the world. Because of differing cultural and political situations, the specific construction of cultural studies differs from place to place. In the United States, for instance, cultural studies

POINT OF VIEW

TEST OF U.S. CULTURAL KNOWLEDGE

This test examines your knowledge of many of the cultures that comprise the contemporary United States.

1. *Lagniappe* is a term used in southern Louisiana for:
   a. Hurricanes
   b. Something free or sometimes a small gift given by a store owner to a customer after a purchase
   c. Inviting someone over for a meal
   d. Helping a friend with home remodeling or yard work

2. What is the name of the dish that features black-eyed peas and rice (although sometimes collards, ham hocks, stewed tomatoes, or other items) and is served in the South, especially on New Year's Day?
   a. Chitlings
   b. Jowls
   c. Hoppin' John
   d. Red rice

3. A very sweet pie made from molasses that originated with the Pennsylvania Dutch:
   a. Mincemeat pie
   b. Sugar pie
   c. Shoofly pie
   d. Lancaster pie

4. Which of the following is *not* the name of a Native American tribe?
   a. Seminole
   b. Apache
   c. Arapaho
   d. Illini

5. The month of Ramadan, a month of fasting for Muslims, ends with which holiday?
   a. Eid ul-Fitr
   b. Allahu Akbar

developed mainly within departments of communication (Grossberg, 1993).

You may sense that the concept of culture that emerged from this

c. Takbir

d. Abu Bakr

6. On June 12 every year, some U.S. Americans celebrate "Loving Day" to commemorate:

    a. Your legal right to love someone of another race

    b. Your legal right to love someone of the same sex

    c. Your legal right to be a single parent

    d. Your legal right to get a divorce

7. The celebration of Buddha's birthday is not held on Christmas, but instead on:

    a. Fourth of July

    b. July 14

    c. Asian Lunar New Year's Day

    d. Hanamatsuri

8. Sometimes viewed as a Scandinavian tortilla, these potato flatcakes are often sold in areas with high Scandinavian American populations:

    a. Lefse

    b. Lutefisk

    c. Aquavit

    d. Fiskepudding

9. This traditional Mexican soup is made mostly from tripe, hominy, and chili:

    a. Tortilla soup

    b. Tomatillo

    c. Chorizo soup

    d. Menudo

10. Like a coconut pudding, this food comes from Hawaii:

    a. Lomi lomi

    b. Poke

    c. Haupia

    d. Kalua

Answers can be found on page 122.

area of inquiry differs markedly from the concept expressed in social science or even interpretive research. However, it is in agreement with concepts found in recent work in anthropology. Many anthropologists have criticized research that categorizes people and characterizes cultural patterns as set, unchanging, and unconnected to issues of gender, class, and history (Keesing, 1994). Recent anthropological research sees cultural processes as dynamic and fluid "organizations of diversity" that extend across national and regional borders within contexts of history and power (Hannerz, 1996).

Communication scholars who embrace the critical notions encourage us to

> *move beyond hegemonic definition of culture as "shared and transmit-ted from generation to generation" that assume that we all experience a "common culture" and . . . is passed down from one generation to the next in a linear and seemingly static fashion. . . . [T]his is a dangerous myth . . . that works in invisible yet extremely powerful ways to suppress and erase marginalized voices and experiences. (Gust Yep, in Collier et al., 2002, p. 231)*

Viewing culture as a contested site or zone helps us understand the struggles of various groups—Native Americans, Asian Americans, Pacific Islanders, African Americans, Latinos/as, women, gays and lesbians, working-class people, and so on—as they attempt to negotiate their relationships and promote their well-being within U.S. society. By studying the communication that springs from these ongoing struggles, we can better understand several intercultural concerns. Consider, for example, Proposition 227 in California, passed by voters in 1998, which eliminated public funding for bilingual education. The controversy surrounding the passage of this proposition illustrates the concerns of many different cultural groups. Similar debates surrounded the prior passage of Propositions 187 and 209 in California.

Viewing culture as a contested site opens up new ways of thinking about intercultural communication. After all, the individuals in a given culture are not identical, which suggests that any culture is replete with cultural struggles. Thus, when we use terms like *Chinese culture* and *French culture*, we gloss over the heterogeneity, the diversity, that resides in that culture. Yet the ways in which various cultures are heterogeneous are not the same elsewhere as in the United States, which means it would be a mistake to map our structure of differences onto other cultures. How sexuality, ethnicity, gender, and class function in other cultures is not necessarily the same as, or even similar to, their function in the United States. By viewing any culture as a contested zone or site of struggle, we can understand the complexities of that culture; we can become more sensitive to how people in that culture live.

Our dialectical approach, though, enables us to accept and see the interrelatedness of these different views. Culture is at once a shared and a learned pattern of beliefs and perceptions that are mutually intelligible and widely accessible. It is also a site of struggle for contested meanings. A dialectic perspective can help facilitate discussions on conflicting cultural notions (e.g., how to reconcile U.S. patriotism and instances of anti-Americanism). Our task in taking a dialectical approach is not to say whose views are right or wrong, but to recognize "the truth in all sides of the conflict and understanding the ways in which multiple realities constitute the whole of the cultural quandary" (Cargile, 2005, p. 117).

WHAT IS COMMUNICATION?

The second component in understanding intercultural communication, **communication**, is as complex as culture. The defining characteristic of communication is meaning, and we could say that communication occurs whenever someone attributes meaning to another person's words or actions. Communication may be understood as a "symbolic process whereby reality is produced, maintained, repaired and transformed" (Carey, 1989, p. 23). This simple definition involves several ideas.

First, communication is *symbolic*. This means that the words we speak and the gestures we make have no inherent meaning but rather gain their significance from an agreed-upon meaning. Thus, when we use symbols to communicate, we assume the other person shares our symbol system. Also, these symbolic meanings are conveyed both verbally and nonverbally. Thousands of nonverbal behaviors—gestures, postures, eye movements, facial expressions, and so on—involve shared meaning. Powerful social symbols—for example, flags, national anthems, and Disney logos—also communicate meaning nonverbally. Many of these symbols are material as well; that is, they have physical consequences in the world. For example, when schoolchildren in the United States bring guns to school and kill schoolmates, the symbolism of these acts communicate something, while the acts themselves are material.

To make things more complicated, each message has more than one meaning, and perhaps many layers of meaning. For example, the message *I love you* may mean, "I'd like to have a good time with you tonight," or "I feel guilty about what I did last night without you," or

---

communication A symbolic process whereby reality is produced, maintained, repaired, and transformed.

"I need you to do me a favor," or "I have a good time when I'm with you," or "I want to spend the rest of my life (or at least the next few hours) with you." When we communicate, we assume that the other person takes the meaning that we intend. However, for individuals from different cultural backgrounds and experiences, this assumption may be faulty.

Second, the *process* by which we negotiate meaning is dynamic. Communication is not a singular event but is ongoing—it relies on other communication events to make sense. When we enter into communication with another person, we simultaneously take in messages through all of our senses. The messages are not discrete and linear; they are simultaneous, with blurry boundaries between beginning and end. When we negotiate meaning, we are creating, maintaining, repairing, or transforming reality. This implies that people are actively involved in the communication process. One person cannot communicate alone.

THE RELATIONSHIP BETWEEN CULTURE AND COMMUNICATION

The relationship between culture and communication is complex. A dialectical perspective assumes that culture and communication are interrelated and reciprocal. That is, culture influences communication, and vice versa. Thus, cultural groups influence the process by which the perception of reality is created and maintained: "All communities in all places at all times manifest their own view of reality in what they do. The entire culture reflects the contemporary model of reality" (Burke, 1985, p. 11). However, we might also say that communication helps create the cultural reality of a community. Let's see how these reciprocal relationships work.

How Culture Influences Communication

Intercultural communication scholars use broad frameworks from anthropology and psychology to identify and study cultural differences in communication. Two of the most relevant were developed by anthropologists Kluckhohn and Strodtbeck (1961) and by social psychologist Hofstede (1984).

Kluckhohn and Strodtbeck Value Orientations Researchers Florence Kluckhohn and Fred Strodtbeck studied contemporary Diné (Navaho) and descendants of Spanish colonists and European Americans in the

Southwest in the 1950s. They emphasized the centrality of **cultural values** in understanding cultural groups. Values are the most deeply felt beliefs shared by a cultural group; they reflect a shared perception of what ought to be, and not what is. Equality, for example, is a value shared by many people in the United States. It refers to the belief that all humans are created equal, even though we must acknowledge that, in reality, there are many disparities, such as in talent, intelligence, or access to material goods.

Intercultural conflicts are often caused by differences in value orientations. For example, some people feel strongly that it is important to consider how things were done in the past. For them, history and tradition help provide guidance. Values often conflict among participants in international assistance projects in which future-oriented individuals show a lack of respect for traditional ways of doing things. And conflicts may be exacerbated by power differentials, with some values privileged over others. Organizational communication scholars have pointed out that many U.S. workplaces reward extremely individualistic relationships and "doing" behaviors at the expense of more collaborative (and equally productive) work (Buzzanell, 1994). Kluckhohn and Strodtbeck suggested that members of all cultural groups must answer the following important questions:

- What is human nature?
- What is the relationship between humans and nature?
- What is the relationship between humans?
- What is the preferred personality?
- What is the orientation toward time?

According to Kluckhohn and Strodtbeck, there are three possible responses to each question as they relate to shared values. (See Table 3.2.) Kluckhohn and Strodtbeck believed that, although all responses are possible in all societies, each society has one, or possibly two, preferred responses to each question that reflect the predominant values of that society. Religious beliefs, for example, may reinforce certain cultural values. The questions and their responses become a framework for understanding broad differences in values among various cultural groups. Although the framework was applied originally to ethnic groups, we can extend it to cultural groups based on gender, class, nationality, and so on.

---

cultural values The worldview of a cultural group and its set of deeply held beliefs.

TABLE 3.2 KLUCKHOHN AND STRODTBECK VALUE ORIENTATIONS			
	Range of values		
Human nature	Basically good	Mixture of good and evil	Basically evil
Relationship between humans and nature	Humans dominate	Harmony exists between the two	Nature dominates
Relationships between humans	Individual	Group oriented	Collateral
Preferred personality	"Doing": stress on action	"Growing": stress on spiritual growth spiritual growth	"Being": stress on who you are
Time orientation	Future oriented	Present oriented	Past-oriented

Source: Adapted from F. Kluckhohn and F. Strodtbeck, *Variations in Value Orientation* (Chicago: Row, Peterson, 1961).

The Nature of Human Nature   As the table shows, there are three possible responses, or solutions, to basic questions about human nature. One solution is a belief in the fundamental goodness of human nature. Legal practices in a society that holds this orientation would emphasize rehabilitating violators of the law; jails and prisons would be seen as places to train violators to rejoin society as contributing citizens. Religions such as Buddhism and Confucianism tend toward this orientation, focusing on improving the natural goodness of humans.

A second solution reflects a perception of a combination of goodness and evil in human nature. Many groups within the United States hold this value orientation, although there has been a shift in views for many U.S. Americans in the past 50 years. With regard to religious beliefs, there is less emphasis on the fundamental evil of humanity, which many European settlers of the Puritan tradition believed (Kohls, 1996). However, the current emphasis is on incarceration and punishment for violators of the law. For example, consider the increase in "three strikes" legislation and the lack of interest in rehabilitation and reform. Given this orientation, not surprisingly, the United States currently has a higher proportion of citizens incarcerated than any other industrialized country.

According to the third orientation, human nature is essentially evil. Societies that hold this belief would be less interested in rehabilitation of criminals than in punishment. We often have trouble understanding torture or the practice of cutting off hands and other limbs—practices prevalent in many societies in the past—without understanding their orientation to human nature. While he lived in Belgium, Tom was

Korean communication scholars Tae-Seop Lim and Soo-Hyang Choi describe the Korean value of collectivism, as expressed in interpersonal relations and communication.

Traditionally, Koreans have valued social relationships more than anything else. Koreans often forgo their own personal interests and the welfare of the groups they belong to for the sake of their interpersonal relationships. Because Koreans emphasize social relationships, the abilities to maintain good interpersonal relationships are also valued. Persons are judged based upon their abilities to maintain successful relationships. Having good relationships with others is considered to reflect one's character as well as competence.

Che-myon is what enables a person to face others with dignity. Part of che-myon, like the Western concept of face, is personalized and negotiated without interaction. The aspect of che-myon *that Koreans are really sensitive to, however, is sociological and normative* chemyon. *This is extended to one in relation to the social position one holds.*

Noon-chi is what makes tacit communication possible. It is a strategy that enables one to figure out the intention, desire, mood, and attitude of the other without exchanging explicit verbal messages. It is similar to the Western notion of "reading between the lines," but is much more complicated than its Western counterpart. Noon-chi sometimes reads something out of nothing; that is, it reads the mind of the other even before the other knows his or her own mind. Noon-chi is often used to protect each other's che-myon. When one needs to perform a certain face-threatening act, if the other figures out one's needs before one expresses them and reacts appropriately, then both parties do not have to endanger their che-myon. . . .

[A] relationship needs mutual jung to be solid. Jung is a type of emotional attachment that grows over time as persons in a relationship make repeated contacts with each other. It functions to make a relationship strongly bonded. As the relationship grows old, love often fades away, but jung usually grows deep.

Source: From T.-S. Lim and S.-H. Choi, "Interpersonal Relationships in Korea." In W. B. Gudykunst et al. (Eds.), *Communication in Personal Relationships Across Cultures* (Thousand Oaks, CA: Sage, 1996), pp. 122–136.

particularly struck by the display of punishments and tortures in the Counts of Flanders Castle in Ghent. Perhaps the key to understanding these cultural practices is an understanding of the Christian view of humans as essentially evil and born in sin.

Relationship Between Humans and Nature   In most of U.S. society, humans dominate nature. For instance, scientists seed clouds when we need rain, and engineers reroute rivers and build dams to meet the needs for water, recreation, and power. We control births with drugs and medical devices, and we make snow and ice for the recreational pastimes of skiing and skating. Certainly, not everyone in the United States agrees that humans should always dominate nature. Conflicts between environmentalists and land developers often center on disagreements over this value orientation. And, of course, there are variations in how these values play out in different societies. For example, a country like Canada, which generally espouses a "humans over nature" orientation, still seems more concerned with environmental issues than does the United States. As described by a student,

> *Canada is very concerned about protecting their environment, and this is very clear even if you are just traveling through. They are concerned about clean water, clean air and not doing too much logging of their trees, keeping streams free of pollution, etc.*

In societies that believe mainly in the domination of nature over humans, decisions are made differently. Families may be more accepting of the number of children that are born naturally. There is less intervention in the processes of nature, and there are fewer attempts to control what people see as the natural order.

Many Native Americans and Japanese believe in the value of humans living in harmony with nature, rather than one force dominating the other. In this value orientation, nature is respected and plays an integral part in the spiritual and religious life of the community. Some societies—for example, many Arab groups—emphasize aspects of both harmony with and domination of nature. This reminds us that values are played out in very complex ways in any cultural group.

Relationships Between Humans   Some cultural groups value individualism, whereas others are more group oriented. The cultural differences pertaining to these values distinguish two types of societies. Individualism, often cited as a value held by European Americans, places importance on individuals rather than on families, work teams, or other groups (Bellah, Madsen, Sullivan, Swidler, & Tipton, 1985).

This characteristic is often cited as the most important European American cultural value. In contrast, people from more collectivistic societies, like those in Central and South America, Asia, and many Arab societies, place a great deal of importance on extended families and group loyalty. In the United States, this is the case in Amish communities and in some Latino/a and Native American communities. A visitor to Mexico described one example of collectivism in that culture:

> *I remember that in public that children always seem to be accompanied by someone older, usually a family member. People went around in family groups—children with older siblings, grandparents, aunts—not nearly so age-segregated as it is here in the U.S.*

The collateral orientation emphasizes the collectivist connection to other individuals (mostly family members) even after death. This orientation is found in cultures in which ancestors are seen as a part of the family and are influential in decisions even though they are not alive. Examples of this include the Asian practice of maintaining a table in the house to honor their ancestors or the Mexican "Day of the Dead" practice of having a picnic near the graves of the family members and leaving food for them.

Values may also be related to economic status or rural–urban distinctions. In the United States, for example, working-class people tend to be more collectivistic than middle- or upper-class people. (Working-class people reportedly donate a higher percentage of their time and money to help others.) Historian Roxanne A. Dunbar (1997), who grew up poor in Oklahoma, describes an encounter with middle-class individualism she had while on an extended car trip with her new husband, Jimmy. They passed several stranded motorists, the women sitting in the shade while the men worked on the cars. She was surprised when her husband didn't stop to help:

> *"Why don't we stop?" I asked. No one in my family would ever have passed up a stranded motorist. . . .*
> *"They're hustlers, rob you blind, highway bandits," Jimmy said.*
> *"How do you know?"*
> *"I just know, they use the kids and old people for bait to get you to stop, then rob you, they're transients, fruit pickers, white trash."*
> *I stared at the sad faces as we passed by and tried to see the con artists and criminals behind the masks. But they merely looked familiar, like my own relatives. (p. 83)*

Two news items in the Belgian newspaper Le Soir show apparently contradictory cultural values. In the first, Yves Berger, a writer and U.S. specialist, was asked to explain the sexual affair of President Bill Clinton.

In any case, it shows to what extent puritanism is ingrained in the American mentality. This might seem unbelievable as Americans, in daily life, give the opposite appearance.

(Elle nous permet en tout cas de mesurer à quel point le puritanisme est une donnée profonde de la mentalité, de la sensibilité américaines. Cela peut évidemment sembler incroyable, tant les Américains donnent quotidiennement le spectacle du contraire.)

Another article in the same newspaper describes the dramatic growth of the U.S. pornography industry.

The adult video market is booming and the business figures on the rental and sale of adult videos rose in 1997 to 4.2 billion dollars, according to the annual guide Adult Video News.

(Le marché de la vidéo pour adults est en plein boom et le chiffre d'affaires de la location et de la vente des films pornographiques s'est élevé en 1997 à 4,2 millards de dollars, selon le guide annuel Adult Video News.)

Sources: From Y. Berger, "A bout portant," Le Soir, January 7, 1998, p. 2; from "Marché porno en expansion aux Etats-Unis," Le Soir, January 7, 1998, p. 11.

These cultural values may influence patterns of communication. For example, people who value individualism *tend* also to favor direct forms of communication and to support overt forms of conflict resolution. People in collectivistic societies *may* employ less direct communication and more avoidance-style conflict resolution. Of course, sometimes people belong to cultural groups that hold contradictory values. For example, most U.S. work contexts require highly individualistic communication, which may conflict with the collectivistic family or ethnic backgrounds of some workers. Workers may find it hard to reconcile and live with these competing values. Consider the experience of Lucia, a Native American college student. When one of her uncles passed away during the first week of school, she was expected to participate in family activities. She traveled out of state with her family to his home, helped cook and feed other family members, and attended the wake and the funeral. Then her mother became ill, and she had to care for her. Thus, she missed the first two weeks of school.

POINT OF VIEW

In an interview that appears in *Le Nouvel Observateur*, François Mas was asked to explain the popularity of the medication Viagra (a remedy for sexual impotence) in the United States. He relates the popularity to the "can do" value of the U.S. American people.

Probably the most revealing is the "can do" attitude. This attitude, inherited from the pioneers, is how American society, in general, deals with existing problems. Centered on the concrete and practical applications, and often seen as naive in the view of older cultures, this approach has the advantage of deploying a kind of energy and rejecting opposition to progress.

(Le plus révélateur étant le "can do." . . . Cette attitude, héritée de pionniers, est celle de la société américaine en général face aux problèmes de l'existence. Centrée sur le réel et les applications pratiques, souvent naïve dans son expression aux yeux de cultures plus anciennes, cette approach a l'avantage de déployer une certaine énergie et de refuser l'immobilisme.)

Source: From F. Mas, "Vers un Renouveau Sexuel," *Le Nouvel Observateur*, May 1998, pp. 21–27.

Some of her professors were sympathetic; others were not. As Lucia describes it, she feels almost constantly torn between the demands of her collectivistic family and the demands of the individualistic professors and administration.

Preferred Forms of Activity   The most common "activity value" in the United States is the "doing" orientation, which emphasizes productivity. (Remember the expression "Idle hands are the devil's workshop"?) Employment reward systems reflect this value in that workers often must document their progress (e.g., in numbers of sales made or numbers of clients seen). In general, the highest status is conferred on those who "do" (sports figures, physicians, lawyers), rather than on those who "think" (philosophers, professors, priests) (Stewart & Bennett, 1991).

The "growing" orientation emphasizes spiritual aspects of life. This orientation seems to be less prevalent than the other two, perhaps practiced only in Zen Buddhism and as a cultural motif in the United States in the 1960s (Stewart & Bennett, 1991). Some societies, as in Japan, combine both "doing" and "growing" orientations, emphasizing action and spiritual growth. The third solution is to emphasize "being," a kind of self-actualization in which the individual is fused with the experience. Some societies in Central and South America, as well aş Greece and Spain, exhibit this orientation.

Orientation to Time   Most U.S. cultural communities—particularly European American and middle class—seem to emphasize the future. Consider the practices of depositing money in retirement accounts or keeping appointment books that reach years into the future. Other societies—for example, in Spain or Greece—seem to emphasize the importance of the present, a recognition of the value of living fully in and realizing the potential of the present moment. One of our friends described her impression of this value difference after a visit toMexico:

> *I had a wonderful experience in Mexico. I liked the energy—there was ALWAYS so much going on in the streets, and in the zocalo, all hours of the day and night. And when I returned to the U.S., the streets seemed so dead—everyone individually alone in their own little houses here. I felt suddenly so sensory-deprived!! I guess I also liked it partly because it is so different, culturally, from the way I grew up. The emphasis of expressing and focusing on life in the present. I don't want to imply that life is a constant thoughtless fiesta in Mexico, because it's not. But there was a kind of joie de vivre and enjoyment of life NOW that certainly was not present in my family's very constrained, restrained, serious lifestyle! And so Mexico seemed a great contrast!*

Many European and Asian societies strongly emphasize the past, believing that knowledge and awareness of history has something to contribute to an understanding of contemporary life. For example, the Leaning Tower of Pisa was closed for 10 years while Italian workers repaired structural damage on this historic building.

Hofstede Value Orientations   Social psychologist Geert Hofstede (1984) extended the work of Kluckhohn and Strodtbeck, based on extensive cross-cultural study of personnel working in IBM subsidiaries in 53 countries. Whereas Kluckhohn and Strodbeck (1961) based their framework on cultural patterns of ethnic communities within the United States, Hofstede and colleagues examined value differences among national societies. Hofstede identified five areas of common problems. One problem type, individualism versus collectivism, appeared in the Kluckhohn and Strodbeck framework. Although the problems were shared by different cultural groups, solutions varied from culture to culture (Hofstede & Hofstede, 2004). As shown in Table 3.3, the problem types are identified as follows:

- Power distance: social inequality, including the relationship with authority
- Femininity versus masculinity: the social implications of having been born male or female
- Ways of dealing with uncertainty, controlling aggression, and exprssing emotions
- Long-term versus short-term orientation to life

Hofstede then investigated how these various cultural values influenced corporate behavior in various countries. Let's examine the other problem types more closely. (See Table 3.3.)

Power distance refers to the extent to which less powerful members of institutions and organizations within a country expect and accept the unequal distribution of power. Denmark, Israel, and New Zealand, for example, value small power distance. Most people there believe that less hierarchy is better and that power should be used only for legitimate purposes. Therefore, the best corporate leaders in those countries are those who minimize power differences. In societies that value large power distance—for example, Mexico, the Philippines, and India—the decision-making process and the relationships between managers and subordinates are more formalized. In addition, people may be uncomfortable in settings in which hierarchy is unclear or ambiguous.

The **masculinity–femininity value** is two-dimensional. It refers to (1) the degree to which gender-specific roles are valued and (2) the degree to which cultural groups value so-called masculine values (achievement, ambition, acquisition of material goods) or so-called feminine values (quality of life, service to others, nurturance, support for the unfortunate). IBM employees in Japan, Austria, and Mexico scored high on the masculine values orientation, expressing a general preference for gender-specific roles, with some roles (e.g., main wage earner) better filled by men and other roles (e.g., homemaker, teacher) by women. In contrast, employees in northern Europe (Denmark, Norway, Sweden, and the Netherlands) tended to rank higher in feminine values orientation, reflecting more gender equality and a stronger belief in the importance of quality of life for all.

---

power distance A cultural variability dimension that concerns the extent to which people accept an unequal distribution of power.
masculinity–femininity value A cultural variability dimension that concerns the degree of being feminine—valuing fluid gender roles, quality of life, service, relationships, and interdependence— and the degree of being masculine—emphasizing distinctive gender roles, ambition, materialism, and independence.

TABLE 3.3 HOFSTEDE VALUE ORIENTATIONS	
Power Distance	
Low power distance Less hierarchy better	High power distance More hierarchy better
Femininity Masulinity	
Femininity Fewer gender-specific roles Value quallity of life, supprt for unfortunate	Masculinity More gende-specific roles Achievement, ambition, acquisition, acquisition of material goods
Uncertainty Avoidance	
Low uncertainty avoidance Dislike rules, accept dissent Less formality	High uncertainty avoidance More extensive rules, limit dissent More formality
Long-term/Short-term Orientation	
Short-term orientation Universal guidelines for good and evil	Long-term orientation Definition of good and evil depends on circumstances
Prefer quick results	Value perseverance and tenacity

Source: Adapted from G. Hofstede and G. J. Hofstede, *Cultures and Organizations: Software of the Mind* (2nd ed.) (Boston: McGraw-Hill, 2004), p. 232.

Uncertainty avoidance concerns the degree to which people who feel threatened by ambiguous situations respond by avoiding them or trying to establish more structure to compensate for the uncertainty. Societies that have a weak uncertainty avoidance orientation (Great Britain, Sweden, and the United States) prefer to limit rules, accept dissent, and take risks. In contrast, those with a strong uncertainty avoidance orientation (Greece, Portugal, and Japan) usually prefer more extensive rules and regulations in organizational settings and seek consensus about goals.

Hofstede's original framework contained only four problem types and was criticized for its predominantly western European bias. In response, a group of Chinese researchers developed and administered a similar, but more Asian-oriented, questionnaire to people in 22 countries around the world (Chinese Culture Connection, 1987). Their questionnaire included ideas related to Confucian-based thinking. In comparing their framework to Hofstede's, they concluded that there was, in fact, a great deal of overlap. Indeed, the three dimensions of individualism—collectivism, power distance, and masculinity—femininity—

uncertainty avoidance A cultural variability dimension that concerns the extent to which uncertainty, ambiguity, and deviant ideas and behaviors are avoided.

seem to be universal. However, uncertainty avoidance seems to be more relevant to Western societies. A fifth dimension that emerged from the Asian study and that seems to apply to both Eastern and Western societies is the **long-term versus short-term orientation**, which reflects a society's search for virtue or truth.

Those with a short-term orientation are concerned with possessing the truth (reflected in the Western religions of Judaism, Christianity, and Islam), focus on quick results in endeavors, and recognize social pressure to conform. Those with a long-term orientation tend to respect the demands of virtue (reflected in Eastern religions such as Confucianism, Hinduism, Buddhism, and Shintoism); to focus more on thrift, perseverance, and tenacity in whatever they attempt; and to be willing to subordinate themselves to a larger purpose.

Limitations of Value Frameworks Identifying cultural values helps us understand broad cultural differences, but it is important to remember that not everyone in a given society holds the dominant value. We shouldn't merely reduce individuals to stereotypes based on these value orientations. After all, not all Amish or Japanese are group oriented, and not all Americans and Australians are individualistic. Remember that cultures are dynamic and heterogeneous. Although people in small rural communities may be more collectively oriented, or more willing to help their neighbors, we cannot say that people in big cities ignore those around them.

Value heterogeneity may be particularly noticeable in a society that is undergoing rapid change. Japan, for example was in economic ruin only 50 years ago, after a stunning military defeat at the end of World War II. It now has one of the world's strongest economies. This rapid social and economic change influences traditional values. Recent research with Japanese college students shows they are now remarkably similar to their U.S. counterparts in their preference for individualism, whereas many of their parents' generation still prefer collectivism (Matsumoto, 2002).

Another limitation of value frameworks is that they tend to "essentialize" people. In other words, people tend to assume that a particular group characteristic is the essential characteristic of a given member at all times and in all contexts. Writers Tim Ambler and Morgan Witzel (2000), who have spent a great deal of time in China, challenge the validity of these frameworks and promote a dialectical perspective:

---

long-term versus short-term orientation A cultural variability dimension that reflects a cultural-group orientation toward virtue or truth. The long-term orientation emphasizes virtue, whereas the short-term orientation emphasizes truth.

*For many people familiar with both China and the overseas Chinese, . . .
this research is not reliable in an oriental context because it falls into the
either/or trap. . . . The Chinese are not either individualist or collective
but both at the same time. (p. 70)*

The cultural–individual dialectic reminds us that these value orientations exist on a continuum and are all present, to a greater or lesser
extent, in all societies. For example, we could characterize the debate
about health care in the United States as a struggle between "masculine"
and "feminine" value orientations. Those with a "masculine" orientation believe that each person should take care of him- or herself and
be free to achieve and to acquire as many material goods as possible.
Others, representing a "feminine" position, believe that everyone
should sacrifice a little for the good of the whole and that everyone
should be assured access to health care and hospitalization.

The differences–similarities dialectic reminds us that, although
people may differ with respect to specific value orientations, they also
may hold other value orientations in common. For example, people
may have different views on the importance of individual or group
loyalty but share a belief in the essential goodness of human nature
and find similarity in religious faith and practice. Finally, a static–dynamic dialectic reminds us that, although group-related values tend to
be relatively consistent, people are dynamic, and their behavior varies
contextually. Thus, they may be more or less individualistic or group-
oriented depending on the context.

How Communication Reinforces Culture

Culture not only influences communication but also is enacted
through, and so is influenced by, communication. Scholars of cultural
communication describe how various aspects of culture are enacted
in speech communities in situ, that is, in contexts. They seek to understand communication patterns that are situated socially and give
voice to cultural identity. Specifically, they examine how the cultural
forms and frames (terms, rituals, myths, and social dramas) are enacted
through structuring norms of conversation and interaction. The patterns are not connected in a deterministic way to any cultural group
(Philipsen, 2002).

Researcher Tamar Katriel (1990) examines "griping," a **communication ritual** that takes place among middle-class Israelis. Using the
SPEAKING framework (scene, participant, end, act sequence, key, instrumentality, norm, and genre), Katriel analyzes the ritual in the follow-

communication ritual A set form of systematic interactions that take place on a regular basis.

ing way: The griping topic must be one related to the domain of public life, and the purpose of the griping is not to solve the problem but to vent pent-up tensions and to affirm the shared reality of being Israeli. The ritual is a deeply felt, widely held, accessible behavioral pattern that affirms the cultural identity of Israelis. Although individuals belonging to other cultural groups may gripe, the activity may not be performed in this systematic cultural way and may not fill the same function.

The instrumentality (or channel) in griping is face-to-face, and the scene (or setting) usually is a Friday night gathering in a private home. Participants may be friends or acquaintances, or even strangers, but not real outsiders. (Katriel describes an embarrassing incident when a couple of gripers discovered that one of the group was merely a visiting Jew and not a native Israeli.) The key (or tone) of this ritual is one of plaintiveness and frustration. The act sequence comprises an initiation phase, when someone voices a complaint; this is followed by the acknowledgment phase, when others comment on the opener, and then a progression of subthemes. Finally, during the termination phase, everyone intellectually sighs and agrees that it is a problem: "It's no joke, things are getting worse all the time," the participants might say.

It is possible to compare different ways in which cultural norms and forms such as griping enact aspects of the culture and construct cultural identity. For example, although Katriel is not interested in making cross-cultural comparisons, she does allude to the difference between the Israeli griping ritual and a similar communication ritual that many white, middle-class U.S. residents engage in (Katriel & Philipsen, 1990). The communication ritual is a form of close, supportive, and flexible speech aimed at solving personal problems and affirming participants' identities. It is initiated when people sit down together, acknowledge the problem, and negotiate a solution. Katriel identifies similarities in these two rituals: Each fills the function of dramatizing major cultural problems, provides a preferred social context for the venting of problems and frustration, and promotes a sense of community identity (Katriel, 1990).

A related approach from cultural communication studies sees culture as **performative**. If we accept this metaphor, then we are not studying any external (cultural) reality. Rather, we are examining how persons enact and represent their culture's worldviews. For example, as Philipsen (1992) reports in his study of Teamsterville, men enact their gender (cultural) roles by remaining silent in many instances, engaging in talk mainly with peers but not with women or children.

---

performative Acting or presenting oneself in a specific way so as to accomplish some goal.

These interpretive studies sometimes use cultural values as a way to explain cultural patterns. Kristine Fitch (1994) conducted a cross-cultural study comparing how people in Bogotá, Colombia, and Boulder, Colorado, got others to do what they wanted, a sociolinguistic form known as a *directive*. Fitch found that directives were seen as a problem in both societies, but as different kinds of problems that reflected and reinforced different value orientations. Individuals in Boulder seemed to think that telling someone what to do should be approached carefully so as not to infringe on that person's autonomy—reflecting a value of individualism. In Bogotá, where collectivistic values reign, directives must be negotiated within relationships; there must be enough *confianza* (respect) or authority that one person is required by the social hierarchy to do the other's bidding. As you can see, cultural values can be used to show how culture influences communication or to explain how communication reinforces cultural values.

Communication as Resistance to the Dominant Cultural System

Resistance is the metaphor used in cultural studies to conceptualize the relationship between culture and communication. Borrowing this metaphor, we can try to discover how individuals use their own space to resist the dominant cultural system. For example, in the fall of 2005, nonwhite French youth rioted for days in the suburbs of Paris to communicate their resistance to the ways the French social system works. They felt that their efforts to integrate into mainstream French society were being thwarted by systematic racial discrimination. Similarly, workers often find ways to resist extreme individualism and competition in the workplace. For example, flight attendants may collaborate to protect each other from the critical gaze of supervisors (Murphy, 1998). Or students may sign their advisers' names on course registration forms, thereby circumventing the university bureaucracy. We can interpret these behaviors as resistance to the dominant cultural system.

THE RELATIONSHIP BETWEEN COMMUNICATION AND CONTEXT

Context typically is created by the physical or social aspects of the situation in which communication occurs. For example, communication may occur in a classroom, a bar, or a church; in each case, the physical characteristics of the setting influence the communication. People communicate differently depending on the context. Context is neither static nor objective, and it can be multilayered. Context may consist of the social, political, and historical structures in which the communication occurs.

Not surprisingly, the social context is determined on the societal level. Consider, for example, the controversy over the Calvin Klein underwear ads in the early 1990s that used young adolescents as models: Many critics viewed the ads as equivalent to pedophilia. The controversy took place in a social context in which pedophilia was seen as perverse or immoral. This meant that any communication that encouraged or fed that behavior or perspective, including advertising, was deemed wrong by the majority of observers. However, pedophilia has not been considered wrong in all societies in all periods of history. To interpret the ads adequately, we would have to know something about the current feelings toward and meanings attached to pedophilia wherever the ads were displayed.

The political context in which communication occurs includes those forces that attempt to change or retain existing social structures and relations. For example, to understand the acts of protesters who throw blood or red paint on people who wear fur coats, we must consider the political context. In this case, the political context would be the ongoing informal debates about animal rights and cruelty to animals farmed for their pelts. In other locales or other eras, the protesters' communicative acts would not make sense or would be interpreted in other ways.

We also need to examine the historical context of communication. For example, the meaning of a college degree depends in part on the particular school's reputation. Why does a degree from Harvard communicate a different meaning than a degree from an obscure state university? Harvard's reputation relies on history—the large endowments given over the years, the important persons who have attended and graduated, and so forth.

THE RELATIONSHIP BETWEEN COMMUNICATION AND POWER

Power is pervasive in communication interactions, although it is not always evident or obvious how power influences communication or what kinds of meaning are constructed. We often think of communication between individuals as being between equals, but this is rarely

Rose Weitz, a communication scholar, describes the importance of hair for women in U.S. society in attracting men. Although some writers say that women who use strategies like the "hair flip" in attracting men do so unconsciously and are just blindly obeying cultural rules, her interviews with women reveal that many are acutely aware of the cultural rules and the power of the "flip." Those who cannot participate feel marginalized.

A young white woman:

I have very long hair and use the hair flip, both consciously and unconsciously. When I do it [consciously], I check the room to see if anyone is looking in my direction but never catch a guy's eye first. I just do it in his line of vision. [I] bend over slightly, pretending to get something from a bag or pick something up) so that some of my hair falls in front of my shoulder. Then I lean back and flip my hair out and then shake my head so my hair sways a little.

A young Latino woman:

In Hispanic culture hair is very important for a woman. It defines our beauty and gives us power over men. Now that I cut my hair short, I miss the feeling of moving my hair around and the power it gave me. . . .

The hair flip is especially aggravating for those black women whose hair will not grow long. As one black graduate student explains,

As an African American woman, I am very aware of non–African American women "flipping" their hair. . . . I will speak only for myself here (but I think it's a pretty global feeling for many African American women), but I often look at women who can flip their hair with envy, wishfulness, perhaps regret?, . . . with my "natural" hair, if I run my fingers through it, it's going to be a mess [and won't] gracefully fall back into place.

Source: R. Weitz, *Rapunzel's Daughters: What Women's Hair Tells Us About Women's Lives.* New York: Farrar, Straus and Giroux, 2004.

the case (Allen, 2004). As communication scholar Mark Orbe (1998) describes it,

In every society a social hierarchy exists that privileges some groups over others. Those groups that function at the top of the social hierarchy determine to a great extent the communication system of the entire society. (p. 8)

Orbe goes on to describe how those people in power, consciously or unconsciously, create and maintain communication systems that reflect, reinforce, and promote their own ways of thinking and communicating. There are two levels of group-related power: (1) the primary dimensions—age, ethnicity, gender, physical abilities, race, and sexual orientation—which are more permanent in nature, and (2) the secondary dimensions—educational background, geographic location, marital status, and socioeconomic status—which are more changeable (Loden & Rosener, 1991). The point is that the dominant communication systems ultimately impede those who do not share the systems. The communication style most valued in college classrooms, for example, emphasizes public speaking and competition (because the first person who raises his or her hand gets to speak). Not all students are comfortable with this style, but those who take to it naturally are more likely to succeed.

Power also comes from social institutions and the roles individuals occupy in those institutions. For example, in the classroom, there is temporary inequality, with instructors having more power. After all, they set the course requirements, give grades, determine who speaks, and so on. In this case, the power rests not with the individual instructor but with the role that he or she is enacting.

Power is dynamic. It is not a simple one-way proposition. For example, students may leave a classroom at any time during a class period, or they may carry on a conversation while the professor is speaking—thus weakening the professor's power over them. They may also refuse to accept a grade and file a grievance with the university administration to have the grade changed. Further, the typical power relationship between instructor and student often is not perpetuated beyond the classroom. However, some issues of power play out in a broader social context (Johnson, 2001). For example, in contemporary society, cosmetic companies have a vested interest in a particular image of female beauty that involves purchasing and using makeup. Advertisements encourage women to feel compelled to participate in this cultural definition. Resistance can be expressed by a refusal to go along with the dominant cultural standards of beauty. Angela, a student from rural Michigan, describes how she resisted the "beauty culture" of her metropolitan university:

> *I came to school, and when I looked around I felt like I was inadequate. I had one of two choices: to conform to what the girls look like here, or to stay the same. I chose to stay true to my "Michigan" self. I felt more confident this way. I still remember looking at all of the blond girls with their fake boobs and black pants, strutting down campus. Four years later, I have a more mature attitude and realized that this culture wasn't for me.*

What happens when someone like Angela decides not to buy into this definition? Regardless of the woman's individual reason for not participating, other people are likely to interpret her behavior in ways that may not match her own reasons. What her unadorned face communicates is understood against a backdrop of society's definitions—that is, the backdrop developed by the cosmetics industry.

Dominant cultural groups attempt to perpetuate their positions of privilege in many ways. However, subordinate groups can resist this domination in many ways too. Cultural groups can use political and legal means to maintain or resist domination, but these are not the only means of invoking power relations. Groups can negotiate their various relations to culture through economic boycotts, strikes, and sit-ins. Individuals can subscribe (or not subscribe) to specific magazines or newspapers, change TV channels, write letters to government officials, or take action in other ways to change the influence of power.

The disempowered can negotiate power in many ways. For instance, employees in a large institution can find ways to reposition themselves or gain power. Students might sign their advisers' signature on their registration schedules if they don't have time to see their advisers.

Power is complex, especially in relation to institutions or the social structure. Some inequities, such as in gender, class, or race, are more rigid than those created by temporary roles such as student or teacher. The power relations between student and teacher, for example, are more complex if the teacher is a female challenged by male students. We really can't understand intercultural communication without considering the power dynamics in the interaction.

A dialectical perspective looks at the dynamic and interrelated ways in which culture, communication, context, and power intersect in intercultural communication interactions. Consider this example: When Tom first arrived in Brussels in January 1998, he asked for a national train schedule from the information office at one of the train stations. Because he does not speak Dutch, he talked to the agent behind the counter in French. The agent gave Tom a copy of the national train schedule in Dutch. When Tom asked if it was available in French, the man politely apologized, saying that it was the end of the season and there were no more available in French. It was clear to Tom that, although both parties followed *la forme de la politesse*, the agent did not want to give him the train schedule in French. Indeed, it was not near the end of the season because the 1997–1998 train schedule ran from June 1 to May 23.

From a communication perspective, it might not be at all clear that an intercultural struggle had taken place. None of the traditional signals of conflict were manifested: no raised voices, no harsh words, no curtness. Indeed, the exchange seemed polite and courteous.

From a cultural perspective, however, with various contexts and power differentials in mind, a different view of this intercultural interaction emerges. Belgium is a nation largely divided by two cultures, Flemish and Walloon, although there is a small German-speaking minority in the far eastern part of the country. Belgium is officially trilingual (Dutch, French, German); that is, each language is the official language in its territory. Dutch is the official language in Flanders, and French is the official language in Wallonia, except in the eastern part, where German is the official language. The only part of Belgium that is officially bilingual is the "Brussels-Capital Region."

There are many historical contexts to consider here. For example, Brussels is historically a Flemish city, located in Flanders (but near the border with Wallonia). Also, the French language dominated in Belgium from the time it gained independence from the Netherlands in 1830 until the early 20th century when Flemish gained parity.

There are social and economic contexts to consider as well. Since the 1960s, Flanders has been more economically powerful than Wallonia. The Brussels-Capital Region, despite being in Flanders, has become increasingly French speaking; some estimates place the current percentage of francophones at 85% to 90%. And nearly 30% of Brussels' residents are foreigners, most of whom are francophones. The increasing migration of city dwellers to the suburbs has also caused tensions because a number of communes located in Flanders now have a francophone majority.

So, although the Brussels-Capital Region is officially bilingual, this is the site of a number of struggles between French and Dutch. Indeed, as many Walloons told Tom, one does not get a sense of the conflict in Wallonia, but it is evident in Brussels. In the context of the various tensions that existed at the time of Tom's arrival in Belgium, the intercultural conflict at the train station is merely a playing out of much larger issues in Belgian society. Tom's entry into that society, as another francophone foreigner, situated his communication interactions in largely prefigured ways.

Although he later secured a French train schedule, he continued to use the Dutch one so he could learn the Dutch names of many Belgian cities as well. In any case, Tom's experience involved various dialectical tensions: (1) being a francophone foreigner versus a traditional Flemish resident, (2) being in an officially bilingual region versus an increasingly francophone one, (3) recognizing the importance of formality and politeness in French versus the nature of this ancient conflict, (4) having abundant opportunities to learn French versus the

POINT OF VIEW

ANSWERS TO THE TEST OF U.S. CULTURAL KNOWLEDGE

1. The correct answer is B. Lagniappe refers to small freebies or sometimes small gifts given by stores when you purchase something. It is used mostly in southern Louisiana and Mississippi but also along the Gulf Coast.
2. The correct answer is C. Hoppin' John is a New Year's tradition across the South. Normally it is simply rice and black-eyed peas, but it can include other items.
3. The correct answer is C. Shoofly pie, traditionally made from molasses, is a very sweet pie.
4. The correct answer is D. The Illini are a nonexistent tribe used as the mascot of the University of Illinois at Urbana-Champaign.
5. The correct answer is A. Also sometimes just called Eid, this is a three-day joyous festival that celebrates family, friendship, community, and the Creator. It is a time of reconciliation.
6. The correct answer is A. It marks the anniversary of the Supreme Court ruling in *Loving v. Virginia* that overturned legal barriers to interracial marriage.
7. The correct answer is D. Hanamatsuri (or flower festival) is in the spring and marks a time of renewal and the birthday of Buddha.
8. The correct answer is A. Lefse is made primarily from potatoes.
9. The correct answer is D. Menudo is traditionally served on New Year's Day.
10. The correct answer is C. Haupia is made from coconut milk.

lack of opportunities to study Dutch in the United States, and (5) illustrating the economic power of the Flemish in Belgium versus that of the francophones in Brussels. From these dialectical tensions and others, Tom attempted to understand and contextualize his intercultural interaction.

There are no simple lists of behaviors that are key to successful intercultural interaction. Instead, we encourage you to understand the contexts and dialectical tensions that arise in your intercultural communication experiences. In this way, you will better understand the constraints you face in your interactions. You will also come to a better understanding of the culture you are in and the culture you are from. Although the dialectical perspective makes the investigation of culture and communication far more complex, it also makes it far more exciting and interesting and leads to a much richer understanding.

DISCUSSION QUESTIONS

1. How have notions of high and low culture infenced people's perspectives on culture?
2. How do the values of a cultural group influence communication with members of other cultural groups?
3. What techniques do people use to assert power in communication interactions?
4. How is culture a contested site?

ACTIVITIES

1. *Cultural Values.* Look for advertisements in newspapers and popular magazines. Analyze the ads to see if you can identify the social values to which they appeal.
2. *Culture: Deeply Felt or Contested Zone?* Analyze the lyrics of songs you listen to and try to identify patterns in the songs. Then think about your own cultural position and discuss which framework— the one proposed by cultural ethnographies (culture as deeply felt) or the one proposed by cultural studies (culture as a contested zone)—more adequately articulates the connection between culture and communication.

REFERENCES

Allen, B. (2004). *Difference matters: Communicating social identity.* Long Grove, IL: Waveland Press.

Ambler, T., & Witzel, M. (2000). *Doing business in China.* New York: Routledge.

Baldwin, J. R., & Lindsley, S. L. (1994). *Conceptualizations of culture.* Tempe: Arizona State University Urban Studies Center.

Bellah, R. N., Madsen, R., Sullivan, W. M., Swidler, A., & Tipton, S. M. (1985). *Habits of the heart: Individualism and commitment in American life.* New York: Harper & Row.

Berger, Y. (1998, January 7). A bout portant. Le Soir, p. 2.

Burke, J. (1985). *The day the universe changed.* Boston: Little, Brown.

Buzzanell, P. M. (1994). Gaining a voice: Feminist organizational communication theorizing. *Management Communication Quarterly, 7,* 339–383.

Carbaugh, D. (1988). Comments on "culture" in communication inquiry. *Communication Reports*, 1, 38–41.

Carey, J. W. (1989). *Communication as culture: Essays on media and society*. Boston: Unwin Hyman.

Cargile, A. (2005). Describing culture dialectically. In W. J. Starosta & G.-M. Chen (Eds.), *Taking stock in intercultural communication: Where to now?* (pp. 99–123). Washington, DC: National Communication Association.

Chinese Culture Connection. (1987). Chinese values and the search for culture-free dimensions of culture. *Journal of Cross-Cultural Psychology*, 18, 143–164.

Collier, M. J., Hegde, R. S., Lee, W., Nakayama, T. K., & Yep, G. A. (2002). Dialogue on the edges: Ferment in communication and culture. In M. J. Collier (Ed.), *Transforming communication about culture (International and Intercultural Communication Annual*, Vol. 24, pp. 219–280). Thousand Oaks, CA: Sage.

Dunbar, R. A. (1997). Bloody footprints: Reflections on growing up poor white. In M. Wray & A. Newitz (Eds.), *White trash: Race and class in America* (pp. 73–86). New York: Routledge.

Fitch, K. L. (1994). A cross-cultural study of directive sequences and some implications for compliance-gaining research. *Communication Monographs*, 61, 185–209.

Geertz, C. (1973). *The interpretation of culture*. New York: Basic Books.

Grossberg, L. (1993). Can cultural studies find true happiness in communication? *Journal of Communication*, 43(4), 89–97.

Gudykunst, W. B. (2002). Issues in cross-cultural communication research. In W. B. Gudykunst & B. Mody (Eds.). *Handbook of international and intercultural communication* (2nd ed., pp. 165–177). Thousand Oaks, CA: Sage.

Hall, B. (1992). Theories of culture and communication. *Communication Theory*, 1, 50–70.

Hall, S. (1992). Cultural studies and its theoretical legacies. In L. Grossberg, C. Nelson, & P. Treichler (Eds.), *Cultural studies* (pp. 277–294). New York: Routledge.

Hannerz, U. (1996). *Transnational connections*. London: Routledge.

Hofstede, G. (1984). *Culture's consequences*. Beverly Hills, CA: Sage.

Hofstede, G., & Hofstede, G. J. (2004). *Cultures and organizations: Software of the mind* (2nd ed.). Boston: McGraw-Hill.

Hymes, D. (1972). Models of the interaction of language and social life. In J. Gumperz & D. Hymes (Eds.), *Directions in sociolinguistics: The ethnography of speaking* (pp. 35–71). New York: Holt, Rinehart & Winston.

Johnson, A. G. (2001). *Privilege, power, and difference*. Boston: McGraw-Hill.

Katriel, T. (1990). "Griping" as a verbal ritual in some Israeli discourse. In D. Carbaugh (Ed.), *Cultural communication and intercultural contact* (pp. 99–112). Hillsdale, NJ: Lawrence Erlbaum.

Katriel, T., & Philipsen, G. (1990). What we need is communication: "Communication" as a cultural category in some American speech. In D. Carbaugh (Ed.), *Cultural communication and intercultural contact* (pp. 77–94). Hillsdale, NJ: Lawrence Erlbaum.

Keesing, R. M. (1994). Theories of culture revisited. In R. Brofsky (Ed.), *Assessing cultural anthropology*. New York: McGraw-Hill.

Kluckhohn, F., & Strodtbeck, F. (1961). *Variations in value orientations*. Chicago: Row, Peterson.

Kohls, L. R. (1996). *Survival kit for*

overseas living. Yarmouth, ME: Intercultural Press.

Loden, M., & Rosener, J. B. (1991). *Workforce American! Managing employee diversity as a vital resource.* Homewood, IL: Business One Irwin.

Martin, J. N., & Nakayama, T. K. (1999). Thinking dialectically about culture and communication. *Communication Theory, 9,* 1–25.

Matsumoto, D. (2002). *The New Japan: Debunking seven cultural stereotypes.* Yarmouth, ME: Intercultural Press.

Murphy, A. G. (1998). Hidden transcripts of flight attendant resistance. *Management Communication Quarterly, 11,* 499–512.

Orbe, M. O. (1998). *Constructing co-cultural theory: An explication of culture, power, and communication.* Thousand Oaks, CA: Sage.

Philipsen, G. (1992). *Speaking culturally: Explorations in social communication.* Albany: State University of New York Press.

Philipsen, G. (2002). Cultural communication. In W. B. Gudykunst & B. Mody (Eds.), *Handbook of international and intercultural communication* (2nd ed., pp. 51–67). Thousand Oaks, CA: Sage.

Singer, M. R. (1987). *Intercultural communication: A perceptual approach.* Englewood Cliffs, NJ: Prentice-Hall.

Stewart, E. C., & Bennett, M. J. (1991). *American cultural patterns: A cross-cultural perspective.* Yarmouth, ME: Intercultural Press.

Williams, R. (1981). The analysis of culture. In T. Bennett, G. Martin, C. Mercer, & J. Woollacott (Eds.), *Culture, ideology and social process: A reader* (pp. 43–52). London: Open University Press.

Williams, R. (1983). *Keywords: A vocabulary of culture and society* (Rev. ed). New York: Oxford University Press.

HISTORY AND INTERCULTURAL COMMUNICATION

CHAPTER OBJECTIVES

After reading this chapter, you should be able to

1. Identify six different types of history.

2. Define "the grand narrative."

3. Explain the relationship between history, power, and intercultural communication.

4. Describe the role of narratives in constructing history.

5. Describe the relationship between history and identity.

6. Identify four types of hidden histories.

7. Identify four antecedents that influence intercultural contact.

8. Explain the contact hypothesis.

9. Identify eight contact conditions that influence positive attitude change.

10. Describe a dialectic perspective in negotiating personal histories.

Frances Fitzgerald (1972), a journalist who has written about the U.S. involvement in the Vietnam War, analyzes the U.S. cultural orientation to the future rather than the past:

Americans ignore history, for to them everything has always seemed new under the sun. The national myth is that of creativity and progress, of a steady climbing upward into power and prosperity, both for the individual and for the country as a whole. Americans see history as a straight line and themselves standing at the cutting edge of it as representatives for all mankind. They believe in the future as if it were a religion; they believe that there is nothing they cannot accomplish, that solutions wait somewhere for all problems.

This difference in orientation to the past framed the conflict in a very narrow way for the United States. This contrasts greatly with the Vietnamese view of history, especially in the context of their struggles against outside aggression over thousands of years.

You may think it odd to find a chapter about history in a book on intercultural communication. After all, what does the past have to do with intercultural interaction? In this chapter, we discuss how the past is a very important facet of intercultural communication.

The history that we know and our views of that history are very much influenced by our culture. When people of different cultural backgrounds encounter one another, the differences among them can become hidden barriers to communication. However, people often overlook such dynamics in intercultural communication. We typically think of "history" as something contained in history books. We may view history as those events and people, mostly military and political, that played significant roles in shaping the world of today. This chapter examines some of the ways in which history is important in understanding intercultural interaction. Many intercultural interactions involve a dialectical interplay between past and present.

We have found, in the classes we teach, that European American students often want to deemphasize history. "Why do we have to dwell on the past? Can't we all move on?" they ask. In contrast, some other students argue that without history it is impossible to understand who they are. How do these different viewpoints affect the communication among such students? What is the possibility for meaningful communication interactions among them?

On a larger scale, we can see how history influences intercultural interaction in many different contexts. For example, the ongoing conflict between the Israelis and the Palestinians makes little sense without an understanding of the historical relations among the different groups that reside in the area. Historical antagonisms help explain the present-day animosity felt by many Pakistanis toward Indians. Disputes over the Kashmir region, Indian participation in the struggle for independence of Bangladesh, and conflicts over the Himalayas underscore deep-rooted bases for strife. Likewise, historical antagonisms (including colonization, discrimination, and starvation) help explain the current animosity felt by many Irish toward the British.

How we think about the past very much influences how we think about ourselves and others even here in the United States. Judith went to college in southern Virginia after growing up in Delaware and Pennsylvania. She was shocked to encounter the antipathy that her dormitory suitemates expressed toward northerners. The suitemates stated emphatically that they had no desire to visit the North; they felt certain that "Yankees" were unfriendly and unpleasant people.

For Judith, the Civil War was a paragraph in a history book; for her suite-mates, that historical event held a more important meaning. It took a while for friendships to develop between Judith and her suitemates. In this way, their interactions demonstrated the present–past dialectic. Indeed, this exemplifies the central focus of this chapter: that various histories contextualize intercultural communication. Taking a dialectical perspective enables us to understand how history positions people in different places from which they can communicate and understand other people's messages.

Early in this book, we set forth six dialectical tensions that we believe drive much intercultural interaction. In this chapter, we focus on the history/past–present/future dialectic. As you will see, culture and cultural identities are intimately tied to history because they have no meaning without history. Yet there is no single version of history; the past has been written in many different ways. For example, your own family has its version of family history that must be placed in dialectical tension with all of the other narratives about the past. Is it important to you to feel positive about who your forebears were and where they came from? We often feel a strong need to identify in positive ways with our past even if we are not interested in history. The stories of the past, whether accurate or not, help us understand why our families live where they do, why they own or lost land there, and so on. We experience this dialectical tension between the past, the present, and the future every day. It helps us understand who we are and why we live and communicate in the ways we do.

In this chapter, we first discuss the various histories that provide the contexts in which we communicate: political, intellectual, social, family, national, and cultural-group histories. We then describe how these histories are intertwined with our various identities, based on gender, sexual orientation, ethnicity, race, and so on. This chapter introduces two identities that have strong historical bases: diasporic and colonial. We pay particular attention to the role of narrating our personal histories. As you read this chapter, think about the importance of history in constructing your own identity and the ways in which the past–present dialectic helps us understand different identities for others in various cultural groups. Finally, we explore how history influences intercultural communication.

FROM HISTORY TO HISTORIES

Many different kinds of history influence our understanding of who we are—as individuals, as family members, as members of cultural groups, and as citizens of a nation. To understand the dialectics in everyday interaction, we need to think about the many histories that help form our different identities. These histories necessarily overlap and influence each other. For example, when Fidel Castro came to power over half a century ago, many Cubans fled to the United States. The families that departed have histories about that experience that help them understand their cultural identity. Political histories tell the story of that exodus but not necessarily the story of every family, even though many families' histories were very much influenced by that event. Understanding all of those histories sheds new light on the conflict surrounding the decision in 2000 to return young Elián González to his father in Cuba, rather than permit him to remain in the United States. Identifying the various forms of historical contexts is the first step in understanding how history affects communication.

Political, Intellectual, and Social Histories

Some people restrict their notion of history to documented events. Although we cannot read every book written, we do have greater access to written history. When these types of history focus on political events, we call them **political histories**. Written histories that focus on the development of ideas are often called **intellectual histories**. Some writers seek to understand the everyday life experiences of various groups in the past; what they document are called **social histories**.

---

political histories Written histories that focus on political events.
intellectual histories Written histories that focus on the development of ideas.
social histories Written histories that focus on everyday life experiences of various groups in the past.

Although these types of history seem more manageable than the broad notion of history as "everything that has happened before now," we must also remember that many historical events never make it into books. For example, the strict laws that forbade teaching slaves in the United States to read kept many of their stories from being documented. **Absent history**, of course, does not mean the people did not exist, their experiences do not matter, or their history has no bearing on us today. To consider such absent histories requires that we think in more complex ways about the past and the ways it influences the present and the future.

Family Histories

Family histories occur at the same time as other histories but on a more personal level. They often are not written down but are passed along orally from one generation to the next. Some people do not know which countries or cities their families emigrated from or what tribes they belonged to or where they lived in the United States. Other people place great emphasis on knowing that their ancestors fought in the Revolutionary War, survived the Holocaust, or traveled the Trail of Tears when the Cherokees were forcibly relocated from the Southeast to present-day Oklahoma. Many of these family histories are deeply intertwined with ethnic-group histories, but the family histories identify each family's participation in these events.

You might talk to members of your own family to discover how they feel about your family's history. Find out, for example, how family history influences their perceptions of who they are. Do they wish they knew more about their family? What things has your family continued to do that your forebears probably also did? Do you eat some of the same foods? Practice the same religion? Celebrate birthdays or weddings in the same way? The continuity between past and present often is taken for granted.

National Histories

The history of any nation is important to the people of that nation. We typically learn **national history** in school. In the United States,

---

absent history Any part of history that was not recorded or that is missing. Not everything that happened in the past is accessible to us today because only some voices were documented and only some perspectives were recorded.

family histories Histories of individual families that are typically passed down through oral stories.

national history A body of knowledge based on past events that influenced a country's development.

we learn about the founding fathers—George Washington, Benjamin Franklin, John Jay, Alexander Hamilton, and so on—and our national history typically begins with the arrival of Europeans in North America in the 16th century.

U.S. citizens are expected to recognize the great events and the so-called great people (mostly men of European ancestry) who were influential in the development of the nation. In history classes, students learn about the Revolutionary War, Thomas Paine, the War of 1812, the Civil War, Abraham Lincoln, the Great Depression, Franklin D. Roosevelt, and so on. They are told stories, verging on myths, that give life to these events and figures. For example, students learn about Patrick Henry's "give me liberty or give me death" speech even though the text of the speech was collected by a biographer who "pieced together twelve hundred words from scattered fragments that ear witnesses remembered from twenty years before" (Thonssen, Baird, & Braden, 1970, p. 335). Students also learn about George Washington having chopped down a cherry tree and confessing his guilt ("I cannot tell a lie"), although there's no evidence of this story's truth.

National history gives us a shared notion of who we are and solidifies our sense of nationhood. Although we may not fit into the national narrative, we are expected to be familiar with this particular telling of U.S. history so we can understand the many references used in communication. It is one way of constructing cultural discourses. Yet U.S. students seldom learn much about the histories of other nations and cultures unless they study the languages of those countries. As any student of another language knows, it is part of the curriculum to study not only the grammar and vocabulary of the language but also the culture and history of the people who speak that language.

Judith and Tom both studied French. Because we learned a great deal about French history, we understand references to the *ancien régime* (the political system prior to the French Revolution in 1789), *les Pieds-noirs* (colonial French who returned to France during the struggle for Algerian independence in the mid-20th century), *la Bastille* (the notorious prison), and other commonly used terms. The French have their own national history, centering on the development of France as a nation. For example, French people know that they live in the *Vème République* (or Fifth Republic), and they know what that means within the grand narrative of French history.

When Judith lived in Algeria, her French friends spoke of *les Événements* (the events), but her Algerian friends spoke of *la Libération*—both referring to the war between France and Algeria that led to Algerian independence. When Tom lived in France, he also heard the expression *la Libération*, but here it referred to the end of the German occupation in France during World War II. Historical contexts shape language, which means we must search for salient historical features in communicating across cultural differences.

Cultural-Group Histories

Although people may share a single national history, each cultural group within the nation may have its own history. The history may be obscure (hidden), but it is still related to the national history. **Cultural-group histories** help us understand the identities of various groups.

Consider, for example, the expulsion of many Acadians from eastern Canada and their migration to and settlement in Louisiana. These historical events are central to understanding the cultural traits of the Cajuns. The forced removal in 1838 of the Cherokees from Georgia to settlements in what eventually became the state of Oklahoma resulted in a 22% loss of the Cherokee population. This event, known as the Trail of Tears, explains much about the Cherokee Nation. The migration in 1846 of 12,000 Latter Day Saints from Nauvoo, Illinois, to the Great Basin region in the western United States was prompted by anti-Mormon attacks. These events explain much about the character of Utah. The northward migration of African Americans in the early part of the 20th century helps us understand the settlement patterns and working conditions in northern cities such as Cleveland, Detroit, Chicago, and New York. These cultural histories are not typically included in our national history, but they are important in the development of group identity, family histories, and contemporary lives of individual members of these co-cultures.

We prefer to view history as the many stories we tell about the past, rather than one story on a single time continuum. Certainly, the events of families, cultural groups, and nations are related. Even world events are related. Ignorance of the histories of other groups makes intercultural communication more difficult and more susceptible to misunderstandings.

HISTORY, POWER, AND INTERCULTURAL COMMUNICATION

Power is a central dynamic in the writing of history. It influences the

---

cultural-group histories The history of each cultural group within a nation that includes, for example, the history of where the group originated, why the people migrated, and how they came to develop and maintain their cultural traits.

content of the history we know and the way it is delivered. Power dictates what is taught and what is silenced, what is available and what is erased. Let's look at what this means.

The Power of Texts

History is extremely important in understanding identity. Think about all of the stories about the past that you have been taught. Yet, as literature professor Fredric Jameson (1981) notes, although history is not a narrative at all, it is accessible to us only in textual, narrative form. However, people do not have equal access to the writing and production of these texts.

Political texts reflect the disparities of access to political participation in various countries at various times in history. Some languages have been forbidden, making the writing of texts difficult if not impossible. For example, U.S. government Indian schools did not permit Native American children to speak their native languages, which makes it more difficult for people today to understand what this experience was about.

With regard to the language we use to understand history, think about the difference between the terms *internment camp* and *concentration camp*. In 1942, at the height of World War II, after President Franklin Roosevelt signed Executive Order 9066, anyone of Japanese ancestry—whether they were U.S. citizens or not—were rounded up from a restricted zone, including parts of Arizona, Oregon, and Washington and all of California, and placed mostly into ten camps. The U.S. federal government used both terms in the 1940s, but the historical weight of the German concentration camps of the same era, in which millions of Jews perished, often casts a shadow over our understanding of the U.S. concentration camps. Denotatively, the use of the term *concentration camp* is correct, but connotatively, it invokes quite different responses. You may wish to keep this in mind as you read Chapter 6, which discusses the importance of language and discourse in intercultural communication.

When U.S. Americans are taught history, they also learn a particular way of looking at the world from their history textbooks. This worldview, as James Loewen (1995) tells us, reinforces a very positive white American identity. In his analysis of history textbooks, he notes, "History is furious debate informed by evidence and reason. Textbooks encourage students to believe that history is facts to be learned" (p. 16). Yet these "facts" are often wrong or portray the past in ways that serve the white American identity. For example, he analyzes the way in which Native Americans are depicted in history texts:

POINT OF VIEW

The internment, or mass imprisonment, of Japanese Americans by the U.S. government in the 1940s has led to much discussion about the right term for these camps. What difference does it make if we call them "concentration camps" or "relocation centers"? This entry from the *Encyclopedia of Japanese American History* provides food for thought.

> **Concentration camps.** *Euphemistically called "relocation centers" by the War Relocation Authority (WRA), the concentration camps were hastily constructed facilities for housing Japanese Americans forcibly removed from their homes and businesses on the West Coast during World War II. Located in isolated areas of the United States on either desert or swampland, the camps were usually surrounded by barbed wire and guarded by armed sentries. Although these sentries were presumably in place to protect the inmates from hostile outsiders, their guns usually pointed into the camps instead of away from them. Most inmates were transported to their camp by train from an assembly center between April and September 1942. In all, over 120,000 Japanese Americans served time in these camps.*

Source: From B. Niiya (Ed.), *Encyclopedia of Japanese American History: An A-to-Z Reference from 1868 to the Present* (New York: Checkmark Books, 2001), p. 142.

Even if no Natives remained among us, however, it would still be important for us to understand the alternatives forgone, to remember the wars, and to learn the unvarnished truths about white–Indian relations. Indian history is the antidote to the pious ethnocentrism of American exceptionalism, the notion that European Americans are God's chosen people. Indian history reveals that the United States and its predecessor British colonies have wrought great harm in the world. We must not forget this—not to wallow in our wrongdoing, but to understand and to learn, that we might not wreak harm again. (p. 136)

But the prevailing value of teaching history lies not in serving the future but in reinforcing a positive cultural identity for white Americans. How does power function in determining which stories are told and how they are told?

The relative availability of political texts and the ways that they reflect powerful inequities are reinscribed in the process of writing history. History writing requires documentation and texts, and, of course, is limited by what is available. In writing history, we often ask ourselves, "What was important?" without asking, "Important to whom? For what purposes?" Once texts are written, they are available for teaching and learning about the past. But the seeming unity of the past, the linear nature of history, is merely the reflection of a **modernist identity**, grounded in the Western tradition.

The Power of Other Histories

We live in an era of rapid change, which causes us to rethink cultural struggles and identities. It may be difficult for you to envision, but at one time a unified story of humankind—the **"grand narrative"**—dominated how people thought of the past, present, and future. The grand narrative refers to the overarching, all-encompassing story of a nation or humankind in general. Because of the way it is built, this grand narrative organizes history into an understandable story that leads to some "truths" over other possible conclusions. In the story of humankind, the grand narrative was one of progress and an underlying assumption that developments in science, medicine, and education would lead to progress and better lives. This is no longer the case. French philosopher Jean-François Lyotard (1984) writes:

> *In contemporary society and culture—postindustrial society, postmodern culture—the grand narrative has lost its credibility, regardless of what mode of unification it uses, regardless of whether it is a speculative narrative or a narrative of emancipation. (p. 37)*

In the wake of continuous wars and global conflicts, global warming, failed promises of liberation, new diseases such as human immunodeficiency virus (HIV) and bird flu, and other events that challenge what we know and what has changed, the master narrative no longer seems as believable to many. In its place are many other narratives that tell different stories. In the context of intercultural communication, the master narratives of many cultures and nations are also undergoing reconsideration, and many new narratives are emerging.

In her work on the constructions of white identity in South Africa, communication scholar Melissa Steyn (2001) notes how the grand narrative in South Africa served white interests and led to the establishment of **apartheid**. Although racially restrictive laws existed in South Africa for many years, the South African government instituted a rigid framework for regulating race in 1948. This system, apartheid,

---

modernist identity The identity that is grounded in the Western tradition of scientific and political beliefs and assumptions— for example, the belief in external reality, democratic representation, liberation, and independent subjects.
grand narrative A unified history and view of humankind.
apartheid A policy that segregated people racially in South Africa.

Since the ending of apartheid in South Africa, there has been a rewriting of the nation's history textbooks in an attempt to forge a new national identity and a different understanding of the past. However, there are strongly contested and very different views about the South African past. Compare, for example, the apartheid view and the postapartheid view of the establishment of separate areas for whites and blacks during the 1950s and 1960s. Think about how any understanding of history is important in creating cultural identity.

> *Apartheid View: The Group Areas Act is passed, dividing the country by race. Apartheid is an absolute necessity, because all nationalisms are mutually exclusive, and it is in the best interest of both races to live separately from one another. Hence black people must be relocated to "some of the best parts of the country."*
>
> *Post-Apartheid View: Tens of thousands of black people are violently removed from their homes, entire neighborhoods are bulldozed, and dispossessed residents are forced to move to some of the least fertile and most remote regions of the country, where employment opportunities are scarce, if not nonexistent. Meanwhile, the white minority secures control of the best land and its mineral wealth.*

Source: From Sasha Polakow-Suransky, "Reviving South African History," *The Chronicle of Higher Education*, June 14, 2002, p. A37.

lasted until it was dismantled from 1990 to 1994, but only after a long struggle against it. Under this apartheid system, everyone was required to register their race in one of four categories: black, white, Indian, and coloured. These categories were used to restrict where people could live (e.g., blacks were permitted to live on only 13% of the land, although they constituted 60% of the population), employment, access to public facilities (e.g., hospitals, ambulances, educational institutions), and other aspects of public life. Although they were numerically a minority, whites dominated this social system and accrued most of the benefits of it. To do so, they needed to tell a master narrative in which this system seemed to make sense. It was only under tremendous domestic and international pressure that the system was dismantled (Bureau of African Affairs, 2005; Guelke, 2005; Thompson, 2001).

The popular film *Cry Freedom* (Attenborough, 1987), starring Denzel Washington as Steven Biko, a black leader, highlights the struggle and consequences of apartheid. Steyn writes:

> *In drawing on the master narrative, interpreting it and adapting it to the particular circumstances in which they found themselves in the country, whites were able to maintain their advantage as the dominating group that controlled the political, material, and symbolic resources of the country for three centuries. (p. 43)*

By telling and retelling one view of the past, white South Africans were able to create a society in which a white minority dominated.

In place of the grand narrative are revised and restored histories that previously were suppressed, hidden, or erased. The cultural movements making this shift possible are empowering to the cultural identities involved. Recovering various histories is necessary to rethinking what some cultural identities mean. It also helps us rethink the dominant cultural identity.

For example, on June 30, 1960, at the signing of the treaty granting independence to the former Belgian colony of the Congo (as Zaire), the king of the Belgians, Baudouin, constructed one way of thinking about the past:

> *All of our thoughts should be turned toward those who founded the African emancipation and after them, those who made the Congo into what it is today. They merit at the same time our admiration and your recognition since it was they who consecrated all of their efforts and even their lives for a grand ideal, bringing you peace and enriching your homeland materially and morally. They must never be forgotten, not by Belgium, not by the Congo. (quoted in Gérard-Libois & Heinen, 1989, p. 143)*

In response, Patrice Lumumba, who would become prime minister, offered a different view of Belgian colonialism:

> *After eighty years of colonial rule, our wounds are still too fresh and too deep to be chased from our memory. . . . We have known the ironies, the insults, the beatings to which we had to submit morning, noon, and night because we were negroes. Who will forget that they spoke to Blacks with "tu" certainly not because of friendship, but because the honorary "vous" was reserved only for speaking to whites. (p. 147)*

Lumumba's words created a different sense of history. These differences were clear to the people of the time and remain clear today. In this way, the grand narrative of Belgian colonialism has been reconfigured and no longer stands as the only story of the Belgian Congo.

Power in Intercultural Interactions

Power is also the legacy, the remnants of the history that leaves cultural groups in particular positions. We are not equal in our intercultural encounters, nor can we ever be equal. Long histories of imperialism, colonialism, exploitation, wars, genocide, and more leave cultural groups out of balance when they communicate.

Regardless of whether we choose to recognize the foundations for many of our differences, these inequalities influence how we think about others and how we interact with them. They also influence how we think about ourselves—our identities. These are important aspects of intercultural communication. It may seem daunting to confront the history of power struggles. Nevertheless, the more you know, the better you will be positioned to engage in successful intercultural interactions.

HISTORY AND IDENTITY

The development of cultural identity is influenced largely by history. In this next section, we look at some of the ways that cultural identities are constructed through understanding the past. Note how different cultural-group identities are tied to history.

Histories as Stories

Faced with these many levels or types of history, you might wonder how we make sense of them in our everyday lives. Although it might be tempting to ignore them all and merely pretend to be "ourselves," this belies the substantial influence that history has on our own identities.

According to communication scholar Walter Fisher (1984, 1985), storytelling is fundamental to the human experience. Instead of referring to humans as *Homo sapiens*, Fisher prefers to call them *Homo narrans* because it underscores the importance of narratives in our lives. Histories are stories that we use to make sense of who we are and who we think others are.

It is important to recognize that a strong element in our cultural

POINT OF VIEW

We can never escape the past, and in the Polish town that was the site of the infamous Auschwitz concentration camp, the preservation of this past is seen as hampering economic development. Much of the town is preserved to mark this horrific history. If they cannot escape the past, what options do the townspeople have in this situation?

Andrzej Czarnik was surprised, but hardly shocked, to learn that his home stood on the site of the first gas chamber Nazis used to kill Jews at Auschwitz.

"In this town," he said, "there are human ashes everywhere."

A year ago, Czarnik agreed to an offer to take another house a mile away so the Auschwitz museum could demolish his and erect a memorial.

"What can you do about it?" he said, sitting on a bench outside his new twostory home. "You can't just plant grass everywhere."

It's a familiar refrain among the 43,000 residents of Oswiecim, a poor industrial town in southern Poland, where remnants of the Auschwitz-Birkenau death camp seem to be everywhere. . . .

Frustrated townspeople say that the preserved remains of the camp are symbol enough and that uncertainty over other so-called martyrdom sites hampers sorely needed investment.

The town is hurting from layoffs that began in 1997 when the communistera Dwory chemicals plant began restructuring. . . .

Jewish appeals to preserve off-camp sites have collided with private-property rights and local fears that Oswiecim could become one big cemetery. . . .

Townspeople say they deserve more understanding, not more off-limits zones.

"We want to live a normal life," said Monika Kos, 21, who has lived all her life in the Pilecki housing block just outside the Auschwitz fence. Built as a camp annex in 1944, the buildings once housed 6,000 female prisoners and a laboratory where some endured sterilization experiments.

Source: From Beata Pasek, "Auschwitz Haunts Town," *The Arizona Republic*, June 9, 2002, p. A24.

attitudes encourages us to forget history at times. French writer Jean Baudrillard (1988) observes:

> *America was created in the hope of escaping from history, of building a utopia sheltered from history. . . . [It] has in part succeeded in that project, a project it is still pursuing today. The concept of history as the transcending of a social and political rationality, as a dialectical, conflictual vision of societies, is not theirs, just as modernity, conceived precisely as an original break with certain history, will never be ours [France's]. (p. 80)*

The desire to escape history is significant in what it tells us about how our culture negotiates its relation to the past, as well as how we view the relations of other nations and cultures to their pasts. By ignoring history, we sometimes come to wrongheaded conclusions about others that only perpetuate and reinforce stereotypes. For example, the notion that Jewish people are obsessed with money and are disproportionately represented in the world of finance belies the history of anti-Semitism, whereby Jews were excluded from many professions. The paradox is that we cannot escape history even if we fail to recognize it or try to suppress it.

Nonmainstream Histories

People from nonmainstream cultural groups often struggle to retain their histories. Theirs are not the histories that everyone learns about in school, yet these histories are vital to understanding how others perceive them and why. Mainstream history has neither the time nor the space nor the inclination to include all **ethnic histories** and **racial histories**. This is especially true given that the histories of cultural groups sometimes seem to question, and even undermine, the celebratory nature of the mainstream national history.

When Tom's parents meet other Japanese Americans of their generation, they are often asked, "What camp were you in?" This question makes little sense outside of its historical context. Indeed, this question is embedded in understanding a particular moment in history, a moment that is not widely understood. Most Japanese Americans were interned in concentration camps during World War II. In the aftermath of the experience, the use of that history as a marker has been important in maintaining cultural identity.

Similarly, for Jewish people, remembering the Holocaust is crucial to their identity. A Jewish colleague recalls growing up in New York

---

ethnic histories The histories of ethnic groups.
racial histories The histories of nonmainstream racial groups.

City in the 1950s and 1960s and hearing stories of Nazi atrocities. Survivors warned that such atrocities could happen again, that being victimized was always a possibility. Recent attempts by revisionists to deny that the Holocaust even happened have met with fierce opposition and a renewed effort to document that tragedy in unmistakable detail. The Holocaust Museum in Washington, D.C., is a memorial to that history for all of us.

Ethnic and racial histories are never isolated; rather, they crisscross other cultural trajectories. We may feel as if we have been placed in the position of victim or victimizer by distant historical events, and we may even seem to occupy both of these positions simultaneously. Consider, for example, the position of German American Mennonites during World War II. They were punished as pacifists and yet also were seen as aggressors by U.S. Jews. To further complicate matters, U.S. citizens of German ancestry were not interned in concentration camps, as were U.S. citizens of Japanese ancestry. How we think about being victims and victimizers is quite complex.

French writer Maurice Blanchot, in confronting the horrors of the Holocaust, the devastation of the atom bomb, and other human disasters, redefines the notion of responsibility, separating it from fault. In *The Writing of the Disaster*, Blanchot (1986) asserts,

> *My responsibility is anterior to my birth just as it is exterior to my consent, to my liberty. I am born thanks to a favor which turns out to be a predestination—born unto the grief of the other, which is the grief of all. (p. 22)*

This perspective can help us face and deal with the different positions that history finds for us.

The displacement of various populations is embedded in the history of every migrating or colonizing people. Whether caused by natural disasters such as the drought in the Midwest during the Great Depression of the 1930s or determined by choice, migrations influence how we live today. Native peoples throughout most of the United States were exterminated or removed to settlements in other regions. The state of Iowa, for example, has few Native Americans and only one reservation. The current residents of Iowa had nothing to do with the events in their state's history, but they are the beneficiaries through the ownership of farms and other land. So, although contemporary Iowans are not in a position of fault or blame, they are, through these benefits, in a position of responsibility. Like all of us, their lives are entangled in the web of history from which there is no escape, only denial and silence.

DNA testing has helped uncover the hidden histories of families. For Hispanics in the Southwest, DNA testing has helped many realize that they are likely descendants of Marranos (Sephardic Jews) who fled the Inquisition over four hundred years ago. Some of these descendants reclaim their Jewish heritage; others do not.

When she was growing up in a small town in southern Colorado, an area where her ancestors settled centuries ago, when it was on the fringes of the northern frontier of New Spain, Bernadette Gonzalez always though some of the stories about her family were unusual, if not bizarre.

Her grandmother, for instance, refused to travel on Saturday and would use a specific porcelain basin to drain blood out of meat before she cooked it. [. . .]

Ms. Gonzalez started researching her family history and concluded that her ancesters were Marranos, or Sephardic Jews, who had fled the Inquisition in Spain and in Mexico more than four centuries ago. Though raised in the Roman Catholic faith, Ms. Gonzalez felt a need to reconnect to her Jewish roots, so she converted to Judaism three years ago. [. . .]

Modern science may now be shedding new light on the history of the crypto-Jews after molecular anthropologists recently developed a DNA test of the male or Y chromosome that can indicate an ancestral connection to the Cohanim, a priestly class of Jews that traces its origin back more then 3,000 years to Aaron, the older brother of Moses. [. . .]

Not everyone who discovers Jewish ancestry, either through genealogical research or DNA testing, has decided to convert to Judaism, but some Hispanics who have found links still feel drawn to incorporate Jewish customs into their life.

Source: Simon Romero, "Hispanics Uncovering Roots as Inquisition's 'Hidden' Jews," *New York Times*, October 29, 2005, p. A17.

Hidden Histories

For people whose histories are outside the mainstream, speaking out is an important step in the construction of personal and cultural identities. Telling our personal narratives offers us an important entry into and means of reconciling with history. These **hidden histories** — gender, sexual, racial and ethnic, diasporic, colonial, and socioeconomic —

---

hidden histories The histories that are hidden from or forgotten by the mainstream representations of past events.

help us understand how others negotiated the cultural attitudes of the past that have relevance for the present.

Gender Histories Feminist scholars have long insisted that much of the history of women has been obliterated, marginalized, or erased. Historian Mei Nakano (1990) notes:

> *The history of women, told by women, is a recent phenomenon. It has called for a fundamental reevaluation of assumptions and principles that govern traditional history. It challenges us to have a more inclusive view of history, not merely the chronicling of events of the past, not dominated by the record of men marching forward through time, their paths strewn with the detritus of war and politics and industry and labor. (p. xiii)*

Although there is much interest in women's history among contemporary scholars, documenting such **gender histories** is difficult because of the traditional restrictions on women's access to public forums, public documents, and public records. Even so, the return to the past to unearth and recover identities that can be adapted for survival is a key theme of writer Gloria Anzaldúa (1987). She presents *la Llorana* (the crying woman) as a cultural and historical image that gives her the power to resist cultural and gender domination. *La Llorana* is well known in northern Mexico and the U.S. Southwest. This legend tells the story of a woman who killed her children and who now wanders around looking for them and weeping for them. Her story has been retold in various ways, and Anzaldúa rewrites the tale to highlight the power that resides in her relentless crying. This mythical image gives her the power to resist cultural and gender domination:

> *My Chicana identity is grounded in the Indian woman's history of resistance. The Aztec female rites of mourning were rites of defiance protesting the cultural changes which disrupted the equality and balance between female and male, and protesting their demotion to a lesser status, their denigration. Like* la Llorana, *the Indian woman's only means of protest was wailing. (p. 21)*

Anzaldúa's history may seem distant to us, but it is intimately tied to what her Chicana identity means to her.

Sexual Orientation Histories In recounting his experiences as a young man whom the police registered as "homosexual," Pierre Seel

---

gender histories The histories of how cultural conventions of men and women are created, maintained, and/or altered.

(1994) recounts how police lists were used by the Nazis to round up homosexuals for internment. The incarceration and extermination of gays, as members of one of the groups deemed "undesirable" by Nazi Germany, is often overlooked by World War II historians. Seel recalls one event in his **sexual orientation history**:

> *One day at a meeting in the SOS Racisme [an antiracism organization] room, I finished by getting up and recounting my experience of Nazism, my deportation for homosexuality. I remarked as well the ingratitude of history which erases that which is not officially convenient for it. (p. 162)*

(Un jour de réunion, dans la salle de SOS Racisme, je finis par me lever et par raconter mon expérience du nazisme, ma déportation pour homosexualité. Je fis également remarquer l'ingratitude de l'histoire qui gomme ce qui ne lui convient pas officiellement.)

This suppression of history reflects attempts to construct specific understandings of the past. If we do not or cannot listen to the voices of others, we miss the significance of historical lessons. For example, a legislative attempt to force gays and lesbians to register with the police in the state of Montana ultimately was vetoed by the governor after he learned of the law's similarities to laws in Nazi Germany.

The late Guy Hocquenghem (Hocquenghem & Blasius, 1980), a gay French philosopher, lamented the letting go of the past because doing so left little to sustain and nurture his community:

> *I am struck by the ignorance among gay people about the past—no, more even than ignorance: the "will to forget" the German gay holocaust. . . . But we aren't even the only ones who remember, we don't remember! So we find ourselves beginning at zero in each generation. (p. 40)*

How we think about the past and what we know about it help us to build and maintain communities and cultural identities. And our relationships with the past are intimately tied to issues of power. To illustrate, the book *The Pink Swastika: Homosexuality in the Nazi Party* attempts to blame the Holocaust on German gays and lesbians ("Under Surveillance," 1995). This book, in depicting gays and lesbians as perpetrators, rather than victims, of Nazi atrocities, presents the gay identity in a markedly negative light. However, stories of the horrendous treatment of gays and lesbians during World War II serve to promote a common history and influence intercultural communication among gays and lesbians in France, Germany, the Netherlands, and other nations. Today, a monument in Amsterdam serves to mark that history,

---

sexual orientation histories The historical experiences of gays and lesbians.

to help ensure that we remember that gays and lesbians were victims of the Nazi Holocaust as well.

Racial and Ethnic Histories   The injustices done by any nation are often swept under the carpet. In an attempt to bring attention to and promote renewed understanding of the internment of Japanese Americans during World War II, academician John Tateishi (1984) collected the stories of some of the internees. He notes at the outset that

> *this book makes no attempt to be a definitive academic history of Japanese American internment. Rather it tries to present for the first time in human and personal terms the experience of the only group of American citizens ever to be confined in concentration camps in the United States. (p. vii)*

Although not an academic history, this collection of oral histories provides insight into the experiences of many Japanese Americans. Because this historical event demonstrates the fragility of our constitutional system and its guarantees in the face of prejudice and ignorance, it is not often discussed as significant in U.S. history. For Japanese Americans, however, it represents a defining moment in the development of their community.

Not all histories are so explicitly suppressed. For example, in recounting his personal narrative, writer René Han (1992) tells us:

> *I was born in France. My parents were both Chinese. I am therefore Chinese because they left on my face the indelible imprint of the race. In life, nationality, when it doesn't match with physical traits, is less important than appearance. But I am French. I have never been anything but French and, for nothing in the world, would I be anything else. (p. 11)*

(Je suis né en France. Mes parents étaient, tous les deux, chinois. Je suis donc chinois parce qu'ils ont laissé, sur mon visage, l'empreinte indélébile de la race. Dans la vie d'un homme la nationalité, quand elle ne concorde pas avec les traits, importe moins que l' apparence. Pourtant, je suis français. Je n'ai jamais été que français et, pour rien au monde, je ne voudrais cesser de l'être.)

Nevertheless, disjointedness is a central theme in Han's life:

> *There is my appearance and there is me. Appearance is the way others look at me. For them, I am above all Chinese. For me, it's my own perception that I have of my being. And I never see myself as anything but a Frenchman living in France among other French people. (p. 12)*

This letter from the president of the United States was sent to all of the surviving Japanese American internees who were in U.S. concentration camps during World War II. In recognizing that there is no way to change mistakes made in the past, what does this letter do? If you were to write this letter, what would you write in the letter? How should we deal with the past to construct better intercultural relations in the future?

THE WHITE HOUSE
WASHINGTON

A monetary sum and words alone cannot restore lost years or erase painful memories; neither can they fully convey our Nation's resolve to rectify injustice and to uphold the rights of individuals. We can never fully right the wrongs of the past. But we can take a clear stand for justice and recognize that serious injustices were done to Japanese Americans during World War II.

In enacting a law calling for restitution and offering a sincere apology, your fellow Americans have, in a very real sense, renewed their traditional commitment to the ideals of freedom, equality, and justice. You and your family have our best wishes for the future.

Sincerely,

GEORGE BUSH
PRESIDENT OF THE UNITED STATES

OCTOBER 1990

(Il y a mon apparence et il y a moi. L'apparence, c'est le regard des autres. Pour eux, je suis, d'abord, un Chinois. Moi, c'est la propre perception que j'ai mon être. Et je ne me suis jamais perçu que comme un Français, un Français vivant en France parmi les autres.)

The intercultural communication problems that arise in negotiating the complexities of how people view both themselves and others are neither unique to France nor rare. The desire to view the world in discrete units, as if people never migrate, presents problems for intercultural contact.

As you will see in Chapter 5, people often confuse "nationality"— a legal status that denotes citizenship in a particular country—with "race" or "ethnicity." Why do you think this confusion occurs? In what ways do we engage in stereotypes when we assume that, say, French citizens or Mexican citizens must look a certain way? We know that we live in a world of transnational and transcontinental migrations, yet we often react as if we believed otherwise. To illustrate, a U.S. American in the Netherlands was surprised to see people of African and Asian ancestry talking and laughing with Europeans in Dutch. What do you think are the ideological and political underpinnings of such thinking?

Diasporic Histories　　The international relationships that many racial and ethnic groups have with others who share their heritage and history are often overlooked in intercultural communication. These international ties may have been created by transnational migrations, slavery, religious crusades, or other historical forces. Because most people do not think about the diverse connections people have to other nations and cultures, we consider these histories to be hidden. In his book *The Black Atlantic*, scholar Paul Gilroy (1993) emphasizes that, to understand the identities, cultures, and experiences of African descendants living in Britain and the United States, we must examine the connections between Africa, Europe, and North America.

A massive migration, often caused by war or famine or persecution, that results in the dispersal of a unified group is called a **diaspora**. The chronicles of these events are **diasporic histories**. A cultural group (or even an individual) that flees its homeland is likely to bring some customs and practices to the new homeland. In fact, diasporic migrations often cause people to cling more strongly to symbols and practices that

---

diaspora A massive migration often caused by war, famine, or persecution that results in the dispersal of a unified group.
diasporic histories The histories of the ways in which international cultural groups were created through transnational migrations, slavery, religious crusades, or other historical forces.

POINT OF VIEW

Many U.S. Americans may not be aware that the United States sent troops into Iraq during World War II. This history has prefigured the contemporary involvement in Iraq. In a 1942 guide for soldiers being sent to Iraq, the U.S. government made a number of intercultural communication suggestions:

> You will enter Iraq (i-RAHK) both as a soldier and as an individual, because on our side a man can be both. That is our strength—if we are smart enough to use it. It can be our weakness if we aren't. As a soldier your duties are laid out for you. As an individual, it is what you do on your own that counts—and it may count for a lot more than you think.
>
> American success or failure in Iraq may well depend on whether the Iraqis (as the people are called) like American soldiers or not. It may not be quite that simple. But then again it could. . . .
>
> Most Americans and Europeans who have gone to Iraq didn't like it at first. Might as well be frank about it. But nearly all of these same people changed their minds, largely on account of the Iraqi people they began to meet. So will you. . . .
>
> But you will find out that the Iraqi is one of the most cheerful and friendly people in the world. If you are willing to go just a little out of your way to understand him, everything will be okay.
>
> Differences? Sure, there are differences. Differences galore! But what of it? You aren't going to Iraq to change the Iraqis. Just the opposite. We are fighting this war to preserve the principle of "live and let live."

Source: From U.S. government, "A Short Guide to Iraq," 1942. Reprinted in *Harper's Magazine*, October 2004. Also reprinted in *L'actualité*, trans. M. Desjardins, November 1, 2005, pp. 94–96. Available at http://www.harpers. org/BluebirdsOverBaghdad.html. Posted October 27, 2005.

reflect their group's identity. Over the years, though, people become acculturated to some degree in their new homelands. Consider, for example, the dispersal of eastern European Jews who migrated during or after World War II to the United States, Australia, South America, Israel, and other parts of the world. They brought their Jewish culture and eastern European culture with them, but they also adopted new cultural patterns as they became New Yorkers, Australians, Argentinians, Israelis, and so on. Imagine the communication differences among these people over time. Imagine the differences between these groups and members of the dominant culture of their new homelands.

History helps us understand the cultural connections among people affected by diasporas and other transnational migrations. Indeed, it is important that we recognize these relationships. But we must also be careful to distinguish between the ways in which these connections are helpful or hurtful to intercultural communication. For example, some cultures tend to regard negatively those who left their homeland. Thus, many Japanese tend to look down on Japanese Canadians, Japanese Americans, Japanese Brazilians, Japanese Mexicans, and Japanese Peruvians. In contrast, the Irish tend not to look down on Irish Americans or Irish Canadians. Of course, we must remember, too, that many other intervening factors can influence diasporic relationships on an interpersonal level.

Colonial Histories As you probably know, throughout history, societies and nations have ventured beyond their borders. Because of overpopulation, limited resources, notions of grandeur, or other factors, people have left their homelands to colonize other territories. It is important to recognize these **colonial histories** so we can better understand the dynamics of intercultural communication today.

Let's look at the significance of colonialism in determining language. Historically, three of the most important colonizers were Britain, France, and Spain. As a result of colonialism, English is spoken in Canada, Australia, New Zealand, Belize, Nigeria, South Africa, India, Pakistan, Bangladesh, Zimbabwe, Singapore, and the United States, among many places in the world. French is spoken in Canada, Senegal, Tahiti, Haiti, Benin, Côte d'Ivoire, Niger, Rwanda, Mali, Chad, and the Central African Republic, among other places. And Spanish is spoken in most of the Western Hemisphere, from Mexico to Chile and Argentina, and including Cuba, Venezuela, Colombia, and Panama.

Many foreign language textbooks proudly display maps that show the many places around the world where that language is commonly spoken. Certainly, it's nice to know that one can speak Spanish or French in so many places. But the maps don't reveal why those languages are widely spoken in those regions, and they don't reveal the legacies of colonialism in those regions. For example, the United Kingdom maintains close relations with many of its former colonies, and the queen of England is also the queen of Canada, Australia, New Zealand, and the Bahamas.

Other languages have been spread through colonialism as well, including Portuguese in Brazil and Angola; Dutch in Angola, Suriname, and Mozambique; and a related Dutch language, Afrikaans, in South

---

colonial histories The histories that legitimate international invasions and annexations.

Africa. Russian is spoken in the former Soviet republics of Kazakhstan, Azerbaijan, and Tajikistan. In addition, many nations have reclaimed their own languages in an effort to resist the influences of colonialism. For example, today, Arabic is spoken in Algeria, and Vietnamese is spoken in Vietnam; at one time, French was widely spoken in both countries. And in the recently independent Latvia, the ability to speak Latvian is a requirement for citizenship.

The primary languages that we speak are not freely chosen by us. Rather, we must learn the languages of the societies into which we are born. Judith and Tom, for example, both speak English, although their ancestors came to the United States from non-English-speaking countries. We did not choose to learn English among all of the languages of the world. Although we don't resent our native language, we recognize why many individuals might resent a language imposed on them. Think about the historical forces that led you to speak some language(s) and not others. Understanding history is crucial to understanding the linguistic worlds we inhabit, and vestiges of colonialism are often part of these histories.

Postcolonialism is useful in helping us understand the relationship between history and the present. In struggling with a colonial past, people have devised many ways of confronting that past. As explained in Chapter 2, postcolonialism is not simply the study of colonialism, but the study of how we might deal with that past and its aftermath, which may include the *ongoing* use of the colonial language, culture, and religion. For example, many companies are locating parts of their businesses in India because of the widespread use of English as a former British colony. How should people in India deal with the ongoing dominance of English, the colonizer's language, but also the language of business?

For example, Hispanics or Latino/as share a common history of colonization by Spain, whether their families trace their origins to Mexico, Puerto Rico, Cuba, and so on. Although Spain is no longer in political control of these lands, how do those who live in the legacy of this history deal with that history? In what ways does it remain important, as a part of this cultural identity, to embrace the colonizer's language (Spanish)? The colonizer's religion (Catholicism)? And are there other aspects of Spanish culture that continue to be reproduced over and over again? Postcolonialism is not simply a call to make a clean break from that colonial past, but "to examine the violent actions and erasures of colonialism" (Shome & Hegde, 2002, p. 250). In this case, that interrogation might even mean reconsidering the category "Hispanic" that incorporates a wide range of groups that share a Spanish colonial history but do not share other histories that constitute their cultures. The legacy of this cultural invasion often lasts much longer than the political relationship.

Socioeconomic Class Histories   Although we often overlook the importance of socioeconomic class as a factor in history, the fact is that economic and class issues prompted many people to emigrate to the United States. The poverty in Ireland in the 19th century, for example, did much to fuel the flight to the United States; in fact, today, there are more Irish Americans than Irish.

Yet it is not always the socioeconomically disadvantaged who emigrate. After the Russian Revolution in 1917, many affluent Russians moved to Paris. Likewise, many affluent Cubans left the country after Castro seized power in 1959. Today, Canada offers business immigration status to investors who own their own businesses and "who have a net worth, accumulated by their own endeavors, of at least CAD [Canadian dollars] $500,000" ("Immigrant Investor Program Redesign," 1998). Although the program varies somewhat from province to province, the policy ensures that socioeconomic class continues to influence some migrations.

The key point here is that socioeconomic class distinctions are often overlooked in examining the migrations and acculturation of groups around the world. Historically, the kinds of employment that immigrants supplied and the regions they settled were often marked by the kinds of capital—cultural and financial—that they were or were not able to bring with them. These factors also influence the interactions and politics of different groups; for example, Mexican Americans and Cuban Americans, as groups, frequently are at odds with the political mainstream.

INTERCULTURAL COMMUNICATION AND HISTORY

One way to understand specific relationships between communication and history is to examine the attitudes and notions that individuals bring to an interaction; these are the antecedents of contact. A second way is to look at the specific conditions of the interaction and the role that history plays in these contexts. Finally, we can examine how various histories are negotiated in intercultural interaction, applying a dialectical perspective to these different histories.

Antecedents of Contact

We may be able to negotiate some aspects of history in interaction, but it is important to recognize that we bring our personal histories to each intercultural interaction. These personal histories involve our prior experience and our attitudes. Social psychologist Richard Brislin (1981) has identified four elements of personal histories that influence interaction.

First, people bring childhood experiences to interactions. For example, both Judith and Tom grew up hearing negative comments about Catholics. As a result, our first interactions with adherents to this faith were tinged with some suspicion. This personal history did not affect initial interactions with people of other religions.

Second, people may bring historical myths to interactions. These are myths with which many people are familiar. The Jewish conspiracy myth—that Jewish people are secretly in control of U.S. government and business—is one example.

Third, the languages that people speak influence their interactions. Language can be an attraction or a repellent in intercultural interactions. For example, many people from the United States enjoy traveling in Britain because English is spoken there. However, these same people may have little desire, or even be afraid, to visit Russia, simply because it is not an English-speaking country.

Finally, people tend to be affected by recent, vivid events. For example, after the bombing of the World Trade Center in New York, interactions between Arab Americans and other U.S. residents were strained, characterized by suspicion, fear, and distrust. The media's treatment of such catastrophic events often creates barriers and reinforces stereotypes by blurring distinctions between Arabs, Persians and Palestinians. Perhaps recent histories, such as the racially motivated riots in Los Angeles in the mid-1990s, are more influential in our interactions than the hidden or past histories, such as the massacre in 1890 of some 260 Sioux Indians at Wounded Knee in South Dakota or the women's suffrage movement around the turn of the 20th century.

The Contact Hypothesis

The **contact hypothesis** is the notion that better communication between groups of people is facilitated simply by bringing them together and allowing them to interact. Although history does not seem to support this notion, many public policies and programs in the United

---

contact hypothesis The notion that better communication between groups is facilitated simply by putting people together in the same place and allowing them to interact.

In this excerpt, intercultural scholar Parker Johnson describes the way in which history affects his everyday experience in the United States. History, although "in the past," continues to affect contemporary cultural experiences.

Racism is a lifelong unlearning and relearning process like alcoholism and sexism; it is not a task to be solved and done within a finite moment. It is not solely about "Black–White" relations; there are many other racial, ethnic, and cultural groups. However, our fixation with the "Black–White paradigm" does reveal our passionate and unreconciled history of slavery which is often subtle and piercing in its manifestations. For example, I drive to Harrisburg [PA] and see the Plantation Inn near the junction of route 15 and the Penn turnpike. Would we ever see a "concentration camp inn" or an "internment camp inn"? We are comfortable with the abominable history of slavery and keep it alive with such symbols. The same is true of the Confederate flag which is so proudly displayed in Gettysburg. It is fundamentally racist to display that flag and ask Black folks to get over slavery with the constant reminder displayed throughout the country. We see slavery with the constant reminder displayed throughout the country. We see no Nazi flags prominently displayed in Germany or the U.S. despite [their] importance to German history. Let's challenge these ideas and reclaim our humanity.

Source: From Parker Johnson, "Eliminating Racism as a Social Disease," *Hanover Evening Sun*, October 21, 1995, p. 2.

States and abroad are based on this hypothesis. Examples include desegregation rulings; the prevalence of master-planned communities like Reston, Virginia; and many international student exchange programs. All of these programs are based on the assumption that simply giving people from different groups opportunities to interact will result in more positive intergroup attitudes and reduced prejudice.

Gordon Allport (1979) and Yehudi Amir (1969), two noted psychologists, have tried to identify the conditions under which the contact hypothesis does and does not hold true. The histories of various groups figure prominently in their studies. Based on these and subsequent studies, psychologists have outlined at least eight conditions that must be met (more or less) to improve attitudes and facilitate intergroup communication (Schwarzwald & Amir, 1996; Stephan & Stephan, 1996). These are particularly relevant in light of increasing

How we commemorate the past can create intercultural conflicts, in that many historical events are entangled in contemporary cultural identities. Note how different views of the past can make a difference in how we assign status to the so-called Old Spanish Trail.

> *The Old Spanish Trail, a main corridor of moving Native American slaves, wool products and livestock between Santa Fe, N.M., and Los Angeles in its heyday, 1829 to 1850, is being considered for adoption into the national trail system. The system already includes such historic routes as the Oregon Trail.*
>
> *Alan Downer, the [Navajo] tribe's historic preservation director, said that he was surprised the measure was being considered and that the Navajos had not even been consulted about the project. The trail snakes through about 100 miles of the [tribe's] reservation near the Four Corners area.*
>
> *"I don't think honoring a European culture like this with which the Navajos had such distrust and hostility will be very popular on the reservations," Downer said. "After all, it was used for slave raids and other unsavory activities during a particularly rough time in the tribe's history."*
>
> *Harry Walters, a history professor at the Navajos' Dine College in Tsalie, said he sees "no value" to Navajo culture in recognizing the trail.*
>
> *"All it does is glorify European expansion and land-grabbing," Walters said.*

Source: From Mark Shaffer, "Navajos Protest National Status for Old Spanish Trail," *The Arizona Republic*, June 9, 2002, pp. B1, B8.

diversity in U.S. society in general and the workforce in particular. The eight conditions are as follows:

1. Group members should be of equal status, both within and outside the contact situation. Communication will occur more easily if there is no disparity between individuals in status characteristics (education, socioeconomic status, and so on). This condition does not include temporary inequality, such as in student–teacher or patient–doctor roles. Consider the implications of this condition for relations among various ethnic groups in the United States. How are we likely to think of individuals from specific ethnic groups if our interactions are characterized by inequality? A good example is the interaction between longtime residents and recent immigrants in the Southwest, where Mexican Americans often provide housecleaning, gardening, and

similar services for whites. It is easy to see how the history of these two groups in the United States contributes to the lack of equality in interaction, leads to stereotyping, and inhibits effective intercultural communication. But the history of relations between Mexican Americans and whites varies within this region. For example, families of Spanish descent have lived in New Mexico longer than other European-descent families, whereas Arizona has a higher concentration of recent immigrants from Mexico. Intergroup interactions in New Mexico are characterized less by inequality (Stephan & Stephan, 1989).

2. Strong normative and institutional support for the contact should be provided. This suggests that, when individuals from different groups come together, positive outcomes do not happen by accident. Rather, institutional encouragement is necessary. Examples include university support for contact between U.S. and international students, or for contact among different cultural groups within the university, and local community support for integrating elementary and high schools. Numerous studies have shown the importance of commitment by top management to policies that facilitate intercultural interaction in the workplace (Brinkman, 1997). Finally, institutional support may also mean government and legal support, expressed through court action.

3. Contact between the groups should be voluntary. This may seem to contradict the previous condition, but it doesn't. Although support must exist beyond the individual, individuals need to feel that they have a choice in making contact. If they believe that they are being forced to interact, as with some diversity programs or affirmative action programs, the intercultural interaction is unlikely to have positive outcomes. For example, an air traffic controller was so incensed by a required diversity program exercise on gender differences that he sued the Department of Transportation for $300,000 (Erbe & Hart, 1994). A better program design would be to involve all participants from the beginning. This can be done by showing the benefits of an inclusive diversity policy—one that values all kinds of diversity, and not merely that based on gender, for example. Equally important is the mounting evidence of bottom-line benefits of diverse personnel who work well together (Harris, 1997).

4. The contact should have the potential to extend beyond the immediate situation and occur in a variety of contexts with a variety of individuals from all groups. This suggests that superficial contact between members of different groups is not likely to have much impact on attitudes (stereotypes, prejudice) or result in productive communication. For instance, simply sitting beside someone from another culture in a class or sampling food from different countries is not likely

to result in genuine understanding of that person or appreciation for his or her cultural background (Stephan & Stephan, 1992). Thus, international students who live with host families are much more likely to have positive impressions of the host country and to develop better intercultural communication skills than those who go on "island programs," in which students interact mostly with other foreigners to the host country.

5. Programs should maximize cooperation within groups and minimize competition. For example, bringing a diverse group of students together should not involve pitting the African Americans against the European Americans on separate sports teams. Instead, it might involve creating diversity within teams to emphasize cooperation. Especially important is having a superordinate goal, a goal that everyone can agree on. This helps diverse groups develop a common identity (Gaertner, Dovidio, & Bachman, 1996). For instance, there is a successful summer camp in Maine for Arab and Jewish youths; the camp brings together members of these historically conflicting groups for a summer of cooperation, discussion, and relationship building.

6. Programs should equalize numbers of group members. Positive outcomes and successful communication will be more likely if members are represented in numerical equality. Research studies have shown that being in the numerical minority can cause stress and that the "solo" minority, particularly in beginning a new job, is subject to exaggerated expectations (either very high or very low) and extreme evaluations (either very good or very bad) (Pettigrew & Martin, 1989).

7. Group members should have similar beliefs and values. A large body of research supports the idea that people are attracted to those whom they perceive to be similar to themselves. This means that, in bringing diverse groups of people together, we should look for common ground—similarities based on religion, interests, competencies, and so on. For example, an international group of mothers is working for peace in the Middle East. Although members represent different ethnic groups, they come together with a shared goal—to protect their children from military action between the warring factions in the region.

8. Programs should promote individuation of group members. This means that they should downplay the characteristics that mark the different groups (such as language, physical abilities, or racial characteristics). Instead, group members might focus on the characteristics that express individual personalities.

This list of conditions can help us understand how domestic and international contexts vary (Gudykunst, 1979). It is easy to see how the history within a nation-state may lead to conditions and attitudes that

are more difficult to facilitate. For example, historical conditions between African Americans and white Americans may make it impossible
to meet these conditions; interracial interactions in the United States
cannot be characterized by equality.

Note that this list of conditions is incomplete. Moreover, meeting all of the conditions does not guarantee positive outcomes when
diverse groups of people interact. However, the list is a starting place,
and it is important to be able to identify which conditions are affected
by historical factors that may be difficult to change and which can be
more easily facilitated by communication professionals.

Negotiating Histories Dialectically in Interaction

How can a dialectical perspective help us negotiate interactions, given
individual attitudes and personal and cultural histories? How can we
balance past and present in our everyday intercultural interactions?
First, it is important to recognize that we all bring our own histories
(some known, some hidden) to interactions. We can try to evaluate the
role that history plays for those with whom we interact.

Second, we should understand the role that histories play in our
identities, in what we bring to the interaction. Communication scholar
Marsha Houston (1997) says there are three things that white people
who want to be her friends should never say: "I don't notice you're
black," "You're not like the others," and "I know how you feel." In her
opinion, each of these denies or rejects a part of her identity that is
deeply rooted in history.

Sometimes it is unwise to ask people where they are "really from."
Such questions assume that they cannot be from where they said they
were from, due to racial characteristics or other apparent features.
Recognizing a person's history and its link to her or his identity in
communication is a first step in establishing intercultural relationships.
It is also important to be aware of your own historical blinders and
assumptions.

Sometimes the past–present dialectic operates along with the
disadvantage–privilege dialectic. The Hungarian philosopher György
Lukács wrote a book titled *History and Class Consciousness* (1971), in
which he argues that we need to think dialectically about history and
social class. Our own recognition of how class differences have influenced our families is very much affected by the past and by the conditions members experienced that might explain whom they married,
why they lived where they did, what languages they do and do not
speak, and what culture they identify with.

Two dialectical tensions emerge here: (1) between privilege and

POINT OF VIEW

Geetha Kothari, a native New Yorker, explains her anger at being asked where she is from. How does this question communicate to her that she is not a U.S. American?

"Where are you from?"

The bartender asks this as I get up from my table. It's quiet at the Bloomfield Bridge Tavern, home of the best pirogies in Pittsburgh. I have just finished eating, just finished telling my boyfriend how much I love this place because it's cheap and simple, not crowded in the early evening, and has good food.

"New York."

He stares at me, but before he can ask another question, I'm down the stairs in the ladies' room, washing my hot face. When I come up again, I glare at him.

"I hate this place," I say to my boyfriend. "That man asked me where I'm from."

The man has no reason to ask me that question. We are not having a conversation. I am not his friend. Out of the blue, having said no other words to me, he feels that it is ok for him, a white man, to ask me where I am from. The only context for this question is my skin color and his need to classify me. I am sure he doesn't expect me to say New York. I look different, therefore it's assumed that I must be from somewhere, somewhere that isn't here, America. It would never occur to him to ask my boyfriend, who is white—and Canadian—where he's from.

Source: From "Where Are You From?" by Geetha Kothari, 1995, *Under Western Eyes: Personal Essays From Asian America*, edited by G. Hongo, pp. 151–173.

disadvantage, and (2) between the personal and the social. Both of these dialectics affect our view of the past, present, and future. As we attempt to understand ourselves and our situations (as well as those of others), we must recognize that we arrived at universities for a variety of reasons. Embedded in our backgrounds are dialectical tensions between privilege and disadvantage, and the ways in which those factors were established in the past and the present. Then there is the dialectical tension between seeing ourselves as unique persons and as members of particular social classes. These factors affect both the present and the future. In each case, we must also negotiate the dialectical tensions between the past and the present, and between the present and the future. Who we think we are today is very much influenced by how we view the past, how we live, and what culture we believe to be our own.

DISCUSSION QUESTIONS

1. What are some examples of hidden histories, and why are they hidden?

2. How do the various histories of the United States influence American's communication with people from other countries?

3. What kinds of histories are likely to influence your interactions with an international student of the same gender and age?

4. What factors in your experience have led to the development of positive feelings about your own cultural heritage and background? What factors have led to negative feelings, if any?

5. When can contact between members of two cultures improve their attitudes toward each other and facilitate communication between them?

6. How do histories influence the process of identity formation?

7. What is the significance of the shift from history to histories? How does this shift help us understand intercultural communication?

8. Why do some people in the United States prefer not to talk about history? What views of social reality and intercultural communication does this attitude encourage?

ACTIVITIES

Cultural-Group History. This exercise can be done by individual students or in groups. Choose a cultural group in the United States that is unfamiliar to you. Study the history of this group, and identify and describe significant events in its history. Answer the following questions:

a. What is the historical relationship between this group and other groups (particularly the dominant cultural groups)?

b. Are there any historical incidents of discrimination? If so, describe them.

c. What are common stereotypes about the group? How did these stereotypes originate?

d. Who are important leaders and heroes of the group?

e. What are notable achievements of the group?

f. How has the history of this group influenced the identity of group members today?

REFERENCES

Allport, G. (1979). *The nature of prejudice.* New York: Addison-Wesley.

Amir, Y. (1969). Contact hypothesis in ethnic relations. *Psychological Bulletin, 71,* 319–343.

Anzaldúa, G. (1987). *Borderlands/La frontera: The new mestiza.* San Francisco: Spinsters/Aunt Lute.

Attenborough, R. (Director). (1987). *Cry Freedom* [Motion picture]. United States: Universal Studios.

Baudrillard, J. (1988). *America* (C. Turner, Trans.). New York: Verso.

Blanchot, M. (1986). *The writing of the disaster* (A. Smock, Trans.). Lincoln: University of Nebraska Press.

Brinkman, H. (1997). Managing diversity: A review of recommendations for success. In C. D. Brown, C. Snedeker, & B. Sykes (Eds.), *Conflict and diversity* (pp. 35–50). Cresskill, NJ: Hampton Press.

Brislin, R. W. (1981). *Cross cultural encounters: Face to face interaction.* New York: Pergamon.

Bureau of African Affairs. (2005, September). Background note: South Africa. United States Department of State. http://www.state.gov/r/pa/ei/bgn/2898.htm#history. Accessed October 30, 2005.

Erbe, B., & Hart, B. (1994, September 16). Employer goes overboard on "gender sensitivity" issue. *The Evansville Courier,* p. A13.

Fisher, W. (1984). Narration as a human communication paradigm: The case of public moral argument. *Communication Monographs, 51,* 1–22.

Fisher, W. (1985). The narrative paradigm: An elaboration. *Communication Monographs, 52,* 347–367.

Fitzgerald, F. (1972). *Fire in the lake: Vietnamese and Americans in Vietnam.* New York: Vintage Books.

Gaertner, S. L., Dovidio, J. F., &

Bachman, B. A. (1996). Revisiting the contact hypothesis: The induction of a common ingroup identity. *International Journal of Intercultural Relations, 20,* 271–290.

Gérard-Libois, J., & Heinen, J. (1989). *Belgique-Congo, 1960.* Brussels: Politique et Histoire.

Gilroy, P. (1993). *The Black Atlantic: Modernity and double consciousness.* New York: Verso.

Gudykunst, W. B. (1979). Intercultural contact and attitude change: A review of literature and suggestions for future research. *International and Intercultural Communication Annual, 4,* 1–16.

Guelke, A. (2005). *Rethinking the rise and fall of apartheid: South Africa and world politics.* New York: Palgrave Macmillan.

Han, R. (1992). *Un chinois de Bourgogne, avant-mémoires.* Paris: Librairie Académique Perrin.

Harris, T. E. (1997). Diversity: Importance, ironies, and pathways. In C. D. Brown, C. Snedeker, & B. Sykes (Eds.), *Conflict and diversity* (pp. 17–34). Cresskill, NJ: Hampton Press.

Hocquenghem, G., & Blasius, M. (1980, April). Interview. *Christopher Street, 8*(4), 36–45.

Houston, M. (1997). When Black women talk with White women: Why dialogues are difficult. In A. González, M. Houston, & V. Chen (Eds.), *Our voices: Essays in ethnicity, culture, and communication* (2nd ed., pp. 187–194). Los Angeles: Roxbury.

Immigrant Investor Program Redesign. (1998, December). Guide for applying for permanent residence in Canada: Business applicants. cicnet.ci.gc.ca/press/98/9865-pre.html

Jameson, F. (1981). *The political un-*

conscious: Narrative as a socially symbolic act. Ithaca, NY: Cornell University Press.

Kothari, G. (1995). Where are you from? In G. Hongo (Ed.), *Under Western eyes: Personal essays from Asian America* (pp. 151–173). New York: Anchor Books/Doubleday.

Loewen, J. W. (1995). *Lies my teacher told me: Everything your American history textbook got wrong.* New York: Touchstone.

Lukács, György. (1971). *History and class consciousness: Studies in Marxist dialectics* (R. Livingstone, Trans.). Cambridge, MA: MIT Press.

Lyotard, J.-F. (1984). *The postmodern condition: A report on knowledge* (G. Bennington & B. Massumi, Trans.). Minneapolis: University of Minnesota Press.

Nakano, M. (1990). *Japanese American women: Three generations, 1890–1990.* Berkeley and San Francisco: Mina Press/National Japanese American Historical Society.

Pettigrew, T. F., & Martin, J. (1989). Organizational inclusion of minority groups: A social psychological analysis. In J. P. VanOudenhoven & T. M. Willemsen (Eds.), *Ethnic minorities: Social psychological perspectives* (pp. 169–200). Amsterdam/Lisse: Swets & Zeitlinger.

Schwarzwald, J., & Amir, Y. (1996). Guest editor's introduction: Special issue on prejudice, discrimination and conflict. *International Journal of Intercultural Relations, 20,* 265–270.

Seel, P., with Bitoux, J. (1994). *Moi, Pierre Seel, déporté homosexual.* Paris: Calmann-Lévy.

Shaffer, M. (2002, June 9). Navajos protest national status for Old Spanish Trail. *The Arizona Republic,* pp. B1, B8.

Shome, R., & Hegde, R. (2002). Postcolonial approaches to communication: Charting the terrain, engaging the intersections. *Communication Theory, 12,* 249–270.

Stephan, C. W., & Stephan, W. G. (1989). Antecedents of intergroup anxiety in Asian Americans and Hispanic Americans. *International Journal of Intercultural Relations, 13,* 203–216.

Stephan, C. W., & Stephan, W. G. (1992). Reducing intercultural anxiety through intercultural contact. *International Journal of Intercultural Relations, 16,* 89–106.

Stephan, W. G., & Stephan, C. W. (1996). *Intergroup relations.* Boulder, CO: Westview Press.

Steyn, M. (2001). *"Whiteness just isn't what it used to be": White identity in a changing South Africa.* Albany: State University of New York Press.

Tateishi, J. (1984). *And justice for all: An oral history of the Japanese American detention camps.* New York: Random House.

Thompson, L. (2001). *A history of South Africa* (3rd ed.). New Haven: Yale University Press.

Thonssen, L., Baird, A. C., & Braden, W. W. (1970). *Speech criticism* (2nd ed.). New York: Ronald Press.

Under surveillance. (1995, December 26). *The Advocate,* p. 14.

PART II
Intercultural Communication Processes

IDENTITY AND INTERCULTURAL COMMUNICATION

CHAPTER OBJECTIVES

After reading this chapter, you should be able to:

1. Identify three communication approaches to identity.

2. Define identity.

3. Explain the relationship between identity and language.

4. Describe phases of minority identity development.

5. Describe phases of majority identity development.

6. Identify and describe nine social and cultural identities.

7. Identify characteristics of whiteness.

8. Explain the relationship among identity, stereotyping, and prejudice.

9. Describe phases of multicultural identity development.

10. Explain the relationship between identity and communication.

Now that we have examined some sociohistorical contexts that shape culture and communication, let us turn to a discussion of identity and its role in intercul-tural communication. Identity serves as a bridge between culture and commu-nication. It is important because we com-municate our identity to others, and we learn who we are through communication. It is through communication—with our family, friends, and others—that we come to understand ourselves and form our identity. Issues of identity are particularly important in intercul-tural interactions.

Conflicts can arise, however, when there are sharp differences be-tween who we think we are and who others think we are. For example, a female college student living with a family in Mexico on a homestay may be treated protectively and chaperoned when she socializes, which may conflict with her view of herself as an independent person. In this case, the person's identity is not confirmed but is questioned or chal-lenged in the interaction.

In this chapter, we describe a dialectical approach to understand-ing identity, one that encompasses three communication approaches: social science, interpretive, and critical. We then explore the impor-tant role language plays in understanding identity and how minority and majority identities develop. We then turn to the development of specific aspects of our social and cultural identity including those re-lated to gender, race or ethnicity, class, religion, and nationality. We describe how these identities are often related to problematic commu-nication—stereotypes, prejudice, and discrimination. We also examine an increasingly important identity—that of multicultural individuals. Finally, we discuss the relationship between identity and communica-tion.

THINKING DIALECTICALLY ABOUT IDENTITY

Identity is a core issue for most people. It is about who we are. The importance of identity is reflected in the seriousness of the growing crimes in the United States—identity theft and the devastation of peo-ple who have their identity "stolen." How do we come to understand who we are? What are the characteristics of **identity**? In this section we use both the static–dynamic and the personal–contextual dialectic in answering these questions.

---

identity The concept of who we are. Characteristics of identity may be understood differ-ently depending on the perspectives that people take—for example, social science, interpretive, or critical perspectives.

There are three contemporary communication perspectives on identity (see Table 5.1). The social science perspective, based largely on research in psychology, views the self in a relatively static fashion, in relation to the various cultural communities to which a person belongs: nationality, race, ethnicity, religion, gender, and so on. The interpretive perspective is more dynamic and recognizes the important role of interaction with others as a factor in the development of the self. Finally, the critical perspective views identity even more dynamically— as a result of contexts quite distant from the individual. As you read this chapter, keep in mind that the relationship between identity and intercultural interaction involves both static and dynamic elements and both personal and contextual elements.

TABLE 5.1 THREE PERSPECTIVES ON IDENTITY AND COMMUNICATION		
Social science	**Interpretive**	**Critical**
Identity created by self (by relating to groups)	Identity formed through communication witht others	Identity shaped through social, historical forces
Emphasizes individualized, familial, and spiritual (cross-culturali self perspective)	Emphasizes avowal and ascribed dimensions	Emphasizes contexts and resisting ascribed identity

The Social Science Perspective

The social science perspective emphasizes that identity is created in part by the self and in part in relation to group membership. According to this perspective, the self is composed of multiple identities, and these notions of identity are culture bound. How, then, do we come to understand who we are? That depends very much on our cultural background. According to Western psychologists like Erik Erikson, our identities are self-created, formed through identity conflicts and crises, through identity diffusion and confusion (Erikson, 1950, 1968). Occasionally, we may need a moratorium, a time-out, in the process. Our identities are created not in one smooth, orderly process but in spurts, with some events providing insights into who we are and long periods intervening during which we may not think much about ourselves or our identities.

Cross-Cultural Perspectives In the United States, young people are often encouraged to develop a strong sense of identity, to "know who they are," to be independent and self-reliant, which reflects an emphasis on the cultural value of individualism. However, this was not always the case, and even today in many countries there is a very different, more collectivist notion of self. Min-Sun Kim (2002), a communication scholar, traces the evolution of the individualistic self. Before 1500, people in Europe as well as in most other civilizations lived in small cohesive communities, with a worldview characterized by the interdependence of spiritual and material phenomena. With the beginning of the industrial revolution in the 1600s came the notion of the world as a machine; this mechanistic view extended to living organisms and has had a profound effect on Western thought. It taught people to think of themselves as isolated egos—unconnected to the natural world and society in general. Thus, according to Kim, a person in the West came to be understood as "an individual entity with a separate existence independent of place in society" (Kim, 2002, p. 12). In contrast, people in many other regions of the world have retained the more interdependent notion of the self.

Cross-cultural psychologist Alan Roland (1988) has identified three universal aspects of identity present in all individuals: (1) an individualized identity, (2) a familial identity, and (3) a spiritual identity. Cultural groups usually emphasize one or two of these dimensions and downplay the other(s). Let's see how this works. The **individualized identity** is the sense of an independent "I," with sharp distinctions between the self and others. This identity is emphasized by most groups in the United States, where young people are encouraged to be independent and self-reliant at a fairly early age—by adolescence.

In contrast, the **familial identity**, evident in many collectivististic cultures, stresses the importance of emotional connectedness to and interdependence with others. For example, in many African and Asian societies, and in some cultural groups in the United States, children are encouraged and expected to form strong, interdependent bonds, first with the family and later with other groups. As one of our students explains,

> *to be Mexican American is to unconditionally love one's family and all it stands for. Mexican-Americans are an incredibly close-knit group of people, especially when it comes to family. We are probably the only culture that can actually recite the names of our fourth cousins by heart. In this respect our families are like clans, they go much further than the immediate family and very deep into extended families. We even have a celebration,* Dia de los Muertos *(Day of the Dead), that honors our ancestors.*

Individualized identity The sense of self as independent and self-reliant.
familial identity The sense of self as always connected to family and others.

POINT OF VIEW

Communication scholar Ge Gao contrasts the Western idea of the independent self with the Chinese notion of the interdependent self.

In the Western world, an "individual" signifies an independent entity with free will, emotions and personality. An individual, however, is not conceptualized in this way in the Chinese culture. . . . The incomplete nature of the self is supported by both Taoism and Confucianism even though they differ in many fundamental ways. Taoism defines self as part of nature. Self and nature together complete a harmonious relationship. Self in the Confucian sense is defined by a person's surrounding relations, which often are derived from kinship networks and supported by cultural values such as filial piety, loyalty, dignity, and integrity. . . .

The other-orientation thus is key to an interdependent self. Congruous with the notion of an interdependent self, the Chinese self also needs to be recognized, defined, and completed by others. The self's orientation to others' needs, wishes, and expectations is essential to the development of the Chinese self.

Source: From Ge Gao, "Self and Other: A Chinese Perspective on Interpersonal Relationships." In W. G. Gudykunst et al. (Eds.), *Communication in Personal Relationships Across Cultures* (Thousand Oaks, CA: Sage, 1996), pp. 83–84.

In these societies, educational, occupational, and even marital choices are made by individuals with extensive family guidance. The goal of the developed identity is not to become independent from others but rather to gain an understanding of and cultivate one's place in the complex web of interdependence with others. Communication scholar Ge Gao (1996) describes the Chinese sense of self:

The other-orientation thus is key to an interdependent self. Congruous with the notion of an interdependent self, the Chinese self also needs to be recognized, defined, and completed by others. The self's orientation to others' needs, wishes, and expectations is essential to the development of the Chinese self. (p. 84)

In addition, the understanding of the familial self may be more connected to others and situation bound. According to studies comparing North Americans' and East Asians' senses of identity, when asked to describe themselves, the North Americans give more abstract, situation-free descriptions ("I am kind," "I am outgoing," "I am quiet in the morning"), whereas East Asians tend to describe their memberships and relationships to others rather than themselves ("I am a mother," "I am the youngest child in my family," "I am a member of a tennis club") (Cross, 2000).

The third dimension is the **spiritual identity**, the inner spiritual reality that is realized and experienced to varying extents by people through a number of outlets. For example, the spiritual self in India is expressed through a structure of gods and goddesses and through rituals and mediation. In Japan, the realization of the spiritual self tends more toward aesthetic modes, such as the tea ceremony and flower arranging (Roland, 1988).

Clearly, identity development does not occur in the same way in every society. The notion of identity in India, Japan, and some Latino/a and Asian American groups emphasizes the integration of the familial and the spiritual self but very little of the more individualized self.

This is not to say there is not considerable individuality among people in these groups. However, the general identity contrasts dramatically with the predominant mode in most U.S. cultural groups, in which the individualized self is emphasized and there is little attention to the familial self. However, there may be some development of the spiritual self among devout Catholic, Protestant, or Jewish individuals.

Groups play an important part in the development of all these dimensions of self. As we are growing up, we identify with many groups, based on gender, race, ethnicity, class, sexual orientation, religion, and nationality (Tajfel, 1981, 1982). And depending on our cultural background, we may develop tight or looser bonds with these groups (Kim, 2002). By comparing ourselves and others with members of these groups, we come to understand who we are. Because we belong to various groups, we develop multiple identities that come into play at different times, depending on the context. For example, in going to church or temple, we may highlight our religious identity. In going to clubs or bars, we may highlight our sexual orientation identity. Women who join social groups exclusive to women (or men who attend social functions just for men) are highlighting their gender identity.

The Interpretive Perspective

The interpretive perspective builds on the notions of identity formation discussed previously but takes a more dynamic turn. That is, it emphasizes that identities are negotiated, co-created, reinforced, and

spiritual identity Identification with feelings of connectedness to others and higher meanings in life.

challenged though communication with others; they emerge when messages are exchanged between persons (Hecht, Warren, Jung, & Krieger, 2005; Ting-Toomey, 2005). This means that presenting our identities is not a simple process. Does everyone see you as you see yourself? Probably not. To understand how these images may conflict, the concepts of avowal and ascription are useful.

Avowal is the process by which individuals portray themselves, whereas **ascription** is the process by which others attribute identities to them. Sometimes these processes are congruent. For example, we (Judith and Tom) see ourselves as professors and hope that students also see us as professors. We also see ourselves as young, but many students do not concur, ascribing an "old person" identity to us. This ascribed identity challenges our avowed identity. And these conflicting views influence the communication between us and our students.

Different identities are emphasized depending on the individuals we are communicating with and the topics of conversation. For example, in a social conversation with someone we are attracted to, our gender or sexual orientation identity is probably more important to us than other identities (ethnicity, nationality). And our communication is probably most successful when the person we are talking with confirms the identity we think is most important at the moment. In this sense, competent intercultural communication affirms the identity that is most salient in any conversation (Collier & Thomas, 1988). For example, if you are talking with a professor about a research project, the conversation will be most competent if the interaction confirms the salient identities (professor and student) rather than other identities (e.g., those based on gender, religion, or ethnicity).

How do you feel when someone does not recognize the identity you believe is most salient? For example, suppose your parents treat you as a child (their ascription) and not as an independent adult (your avowal). How might this affect communication? One of our students describes how he reacts when people ascribe a different identity than the one he avows:

> *Pretty much my entire life I was seen not as American but as half Mexican. In reality I am 50% Mexican and 50% Dutch. So technically I am half Mexican and half Dutch American. I always say it like that but it was obvious that not everybody saw it like that. I was asked if I was Hawaiian, Persian, and even Italian, but I was able to politely tell them about myself.*

---

avowal The process by which an individual portrays himself or herself.
ascription The process by which others attribute identities to an individual.

Central to the interpretive perspective is the idea that our identities are expressed communicatively—in core symbols, labels, and norms. **Core symbols** (or cultural values) tell us about the fundamental beliefs and the central concepts that define a particular identity. Communication scholar Michael Hecht and his colleagues (Hecht, 1998; Hecht, Jackson, & Ribeau, 2003) have identified the contrasting core symbols associated with various ethnic identities. For example, core symbols of African American identity may be positivity, sharing, uniqueness, realism, and assertiveness. Individualism is often cited as a core symbol of European American identity. Core symbols are not only expressed but also created and shaped through communication. Labels are a category of core symbols; they are the terms we use to refer to particular aspects of our own and others' identities—for example, *African American, Latino, white,* or *European American.*

Finally, some norms of behavior are associated with particular identities. For example, women may express their gender identity by being more concerned about safety than men. They may take more precautions when they go out at night, such as walking in groups. People might express their religious identity by participating in activities such as going to church or Bible study meetings.

The Critical Perspective

Like the interpretive perspective, the critical perspective emphasizes the dynamic nature of identities, but in addition, it emphasizes the contextual and often conflictual elements of identity development. This perspective pays particular attention to the societal structures and institutions that constrain identities and are often the root of injustice and oppression (Collier, 2005).

Contextual Identity Formation The driving force behind a critical approach is the attempt to understand identity formation within the contexts of history, economics, politics, and discourse. To grasp this notion, ask yourself, How and why do people identify with particular groups and not others? What choices are available to them?

We are all subject to being pigeonholed into identity categories, or contexts, even before we are born. Many parents ponder a name for their unborn child, who is already part of society through his or her relationship to the parents. Some children have a good start at being, say, Jewish or Chicana before they are even born. We cannot ignore

---

core symbols The fundamental beliefs that are shared by the members of a cultural group. Labels, a category of core symbols, are names or markers used to classify individual, social, or cultural groups.

the ethnic, socioeconomic, or racial positions from which we start our identity journeys.

To illustrate, French psychoanalyst Jacques Lacan (1977) offers the example of two children on a train that stops at a station. Each child looks out a window and identifies the location: One says that they are in front of the door for the ladies' bathroom; the other says they are in front of the gentlemen's. Both children see and use labels from their seating position to describe where they are; they are on the same train, but they describe their locations differently. Just as we are never "out" of position, we are never "outside" of language and its system that helps define us. And, like the two children, where we are positioned—by language and by society—influences how and what we see and, most importantly, what it means.

The identities that others may ascribe to us are socially and politically determined. They are not constructed by the self alone. We must ask ourselves what drives the construction of particular kinds of identities. For example, the label "heterosexual" is a relatively recent one, created less than a hundred years ago (Katz, 1995). Today, people do not hesitate to identify themselves as "heterosexuals." A critical perspective insists on the constructive nature of this process and attempts to identify the social forces and needs that give rise to these identities.

These contextual constraints on identity are also reflected in the experience of a Palestinian woman who describes her feelings of not having a national "identity" as represented by a passport—because of political circumstances far beyond her control:

> I am Palestinian but I don't have either a Palestinian passport or an Israeli passport. . . . If I take the Palestinian passport, the Israeli government would prevent me from entering Jerusalem and Jerusalem is a part of my soul. I just can't NOT enter it. And of course I'm not taking an Israeli passport, so . . . I get frustrated when I talk to people WITH identity, especially Palestinians with Israeli identity. I just get like kind of offended because I think they're more comfortable than me. (Collier, 2005, p. 243)

Resisting Ascribed Identities When we invoke such discourses about identity, we are pulled into the social forces that feed the discourse. We might resist the position they put us in, and we might try to ascribe other identities to ourselves. Nevertheless, we must begin from that position in carving out a new identity.

French philosopher Louis Althusser (1971) uses the term **inter-**

pellation to refer to this process. He notes that we are pushed into this system of social forces

> *by that very precise operation which I have called interpellation or hailing, and which can be imagined along the lines of the most commonplace everyday police (or other) hailing: "Hey you there!"* . . . *Experience shows that the practical telecommunication of hailings is such that they hardly ever miss their man: verbal call or whistle, the one hailed always recognizes that it is really him who is being hailed. And yet it is a strange phenomenon, and one which cannot be explained solely by "guilt feelings."* (p. 163)

This hailing process that Althusser describes operates in intercultural communication interactions. It establishes the foundation from which the interaction occurs. For example, occasionally, someone will ask Tom if he is Japanese, a question that puts him in an awkward position. He does not hold Japanese citizenship, nor has he ever lived in Japan. Yet the question probably doesn't mean to address these issues. Rather, the person is asking what it means to be "Japanese." How can Tom reconfigure his position in relation to this question?

The Dynamic Nature of Identities The social forces that give rise to particular identities are never stable but are always changing. Therefore, the critical perspective insists on the dynamic nature of identities. For example, the emergence of the European Union has given new meaning to the notion of being "European" as an identity. Similarly, the terrorist attacks of September 11, 2001, have caused many Americans to reconsider what it means to be "American." And the various and sometimes contradictory notions of what it means to be an American highlights the fluidity and dynamic nature of identities. For some, being "American" now means having a renewed patriotism, as described by one of our students:

> *To be an American is to be proud. After September 11, a sense of patriotism swept through this country that I have never felt before. Growing up I heard about how patriotic the United States was during WW I and WW II, but I had never experienced it personally. After that day, it was as if racial, religious, and democratic differences had stopped. Even if that tension only stopped temporarily, the point is that it did stop. Our country came together to help, pray, and donate. The feeling of being an American is a sense of feeling and strength and pride.*

---

interpellation The communication process by which one is pulled into the social forces that place people into a specific identity.

For others, the events of 9/11 led to more ambivalence about being "American":

> *The media showed negative responses that other countries displayed toward Americans. This makes me ponder what I've done, as a white mutt American to make people feel this way. I know it is not necessarily my fault but actually American beliefs as a whole. . . . The "cop in the head" feeling occurs in me whenever I see a group of people gathered around speaking a foreign language and staring at me. Maybe it is an insecurity issue within me, aided by rumors I've heard, that initiates this uneasy feeling. I really hope Americans, as a whole, become more accepting of each other so that other countries will see that we can work together with such diversity.*

For another example, look at the way that identity labels have changed from "colored" to "Negro" to "black" to "Afro-American" to "African American." Although the labels seem to refer to the same group of people, the political and cultural identities of those so labeled are different. Indeed, the contexts in which the terms developed and were used vary considerably.

IDENTITY AND LANGUAGE

The labels that refer to particular identities are an important part of intercultural communication. These labels do not, of course, exist outside of their relational meanings. It is the relationships—not only interpersonal but social—that help us understand the importance of the labels.

Communication scholar Dolores Tanno (2000) describes her own multiple identities reflected in the various labels applied to her. For instance, the label "Spanish" was applied by her family and designates an ancestral origin in Spain. The label "Mexican American" reflects two important cultures that contribute to her identity. "Latina" reflects cultural and historical connectedness with others of Spanish descent (e.g., Puerto Ricans and South Americans), and "Chicana" promotes political and cultural assertiveness in representing her identity. She stresses that she is all of these, that each one reveals a different facet of her identity: symbolic, historical, cultural, and political.

In emphasizing the fluidity and relational nature of labels, communication scholar Stuart Hall (1985) notes that,

Writer Philippe Wamba describes how his multicultural identity developed across several continents and languages. His father (from the Democratic Republic of Congo, formerly Zaire) and mother (an African American midwesterner) met and married while attending college in Michigan. His father's career took the family first to Boston (where Philippe was one of only a few blacks in his school), then to Dar es Salaam, Tanzania, where he learned flawless Swahili and added a third heritage to his cultural background: "half American, half Zairean, and half Tanzanian." Now an adult, he describes his answer to the question "Where are you from?"

I used to try to find succinct ways of responding to the question "Where are you from"—simple one-word answers that would satisfy the curious. I envied my friends their ability to state one place confidently and simply say "New York" or "Kenya." . . . For a period, I even referred to myself as a "a citizen of the world," a high-minded moniker, bred of my own boredom and frustration, that used to annoy people. . . . Now I have decided that the succinct answer is always inadequate and that the story of origin is always a complex saga. . . . I have come to reject the idea of a simple, dualized family heritage and the simple bicultural understanding of self I internalized as a child. . . . For a time I lived as a sophisticated cultural chameleon, attempting to blend with my shifting surroundings by assuming the appearance and habits of those around me. . . . In the end I am both African and African American and therefore neither. I envy others their hometowns and unconflicted patriotism, but no longer would I exchange them for my freedom to seek multiple homes and nations and to forge my own.

Source: From P. Wamba, "A Middle Passage." In C. C. O'Hearn (Ed.), *Half and Half: Writers on Growing up Biracial + Bicultural* (New York: Pantheon Books, 1998), pp. 168–169.

at different times in my thirty years in England, I have been "hailed" or interpellated as "coloured," "West-Indian," "Negro," "black," "immigrant." Sometimes in the street; sometimes at street corners; sometimes abusively; sometimes in a friendly manner; sometimes ambiguously. (p. 108)

Hall underscores the dynamic and dialectic nature of identity and the self as he continues:

In fact I "am" not one or another of these ways of representing me, though I have been all of them at different times and still am some of them to some degree. But, there is no essential, unitary "I"—only the fragmentary, contradictory subject I become. (pp. 108–109)

These and other labels construct relational meanings in communication situations. The interpersonal relationships between Hall and the other speakers are important, but equally important are such labels' social meanings.

Like culture, labels also change over time. At one time, it was acceptable to use the label *oriental* to refer to people, but today the social meaning of that term is considered negative. There are many terms that you may not know are considered offensive, but as you interact with others around the world, you should be aware that you need to learn what terms to use and what terms to avoid. For example, referring to Quebeckers, especially French-speaking Quebeckers, as *pepsi's* may get you in trouble. Pepsi is considered a derogatory term for Quebeckers. Québec is reputedly one of the few places around the world where Pepsi outsells Coca-Cola, which may be because of the bottle size, but the term may also come from the Pepsi's glass bottles that were empty from the neck up. Other terms are still contested. For example, some gays and lesbians do not like the term *queer*; others have embraced it. Cultures change over time, as do languages. It is important that you stay aware of these changes as much as possible so you do not unintentionally offend others.

IDENTITY DEVELOPMENT ISSUES

People can identify with a multitude of groups: gender, age, religion, nationality, to name only a few. How do we come to develop a sense of identities? As we noted earlier, our identities develop over a period of time and always through interaction with others. How an individual's identity develops depends partly on the relative position or location of the identity within the societal hierarchy. Some identities have a higher position on the social hierarchy. For example, a heterosexual identity has a more privileged position than a homosexual identity; a Christian religious identity is generally more privileged than a Jewish or Muslim religious identity in the United States. To distinguish between the various positions, we label the more privileged identities "majority identities" and label the less privileged "minority identities." This terminology refers to the relative dominance or power of the identity position, not the numerical quantity.

Social science researchers have identified various models that describe how minority and majority identities develop. Although the models center on racial and ethnic identities, they may also apply to other identities such as class, gender, or sexual orientation (Ponterotto & Pedersen, 1993). It is also important to remember that, as with any model, these represent the experience of many people, but the stages are not set in stone. Identity development is a complex process; not everyone experiences these phases in exactly the same way. Some people spend more time in one phase than do others; individuals may experience the phases in different ways, and not everyone reaches the final phase.

Minority Identity Development

In general, minority identities tend to develop earlier than majority identities. For example, straight people tend often do not think about their sexual orientation identity, whereas gay people are often acutely aware of their sexual orientation identity being different from the majority, and develop a sense of sexual orientation identity earlier than people who are straight. Similarly, while whites may develop a strong ethnic identity, they often do not think about their racial identity, whereas members of racial minority groups are aware of their racial identities at an early age (Ferguson, 1990).

Minority identity often develops in the following stages:

Stage 1: Unexamined Identity   This stage is characterized by the lack of exploration of identity, be it racial, ethnic, sexual orientation, gender, or whatever. At this stage, individuals may simply lack interest in the identity issue. As one African American woman put it, "Why do I need to learn about who was the first black woman to do this or that? I'm just not too interested." Or minority group members may initially accept the values and attitudes of the majority culture, expressing positive attitudes toward the dominant group and negative views of their own group. Young girls may idolize their successful professional fathers and disparage their stay-at-home mothers. Gay young people may try very hard to act "straight" and may even participate in "gay bashing."

Stage 2: Conformity   This stage is characterized by the internaliza-

---

minority identity A sense of belonging to a nondominant group.

tion of the values and norms of the dominant group and a strong desire to assimilate into the dominant culture. Individuals in this phase may have negative, self-deprecating attitudes toward both themselves and their group. As one young Jewish woman said, "I tried very hard in high school to not let anyone know I was Jewish. I'd talk about Christmas shopping and Christmas parties with my friends even though my parents didn't allow me to participate at all in any Christmas celebration."

Individuals who criticize members of their own ethnic or racial group may be given negative labels such as "Uncle Tom" or "oreo" for African Americans, "banana" for Asian Americans, "apple" for Native Americans, and "Tio Taco" for Chicanos. Such labels condemn attitudes and behaviors that support the dominant white culture. This stage often continues until they encounter a situation that causes them to question predominant culture attitudes, which initiates the movement to the next stage.

Stage 3: Resistance and Separatism   Many kinds of events can trigger the move to the third stage, including negative ones such as encountering discrimination or name-calling. A period of dissonance, or a growing awareness that not all dominant group values are beneficial to minorities, may also precede this stage. For example, Tomiko, a young professional woman, never thought much about her gender identity. However, she became more self-reflective and was propelled into this stage of identity development after discovering that she could not join the country club that many of her male colleagues belonged to—where they often discussed important job-related issues—because of her gender. And she then learned that the leave policies at her firm were such that if she decided to have a child she would likely be penalized professionally. Her gender identity then became very important to her, and she moved to the resistance and separation stage. For a time she decided only to patronize businesses where women were treated equally. She selected a female doctor as her primary care physician, shopped at a hardware store owned by a group of women, and when she tackled a home remodeling project she solicited bids only from female construction firms.

International students sometimes develop their national identity as a minority identity when they study overseas. Dewi, an Indonesian student, reported that when she first arrived in the United States, she thought little of her national identity (because this was a majority identity in *her* country). She told everyone she thought the United States was the greatest place and really tried hard to use American slang, dress American, and fit in. After several experiences with discrimination, she moved to a more separate stage where she only socialized with other Indonesian or other international students for a time. For writer Ruben Martinez (1998), a defining moment was when he was rather cruelly rejected by a white girl whom he had asked to dance at a high school prom:

> *I looked around me at the dance floor with new eyes: Mexicans danced with Mexicans, blacks with blacks, whites with whites. Who the hell did I think I was? Still, it would take a while for the gringo-hater in me to bust out. It was only a matter of time before I turned away from my whiteness and became the ethnic rebel. It seemed like it happened overnight, but it was the result of years of pent-up rage in me. (p. 256)*

Sometimes the move to this phase happens because individuals who have been denying their identity meet someone from that group who exhibits a strong identity. This encounter may result in a concern to clarify their own identity. So the young woman who was ashamed of being Jewish and tried hard to act "Christian" met a dynamic young man who was active in his synagogue and had a strong Jewish faith. Through their relationship she gained an appreciation of her own religious background, including the Jewish struggle for survival throughout the centuries. As often happens in this stage, she wholeheartedly endorsed the values and attitude attribute to the minority (Jewish) group and rejected the values and norms associate with the dominant group—she dropped most of her Christian friends and socialized primarily with her Jewish friends.

This stage may be characterized by a blanket endorsement of one's group and all the values and attitudes attributed to the group. At the same time, the person may reject the values and norms associated with the dominant group.

Stage 4: Integration According to this model, the ideal outcome of the identity development process is the final stage—an achieved identity. Individuals who have reached this stage have a strong sense of their own group identity (based on gender, race, ethnicity, sexual orientation, and so on) and an appreciation of other cultural groups. In this stage, they come to realize that racism and other forms of oppression occur, but they try to redirect any anger from the previous stage in more positive ways. The end result is individuals with a confident and secure identity characterized by a desire to eliminate all forms of injustice, and not merely oppression aimed at their own group.

Brenda: I had a hard time accepting my "old age identity." And for a while, I didn't even want to be around younger people. However, now I realize there will always be some discrimination against older women. We're really just invisible. I walk into a store and if there is anyone younger and more attractive, salespeople will often look right though me. However, I accept that this is the way our society is. And I can enjoy being around younger people now—I love their energy and their optimism. And I know that there are positive things about being older. Like, many things I just don't worry about anymore.

Ryan: Because my name is Irish, people generally assume I'm Catholic, but my family has always been Protestant. I knew from an early age that we were different from other Irish. I didn't really understand anything about the history of Ireland, and I always thought of myself as just an American. Now that I know more about this history and my family's history, I feel comfortable being a Protestant and Irish American. I'm happy to be both and different from other Irish Americans.

Sam(antha): I never liked to wear dresses and play with makeup. I knew I was different from a very young age, but I never understood what any of that meant. I used to deny who I was—loudly. Today, I still avoid wearing dresses, hose, heels, and makeup, but I no longer worry if people will think I'm a lesbian. I *am* a lesbian and I prefer that others know, so that men, in particular, don't approach me assuming that I might be interested.

Majority Identity Development

Rita Hardiman (1994, 2003), educator and pioneer in antiracism training, presents a model of **majority identity** development that has similarities to the model for minority group members. Although she intended the model to represent how white people develop a sense of healthy racial identity, it can also be helpful in describing how other majority identities develop—straight sexual orientation, Christian religious identity, male gender identity, middle-class identity, and so on. Again, remember that majority identity, like minority identity, develops in a complex process. And this model—unlike some other identity development models—is prescriptive. In other words, it outlines the way some scholars think a majority identity *should* develop, from accepting societal hierarchies that favor some identities and diminish others to resisting these inequities.

Hardiman (1993, 2004) outlines five stages:

---

majority identity A sense of belonging to a dominant group.

Stage 1: Unexamined Identity   This first stage is the same as for minority identities. In this case, individuals may be aware of some physical and cultural differences, but they do not fear the other or think much about their own identity. There is no understanding of the social meaning and value of gender, sexual orientation, religion, and so on. Although young boys may develop a sense of what it means to be a male by watching their fathers or other males, they are not aware of the social consequences of being born male over female. Those with majority identities, unlike those with minority identities, may stay in this stage for a long time.

Stage 2: Acceptance   The second stage represents the internalization, conscious or unconscious, of a racist (or otherwise biased) ideology. This may involve passive or active acceptance. The key point is that individuals are not aware that they have been programmed to accept this worldview.

In the passive acceptance stage, individuals have no conscious identification with being white, straight, male, etc. However, they may hold some assumptions based on an acceptance of inequities in the larger society. In general, the social hierarchy is experienced as "normal" for the dominant group, and they may view minority groups as being unduly sensitive and assume that if the minority members really wanted to change their lot in life they could. Here are some possible assumptions.

Being male in this stage may involve the following (sometime unconscious) assumptions:

- Men and women may be different, but they are basically equal. Kyle, a student, tells us, "I never heard so much whining from 'feminists' until I came to college. Frankly, it is a little much. Although women may have faced barriers in the past, that's in the past. Women can pretty much do whatever they want in society today. If they want to be doctors, lawyers, police officers, firefighters, or anything else, they just need to set their minds to it and do it."

- If women really want to make it professionally, they can work as hard as men work and they will succeed.

Being straight may involve these assumptions:

- Gay people choose to be gay.
- Gay people whine a lot, unfairly, about discrimination. There is

no recognition of the many privileges given to those who are straight.

- Gay people put their gayness in straight people's faces. At this stage there is no recognition of the vast societal emphasis on heterosexuality.

Being white may involve these assumptions:

- Minority groups are culturally deprived and need help to assimilate.
- Affirmative action is reverse discrimination because people of color are being given opportunities that whites don't have.
- White culture—music, art, and literature—is "classical"; works of art by people of color are folk art or "crafts."
- People of color are culturally different, whereas whites have no group identity or culture or shared experience of racial privilege.

Individuals in this stage usually take one of two positions with respect to interactions with minorities: (1) They avoid contact somewhat with minority group members, or (2) they adopt a patronizing stance toward them. Both positions are possible at the same time.

In contrast, those in the active acceptance stage are conscious of their privileged position and may express their feelings of superiority collectively (e.g., join male-only clubs). Some people never move beyond this phase—whether it is characterized by passive or active acceptance. And if they do, it is usually a result of a number of cumulative events. For example, Judith gradually came to realize that her two nieces, who are sisters—one of whom is African American and one of whom is white—had very different experiences growing up. Both girls lived in middle-class neighborhoods, both were honor students in high school, and both went to Ivy League colleges. However, they often had very different experiences. On more than one occasion, the African American girl was followed by security while shopping; she also was stopped several times by police while driving her mother's sports car. Her white sister never had these experiences. Eventually, awareness of this reality prodded Judith to the next stage. As was true with Judith, the move to the next stage often comes because of personal relationships.

I realized how difficult it is for gay people when I became good friends with a gay colleague. I had never realized how many cheap jokes about gays there are in movies, how many financial benefits I had because I was straight. Since I'm married, my spouse and I can have joint health benefits, death benefits, hospital visitation rights when my spouse is in ICU,

POINT OF VIEW

This essay describes some of the controversy surrounding the increasing diversity in dolls.

One girl is black, the second white. But Allister Byrd and Samantha Arvin say the same thing when it comes to playing with dolls. They love them in any color—black, white, brown, you name it.

Toy makers are taking note with new doll lines that are more diverse than ever, including the first multiracial Barbie, which was on display last week at the American International Toy Fair in New York. A Mattel spokeswoman says the new Barbie could be viewed as black, Asian and Hispanic—a "mix of cultures in one doll."

. . . Some dolls of different races and ethnicities, including black Barbie, have been around for years, but industry experts say an increased demand and awareness of other cultures has spawned a new wave of diverse dolls.

. . . At least one line, called the Ghetto Kids, was criticized by some parents and TV commentators because its packaging included hard-hitting doll "biographies" that mentioned parents who were drug addicts or who abandoned and even sold their children.

Officials at Chicago-based Teddi's Toys, who created the dolls, have since removed some of the made-up doll background. But they're keeping the Ghetto Kids name as an attention grabber. They also hope information on their Website, including a cartoon series, will spur parents to talk to kids about such topics as smoking, guns, and teen-age pregnancy.

to say nothing of the fact that I can always refer to my husband in any conversation without anyone lifting an eyebrow or looking at me weird.

This model recognizes that it is very difficult to escape the societal hierarchy that influences both minority and majority identity development because of its pervasive, systemic, and interlocking nature. The hierarch is a by-product of living within and being impacted by the institutional and cultural systems that surrounds us.

Stage 3: Resistance The next stage represents a major paradigm shift. It involves a move from blaming minority members for their condition to naming and blaming their own dominant group as a source of problems. This resistance may take the form of passive resistance, with little behavioral change, or active resistance—trying to reduce, eliminate,

"It's real life, real time," says company founder Tommy Perez, who unveiled a Jewish Ghetto Kid at the New York toy fair. "It doesn' t pull many punches."

Some parents say the race issue alone can be touchy, even if diversity among dolls is expanding.

Rob Whitehouse, a father from Akron, Ohio, says he's noticed the looks his fair-haired, fair-skinned 5 year old gets when she totes around her favorite companion, a black Addy doll. . . . "I just say, 'yeah, she loves it'" Whitehouse says. "It's best just to be very matter-of-fact about it."

Marguerite Wright, a clinical psychologist from Oakland, Calif., says that's a good way to handle it. But sometimes, she says, parents insist that their children play with dolls of a certain race, usually their own. "It's just a small step between forcing children to choose dolls according to skin color and forcing them to choose friends according to skin color," say Wright, who addresses the doll issue in her book "I'm Chocolate, You're Vanilla: Raising Healthy Black and Biracial Children in a Race-Conscious World."

Some parents say their children still don't have much choice in dolls because the selection remains overwhelmingly white. Phyllis Redus, who is black, says she often has a hard time finding anything but white dolls in her hometown of Huntsville, Ala. . . .

Source: From "Dolls Getting More Racially Diverse," *Pittsburgh Tribune-Review*, February 20, 2002, www.pittsburghlive.com/x/tribune-review/entertainment/ s_18297.html.

or challenge the institutional hierarchies that oppress. In reference to one's own identity, this stage is often characterized by embarrassment about one's own privileged position, guilt, shame, and a need to distances oneself from the dominant group.

Our student, Kayla, says: I was raised as a Christian, so I was never taught to question our beliefs. Since I've left home, I have met gay and lesbian students and I no longer understand why my church has such a problem with homosexuality. I get angry and sometimes I speak out when I'm at home and my parents get upset, but I don't want to stand around and let bigots take over my church. I have begun to question my Christian values, as I no longer know if they are compatible with my sense of right and wrong.

Kevin says that:

> For a while, I couldn't stand to be around white people, even though I'm white. After I learned more about how we tried to exterminate Indians, put Japanese Americans (but not German Americans) in internment camps during World War II and how many people of color are still subjected to incidents of racism and discrimination even today, I felt so awful and depressed. I started just hanging around with people who weren't white, listening to their music and going to their parties.

Stage 4: Redefinition In the fourth stage, people begin to refocus or redirect their energy toward redefining their identity in a way that recognizes their privilege and works to eliminate oppression and inequities. They realize that they don't have to accept uncritically the definitions of being white, straight, male, Christian, U.S. American that society has instilled in them. For example, Nick tells us, "As a straight white guy, I often find myself in social situations in which people feel free to make offhand remarks or jokes that are somewhat racist, heterosexist, or sexist. They assume that I would agree with them, since I'm not a minority, gay, or a woman, but I don't. I am happy to be who I am, but this doesn't mean that being a straight white man means I need to be racist, sexist, or homophobic. I am proud to be who I am, but I don't think that means I have to put down others."

Stage 5: Integration As in the final stage of minority identity development, majority group individuals now are able to internalize their increased consciousness and integrate their majority identities into all other facets of their identity. They not only recognize their identity as white but also appreciate other groups. This integration affects other aspects of social and personal identity, including religion and gender.

Hardiman (2003) acknowledges that this model is rather simplistic in explaining the diverse experiences of people. It does not acknowledge the impact of diverse environments and socialization processes that influence how people experience their dominant identities or the realities of interlocking identities.

Systems of privilege are complicated; this is one reason why people can belong to a privileged category and not feel privileged. You may have several identities that are more privileged and several that are less privileged. So, for example, a middle-class white lesbian, benefiting from and yet unaware of the privileges of race or class, may think that her experience of sexual orientation and gender inequality enables her to understand what she needs to know about other forms of privilege and oppression. Or a straight working-class white man may be annoyed at the idea that his sexual orientation, whiteness, and maleness somehow gives him access to privilege. As a member of the working class, he may feel insecure in his job, afraid of being outsourced, downsized, and feel not at all privileged (Johnson, 2001).

To make it more complicated, our multiple identities exist all at once in relation to one another. People never see us solely in terms of race or gender or nationality—they see us as a complex of identities. So it makes no sense to talk about the experience of one identity—being white, for example—without looking at other identities. A dialectical perspective helps here in avoiding falling into the trap of thinking we are or are not privileged. Most of us are both.

SOCIAL AND CULTURAL IDENTITIES

People can identify with a multitude of groups. This section describes some of the major types of groups.

Gender Identity

We often begin life with gender identities. When newborns arrive in our culture, they may be greeted with clothes and blankets in either blue for boys or pink for girls. To establish a **gender identity** for the newborn, visitors may ask if the baby is a boy or a girl. But gender is not the same as biological sex. This distinction is important in understanding how our views on biological sex influence gender identities.

What it means to be a man or a woman in our society is heavily influenced by cultural notions. For example, some activities are considered more masculine or more feminine. Thus, whether people hunt or sew or fight or read poetry can transform the ways that others view them. Similarly, the programs that people watch on television—soap operas, football games, and so on—affect how they socialize with others, contributing to gendered contexts.

As culture changes, so does the notion of what we idealize as masculine or feminine. Cultural historian Gail Bederman (1995) observes,

> *Even the popular imagery of a perfect male body changed. In the 1860s, the middle class had seen the ideal male body as lean and wiry. By the*

---

gender identity The identification with the cultural notions of masculinity and femininity and what it means to be a man or a woman.

1890s, however, an ideal male body required physical bulk and well-defined muscles. (p. 15)

In this sense, the male body, as well as the female body, can be understood not in its "natural" state but in relation to idealized notions of masculinity and femininity. To know that this man or that woman is particularly good looking requires an understanding of the gendered notions of attractiveness in a culture.

Our notions of masculinity and femininity change continually, driven by commercial interests and other cultural forces. For example, there is a major push now to market cosmetics to men. However, advertisers acknowledge that this requires sensitivity to men's ideas about makeup:

Unlike women, most men don't want to talk about makeup, don't want to go out in public to shop for makeup and don't know how to use makeup. The first barrier is getting men to department stores or specialty shops to buy products. (Yamanouchi, 2002, p. D1)

Our expression of gender not only communicates who we think we are but also constructs a sense of who we want to be. Initially, we learn what masculinity and femininity mean in our culture. Communication scholar Julia T. Wood (2005) has identified feminine and masculine themes in U.S. society. These are the femininity themes: appearance still counts; be sensitive and caring; accept negative treatment by others; and be a superwoman. The masculinity themes are don't be female; be successful; be aggressive; be sexual; and be self-reliant. Masculinity themes are often the opposite of what it means to be a woman or a gay man. According to Wood, U.S. American men are socialized that first and foremost, being a man is about *not* being a woman. Then, through various media, we monitor how these notions shift and negotiate to communicate our gendered selves to others.

Consider, for example, the contemporary trend in the United States for women to have very full lips. If one's lips are not naturally full, there is always the option of getting collagen injections or having other body fat surgically inserted into the lips. In contrast, our Japanese students tell us that full lips are not considered at all attractive in Japan. The dynamic character of gender reflects its close connection to culture. Society has many images of masculinity and femininity; we do not all seek to look and act according to a single ideal. At the same time, we *do* seek to communicate our gendered identities as part of who we are.

Gender identity is also demonstrated by communication style. For example, women's communication style is often described as support-ive, egalitarian, personal, and disclosive, whereas men's is characterized as competitive and assertive (Wood, 2005). However, these differences may be more perception than fact. Results of recent research sug-gest that women's and men's communication styles are more similar than they are different (Canary & Hause, 1993; Pennebaker, Mehl, & Niederhoffer, 2003). And yet these stereotypes of gender differences persist, maybe partly because of the stereotypical depictions of men and women in magazines, on television, and in movies.

However, what it means to be feminine and masculine are not stable, clear-cut identity categories. Rather, these notions are created, reinforced, and reconstructed by society through communication and overlap with our other identities.

Age Identity

As we age, we also play into cultural notions of how individuals our age should act, look, and behave; that is, we develop an **age identity**. As we grow older, we sometimes look at the clothes displayed in store windows or advertised in newspapers and magazines and feel that we are either too old or too young for that "look." These feelings stem from an understanding of what age means and how we identify with people that age.

Some people feel old at 30; others feel young at 40 or 50. Nothing inherent in age tells us we are young or old. Rather, our notions of age and youth are all based on cultural conventions. The United States is an age-conscious society. One of the first things we teach children is to tell their age. And children will proudly tell their age, until about the mid 20s on, when people rarely mention their age. In contrast, people older than 70 often brag about their age. Certain ages have special significance in some cultures. Latino families sometimes celebrate a daughter's 15th birthday with a *quinceañera* party—marking the girl's entry into womanhood. Some Jewish families celebrate with a bat mitz-vah ceremony for daughters and a bar mitzvah for sons on their 13th birthday (Allen, 2004). These same cultural conventions also suggest that it is inappropriate to engage in a romantic relationship with some-one who is too old or too young.

Our notions of age often change as we grow older ourselves. When we are quite young, someone in college seems old; when we are in college, we do not feel so old. Yet the relative nature of age is only one part of the identity process. Social constructions of age also play

age identity The identification with the cultural conventions of how we should act, look, and behave according to our age.

a role. Different generations often have different philosophies, values, and ways of speaking. For example, recent data show that today's college freshmen are more liberal politically and more interested in volunteer work and civic responsibility than were Gen Xers. Scholars who view generations as "cultural groups" say that these characteristics make them similar to the World War I generation—politically curious and assertive, and devoted to a sense of personal responsibility (Sax, Lindholm, Astin, Korn, & Mahoney, 2001).

Sometimes these generational differences can lead to conflict in the workplace. For example, young people who entered the job market during the "dot.com" years have little corporate loyalty and think nothing of changing jobs when a better opportunity comes along. This can irritate baby boomer workers, who emphasize the importance of demonstrating corporate loyalty, of "paying one's dues" to the establishment while gradually working one's way "up the corporate ladder" (Zemke, Raines, & Filipczak, 2000). Although not all people in any generation are alike, the attempt to find trends across generations reflects our interest in understanding age identity.

Racial and Ethnic Identities

Racial Identity   Race consciousness, or **racial identity**, is largely a modern phenomenon. In the United States today, the issue of race is both controversial and pervasive. It is the topic of many public discussions, from television talk shows to talk radio. Yet many people feel uncomfortable talking about it or think it should not be an issue in daily life. Perhaps we can better understand the contemporary issues if we look at how the notion of race developed historically in the United States.

Current debates about race have their roots in the 15th and 16th centuries, when European explorers encountered people who looked different from themselves. The debates centered on religious questions of whether there was "one family of man." If so, what rights were to be accorded to those who were different? Debates about which groups were "human" and which were "animal" pervaded popular and legal discourse and provided a rationale for slavery. Later, in the 18th and 19th centuries, the scientific community tried to establish a classification system of race, based on genetics and cranial capacity. However, these efforts were largely unsuccessful.

Today, most scientists have abandoned a strict biological basis for

---

racial identity Identifying with a particular racial group. Although in the past racial groups were classified on the basis of biological characteristics, most scientists now recognize that race is constructed in fluid social and historical contexts.

classifying racial groups, deferring instead to a social science approach to understanding race. They recognize that racial categories like white and black are constructed in social and historical contexts.

Several arguments refute the physiological basis for race. First, racial categories vary widely throughout the world. In general, distinctions between white and black are fairly rigid in the United States, and many people become uneasy when they are unable to categorize individuals. In contrast, Brazil recognizes a wide variety of intermediate racial categories in addition to white and black. These variations indicate a cultural, rather than a biological, basis for racial classification (Omi & Winant, 2001). Terms like *mulatto* and *Black Irish* demonstrate cultural classifications; terms like *Caucasoid* and *Australoid* are examples of biological classification.

Second, U.S. law uses a variety of definitions to determine racial categories. A 1982 case in Louisiana reopened debates about race as socially created rather than biologically determined. Susie Phipps applied for a passport and discovered that under Louisiana law she was black because she was 1/32 African (her great grandmother had been a slave). She then sued to be reclassified as white. Not only did she consider herself white, inasmuch as she grew up among whites, but she also was married to a white man. And because her children were only 1/64 African, they were legally white. Although she lost her lawsuit, the ensuing political and popular discussions persuaded Louisiana lawmakers to change the way the state classified people racially. It is important that the law was changed, but this legal situation does not obscure the fact that social definitions of race continue to exist (Hasian & Nakayama, 1999).

A third example of how racial categories are socially constructed is illustrated by their fluid nature. As more and more southern Europeans immigrated to the United States in the 19th century, the established Anglo and German society tried to classify these newcomers (Irish and Jewish, as well as southern European) as nonwhite. However, this attempt was not successful because, based on the narrower definition, whites might have become demographically disempowered. Instead, the racial line was drawn to include all Europeans, and people from outside of Europe (e.g., immigrants from China) were designated as non-White (Roediger, 2005).

Racial categories, then, are based to some extent on physical characteristics, but they are also constructed in fluid social contexts. It probably makes more sense to talk about racial *formation* than racial *categories*, thereby casting race as a complex of social meanings rather than as a fixed and objective concept. How people construct these meanings and think about race influences the ways in which they communicate.

Ethnic Identity   In contrast to racial identity, **ethnic identity** may be seen as a set of ideas about one's own ethnic group membership. It typically includes several dimensions: (1) self-identification, (2) knowledge about the ethnic culture (traditions, customs, values, and behaviors), and (3) feelings about belonging to a particular ethnic group. Ethnic identity often involves a shared sense of origin and history, which may link ethnic groups to distant cultures in Asia, Europe, Latin America, or other locations.

Having an ethnic identity means experiencing a sense of belonging to a particular group and knowing something about the shared experience of group members. For instance, Judith grew up in an ethnic community. She heard her parents and relatives speak German, and her grandparents made several trips back to Germany and talked about their German roots. This experience contributed to her ethnic identity.

For some U.S. residents, ethnicity is a specific and relevant concept. They see themselves as connected to an origin outside the United States—as Mexican American, Japanese American, Welsh American, and so on—or to some region prior to its being absorbed into the United States—Navajo, Hopi, and so on. As one African American student told us, "I have always known my history and the history of my people in this country. I will always be first African American and then American. Who I am is based on my heritage." For others, ethnicity is a vague concept. They see themselves as "American" and reject the notion of **hyphenated Americans**. One of our students explains:

> *I am American. I am not German American or Irish American or Native America. I have never set foot on German or Irish land. I went to Scotland a couple years ago and found a Scottish plaid that was my family crest. I still didn't even feel a real connection to it and bought it as more of a joke, to say, "Look! I'm Scottish!" even though in my heart I know I'm not.*

We discuss the issues of ethnicity for white people later.

What, then, does *American* mean? Who defines it? Is there only one meaning, or are there many different meanings? It is important

---

ethnic identity (1) A set of ideas about one's own ethnic group membership; (2) a sense of belonging to a particular group and knowing something about the shared experience of the group.
hyphenated Americans U.S. Americans who identify not only with being U.S. citizens but also as members of ethnic groups.

to determine what definition is being used by those who insist that we should all simply be "Americans." If one's identity is "just American," how is this identity formed, and how does it influence communication with others who see themselves as hyphenated Americans (Alba, 1985, 1990; Carbaugh, 1989)?

Racial Versus Ethnic Identity Scholars dispute whether racial and ethnic identity are similar or different. Some suggest that ethnic identity is constructed by both selves and others but that racial identity is constructed solely by others. They stress as well that race overrides ethnicity in the way people classify others (Cornell & Hartmann, 1998). The American Anthropological Association has suggested that the U.S. government phase out use of the term *race* in the collection of federal data because the concept has no scientific validity or utility.

On the one hand, discussions about ethnicity tend to assume a "melting pot" perspective on U.S. society. On the other hand, discussions about race as shaped by U.S. history allow us to talk about racism. If we never talk about race, but only about ethnicity, can we consider the effects and influences of racism?

Bounded Versus Dominant Identities One way to sort out the relationship between ethnicity and race is to differentiate between bounded and dominant (or normative) identities (Frankenburg, 1993; Trinh, 1986/1987). Bounded cultures are characterized by groups that are specific but not dominant. For most white people, it is easy to comprehend the sense of belonging in a bounded group (e.g., an ethnic group). Clearly, for example, being Amish means following the *ordnung* (community rules). Growing up in a German American home, Judith's identity included a clear emphasis on seriousness and very little on communicative expressiveness. This identity differed from that of her Italian American friends at college, who seemed much more expressive.

However, what it means to belong to the dominant, or normative, culture is more elusive. *Normative* means "setting the norm for a society." In the United States, whites clearly are the normative group in that they set the standards for appropriate and effective behavior. Although it can be difficult for white people to define what a normative white identity is, this does not deny its existence or importance. It is often not easy to see what the cultural practices are that link white people together. For example, we seldom think of Thanksgiving or Valentine's Day as white holidays.

Our sense of racial or ethnic identity develops over time, in stages,

POINT OF VIEW

This press release from the American Anthropological Association questions the utility of the term *race* and suggests that the government eliminate it from its data gathering.

The government should phase out use of the term "race" in the collection of federal data because the concept has no scientific justification in human biology, according to a statement released today by the American Anthropological Association (AAA).

Instead of race, ethnic categories, which better reflect the diversity of the US population, should be used. The AAA statement includes five recommendations for changes in the way the government collects information about its citizens. It addresses the federal Office of Management and Budget (OMB) Directive 15, which designates racial and ethnic categories used in the US census and in innumerable other public and private research projects.

The recommendations outlined by the AAA include the immediate need for the OMB to combine the now-separate "race" and "ethnicity" questions into one question for the 2000 Census and to eliminate "race" by the time planning begins for the 2010 Census. Respondents should be allowed to identify more than one category in reporting their ancestry. Additionally, the AAA advocates more research to determine what terms best capture human variability in ways best understood by the American people.

. . . Probably the clearest data on human variation come from genetic studies. Genetic data do show differences between groups and these can potentially trace an individual's likely geographic origin. This can be helpful in such applications as health screening. Nevertheless, the data also show that any two individuals within a particular population are as different genetically as any two people selected from any two populations in the world. . . .

Source: From "AAA Recommends Race Be Scrapped; Suggests New Government Categories," press release/OMB15, September 1997, www.aaanet. org/gvt/obmnews.htm.

and through communication with others. These stages seem to reflect our growing understanding of who we are and depend to some extent on the groups we belong to. Many ethnic or racial groups share the experience of oppression. In response, they may generate attitudes and behaviors consistent with a natural internal struggle to develop a strong sense of group identity and self-identity. For many cultural groups, these strong identities ensure their survival.

Characteristics of Whiteness

What does it mean to be white in the United States? What are the characteristics of a white identity? Is there a unique set of characteristics that define whiteness, just as other racial identities have been described? The film *The Color of Fear*, produced in the early 1990s, addresses these issues by examining the real-life experiences of men from a variety of ethnic and racial backgrounds. Let's look at the dialogue between Victor, who is African American, and David, who is white.

Victor: What I hear from white people is, they talk about being human. They don't talk about themselves as white people. What I want to know is what it means to be white.

David: We don't look at ourselves as part of an ethnic group. I think that's what you're looking for and you're not going to find it.

Victor: Do you know that that means something? The fact that you have no answer to that?

It may be difficult for most white people to describe exactly what cultural patterns are uniquely white, but scholars have tried to do so. For example, scholar Ruth Frankenburg (1993) says that whiteness may be defined not only in terms of race or ethnicity but also as a set of linked dimensions. These dimensions include (1) normative race privilege, (2) a standpoint from which white people look at themselves, others, and society, and (3) a set of cultural practices (often unnoticed and unnamed).

Normative Race Privilege   Historically, whites have been the normative (dominant) group in the United States and, as such, have benefited from privileges that go along with belonging to the dominant group. However, not all whites have power, and not all have equal access to power. In fact, at times during U.S. history, some white communities were not privileged and were viewed as separate, or different, if not inferior. Examples include the Irish and Italians in the early 20th century and German Americans during World War II. And as scholars point out, the memory of marginality outlasts the marginality. For example, memories of discrimination may persist in the minds of some Italian Americans although little discrimination exists today. There also are many white people in the United States who are poor and so lack economic power.

There is an emerging perception that being white no longer means automatic privilege, particularly as demographics change in the United States and as some whites perceive themselves to be in the minority. This has led some whites to feel threatened and "out of place." Charles

A. Gallagher (1994), a sociologist, conducted a study in the early 1990s on what it means to be white in the United States today. He surveyed students at Temple University in Philadelphia, asking them how they felt about being white. He also asked the students to estimate the ratio of whites to blacks on campus. Many students reported that they thought the ratio was 30% white and 70% black; that is, they perceived themselves to be in the minority. The actual ratio was 70% white and 30% black. Students' perceptions affected their sense of identity, which, in turn, can affect intercultural communication.

Gallagher found that many of the students, mostly from working-class families, were very aware of their whiteness. Further, they believed that being white was a liability, that they were being prejudged as racist and blamed for social conditions they personally did not cause. They also claimed that they were denied opportunities that were unfairly given to minority students. One of our white students describes this feeling:

> *When I was trying to get into college I had to fight for every inch. I didn't have a lot of money to go to school with, so to get a scholarship was of great importance to me. So I went out and bought a book titled* The Big Book of Scholarships. *Ninety percent of the scholarships that this book contained didn't apply to me. They applied to the so-called minorities. . . . I think this country has gone on so long with the notion that white equals wealth or with things like affirmative action, that it has lost sight of the fact that this country is not that way any longer.*

In addition, because of corporate downsizing and the movement of jobs overseas in recent decades, increasing numbers of middle-aged white men have not achieved the degree of economic or professional success they had anticipated. They sometimes blame their lack of success on immigrants who will work for less or on the increasing numbers of women and minorities in the workplace. In these cases, whiteness is not invisible; it is a salient feature of the white individuals' identities. A more recent study by communication scholars Bahk and Jandt (2004) revealed significant difference in perceptions of white privilege by whites and nonwhites. They surveyed 700 students, asking them to indicate how strongly they agreed or disagreed with various statements regarding the meaning of whiteness. Nonwhites indicated high agreement with the following statements, whereas whites agreed significantly less:

- "White people have privilege in the United States."
- "When people refer to 'Americans,' it is usually whites they have in mind."

- "White people are regarded as superior to people of other racial groups."

The study shows that although whites may not perceive their racial privilege, it is quite clearly seen by those who are not white.

There was also interesting differences in perceptions regarding whites' communication behavior. This same study revealed that nonwhites perceive that whites tend to distance themselves from other racial groups, that they choose to interact with other whites rather than nonwhites in social situations, and that they tend to mingle much better with whites than other groups (Bahk & Jandt, 2004).

The point is not whether these perceptions are accurate. Rather, the point is that identities are negotiated and challenged through communication. People act on their perceptions, not on some external reality. As the nation becomes increasingly diverse and whites no longer form a majority in some regions, there will be increasing challenges for all of us as we negotiate our cultural identities. There may be many whites who feel like the students in Gallagher's study: threatened and outnumbered. How can whites in the United States incorporate the reality of not belonging to a majority group? Will whites find inclusive and productive ways to manage this identity change? Or will they react in defensive and exclusionary ways?

One reaction to feeling outnumbered and being a "new member" of an ethnic minority group is to strengthen one's own ethnic identity. For example, white people may tend to have stronger white identities in those U.S. states that have a higher percentage of nonwhites (e.g., Mississippi, South Carolina, Alabama). In these states, the white population traditionally has struggled to protect its racial privilege in various ways. As other states become increasingly less white, we are beginning to see various moves to protect whiteness, as in California with a series of propositions (187, prohibiting undocumented workers from receiving public services; 209, making affirmative action programs illegal in public universities; and 227, banning bilingual education in public schools) and increasing concerns about immigration. Historically, California has enacted measures to ensure that whites retained dominance in population, as well as in politics, economics, and so on. It is unclear what will happen in California and other states if, as predicted, whites become a demographic minority group. How do you think that whites will respond?

A Standpoint From Which to View Society Opinion polls reveal significant differences in how whites and blacks view many issues. For example, according to polls, most African Americans doubted

O. J. Simpson's guilt or had no faith in the legal system, whereas most whites thought Simpson was guilty of murdering two people.

TABLE 5.2 KATRINA THROUGH THE PRISM OF RACE			
	Total %	White %	Black %
Gov't response if most victims had been white?			
Faster	26	17	66
The same	68	77	27
Don't know	6	6	6
	100	100	100
Shows racial inequality still a major problem?			
Yes	38	32	71
No	50	56	22
Don't know	12	12	7
	100	100	100
Number of cases	(1,000)	(712)	(211)

Note: In order to gain enough interviews to report on this group accurately, the survey includes an oversample of African Americans. For all results based on the total population, statistical adjustments (weighting) are used to ensure that the correct national racial and ethnic characteristics are met.
Source: From Pew Research Center, http://people-press.org/reports/pdf/255.pdf

According to a survey conducted by the Pew Research Center (2005), the aftermath of Hurricane Katrina in the fall of 2005 revealed continuing significant differences in black and white perception. For example, as shown in Table 5.2, blacks and whites drew very different lessons from the Katrina tragedy. Seven in ten blacks (71%) said the disaster showed that racial inequality remains a major problem in the country, compared to only 32% of whites. More striking was the disagreement over whether the government's response to the crisis would have been faster if most of the storm's victims had been white; 66% of African Americans expressed that view, compared to 17% of whites (http://people-press.org/reports/pdf/255.pdf); see Table 5.2.

In another study, Frankenburg (1993) interviewed a number of white women, some of whom reported that they viewed being white as less than positive—as artificial, dominant, bland, homogeneous, and sterile. These respondents also saw white culture as less interesting and less rich than nonwhite culture. In contrast, other women viewed being white as positive, representing what was "civilized," as in classical music and fine art.

A Set of Cultural Practices   Is there a specific, unique "white" way of viewing the world? As noted previously, some views held consistently by whites are not necessarily shared by other groups. And some cultural practices and core symbols (e.g., individualism) are expressed primarily by whites and significantly less by members of minority groups. We need to note here that not everyone who is white shares all cultural practices. For example, recent immigrants who are white, but not born in the United States, may share in the privilege accorded all white people in the United States; however, they might not necessarily share in the viewpoints or the set of cultural practices of whites whose families have been in the United States for many generations. It is important to remember that some whites may identify fairly strongly with their European roots, especially if their families are more recent immigrants and they still have family members in Europe; other whites may not feel any connection to Europe and feel completely "American." These cultural practices are most clearly visible to those who are not white, to those groups who are excluded (Helms, 1994). For example, in the fairy tale of Snow White, the celebration of her beauty—emphasizing her beautiful, pure white skin—is often seen as problematic by people who are not white.

Religious Identity

Religious identity can be an important dimension of many people's identities, as well as an important site of intercultural conflict. Religious identity often is conflated with racial or ethnic identity, which makes it difficult to view religious identity simply in terms of belonging to a particular religion. For example, when someone says, "I am Jewish," does it mean that he practices Judaism? That he views Jewish identity as an ethnic identity? Or when someone says, "She has a Jewish last name," is it a statement that recognizes religious identity? With a historical view, we can see Jews as a racial group, an ethnic group, and a religious group.

Drawing distinctions between various identities—racial, ethnic, class, national, and regional—can be problematic. For example, Italians and Irish are often viewed as Catholics, and Episcopalians are frequently seen as belonging to the upper classes. Issues of religion and ethnicity have come to the forefront in the war against Al-Qaeda

---

religious identity A sense of belonging to a religious group.

and other militant groups. Although those who carried out the attacks against the Pentagon and the World Trade Center were Muslims and Arabs, it is hardly true that all Muslims are Arabs or that all Arabs are Muslims (Feghali, 1997).

Religious differences have been at the root of contemporary conflicts from the Middle East to Northern Ireland, and from India and Pakistan to Bosnia-Herzegovina. In the United States, religious conflicts caused the Mormons to flee the Midwest for Utah in the mid-19th century. More recently, religious conflicts have become very real for some Arab Americans as the U.S. government presses the war against terrorism, with many of those people subject to suspicion if not persecution. And militant Muslims in the Middle East and elsewhere see their struggle against the United States as a very serious endeavor and are willing to die for their religious beliefs.

In the United States, we often believe that people should be free to practice whatever religion they wish. Conflicts arise, however, when the religious beliefs of some individuals are imposed on others who may not share those beliefs. For example, some Jews see the predominance of Christmas trees and Christian crosses as an affront to their religious beliefs.

People in some religions communicate and mark their religious differences by their clothing. For example, Hassidic Jews wear traditional, somber clothing, and Muslim women are often veiled according to the Muslim guideline of female modesty. Of course, most religions are not identified by clothing. For example, you may not know if someone is Buddhist, Catholic, Lutheran, or atheist based upon the way he or she dresses. Because religious identities are less salient, everyday interactions may not invoke religious identity.

Class Identity

We don't often think about socioeconomic class as an important part of our identity. Yet scholars have shown that class often plays an important role in shaping our reactions to and interpretations of culture. For example, French sociologist Pierre Bourdieu (1987) studied the various responses to art, sports, and other cultural activities of people in different French social classes. According to Bourdieu, working-class people prefer to watch soccer, whereas upper-class individuals like tennis, and middle-class people prefer photographic art, whereas upper-class individuals favor less representational art. As these findings reveal, class distinctions are real and can be linked to actual behavioral practices and preferences.

English professor Paul Fussell (1992) shows how similar signs of

POINT OF VIEW

Communication scholar Kathleen Wong (Lau) describes how she gradually became aware of the intersections of race, class, and ethnicity through her own life experiences. Her parents were Chinese immigrant factory workers. She entered an elite college where the students were mostly white and children of teachers, attorneys, doctors, and other professionals.

It took me many years to understand the many dimensions of alienation I felt as a young Asian American woman coming of age. I didn't understand the complexity and muddiness of my own internalized oppression that had rendered me silent about my Chinese American parents, their occupations and about my working-class neighborhood. With the hindsight of time, I can see that I muddled through my earlier undergraduate education not understanding the complex terms of my own minority identity. I learned about internalized oppression along with dimensions of race, ethnicity and gender, but didn't understand how the dimensions of one's marginalized identities are interwoven so tightly that at times, one doesn't recognize the different threads.

I spent most of my undergraduate career in total culture shock entering an institution and community that was considerably whiter than the one in which I had grown up.... It was in this university setting that I first began to see the essential intersectionality of my ethnic, racial, gender, and working class identity. But I didn't recognize this distinction until I became socially acquainted with some of my Asian American friends and spent time with their families. I remember the familiar awkwardness of silence when asked about my parents' occupations... I found I had little in common with my Chinese American friends in terms of ethnic culture. Some of the distinctly Chinese practices in which my family engaged were seen by their parents as very "village", quaint and cute. Somehow I had grown up thinking our practices were universally Chinese immigrant. I had grown up paradoxically aware of class and at the same time totally unaware of how my own ethnic culture was shaped by class.... Race, ethnicity, and class had become so intertwined that I couldn't separate them. In trying to erase class, I was erasing my own ethnic and racial identity... with each new [experience] I understand [more about] the connectedness of the many parts of my identities and how these parts cannot be separate from one another.

Source: From K. Wong (Lau), "Working Through Identity: Understanding Class in the Context of Race, Ethnicity and Gender." In A. Gonzalez et al. (Eds.), *Our voices: Essays in culture, ethnicity and communication* (Los Angeles: Roxbury, 2004), pp. 256–263.

class identity operate in U.S. society. According to Fussell, the magazines we read, the foods we eat, and the words we use often reflect our social class position. At some level, we recognize these class distinctions, but we consider it impolite to ask directly about a person's class background. Therefore, we may use communication strategies to place others in a class hierarchy. Unfortunately, these strategies don't always yield accurate information. For example, people may try to guess your class background by the foods you eat. Some foods are seen as "rich folk's food"—for instance, lamb, white asparagus, brie, artichokes, goose, and caviar. Do you feel as if you are revealing your class background if you admit that these foods are unfamiliar to you? Perhaps not admitting your unfamiliarity is a form of "passing," of representing yourself as belonging to a group you really don't belong to. Another strategy that people may use to guess a person's class background is to ask where that person did her or his undergraduate work.

Most people in the United States recognize class associations even as they may deny that such class divisions exist. What does this apparent contradiction indicate? Most importantly, it reveals the complexities of class issues, particularly in the United States. We often don't really know the criteria for inclusion in a given social class. Is membership determined by financial assets? By educational level? By profession? By family background? These factors may or may not be indicators of class.

Another reason for this apparent contradiction is that people in the majority or normative class (the middle class) tend not to think about class, whereas those in the working class are often reminded that their communication styles and lifestyle choices are not the norm. David Engen (2004), a communication scholar, describes his own experience of entering college from a working-class background and feeling like he had entered a new culture. For one thing, the working-class communication style he was accustomed to was very different from the proper English required in his classes. "I vividly recall coming to college saying things such as 'I seen that,' 'I ain't worried about that' and 'that don't mean nothing to me.' I am glad my professors and friends helped me acquire a language that allowed me to succeed in mainstream American society" (p. 253). And the philosophical conversations expected in class were a challenge. As he describes it, working-class communication is about getting things done, very different from the abstract conversations he was expected to participate in—designed to broaden perspective rather than to accomplish any particular task. In this respect, class is like race. For example, terms like *trailer trash*

---

class identity A sense of belonging to a group that shares similar economic, occupational, or social status.

and *white trash* show the negative connotations associated with people who are not middle class (Moon & Rolison, 1998).

A central assumption of the American dream is that, with hard work and persistence, individuals can improve their class standing, even in the face of overwhelming evidence to the contrary. And the American dream seems alive and well. An estimated 94% of Americans still think that "people who work full time should be able to earn enough to keep their families out of poverty" (Allen, 2004, p. 105). Yet the reality is shown dramatically by Barbara Ehrenreich's (2001) study. Ehrenreich, a journalist, wanted to see how people can survive on minimum wage. She left her home, accepted whatever jobs she could get, staying in the cheapest lodging and working around the country as a waitress, hotel maid, cleaning woman, and nursing home aide. In her book, she describes how much of the "unskilled" work was mentally and physically exhausting, and concludes that one minimum-wage job is not enough; you need two if you want a roof over your head.

The mobility myth, like the American dream, is just that, a myth. The United States has the most unequally distributed wealth and income in the world. Approximately 40% of families have little or no wealth (Lott & Bullock, 2001). As we described in Chapter 1, the gap between the rich and poor is growing increasingly wider (see Figure 5.1). American workers have been hit hard economically, a result of globalization, improvements in technology, outsourcing, and the decline of manufacturing. At the same time, the richest are getting richer. For example, in 2005, the chief executives at California's largest 100 companies made a collective $1.1 billion, in contrast to the 2.9% raise of the average California worker in the same time period (Herbert, 2005).

However, holding on to such a myth has consequences. According to Allen (2004), the ideology underlying the myth persuades us that poor people are the ones to blame for being poor, that "poor people collectively exhibit traits that keep them down. . . . [It] blames the poor for their plight and ignores the fact that many wealthy people have inherited their wealth and resources or that they were better positioned to attain the American dream. This does not acknowledge that economic, cultural and social capital can tilt the playing field in favor of those who have accumulated wealth, knowledge, and/or connections" (p. 105). And the media often reinforce these notions. As Leonardo DiCaprio's character in the movie *Titanic* shows us, upward mobility is easy enough—merely a matter of being opportunistic, charming, and a little bit lucky.

Working-class individuals who aren't upwardly mobile are often portrayed in TV sitcoms and movies as unintelligent, criminal, or unwilling to do what they have to do to better their lot in life. (Consider, for example, the TV show *Married With Children*.) Members of the real working class, as frequent guests on television talk shows like *Rikki Lake* and *Jerry Springer* and on court shows like *Judge Judy* and *Judge Joe Brown*, are urged to be verbally contentious and even physically aggressive with each other.

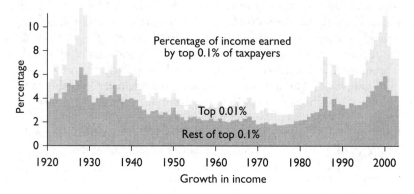

Growth in income

Number of households	All households	Households with inflation-adjusted net worth of:		
		$1–5 million	$5–10 million	$10 million
1983	84 million	2.2 million	180,500	66,500
2001	106 million	4.8 million	729,400	338,400
Percent increase	+27%	+123%	+304%	+409%

Growth in wealth

FIGURE 5.1   These graphs show how the wealthiest Americans have accumulated more assets and more income far more rapidly than the vast majority of Americans.

The point is that, although class identity is not as readily apparent as, say, gender identity, it still influences our perceptions of and communication with others. Race, class, and sometimes gender identity are interrelated. For example, statistically speaking, being born African American, poor, and female increases one's chances of remaining in poverty. But, of course, race and class are not synonymous. There are many poor whites, and there are increasing numbers of wealthy African Americans. In this sense, these multiple identities are interrelated but not identical.

National Identity

Among many identities, we also have a **national identity**, which

---

national identity National citizenship.

should not be confused with racial or ethnic identity. Nationality, un-like racial or ethnic identity, refers to one's legal status in relation to a nation. Many U.S. citizens can trace their ethnicity to Latin America, Asia, Europe, or Africa, but their nationality, or citizenship, is with the United States.

Although national identity may seem to be a clear-cut issue, this is not the case when the nation's status is unclear. For example, bloody conflicts erupted over the attempted secession in the mid-1800s of the Confederate States of America from the United States. Similar conflicts erupted in more recent times when Eritrea tried to separate from Ethiopia, and Chechnya from Russia. Less bloody conflicts that involved nationhood led, in the former Czechoslovakia, to the separation of Slovakia and the Czech Republic.

Contemporary nationhood struggles are being played out as Quebec attempts to separate from Canada and as Corsica and Tahiti attempt to separate from France. Sometimes nations disappear from the political map but persist in the social imagination and eventually reemerge, such as Poland, Ukraine, Latvia, Lithuania, and Estonia. Other times national identity may shift in significant ways, as in the United States after the attacks of September 11, 2001, when ideas about national identity seemed to incorporate increased expressions of patriotism. One of our Japanese graduate students explains how her feeling of national identity is much different from what she sees in the United States:

> *I have seen so many "God bless America," "Proud to be American" messages EVERYWHERE as I have lived here as a Japanese sojourner. . . . Coming from Japan, I don't think I have the same notion of "I am proud about my country." I love my culture, the beauty, the meanings, the spirituality that surround it. But I feel that I have been consciously or subconsciously taught that being proud of your country can be* dangerous, misleading, blinding. *Look at what happened before 1945—how many people in my country thought about their country and framed the "cause" which led to a disaster (WW II). In fact, I have talked to my Japanese friends about this sentiment and mixed emotion I feel about the concept of "patriotism," and almost all of them agreed with me—we were not taught to be proud of our country in the post–WW II era. Of course, each country has a different history, political situation, so what I am saying here doesn't necessarily translate to other people in other cultures.*
>
> *It may sound funny, but one thing I would say I am proud of about my country is that I don't have to say I am proud of my country. I am proud that I can see both beautiful and ugly sides of my country's history. I feel free there, for not being pressured by anyone to say that I am proud of my country.*

In sum, people have various ways of thinking about nationality, and they sometimes confuse nationality and ethnicity. Thus, we have overheard students asking minority students, "What is your nationality?" when they actually meant, "What is your ethnicity?" This confusion can lead to—and perhaps reflects—a lack of understanding about differences between, say, Asian Americans (ethnic group) and Asians (nationality groups). It can also tend to alienate Asian Americans and others who have been in the United States for several generations but are still perceived as foreigners.

Regional Identity

Closely related to nationality is the notion of **regional identity**. Many regions of the world have separate, but vital and important, cultural identities. The Scottish Highlands is a region of northern Scotland that is distinctly different from the Lowlands, and regional identity remains strong in the Highlands.

Here in the United States, regional identities remain important, but perhaps less so as the nation moves toward homogeneity. Southerners, for example, often view themselves, and are viewed by others, as a distinct cultural group. Similarly, Texas advertises itself as "A Whole Other Country," promoting its regional identity. Although some regional identities can fuel national independence movements, they more often reflect cultural identities that affirm distinctive cuisines, dress, manners, and language. These identities may become important in intercultural communication situations. For example, suppose you meet someone who is Chinese. Whether the person is from Beijing, Hong Kong, or elsewhere in China may raise important communication issues. After all, Mandarin is not always understood by Cantonese speakers, although both are dialects of the Chinese language. Indeed, there are many dialects in China, and they certainly are not understood by all other Chinese speakers.

One fairly recent variation in regional identities has to do with the degree of diversity within certain parts of the United States. Data from the 2000 census reveal that the South and the West are the most diverse, along with the coastal Northeast. The Midwest, in contrast, with a few exceptions, remains relatively homogenous (Brewer & Suchan, 2001, pp. 22–23). In addition, the overwhelming majority of multiracial individuals (67%) live in the South and the West (pp. 87–89). What are the implications for identity and intercultural communication? It could mean that people in these areas have more opportunities

---

regional identity Identification with a specific geographic region of a nation.

for understanding and practicing intercultural communication, and so benefit from the diversity. Or they may withdraw into their own groups and protect their racial and ethnic "borders."

Personal Identity

Many issues of identity are closely tied to our notions of self. Each of us has a **personal identity,** but it may not be unified or coherent. A dialectical perspective allow us to see identity in a more complex way. We are who we think we are; at the same time, however, contextual and external forces constrain and influence our self-perceptions. We have many identities, and these can conflict. For example, according to communication scholar Victoria Chen (1992), some Chinese American women feel caught between the traditional values of their parents' culture and their own desire to be Americanized. From the parents' point of view, the daughters are never Chinese enough. From the perspective of many people within the dominant culture, though, it is difficult to relate to these Chinese American women simply as "American women, born and reared in this society" (p. 231). The dialectical tension related to issues of identity for these women reveals the strain between feeling obligated to behave in traditional ways at home and yet holding a Western notion of gender equality. A dialectical perspective sees these contradictions as real and presenting challenges in communication and everyday life.

Our personal identities are important to us, and we try to communicate them to others. We are more or less successful depending on how others respond to us. We use the various ways that identity is constructed to portray ourselves as we want others to see us.

IDENTITY, STEREOTYPES, AND PREJUDICE

The identity characteristics described previously sometimes form the basis for stereotypes, prejudice, and racism. The origins of these have both individual and contextual elements. To make sense out of the overwhelming amount of information we receive, we necessarily categorize and generalize, sometimes relying on **stereotypes**— widely held beliefs about some group. Stereotypes help us know what to expect from others. They may be positive or negative. For example, Asian Americans have often been subjected to the positive **"model**

---

personal identity Who we think we are and who others think we are.
stereotypes Widely held beliefs about a group of people.

minority" stereotype, which characterizes all Asians and Asian Americans as hardworking and serious. This stereotype became particularly prevalent in the United States during the civil rights movement of the 1960s and 1970s. At that time, Asian Americans were seen as the "good" minority—in contrast to African Americans, who were often confrontative and even militant in their fight for equality.

Even positive stereotypes can be damaging in that they create unrealistic expectations for individuals. Simply because someone is Asian American (or pretty, or smart) does not mean that he or she will excel in school or be outgoing and charming. Stereotypes become particularly detrimental when they are negative and are held rigidly. Research has shown that, once adopted, stereotypes are difficult to discard. In fact, people tend to remember information that supports a stereotype but may not retain information that contradicts it (Hamilton, Sherman, & Ruvolo, 1990).

We pick up stereotypes in many ways, including from the media. In TV shows and movies, older people often are portrayed as needing help, and Asian Americans, African Americans, or Latino/as rarely play leading, assertive roles. Current research also shows that although obvious negative stereotypes of Native American Indians are less common in the media, they are still commonly represented in print media as degraded outsiders, often "corrupt, alcoholic and doomed objects of pity" (Miller & Ross, 2004, p. 255) or as either the "good" or "bad" Indians. Communication scholar Bishetta D. Merritt (2000) analyzes portrayals of African American women on television shows and decries the lack of multidimensional roles. She identifies the kinds of roles that perpetuate stereotypes:

> *Portrayals that receive little or no attention today are the background characters that merely serve as scenery on television programs. These characters include the homeless person on the street, the hotel lobby prostitute, or the drug user making a buy from her dealer. They may not be named in the credits or have recurring roles, but their mere appearance can have an impact on the consciousness of the viewer and, as a result, an impact on the imagery of the African American women. (p. 52)*

We may learn stereotypes from our families and peers. One student described how she learned stereotyping and prejudice from her classmates:

---

model minority A stereotype that characterizes all Asians and Asian Americans as hardworking and serious and so a "good" minority.

This essay describes how one group, a basketball team with several Native American players, resists an ascribed identity and a stereotype they feel is offensive.

Unable to persuade a local school to change a mascot name that offends them, a group of American Indian students at the University of Northern Colorado named their intramural basketball team "The Fighting Whities."

The team chose a white man as its mascot to raise awareness of stereotypes that some cultures endure. "The message is, let's do something that will let people see the other side of what it's like to be a mascot" said Solomon Little Owl, a member of the team and director of Native American Student Services at the university.

The team, made of American Indians, Hispanics and Anglos, wears jerseys that say "Every thang's going to be all white."

The students are upset with Eaton High School for using an American Indian caricature on the team logo. The team is called the Reds.

"It's not meant to be vicious, it is meant to be humorous," said Ray White, a Mohawk American Indian on the team. "It puts people in our shoes."

Eaton School District superintendent John Nuspl said the school's logo is not derogatory and called the group's criticism insulting. "There's no mockery of Native Americans with this," he said.

Source: From Associated Press, "Fighting Whities' Mock School's Indian Mascot," March 11, 2002, www.azcentral.com/news/articles/0311fightingwhities-ON.html.

One of my earliest experiences with a person ethnically diverse from me was when I was in kindergarten. A little girl in my class named Adelia was from Pakistan. I noticed that Adelia was a different color from me, but I didn't think it was a bad thing. I got along with her very well. We played the same games, watched the same cartoons, and enjoyed each other's company. Soon I discovered that my other friends didn't like Adelia as much as I did. They didn't want to hold hands with her, and they claimed that she was different from us. When I told them that Adelia was my friend, they didn't want to hold hands with me either. They started to poke fun at me and excluded me from their games. This hurt me so much that I stopped playing with Adelia, and I joined my friends in avoiding her. As a result, Adelia began to resent me and labeled me prejudiced.

Stereotypes can also develop out of negative experiences. If we have unpleasant encounters with people, we may generalize that unpleasantness to include all members of that group, whatever group characteristic we focus on (e.g., race, gender, or sexual orientation). This was demonstrated repeatedly after the attacks of September 11, 2001. Many people of Middle Eastern descent became victims of stereotyping, particularly when traveling. For example, one Arab American software developer from Dallas who was waiting for his flight home from Seattle to leave the gate was told by a flight attendent to take his belongings and get off the plane. Apparently, the pilot had been suspicious of his looks. He was questioned for more than an hour by authorities before being allowed to proceed.

Because stereotypes often operate at an unconscious level and so are persistent, people have to work consciously to reject them. First, they must recognize the stereotype, and then they must obtain information to counteract it. This is not easy because, as noted previously, we tend to "see" behavior that fits our stereotypes and to ignore that which doesn't. For example, if you think that most women are bad drivers, you will tend to notice when a female motorist makes a mistake but to ignore bad male driving. To undo this stereotype, you have to be very vigilant and do something that isn't "natural"—to be very conscious of how you "see" and categorize bad driving, and to note bad driving by both males and females.

Prejudice is a negative attitude toward a cultural group based on little or no experience. It is a prejudgment of sorts. Whereas stereotypes tell us what a group is like, prejudice tells us how we are likely to feel about that group (Newberg, 1994). Scholars disgree somewhat on the origins of prejudice and its relationship to stereotyping. Prejudice may arise from personal needs to feel positive about our own groups and negative about others, or it may arise from perceived or real threats (Hecht, 1998). Researchers Walter Stephan and Cookie Stephan (1996) have shown that tension between cultural groups and negative previous contact, along with status inequalities and perceived threats, can lead to prejudice.

Why do people hold prejudices? Psychologist Richard Brislin (1999) suggests that, just as stereotyping arises from normal cognitive functioning, holding prejudices may serve understandable functions. These functions may not excuse prejudice, but they do help us understand why prejudice is so widespread. He identifies four such functions:

1. The utilitarian function. People hold certain prejudices because they can lead to rewards. For example, if your friends or family hold preju-

---

prejudice An attitude (usually negative) toward a cultural group based on little or no evidence.

dices toward certain groups, it will be easier for you simply to share those attitudes, rather than risk rejection by contradicting their attitudes.

2. The ego-defensive function. People hold certain prejudices because they don't want to believe unpleasant things about themselves. For example, if either of us (Judith or Tom) is not a very good teacher, it will be useful for us to hold negative stereotypes about students, such as that they are lazy and don't work hard. In this way, we can avoid confronting the real problem—our lack of teaching skills. The same kind of thing happens in the workplace: It is easier for people to stereotype women and minorities as unfit for jobs than to confront their own lack of skill or qualifications for a job.

3. The value-expressive function. People hold certain prejudices because they serve to reinforce aspects of life that are highly valued. Religious attitudes often function in this way. Some people are prejudiced against certain religious groups because they see themselves as holding beliefs in the one true God, and part of their doctrine is the belief that others are wrong. For instance, Judith's Mennonite family held prejudices against Catholics, who were viewed as misguided and wrong. This may also be operating today as some U.S. Americans search for validation of prejudices again Muslims. A more extreme example involves the atrocities committed against groups of people by others who want to retain the supposed values of a pure racial stock (e.g., "ethnic cleansing" by Serbs against Muslims in the former Yugoslavia).

4. The knowledge function. People hold certain prejudices because such attitudes allow them to organize and structure their world in a way that makes sense to them—in the same way that stereotypes help us organize our world. For example, if you believe that members of a certain group are flaky and irresponsible, then you don't have to think very much when meeting someone from that group in a work situation. You already know what they're like and so can react to them more automatically.

Prejudices can serve several of these functions over the life span. Thus, children may develop a certain prejudice to please their parents (utilitarian) and continue to hold the prejudice because it helps define who they are (value-expressive). Brislin (1999) points out that many remedial programs addressing the problem of prejudice fail because of a lack of recognition of the important functions that prejudice fill in our lives. Presenting people with factual information about groups addresses only one function (knowledge) and ignores the more complex reasons that we hold prejudices.

The behaviors that result from stereotyping or prejudice—overt actions to exclude, avoid, or distance—are called **discrimination** (see

discrimination Behaviors resulting from stereotypes or prejudice that cause some people to be denied equal participation or rights based on cultural-group membership, such as race.

Point of View). Discrimination may be based on race (racism), gender (sexism), or any of the other identities discussed in this chapter. It may range from subtle nonverbal behavior such as lack of eye contact or exclusion from a conversation, to verbal insults and exclusion from jobs or other economic opportunities, to physical violence and systematic exclusion. To see how exclusion and avoidance can be subtle, consider all the communication choices people can make that affect whether other people feel welcome or valued or like outsiders who don't belong (Johnson, 2001, p. 59):

- Whether we look at people when we talk with them
- Whether we smile at people when they walk into the room, or stare as if to say "What are you doing?" or stop the conversation with a hush they have to wade through to be included in the smallest way
- Whether we listen and respond to what people say, or drift away to someone or something else; whether we talk about things they know about, or stick to what's peculiar to the "in-group"
- Whether we acknowledge people's presence, or make them wait as if they weren't there; whether we avoid touching their skin when giving or taking something; how closely we watch them to see what they're up to
- Whether we avoid someone walking down the street, giving them a wide berth when we pass or even cross to the other side
- Whether we share with new colleagues the informal rules that you have to know to succeed, belong, or get along—or turn the conversation to something light and superficial when they're around
- Whether we invite people to our home or out for a drink and talk

Discrimination may be interpersonal, collective, or institutional. In recent years, interpersonal racism has become not only more subtle and indirect but also more persistent. Equally persistent is institutionalized or collective discrimination whereby individuals are systematically denied equal participation in society or equal access to rights in informal and formal ways (Maluso, 1995).

A study by the U.S. Justice Department found that black, Latino/a, and white motorists are equally likely to pulled over by police, but blacks and Latinos are much more likely to be searched, handcuffed, arrested, and subjected to force or the threat of it. Handcuffs were used on a higher percentage of black (6.4%) and Latino/a motorists (5.6%) than white (2%). Also, blacks (2.7%) and Latinos (2.4%) were far more likely than whites (0.8%) to report that police used force or the threat of force (Sniffen, 2005).

SOCIAL VERSUS PSYCHOLOGICAL DEFINITIONS OF RACISM: THE LESSONS OF KATRINA

Of the many sorry things about the contemporary United States that Hurricane Katrina made plain, perhaps none was more depressing than what it showed about the profound divide in how Americans think about race and racism. The brute, tangible facts of the case were evident to the naked eye: the televised and photographed spectacle of Katrina's aftermath in New Orleans revealed that the vast majority of those crowded into the squalid shelters in the middle of the city were black, in numbers disproportionate even to the large percentage of blacks residing in New Orleans. At first the mainstream media restricted themselves to muttering nervously about this fact, but what finally brought the racial dimension (and divide) into open debate was rapper Kanye West's declaration on live TV, during an off-script moment at a Katrina fundraiser, that, "George Bush doesn't care about black people." The inevitable partisan firestorm that erupted exposed deep disagreements about the contours of racism in the contemporary United States.

To what extent was West's statement fair? What exactly would it mean to ascribe the racial profile of Katrina's victims to "racism"? This essay suggests that the debate over the racial meaning of Katrina exposes a public disagreement about the meaning of racism itself. The fundamental divide in the debate over racism in the United States today is between those who regard racism as essentially a question of individual psychology as opposed to those who consider it a social, structural phenomenon.

One of the things that makes discussing racism fundamentally challenging is the tendency (most commonly found on the Right and among whites) to equate racism with racial prejudice. People of this persuasion consider racism as identical to (and, crucially, limited to) ethnophobia—*that is, disdain for other people on the basis of their supposed racial characteristics. In this definition, racism is not a social condition but rather is something that exists* in the minds of "racists."

It is widely and correctly observed that this sort of racial prejudice, or bigotry, has abated greatly in the last half century. Though racial prejudice certainly still exists, many fewer people despise others simply because of their skin color. This is true not only in terms of a reduction of the number of bigots, but also in terms of a steady restriction of the social settings in which prejudice manifests itself. Even subtle displays of bigotry are today widely regarded as illegitimate not just in the political arena, but also at work or even in private social circles. While many whites may still cavil at their daughters marrying a black man, the vast majority of whites no longer actively or even passively refuse to work alongside people of color; and that someone might be

(continued)

refused service on public transportation because of their skin color is close to unimaginable. It is impossible to overstate what huge progress the curbing of bigotry represents for the United States. Indeed, the tabooification of active racial hatred has misled some into believing that "racism" is no longer a significant problem for American society.

If rolling back bigotry is a necessary condition for eliminating racism, it is alas not a sufficient condition. The problem with equating racism with prejudice is that such a definition of racism fails to address the fact that racial discrimination takes place not merely through intentional (though perhaps unselfconscious) interactions between individuals, but also as a result of deep social and institutional practices and habits. *That is, historical patterns of race-based exclusion do not disappear in lock-step with the diminishment of the chthonic prejudices that underpinned the original race-based exclusions. Long after most white people have ceased to dislike or actively discriminate against racial minorities, there persist social patterns and habits—where people live, which social organizations they belong to, what schools they attend, and so on—that were constructed during the hundreds of years when active racial prejudice was the fact of ethnic life in America. These social and institutional structures and practices, in other words, rest on prejudicial racialist foundations. As such, they are bearers of the racist past, even though they may today no longer be populated by active bigots. This social and economic exclusion on the basis of race is what "racism" is really all about.*

The continued exclusion of blacks from certain prestigious, purely social organizations is the archetype for this sort of racism. Consider the stereotype of the all-white country club. The barrier to entry for blacks into these sorts of institutions is rarely an active rule *banning blacks from joining. Rather, what excludes blacks is that the club members know few if any black people as social equals outside the club. Now, it would be a mistake to conclude from this lack of black friends that the club members are necessarily prejudiced against black people. Rather, the club is simply an institutional manifestation of a longstanding social network of upper-class whites. For such a social set, it's not that they're against socializing with blacks (though maybe their parents or grandparents were), it's just that* as a matter of fact they don't *socialize with blacks. In the meanwhile, the club facilitates the making of money (within its narrow social circle), the reproduction of the elite (within the same narrow social circle), and thus generally works to assure the social replication of the longstanding racialist pattern,* all without a discriminatory thought ever entering anyone's head.

Moreover, it should be stressed that racism can replicate itself via a mere unwillingness to challenge such racialized institutions and patterns.

Undoubtedly the majority of white Americans regard themselves as post prejudicial; yet many continue to consider the impact of racialist patterns of exclusion as something that the individual victims of those patterns must take "personal responsibility" for redressing. In the case of Katrina, the result was a huge gap between blacks and whites in their understanding of the meaning of the catastrophe: for blacks, the visible disproportion of blacks among Katrina's victims signified how the government and the American people systematically ignore the plight of their communities; by contrast, the large majority of whites considered race to be more or less irrelevant to the meaning of Katrina.

Here we arrive at the fulcrum of the contemporary political debate about racism. It cannot be repeated often enough that racial exclusion, e.g. racism, today happens not so much through active bigotry as it does through the tacit exclusions created by these sorts of unstated, unconsidered social habits. The fundamental point is one that is deeply uncomfortable for large sectors of this country: if your social network is, for purely historical reasons, defined by color lines that were drawn long ago in a different and undeniably widely bigoted age, then you don't have to be a bigot yourself to be perpetuating the institutional structures of racial exclusion, e.g. racism. *This was exactly Illinois Senator Barack Obama's point when he declared on the Senate floor that the poor response to Katrina was not "evidence of active malice," but merely the result of "a continuation of passive indifference."*[1]

*The social definition of racism underpins the argument that while anyone can be prejudiced or bigoted toward anyone else on account of their skin color (including blacks who hate whites), racism is something that applies only to blacks and other ethnic minorities. Since racism is a matter of racially-coded social exclusion from positions of power, and since white people are not sys-*tematically *so excluded, white people cannot be victims of racism. Yes, a white person can be a victim of bigotry, and a black person can be a bigot, but it is only society itself that is racist. Individuals can only meaningfully be described as "racists" insofar as their prejudices actively perpetuate society's racism.*

When two thirds of blacks believe that "racism continues to be a problem" in this country, while two thirds of whites believe that it is not, the divide in good measure can be explained by the competing understandings of what constitutes racism. To quote the Wall Street Journal's *op-ed page, "For white Americans in general. . . . as the proportion of whites who supported or were complicit in Jim Crow segregation or other racist institutions declines . . . the question of race becomes less fraught with every passing year."*[2] *By contrast, black people find themselves systematically outside the centers of power and privilege, and conclude that the lovely thoughts inside white people's heads aren't the salient issue.*

(continued)

Put in terms of this social understanding of racism, we can now see how Kanye West's blurted remark seems entirely and precisely accurate: George Bush's lack of "care" for black people was not so much about a failure of personal sympathy for the individual victims of Katrina, as it was about a cognitive failure to recognize blacks and blackness as meaningful social categories that structured the experience of Katrina. Or to put it another way: the reason disproportionately many black folks suffered at the hands of Katrina was not because white people (or George Bush) disliked the black people in New Orleans; it was because they didn't regard blacks and blackness as a meaningful social categories worthy of special attention. It was precisely that history of neglect, that failure to care, that underpinned the racial aspect of the Katrina disaster.

Many people are deeply troubled by the argument that racism is not a matter of individual psychology but rather a social condition. They sense that this definition of racism flies in the face of the idea that America is a land of unlimited individual opportunity. And they suspect, for good reason, that defining racism as larger and longer-lived than the bigotry of individuals leads nolens volens to the idea that ending racism requires structural reform. For if dissolving racism cannot take place simply by adjusting individuals' "preference sets" to non-bigoted settings, then the solution to racism cannot happen exclusively in the marketplace, but instead must be mediated by an institution outside the market. Moreover, to be effective, such an institution needs to have society-wide reach, and the authority and power to make the necessary social interventions. This, of course, is the moral starting point for state-enforced regulations that aim to break the cycle of structural social exclusion— regulations such as preferential treatment for minority-owned businesses that bid for government contracts and so-called "affirmative action" in hiring and academic admissions. The point of these regulations has been to break the tacit patterns of social exclusion.

In sum, Katrina provides an unprecedented opportunity to communicate that "racism" is not just a matter of the psychology of hatred but is instead also a matter of the racial structure of political and economic inclusion and exclusion. Moreover, we should not blinker ourselves: this message is one that is deeply opposed by powerful political forces in the United States today. Those who deny the social nature of racism may not be bigots, but they are undoubtedly abettors of racism in the social sense of the word.

1. "Statement of Senator Barack Obama on Hurricane Katrina Relief Efforts," http://obama.senate.gov/statement/050906-statement_of_senator_barack_obama_on_hurricane_katrina_relief_efforts/(September 6, 2005).
2. James Taranto, "The Best of the Web Today," Opinion Journal, September 8, 2005.
Source: From N. Gilman, "What Katrina Teaches About the Meaning of Racism." Social Science Research Council, September 14, 2005. Available from http://understandingkatrina.ssrc.org/Gilman/.

MULTICULTURAL PEOPLE

Multicultural people, a group currently dramatically increasing in number, are those who live "on the borders" of two or more cultures. They often struggle to reconcile two very different sets of values, norms, worldviews, and lifestyles. Some are multicultural as a result of being born to parents from different racial, ethnic, religious, or national cultures or they were adopted into families that are racially different from their own family of origin. Others are multicultural because their parents lived overseas and they grew up in cultures different from their own, or because they spent extended time in another culture as an adult or married someone from another cultural background. Let's start with those who are born into biracial or multiracial families.

According to the most recent census, the United States has almost 7 million multiracial people—that is, people whose ancestry includes two or more races (Brewer & Suchan, 2001). The 2000 census was the first one in which people were given the option of selecting several categories to indicate their racial identities. This rapidly growing segment of our population must be understood in its historical context. The United States has a long history of forbidding miscegenation (the mixing of two races). The law sought not to prevent *any* interracial marriage but to protect "whiteness"; interracial marriage between people of color was rarely prohibited or regulated (Root, 2001). Thus, in 1957, the state of Virginia ruled the marriage of Mildred Jeter (African American and Native American heritage) and Peter Loving (white) illegal. The couple fought to have their marriage legalized for almost 10 years. Finally, in 1967, the Supreme Court ruled in their favor, in *Loving v. Virginia*, overturning 200 years of antimiscegenation legislation.

The development of racial identity for the children of parents like the Lovings is a fluid process of complex transactions between the child and the broader social environment (Nance & Foeman, 2002). Whereas majority and minority identities seem to develop in a fairly linear fashion, biracial children may cycle through three stages: (1) awareness of differentness and resulting dissonance, (2) struggle for acceptance, and (3) self-acceptance and self-assertion. And as they mature, they may experience the same three phases with greater intensity and awareness.

In the first stage, multiracial children realize that they are different from other children—they may feel that they don't fit in anywhere. Tiffany, whose mother is white and father is black, describes her experience:

Growing up I had kids make fun of me because they said I did not know what color I was. That really hurt me as a kid because even at a young age, I started questioning my own race.

At the next stage, struggle for acceptance, multiracial adolescents may feel that they have to choose one race or the other—and indeed this was Tiffany's experience:

During my teenage years I still was a little confused about my race because I would only choose one side. When people asked me what color I was I would tell them I was black because I was embarrassed about being mixed. I was afraid of not being accepted by the black community if I said I was mixed. . . . I would go around telling people that I am black and would get mad if someone said I was white. I never thought about being mixed with both black and white.

After being torn between the two (or more) races, multiracial individuals may reach the third stage, of self-acceptance and self-assertion. Tiffany describes how this happened for her:

I can recall a time when I had to spend Christmas with my mother's side of the family. This was the first time I met her side of the family and I felt myself being scared. Honestly, I have never been around a lot of white people, and when I was there I realized that I am mixed and this is who I am and I cannot hide it anymore. . . . From then on I claimed both sides.

And she goes on to demonstrate her self-acceptance and self-assertion:

Being mixed is wonderful, and most importantly, being mixed taught me many things especially growing up. It taught me how to be strong, not to worry about what other people think and to just be myself. It also taught me not to like only one color and that all colors are beautiful. My race made me who I am today. I am strong and I know my race. I no longer have to deny what my race is or who I am.

As you might imagine, many positive aspects are associated with having a biracial identity. In one recent study, the majority of biracial respondents "did not express feelings of marginality as suggested by traditional theories of bicultural identity. Instead, these youth exhibited a clear understanding and affiliation with both groups' cultures and values" (Miller, Watling, Staggs, & Rotheram-Borus, 2003, p. 139). Later in the chapter we discuss further the important role that multicultural people can play in intercultural relations.

In addition to multicultural identities based on race and ethnicity, there are multicultural identities based on religion, sexual orientation, or other identities. For example, children growing up with a Jewish and a Christian parent may feel torn between the two and follow some of the same identity development phases as biracial children—where they feel different, forced to choose between one or the other. Teresa says, "My father is Mexican American and my mother is white, so I have a Latino last name. When I was younger, some kids would tease me with racial slurs about Mexicans. My mother totally didn't understand and just said that I should ignore them, but my father understood much better. He faced the same taunting as a child in Indiana." A straight child of gay parents may have similar feelings of needing to negotiate between straight and gay worldviews.

Individuals develop multicultural identities for other reasons. For example, **global nomads** grow up in many different cultural contexts because their parents moved around a lot (e.g., missionaries, international business employees, or military families). Children of foreign-born immigrants may also develop multicultural identities. Foreign-born immigrants in the United States represent one of the fastest-growing segments—almost a *third of the current foreign-born* population arrived in the United States since 1990. These include refugees from war zones like Kosovo and the Balkans, and migrants who come to the United States to escape dire economic conditions. They often struggle to negotiate their identities, torn between family expectations and their new American culture. Khoa, a first-generation Vietnamese American, describes how important his family's values are:

> *What does it mean to be "Asian" then? Being Asian is being proud of my heritage, my family, and the values that they have passed down to you. I am proud of my parents' discipline upon me. . . . I learned very early in life the differences between right and wrong. . . . I am proud that my parents taught me to respect my elders. I value the time I spend with my grandparents. I love the time I spend with my uncles and aunts, and my cousins. Having a deep love and honest respect for my family, both immediate and extended, is what being "Asian" means to me.*

Then he recounts the struggle to reconcile being both Vietnamese and American:

> *There are a few things, though, that my parents believe in that I do not agree with. I think it is important that you know where you came from and to have pride in your nationality. However, I do not think that just*

---

global nomads People who grow up in many different cultural contexts because their parents relocated.

This essay describes some of the complexities and controversies surrounding the "new" multiracial category used for the first time in the 2000 census, illustrating how race is a dynamic notion that changes depending on individuals and context.

The 2000 Census marked a fundamental change in how we measure race in the United States. Rather than insist that every person in the country identify with only one racial group, as have all previous U.S. censuses, it invited multiracial identification. . . . Yet the first census count of the multiracial population will be far from definitive.

My reasons for believing this are both personal and professional. Consider the following reactions to my 3 year old daughter. When she and my wife were at a hospital in New Mexico, a white nurse asked if she spoke Spanish. While they waited in line at a grocery store in Ann Arbor, an African American bagger leaned over to my daughter and said, "I know you've got soul." As they made their way through O'Hare International Airport in Chicago, a white airline worker commented to my wife that our daughter "has a great tan."

The nurse in New Mexico saw a white woman with a bronze-skinned child and concluded that, like many people in the Southwest, our daughter was part Latino. In the predominantly black-and-white context of Michigan, the grocery store bagger interpreted these same cues as indicative of black heritage. By contrast, the white airline worker, who for historical reasons has probably had little personal experience with multiracial children, used the more salient frame of sun tanning to reconcile the incongruity between my wife and daughter's physical characteristics.

Now consider the results from a national survey of adolescents. When more than 10,000 middle and high school students were asked to report their race on separate school and home surveys, about 12 percent failed to provide consistent responses. Seven percent reported being multiracial on only one of the surveys and nearly 3 percent of the youth switched between single-race groups. Multiracial reports were almost

because I am Vietnamese I am obligated to marry a Vietnamese girl. A Vietnamese girl is not any better or worse than any other girl of another nationality.

Like Khoa, multicultural adolescents often feel pulled in different directions as they develop their own identities.

A final category of multicultural people includes those who have twice as likely on the school survey, which was self-administered, as on the home survey, which was administered by an interviewer.

These examples illustrate that rather than being a fixed characteristic, one's race is constantly being negotiated. Race depends not just on ancestry—my wife identifies as white and I as black—but also on the verbal, physical and cultural cues we project to others, their interpretation of these cues and the setting in which this exchange occurs. . . . Although most people who answered the 2000 Census probably did not give the race question much thought, its new wording certainly caused some people to contemplate which response they should give for the racially mixed members of their household. . . .

So as the Census Bureau begins releasing its official count of multiracial Americans, we should all be a little skeptical about the numbers. If the 2000 race question had specifically asked for all of the racial groups known to be in a person's background, the count of multiracials would be much larger. Alternatively, if it had asked for the race or races that others most often consider this person to be, then the count of multiracials would almost certainly be much smaller.

This is not to say that the limited space available on the census could have been used to capture all of the complexities of race. Rather, my point is that because race can and, from people like my daughters, does vary across observers and contexts, we must employ more sophisticated ways of measuring race if we hope to understand the multiracial population. More complex approaches will likely show that the size and characteristics of the multiracial population vary significantly from Census 2000 estimates. We should all keep this is mind before using the census count of multiracials to support statements about the social, political and legal consequences of race in contemporary American society.

Source: From D. R. Harris, "The Multiracial Count," *Washington Post*, March 24, 2001, p. A21.

intense intercultural experiences as adults—for example, people who maintain long-term romantic relationships with members of another ethnic or racial group or who spend extensive time living in other cultures. Miguel tells us, "My father is an American, but my mother is from Chile. Because they divorced when I was young and my father returned to the United States, I spent a lot of time traveling back and forth and learning to adapt to two different cultures and languages. I don't feel completely Chilean or American, but I feel like I am both. I have family and friends in both places and I feel connected in different ways."

All multicultural people may feel as if they live in cultural margins, struggling with two sets of cultural realities: not completely part of the dominant culture but not an outsider, either.

Social psychologist Peter Adler (1974) describes the multicultural person as someone who comes to grips with a multiplicity of realities. This individual's identity is not defined by a sense of belonging; rather, it is a new psychocultural form of consciousness. Milton Bennett (1993) describes how individuals can develop an "ethnorelative" perspective based on their attitudes toward cultural difference. The first, and most ethnocentric, stage involves the denial or ignoring of difference. The next stage occurs when people recognize difference but attach negative meaning to it. A third stage occurs when people minimize the effects of difference—for example, with statements like "We're really all the same under the skin" and "After all, we're all God's children." Bennett recognizes that minority and majority individuals may experience these phases differently. In addition, minority individuals usually skip the first phase. They don't have the option to deny difference; they are often reminded by others that they are different.

The remainder of the stages represent a major shift in thinking—a paradigm shift—because positive meanings are associated with difference. In the fourth phase (acceptance), people accept the notion of cultural difference; in the fifth phase (adaptation), they may change their own behavior to adapt to others. The final phase (integration) is similar to Peter Adler's (1974) notion of a "multicultural person."

According to Adler, multicultural individuals may become **culture brokers**—people who facilitate cross-cultural interaction and reduce conflict. And, indeed, there are many challenges and opportunities today for multicultural people, who can reach a level of insight and cultural functioning not experienced by others. One of our students, who is Dutch (ethnicity) and Mexican (nationality), describes this:

> *Being the makeup I am to me means I come from two extremely proud cultures. The Dutch in me gives me a sense of tradition and loyalty. The Mexican side gives me a rich sense of family as well as closeness with not only my immediate family, with my aunts, uncles, and cousins as well. My unique mix makes me very proud of my identity. To me it means that I am proof that two parts of the world can unite in a world that still believes otherwise.*

---

culture brokers Individuals who act as bridges between cultures, facilitating cross-cultural interaction and conflict.

However, Adler (1974) also identifies potential stresses and tensions associated with multicultural individuals:
They may confuse the profound with the insignificant, not sure what is really important.
They may feel multiphrenic, fragmented.
They may suffer a loss of their own authenticity and feel reduced to a variety of roles.
They may retreat into existential absurdity. (p. 35)

Communication scholar Janet Bennett (1993) provides insight into how being multicultural can be at once rewarding *and* challenging. She describes two types of multicultural individuals: (1) *encapsulated marginals*, who become trapped by their own marginality, and (2) *constructive marginals*, who thrive in their marginality.
Encapsulated marginals have difficulty making decisions, are troubled by ambiguity, and feel pressure from both groups. They try to assimilate but never feel comfortable, never feel "at home." In contrast, constructive marginal people thrive in their marginal existence and, *at the same time*, they recognize the tremendous challenges. They see themselves (rather than others) as choice makers. They recognize the significance of being "in between," and they are able to make commitments within the relativistic framework. Even so, this identity is constantly being negotiated and explored; it is never easy, given society's penchant for superficial categories. Writer Ruben Martinez (1998) describes the experience of a constructive marginal:

And so I can celebrate what I feel to be my cultural success. I've taken the far-flung pieces of myself and fashioned an identity beyond that ridiculous, fraying old border between the United States and Mexico. But my "success" is still marked by anxiety, a white noise that disturbs whatever raceless utopia I might imagine. I feel an uneasy tension between all the colors, hating and loving them all, perceiving and speaking from one and many perspectives simultaneously. The key word here is "tension": nothing, as yet, has been resolved. My body is both real and unreal, its color both confining and liberating. (p. 260)

IDENTITY AND COMMUNICATION

Identity has a profound influence on intercultural communication processes. We can employ some of the dialectics identified in earlier chapters to illuminate this relationship. First, we can use the individual–

cultural dynamic to examine the issues that arise when we encounter people whose identities we don't know. In intercultural communication interactions, mistaken identities are often exacerbated and can create communication problems.

Sometimes we assume knowledge about another person's identity based on his or her membership in a particular cultural group. When we do so, we are ignoring the individual aspect. Taking a dialectical perspective can help us recognize and balance both the individual and the cultural aspects of another's identity. This perspective can guide the ways that we communicate with that person (and conceivably with others). "The question here is one of identity: Who am I perceived to be when I communicate with others? . . . My identity is very much tied to the ways in which others speak to me and the ways in which society represents my interests" (Nakayama, 2000, p. 14).

Think about the assumptions you might make about others based on their physical appearance. What do you "know" about people if you know only that they are from, say, the South, or Australia, or Pakistan? Perhaps it is easier to think about the times that people have made erroneous assumptions about you based on limited information—assumptions that you became aware of in the process of communication. Focusing solely on someone's nationality, place of origin, education, religion, and the like, can lead to mistaken conclusions about the person's identity.

Another way to understand how we communicate our identities comes from the study of performance. Although we can look at someone's individual performance of identity to better understand how they understand who they think they are, we can also look at cultural performance to understand cultural identities. For example, in her essay on martyrdom in Islam, Lindsay Calhoun (2004) explains the importance of this performance as a part of national identity and religious identity. Noting that martyrdom is "found in nearly all the world's major religious traditions" (p. 328), Calhoun notes that in the West, we see martyrs "as fanatics and terrorists" (p. 328). She explores this performance more closely to see that it is "a strategic performance of resistance and/or reification meant to exact both a cost and a reward upon the martyr, his or her supporters, and oppressors" (p. 344). It is a kind of performance that helps the martyr communicate an Islamic identity, but also a national identity. Through this performance of identity, the martyr is reconfigured in a new way.

Sometimes a focus on the performance if identity can help us better understand parts of our cultural past that we would have difficult understanding today. One part of U.S. history often hidden is the horrific practice of lynching. Yet we must acknowledge that lynching was a widespread and common practice in U.S. culture, and we can often be confused when we see many of the perpetrators smiling in these photos because it seems incomprehensible that they were not horrified by this event.

Performance studies scholar Kirk Fuoss (1999) suggests that a performance perspective can help us better understand how people can participate in these atrocities and the purpose of these lynchings for the perpetrators. For example, Fuoss argues that lynching in the United States functioned as a cultural performance that served to reinforce a particular kind of racial order for those who participated in or heard about the lynching. Lynchings took place outside of the legal system, and therefore a belief in the evilness of the victim substituted for a proof or evidence of guilt. This inversion of right and wrong served to relieve the group identity of the lynchers from their own evil behavior. These murders reflect aspects of our culture that have deep historical roots. By examining these performative acts, we can begin to see what they communicate to others and the kinds of social order they encourage. Thus, lynchings are a public act that serve to communicate the positions of various cultural groups in society. It is important to remember that performances are not only artistic and interesting, but they can also be horrific. In both cases, performances of identity can offer insights into our culture.

Now let's turn to the static–dynamic dialectic. The problem of erroneous assumptions has increased during the information age, due to the torrent of information about the world and the dynamic nature of the world in which we live. We are bombarded daily with information from around the globe about places and people. This glut of information and intercultural contacts has heightened the importance of developing a more complex view of identity.

Given the many identities that we all negotiate for ourselves in our everyday interactions, it becomes clear how our identities and those of others make intercultural communication problematic. We need to think of these identities as both static and dynamic. We live in an era of information overload, and the wide array of communication media only serve to increase the identities we must negotiate. Consider the relationships that develop via e-mail, for example. Some people even create new identities as a result of online interactions. We change who we are depending on the people we communicate with and the manner of our communication. Yet we also expect some static characteristics from the people with whom we communicate. We expect others to express certain fixed qualities; these help account for why we tend to like or dislike them and how we can establish particular communication patterns with them. The tensions that we feel as we change identities from e-mail to telephone to mail to fax and other communication media demonstrate the dynamic and static characters of identities.

Finally, we can focus on the personal–contextual dialectic of identity and communication. Although some dimensions of our identities are personal and remain fairly consistent, we cannot overlook the contextual constraints on our identity.

DISCUSSION QUESTIONS

1. How do our perceptions of our own cultural identity influence our communication with others?
2. What are some ways in which we express our identities?
3. How does being white affect one's experience in the United States?
4. What are the roles of avowal and ascription in the process of identity formation?
5. What are some of the ways in which members of minority cultures and members of majority cultures develop their cultural identities?

ACTIVITIES

1. *Stereotypes in Your Life*. List some of the stereotypes you have heard about U.S. Americans. Then answer the following questions:

   a. How do you think these stereotypes developed?

   b. How do they influence communication between U.S. Americans and people from other countries?

2. *Stereotypes in Prime-Time TV*. Watch four hours of television during the next week, preferably during evening hours when there are more commercials. Record the number of representatives of different identity groups (ethnic, racial, gender, age, class, and so on) that appear in the commercials; also record the role that each person plays. Answer the following questions:

   a. How many different groups were represented?

   b. What groups were most represented? Why do you think this is so?

   c. What groups were least represented? Why do you think this is so?

   d. What differences (if any) were there in the roles that members of the various groups played? Did one group play more sophisticated or more glamorous roles than others?

   e. In how many cases were people depicted in stereotypical

roles—for example, African Americans as athletes, or women as homemakers?

f. What stereotypes were reinforced in the commercials?

g. What do your findings suggest about the power of the media and their effect on identity formation and intercultural communication? (Think about avowal, ascription, and interpellation.)

REFERENCES

Adler, P. (1974). Beyond cultural identity: Reflections on cultural and multicultural man. *Topics in culture learning* (Vol. 2, pp. 23–40). Honolulu: East-West Center.

Alba, R. D. (1985). The twilight of ethnicity among Americans of European ancestry: The case of Italians. *Ethnic and Racial Studies, 8*, 134–158.

Alba, R. D. (1990). *Ethnic identity: The transformation of white America.* New Haven, CT: Yale University Press.

Allen, B. (2004). *Difference matters: Communicating social identity.* Waveland Press.

Althusser, L. (1971). Ideology and ideological state apparatuses (notes towards an investigation). In B. Brewster (Trans.), *Lenin and philosophy and other essays* (pp. 134–165). London: NLB.

Bahk, C. M., & Jandt, F. E. (2004). Being white in America: Development of a scale. *The Howard Journal of Communications, 15*, 57–68.

Bederman, G. (1995). *Manliness and civilization: A cultural history of gender and race in the United States, 1880–1917.* Chicago: University of Chicago Press.

Bennett, J. M. (1993). Cultural marginality: Identity issues in intercultural training. In R. M. Paige (Ed.), *Education for the intercultural experience* (pp. 109–136). Yarmouth, ME: Intercultural Press.

Bennett, M. J. (1993). Towards eth-norelativism: A developmental model of intercultural sensitivity. In R. M. Paige (Ed.), *Education for the intercultural experience* (pp. 21–72). Yarmouth, ME: Intercultural Press.

Bourdieu, P. (1987). *Distinction: A social critique of the judgment of taste* (R. Nice, Trans.). Cambridge, MA: Harvard University Press.

Brewer, C. A., & Suchan, T. A. (2001). *Mapping Census 2000: The geography of U.S. diversity* (U.S. Census Bureau, Census Special Reports, Series CENSR/01-1). Washington, DC: U.S. Government Printing Office.

Brislin, R. (1999). *Understanding culture's influence on behavior* (2nd ed.). Belmont, CA: Wadsworth.

Calhoun, L. R. (2004). Islamic martyrdom in the postcolonial condition. *Text and Performance Quarterly, 24*, 327–347.

Canary, D. J., & Hause, K. S. (1993). Is there any reason to research sex difference in communication? *Communication Quarterly, 41*, 129–144.

Carbaugh, D. (1989). *Talking American: Cultural discourse on Donahue.* Norwood, NJ: Ablex.

Chen, V. (1992). The construction of Chinese American women's identity. In L. F. Rakow (Ed.), *Women making meaning* (pp. 225–243). New York: Routledge.

Collier, M. J. (2005). Theorizing cultural identification: Critical updates and continuing evolution. In W. B. Gudykunst (Ed.), *Theorizing about intercultural communication* (pp. 235–256). Thousand Oaks, CA: Sage.

Collier, M. J., & Thomas, M. (1988). Cultural identity: An interpretive perspective. In Y. Y. Kim & W. B. Gudykunst (Eds.), *Theories in intercultural communication* (pp. 99–122). Newbury Park, CA: Sage.

Cornell, S., & Hartmann, D. (1998). *Ethnicity and race: Making identities in a changing world.* Thousand Oaks, CA: Pine Forge Press.

Cross, S. E. (2000). What does it mean to "know thyself" in the United States and Japan?: The cultural construction of the self. In T. J. Owens (Ed.), *Self and identity through the life course in cross-cultural perspective* (pp. 159–180). Stamford, CT: JAI Press.

Engen, D. (2004). Invisible identities: Notes on class and race. In A. Gonzalez, M. Houston, & V. Chen (Eds.), *Our voices: Essays in culture, ethnicity and communication* (pp. 250–255). Los Angeles: Roxbury.

Ehrenreich, B. (2001). *Nickel and dimed: On (not) getting by in America.* New York: Metropolitan Books.

Erikson, E. (1950). *Childhood and society.* New York: Norton.

Erikson, E. (1968). *Identity: Youth and crisis.* New York: Norton.

Feghali, E. (1997). Arab cultural communication patterns. *International Journal of Intercultural Relations, 21,* 345–378.

Ferguson, R. (1990). Introduction: Invisible center. In R. Ferguson, M. Gever, T. M. Trinh, & C. West (Eds.), *Out there: Marginalization and contemporary cultures* (pp. 9–14). New York and Cambridge: New Museum of Contemporary Art/MIT Press.

Frankenburg, R. (1993). *White women, race matters: The social construction of whiteness.* Minneapolis: University of Minnesota Press.

Fuoss, K. W. (1999). Lynching performances, theaters of violence. *Text and Performance Quarterly, 19,* 1–37.

Fussell, P. (1992). *Class: A guide through the American status system.* New York: Touchstone Books. (Original work published 1979)

Gallager, C. A. (1994). White construction in the university. *Socialist Review, 1/2,* 167–187.

Gao, G. (1996). Self and other: A Chinese perspective on interpersonal relationships. In W. G. Gudykunst, S. Ting-Toomey, & T. Nishida (Eds.), *Communication in personal relationships across cultures* (pp. 81–101). Thousand Oaks, CA: Sage.

Hall, S. (1985). Signification, representation, ideology: Althusser and the poststructuralist debates. *Critical Studies in Mass Communication, 2,* 91–114.

Hamilton, D. L., Sherman, S. J., & Ruvolo, C. M. (1990). Stereotype-based expectancies: Effects on information processing and social behavior. *Journal of Social Issues, 46,* 35–60.

Hardiman, R. (1994). White racial identity development in the United States. In E. P. Salett & D. R. Koslow (Eds.), *Race, ethnicity and self: Identity in multicultural perspective* (pp. 117–142). Washington, DC: National MultiCultural Institute.

Hardiman, R. (2003). White racial identity development in the United States. In E. P. Salett & D. R. Koslow (Eds.), *Race, ethnicity and self* (2nd ed., pp. 117–136). Washington, DC: National MultiCultural Institute.

Hasian, M., Jr., & Nakayama, T. K. (1999). Racial fictions and cultural identity. In J. Sloop & J. McDaniels (Eds.), *Treading judgment.* Boulder, CO: Westview Press.

Hecht, M. L. (1998). Introduction. In M. L. Hecht (Ed.), *Communicating prejudice* (pp. 3–23). Thousand Oaks, CA: Sage.

Hecht, M. L., Jackson, R. L. III, & Ribeau, S. A. (2003). *African American communication: Exploring identity and culture* (2nd ed.). Mahwah, NJ: Lawrence Erlbaum.

Hecht, M. L., Warren, J. R., Jung, E., & Krieger, J. L. (2005). A communication theory of identity: Development, theoretical perspective and future directions. In W. B. Gudykunst (Ed.), *Theorizing about intercultural communication* (pp. 257–278). Thousand Oaks, CA: Sage.

Helms, J. (1994). *A race is a nice thing to have: A guide to being a white person.* Topeka, KS: Content Communication.

Herbert, B. (2005, June 6). *The mobility myth.* New York Times. Available at http://www.commondreams.org/views05/0606-27.htm

Johnson, A. (2001). *Privilege, power and difference.* Boston: McGraw-Hill.

Katz, J. (1995). *The invention of heterosexuality.* New York: Dutton.

Kim, M.-S. (2002). *Non-western perspectives on human communication.* Thousand Oaks, CA: Sage.

Lacan, J. (1977). The agency of the letter in the unconscious or reason since Freud. In A. Sheridan (Trans.), *Écrits: A selection* (pp. 146–178). New York: Norton. (Original work published 1957)

Leonard, M. F. (2004). Struggling for identity: Multiethnic and biracial individuals in America. In A. Gonzalez, M. Houston, & V. Chen (Eds.), *Our voices* (pp. 228–239). Los Angeles: Roxbury.

Lott, B., & Bullock, H. E. (2001). Who are the poor? *Journal of Social Issues, 57,* 189–206.

Maluso, D. (1995). Shaking hands with a clenched fist: Interpersonal racism. In B. Lott & D. Maluso (Eds.), *The social psychology of interpersonal discrimination* (pp. 50–79). New York: Guilford.

Martinez, R. (1998). Technicolor. In C. C. O'Hearn (Ed.) *Half and half: Writers on growing up biracial + bicultural* (pp. 245–264). New York: Pantheon Books.

Mehl, M. R., & Pennebaker, J. W. (2003). The sounds of social life: A psychometric analysis of students' daily social environments and natural conversations. *Journal of Personality and Social Psychology, 84,* 857–870.

Merritt, B. D. (2000). Illusive reflections: African American women on primetime television. In A. Gonzalez, M. Houston, & V. Chen (Eds.), *Our voices: Essays in culture, ethnicity and communication* (3rd ed., pp. 47–53). Los Angeles: Roxbury.

Miller, A., & Ross, S. D. (2004). They are not us: Framing of American Indians by the *Boston Globe. The Howard Journal of Communications, 15,* 245–259.

Miller, R. L., Watling, J. R., Staggs, S. L., & Rotheram-Borus, M. J. (2003). Growing up biracial in the United States. In E. P. Salett & D. R. Koslow (Eds.), *Race, ethnicity and self* (2nd ed., pp. 139–168). Washington, DC: National Multi-Cultural Institute.

Moon, D. G., & Rolison, G. L. (1998). *Communication of classism.* In M. L. Hecht (Ed.), *Communicating prejudice* (pp. 122–135). Thousand Oaks, CA: Sage.

Morin, R. (2001, July 11). Misperceptions cloud whites' view of blacks. *The Washington Post,* p. A01.

Nakayama, T. K. (2000). Dis/orienting identities: Asian Americans, history, and intercultural communication. In A. González, M. Houston, & V. Chen (Eds.), *Our voices: Essays in ethnicity, culture, and communication* (3rd ed., pp. 13–20). Los Angeles: Roxbury.

Nance, T. A., & Foeman, A. K. (2002). On being biracial in the United States. In J. N. Martin, T. K. Nakayama, & L. A. Flores (Eds.), *Readings in intercultural communication: Experiences and contexts* (pp. 53–62). Boston: McGraw-Hill.

Newberg, S. L. (1994). Expectancy-confirmation processes in stereotype-tinged social encounters: The moderation of social goals. In M. P. Zanna & J. M. Olson (Eds.), *Ontario symposium on personality and social psychology: Vol 7. The psychology of prejudice* (pp. 103–130). Hillsdale, NJ: Lawrence Erlbaum.

Omi, M., & Winant, H. (1998). Racial formation. In P. S. Rothenberg (Ed.), *Race, class and gender in the United States* (pp. 26–35). New York: St. Martin's Press.

Omi, M., & Winant, H. (2001). Racial formation. In P. S. Rothenberg (Ed.), *Race, class and gender in the United States* (pp. 11–21). New York: Worth.

Pennebaker, J. W., Mehl, M. R., & Niederhoffer, K. G. (2003). Psychological aspects of natural language use: Our words, our selves. *Annual Review of Psychology, 54,* 547–577.

Pew Research Center for the People & the Press. (2005, September 8). Hugh racial divide over Katrina and its consequences. News release. Available from http://people-press.org/reports/pdf/255.pdf

Phinney, J. S. (1993). A three-stage model of ethnic identity development in adolescence. In M. E. Bernal & G. Knight (Eds.), *Ethnic identity* (pp. 61–79). Albany: State University of New York Press.

Ponterotto, J. G., & Pedersen, P. B. (1993). *Preventing prejudice* (Chaps. 4 & 5). Newbury Park, CA: Sage.

Roediger, D. R. (2005). *Working toward whiteness: How America's immigrants became white.* New York: Basic Books.

Roland, A. (1988). *In search of self in India and Japan: Towards a cross-cultural psychology.* Princeton, NJ: Princeton University Press.

Root, M. P. P. (2001). *Love's revolution: Interracial marriage.* Philadelphia: Temple University Press.

Sax, L. J., Lindholm, J. A., Astin, A. W., Korn, W. S., & Mahoney, K. M. (2001). *The American freshman: National norms for fall 2001.* Los Angeles: UCLA Graduate School of Education and Information Studies.

Sniffen, M. J. (2005, August 24). Race disparity seen during traffic stops. The Associated Press News Service.

Stephan, W., & Stephan, C. (1996). Predicting prejudice: The role of threat. *International Journal of Intercultural Relations, 20,* 409–426.

Tajfel, H. (1978). Social categorization, social identity and social comparison. In H. Tajfel (Ed.), *Differentiation between social groups* (pp. 61–76). London: Academic Press.

Tajfel, H. (1981). *Human categories and social groups.* Cambridge: Cambridge University Press.

Tajfel, H. (1982). *Social identity and intergroup relations.* Cambridge: Cambridge University Press.

Tanno, D. (2000). Names, narratives, and the evolution of ethnic identity. In A. González, M. Houston, & V. Chen (Eds.), *Our voices: Essays in ethnicity, culture, and communication* (3rd ed., pp. 25–28). Los Angeles: Roxbury.

Ting-Toomey, S. (2005). Identity negotiation theory: Crossing cultural boundaries. In W. B. Gudykunst (Ed.), *Theorizing about intercultural communication* (pp. 211–233). Thousand Oaks, CA: Sage.

Trinh, T. M. (1986/1987). Difference: A special third world women issue. *Discourse, 8.*

Witteborn, S. (2004). Of being an

Arab woman before and after September 11: The enactment of communal identities in talk. *Howard Journal of Communications, 15*, 83–98.

Wood, J. T. (2005). *Gendered lives: Communication, gender and culture* (6th ed). Belmont, CA: Wadsworth.

Yamanouchi, K. (2002, May 19). Cosmetic companies market products aimed at men, *Arizona Republic*, p. D1.

Zemke, R., Raines, C., & Filipczak, B. (2000). *Generations at work: Managing the clash of veterans, boomers, xers, and nexters in your workplace.* New York: AMACOM.

6

LANGUAGE AND INTERCULTURAL COMMUNICATION

CHAPTER OBJECTIVES

After reading this chapter, you should be able to:

1. Understand how language and discourse differ.

2. Define the components of semiotics.

3. Be able to discuss the four components of language.

4. Explain the nominalist, relativist, and qualified relativist positions on language and perception.

5. Be able to explain variations in communication style.

6. Explain the power of labels.

7. Understand the challenges of multilingualism.

8. Explain the difference between translation and interpretation.

9. Understand the phenomenon of code switching and interlanguage.

10. Discuss the complexities of language policies.

When many people travel abroad, one of the first things they encounter are language differences. Surrounded by people who are speaking a different language can be bewildering, and some people may think that learning another language covers everything they need to know about intercultural communication.

As this book shows, intercultural communication involves far more than merely language, but language clearly cannot be overlooked as a central element in the process. This chapter focuses on the verbal aspects of intercultural communication; the next chapter focuses on the nonverbal elements.

The social science approach generally focuses on language and its relation to intercultural communication, the interpretive approach focuses on contextual uses of linguistic codes, and the critical approach emphasizes the relations between discourse and power. This chapter uses a dialectical perspective to explore how language works dynamically in intercultural contexts. With the personal– contextual dialectic, we can consider not only how language use operates on an individual level but also how it is influenced by context. We also use the static– dynamic dialectic to distinguish between language and discourse, to identify the components of language, and to explore the relationship among language, meaning, and perception. Although it may seem that the components of language are static, the *use* of language is a dynamic process.

In this chapter, we also explore cultural variations of language. Then we discuss the relationship between language and power, and between language and identity, and examine issues of multilingualism, translation, and interpretation. Finally, we look at language policies and politics.

THE STUDY OF LANGUAGE: THINKING DIALECTICALLY

Language Versus Discourse

Ferdinand de Saussure laid the early foundations for the structural study of language while he was a Swiss language professor whose students pulled together his lecture notes and published a *Course in General Linguistics* (1966). His lectures notes lay out a structural approach to studying language in general, rather than a specific language. He made an important distinction between *la langue* and *la parole*. *La langue* refers to the entire system of **language**—its theoretical conceptualization. For example, when we consider what is English, should we include the various forms of English spoken around the world—for instance, in South Africa, Ireland, Zimbabwe, Australia, New Zealand, Singapore, China, Nigeria, and Kenya? Do we include the different kinds of English that have been spoken in the past, such as Old English and Middle English? How about the various forms of **pidgin** or **creole**? As you can see, thinking about English is very complex indeed.

In contrast, *la parole* refers to language in use, or **discourse.** We think about discourse by focusing on how language is actually used by particular communities of people, in particular contexts, for particular purposes. Because there are so many different ways of expressing a given idea, the selection of one approach over another is critical to the study of communication. To illustrate, think about the discourse that you typically use to communicate with your parents. How does it differ from the discourse you use with your friends? How does your discourse change when you speak at a wedding or a funeral? Note that the changing communities and contexts influence the discourse that you use. What other com-munities and contexts can you identify that might invoke particular discursive patterns?

Sometimes specific words and phrases are embedded with a specific history that listeners may find problematic. Consider expressions like "I'm not your slave," "Boy, this job is like slave labor," and "My professor is a nazi." The experience of slavery or the Holocaust—or other horrific historical events—is not always taken so metaphorically.

The Components of Language

Linguistics is just one of many ways to think about language. Linguists generally divide up the study of language into four parts: semantics, syntactics, pragmatics, and phonetics. Each part highlights a different aspect of the way language works.

---

la langue The entire system of a language. (Compare with **la parole**.)
la parole In linguistics or semiotics, a term that means discourse or language in use. (Compare with **la langue**.)
pidgin A mixed language incorporating the vocabulary of one or more languages, having a very simplified form of the grammatical system of one of these, and not used as the main language of any of its speakers.
creole The form of language that emerges when speakers of several languages are in long-lasting contact with each other; creole has characteristics of both languages.
discourse The ways in which language is actually used by particular communities of people, in particular contexts, for particular purposes.

Semantics is the study of meaning—that is, how words communicate the meanings we intend in our communication. The emphasis in semantics is on the generation of meaning, focusing on a single word. For example, think about a chair. Do we define *chair* by its shape? Does a throne count as a chair? Do we define it by its function? If we sit on a table, does that make it a chair?

Syntactics is the study of the structure, or grammar, of a language—the rules for combining words into meaningful sentences. One way to think of syntactics is to consider how the order of the words in a sentence creates a particular meaning. For example, the word order in "The red car smashed into the blue car" makes a big difference in the meaning of the sentence. "The blue car smashed into the red car" means something else entirely.

In French, there is a difference between *Qu'est-ce que c'est?* and *Qu'est-ce que c'est que ça?* and *C'est quoi, ça?* Although all three questions mean "What is that?" they each emphasize something different. (Most accurately translated, they mean "What's that?" "What's *that?*" and "That is *what?*") This illustrates that in French meaning often depends more on syntax than on the emphasis of single words in a sentence; this is often the case for English as well.

Pragmatics is the study of how meaning is constructed in relation to receivers, how language is actually used in particular contexts in language communities. For example, if someone says, "That's a cool outfit," you might interpret it variously depending on the intonation, your relationship with the speaker, the locale, and so on. The person might be mocking the outfit, or flirting with you, or simply giving a compliment. The meaning does not come from the words or the word order alone.

Phonetics is the study of the sound system of language—how words are pronounced, which units of sounds (phonemes) are meaningful for a specific language, and which sounds are universal. Because different languages use different sounds, it is often difficult for nonnative speakers to learn how to pronounce some sounds.

French, for example, has no equivalent for the voiced "th" sound (as in *mother*) or the unvoiced "th" sound (as in *think*) in English. French speakers often substitute similar sounds to pronounce English words containing "th." In contrast, English speakers often have a difficult

---

semantics The study of words and meanings.
syntactics The study of the structure, or grammar, of a language.
pragmatics The study of how meaning is constructed in relation to receivers and how language is actually used in particular contexts in language communities.
phonetics The study of the sound system of a language.

time pronouncing the French "r" (as in *la fourrure*), which is produced further back in the mouth than in English.

The Japanese language has a sound that is between the English "r" and "l." This makes it difficult for Japanese speakers to pronounce some English words, especially those in which the "r" and "l" sounds are both used—for example, the word *gorilla*. It also is difficult for English speakers to pronounce Japanese words that contain the "r/l" sound—for example, *ramen* and *karaoke*.

The **International Phonetic Alphabet (IPA)** helps linguists transcribe the pronunciation of words in different languages. The IPA was developed in 1889 by linguists who realized that it was impossible to transcribe unfamiliar languages without a common notation system. It is based primarily on the Latin alphabet but has been modified over the years to accommodate sounds that weren't easily represented by the Latin alphabet. Most languages have from 15 to 50 meaningful sound units, but the total number of all sound units for all languages is in the hundreds (West, 1975).

Semiotics

The study of **semiotics**, or semiology, offers a useful approach to examining how different discursive units communicate meaning. The process of producing meaning is called **semiosis**. A particularly useful framework for understanding semiosis comes from literary critic Roland Barthes (1980). In his system, meaning is constructed through the interpretation of **signs**—combinations of signifiers and signifieds. **Signifiers** are the culturally constructed, arbitrary words or symbols we use to refer to something else, the **signified**. For example, the word *man* is a signifier that refers to some signified, an adult male human being.

Obviously, *man* is a general signifier that does not refer to any particular individual. The relationship between this signifier and the sign (the meaning) depends on how the signifier is used (e.g., as in the sentence "There is a man sitting in the first chair on the left") or on our general sense of what *man* means. The difference here between the

---

International Phonetic Alphabet (IPA) An alphabet developed to help linguists transcribe the pronunciation of words in different languages.

semiotics The analysis of the nature of and relationships between signs in language.

semiosis The process of producing meaning.

signs In semiotics, the meanings that emerge from the combination of signifiers and signifieds. (See **semiotics**, **signified**, and **signifiers**.)

signifiers In semiotics, the culturally constructed, arbitrary words or symbols that people use to refer to something else. (See **semiotics**.)

signified In semiotics, anything that is expressed in arbitrary words, or signifiers. (See **semiotics** and **signifiers**.)

signifier and the sign rests on the difference between the word *man* and the meaning of that word. At its most basic level, *man* means an adult human male, but the semiotic process does not end there because *man* carries many other layers of meaning. Barthes calls these layers **myths**. The expression "Man is the measure of all things," for example, has many levels of meaning, including the centering of male experience as the norm. *Man* may or may not refer to any particular adult male, but it provides a concept we can use to construct particular meanings based on the way the sign *man* functions. What does *man* mean when someone says, "Act like a real man!"

What comes to mind when you think of the term *man?* How do you know when to use this signifier (and when not to use it) to communicate to others? Think of all of the adult males you know: How do they "fit" under this signifier? In what ways does the signifier reign over their behaviors, both verbal and nonverbal, to communicate particular ideas about them?

Intercultural communication is not concerned solely with the cultural differences in verbal systems, although that is certainly a central interest. Semiotics can be useful in unraveling the ways that the cultural codes regulate verbal and nonverbal communication systems, as we will see in the next chapter. That is, semiotics allows us one way to "crack the codes" of other cultural frameworks. The goal is to establish entire systems of semiosis and the means by which those systems create meaning. We are not so much interested in the discrete, individual signifiers, as in the ways that signifiers are combined and configured.

The use of these semiotic systems relies on many codes taken from a variety of sources: economics, history, politics, religion, and so on. For example, when a Nazi swastika was spray-painted on a sign in Harwich on Cape Cod, Massachusetts, in December 2005, the power of this message and what it communicates relied on semiotic systems from the past. The history of the Nazi persecution of Jews, homosexuals, Gypsies, and others during World War II is well known: The power behind the signifier, the swastika, comes from that historical knowledge and the codes of its ideology that communicate its message. Taken with a cross-burning incident three months earlier in September in nearby Sandwich, some residents are concerned (Karlson, 2005). The practice of cross burning has a different history than the swastika, but understanding that history and the terror of the Ku Klux Klan helps us understand the power of this signifier and its message. Historical relations from the past can influence the construction, maintenance, and perpetuation of intercultural relations in the present.

myths (1) Theories or stories that are widely understood and believed; (2) in semiotics, the layers of meaning beneath a signifier. (See **semiotics**, **signified**, and **signifier**.)

Because we seek the larger semiotic systems, we need to be aware of the cultural contexts that regulate the semiotic frameworks. When we are in different cultural contexts, the semiotic systems transform the communication situations. Consider the following observation by writer Edmundo Desnoes (1985), who discusses the work of photographer Susan Meiselas on her trip to Nicaragua. Desnoes notes that Meiselas "discovered one of the keys to understanding Latin America: a different context creates a different discourse. What she saw and what she shot in Nicaragua could not be plucked away and packaged in New York" (p. 39). That is, the photographs that Meiselas took could not communicate what she saw and experienced and wanted to express. The U.S. context necessarily would be regulated by a different semiotic system that would construct different signs and assign different meanings for the images.

It is wise to be sensitive to the many levels of cultural context that are regulated by different semiotic systems. In other words, it's a good idea to avoid framing the cultural context simply in terms of a "nation." Nation-states have other cultural contexts within their borders—for example, commercial and financial districts, residential areas, and bars, which are all regulated by their own semiotic systems. Consider the clothes that people might wear to a bar; wearing the same clothes in a business setting would not communicate the same message.

Language and Perception

How much of our perception is shaped by the particular language we speak? Do English speakers see the world differently from, say, Arabic speakers? Is there anything about the particular language we speak that constrains or shapes our perception of the world? These questions are at the heart of the "political correctness" debate. We can address these questions from two points of view: the nominalist and the relativist.

The Nominalist Position According to the **nominalist position**, perception is not shaped by the particular language we speak. Language is simply an arbitrary "outer form of thought." Thus, we all have the same range of thoughts, which we express in different ways with different languages. This means that any thought can be expressed in any language, although some may take more or fewer words. The existence of different languages does not mean that people have different thought processes or inhabit different perceptual worlds. After all, a

---

nominalist position The view that perception is not shaped by the particular language one speaks. (Compare with **relativist position** and **qualified relativist position**.)

tree may be an *arbre* in French and an arbol in Spanish, but we all perceive the tree in the same way.

The Relativist Position   According to the **relativist position,** the particular language we speak, especially the structure of that language, determines our thought patterns, our perceptions of reality, and, ultimately, important cultural components. This position is best represented by the Sapir-Whorf hypothesis. As you may recall from Chapter 2, this hypothesis was proposed by Edward Sapir (1921), a linguist, and his student, Benjamin Whorf (1956), based on linguistic research they conducted in the 1930s and 1940s on Native American languages. They proposed that language is not merely an "instrument for voicing ideas but is itself the shaper of ideas, the guide for the individual's mental activity" (Hoijer, 1994, p. 194). According to the Sapir-Whorf hypothesis, language defines our experience. For example, there are no possessives (*his/her/our/your*) in the Diné (Navajo) language; we might conclude, therefore, that the Diné think in a particular way about the concept of possession. Another example is the variation in verb forms in English, Spanish, and French. In English and Spanish, the present continuous verb form is frequently used; thus, a student might say, "I am studying" or "*Estoy estudiando.*" A French speaker, in contrast, would use the simple present form, "*J'étudie.*" The Sapir-Whorf hypothesis suggests that, based on this variation in verb form, French, English, and Spanish speakers may think differently about movement or action.

Another frequently cited example involves variation in color vocabulary. The Diné use one word for blue and green, two words for two different colors of black, and one word for red; these four words form the vocabulary for primary colors in Diné culture. The Sapir-Whorf hypothesis suggests that English and Diné speakers perceive colors differently. Other examples of variations in syntax and semantics reflect differences in perception.

The Sapir-Whorf hypothesis has had tremendous influence on scholarly thinking about language and its impact on everyday communication. It questions the basic assumption that we all inhabit the same perceptual world, the same social reality.

More recently, the Sapir-Whorf hypothesis position has been critiqued by a number of studies that challenge the connection between language and how we think. After looking at a number of these studies, some of which included people who were deaf and raised without

---

relativist position The view that the particular language individuals speak, especially the structure of the language, shapes their perception of reality and cultural patterns. (Compare with **nominalist position** and **qualified relativist position**.)

language, Steven Pinker, a professor of brain and cognitive sciences, concludes, "People do not think in English or Chinese or Arabic; they think in a language of thought. This language of thought probably looks a bit like all these languages" (1994, p. 72). He believes that people think in "mentalese" that are not specific to any language but outside of language.

In contrast, George Lakoff (1989) maintains that color concepts, for example, are explained by three factors: a neurophysiological apparatus, a universal cognitive apparatus, and culturally determined choices that apply to the input of the universal cognitive apparatus (p. 104). The neurophysiological apparatus refers to the biological process of seeing certain pure hues such as red, blue, white, and black. The universal cognitive apparatus refers to the way that we compute other colors, such as orange or purple. The culturally determined choices refer to the way that we organize these colors because different languages have different ways of categorizing all of these colors. Lakoff then combines the physiological aspects with the cultural aspects of our relationship to the world.

The **qualified relativist position** takes a more moderate view of the relationship between language and perception. Proponents recognize the power of language but see language as a tool rather than a mirror of perception. This view allows for more freedom than the Sapir-Whorf hypothesis. As you read the research findings that follow, you may see the wisdom of the qualified relativist position.

Recent Research Findings

Communication scholar Thomas M. Steinfatt (1989) summarizes three areas of research that investigate the Sapir-Whorf hypothesis: (1) children's **language acquisition,** (2) cross-cultural differences in language, and (3) cognitive development of children who are deaf. As you will see, most of the research in these areas does not support a strict interpretation of the Sapir-Whorf hypothesis.

Language Acquisition in Children   If language structures thought, then language must precede, and only subsequently influence, thought. This raises the question of whether it is possible to think without language. B. F. Skinner, Jean Piaget, Lev Vygotsky, and other psychologists have long wrestled with this question. As their works indicate,

---

qualified relativist position A moderate view of the relationship between language and perception. This position sees language as a tool rather than a prison. (Compare with **nominalist position** and **relativist position**.)
language acquisition The process of learning language.

they seem to conclude that language and thought are so closely related that it is difficult to speak of one as initiating influence over the other. Their works thus do not provide evidence for a strong relativist position.

Cross-Cultural Differences in Language Do groups with different language labels perceive the world in different ways? One study compared perception of color variations in U.S. English speakers and the Dani of western New Guinea, who classify colors into roughly two groups, light and dark (Heider & Oliver, 1972). The researchers showed a paint chip to an individual, removed the paint chip, showed the person the same chip along with others, and then asked her or him to identify the original paint chip. There was little difference in the responses of the U.S. English speakers and the Dani, who were able to identify the original paint chip even though their language may not contain a word for that color.

Consider a more familiar example. Many men in the United States might identify someone's shirt as "red," whereas women viewing the same shirt might call it "cranberry" or "cherry" or "scarlet." Both the men and the women recognize the color distinctions, but men tend to use fewer words than women to distinguish colors.

Another example of cross-cultural research involves variations in verb forms. The Chinese language has no counterfactual verb form (illustrated by "If I had known, I *would have gone*, but I did not"). Researchers constructed stories using the counterfactual form and found that the Chinese respondents understood the concept of counterfactual and could answer questions appropriately even though this structure is not present in Chinese (Au, 1983, 1984, 1985; Bloom, 1981, 1984). No evidence indicates that Chinese speakers are unable to think in terms of counterfactuals; rather, they simply do not normally express thoughts using such constructions. Although these research examples do not support the nominalist position, they do not provide strong evidence for the relativist position either.

Cognition of Children Who Are Deaf Researchers have also tried to determine if children who are deaf or who have limited language use have diminished ability in perception or logical thinking. The children with disabilities had the same semantic or categorizing competence, and the same level of cognitive skill, as those children who could hear. The children were deficient in purely linguistic skills and short-term memory storage. The researchers concluded that children who are deaf do not seem to have a different worldview (Rhodda & Grove, 1987).

CULTURAL VARIATIONS IN LANGUAGE

Language is powerful and can have tremendous implications for people's lives. For example, uttering the words I *do* can influence lives dramatically. Being called names can be hurtful and painful, despite the old adage "Sticks and stones can break my bones, but words will never hurt me."

The particular language we use predisposes us to think in particular ways and not in others. For example, the fact that English speakers do not distinguish between a formal and an informal *you* (as in German, with *du* and *Sie*, or in Spanish, with *tu* and *usted*) may mean that English speakers think about formality and informality differently than do German or Spanish speakers. In Japanese, formality is not simply noted by *you*; it is part of the entire language system. Nouns take the **honorific** "o" before them, and verbs take more formal and polite forms. Thus, "*Doitsu-go ga dekimasen* [I—or you, he, she, we, they—don't speak German]" is more polite and formal than "*Doitsu-go ga dekinai.*"

In other languages, the deliberate use of nonformal ways of speaking in more formal contexts can be insulting to another person. For example, French speakers may use the "tu" form when speaking to their dog or cat, but it can be insulting to use the "tu" form in a more formal setting when speaking to relative strangers. Yet it may be permissible to use the "tu" form in more social settings with relative strangers, such as at parties or in bars. Here, pragmatics becomes important. That is, we need to think about what else might be communicated by others and whether they shift to more informal ways of speaking.

Variations in Communication Style

Communication style combines both language and nonverbal communication. It is the **tonal coloring**, the **metamessage**, that contex-

---

honorific A term or expression that shows respect.
communication style The metamessage that contextualizes how listeners are expected to accept and interpret verbal messages.
tonal coloring See **metamessage**.
metamessage The meaning of a message that tells others how they should respond to the content of our communication based on our relationship to them; also known as **tonal coloring**.

POINT OF VIEW

A British journalist for *The Economist* found this guide on an office wall in the European Court of Justice. Note the differences between what is said, what is interpreted by the listener, and what is meant. Where should we look for the meaning of language?

What they say: I'm sure it's my fault.
What is understood: It is his fault.
What they mean: It is your fault.

What they say: I'll bear it in mind.
What is understood: He will probably do it.
What they mean: I will do nothing about it.

What they say: I was a bit disappointed that . . .
What is understood: It doesn't really matter.
What they mean: I am most upset and cross.

What they say: By the way/Incidentally . . .
What is understood: This is not very important.
What they mean: The primary purpose of our discussion is . . .

What they say: I hear what you say.
What is understood: He accepts my point of view.
What they mean: I disagree and do not want to discuss it any further.

What they say: Correct me if I'm wrong.
What is understood: Tell me what you think.
What they mean: I know I'm right—please don't contradict me.

What they say: With the greatest respect . . .
What is understood: He is listening to me.
What they mean: I think you are wrong, or a fool.

What they say: That is an original point of view.
What is understood: He likes my ideas.
What they mean: You must be crazy!

What they say: Very interesting.
What is understood: He is impressed.
What they mean: I don't agree, or I don't believe you.

What they say: You must come for dinner sometime.
What is understood: I will get an invitation soon.
What they mean: Not an invitation, just being polite.

What they say: Quite good.
What is understood: Quite good.
What they mean: A bit disappointing.

Source: From "English as a Second Language," *Harper's Magazine*, December 2004, pp. 27–28.

POINT OF VIEW

Because we live in a more global world, think about the impact of language differences in hospital emergency rooms, as well as other everyday needs, such as fire departments, police departments, and so on. How can we ensure adequate services for everyone?

When a Spanish-speaking hospital receptionist refused to interpret during her lunch hour, doctors at St. Vincent's Staten Island Hospital turned to a 7-year-old child to tell their patient, an injured construction worker, that he needed an emergency amputation.

With no one to bridge the language gap for another patient, a newly pregnant immigrant from Mexico with life-threatening complications, doctors pressed her to sign a consent form in English for emergency surgery. Understanding that the surgery was needed "to save the baby," the young married woman awoke to learn that the operation had instead left her childless and sterile. [. . .]

Among the cases cited was that of a Korean woman taken by ambulance to Flushing Hospital Medical Center last year after being beaten in the head with a brick in a street robbery. Doctors used 30 stitches for her head wound, but when the woman, a 45-year-old manicurist, returned for follow-up care a few days later, she was handed a piece of paper stating in English that to be seen by a doctor she had to pay $95 and bring a photo ID. The robbery had left her with neither.

"I felt helpless," said the woman, who works in a nail salon in Great Neck, on Long Island, speaking by telephone through a translator on the condition that she be identified only as Ms. N. "I was crying

tualizes how listeners are expected to receive and interpret verbal messages. A primary way in which cultural groups differ in communication style is in a preference for high- versus lowcontext communication. A **high-context communication** style is one in which "most of the information is either in the physical context or internalized in the person, while very little is in the coded, explicit, transmitted part of the message" (Hall, 1976, p. 79). This style of communication emphasizes understanding messages without direct verbal communication. People in long-term relationships often communicate in this style. For example, one person may send a meaningful glance across the room at a

---

high-context communication A style of communication in which much of the information is contained in the contexts and nonverbal cues rather than expressed explicitly in words. (Compare with **low-context communication**.)

at home." Seongho Kim, then a social worker with Korean Community Services, returned with her to the hospital, where he pointed out that Ms. N.'s care would be covered by the New York State Crime Victims Fund. Only then did an employee agree to let her be seen by a Korean-speaking doctor, Mr. Kim said. "People are dying because of their language." [. . .]

In some cases, the monitors themselves witnessed the medical consequences of communication failures. Ana Maria Archila, executive director of the Latin American Integration Center, an immigrant rights and social service agency, said she and two others overheard doctors at St. Vincent's telling a construction worker, through his 7-year-old cousin, that the worker needed an amputation.

"The child said, 'I'm not sure if they said foot or said toe,'" Ms. Archila recalled. "This worker, he was about to cry."

The monitors later learned that it was the man's third trip to the emergency room after a construction accident that had crushed his toe weeks earlier. Unable to explain his symptoms in English, he reported, he had been handled dismissively until he returned with his big toe blackened by gangrene.

Later, after the toe was amputated, Ms. Archila added, he had to rely on a patient in the next bed to translate the doctors' instructions for post-operative care.

Source: From N. Bernstein, "Language Barrier Called Health Hazard in E.R.," *New York Times*, April 21, 2005, p. B1.

party, and his or her partner will know from the nonverbal clue that it is time to go home.

In contrast, in **low-context communication**, the majority of meaning and information is in the verbal code. This style of communication, which emphasizes explicit verbal messages, is highly valued in many settings in the United States. Interpersonal communication textbooks often stress that we should not rely on nonverbal, contextual information. It is better, they say, to be explicit and to the point, and not to leave things ambiguous. However, many cultural groups around the world value high-context communication. They encourage children and adolescents to pay close attention to contextual cues (body

low-context communication A style of communication in which much of the information is conveyed in words rather than in nonverbal cues and contexts. (Compare with **high-context communication**.)

language, environmental cues), and not simply the words spoken in a conversation (Gudykunst & Matsumoto, 1996).

William Gudykunst and Stella Ting-Toomey (2003) identify two major dimensions of communication styles: direct versus indirect and elaborate versus understated.

Direct Versus Indirect Styles This dimension refers to the extent to which speakers reveal their intentions through explicit verbal communication and emphasizes low-context communication. A direct communication style is one in which verbal messages reveal the speaker's true intentions, needs, wants, and desires. An indirect style is one in which the verbal message is often designed to camouflage the speaker's true intentions, needs, wants, and desires. Most of the time, individuals and groups are more or less direct depending on the context.

Many English speakers in the United States favor the direct speech style as the most appropriate in most contexts. This is revealed in statements like "Don't beat around the bush," "Get to the point," and "What exactly are you trying to say?" Although "white lies" may be permitted in some contexts, the direct style emphasizes honesty, openness, forthrightness, and individualism.

However, some cultural groups prefer a more indirect style, with the emphasis on high-context communication. Preserving the harmony of relationships has a higher priority than being totally honest. Thus, a speaker might look for a "soft" way to communicate that there is a problem in the relationship, perhaps by providing contextual cues (Ueda, 1974). Some languages have many words and gestures that convey the idea of "maybe." For example, three Indonesians studying in the United States were invited by their adviser to participate in a cross-cultural training workshop. They did not want to participate, nor did they have the time. But neither did they want to offend their professor, whom they held in high regard. Therefore, rather than tell him they couldn't attend, they simply didn't return his calls and didn't show up to the workshop.

An international student from Tunisia told Judith and Tom that he had been in the United States for several months before he realized that if someone was asked for directions and didn't know the location of the place, that person should tell the truth instead of making up a response. He explained that he had been taught that it was better to engage in conversation, to give *some* response, than to disappoint the person by revealing he didn't know.

Different communication styles are responsible for many problems that arise between men and women and between persons from different ethnic groups. These problems may be caused by different priorities for truth, honesty, harmony, and conflict avoidance in relationships.

Elaborate Versus Understated Styles This dimension of communication styles refers to the degree to which talk is used. The elaborate style involves the use of rich, expressive language in everyday talk. For example, the Arabic language has many metaphorical expressions used in everyday speech. In this style, a simple assertive statement means little; the listener will believe the opposite.

In contrast, the understated style values succinct, simple assertions, and silence. Amish people often use this style of communication. A common refrain is, "If you don't have anything nice to say, don't say anything at all." Free self-expression is not encouraged. Silence is especially appropriate in ambiguous situations; if one is unsure of what is going on, it is better to remain silent.

The exact style falls between the elaborate and the understated, as expressed in the maxim "Verbal contributions should be no more or less information than is required" (Grice, 1975). The exact style emphasizes cooperative communication and sincerity as a basis for interaction.

In international negotiations, visible differences in style can contribute to misperceptions and misunderstandings. For example, if we look at two open letters addressed to the Iraqi people in April 2003, we can see striking differences in the styles used by the British prime minister Tony Blair and the former Iraqi leader, Saddam Hussein. Saddam Hussein was not captured by U.S. forces until December 2003. On April 4, 2003, in a leaflet to be distributed to the Iraqi people, Mr. Blair writes:

From Tony Blair

As soon as Saddam Hussein's regime falls, the work to build a new free and united Iraq will begin. A peaceful, prosperous Iraq which will be run by and for the Iraqi people. Not by America, not by Britain, not by the UN—though all of us will help—but by you the people of Iraq.

For the first time in 25 years you will be free from the shadow of Saddam and can look forward to a new beginning for your families and your country.

That is already starting to happen in those parts of your country that have been liberated. But you want to know that we will stay to get the job done. You want to know that Saddam will be gone.

I assure you: he will be. Then, coalition forces will make the country safe, and will work with the United Nations to help Iraq get back on its feet. We will continue to provide immediate humanitarian aid, and we will help with longer-term projects.

Our troops will leave as soon as they can. They will not stay a day longer than necessary. (http://www.guardian.co.uk/Iraq/Story/0,2763,929934,00.html)

In contrast, Saddam Hussein spoke in a more indirect and elaborate style in his open letter to the Iraqi people on April 30, 2003:

From Saddam Hussein to the great Iraqi people, the sons of the Arab and Islamic nation, and honourable people everywhere.

Peace be upon you, and the mercy and blessings of God.

Just as Hulaku entered Baghdad, the criminal Bush entered it, with Alqami, or rather, more than one Alqami.

They did not conquer you—you who reject the occupation and humiliation, you who have Arabism and Islam in your hearts and minds—except through betrayal.

Indeed, it is not a victory while there is still resistance in your souls.

What we used to say has now become reality, for we do not live in peace and security while the deformed Zionist entity is on our Arab land; therefore there is no rift in the unity of the Arab struggle.

Sons of our great people:

Rise up against the occupier and do not trust anyone who talks of Sunni and Shia, because the only issue that the homeland—your great Iraq—faces now is the occupation.

There are no priorities other than driving out the infidel, criminal, cowardly occupier. No honourable hand is held out to shake his, but, rather, the hand of traitors and collaborators.

I say to you that all the countries surrounding you are against your resistance, but God is with you because you are fighting unbelief and defending your rights. (http://www.guardian.co.uk/Iraq/Story/0,2763,946805,00.html)

These different uses of language communicate different things to their culturally disparate audiences. As they also demonstrate, it is not easy to interpret language use from other people's perspectives.

Taking a dialectical perspective, though, should help us avoid stereotyping specific groups (such as Arabic or English speakers) in terms of communication style. We should not expect any group to use a particular communication style all the time. Instead, we might recognize that style operates dynamically and is related to context, historical forces, and so on. Furthermore, we might consider how tolerant we are when we encounter others who communicate in very different ways and how willing or able we are to alter our own style to communicate better.

Variations in Contextual Rules

Understanding some of the cultural variations in communication style is useful. A dialectical perspective reminds us that the particular style we use may vary from context to context. Think of the many contexts in which you communicate during the day—classroom, family, work, and so on—and about how you alter your communication to suit these contexts. You may be more direct with your family and less direct in classroom settings. Similarly, you may be more instrumental in task situations and more affective when socializing with your friends.

Many research studies have examined the rules for the use of socially situated language in specific contexts. They attempt to identify contexts and then "discover" the rules that apply in these contexts for a given speech community. Researchers Jack Daniel and Geneva Smitherman (1990) studied the communication dynamics in black churches. They first identified the priorities among congregation members: unity between the spiritual and the material, the centrality of religion, the harmony of nature and the universe, and the participatory, interrelatedness of life. They then described a basic communication format, the call-response, in both the traditional religious context and secular life contexts. In church, the speaker and audience interact, with sermons alternating with music. In secular life, call-response takes the form of banter between the rapper (rhetor) and others in the social group.

Daniel and Smitherman (1990) go on to discuss problems that can occur in black–white communication:

When the Black person is speaking, the white person, because call-response is not in his cultural heritage, obviously does not engage in the response process, remaining relatively passive, perhaps voicing an occasional, subdued, "mmmmmmmhm." Judging from the white individual's seeming lack of involvement in the communication, the Black communicator gets the feeling that the white isn't listening to him . . . and the white person gets the feeling that the Black person isn't listening because he keeps interrupting. (p. 39)

People communicate differently in different speech communities.

English is spoken in many different ways around the world by native speakers of English, and there are even more non-native speakers of English. How important is it to learn to listen to the many different world Englishes to be a better intercultural communicator?

There are now many times more nonnative speakers of English in the world than there are native speakers of English, and the gap is likely to widen. But higher education is heading in that direction much faster than are most Midwestern towns. [. . .]

The question is, do such academic breakdowns happen because universities aren't doing enough to prepare international teaching assistants for the classroom, or because American undergraduates, the beleaguered consumers themselves, simply tune out when faced with someone who is sufficiently different from them? [. . .]

In 1988 Donald L. Rubin, a professor of education and speech communication at the University of Georgia, began toying with an experimental model that would occupy him for the next several years: He gathered American undergraduates inside a classroom and then played a taped lecture for them over high-fidelity speakers. The lecture—an introduction to the Mahabharata, say, or a discourse on the growing scarcity of helium—was delivered in the voice of a man from central Ohio.

While the undergraduates sat and listened, they faced an image projected onto the classroom wall in front of them: Half the time, it was a photograph of an American man ("John Smith from Portland"), standing at a chalkboard and staring back at them. For the other half of the testing groups, the slide projected before them was that of an Asian man ("Li Wenshu from Beijing"), standing at the same chalkboard. The two figures were dressed, posed, and groomed as similarly as possible.

Now for the interesting part: When the students were asked to fill in missing words from a printed transcript of the central Ohioan's taped speech, they made 20 percent more errors when staring at the Asian man's image than they did when staring at a picture of "John Smith."

What did that mean? [. . .]

"All the pronunciation improvement in the world," he says, "will not by itself halt the problem of students' dropping classes or complaining about their instructors' language." [. . .]

Mr. Rubin, however, prefers to think of the issue in terms of prerequisites—worldly listening skills are a requirement for graduation. "I consider the ability to listen to and comprehend world Englishes a prerequisite to success in a wide variety of enterprises."

Source: From J. Gravois, "Teaching Impediment: When the Student Can't Understand the Instructor, Who Is to Blame?" *Chronicle of Higher Education,* April 8, 2005, pp. A10, A11, A12.

Thus, the context in which the communication occurs is a significant part of the meaning. Although we might communicate in one way in one speech community, we might change our communication style in another. Understanding the dynamics of various speech communities helps us see the range of communication styles.

DISCOURSE: LANGUAGE AND POWER

Recall that discourse refers to language in use. This means that all discourse is social. The language used—the words and the meanings that are communicated—depends not only on the context but also on the social relations that are part of that interaction. For example, bosses and workers may use the same words, but the meanings communicated are not always the same. A boss and a worker may both refer to the company personnel as a "family." To the boss, this may mean "one big happy family," whereas to a disgruntled employee, it may mean a "dysfunctional family." To some extent, the disparity is related to the inequality between boss and worker, to the power differential.

In Chapter 2, we introduced communication accommodation theory. There are different ways that people accommodate or resist accommodating, depending on the situation. One such theory that encompasses various approaches is co-cultural communication, which we examine next.

Co-Cultural Communication

The co-cultural communication theory, proposed by communication scholar Mark Orbe (1998), describes how language works between dominant and nondominant groups—or **co-cultural groups**. Groups that have the most power (whites, men, heterosexuals) consciously or unconsciously formulate a communication system that supports their perception of the world. This means that co-cultural group members (ethnic minorities, women, gays) must function in communication systems that often do not represent their experiences. Nondominant groups thus find themselves in dialectical struggles: Do they try to adapt to the dominant communication style, or do they maintain their own styles? Women in large male-dominated corporations often struggle with these issues. Do they adapt a male corporate style of speaking, or do they assert their own style?

---

co-cultural group Nondominant cultural groups that exist in a national culture, such as African American or Chinese American.

In studying how communication operates with many different dominant and co-cultural groups, Orbe has identified three general orientations: nonassertive, assertive, and aggressive. Within each of these orientations, co-cultural individuals may emphasize assimilation, accommodation, or separation in relation to the dominant group. These two sets of orientations result in nine types of strategies (Table 6.1). The strategy chosen depends on many things, including preferred outcome, perceived costs and rewards, and context. These nine types of strategies vary from nonassertive assimilation, in which co-cultural individuals emphasize commonalities and avert controversy, to nonassertive separation, in which they avoid or maintain interpersonal barriers. Assertive assimilation strategies include manipulating stereotypes; assertive accommodation strategies include educating others, using liaisons, and communicating self. Aggressive assimilation involves strategies like ridiculing self and mirroring; aggressive accommodating involves confronting others; and aggressive separation involves attacking or sabotaging others.

TABLE 6.1 CO-CULTURAL COMMUNICATION ORIENTATIONS

	Separation	Accommodation	Assimilation
Nonassertive	Avoiding Maintaining interpersonal barriers	Increasing visibility Dispelling stereotypes	Emphasizing commonalities Developing positive face Censoring self Averting controversy
Assertive	Communicating self Intragroup networking Exemplifying strengths Embracing stereotypes	Communicating self Intragroup networking Using liaisons Educating others	Extensive preparation Overcompensating Manipulating stereotypes Bargaining
Aggressive	Attacking Sabotaging others	Confronting Gaining advantage	Dissociating Mirroring Strategic distancing Ridiculing self

Source: From M. Orbe, *Constructing Co-Cultural Theory: An Explication of Culture, Power, and Communication* (Thousand Oaks, CA: Sage, 1998), p. 110.

The point here is that there are both costs and benefits for co-cultural members when they choose which of these strategies to use. Because language is structured in ways that do not reflect their experiences, they must adopt some strategy for dealing with the linguistic framework. For example, if Mark wants to refer to his relationship with Kevin, does he use the word "boyfriend," "friend," "roommate," "husband," "partner," or some other word? If Mark and Kevin were married where it is legal, (e.g., Massachusetts, Canada, Belgium), should they refer to their "husband" when they are in places that explicitly say they do not recognize same-sex marriages from elsewhere, (e.g., Arizona, Michigan, Texas, or Colorado)? What about work? Thanksgiving dinner with the family? Let's look at how these strategies might work, the costs and the benefits of them.

Assimilation Strategies   The three assimilation strategies are nonassertive, assertive, and aggressive. Some co-cultural individuals tend to use nonassertive assimilation strategies. These strategies emphasize trying to fit and be accepted by the dominant group. This strategy might be taken if the individual perceives that it is important not to "make waves" in this context. For example, in some work situations, people may benefit by keeping their jobs and feeling more accepted by co-workers. If these individuals hear the boss using sexist language, being insensitive to other religious holidays, joking about gays/lesbians, and so on, they may keep quiet or pretend not to hear what the boss said. There are potential costs to this approach, because these co-cultural individuals may feel they cannot be honest about themselves and may also feel uncomfortable reinforcing the dominant group's worldview and power.

The second assimilation strategy is assertive assimilation. Co-cultural individuals taking this strategy may downplay co-cultural differences and try to fit into the existing structures. Unlike the nonassertive assimilation strategy, this individual will try to fit in but also let people know how she or he feels from time to time. However, this strategy can promote an us-versus-them mentality, and some people find it difficult to maintain this strategy for very long.

The third assimilation strategy is aggressive assimilation. This strategy emphasizes fitting in, and co-cultural members who take this approach can go to great lengths to prove they are like members of the dominant group. Sometimes this means distancing themselves from other members of their co-culture, mirroring (dressing and behaving like the dominant group), or self-ridiculing. The benefit of this strategy is that the co-cultural member is not seen as "typical" of members of that co-culture. The cost may entail ridicule from members of that co-culture who may accuse this individual of acting white, thinking like a man, or "straight." This may lead to ostracizing of this person from the co-culture.

Accommodation Strategies Like assimilation strategies, there are three accommodation strategies: nonassertive, assertive, and aggressive. Nonassertive accommodation emphasizes blending into the dominant culture but tactfully challenging the dominant structure to recognize co-cultural practices. For example, a Jewish co-worker may want to put up a menorah near the company's Christmas tree as a way of challenging the dominant culture. By gently educating the organization about other religious holidays, the co-cultural member may be able to change their presumptions about everyone celebrating Christmas. Using this strategy, the co-cultural individual may be able to influence group decision making while still showing loyalty to the larger organization's goals. The cost of this strategy may be that others feel that she or he is not pushing hard enough to change larger structural issues in the organization. Also, this strategy does not really promote major changes in organizations to make them more inclusive and reflective of the larger society.

Assertive accommodation tries to strike a balance between the concerns of co-cultural and dominant group members. These strategies involve communicating self, doing intragroup networking, using liaisons, and educating others. For example, Asian American co-workers may share information about themselves with their co-workers, but they also share information about words that are offensive, such as "Oriental" and "slope."

Aggressive accommodation strategies involve moving into the dominant structures and then working from within to promote significant changes—no matter how high the personal cost. Although it may seem as if co-cultural workers who use these strategies are confrontational or self-promoting, they also reflect a genuine desire to work with and not against dominant group workers. For example, a disabled co-worker may consistently remind others that facilities need to be more accessible, such as door handles, bathrooms that can accommodate wheelchairs, and so on.

Separation Strategies The three types of separation strategies are nonassertive, assertive, and aggressive. Nonassertive separation strategies are often used by those who assume that some segregation is part of everyday life in the United States. For those in dominant groups, it is easier to live, work, learn, socialize, and pray with those who are like them. For co-cultural group members, it may take more effort to live as much as possible among those like them. So although it may not be possible for gay people to live only in a gay world, they can try to socialize as much as possible with other gays. The benefit of this approach is that co-cultural members do not have to deal with any negative feelings or stereotypes about their group, but the cost is that they cannot network and make connections with those in power positions.

Assertive separation strategies are used when a more conscious decision is made to maintain distance between dominant and co-cultural group members. Typical strategies my include stressing strengths and embracing stereotypes, as well as intragroup networking. One of the benefits of this approach, like the nonassertive separation strategy, is that it promotes co-cultural unity and self-determination. The cost, however, is that co-cultural group members must try to survive without having access to resources controlled by the dominant group.

Aggressive separation strategies are used by those who feel that is a high priority for dominant group or co-cultural group members. These strategies can include criticizing, attacking, and sabotaging others. The benefit of this approach for co-cultural members is that it enables them to confront pervasive, everyday, assumed discriminatory practices and structures. The cost may be that the dominant group retaliates against this open exposure of the presumed way of doing things.

Again, when confronted with various situations, dominant and co-cultural group members need to think carefully about how they wish to respond. There are benefits and costs to all of the decisions made. Although dominant group members are like to be less harmed than co-cultural group members, everyone may suffer in the end. If Miguel is "cut out of the loop" at work and not told about an important meeting that affects his job, how should he handle this situation? He could pursue an assertive accommodation strategy and remind his co-workers that he needs to be included by pointing out when he is excluded. This could work and produce a more inclusive work environment, or the exclusion may continue because he is ignored. Or he could adopt a more aggressive accommodation strategy and meet with the manager and insist he be included. What are the costs and benefits of this approach? There are no easy answers, but it is important to consider what verbal communication strategy you may want to use when interacting in intercultural communication situations.

Discourse and Social Structure

Just as organizations have particular structures and specific positions within them, societies are structured so that individuals occupy social positions. Differences in **social positions** are central to understanding intercultural commu-nication. For one thing, not all positions within

---

social positions The places from which people speak that are socially constructed and thus embedded with assumptions about gender, race, class, age, social roles, sexuality, and so on.

the structure are equivalent; everyone is not the same. When men whistle at an attractive woman walking by, it has a different force and meaning than if women were to whistle at a man walking by.

Power is a central element, by extension, of this focus on social position. For instance, when a judge in court says what he or she thinks *freedom of speech* means, it carries much greater force than when a neighbor or a classmate gives an opinion about what the phrase means. When we communicate, we tend to note (however unconsciously) the group membership and positions of communication participants. To illustrate, consider the previous example. We understand how communication functions, based on the group membership of the judge (as a member of the judicial system) and of the neighbors and classmates; we need know nothing about their individual identities.

Groups also hold different positions of power in the social structure. Because intercultural contact occurs between members of different groups, the positions of the groups affect communication. Group differences lend meaning to intercultural communication because, as noted previously, the concept of differences is key to language and the semiotic process.

The "Power" Effects of Labels

We often use labels to refer to other people and to ourselves. Labels, as signifiers, acknowledge particular aspects of our social identity. For example, we might label ourselves or others as "male" or "female," indicating sexual identity. Or we might say we are "Canadian" or a "New Englander," indicating a national or regional identity. The context in which a label is used may determine how strongly we feel about the label. On St. Patrick's Day, for example, someone may feel more strongly about being an Irish American than about being a woman or a student or a Texan.

Sometimes people feel trapped or misrepresented by labels. They might complain, "Why do we have to have labels? Why can't I just be me?" These complaints belie the reality of the function of discourse. It would be nearly impossible to communicate without labels. People rarely have trouble when labeled with terms they agree with—for example, "man," "student," "Minnesotan," or "Australian." Trouble arises, however, from the use of labels that they don't like or that they feel describe them inaccurately. Think about how you feel when someone describes you using terms you do not like.

Labels communicate many levels of meaning and establish particular kinds of relationships between speaker and listener. Sometimes people use labels to communicate closeness and affection for others. Labels like "friend," "lover," and "partner" communicate equality. Sometimes people intentionally invoke labels to establish a hostile relationship. Labels like "white trash" and "redneck" intentionally communicate inequality. Sometimes people use labels that are unintentionally offensive to others. When this happens, it demonstrates the speaker's ignorance, lack of cultural sensitivity, and connection to the other group. The use of terms such as "Oriental" and "homosexual" communicates negative characteristics about the speaker and establishes distance between the speaker and listener.

Discourse is tied closely to social structure, so the messages communicated through the use of labels depend greatly on the social position of the speaker. If the speaker and listener are close friends, then the use of particular labels may not lead to distancing in the relationship or be offensive. But if the speaker and listener are strangers, then these same labels might invoke anger or close the lines of communication.

Furthermore, if the speaker is in a position of power, then he or she has potentially an even greater impact. For example, when politicians use discourse that invokes racist, anti-Semitic, or other ideologies of intolerance, many people become concerned because of the influence they may have. These concerns were raised in the 2002 presidential elections in France over candidate Jean-Marie Le Pen, whose comments over the years have raised concerns about anti-immigrant, anti-Semitic discourse. Similar concerns have arisen over the political discourse of Austria's Joerg Haider and Louisiana's David Duke. Of course, political office is not the only powerful position from which to speak. Fundamentalist Christian leaders have caused concern with their antigay discourse.

Judith and Tom collaborated on a study about reactions to labeling. We asked white students which of the following they preferred to be called: white, Caucasian, white American, Euro-American, European American, Anglo, or WASP. They did not favor such specific labels as "WASP" or "European American" but seemed to prefer a more general label like "white." We concluded that they probably had never thought about what labels they preferred to be called. As we noted in Chapter 5, the more powerful aspects of identity seem to go unnoticed; for many people, whiteness just "is," and the preferred label is a general one that does not specify origin or history. Individuals from powerful groups generally do the labeling of others; they themselves do not get labeled (Martin, Krizek, Nakayama, & Bradford, 1996). For example, when men are asked to describe their identities, they often forget to specify gender as part of their identity. Women, in contrast, often include gender as a key element in their identity. This may mean that men are the defining norm and that women exist in relation to this norm. We can see this in the labels we use for men and women and for people of color. We rarely refer to a "male physician" or a "white physician," but we do refer to a "female doctor" or a "black doctor."

This "invisibility" of being white may be changing. Apparently, whites are becoming increasingly more conscious of their white identity, which may change the practice of labeling. Perhaps as the white norm is challenged by changing demographics, by increased interaction in a more diverse United States, and by racial politics, more whites may think about the meaning of labels for their own group.

MOVING BETWEEN LANGUAGES

Multilingualism

People who speak two languages are often called **bilingual**; people who speak more than two languages are considered **multilingual**. Rarely do bilinguals speak both languages with the same level of fluency. More commonly, they prefer to use one language over another, depending on the context and the topic.

Sometimes entire nations are bilingual or multilingual. Belgium, for example, has three national languages (Dutch, German, and French), and Switzerland has four (French, German, Italian, and Romansh).

On either the individual or the national level, multilinguals must engage in language negotiation. That is, they need to work out, whether explicitly or implicitly, which language to use in a given situation. These decisions are sometimes clearly embedded in power relations. For example, French was the court language during the reign of Catherine the Great in 18th-century Russia. French was considered the language of culture, the language of the elite, whereas Russian was considered a vulgar language, the language of the uneducated and the unwashed. Special-interest groups in many U.S. states, especially Arizona and California, have attempted to pass laws declaring English the official language. These attempts reflect a power bid to determine which language will be privileged.

Sometimes a language is chosen as a courtesy to others. For example, Tom joined a small group going to see the fireworks display at the Eiffel Tower on Bastille Day one year. (Bastille Day is a French national holiday, celebrated on July 14, to commemorate the storming of the Bastille prison in 1789 and the beginning of the French

bilingual The ability to speak two languages fluently or at least competently.
multilingual The ability to speak more than two languages fluently or at least competently.

Chris Matthews, host of MSNBC's *Hardball*, explains how he came to realize he had an accent in an interview with Blake Miller of Philadelphia Magazine. How do you know if you have an accent?

I don't think I ever realized I had a Philadelphia accent until I was away for a while in college and I began to understand that we really did talk differently than most people. Then I went to work in Washington for my first job in the Senate, and I remember meeting some people from out West, from Utah, and I would say 'wooder' and they would say 'wah-ter.' It was like I was talking to cowboys.

We're the only city on the East Coast that pronounces our R's. They don't do it in Boston, certainly. They don't do it in New York. But we do it in Philly. We are loyal to the R.

We add an extra syllable to words, like Act-a-me. It's the extra, unexplained syllable that I think is the heart of the Philadelphia accent. It separates us from the lesser forms out there.

Source: From "Accent on Chris Matthews," *Philadelphia Magazine*, September 2005, p. 100.

Revolution.) One woman in the group asked, "*Alors, on parle français ou anglais?* [Are we speaking French or English?]" Because one man felt quite weak at English, French was chosen as the language of the evening.

The reasons that people become bilingual reflect trends identified in Chapter 1—changes that drive the need for intercultural communication. Bilingualism results from these imperatives, as people move from one country to another, as businesses expand into international markets, and so on. More personal imperatives also drive people to become bilingual. Alice Kaplan (1993), a French professor at Duke University, notes, "Speaking a foreign language is, for me and my students, a chance for growth, for freedom, a liberation from the ugliness of our received ideas and mentalities" (p. 211). Many people use foreign languages to escape from a legacy of oppression in their own languages.

Perhaps it is easier to think of language as a "prisonhouse," to borrow Fredric Jameson's (1972) metaphor. All of the semantic, syntactic, pragmatic, and phonetic systems are enmeshed in a social system from which there is no escape, except through the learning of another language. Consider the case of Sam Sue (1992), a Chinese American born and raised in Mississippi, who explains his own need to negotiate these social systems—often riddled by stigmatizing stereotypes—by changing the way he speaks:

> *Northerners see a Southern accent as a signal that you're a racist, you're stupid, or you're a hick. Regardless of what your real situation is. So I reacted to that by adapting the way I speak. If you talked to my brother, you would definitely know he was from the South. But as for myself, I remember customers telling my dad, "Your son sounds like a Yankee."*
> *(p. 4)*

Among the variations in U.S. English, the southern accent unwittingly communicates many negative stereotypes. Escaping into another accent is, for some, the only way to escape the stereotypes.

Learning another language is never easy, but the rewards of knowing another language are immense. Language acquisition studies have shown that it is nearly impossible for individuals to learn the language of a group of people they dislike. For instance, Tom was talking to a student about meeting the program's foreign language requirement. The student said, "I can't take Spanish. I'm from California." When Tom said that he did not understand what she meant, she blurted that she hated Mexicans and wouldn't take Spanish under any circumstances. As her well-entrenched racism suggested, she would indeed never learn Spanish.

An interesting linguistic phenomenon known as **interlanguage** has implications for the teaching and learning of other languages. Interlanguage refers to a kind of communication that emerges when speakers of one language are speaking in another language. The native language's semantics, syntactics, pragmatics, and phonetics often overlap into the second language and create a third way of communicating. For example, many English-speaking female students of German might say, "*Ich bin ein Amerikanerin*," which is incorrect German but is structured on the English way of saying, "I am an American." The correct form is "*Ich bin Amerikanerin*." The insertion of "*ein*" reveals the English language overlap.

In his work on moving between languages, Tom has noted that this creation of other ways of communicating can offer ways of resisting dominant cultures. He notes that "the powerful potential of translation for discovering new voices can violate and disrupt the systemic rules of both languages" (Nakayama, 1997, p. 240). He gives the example of "shiros," which is used by some Japanese Americans to refer to whites.

---

interlanguage A kind of communication that emerges when speakers of one language are speaking in another language. The native language's semantics, syntactics, pragmatics, phonetics, and language styles often overlap and create a third way of communicating.

Shiro is the color white, and adding an s at the end is the English grammatical way to pluralize words. Tom explains,

> Using the color for people highlights the overlay of the ideology of the English language onto Japanese and an odd mixing that probably would not make sense to people who speak only English or Japanese, or those who do not live in the spaces between them. (p. 242n)

Different people react differently to the dialectical tensions of a multilingual world. Some work hard to learn other languages and other ways of communicating, even if they make numerous errors along the way. Others retreat into their familiar languages and ways of living. The dialectical tensions that arise over different languages and different systems of meaning are played out around the world. But these dialectical tensions never disappear; they are always posing new challenges for intercultural communicators.

Translation and Interpretation

Because no one can learn all of the languages in the world, we must rely on translation and interpretation—two distinct but important means of communicating across language differences. The European Union (EU), for example, has a strict policy of recognizing all of the languages of its constituent members. Hence, many translators and interpreters are hired by the EU to help bridge the linguistic gaps.

Translation generally refers to the process of producing a written text that refers to something said or written in another language. The original language text of a translation is called the **source text**; the text into which it is translated is the **target text**.

Interpretation refers to the process of verbally expressing what is said or written in another language. Interpretation can either be simultaneous, with the interpreter speaking at the same time as the original speaker, or consecutive, with the interpreter speaking only during the breaks provided by the original speaker.

As we know from language theories, languages are entire systems of meaning and consciousness that are not easily rendered into another language in a word-for-word equivalence. The ways in which different

---

translation The process of producing a written text that refers to something said or written in another language.
source text The original language text of a translation. (See also **target text**.)
target text The new language text into which the original language text is translated. (See also **source text**.)
interpretation The process of verbally expressing what is said or written in another language.

languages convey views of the world are not equivalent, as we noted previously. Consider the difficulty involved simply in translating names of colors. The English word *brown* might be translated as any of these French words, depending on how the word is used: *roux, brun, bistre, bis, marron, jaune,* and *gris* (Vinay & Darbelnet, 1977, p. 261).

Issues of Equivalency and Accuracy Some languages have tremendous flexibility in expression; others have a limited range of words. The reverse may be true, however, for some topics. This slippage between languages is both aggravating and thrilling for translators and interpreters. Translation studies traditionally have tended to emphasize issues of **equivalency** and accuracy. That is, the focus, largely from linguistics, has been on comparing the translated meaning with the original meaning. However, for those interested in the intercultural communication process, the emphasis is not so much on equivalence as on the bridges that people construct to cross from one language to another.

Many U.S. police departments are now hiring officers who are bilingual, because they must work with a multilingual public. In Arizona, like many other states, Spanish is a particularly important language. Let's look at a specific case in which a police detective for the Scottsdale (Arizona) Police Department explained an unusual phrase:

> *Detective Ron Bayne has heard his share of Spanish phrases while on the job. But he recently stumped a roomful of Spanish-speaking police officers with an unusual expression.*
>
> *A suspect said, "Me llevaron a tocar el piano [They took me to play the piano]."*
>
> *"I knew it couldn't mean that," said Bayne, a translator for the Scottsdale Police Department. "But I had no idea what it really meant." (Meléndez, 2002, p. B1)*

This slang term, popular with undocumented aliens, highlights the differences between "street" Spanish and classroom Spanish. It also points to the importance of context in understanding meaning. In this context, we know that the police did not take a suspect to play a piano. Instead, this suspect was saying that the police had fingerprinted him. The varieties of expression in Spanish reflect social class and other differences that are not always communicated through translation or interpretation.

Yet the context for interpreters and translators must also be rec-

---

equivalency An issue in translation, the condition of being equal in meaning, value, quantity, and so on.

ognized. The need for Spanish speakers in the U.S. Southwest represents only the tip of the "linguistic iceberg." The recent attacks on the World Trade Center have created another need for translators and interpreters:

> *The CIA is looking for a few good speakers of Pashto. And Farsi, Dari and Arabic, too.*
>
> *Backed with new funds from the White House in the wake of the Sept. 11 terrorist attacks, the spy agency has embarked on an urgent mission to reinforce its depleted ranks of specialists in the languages and cultures of other central Asia nations.*
>
> *It is a part of the world the United States virtually ignored for the last decade. (Strobel, 2001)*

The changing context for intelligence work has changed the context for translators and interpreters as well, to say nothing of the languages that are highly valued. These issues, although beyond the scope of equivalency and accuracy, are an important part of the dynamic of intercultural communication.

The Role of the Translator or Interpreter We often assume that translators and interpreters are "invisible," that they simply render into the target language whatever they hear or read. The roles that they play as intermediaries, however, often regulate how they render the original. Tom believes that it is not always appropriate to translate everything that one speaker is saying to another, in exactly the same way, because the potential for misunderstanding because of cultural differences might be too great. Translation is more than merely switching languages; it also involves negotiating cultures. Writer Elisabeth Marx (1999) explains,

> *It is not sufficient to be able to translate—you have to comprehend the subtleties and connotations of the language. Walter Hasselkus, the German chief executive of Rover, gave a good example of this when he remarked: "When the British say that they have a 'slight' problem, I know that it has to be taken seriously." There are numerous examples of misunderstandings between American English and British English, even though they are, at root, the same language. (p. 95)*

It might be helpful to think of translators and interpreters as cultural brokers who must be highly sensitive to the contexts of intercultural communication.

We often assume that anyone who knows two languages can be a

POINT OF VIEW

Translation can create amusing and interesting intercultural barriers. Consider the following translation experiences.

1. A Canadian importer of Turkish shirts destined for Quebec used a dictionary to help him translate into French the label "Made in Turkey." His final translation: "Fabriqué en Dinde." True, "dinde" means "turkey." But it refers to the bird, not the country, which in French is Turquie.

2. An Otis Engineering Corp. display at a Moscow exhibition produced as many snickers among the Russians as it did praise. Company executives were not happy to learn that a translator had rendered in Russian a sign identifying "completion equipment" as "equipment for orgasms."

3. Japan's Olfa Corp. sold knives in the United States with the warning "Caution: Blade extremely sharp. Keep out of children."

4. In one country, the popular Frank Perdue Co. slogan, "It takes a tough man to make a tender chicken," read in local language something akin to "It takes a sexually excited man to make a chicken affectionate."

5. One company in Taiwan, trying to sell diet goods to expatriates living there, urged consumers to buy its product to add "roughage" to their systems. The instructions claimed that a person should consume enough roughage until "your tool floats." Someone dropped the "s" from "stool."

6. How about the Hong Kong dentist who advertised "Teeth extracted by the latest Methodists."

7. Or the hotel in notoriously polluted Mexico City that proclaimed: "The manager has personally passed all the water served here."

8. General Motors Corp.'s promotion in Belgium for its car that had a "body by Fisher" turned out to be, in the Flemish translation, "corpse by Fisher."

Source: From Laurel Delaney, "8 Global Marketing Gaffes," 2002. http://www.marketingprofs.com/2/delany2.asp

translator or an interpreter. Research has shown, however, that high levels of fluency in two languages do not necessarily make someone a good translator or interpreter. The task obviously requires the knowledge of two languages. But that's not enough. Think about all of the people you know who are native English speakers. What might account for why some of them are better writers than others? Knowing English, for example, is a prerequisite for writing in English, but this knowledge does not necessarily make a person a good writer. Because of the complex relationships between people, particularly in intercultural situations, translation and interpretation involve far more than linguistic equivalence, which traditionally has been the focus.

In his 1993 book *Contemporary Translation Theories*, linguist Edwin Gentzler speculates that the 1990s "might be characterized as experiencing a boom in translation theory" (p. 181). In part, this "boom" was fueled by a recognition that the traditional focus in translation studies is too limiting to explain the wide variety of ways that meanings might be communicated. Gentzler concludes, "With such insight, perhaps we will be less likely to dismiss that which does not fit into or measure up to our standards, and instead open ourselves to alternative ways of perceiving—in other words, to invite real intra- and intercultural communication" (p. 199).

The field of translation studies is rapidly becoming more central to academic inquiry as it moves from the fringes to an area of inquiry with far-reaching consequences for many disciplines. These developments will have a tremendous impact on how academics approach intercultural communication. Perhaps intercultural communication scholars will begin to play a larger role in the developments of translation studies.

LANGUAGE AND IDENTITY

In the previous chapter, we discussed cultural identity and its complexities. One part of our cultural identity is tied to the language(s) that we speak. As U.S. Americans, we are expected to speak English. If we travel to Nebraska, we assume the people there speak English. When we travel around the world, we expect Russians to speak Russian, Koreans to speak Korean, and Indonesians to speak Indonesian. But things get more involved, as we noted in Chapter 4, when we consider why Brazilians speak Portuguese, Congolese speak French, and Australians speak English. The relationship between language and culture becomes more complicated when we look at the complexity of cultural identities at home and abroad.

Language and Cultural Group Identity

When Tom was at the Arizona Book Festival recently, a white man held up a book written in Chinese and asked Tom what it was about. "I don't read Chinese," Tom replied. "Well, you should," he retorted and walked away. Two assumptions seem to be at work here: (1) Anyone who looks Asian must be Chinese, and (2) Asian Americans should be able to speak their ancestral languages. This tension has raised important identity questions for Asian Americans. Writer Henry Moritsugu (1992), who was born and raised in Canada and who later immigrated to the United States, explains,

> *There is no way we could teach our children Japanese at home. We speak English. It wasn't a conscious effort that we did this. . . . It was more important to be accepted. . . . I wish I could speak the language better. I love Japanese food. I love going to Japanese restaurants. Sometimes I see Japanese groups enjoying themselves at karaoke bars . . . I feel definitely Western, more so than Asian. . . . But we look Asian, so you have to be aware of who you are. (p. 99)*

The ability to speak another language can be important in how people view their group membership.

Many Chicana/os also have to negotiate a relationship to Spanish, whether or not they speak the language. Communication scholar Jacqueline Martinez (2000) explains,

> *It has taken a long time for me to come to see and feel my own body as an ethnic body. Absent the capacity to express myself in Spanish, I am left to reach for less tangible traces of an ethnic self that have been buried under layers of assimilation into Anglo culture and practice. . . . Yet still there is a profoundly important way in which, until this body of mine can speak in Spanish, gesture in a "Spanishly" way, and be immersed in Spanish-speaking communities, there will remain ambiguities about its ethnic identification. (p. 44)*

Although some people who migrate to the United States retain the languages of their homelands, many other U.S. American families no longer speak the language of their forebears. Historically, bilingualism was openly discouraged in the United States. Writer Gloria Anzaldúa (1987) recalls how she was discouraged from speaking Spanish:

> *I remember being caught speaking Spanish at recess—that was good for three licks on the knuckles with a sharp ruler. I remember being sent to the corner of the classroom for "talking back" to the Anglo teacher when all I was trying to do was tell her how to pronounce my name. If you*

Languages develop in relation to their environments. Changes in the global climate are bringing vast changes to the environment of the Arctic regions. Note how the indigenous languages are working to adapt to these changes.

What are the words used by indigenous peoples in the Arctic for "hornet," "robin," "elk," "barn owl" or "salmon?"

If you don't know, you're not alone.

Many indigenous languages have no words for legions of new animals, insects and plants advancing north as global warming thaws the polar ice and lets forests creep over tundra.

"We can't even describe what we're seeing," said Sheila Watt-Cloutier, chair of the Inuit Circumpolar Conference, which says it represents 155,000 people in Canada, Alaska, Greenland and Russia.

In the Inuit language Inuktitut, robins are known just as the "bird with the red breast," she said. Inuit hunters in north Canada recently saw some ducks but have not figured out what species they were, in Inuktitut or any other language.

[. . .]

In Arctic Europe, birch trees are gaining ground and Saami reindeer herders are seeing roe deer or even elk, a forest-dwelling cousin of moose, on former lichen pastures.

"I know about 1,200 words for reindeer—we classify them by age, sex, color, antlers," said Nils Isak Eira, who manages a herd of 2,000 reindeer in north Norway.

"I know just one word for elk—'sarvva'," said 50-year-old Eira. "But the animals are so unusual that many Saami use the Norwegian word 'elg.' When I was a child it was like a mythical creature."

Source: From A. Doyle, "As Ice Melts, Arctic People at Loss for Words." MSNBC, November 24, 2004. Available at http://www.msnbc.msn.com/id/6530026.

want to be American, speak "American." If you don't like it, go back to Mexico where you belong. (p. 53)

Even today we often hear arguments in favor of making English the official language of the nation. The interconnections between cultural identity and language are indeed strong.

What about the challenges facing cultural groups whose languages are nearing extinction? Whereas millions of people speak Chinese,

Japanese, and Spanish, some languages are spoken by only a handful of people. One Osage Indian laments,

> *Even though I am painfully aware of what needs to be said and how to say it, my words usually fall upon noncomprehending ears, for only a handful of Osage Indians can speak or understand our tribal language. And, after each such occasion, I often silently lament that this may be the last time the Osage language is publicly spoken and that within a mere 10 years it might not ever be heard again. (quoted in Pratt & Buchanan, 2000, p. 155)*

Many Native American tribes are currently working to save their tribal languages, but they face enormous challenges. Yet it is their culture and identity that are at risk.

The languages we speak and the languages others think we should speak can create barriers in intercultural communication. Why might some U.S. Americans assume that someone whose ancestors came from China continues to speak Chinese, while someone whose ancestors came from Germany or Denmark is assumed to no longer speak German or Dutch? Here, again, we can see how identity, language, and history create tensions between who we think we are and who others think we are.

Code Switching

Code switching is a technical term in communication that refers to the phenomenon of changing languages, dialects, or even accents. People code switch for several reasons: (1) to accommodate the other speakers, (2) to avoid accommodating others, or (3) to express another aspect of their cultural identity.

Linguistics professor Jean-Louis Sauvage (2002) studied the complexity of code switching in Belgium, which involves not only dialects but languages as well. He explains the practical side of code switching:

> *For example, my house was built by a contractor who sometimes resorted to Flemish subcontractors. One of these subcontractors was the electrician. I spoke Dutch to him but had to use French words when I referred to technical notions that I did not completely understand even in French. This was not a problem for the electrician, who knew these terms in Dutch as well as in French but would have been unable to explain them to me in French. (p. 159)*

---

code switching A technical term in communication that refers to the phenomenon of changing languages, dialects, or even accents.

Given the complex language policies and politics in Belgium, code switching takes on particularly important political meaning. Who code switches and who does not is a frequent source of contestation. In her work on code switching, communication scholar Karla Scott (2000) discusses how the use of different ways of communicating creates different cultural contexts and different relationships between the conversants. Based on a series of interviews with black women, she notes "the women's shared recognition that in markedly different cultural worlds their language use is connected to identity" (p. 246). She focuses on the use of the words *girl* and *look* as they relate to communicative practices in different contexts. She identifies three areas in which code switching occurs with *girl*: "(1) in discourse about differences between Black and White women's language use, (2) in discourse about being with other Black women, and (3) in uses of '*girl*' as a marker in discourse among participants during the interview" (p. 241). The use of *look* in code switching occurs in three contexts as well: "(1) in discussions and descriptions of talking like a Black woman versus White women's talk, (2) in the women's reports of interactions with Whites, both male and female, and (3) in the women's reports of interactions with Black men" (p. 243). *Girl* creates a sense of solidarity and shared identity among black women, whereas *look* is particularly important in white-dominated contexts because it asserts a different identity. Thus, code switching between these two words reflects different ways of communicating and different identities and relationships among those communicating.

LANGUAGE POLITICS AND POLICIES

Nations can enact laws recognizing an official language, such as French in France or Irish in Ireland (despite the fact that more Irish speak English than Irish). Some nations have multiple official languages. For instance, Canada has declared English and French to be the official languages. Here in the United States, there is no official national language, although English is the de facto national language. Yet the state of Hawai'i has two official languages, English and Hawaiian. Other U.S. entities have also declared official languages, such as Guam (Chamorro and English), New Mexico (English and Spanish), and Samoa (English and Samoan). Laws or customs that determine which language is spoken where and when are referred to as **language policies**. These

---

language policies Laws or customs that determine which language will be spoken, when and where.

policies often emerge from the politics of language use. As mentioned previously, the court of Catherine the Great of Russia used not Russian but French, which was closely tied to the politics of social and economic class. The history of colonialism also influences language policies. Thus, Portuguese is the official national language of Mozambique, and English and French are the official national languages of Cameroon.

Language policies are embedded in the politics of class, culture, ethnicity, and economics. They do not develop as a result of any supposed quality of the language itself. There are different motivations behind the establishment of language policies that guide the status of different languages in a place. Sometimes nations decide on a national language as part of a process of driving people to assimilate into the national culture. If the state wishes to promote assimilation, language policies that encourage everyone to speak the official language and conduct business in that language are promoted. One such group, U.S. English, Inc., has been advocating for the establishment of English as the official language of the United States.

Sometimes nations develop language policies as a way of protecting minority languages so these languages do not disappear. Welsh in Wales is one example, but Irish in Ireland and Frisian in Germany and the Netherlands are legally protected languages. Some language policies recognize the language rights of its citizens wherever they are in the nation. One example of this is Canada (English and French). Another is Kenya (Swahili and English). Government services are available in either language throughout the nation.

Other language policies are governed by location. In Belgium, Dutch (Flemish) is the official language in Flanders in the north part of the country. French is the official language in Wallonia in the South, and German is the official language in the Eastern Cantons bordering Germany. Thus, if you are boarding a train to go from Antwerp to Liège, you would need to look for "Luik" in the Antwerp train station. When you returned to the train station in Liège to go back, you would look for the train to "Anvers." The signs would not be posted in both languages, except in the Brussels-Capital region (the only bilingual part of the nation).

Sometimes language policies are developed with language parity, but the implementation is not equal. In Cameroon, for example, English and French are both official languages, although 247 indigenous languages are also spoken. Although German was the initial colonizer of Cameroon, Britain and France took over in 1916—with most of the territory going to France—and these "new colonial masters then sought to impose their languages in the newly acquired territory"

(Echu, 2003, p. 34). At independence in 1960, French Cameroon established French as its official language and English became the official language in the former British Cameroon areas once they joined together to form Cameroon. Once united in 1961, Cameroon established both languages as official languages. Because French speakers are far more numerous than English speakers, "French has a de facto dominance over English in the areas of administration, education and the media. In fact, it is not an exaggeration to say that French influence as expressed in language, culture and political policy prevails in all domains" (p. 39). So although Cameroon is officially bilingual, French dominates in nearly all domains, because most of the people are French speakers. Thus, "what appears to be a language policy for the country is hardly clearly defined, in spite of the expressed desire to promote English-French bilingualism and protect the indigenous languages" (p. 44). European colonialism has left its mark in this African nation, and the language policy and language realities remain to be worked out.

We can view the development of language policies as reflecting the dialectical tensions between the nation's history and its future, between the various language communities, and between economic and political relations inside and outside the nation. Language policies can help resolve or exacerbate these tensions.

LANGUAGE AND GLOBALIZATION

In a world in which people, products, and ideas can move easily around the globe, rapid changes are being made in the languages spoken and learned. Globalization has sparked increased interest in some languages while leaving others to disappear.

The dream of a common international language has long marked Western ways of thinking. Ancient Greeks viewed the world as filled with Greek speakers or those who were *barbaroi* (barbarians). The Romans attempted to establish Latin and Greek, which led to the subsequent establishment of Latin as the learned language of Europe. Latin was eventually replaced by French, which was spoken, as we have noted, throughout the elite European communities and became the **lingua franca** of Europe. More recently, Esperanto was created as an international language, and although there are Esperanto speakers, it has not attained wide international acceptance. Today, Ancient Greek and Latin, as well as French, still retain some of their elite status, but

---

lingua franca A commonly shared language that is used as a medium of communication between people of different languages.

POINT OF VIEW

Harumi Befu, emeritus professor at Stanford University, discusses the consequences of English domination for monolingual Americans.

Instead of language enslavement and intellectual imperialism, however, one more often is told of the benefit of learning a second language, such as English. For example, non-native English speakers can relativize their own language and appreciate each language on its own terms. It was Goethe who said that one who does not know a foreign language does not know his/her own language. . . .

Thanks to the global dominance of their country, American intellectuals have acquired the "habitus" (Bourdieu) of superiority, whereby they exercise the license of expressing their thoughts in English wherever they go instead of showing respect to locals through expending efforts to learn their language. This privileged position, however, spells poverty of the mind.

For their minds are imprisoned in a single language; they are unable to liberate their minds through relativizing English. In short, other things being equal, monolingual Americans (not all Americans are monolingual) are the most provincial and least cosmopolitan among those who traffic in the global interlinguistic community—a price they pay for the strength of the country backing them.

Source: From H. Befu, "English Language Intellectual Imperialism and Its Consequences," *Newsletter: Intercultural Communication*, 37 (Intercultural Communication Institute, Kanda University of International Studies, Japan), June 2000, p. 1.

"English is the de facto language of international communication today" (Tsuda, 1999, p. 153).

Many native English speakers are happy with the contemporary status of the language. They feel much more able to travel around the world, without the burden of having to learn other ways of communicating, given that many people around the world speak English. Having a common language also facilitates intercultural communication, but it can also create animosity among those who must learn the other's language. Dominique Noguez (1998) explains,

In these language affairs, as in many other moral or political affairs— tolerance, for example—is the major criteria for reciprocity. Between comparable languages and equal countries, this must be: I speak and learn your language and you speak and learn mine. Otherwise, it's sadomasochism and company—the sadist being simply the one with the gall to say to another: "I am not speaking your language, therefore speak mine!" This is what Anglo-Saxons have been happily doing since at least 1918. (p. 234)

(En ces affaires de langue, comme en bien d'autres affaires morales ou politiques—la tolérance, par exemple—le critère majeur, c'est la réciprocité. Entre langues comparables et pays égaux, ce devrait être: je parle et enseigne votre langue et vous parlez et enseignez la mienne. Autrement, c'est sadomasochisme et compagnie—le sadique étant tout simplement celui qui l'aplomb de declarer à l'autre: "Je ne parle pas votre langue, parlez donc la mienne!" C'est ce que font, avec assez de bonheur, les Anglo-Saxons depuis au moins 1918.)

Learning a foreign language is never easy, of course, but the dominance of English as the lingua franca raises important issues for intercultural communication.

What is the relationship between our four touchstones and this contemporary linguistic situation? That is, how do culture, communication, power, and context play out in the domination of English? First, the intimate connections between language and culture mean that the diffusion of English is tied to the spread of U.S. American culture around the world. Is this a new form of colonialism? If we consider issues of power, what role does the United States play in the domination of English on the world scene? How does this marginalize or disem-power those who are not fluent in English in intercultural communication? What kinds of resentment might be fostered by forcing people to recognize their disempowerment?

In what intercultural contexts is it appropriate to assume that others speak English? For English speakers, this is a particularly unique context. Latvians, for example, cannot attend international meetings and assume that others will speak Latvian; and Albanians will have difficulty transacting international trade if they assume that others know their language.

In his study of the developing use of English in Switzerland, Christof Demont-Heinrich (2005) focused on Switzerland in global and local contexts, cultural and national identity issues, power, and communication. The nation recognizes four national languages— French, German, Italian, and Romansh. Three of these are recognized as official languages—German, French, and Italian—which means that all national government materials are available in the three official languages. Some of the power differences among these language communities are reflected in the demographics from the 2000 census in which "63.9% of respondents named German, 19.5% listed French, 6.6% claimed Italian, and 0.5% named Romansch as their first language" (p. 72). In this context, English has become more influential,

Colonial histories have influenced how people communicate. In Brazil, colonialists developed their own language to communicate across the many indigenous communities they colonized. Although imposed by colonists, today this general language is used to resist domination by Portuguese. How does a language serve political ends? What are the politics of speaking English in the world today?

When the Portuguese arrived in Brazil five centuries ago, they encountered a fundamental problem: the indigenous peoples they conquered spoke more than 700 languages. Rising to the challenge, the Jesuit priests accompanying them concocted a mixture of Indian, Portuguese and African words they called "língua geral," or the "general language," and imposed it on their colonial subjects.

Elsewhere in Brazil, língua geral as a living, spoken tongue died off long ago. But in this remote and neglected corner of the Amazon where Brazil, Colombia and Venezuela meet, the language has not only managed to survive, it has made a remarkable comeback in recent years. [. . .]

Two years ago, in fact, Nheengatú, as the 30,000 or so speakers of língua geral call their language, reached a milestone. By vote of the local council, São Gabriel da Cachoeira became the only municipality in Brazil to recognize a language other than Portuguese as official, conferring that status on língua geral and two local Indian tongues.

As a result, Nheengatú, which is pronounced neen-gah-TOO and means "good talk," is now a language that is permitted to be taught in local schools, spoken in courts and used in government documents. People who can speak língua geral have seen their value on the job market rise and are now being hired as interpreters, teachers and public health aides. [. . .]

"Nheengatú came to us as the language of the conqueror," explained Renato da Silva Matos, a leader of the Federation of Indigenous Organizations of the Rio Negro. "It made the original languages die out" because priests and government officials punished those who spoke any language other than Portuguese or Nheengatú.

But in modern times, the language acquired a very different significance. As the dominion of Portuguese advanced and those who originally imposed the language instead sought its extinction, Nheengatú became "a mechanism of ethnic, cultural and linguistic resistance," said Persida Miki, a professor of education at the Federal University of Amazonas.

Source: From L. Rohter, "Language Born of Colonialism Thrives Again in Amazon," *New York Times*, August 28, 2005, p. A6.

not only among the banking and financial sectors, but increasingly in "consumer and pop culture" (p. 74). Recently, as the initiation of the Zürich canton, a proposal was proposed to allow English to be the first foreign language taught in school (rather than one of the national languages), and eight other German-speaking cantons quickly aligned themselves with this idea. The Swiss Conference of Cantonal Ministers of Education decided that by 2012 all Swiss students must study two foreign languages, but only one must be a national language. Given the value of English in the global economy and the use of English to communicate with other Swiss, one can see why there would be support for the Zürich position. Given the importance of Swiss national identity and their multilingual identity that is shaped by the languages spoken by other Swiss, one can also see why some French-speaking politicians preferred a policy where one of the other national languages would be the first foreign language. Zürich and other cantons are now proposing a ballot initiative that would "require just one foreign language to be taught, ideally English, at the primary school level" (p. 76), which would leave the other national language to be taught in secondary school. Demont-Heinrich concludes by noting that Romansh is likely headed for linguistic extinction, but what will happen to Switzerland? Can Swiss national identity be maintained with English? And what about the world? "Can such a colossal human social order sustain the diverse forms of human linguistic expression" (p. 81), or must humanity reduce its linguistic expression to a few dominant languages that facilitate economic trade? In the era of globalization, where economic growth is driven by external relations and trade, should we be studying Chinese?

DISCUSSION QUESTIONS

1. Why is it important for intercultural communication scholars to study both language and discourse?
2. What is the relationship between our language and the way we perceive reality?
3. What are some cross-cultural variations in language use and communication style?
4. What aspects of context influence the choice of communication style?
5. What does a translator or an interpreter need to know to be effective?
6. Why is it important to know the social positions of individuals and groups involved in intercultural communication?

7. Why do some people say that we should not use labels to refer to people but should treat everybody as individuals? Do you agree?

8. Why do people have such strong reactions to language policies, as in the "English-only" movement?

9. In what ways is the increasing and widespread use of English around the world both a positive and a negative change for U.S. Americans?

ACTIVITIES

1. *Regional Language Variations.* Meet in small groups with other class members and discuss variations in language use in different regions of the United States (accent, vocabulary, and so on). Identify perceptions that are associated with these variations.

2. *"Foreigner" Labels.* Meet in small groups with other class members and generate a list of labels used to refer to people from other countries who come to the United States—for example, "immigrants" and "aliens." For each label, identify a general connotation (positive, negative, mixed). Discuss how connotations of these words may influence our perceptions of people from other countries. Would it make a difference if we referred to them as "guests" or "visitors"?

3. *Values and Language.* Although computer-driven translations have improved dramatically over earlier attempts, translation is still intensely cultural. Communication always involves many layers of meaning, and when you move between languages, there are many more opportunities for misunderstanding. Try to express some important values that you have (e.g., freedom of the press) on this Web site, and see how they are retranslated in five different languages: http://www.tashian.com/multibabel/

REFERENCES

Anzaldúa, G. (1987). *Borderlands/la frontera: The new mestiza.* San Francisco: Spinsters/Aunt Lute.

Au, T. K. (1983). Chinese and English counterfactuals: The Sapir-Whorf hypothesis revisited. *Cognition, 15,* 155–187.

Au, T. K. (1984). Counterfactuals: In reply to Alfred Bloom. *Cognition, 17,* 239–302.

Au, T. K. (1985). Language and cognition. In L. L. Lloyd & R. L. Schiefelbusch (Eds.), *Language perspectives II.* Baltimore: University Park Press.

Barthes, R. (1980). *Elements of semiology* (A. Lavers & C. Smith, Trans.). New York: Hill & Wang. (Original work published 1968)

Befu, H. (2000, June). English language intellectual imperialism and its consequences. *Newsletter: Intercultural Communication, 37* (Intercultural Communication Institute, Kanda University of International Studies, Japan), p. 1.

Bloom, A. (1981). *The linguistic shaping of thought: A study in the impact of language on thinking in China and the West.* Hillsdale, NJ: Lawrence Erlbaum.

Bloom, A. (1984). Caution—the words you use may affect what you say: A response to Terry Kitfong Au's "Chinese and English counterfactuals: The Sapir-Whorf hypothesis revisited." *Cognition, 17,* 275–287.

Daniel, J. L., & Smitherman, G. (1990). How I got over: Communication dynamics in the Black community. In D. Carbaugh (Ed.), *Cultural communication and intercultural contact* (pp. 27–40). Hillsdale, NJ: Lawrence Erlbaum.

Demont-Heinrich, C. (2005). Language and national identity in the era of globalization: The case of English in Switzerland. *Journal of Communication Inquiry, 29,* 66–84.

Desnoes, E. (1985). The death system. In M. Blonsky (Ed.), *On signs* (pp. 39–42). Baltimore: Johns Hopkins University Press.

Echu, G. (2003). Coping with multilingualism: Trends in the evolution of language policy in Cameroon. *PhiN, 25, 31–46.* Available at http://web.fuberlin.de/phin/ phin25/p25t2.htm#ech99b

Gentzler, E. (1993). *Contemporary translation theories.* New York: Routledge.

Grice, H. (1975). Logic and conversation. In P. Cole & J. Morgan (Eds.), *Syntax and semantics: Vol. 3. Speech acts.* New York: Academic Press.

Gudykunst, W. B., & Matsumoto, Y. (1996). Crosscultural variability of communication in personal relationships. In W. B. Gudykunst, S.

Ting-Toomey, & T. Nishida (Eds.), *Communication in personal relationships across cultures* (pp. 19–56). Thousand Oaks, CA: Sage.

Gudykunst, W. B., & Ting-Toomey, S. (2003). *Communicating with strangers: An approach to intercultural communication* (4th ed.). New York: McGraw-Hill.

Hall, E. T. (1976). *Beyond culture.* Garden City, NY: Doubleday.

Heider, E. R., & Oliver, D. C. (1972). The structure of the color space in naming and memory for two languages. *Cognitive Psychology, 8,* 337–354.

Hoijer, H. (1994). The Sapir-Whorf hypothesis. In L. Samovar & R. E. Porter (Eds.), *Intercultural communication: A reader* (pp. 194–200). Belmont, CA: Wadsworth.

Jameson, F. (1972). *The prisonhouse of language.* Princeton, NJ: Princeton University Press.

Kaplan, A. (1993). *French lessons: A memoir.* Chicago: University of Chicago Press.

Karlson, D. (2005, December 2). Swastika on sign unnerves residents. *The Cape Codder.* http:// www.townonline.com/brewster/ localRegional/view.bg?articleid=38 2002&format=&page=1

Lakoff, G. (1989). Some empirical results about the nature of concepts. *Mind & Language, 4,* 103–129.

Martin, J. N., Krizek, R. L., Nakayama, T. K., & Bradford, L. (1996). Exploring whiteness: A study of self-labels for White Americans. *Communication Quarterly, 44,* 125–144.

Martinez, J. (2000). *Phenomenology of Chicana experience and identity: Communication and transformation in praxis.* Lanham, MD: Rowan & Littlefield.

Marx, E. (1999). *Breaking through culture shock.* London: Nicholas Brealey.

Meléndez, M. (2002, April 7). Police

try to connect, reach out in Spanish. *The Arizona Republic*, p. B1.

Moritsugu, H. (1992). To be more Japanese. In J. F. J. Lee (Ed.), *Asian Americans* (pp. 99–103). New York: New Press.

Nakayama, T. K. (1997). Les voix de l'autre. *Western Journal of Communication*, 61(2): 235–242.

Noguez, D. (1998). *La colonisation douce: Feu la langue française, carnets, 1968–1998*. Paris: Arléa.

Orbe, M. P. (1998). *Constructing co-cultural theory: An explication of culture, power, and communication*. Thousand Oaks, CA: Sage.

Pinker, S. (1994). *The language instinct: How the mind creates language*. New York: HarperCollins.

Pratt, S. B., & Buchanan, M. C. (2000). Wa-zha-zhe-i-e: Notions on a dying ancestral language. In A. Gonzàley, M. Houston, & U. Chen (Eds.), *Essays in culture, ethnicity, and communication* (3rd ed., pp. 155–163). Los Angeles: Roxbury.

Rhodda, M., & Grove, C. (1987). *Language, cognition, and deafness*. Hillsdale, NJ: Lawrence Erlbaum.

Sapir, E. (Ed.). (1921). *Language: An introduction to the study of speech*. New York: Harcourt, Brace & World.

Saussure, F. de. (1966). *Course in general linguistics* (C. Bally & A. Sechehaye, Eds. W. Baskin, Trans.). New York: McGraw-Hill.

Sauvage, J.-L. (2002). Code-switching: An everyday reality in Belgium. In J. N. Martin, T. K. Nakayama, & L. A. Flores (Eds.), *Readings in intercultural communication: Experiences and contexts* (2nd ed., pp. 156–161). New York: McGraw-Hill.

Scott, K. D. (2000). Crossing cultural borders: "Girl" and "look" as markers of identity in Black women's language use. *Discourse & Society*, 11(2): 237–248.

Steinfatt, T. M. (1989). Linguistic relativity: Toward a broader view.

In S. Ting-Toomey & F. Korzenny (Eds.), *Language, communication and culture* (pp. 35–78). Newbury Park, CA: Sage.

Strobel, W. P. (2001, November 16). Language, cultural void: CIA urgently seeks Afghan, central Asian linguists. *Detroit Free Press*. www.freep.com/news/ nw/terror2001/ spies16_20011116.htm

Sue, S. (1992). Growing up in Mississippi. In J. F. J. Lee (Ed.), *Asian Americans* (pp. 3–9). New York: New Press.

Tsuda, Y. (1999). The hegemony of English and strategies for linguistic pluralism: Proposing the ecology of language paradigm. In M. Tehranian (Ed.), *Worlds apart: Human security and global governance* (pp. 153–167). New York: Tauris.

Ueda, K. (1974). Sixteen ways to avoid saying "no" in Japan. In J. C. Condon & M. Saito (Eds.), *Intercultural encounters with Japan* (pp. 185–192). Tokyo: Simul Press.

Vinay, J. P., & Darbelnet, J. (1977). *Stylistique comparée du français et de l' anglais: Méthode de traduction*. Paris: Marcel Didier.

West, F. (1975). *The way of language: An introduction*. New York: Harcourt Brace Jovanovich.

Whorf, B. L. (1956). *Language, thought and reality*. Cambridge, MA: MIT Press.

NONVERBAL CODES AND CULTURAL SPACE

CHAPTER OBJECTIVES

After reading this chapter, you should be able to

1. Understand how verbal and nonverbal communication differ.

2. Discuss the types of messages that are communicated nonverbally.

3. Identify cultural universals in nonverbal communication.

4. Explain the limitations of some cross-cultural research findings.

5. Define and give an example of cross-cultural differences in facial expressions, proxemics, gestures, eye contact, chronemics, and silence.

6. Discuss the relationship between nonverbal communication and power.

7. Define cultural space.

8. Describe how cultural spaces are formed.

9. Explain why it is important to understand cultural spaces in intercultural communication.

10. Understand the differences between the modernist and postmodern views of cultural spaces.

Nonverbal elements of cultural communication are highly dynamic and play an important role in understanding intercultural communication. Reading nonverbal communication within various cultural spaces can be a key to survival, depending upon the situation. Consider the following scenario:

> *"It's your first day with your FTO (Field Training Officer). He drives the squad. You're too nervous to drive. You don't know where you're going anyway. And all this stuff is coming at you. The police radio's on; you can't make sense out of it; your FTO's talking to you constantly; you're hearing all these sounds from the street, languages you've never heard. You're seeing things you've never seen before. You're confused as hell.*
>
> *"Suddenly, your FTO stops the squad and says, 'Okay, let's get out, kid.' He jumps out and flings somebody against the wall and takes a gun off of him.*
>
> *"You're looking at him in total disbelief. How'd he know that? This guy must be the Great [Karnak]. Ten years later you've got a kid driving with you and you see something and you fling somebody against a wall. And the kid's looking at you like how did he know? And you know it's not magic." (quoted in Fletcher, 1992, pp. 137–139)*

Communication scholar Connie Fletcher goes on to note, "Urban police officers are one group for whom taking 'everyday life' for granted by screening out the discomfiting or confusing elements can have tragic consequences for both cops and citizens" (p. 135).

You may never become a police officer, but you certainly will find yourself in many intercultural communication situations and cultural spaces. Your own nonverbal communication may create additional problems and, if the behaviors are inappropriate for the particular cultural space, may exacerbate existing tensions. In other cases, your use of nonverbals might reduce tension and confusion.

The first part of this chapter focuses on the importance of understanding nonverbal aspects of intercultural communication. We can examine nonverbal communication in terms of the personal–contextual and the static–dynamic dialectics. Although nonverbal communication can be highly dynamic, personal space, gestures, and facial expressions are fairly static patterns of specific nonverbal communication codes. These patterns are the focus of the second part of this chapter. Finally, we investigate the concept of cultural space and the ways in which cultural identity is shaped and negotiated by the cultural spaces (home, neighborhood, and so on) that people occupy.

As urban police officers know, there is no guidebook to "reading the streets." The nonverbals of the street change constantly. For the same reason, we believe it is useless to list nonverbals to memorize. Instead, it will be more beneficial for you to learn the framework of nonverbal communication and cultural spaces so you can tap into the nonverbal systems of whatever cultural groups become relevant to your life. Understanding communication is a matter of understanding how to think dialectically about *systems* of meaning, and not discrete elements. Nonverbal intercultural communication is no exception.

THINKING DIALECTICALLY ABOUT NONVERBAL COMMUNICATION: DEFINING NONVERBAL COMMUNICATION

In this chapter, we discuss two forms of communication beyond speech. The first includes facial expression, personal space, gestures, eye contact, use of time, and conversational silence. (What is not said is often as important as what is spoken.) The second includes the cultural spaces that we occupy and negotiate. **Cultural spaces** are the social and cultural contexts in which our identity forms—where we grow up and where we live (not necessarily the physical homes and neighborhoods, but the cultural meanings created in these places).

In thinking dialectically, we need to consider the relationship between the nonverbal behavior and the cultural spaces in which the behavior occurs, and between the nonverbal behavior and the verbal message. Although there are patterns to nonverbal behaviors, they are not always culturally appropriate in all cultural spaces. Remember, too, that some nonverbal behaviors are cultural, whereas others are idiosyncratic, that is, peculiar to individuals.

Comparing Verbal and Nonverbal Communication

Recognizing Nonverbal Behavior Both verbal and nonverbal communication are symbolic, communicate meaning, and are patterned—that is, they are governed by contextually determined rules. Societies have different nonverbal languages, just as they have different spoken languages. However, some differences between nonverbal and verbal communication codes have important implications for intercultural interaction.

Let's look at some examples of these differences. The following incident occurred to Judith when she was new to Algeria, where she

---

cultural space The particular configuration of the communication that constructs meanings of various places.

lived for a while. One day she stood at her balcony and waved to one of the young Algerian teachers, who was walking across the school yard. Several minutes later, the young teacher knocked on the door, looking expectantly at Judith, as if summoned. Because Judith knew that it was uncommon in Algeria for men to visit women they didn't know well, she was confused. Why had he come to her door? Was it because she was foreign? After a few awkward moments, he left. A few weeks later, Judith figured it out. In Algeria (as in many other places), the U.S. "wave" is the nonverbal signal for "come here." The young teacher had assumed that Judith had summoned him to her apartment. As this example illustrates, rules for nonverbal communication vary among cultures and contexts.

Let's consider another example. Two U.S. students attending school in France were hitchhiking to the university in Grenoble for the first day of classes. A French motorist picked them up and immediately started speaking English to them. They wondered how he knew they spoke English. Later, when they took a train to Germany, the conductor walked into their compartment and berated them in English for putting their feet on the opposite seat. Again, they wondered how he had known that they spoke English. As these examples suggest, nonverbal communication entails more than gestures—even our appearance can communicate loudly. The students' appearance alone probably was a sufficient clue to their national identity. One of our students explains,

> When I studied abroad in Europe, London more specifically, our clothing as a nonverbal expression was a dead giveaway that we were from America. We dressed much more casual, wore more colors, and had words written on our T-shirts and sweatshirts. This alone said enough; we didn't even have to speak to reveal that we were Americans.

As these examples also show, nonverbal behavior operates at a subconscious level. We rarely think about how we stand, what gestures we use, and so on. Occasionally, someone points out such behaviors, which brings them to the conscious level. Consider one more example, from our student Suzanne:

> I was in Macedonia and I was traveling in a car, so I immediately put on my seat belt. My host family was very offended by this because buckling my seat belt meant I didn't trust the driver. After that I rode without a seat belt.

When misunderstandings arise, we are more likely to question our verbal communication than our nonverbal communication. We can search for different ways to explain verbally what we mean. We can also look up words in a dictionary or ask someone to explain unfamiliar words. In contrast, it is more difficult to identify nonverbal miscommunications or misperceptions.

Learning Nonverbal Behavior   Whereas we learn rules and meanings for language behavior in grammar and language arts lessons, we learn nonverbal meanings and behaviors by more implicit socialization. No one explains, "When you talk with someone you like, lean forward, smile, and touch the person frequently, because that will communicate that you really care about him or her." In many contexts in the United States, such behaviors communicate immediacy and positive meanings (Jones, 2004; Rocca, 2004). But how is it interpreted if someone does not display these behaviors?

Sometimes, though, we learn strategies for nonverbal communication. Have you ever been told to shake hands firmly when you meet someone? You may have learned that a limp handshake indicates a weak person. Likewise, many young women learn to cross their legs at the ankles and to keep their legs together when they sit. These strategies combine socialization and the teaching of nonverbal codes.

Coordinating Nonverbal and Verbal Behaviors   Nonverbal behaviors can reinforce, substitute for, or contradict verbal behaviors. For example, when we shake our heads and say "no," we are reinforcing verbal behavior. When we point instead of saying "over there," we are substituting nonverbal behavior for verbal communication. If we tell a friend, "I can't wait to see you," and then don't show up at the friend' s house, our nonverbal behavior is contradicting the verbal message. Because nonverbal communication operates at a less conscious level, we tend to think that people have less control over their nonverbal behavior. Therefore, we often think of nonverbal behaviors as conveying the "real" messages.

What Nonverbal Behavior Communicates

Although language is an effective and efficient means of communicating explicit information, nonverbal communication conveys **relational messages**—how we really feel about other people. Nonverbal behav-

---

relational messages Messages (verbal and nonverbal) that communicate how we feel about others.

ior also communicates **status** and power. For example, a supervisor may be able to touch subordinates, but it is usually unacceptable for subordinates to touch a supervisor. Broad, expansive gestures are associated with high status; conversely, holding the body in a tight, closed position communicates low status.

In addition, nonverbal behavior communicates **deception**. Early researchers believed that some nonverbal behaviors (e.g., avoiding eye contact or touching or rubbing the face) indicated lying. However, as more recent research has shown, deception is communicated by fairly idiosyncratic behaviors and seems to be revealed more by inconsistency in nonverbal communication than by specific nonverbal behaviors (Henningsen, Cruz, & Morr, 2000; Lock, 2004; Vrij, 2004).

Most nonverbal communication about affect, status, and deception happens at an unconscious level. For this reason, it plays an important role in intercultural interactions. Both pervasive and unconscious, it communicates how we feel about each other and about our cultural groups.

THE UNIVERSALITY OF NONVERBAL BEHAVIOR

Most traditional research in intercultural communication focuses on identifying cross-cultural differences in nonverbal behavior. How do culture, ethnicity, and gender influence nonverbal communication patterns? How universal is most nonverbal communication? Research traditionally has sought to answer these questions.

As we have observed in previous chapters, it is neither beneficial nor accurate to try to reduce individuals to one element of their identity (gender, ethnicity, nationality, and so on). Attempts to place people in discrete categories tend to reduce their complexities and to lead to major misunderstandings. However, we often classify people according to various categories to help us find universalities. For example, although we may know that not all Germans are alike, we may seek information about Germans in general to help us communicate better with individual Germans. In this section, we explore the extent to which nonverbal communication codes are universally shared. We also look for possible cultural variations in these codes that may serve as tentative guidelines to help us communicate better with others.

---

status The relative position an individual holds in social or organizational settings.
deception The act of making someone believe what is not true.

Recent Research Findings

Research investigating the universality of nonverbal communication has focused on four areas: (1) the relationship of human behavior to that of primates (particularly chimpanzees), (2) nonverbal communication of sensory-deprived children who are blind or deaf, (3) facial expressions, and (4) universal functions of nonverbal social behavior.

Chimpanzees and humans share many nonverbal behaviors. For example, both exhibit the eyebrow flash—a slight raising of the eyebrow that communicates recognition—one of the most primitive and universal animal behaviors. Primates and humans also share some facial expressions. Researcher Stephan Suomi (1988) concluded, after many animal studies, that "there are compelling parallels between specific facial expressions universally displayed by rhesus monkey infants and those expressed by human infants and young children and universally interpreted as indicative of basic emotional states" (p. 136). However, communication among monkeys, with fewer facial blends, or combinations of expressions, appears to be less complex than that among humans (Preuschoft, 2000).

Recent studies compared the facial expressions of children who were blind with those of sighted children and found many similarities. Even though the children who were blind couldn't see the facial expressions of others to mimic them, they still made the same expressions. This suggests some innate, genetic basis for these behaviors (Galati, Sini, Schmidt, & Tinti, 2003).

Indeed, many cross-cultural studies support the notion of some universality in nonverbal communication, particularly in **facial expressions**. Several facial gestures seem to be universal, including the eyebrow flash just described, the nose wrinkle (indicating slight social distancing), and the "disgust face" (a strong sign of social repulsion). It is also possible that grooming behavior is universal (as it is in animals), although it seems to be somewhat suppressed in Western societies (Schiefenhovel, 1997). Recent findings indicate that at least six basic emotions—including happiness, sadness, disgust, fear, anger, and surprise—are communicated by similar facial expressions in most societies. Expressions for these emotions are recognized by most cultural groups as having the same meaning (Ekman, 2003; Matsumoto, Franklin, Choi, Rogers, & Tatani, 2002).

Recent research on the universality of nonverbal behavior has also focused on how some nonverbal behavior fills universal human social needs for promoting social affiliation or bonding. For example, according to this research, laughter is not just a message about the positive

facial expressions Facial gestures that convey emotions and attitudes.

feeling of the sender but an attempt to influence others, to make them feel more positive toward the sender. Similarly, the social purpose of mimicry—when interaction partners adopt similar postures, gestures, and mannerisms—is to create an affective or social bond with others. Researchers point out that people in all cultures use these nonverbal behaviors to influence others, and over time, these behaviors that contributed to positive relationships were favored and eventually became automatic and nonconscious (Montepare, 2003; Patterson, 2003).

Although research may indicate universalities in nonverbal communication, some variations exist. The evoking stimuli (i.e., what causes the nonverbal behavior) may vary from one culture to another. Smiling, for example, is universal, but what prompts a person to smile may be culture specific. Similarly, there are variations in the rules for nonverbal behavior and the contexts in which nonverbal communication takes place. For example, people kiss in most cultures, but there is variation in who kisses whom and in what contexts. When French friends greet each other, they often kiss on both cheeks but never on the mouth. Friends in the United States usually kiss on greeting only after long absence, with the kiss usually accompanied by a hug. The rules for kissing also vary along gender lines.

Finally, it is important to look for larger cultural patterns in the nonverbal behavior, rather than trying simply to identify all of the cultural differences. Researcher David Matsumoto (1990) suggests that, although cultural differences in nonverbal patterns are interesting, noting these differences is not sufficient. Studying and cataloging every variation in every aspect of nonverbal behavior would be an overwhelming task. Instead, he recommends studying nonverbal communication patterns that vary with other cultural patterns, such as values.

For example, Matsumoto links cultural patterns in facial expressions with cultural values of power distance and individualism versus collectivism. Hypothetically, cultural groups that emphasize status differences will tend to express emotions that preserve these status differences. Matsumoto also suggests that within individualistic cultures the degree of difference in emotional display between in-groups and out-groups is greater than the degree of difference between the same groups in collectivistic societies. If these theoretical relationships hold true, we can generalize about the nonverbal behavior of many different cultural groups.

Nonverbal Codes

Facial Expressions   As noted earlier, there have been many investigations of the universality of facial expressions. Psychologists Paul

Ekman and Wallace Friesen (1987) conducted extensive and systematic research in nonverbal communication. They showed pictures of U.S. Americans' facial expressions reflecting six emotions thought to be universal to people in various cultural groups. They found that people in these various cultures consistently identified the same emotions reflected in the facial expressions in the photographs.

However, Ekman and Friesen's studies have been criticized for a few reasons. First, the studies don't tap into universality; that is, people may be able to recognize and identify the six emotions because of exposure to media. Also, the researchers presented a limited number of responses (multiple-choice answers) when they asked respondents to identify emotions expressed.

Later studies improved on this research. Researchers took many photographs, not always posed, of facial expressions of members from many different cultural groups; then they asked the subjects to identify the emotion conveyed by the facial expression. They showed these photographs to many different individuals in many different countries, including some without exposure to media. Their conclusion supports the notion of universality of facial expressions. Specifically, basic human emotions are expressed in a fairly finite number of facial expressions, and these expressions can be recognized and identified universally (Boucher & Carlson, 1980; Ekman, 2003).

Proxemics Unlike facial expressions, the norms for personal space seem to vary considerably from culture to culture. As you may recall from Chapter 2, proxemics is the study of how people use personal space, or the "bubble" around us that marks the territory between ourselves and others. O. M. Watson (1970), a proxemics specialist, investigated nonverbal communication between Arab and U.S. students after hearing many complaints from each group about the other. The Arab students viewed the U.S. students as distant and rude; the U.S. students saw the Arab students as pushy, arrogant, and rude. As Watson showed, the two groups were operating with different rules concerning personal space. Watson's research supports Edward Hall's (1966) observations about the cultural variations in how much distance individuals place between themselves and others. Hall distinguished contact cultures from noncontact cultures. He described **contact cultures** as those societies in which people stand closer together while talking, engage in more direct eye contact, use face-to-face body orientations more often while talking, touch more frequently, and speak in louder voices.

---

contact cultures Cultural groups in which people tend to stand close together and touch frequently when they interact—for example, cultural groups in South America, the Middle East, and southern Europe. (See **noncontact cultures**.)

He suggested that societies in South America and southern Europe are contact cultures, whereas those in northern Europe, the United States, and the Far East are **noncontact cultures**—in which people tend to stand farther apart when conversing, maintain less eye contact, and touch less often. Subsequent research seems to confirm Hall's and Watson's early studies (Andersen, Hecht, Hoobler, & Smallwood, 2002).

Of course, many other factors besides regional culture determine how far we stand from someone. Gender, age, ethnicity, context, and topic all influence the use of personal space. In fact, some studies have shown that regional culture is perhaps the least important factor. For example, in many Arab and Muslim societies, gender may be the over-riding factor, because unmarried men and women rarely stand close together, touch each other, or maintain direct eye contact. In contrast, male friends may stand very close together, kiss on the cheek, and even hold hands—reflecting loyalty, great friendship, and, most important, equality in status, with no sexual connotation (Fattah, 2005; Khuri, 2001).

Gestures   Gestures, perhaps even more so than personal space, vary greatly from culture to culture. The consequences for this variation can be quite dramatic, as President G. W. Bush discovered when he gave the "hook 'em horns" greeting to the University of Texas Longhorn marching band during his inauguration. The photos of this greeting were met with confusion in Norway, where the gesture is considered a salute to Satan ("Norwegians Confused by Bush 'Horns' Salute," 2005).

Researcher Dane Archer (1997) describes his attempt to catalogue the various gestures around the world on video. He began this video project with several hypotheses: first, that there would be great varia-tion, and this he found to be true. However, more surprising, his as-sumption regarding the existence of some universal gestures or at least some universal *categories* of gestures (e.g., every culture must have an obscene gesture) was not confirmed.

He gathered his information by visiting English as a Second Lan-guage classes and asking international students to demonstrate ges-tures from their home cultures, resulting in the documentary *A World of Gestures: Culture and Nonverbal Communication*. He drew several conclusions from his study: first, that gestures and their meaning can be very subtle (see the box "Potentially Embarrassing Gestural Mix-

---

noncontact cultures Cultural groups in which people tend to maintain more space and touch less often than people do in contact cultures. For instance, Great Britain and Japan tend to have noncontact cultures. (See **contact cultures**.)

POINT OF VIEW

POTENTIALLY EMBARRASSING GESTURAL MIX-UPS

1. "Good-bye" (U.S.) = "Come here" (Japan)
2. Good luck (U.S.) = "Boyfriend" (Japan)
3. "Screw you" (U.S.) = I don't believe you" (Uruguay)
4. "I'm angry" (Nepal) = "You are afraid" (Mexico)
5. "OK" (U.S.) = "Money" (Japan)
6. "OK" (U.S.) = "Sex" (Mexico)
7. "OK" (U.S.) = "Homosexual" (Ethiopia)
8. "Killed/dead" (U.S. throat slash) = "Lost a job" (Japan)

Source: From D. Archer, "Unspoken Diversity: Cultural Differences in Gestures," *Qualitative Sociology, 20* (1997), p. 81.

ups"). His work "often elicited gasps of surprise, as ESL students from one culture discovered that what at first appeared to be a familiar gesture actually means something radically different in another society" (p. 87). For example, in Germany, and many other European cultures, the gesture for "stupid" is a finger on the forehead, the American gesture for "smart" is nearly identical, but the finger is held an inch to the side, at the temple. Similarly, the American raised thumb gesture of "way to go" is a vulgar gesture, meaning "sit on this" in Sardinia and "screw you" in Iran. And of course, we've already mentioned the difference between the the "hook 'em horns" gesture and the salute to Satan.

Second, Archer emphasizes that gestures are different from many other nonverbal expressions in that they are accessible to conscious awareness—they can be explained, illustrated, and taught to outsiders. Finally, as noted earlier, he had assumed there would be some universal categories—a gesture for "very good," a gesture for "crazy," an obscene gesture. Not so. A number of societies (e.g., the Netherlands, Norway, Switzerland) have no such gesture. In the end, he concludes that through making the video, "We all acquired a deeply enhanced sense of the power, nuances, and unpredictability of cultural differences" (p. 87). And the practical implication of the project was to urge travelers to practice "gestural humility"—assuming that the familiar gestures of our home culture will not mean the same things abroad and also "that we cannot infer or intuit the meaning of any gestures we observe in other cultures" (p. 80).

Eye Contact **Eye contact** often is included in proxemics because it regulates interpersonal distance. Direct eye contact shortens the distance between two people, whereas less eye contact increases the distance. Eye contact communicates meanings about respect and status and often regulates turn-taking.

Patterns of eye contact vary from culture to culture. In many societies, avoiding eye contact communicates respect and deference, although this may vary from context to context. For many U.S. Americans, maintaining eye contact communicates that one is paying attention and showing respect.

When they speak with others, most U.S. Americans look away from their listeners most of the time, looking at their listeners perhaps every 10 to 15 seconds. When a speaker is finished taking a turn, he or she looks directly at the listener to signal completion. However, some cultural groups within the United States use even less eye contact while they speak. For example, some Native Americans tend to avert eye gaze during conversation.

Chronemics **Chronemics** concerns concepts of time and the rules that govern its use. There are many cultural variations regarding how people understand and use time. Edward Hall (1966) distinguished between monochronic and polychronic time orientation. People who have a **monochronic** concept of time regard it as a commodity: time can be gained, lost, spent, wasted, or saved. In this orientation, time is linear, with one event happening at a time. In general, monochronic cultures value being punctual, completing tasks, and keeping to schedules. Most university staff and faculty in the United States maintain a monochronic orientation to time. Classes, meetings, and office appointments start when scheduled; faculty members see one student at a time, hold one meeting at a time, and keep appointments except in the case of emergency. Family problems are considered poor reasons for not fulfilling academic obligations—for both faculty and students.

In contrast, in a **polychronic** orientation, time is more holistic, and perhaps more circular: several events can happen at once. Many international business negotiations and technical assistance projects falter and even fail because of differences in time orientation. For example, U.S. businesspeople often complain that meetings in the Middle East do not start "on time," that people socialize during meetings, and that

eye contact A nonverbal code, eye gaze, that communicates meanings about respect and status and often regulates turn-taking during interactions.
chronemics The concept of time and the rules that govern its use.
monochronic An orientation to time that assumes it is linear and is a commodity that can be lost or gained.
polychronic An orientation to time that sees it as circular and more holistic.

meetings may be canceled because of personal obligations. Tasks often, are accomplished *because* of personal relationships, not in spite of them. International students and business personnel observe that U.S. Americans seem too tied to their schedules; they suggest that U.S. Americans do not care enough about relationships and often sacrifice time with friends and family to complete tasks and keep appointments.

Silence   Cultural groups may vary in the degree of emphasis placed on silence, which can be as meaningful as language. One of our students recalls his childhood:

> *I always learned while growing up that silence was the worst punishment ever. For example, if the house chore stated clearly that I needed to take the garbage out, and I had not done so, then my mother would not say a word to me. And I would know right away that I had forgotten to do something.*

In most U.S. American contexts, silence is not highly valued. Particularly in developing relationships, silence communicates awkwardness and can make people feel uncomfortable. According to scholar William B. Gudykunst's (1985, 2005) uncertainty reduction theory, the main reason for communicating verbally in initial interactions is to reduce uncertainty. In U.S. American contexts, people employ active uncertainty reduction strategies, such as asking questions. However, in many other cultural contexts, people reduce uncertainty using more passive strategies—for example, remaining silent, observing, or perhaps asking a third party about someone's behavior.

In a classic study on the rules for silence among the western Apache in Arizona, researcher Keith Basso (1970) identified five contexts in which silence is appropriate: (1) meeting strangers, (2) courting someone, (3) seeing friends after a long absence, (4) getting cussed out, and (5) being with people who are grieving. Verbal reticence with strangers is directly related to the conviction that the establishment of social relationships is a serious matter that calls for caution, careful judgment, and plenty of time.

Basso hypothesized that the underlying commonality in these social situations is that participants perceive their relationships vis-à-vis one another to be ambiguous and/or unpredictable and that silence is an appropriate response to uncertainty and unpredictability. He also suggested that this same contextual rule may apply to other cultural groups.

Communication scholar Charles Braithwaite (1990) tried to find out if Basso's rule applied to other communities. He compiled ethnographic accounts from 13 speech communities in which silence seems to play a similar role; these groups included Warm Springs (Oregon) Indians, Japanese Hawaiians, and 17th-century Quakers. Braithwaite extended Basso's rule when he determined that in many communities silence is not simply associated with uncertainty. Silence also is associated with social situations in which a known and unequal distribution of power exists among participants.

Recent research has found similar patterns in other cultures. For example, researchers have described the *Asaillinen* (matter-of-fact) verbal style among Finnish people that involves a distrust of talkativeness as "slickness" and a sign of unreliability (Carbaugh & Berry, 2001; Sajavaara & Lehtonen, 1997). Silence, for Finns, reflects thoughtfulness, appropriate consideration, and intelligence, particularly in public discourse or in educational settings like a classroom. In an ethnographic study investigating this communication pattern, Wilkins (2005) reports two excerpts from interviews that illustrate this pattern—one interview with a Finnish student and one with an American student:

Excerpt 1

Finnish Student: I have been to America.

Wilkins: Can you tell me what the experience was like?

Student: The people and the country were very nice.

Wilkins: Did you learn anything?

Student: No.

Wilkins: Why not?

Student: Americans just talk all the time.

Excerpt 2

Wilkins: Do you like Finland?

American Student: Oh yes, I like it a lot.

Wilkins: How about the people?

Student: Sure, Finns are very nice.

Wilkins: How long have you been at the university?

Student: About nine months already.

Wilkins: Oh, have you learned anything?

Student: No, not really.

Wilkins: Why not?

Student: Finns do not say anything in class.

In addition to a positive view of silence, nonverbal facial expressions in the *Asaillinen* style tend to be rather fixed—and expressionless.

The American student, of course, did not have the cultural knowledge to understand what can be accomplished by thoughtful activity and silence. Other scholars have reported similar distrust of talk in Japanese and Chinese cultures influenced by Confucianism and Taoism. Confucius rejected eloquent speaking and instead advocated hesitancy and humble talk in his philosophy of the ideal person (Chang, 1997; Kim, 2001). As one of our Taiwanese students told us, "In America, sometimes students talk about half the class time. Compared to my classes in Taiwan, if a student asked too many questions or expressed his/her opinions that much, we would say that he or she is a show-off."

Cultural Variation or Stereotype?

As noted previously, one of the problems with identifying cultural variations in nonverbal codes is that it is tempting to overgeneralize these variations and stereotype people. For example, psychologist Helmut Morsbach (1988) cautions us about comparing Japanese and Western attitudes toward silence. Based on his research and extensive experience in Japan, he identifies some of the subtleties of cultural patterns of silence. For instance, the television is on continuously in many Japanese homes, and tape-recorded comments about beauty are transmitted at Zen gardens. So, although many scholars suggest that silence might be a cultural ideal, things may be different in practice. In very specific situations (such as in mother–daughter relationships or in the hiding of true feelings), there may be more emphasis on silence in Japan than in comparable U.S. situations. Also, when communicating with strangers, the Japanese view silence as more negative than it is in the United States (Hasegawa & Gudykunst, 1998).

In any case, we would be wise to heed Morsbach's warning about generalizations. Cultural variations are tentative guidelines that we can use in intercultural interaction. They should serve as examples, to help us understand that there is a great deal of variation in nonverbal behavior. Even if we can't anticipate how other people's behavior may differ from our own, we can be flexible when we do encounter differences in how close someone stands or how she or he uses eye contact or conceptualizes time.

Prejudice is often based on nonverbal aspects of behavior. That is, the negative prejudgment is triggered by physical appearances or behavior. The following report from a Web site that tracks hate crimes underscores the importance of physical appearances in prejudice:

On September 26, 2005, in Marysville, California, Daniel J. Farris, 18, was charged with assault with a deadly weapon, causing pain, suffering or injury to an elder or dependent adult and hate crime for allegedly beating an elderly black man while yelling racial slurs. (accessed at http.//www.splcenter.org/intel/hatewatch/fortherecord.jsp)

As in many instances of hate crimes, the victim's appearance was more significant than his specific cultural heritage. From these kinds of experiences with prejudice, victims can often spot prejudicial behavior and people with surprising accuracy. In an interesting study, blacks were able to detect prejudiced people (identified previously by objective survey measurement) after only 20 seconds of observation, with much higher accuracy than whites (Richeson & Shelton, 2005). Victims may also then develop imaginary "maps" that tell them where they belong and where they are likely to be rejected. They may even start to avoid places and situations in which they do not feel welcome (Marsiglia & Hecht, 1998). Can you identify places you've been where you or others were not welcome?

Semiotics and Nonverbal Communication

In Chapter 6, we introduced semiotics—the study of the signs and symbols of communication and their meanings. Semiotics is a useful tool for examining the various ways that meaning is created in advertisements, clothing, tattoos, and other cultural artifacts. Semioticians have been attentive to the context in which the signifiers (words and symbols) are placed to understand which meanings are being communicated. For example, wearing certain kinds of clothes in specific cultural contexts may communicate unwanted messages.

Yet cultural contexts are not fixed and rigid. Rather, they are dynamic and fleeting, as Marcel Proust (1981) noted in writing about Paris in *Remembrance of Things Past:*

> *The reality that I had known no longer existed. It sufficed that Mme Swann did not appear, in the same attire and at the same moment, for the whole avenue to be altered. The places we have known do not belong only to the world of space on which we map them for our own convenience. None of them was ever more than a thin slice, held between the contiguous impressions that composed our life at that time; the memory of a particular image is but regret for a particular moment; and houses, roads, avenues are as fugitive, alas, as the years. (p. 462)*

As this excerpt shows, there is no "real" Paris. The city has different meanings at different times for different people, and for different reasons. For example, executives of multinational corporations moving into Paris see the city quite differently from immigrants arriving in Paris for personal reasons. Remember the tremendous unrest in the suburbs of Paris in the fall of 2005? Therefore, to think about cultural contexts as dynamic means that we must often think about how they change and in whose interests they change.

DEFINING CULTURAL SPACE

At the beginning of this book, we provided some background information about where we grew up. Our individual histories are important in understanding our identities. As writer John Preston (1991) explains, "Where we come from is important to who we are" (p. xi). There is nothing in the rolling hills of Delaware and Pennsylvania or the red clay of Georgia that biologically determined who Judith and Tom are. However, our identities are constructed, in part, in relation to the cultural milieu of the Mid-Atlantic region or the South. Each region has its own histories and ways of life that help us understand who we are. Our decision to tell you where we come from was meant to communicate something about who we think we are. So, although we can identify precisely the borders that mark out these spaces and make them real, or material, the spaces also are cultural in the ways that we imagine them to be.

The discourses that construct the meanings of cultural spaces are dynamic and ever changing. For example, the Delaware that Judith left behind and the Georgia that Tom left behind are not characterized by the same discourses that construct those places now. In addition, the relationship between those cultural spaces and our identities is negotiated in complex ways. For example, both of us participated in other, overlapping cultural spaces that influenced how we think about who we are. Thus, just because someone is from, say, Rhode Island or Samoa or India does not mean that his or her identity and communication practices are reducible to the history of those cultural spaces.

What is the communicative (discursive) relationship between cultural spaces and intercultural communication? Recall that we define cultural space as the particular configuration of the communication (discourse) that constructs meanings of various places. This may seem like an unwieldy definition, but it underscores the complexity of cultural spaces. A cultural space is not simply a particular location that has culturally constructed meanings. It can also be a metaphorical place from which we communicate. We can speak from a number of social locations, marked on the "map of society," that give added meaning to our communication. Thus, we may speak as parents, children, colleagues, siblings, customers, Nebraskans, and a myriad of other "places." All of these are cultural spaces.

Cultural Identity and Cultural Space

Home Cultural spaces influence how we think about ourselves and others. One of the earliest cultural spaces we experience is our home. As noted previously, nonverbal communication often involves issues of status. The home is no exception. As English professor Paul Fussell (1983) notes, "Approaching any house, one is bombarded with class signals" (p. 82). Fussell highlights the semiotic system of social class in the American home—from the way the lawn is maintained, to the kind of furniture within the home, to the way the television is situated. These signs of social class are not always so obvious from all class positions, but we often recognize the signs.

Even if our home does not reflect the social class to which we aspire, it may be a place of identification. We often model our own lives on the patterns from our childhood homes. Although this is not always the case, the home can be a place of safety and security. African American writer bell hooks (1990) remembers:

> *When I was a young girl the journey across town to my grandmother's house was one of the most intriguing experiences. . . . I remember this journey not just because of the stories I would hear. It was a movement away from the segregated blackness of our community into a poor white neighborhood [where] we would have to pass that terrifying whiteness—those white faces on porches staring down on us with hate. . . . Oh! that feeling of safety, of arrival, of homecoming when we finally reached the edges of her yard. (p. 41)*

Home, of course, is not the same as the physical location it occupies or the building (the house) at that location. Home is variously defined in terms of specific addresses, cities, states, regions, and even nations. Although we might have historical ties to a particular place, not everyone has the same relationship between those places and their own identities. Indeed, the relationship between place and cultural identity varies. Writer Steven Saylor (1991) explains,

> *Texas is a long way, on the map and otherwise, from San Francisco. "Steven," said my mother once, "you live in another country out there."*

She was right, and what I feel when I fly from California to Texas must be what an expatriate from any country feels returning to his childhood home. . . . Texas is home, but Texas is also a country whose citizenship I voluntarily renounced. (p. 119)

The discourses surrounding Texas and giving meaning to Texas no longer "fit" Saylor's sense of who he is or wants to be. We all negotiate various relationships to the cultural meanings attached to the particular places or spaces we inhabit. Consider writer Harlan Greene's (1991) relationship to his hometown in South Carolina:

Now that I no longer live there, I often think longingly of my hometown of Charleston. My heart beats faster and color rushes to my cheek whenever I hear someone mentioning her; I lean over and listen, for even hearing the name casts a spell. Mirages rise up, and I am as overcome and drenched in images as a runner just come from running. I see the steeples, the streets, the lush setting. (p. 55)

Despite his attachment to Charleston, Greene does not believe that Charleston feels the same way toward him. He explains, "But I still think of Charleston; I return to her often and always will. I think of her warmly. I claim her now, even though I know she will never claim me" (p. 67).

The complex relationships we have between various places and our identities resist simplistic reduction. These three writers—hooks, Saylor, and Greene—have negotiated different sentiments toward "home." In doing so, each demonstrates the complex dialectical tensions that exist between identity and location.

Neighborhood   One significant type of cultural space that emerged in U.S. cities in the latter 19th and early 20th centuries was the ethnic or racial neighborhood. Historical studies show, however, that the ethnic neighborhoods of the European immigrants were rarely inhabited by only one ethnic group, despite memories to the contrary. According to labor historian D. R. Roediger (2005), even the heart of Little Italy in Chicago was 47% nonItalian, and "No single side of even one square block in the street between 1890 and 1930 was found to be 100 percent Italian. . . . The percentage of Russians, Czechs, Italians and Poles living in segregated neighborhoods ranged from 37 percent to 61 percent" (p. 164). However, this type of real segregation was reserved for the African Americans—where 93 percent of African Americans lived in ghettos. By law and custom, and under different political pressures, some cities developed segregated neighborhoods. Malcolm X (Malcolm

X & Haley, 1964), in his autobiography, tells of the strict laws that governed where his family could live after their house burned down:

> *My father prevailed on some friends to clothe and house us temporarily; then he moved us into another house on the outskirts of East Lansing. In those days Negroes weren't allowed after dark in East Lansing proper. There's where Michigan State University is located; I related all of this to an audience of students when I spoke there in January, 1963. . . . I told them how East Lansing harassed us so much that we had to move again, this time two miles out of town, into the country. (pp. 3–4)*

The legacy of "white-only" areas pervades the history of the United States and the development of its cultural geography. The segregation of African Americans was not accidental. Beginning in 1890 until the late 1960s (the fair-housing legislation), whites in America created thousands of whites-only towns, commonly known as "sundown towns," a reference to the signs often posted at their city limits that warned, as one did in Hawthorne, California, in the 1930s: "Nigger, Don't Let the Sun Set on you in Hawthorne." In fact, historian J. Loewen (2005) claims that, during that 70-year period, "probably a majority of all incorporated places [in the United States] kept out African Americans."

Neighborhoods exemplify how power influences intercultural contact. Thus, some cultural groups defined who got to live where and dictated the rules by which other groups lived. These rules were enforced through legal means and by harassment. For bell hooks and Malcolm X, the lines of segregation were clear and unmistakable.

In San Francisco, different racial politics constructed and isolated Chinatown. The boundaries that demarcated the acceptable place for Chinese and Chinese Americans to live were strictly enforced through violence:

> *The sense of being physically sealed within the boundaries of Chinatown was impressed on the few immigrants coming into the settlement by frequent stonings which occurred as they came up Washington or Clay Street from the piers. It was perpetuated by attacks of white toughs in the adjacent North Beach area and downtown around Union Square, who amused themselves by beating Chinese who came into these areas. "In those days, the boundaries were from Kearny to Powell, and from California to Broadway. If you ever passed them and went out there, the white kids would throw stones at you," Wei Bat Liu told us. (Nee & Nee, 1974, p. 60)*

In contrast to Malcolm X's exclusion from East Lansing, the Chinese of San Francisco were forced to live in a marked-off territory. Yet we must be careful not to confuse the experience of Chinese in San Francisco with the experiences of all Chinese in the United States. For example, a different system developed in Savannah, Georgia, around 1900:

> *Robert Chung Chan advised his kinsmen and the other newly arrived Chinese to live apart from each other. He understood the distrust of Chinatowns that Caucasians felt in San Francisco and New York. . . . Robert Chung Chan, probably more than anyone else, prevented a Chinatown from developing in Savannah. (Pruden, 1990, p. 25)*

Nor should we assume that vast migrations of Chinese necessarily led to the development of Chinatowns in other cities around the world. The settlement of Chinese immigrants in the 13th Arrondissement of Paris, for example, reflects a completely different intersection between cultures: "There is no American-style Chinatown [*Il n'y a pas de Chinatown à la américaine*]" in Paris (Costa-Lascoux & Yu-Sion, 1995, p. 197).

Within the context of different power relations and historical forces, settlement patterns of other cultural groups created various ethnic enclaves across the U.S. landscape. For example, many small towns in the Midwest were settled by particular European groups. Thus, in Iowa, Germans settled in Amana, Dutch in Pella, and Czechs and Slovaks in Cedar Rapids. Cities, too, have their neighborhoods, based on settlement patterns. South Philadelphia is largely Italian American, South Boston is largely Irish American, and Overtown in Miami is largely African American. Although it is no longer legal to mandate that people live in particular districts or neighborhoods based on their racial or ethnic backgrounds, the continued existence of such neighborhoods underscores their historical development and ongoing functions. This is especially true in Detroit, Michigan—the most segregated metropolitan region in the country—where the 8-mile road was made famous by the title and the location of the film starring Detroit hip-hop artist Eminem. The eight-mile, eight-lane road separates one city that is 91% white from the other that is overwhelmingly African American (Chinni, 2002). See Point of View box. Economics, family ties, social needs, and education are some factors in the perpetuation of these cultural spaces.

Similar spaces exist in other countries as well. Remember the days of rioting and car burning that took place in the Parisian suburbs in the fall of 2005? Guillaume Parmentier, the head of the French Institute, commented on the relationship between place and human rela-

EIGHT MILE ROAD

Sometimes called Detroit's mini Berlin Wall, sometimes called the Wailing Wall, the seemingly innocent looking wall in Joe Louis Park does little to betray its shameful past.

After World War I, some black residents of Detroit moved into a then rural and vacant area near the intersection of Wyoming and Eight Mile. In 1940, a developer sought to build homes for middle income whites in a nearby area. However, the Federal Housing Administration's policies of that era precluded their approving loans in racially mixed areas. To secure FHA approval, this developer put up a wall six feet high, one foot in width and one half mile in length, to clearly demark the white and black areas. His wall led FHA to approve loans for his project.

Source: http://detroityes.com/webisodes/2002/8mile/021106-04-8mile-berlin-wall.htm

tions: "We are the victims of our architecture," he said, referring to the sterile high-rise ghettos populated by France's Muslim immigrants. They are the French equivalent of ghettos or *"zones de no-droit"* (lawless areas) where police do not go as a matter of policy. Instead there are check points on the perimeter of these high-rise islands, and those who live there are left to fend for themselves (Hoagland, 2005).

The relationships among identity, power, and cultural space are quite complex. Power relations influence who (or what) gets to claim who (or what), and under what conditions. Some subcultures are accepted and promoted within a particular cultural space, others are tolerated, and still others may be unacceptable. Identifying with various cultural spaces is a negotiated process that is difficult (and sometimes impossible) to predict and control. The key to understanding the relationships among culture, power, people, and cultural spaces is to think dialectically.

Regionalism Ongoing regional and religious conflict, as well as nationalism and ethnic revival, point to the continuing struggles over who gets to define whom. Such conflicts are not new, though. In fact, some cultural spaces (such as Jerusalem) have been sites of struggle for many centuries.

Although regions are not always clearly marked on maps of the world, many people identify quite strongly with particular regions.

POINT OF VIEW

This writer describes the ongoing debate over the "meaning" of the Confederate flag—whether it represents hallowed traditions or symbolizes racism.

The flag has always been around but grew into a prominent symbol among students during the 1960s, as the civil rights movement and its demand for racial equality swept the South. Then the confederate flag became an expression of defiance across Dixie and, at Ole Miss, it really took off after enrollment of the school's first black student, James Meredith, in 1962. . . .

Carmen Hoskins, a black graduate student, calls the flag "the symbol I hate. To them, it represents tradition, but it was one of hatred and slavery. They all swear it doesn't represent that anymore. But I don't care how many 'heritage—not hate' T-shirts I see; things have not changed that much. Get real." . . .

But at the alumni association meeting, no one was predicting an easy solution. As he was sworn in, newly elected association president Frank Triplett, who graduated in 1955, also appealed for students and graduates to move on.

"Change is inevitable," said Triplett, who noted in his invocation that "there is no progress without pain." But, he noted later, "This is painful for a lot of people."

Source: From Donald P. Baker, "Waving the Past in the Future's Face," *The Washington Post National Weekly Edition*, October 13, 1997, p. 30.

Regionalism can be expressed in many ways, from symbolic expressions of identification to armed conflict. Within the United States, people may identify themselves or others as southerners, New Englanders, and so on. In Canada, people from Montreal might identify more strongly with the province of Quebec than with their country. Similarly, some Corsicans might feel a need to negotiate their identity with France. Sometimes people fly regional flags, wear particular kinds of clothes, celebrate regional holidays, and participate in other cultural activities to commu-nicate their regional identification. However, regional expressions are not always simply celebratory, as the conflicts in Kosovo, Chechnya, Eritrea, and Northern Ireland indicate.

National borders may seem straightforward, but they often conceal conflicting regional identities. To understand how intercultural communication may be affected by national borders, we must consider

regionalism Loyalty to a particular region that holds significant cultural meaning for that person.

how history, power, identity, culture, and context come into play. Only by understanding these issues can we approach the complex process of human communication.

Changing Cultural Space

In this chapter, we want to focus on some of the driving needs of those who change cultural spaces.

Travel   We often change cultural spaces when we travel. Traveling is frequently viewed as an unimportant leisure activity, but it is more than that. In terms of intercultural communication, traveling changes cultural spaces in ways that often transform the traveler. Changing cultural spaces means changing who you are and how you interact with others. Perhaps the old saying "When in Rome, do as the Romans do" holds true today as we cross cultural spaces more frequently than ever.

On a recent trip to Belgium, Tom flew nonstop on British Airways from Phoenix to London and then on to Brussels. Because the entire flight was conducted in English, Tom did not have a sense of any transition from English to French. Unlike flying the now defunct Sabena (Belgian National Airlines) from the United States to Belgium, flying British Airways provided no cultural transition space between Arizona and Belgium. Thus, when he got off the plane in Brussels, Tom experienced a more abrupt cultural and language transition, from an English environment to a Flemish/French environment.

Do you alter your communication style when you encounter travelers who are not in their traditional cultural space? Do you assume they should interact in the ways prescribed by your cultural space? These are some of the issues that travel raises.

Migration   People also change cultural spaces when they relocate. Moving, of course, involves a different kind of change in cultural spaces than traveling. In traveling, the change is fleeting, temporary, and usually desirable; it is something that travelers seek out. However, people who migrate do not always seek out this change. For example, in recent years, many people have been forced from their strife-torn homelands in Rwanda and in Bosnia and have settled elsewhere. Many immigrants leave their homelands simply so they can survive. But they often find it difficult to adjust to the change, especially if the language and customs of the new cultural space are unfamiliar.

Even within the United States, people may have trouble adapting to new surroundings when they move. Tom remembers that when northerners moved to the South they often were unfamiliar with the custom of banks closing early on Wednesday or with the traditional New Year's Day foods of black-eyed peas and collards. Ridiculing the customs of their new cultural space simply led to further intercultural communication problems.

Postmodern Cultural Spaces

Space has become increasingly important in the negotiation of cultural and social identities, and so to culture more generally. As Leah Vande Berg (1999) explains, scholars in many areas "have noted that identity and knowledge are profoundly spatial (as well as temporal), and that this condition structures meaningful embodiment and experience" (p. 249). **Postmodern cultural spaces** are places that are defined by cultural practices—languages spoken, identities enacted, rituals performed—and they often change as new people move in and out of these spaces. Imagine being in a small restaurant when a large group of people arrives, all of whom are speaking another language. How has this space changed? Whose space is it? As different people move in and out of this space, how does the cultural character change?

In his study of listening among the Blackfeet, Donal Carbaugh (1999) reports that listening is intimately connected to place as a cultural space. It is both a physical location and a cultural phenomenon. Through his cultural informant, Two Bears, Carbaugh notes that

> *in his oral utterance to us about "listening," in this landscape, he is commenting about a non-oral act of listening to this landscape. This nonverbal act is itself a deeply cultural form of action in which the Blackfeet persona and the physical place become intimately linked, in a particularly Blackfeet way. (p. 257)*

But these places are dynamic, and "listening" is not limited to fixed locations: "Some kinds of places are apparently more appropriate for this kind of Blackfeet 'listening' than are others, although—according to Two Bears—'just about anywhere' might do" (p. 257). Physical place, in this sense, can become a cultural space in that it is infused with cultural meanings. Think about how the same physical place might have a different meaning to someone from a different cultural group.

Another set of postmodern spaces that are quite familiar are those of the Internet. There are MOOs (multi-object domains) and MUDs

---

postmodern cultural spaces Places that are defined by cultural practices—languages spoken, identities enacted, rituals performed—and that often change as new people move in and out of these spaces.

POINT OF VIEW

Inspired by her experiences in various airports around the world, Elisabeth Marx uses airport architecture as a type of cultural lens to understand each culture. How do these physical spaces reflect the cultures that built them? What can we learn about cultural space by thinking about airports? If you know of people who have traveled to other airports, what have they told you about them? How does your city's airport reflect your area's culture?

GERMANY

I always find it interesting to look at airports, airport architecture, the way the services are handled and the general atmosphere to get a first impression of a country, its society and culture. Landing at Frankfurt Airport, particularly the new Terminal 2, is impressive: it is glitzy and big, with glass walls, expensive materials, generous planning and a logical layout—everything you would expect in Germany. However, it takes ages to get through passport control: every single passport is scrutinized and put through an electronic detection system, resulting in large queues of people waiting to get to the luggage area and out of the airport. Is this a colossal system that does not seem to be terribly efficient at times, or is efficiency simply defined in a different way?

FRANCE

Landing at Charles de Gaulle Airport is like being in a 1960s science fiction movie. Its interesting, space-age design illustrates France's affinity for technical advances and modernist architecture and the importance of engineering within its culture. But is design more important than efficiency? To the newcomer, the airport is slightly

(multi-user domains) and chat rooms where people meet in real time and interact primarily for recreational purposes—assuming their own or another identity (Herring, 2004). There are other Internet spaces like message boards, instant messengers (IMs), for asynchronous communication. People meet in these places for fun, to gain information, or as a place to experience a supportive community (e.g., an online chat room where Japanese elderly meet for support [Kanayama, 2003], or a bulletin board where gay, lesbian, and transgendered people can offer support and exchange useful information). And increasingly, blogs are spaces where people come to visit you (Herring, 2004).

Communication scholars have investigated how these virtual

confusing as you have the impression of running round in circles. However, there is no doubt that there is always an interesting and surprising angle to consider.

UK

"Arriving at Heathrow is like arriving in a third world country," commented a self-critical British friend. The main Heathrow building with its three terminals always seems to be in a state of chaos with permanent attempts at improvement, leaving the traveler in a similar state of confusion. Although Heathrow has improved dramatically over the years and has extensive shopping facilities, its rather slapdash approach towards airport architecture may reflect the UK's "layperson" approach. The British are pragmatic and have a low-key attitude to adversity: they don't get too upset and may not seek perfectionism at all costs; they are also prepared to change and to be flexible. This may be one of their strong points when it comes to business.

USA

Landing at San Francisco Airport is at first a pleasant experience—a great location for an airport and a smooth transition through immigration; there are efforts to show off the Californian flora and a distinctly personal touch in a greeting from the city's mayor. However, this personal greeting is a continuous tape and when you have to hear it for the third time in three minutes, you are getting slightly tired of this noise pollution—is this a symptom of the automatized, "have a nice day" service orientation in the USA?

Source: From Elisabeth Marx, *Breaking Through Culture Shock* (London: Nicolas Brealey, 1999), pp. 79, 82, 84–85, 88, 91.

place/spaces affect the communication that occurs there. Teske (2002) explores the implications of this communication that is disembodied—unconnected to time and physical space—and suggests that interacting in these spaces makes us increasingly individualistic and isolated, in spite of *communicating* through a great medium for connecting people. Others suggest that virtual spaces offer a different space for interacting and that cyber relationships are formed, maintained, and dissolved in much the same way (Carter, 2004). We'll explore cyber relationships further in Chapter 9.

The fluid and fleeting nature of cultural space stands in sharp contrast to the 18th- and 19th-century notions of space, which promoted land ownership, surveys, borders, colonies, and territories. No passport is needed to travel in the postmodern cultural space, because there are no border guards. The dynamic nature of postmodern cultural spaces underscores its response to changing cultural needs. The space exists only as long as it is needed in its present form.

Postmodern cultural spaces are both tenuous and dynamic. They are created within existing places, without following any particular guide. There is no marking off of territory, no sense of permanence or official recognition. The postmodern cultural space exists only while it is used.

The ideology of fixed spaces and categories is currently being challenged by postmodernist notions of space and location. Phoenix, for example, which became a city relatively recently, has no Chinatown, or Japantown, or Koreatown, no Irish district, or Polish neighborhood, or Italian area. Instead, people of Polish descent, for example, might live anywhere in the metropolitan area but congregate for special occasions or for specific reasons. On Sundays, the Polish Catholic Mass draws many people from throughout Phoenix. When people want to buy Polish breads and pastries, they can go to the Polish bakery and also speak Polish there. Ethnic identity is only one of several identities that these people negotiate. When they desire recognition and interaction based on their Polish heritage, they can meet that wish. When they seek other forms of identification, they can go to places where they can be Phoenix Suns fans, or community volunteers, and so on. Ethnic identity is neither the sole factor nor necessarily the most important one at all times in their lives.

The markers of ethnic life in Phoenix are the urban sites where people congregate when they desire ethnic cultural contact. At other times, they may frequent different locations in expressing aspects of their identities. In this sense, the postmodern urban space is dynamic and allows people to participate in the communication of identity in new ways (Drzewiecka & Nakayama, 1998).

Cultural spaces can also be metaphorical, with historically defined places serving as sources of contemporary identity negotiation in new spaces. In her study of academia, Olga Idriss Davis (1999) turns to the historical role of the kitchen in African American women's lives and uses the kitchen legacy as a way to rethink the university. She notes that "the relationship between the kitchen and the Academy [university] informs African American women's experience and historically interconnects their struggles for identity" (p. 370). In this sense, the kitchen is a metaphorical cultural space that is invoked in an entirely new place, the university. Again, this postmodern cultural space is not material but metaphoric, and it allows people to negotiate their identities in new places.

DISCUSSION QUESTIONS

1. How does nonverbal communication differ from verbal communication?
2. What are some of the messages that we communicate through our nonverbal behaviors?
3. Which nonverbal behaviors, if any, are universal?
4. How do our cultural spaces affect our identities?
5. What role does power play in determining our cultural spaces?
6. What is the importance of cultural spaces to intercultural communication?
7. How do postmodern cultural spaces differ from modernist notions of cultural space?

ACTIVITIES

1. *Cultural Spaces.* Think about the different cultural spaces in which you participate (clubs, churches, concerts, and so on). Select one of these spaces and describe when and how you enter and leave it. As a group, discuss the answers to the following questions:
    a. Which cultural spaces do many students share? Which are not shared by many students?
    b. Which cultural spaces, if any, are denied to some people? .
    c. What factors determine whether a person has access to a specific cultural space?
2. *Nonverbal Rules.* Choose a cultural space that you are interested in studying. Visit this space on four occasions to observe how people there interact. Focus on one aspect of nonverbal communication (e.g., eye contact or proximity). List some rules that seem to govern this aspect of nonverbal communication. For example, if you are focusing on proximity, you might describe, among other things, how far apart people tend to stand when conversing. Based on your observations, list some prescriptions about proper (expected) nonverbal behavior in this cultural space. Share your conclusions with the class. To what extent do other students share your conclusions? Can we generalize about nonverbal rules in cultural spaces? What factors influence whether an individual follows unspoken rules of behavior?

REFERENCES

Andersen, P. A., Hecht, M. L., Hoobler, G. D., & Smallwood, M. (2002). Nonverbal communication across cultures. In W. B. Gudykunst & B. Mody (Eds.), *Handbook of international and intercultural communication* (2nd ed., pp. 89–106). Thousand Oaks, CA: Sage.

Archer, D. (1997). Unspoken diversity: Cultural differences in gestures. *Qualitative Sociology, 20,* 79–105.

Basso, K. (1970). "To give up on words": Silence in western Apache culture. *Southwestern Journal of Anthropology, 26,* 213–320.

Boucher, J. D., & Carlson, G. E. (1980). Recognition of facial expression in three cultures. *Journal of Cross Cultural Psychology, 11,* 263–280.

Braithwaite, C. A. (1990). Communicative silence: A cross-cultural study of Basso's hypothesis. In D. Carbaugh (Ed.), *Cultural communication and intercultural contact* (pp. 321–327). Hillsdale, NJ: Lawrence Erlbaum.

Carbaugh, D. (1999). "Just listen": "Listening" and landscape among the Blackfeet. *Western Journal of Communication, 63*(3), 250–270.

Carbaugh, D., & Berry, M. (2001). Communicating history, Finnish and American discourses: An ethnographic contribution to intercultural communication inquiry. *Communication Theory, 11,* 352–366.

Carter, D. M. (2004). Living in virtual communities: Making friends online. *Journal of Urban Technology, 11,* 109–136.

Chang, H. (1997). Language and words: Communication in the analects of Confucius. *Journal of Language and Social Psychology, 16,* 107–131.

Chinni, D. (2002, November 15). Along Detroit's Eight Mile Road, a stark racial split. *Christian Science Monitor.* Accessed at http://www.csmonitor.com/2002/1115/p01s02-ussc.htm

Costa-Lascoux, J., & Yu-Sion, L. (1995). *Paris-XIIIe, lumières d'Asie.* Paris: Éditions Autrement.

Davis, O. I. (1999). In the kitchen: Transforming the academy through safe spaces of resistance. *Western Journal of Communication, 63*(3), 364–381.

Drzewiecka, J. A., & Nakayama, T. K. (1998). City sites: Postmodern urban space and the communication of identity. *Southern Communication Journal, 64,* 20–31.

Ekman, P. (2003). *Emotions revealed: Recognizing faces and feelings to improve communication and emotional life.* New York: Times Books.

Ekman, P., & Friesen, W. V. (1987). Universals and cultural differences in the judgments of facial expressions of emotion. *Journal of Personality and Social Psychology, 53,* 712–717.

Fattah, H. M. (2005, May 1). Why Arab men hold hands. *New York Times,* Week in Review, 2.

Fletcher, C. (1992). The semiotics of survival: Street cops read the street. *Howard Journal of Communications, 4*(1, 2), 133–142.

Fussell, P. (1983). *Class.* New York: Ballantine Books.

Galati, D., Sini, B., Schmidt, S., & Tinti, C. (2003). Spontaneous facial expressions in congenitally blind and sighted children aged 8–11. *Journal of Visual Impairment and Blindness, 97,* 418–428.

Greene, H. (1991). Charleston, South Carolina. In J. Preston (Ed.), *Hometowns: Gay men write about where they belong* (pp. 55–67). New York: Dutton.

Gudykunst, W. B. (1985). A model of uncertainty reduction in intergroup encounters. *Journal of Language and Social Psychology, 4,* 79–98.

Gudykunst, W. B. (2005). An anxiety/uncertainty management (AUM) theory of effective communication: Making the mesh of the net finer. In W. B. Gudykunst (Ed.), *Theorizing about intercultural communication* (pp. 281–323). Thousand Oaks, CA: Sage.

Hall, E. T. (1966). *The hidden dimension.* New York: Anchor Books.

Harper, M., & Jones, T. (2005, November 23). Blackface costumes spark Stetson diversity lesson. *Daytona Beach News-Journal* online. Accessed at http://www.news-journalonline.com/News-JournalOnline/News/Headlines/03NewsHEAD04112305.htm

Hasegawa, T., & Gudykunst, W. B. (1998). Silence in Japan and the United States. *Journal of Cross-Cultural Psychology, 29,* 668–684.

Henningsen, D. D., Cruz, M. G., & Morr, M. C. (2000). Pattern violations and perceptions of deception. *Communication Reports, 13,* 1–9.

Herring, S. C. (2004). Slouching toward the ordinary: Current trends in computer mediated communication. *New Media & Society, 6,* 26–31.

Hoagland, J. (2005, November 9). French lessons. *The Washington Post,* p. A31. Accessed at http://www.washingtonpost.com/wp-dyn/content/article/ 2005/11/08/AR2005110801257

hooks, b. (1990). *Yearning: Race, gender, and cultural politics.* Boston: South End Press.

Jones, S. (2004). Putting the person into person-centered and immediate emotional support: Emotional change and perceived helper competence as outcomes of comforting in helping situations. *Communication Research, 31,* 338–360.

Kanayama, T. (2003). Ethnographic research on the experience of Japanese elderly people online. *New Media & Society, 5,* 267–288.

Kim, M.-S. (2001). *Non-Western perspectives on human communication.* Thousand Oaks, CA: Sage.

Khuri, F. I. (2001). *The body in Islamic culture.* London: Saqi Books.

Lock, C. (2004, July 31). Deception detection. *Science News, 166,* 72–73.

Loewen, J. (2005). *Sundown towns: A hidden dimension of American racism.* New York: New Press.

Malcolm X, & Haley, A. (1964). *The autobiography of Malcolm X.* New York: Grove Press.

Marsiglia, F. F., & Hecht, M. L. (1998). Personal and interpersonal interventions. In M. L. Hecht (Ed.), *Communicating prejudice* (pp. 287–301). Thousand Oaks, CA: Sage.

Matsumoto, D. (1990). Cultural influences on facial expressions of emotion. *Southern Communication Journal, 56,* 128–137.

Matsumoto, D., Franklin, B., Choi, J.-W., Rogers, D., & Tatani, H. (2002). Cultural influences in the expression and perception of emotion. In W. B. Gudykunst & B. Mody (Eds.), *Handbook of international and intercultural communication* (2nd ed., pp. 107–127). Thousand Oaks, CA: Sage.

Montepare, J. M. (2003). Evolution and nonverbal behavior: Adaptive social interaction strategies. *Journal of Nonverbal Behavior, 27,* 141–143.

Morsbach, H. (1988). The importance of silence and stillness in Japanese nonverbal communication: A cross cultural approach. In F. Poyatos (Ed.), *Cross cultural perspectives in nonverbal communication* (pp. 201–215). Lewiston, NY: Hogrefe.

Nee, V. G., & Nee, B. D. B. (1974). *Longtime Californ': A documentary study of an American Chinatown.* Boston: Houghton Mifflin.

Norwegians confused by Bush "homs" salute. (2005, December 1). *USAToday*. Accessed at http://www.usatoday.com/news/washington/2005-01-21-bush-norwegians_x.htm?csp=34& POE=click-refer

Patterson, M. L. (2003). Commentary: Evolution and nonverbal behavior: Functions and mediating processes. *Journal of Nonverbal Behavior, 27*, 201–207.

Preston, J. (1991). Introduction. In J. Preston (Ed.), *Hometowns: Gay men write about where they belong* (pp. xi–xiv). New York: Dutton.

Preuschoft, S. (2000). Primate faces and facial expressions. *Social Research, 67*, 245–271.

Proust, M. (1981). *Swann in love: Remembrance of things past* (C. K. S. Moncrieff & T. Kilmartin, Trans.). New York: Vintage.

Pruden, G. B., Jr. (1990). History of the Chinese in Savannah, Georgia. In J. Goldstein (Ed.), *Georgia's East Asian connection: Into the twenty-first century: Vol. 27. West Georgia College studies in the social sciences* (pp. 17–34). Carrollton: West Georgia College.

Richeson, J., & Shelton, J. N. (2005). Brief report: Thin slices of racial bias. *Journal of Nonverbal Behavior, 29*, 75–86.

Rocca, K. (2004). College student attendance: Impact of instructor immediacy and verbal aggression. *Communication Education, 53*, 185–195.

Roediger, D. R. (2005). *Working toward whiteness: How America's immigrants became white*. New York: Basic Books, 2005.

Sajavaara, K., & Lehtonen, J. (1997). The silent Finn revisited. In A. Jaworski (Ed.), *Silence: Interdisciplinary perspectives* (pp. 263–23). New York: Mouton de Gruyter.

Saylor, S. (1991). Amethyst, Texas. In J. Preston (Ed.), *Hometowns: Gay men write about where they belong* (pp. 119–135). New York: Dutton.

Schiefenhovel, W. (1997). Universals in interpersonal interactions. In U. Segerstråle & P. Molnár (Eds.), *Nonverbal communication: Where nature meets culture* (pp. 61–79). Mahwah, NJ: Lawrence Erlbaum.

Sudip, M. (2004, January 26). A hairy situation. *Newsweek*, p. 12.

Suomi, S. J. (1988). Nonverbal communication in nonhuman primates: Implications for the emergence of culture. In U. Segerstråle & P. Molnár (Eds.), *Nonverbal communication: Where nature meets culture* (pp. 131–150). Mahwah, NJ: Lawrence Erlbaum.

Teske, J. A. (2002). Cyberpsychology, human relationships and our virtual interiors. *Zygon, 37*, 677–700.

Vande Berg, L. R. (1999). An introduction to the special issue on "spaces." *Western Journal of Communication, 63* (3), 249.

Vrij, A. (2004). Why professionals fail to catch liars and how they can improve. *Legal and Criminological Psychology, 9*, 159–181.

Watson, O. M. (1970). *Proxemic behavior: A cross cultural study*. The Hague: Mouton.

Wilkins, R. (2005). The optimal form: Inadequacies and excessiveness within the *Asiallinen* [matter of fact] nonverbal style in public and civic settings in Finland. *Journal of Communication, 55*, 383–401.

PART III
Intercultural Communication Applications

POPULAR CULTURE AND INTERCULTURAL COMMUNICATION

CHAPTER OBJECTIVES

After reading this chapter, you should be able to:

1. Differentiate between high and low culture.

2. Discuss the importance of popular culture as a public forum.

3. Identify the four characteristics of popular culture.

4. Identify some patterns of how people consume popular culture.

5. Identify some ways that people resist popular culture.

6. Describe some of the ways that popular culture influences how people understand another culture.

7. Explain the role of popular culture in stereotyping.

8. Explain how the global movement of popular culture influences people around the world.

9. Discuss the concerns of some governments about the influence of foreign media in their countries.

Although we often think of museums as repositories of culture, we know that many facets of our culture are not displayed in museums. For example, museums of fine arts are filled with paintings, sculptures, and other artwork, but these pieces reveal little about the lifestyles or values of the cultural groups that created them. Even contemporary art installations provide little evidence of how people live today.

This chapter explores one type of culture that is often overlooked by intercultural communication scholars but that plays an important role in the construction, maintenance, and experience of culture, particularly in intercultural interactions. This type of culture is popular culture.

LEARNING ABOUT CULTURES WITHOUT PERSONAL EXPERIENCE

People can experience and learn about other cultures by traveling to and relocating and living in other regions. But there will always be many places around the world that we have not visited and where we have not lived. How do we know about places we have never been? Much of what we know probably comes from popular culture—the media experience of films, television, music, videos, books, and magazines that most of us know and share. How does this experience affect intercultural communication?

The Power of Popular Culture

Neither Tom nor Judith has ever been to Brazil, Nigeria, India, Russia, or China. Yet both of us hold tremendous amounts of information about these places from the news, movies, TV shows, advertisements, and more. The kind and quality of information we all have about other places are influenced by popular culture. But the views that the media portray supplement the information we get from other sources. For example, audiences that see the movie *Jarhead* are likely to be familiar with the military mission in Iraq, even if they have not been in military service there. In this sense, popular culture is pervasive.

The complexity of popular culture is often overlooked. People express concern about the social effects of popular culture—for example, the influence of television violence on children, the role of certain kinds of music in causing violent behavior by some youths, and the relationship between heterosexual pornography and violence against women. Yet most people look down on the study of popular culture, as if this form of culture conveys nothing of lasting significance. So, on the one hand, we are concerned about the power of popular culture; on the other, we don't look on popular culture as a serious area of academic research. This inherent contradiction can make it difficult to investigate and discuss popular culture.

As U.S. Americans, we are in a unique position in relationship to popular culture. Products of U.S. popular culture are well known and circulate widely on the international market. The popularity of U.S. movies such as *Crash* and *Mission Impossible III*, of U.S. music stars such as Jennifer Lopez and Madonna, and of U.S. television shows from *I Love Lucy* to *CSI* and *Las Vegas* creates an uneven flow of texts between the United States and other nations. Scholars Elihu Katz and Tamar Liebes (1987) have noted the "apparent ease with which American television programs cross cultural and linguistic frontiers. Indeed, the phenomenon is so taken for granted that hardly any systematic research has been done to explain the reasons why these programs are so successful" (p. 419).

In contrast, U.S. Americans are rarely exposed to popular culture from outside the United States. Exceptions to this largely one-way movement of popular culture include pop music stars who sing in English, such as Ricky Martin (Puerto Rican), Shakira (Colombian), and Céline Dion (French Canadian). Consider how difficult it is to find foreign films or television programs throughout most of the United States. Even when foreign corporations market their products in the United States, they almost always use U.S. advertising agencies—collectively known as "Madison Avenue." The apparent imbalance of cultural texts globally not only renders U.S. Americans more dependent on U.S.-produced popular culture but also can lead to cultural imperialism, a topic we discuss later in this chapter.

The study of popular culture has become increasingly important in the communication field. Although intercultural communication scholars traditionally have overlooked popular culture, we believe that it is a significant influence in intercultural interaction.

What Is Popular Culture?

The 19th-century essayist and poet Matthew Arnold, who expressed concern with protecting civilization, defined *culture* as "the best that has been thought and said in the world"—a definition that emphasizes quality. In this context, many Western societies distinguish "high culture" from "low culture."

High culture refers to those cultural activities that are often the domain of the elite or the well-to-do: ballet, symphony, opera, great literature, and fine art. These activities sometimes are framed as *international* because supposedly they can be appreciated by audiences in other places, from other cultures, in different time periods. Their cultural value is seen as transcendent and timeless. To protect these cultural treasures, social groups build museums, symphony halls, and theaters. In fact, universities devote courses, programs, and even entire departments to the study of aspects of high culture.

In opposition to high culture is low culture, which refers to the activities of the nonelite: music videos, game shows, professional wrestling, stock car racing, graffiti art, TV talk shows, and so on. Traditionally, low-culture activities have been seen as unworthy of serious study—and so of little interest to museums or universities. The cultural values embedded in these activities were considered neither transcendent nor timeless.

The elitism reflected in the distinction between high and low culture points to the tensions in Western social systems. In recent decades, however, this distinction has begun to break down. Rapid social changes propelled universities to alter their policies and also have affected how we study intercultural communication. For example, the turbulent 1960s brought to the university a powerful new interest in ethnic studies, including African American studies and women's and gay and lesbian issues. These areas of study did not rely on the earlier distinctions between high and low culture. Rather, they contributed to a new conceptual framework by arguing for the legitimacy of other cultural forms that traditionally would have been categorized as low culture but were now framed as **popular culture**. Because of this elitist view of culture, the distinction between "high culture" and "low culture" has led to low culture being reconceptualized as popular culture. Barry Brummett (1994), a contemporary rhetorician, offers the following definition: "Popular culture refers to those systems or artifacts that most people share and that most people know about" (p. 21). According to this definition, television, music videos, and popular magazines are systems of popular culture. In contrast, the symphony and the ballet do not qualify as popular culture because most people cannot identify much about them.

So, popular culture often is seen as populist—including forms of contemporary culture that are made popular by and for the people. John Fiske (1989), professor of communication arts, explains,

> To be made into popular culture, a commodity must also bear the interests of the people. Popular culture is not consumption, it is culture—the ac-

---

popular culture A new name for *low culture*, referring to those systems or artifacts that most people share and know about, including television, music, videos, and popular magazines.

tive process of generating and circulating meanings and pleasures within a social system: culture, however industrialized, can never be adequately described in terms of the buying and selling of commodities. (p. 23)

In his study of popular Mexican American music in Los Angeles, ethnic studies professor George Lipsitz (1990) highlights the innovative, alternative ways that marginalized social groups are able to express themselves. In this study, he demonstrates how popular culture can arise by mixing and borrowing from other cultures: "The ability of musicians to learn from other cultures played a key role in their success as rock-and-roll artists" (p. 140). The popular speaks to—and resonates from—the people, but it does so through multiple cultural voices. Lipsitz continues,

The marginality of Chicano rock-and-roll musicians has provided them with a constant source of inspiration and a constant spur toward innovation that gained them the attention of mainstream audiences. But this marginal sensibility amounts to more than novelty or personal eccentricity; it holds legitimacy and power as the product of a real historical community's struggle with oppression. . . . As Chicano musicians demonstrate in their comments about their work, their music reflects a quite conscious cultural politic that seeks inclusion in the American mainstream by transforming it. (p. 159)

Intercultural contact and intercultural communication play a central role in the creation and maintenance of popular culture. Yet, as Lipsitz points out, the popular is political and pleasurable, which further complicates how we think about popular culture.

There are four significant characteristics of popular culture: (1) It is produced by culture industries, (2) it differs from **folk culture**, (3) it is everywhere, and (4) it fills a social function. As Fiske (1989) points out, popular culture is nearly always produced within a capitalist system that sees the products of popular culture as commodities that can be economically profitable. They are produced by what are called **culture industries**. The Disney Corporation is a noteworthy example of a culture industry because it produces amusement parks, movies, cartoons, and a plethora of associated merchandise.

More recently, communication scholars Joshua Gunn and Barry Brummett (2004) have challenged the second point that there is an important difference between folk culture and popular culture. They suggest, "We write as if there is a fundamental difference between a

---

folk culture Traditional and nonmainstream cultural activities that are not financially driven.
culture industries Industries that produce and sell popular culture as commodities.

mass-produced and mass-marketed culture and a more authentic 'folk' culture or subculture. Such a binary is dissolving into a globally marketed culture. A few remaining pockets of folk culture remain here and there: on the Sea Islands, in Amish country, in departments of English. The rest of folk culture is now 50% off at Wal-Mart" (p. 707). In the new context of globalization, whatever happened to folk traditions and artifacts? Have they been unable to escape being mass produced and marketed around the globe? Where would you look for folk culture today? Whatever happened to traditional folk dancing, quilting bees, and other forms of folk culture?

Popular culture is ubiquitous. We are bombarded with it, every day and everywhere. On average, U.S. Americans watch more than 40 hours of television per week. Movie theaters beckon us with the latest multimillion-dollar extravaganzas, nearly all U.S. made. Radio stations and music TV programs blast us with the hottest music groups performing their latest hits. And we are inundated with a staggering number of advertisements and commercials daily.

It is difficult to avoid popular culture. Not only is it ubiquitous, but it also serves an important social function. How many times have you been asked by friends and family for your reaction to a recent movie or TV program? Academicians Horace Newcomb and Paul Hirsch (1987) suggest that television serves as a cultural forum for discussing and working out our ideas on a variety of topics, including those that emerge from the programs themselves. Television, then, has a powerful social function—to serve as a forum for dealing with social issues.

In his study of the role of the local newspaper, *The Newsboy*, in restoring the image of Jasper, Texas, after the dragging murder of James Byrd, Jr., Jack Glascock (2004) found that the newspaper's editorials played an important role in guiding the community response to the hate crime. He notes that the "paper's involvement in community affairs at the outset allowed it to convey the agreed-upon objectives of the crisis discourse to the rest of the community. As the crisis played out the paper extended its leadership role by continuing, dropping or modifying its strategies. The paper's opinion pages also provided a forum for the community to participate, primarily by bolstering the town's image, both within the community [and] to outsiders" (p. 45). In this case, the paper is both a forum for public discussion and a leader in community restoration.

In a similar study, communication scholars Dreama Moon and Tom Nakayama (2005) analyzed newspaper accounts of the murder of Arthur "J. R." Warren in West Virginia. Although the small town where he was murdered did not have a local paper, they found that the media coverage did highlight significant differences in how African

Americans, gays and lesbians, and white heterosexual residents experienced and perceived life there. Through the media, African Americans and gays and lesbians were able to offer an alternative view that differed from the dominant view of idealized small town life. Again, newspapers served as a forum for discussion of this tragic event and related aspects of everyday life and community in this small West Virginia town.

In contrast, not all popular culture may serve as a forum for public deliberation. In his study of baseball tributes in ballparks after the attacks of September 11, 2001, Michael Butterworth (2005) found that these rituals tended to discourage expression of opinions that differed from a nationalistic patriotism at the expense of democratic deliberation. Butterworth describes these baseball tributes and notes, "If baseball can be understood as a representative institution of American democratic culture, then the ways in which it performs (or fails to perform) democratically merit scrutiny and criticism. In the aftermath of unprecedented tragedy (for Americans), baseball could have been a site not only for communal healing but also for productively engaging the pluralism that the game does or should represent" (p. 122). Baseball tributes, then, are a form of popular culture that does not serve a cultural forum for the democratic exchange of ideas.

The ways that people negotiate their relationships to popular culture are complex, and it is this complexity that makes understanding the role of popular culture in intercultural communication so difficult. Clearly, we are not passive recipients of this deluge of popular culture. We are, in fact, quite active in our consumption of or resistance to popular culture, a notion that we turn to next.

CONSUMING AND RESISTING POPULAR CULTURE

Consuming Popular Culture

Faced with this onslaught of **cultural texts**, people negotiate their ways through popular culture in quite different ways. Popular culture texts do not have to win over the majority of people to be "popular." People often seek out or avoid specific forms of popular culture. For example, romance novels are the best-selling form of literature, but many readers have no interest in such books. Likewise, whereas many people enjoy watching soap operas or professional wrestling, many others find no pleasure in those forms of popular culture.

Stuart Hall's (1980) encoding/decoding model might be helpful

---

cultural texts Popular culture messages whether television shows, movies, advertisements, or other widely disseminated messages.

here. Hall is careful to place "meaning" at several stages in the communication process, so that it is never fixed but is always being constructed within various contexts. Thus, in his model, he places **encoding**—or the construction of textual meaning by popular culture institutions—within specific social contexts. **Decoding**—the interpretation of the text's meaning by receivers—is performed by various audiences in different social contexts, whose members have different interests at stake. In this way, the meaning(s) of various popular culture texts can be seen as negotiated throughout the communication process. The "real meaning" of any popular culture text cannot simply be located in either the senders or the receivers. Although this model may seem to suggest tremendous unpredictability in popular culture, people do not create just any meaning out of these texts. We are always enmeshed in our social identities, which help guide our interpretations as decoders. Encoders, in turn, rely on these larger identity formations to help them fashion their texts to sell to particular markets. (See Figure 8.1.)

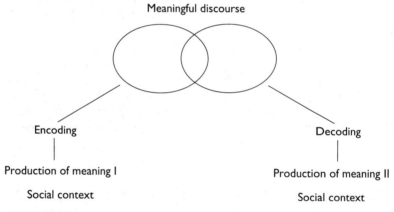

Meaningful discourse

Encoding   Decoding

Production of meaning I   Production of meaning II

Social context   Social context

FIGURE 8.1   Stuart Hall's encoding/decoding model. Try to use this model to discuss how different people might arrive at different interpretations of your favorite TV show.

For example, communication researcher Antonio La Pastina (2004) did an interpretive study of how people in a rural Brazilian community, Macambira in northeastern Brazil, decoded the meanings of the telenovela *The Cattle King*. This telenovela is set in urban Brazil and features many melodramatic stories about socioeconomic class, romance, and sexuality. In interviewing the people of this very rural and isolated community, he found that these viewers tended to interpret

---

encoding The process of creating a message for others to understand.
decoding The process of interpreting a message.

the telenovelas based on their own cultural values about gender, relationships, and sexuality. He also found that these telenovelas tended to shape how the viewers saw urban life in Brazil. Although the producers of this telenovela may not have encoded the shows with this audience in mind when they wrote and produced these narratives, the viewers in this community used their own cultural values to decode their own meanings of the shows.

There is some unpredictability in how people navigate popular culture. After all, not all men enjoy watching football, and not all women like to read romance novels. However, some profiles emerge. Advertising offices of popular magazines even make their **reader profiles** available to potential advertisers. These reader profiles portray what the magazine believes its readership "looks" like. Although reader profiles do not follow a set format, they generally detail the average age, gender, individual and household incomes, and so on, of their readership. The reader profile for *Vogue*, for example, will not look like the reader profile for *Esquire*.

Each magazine targets a particular readership and then sells this readership to advertisers. The diversity of the U.S. American population generates very different readerships among a range of magazines, in several ways. Let's explore some of the ways this diversity is played out in the magazine market.

How Magazines Respond to the Needs of Cultural Identities A wide range of magazines respond to the different social and political needs of groups with different cultural identities. You may already be familiar with magazines geared toward a male or a female readership. But many other kinds of magazines serve important functions for other cultural groups. For example, *Ebony* is one of many magazines that cultivate an African American readership. Similar magazines exist for other cultural identities. *Hispanic Magazine*, published in Florida, targets a Latino/an audience; *The Advocate* claims to be the national newsmagazine for gays and lesbians. These magazines offer information and viewpoints that are generally unavailable in other magazines. They function as a discussion forum for concerns that mainstream magazines often overlook. They also tend to affirm, by their very existence, these other cultural identities, which sometimes are invisible or are silenced in the mainstream culture.

In addition, many non-English-language newspapers circulate among readers of specific ethnic groups, serving the same functions as the magazines just mentioned. However, because their production

---

reader profiles Portrayals of readership demographics prepared by magazines.

costs are low, they are better able to survive and reach their limited readerships. For instance, newspapers printed in Cantonese, Spanish, Vietnamese, Japanese, French, Korean, Arabic, Polish, Russian, and other languages reach non-English-speaking readers in the United States.

How Readers Negotiate Consumption Readers actively negotiate their way through cultural texts such as magazines—consuming those that fulfill important cultural needs and resisting those that do not. Hence, it is possible to be a reader of magazines that reflect various cultural configurations; that is, someone might read several women's magazines and Spanish-language newspapers and magazines, as well as *Newsweek* and *Southern Living*.

Cultural Texts Versus Cultural Identities We must be careful not to conflate the magazines with the cultural identities they are targeting. After all, many publications offer different points of view on any given topic. Thus, there is no single, unified "Asian American position" on immigration reform or any "Latino position" on affirmative action. Rather, there can be a preponderance of opinions on some issues. These often are played out through popular culture forums.

People come together through cultural magazines and newspapers to affirm and negotiate their relationships with their cultural identities. In this way, the texts resemble cultural spaces, which we discussed in Chapter 7. However, magazines are but one example of how popular culture can function. Not all popular culture texts are easily correlated to particular cultural groups. Think about the various TV programs, movies, mass-market paperbacks, and tabloids that flood our everyday lives. The reasons that people enjoy some over others cannot easily be determined. People negotiate their relationships to popular culture in complex ways.

Resisting Popular Culture

Sometimes people actively seek out particular popular culture texts to consume; other times they resist cultural texts. But resistance to popular culture is a complex process. Avoiding certain forms of popular culture is one kind of resistance, but resistance can occur in a variety of ways.

Let's look at the ongoing controversy over the use of the logo of the University of North Dakota's Fighting Sioux. In August 2005, the National Collegiate Athletic Association (NCAA) placed "a ban on Indian imagery that it considers 'hostile or abusive'" (Borzi, 2005, p. B15) in postseason play. The University of North Dakota is one of the 18 institutions listed by the NCAA that would be impacted by this decision. Although the university is appealing this ban, many people are embracing the logo, and others are actively resisting it.

Let's look at how this logo creates strong feelings on both sides and how people are responding to the NCAA decision. There is mixed reaction to the meaning of the way the logo is used. Among American Indians as well there is disagreement about the use of the logo. It is important to recognize that all members of any cultural group have diverse reactions to popular images. For example, not all women are offended by the Hooters restaurant/bar chain that features scantily clad waitresses. Some women, however, do not like the way that women are represented at Hooters.

If we return to our touchstones to examine this controversy, we can see how communication, culture, power, and context play out in this example. American Indians are a relatively small segment of the population. At the University of North Dakota, there were 378 American Indian students out of 12,954 students in the 2005–2006 academic year (http://www.und.edu/profile/). They are the largest minority group at UND, but only about 3% of the student population. The U.S. census taken in 2000 shows that 642,200 people live in the state of North Dakota, and 31,329 are American Indian or about 4.9% of the population (http://www.census.gov/prod/2002pubs/c2kbr01-15.pdf). To whom, then, is this logo communicating? Which groups have a dominant voice in how the logo is interpreted? Think about who is communicating with whom. What kind of power differential is at work here when primarily non–American Indians choose and circulate these images to mostly non–American Indians?

The University of North Dakota's Web page describes the image in this way: "Since the early 1930s, the University of North Dakota athletic teams have been known as the Fighting Sioux and have used an American Indian head representation as their symbol. UND officially adopted the name 'Fighting Sioux' in honor of the first inhabitants of the region and some of the American Indian tribes of the state" (http://www.universityrelations.und.edu/logoappeal/history.html). The president of the university, Charles Kupchella, says, "I don't have a clue why anyone would take offense to something done respectfully and clearly meant as an honor" (quoted in Borzi, p. B16).

The context is important as well. As we noted earlier in this book, we need to consider the historical context as one important frame that helps us understand how meaning is created in intercultural contexts. The history of American Indian imagery is reflected in a distorted media image: "The Hollywood Indian is a mythological being who exists nowhere but within the fertile imaginations of its movie actors, producers, and directors" (Jojola, 1998, p. 12). How might these other distorting images influence the reading of this logo?

Because some of these stereotypes are negative, they have negative consequences for members of that social group. In his study of the controversy at the University of North Dakota over their mascot, the Fighting Sioux, communication scholar Raúl Tovares (2002) points to the climate at sporting events, which highlights the ways in which stereotypes, cultural values, and popular culture images can come together. He explains,

> *Hockey and football games have become sites where offensive images of Native Americans are common. Students from NDSU show up at athletic events with cartoonish images of bison forcing themselves sexually on Native Americans. At "sporting" events, it is not uncommon to hear phrases such as "kill the Sioux," "Sioux suck," "f———k the Sioux," and "rape Sioux women." Such phrases, many Native American students claim, are a direct result of the Fighting Sioux logo. (p. 91)*

Think about the ways that this mascot might circulate on jackets, T-shirts, cartoons, and other popular culture forms. How does popular culture represent an important site for negotiating this cultural identity? Why do non–Native Americans have a dominant voice and more power in these representations?

Finally, an interpretivist who is studying the logo controversy might go to the University of North Dakota and speak to the people there. One professor highlights this aspect of the controversy: "'Unless you're here, you don't know what it's like and how nasty it can get,' said a psychology professor, Doug McDonald, who is Sioux. 'I've had students in my office in tears because of the harassment we get'" (quoted in Borzi, 2005, pp. B15–B16). The logo and associated meaning (e.g., the sale of "Sioux-per dogs") create an environment in which some students clearly see negative meanings.

Here we saw a clear example of a group's resistance to popular culture and popular images because they construct American Indian identity in undesirable ways. Indeed, people often resist particular forms of popular culture by refusing to engage in them. For example, some people feel the need to avoid television and even decide not to own televisions. Some people refuse to go to movies that contain violence or sexuality because they do not find pleasure in such films. In this case, these kinds of conscious decisions are often based on concerns about the ways that cultural products should be understood as political.

POINT OF VIEW

NIKE IN CHINA

Consider again the Nike ad covered in Chapter 1. To understand why the Chinese government and many Chinese people were upset by this advertisement, think about the history of European imperialism in China as one frame for understanding this controversy. If people are upset about an advertisement in the United States, how might they appeal to get an advertisement pulled?

China has banned a Nike television commercial showing U.S. basketball star LeBron James in a battle with an animated cartoon kung fu master, saying the ad insults Chinese national dignity.

The commercial, titled Chamber of Fear, was broadcast on local Chinese stations and on state television's national sports channel before being pulled last month. It shows James, the Cleveland Cavaliers' reigning NBA rookie of the year, in a video game-style setting defeating the kung fu master, two women in traditional Chinese attire and a pair of dragons, considered a sacred symbol in traditional Chinese culture.

The advertisement "violates regulations that mandate that all advertisements in China should uphold national dignity and interest and respect the motherland's culture," the State Administration for Radio, Film and Television said on a statement posted Monday on its Web site.

"It also goes against the rules that require ads not to contain content that blasphemes national practices and cultures."

The statement added: "The ad has received an indignant response from Chinese viewers."

Source: From Audra Ang, "China Bans Nike Commercial," *Miami Herald*, December 7, 2004, p. 5C.

Resistance to popular culture can also be related to social roles. Likewise, some people have expressed concern about the supposedly homophobic or racist ideologies embedded in Disney films such as *Aladdin* (Boone, 1995). *Aladdin* plays into Western fears of homosexuality and the tradition of projecting those concerns on Arab culture. Resistance stems mainly from concerns about the representation of various social groups. Popular culture plays a powerful role in how we think about and understand other groups. The Disney film *Pocahontas* was criticized for its rewriting of the European encounters with Native Americans. According to communication scholars Derek Buescher and

Kent Ono (1996), this film "helps audiences unlearn the infamous history of mass slaughter by replacing it with a cute, cuddly one" (p. 128).

REPRESENTING CULTURAL GROUPS

As noted at the beginning of this chapter, people often are introduced to other cultures through the lens of popular culture. These introductions can be quite intimate, in ways that tourists may not experience. For example, movies may portray romance, familial conflict, or a death in the family; the audience experiences the private lives of people they do not know, in ways that they never could simply as tourists.

Yet we must also think about how these cultural groups are portrayed through that lens of popular culture. Not everyone sees the portrayal in the same way. For example, you may not think that the TV shows *Desperate Housewives* and *Two and a Half Men* represent quintessential U.S. American values and lifestyles. But some viewers may see it as their entree into how U.S. Americans (or perhaps European Americans) live.

In a social science study on television coverage of affirmative action and African Americans, communication researchers Alexis Tan, Yuki Fujioka, and Gerdean Tan (2000) found that more negative coverage increased negative stereotypes about African Americans. However, they also found that "positive TV portrayals did not lead to positive stereotypes, nor did they influence opinions" (p. 370). They conclude that "negative portrayals are remembered more than positive portrayals, are more arousing and therefore are more influential in the development of stereotypes" (p. 370). Given this dynamic, it is clear how TV news coverage can continue to marginalize and reinforce negative stereotypes, even if the reports also present positive information about minority groups.

In a more recent social science study, Mary Beth Oliver and her colleagues (2004) examined news readers' memories of racial facial features of people in the news. They presented one of four different kinds of news stories—nonstereotyped, stereotyped/noncrime, nonviolent crime, and violent crime—with the same photograph of the individual in the story. Participants were asked to recall this individual's facial features on a computer screen. They conclude, in part, that "[w]hen the stories pertained to crime, Afrocentric features were significantly more pronounced than the actual photograph depicted, whereas when the stories were unrelated to crime, the selected features did not differ significantly from the photograph actually seen" (p. 99). They suggest that certain topics might activate stereotypes and thus influence how these news stories are interpreted.

Migrants' Perceptions of Mainstream Culture

Ethnographers and other interpretive scholars have crossed international and cultural boundaries to examine the influence of popular culture. In an early study, Elihu Katz and Tamar Liebes (1987) set up focus groups to see how different cultural groups perceived the popular 1980s TV drama *Dallas:*

> *There were ten groups each of Israeli Arabs, new immigrants to Israel from Russia, first and second generation immigrants from Morocco, and kibbutz members. Taking these groups as a microcosm of the worldwide audience of Dallas, we are comparing their readings of the program with ten groups of matched Americans in Los Angeles. (p. 421)*

Katz and Liebes found that the U.S. Americans in Los Angeles were much less likely to perceive *Dallas* as portraying life in the United States. In contrast, the Israelis, Arabs, and immigrants were much more inclined to believe that this television show was indeed all about life in the United States. Katz and Liebes note, "What seems clear from the analysis, even at this stage, is that the non-Americans consider the story more real than the Americans. The non-Americans have little doubt that the story is about 'America'; the Americans are less sure" (p. 421). The results of this study are not surprising, but we should not overlook what they tell us about the intercultural communication process. We can see that these popular culture images are often more influential in constructing particular ways of understanding other cultural groups than our own.

Another study (Lee & Cho, 1990) that focused on immigrants to the United States yielded similar results. The researchers asked female Korean immigrants why they preferred watching Korean TV shows (which they had to rent at the video store) instead of U.S. programs. The respondents stated that, because of the cultural differences, the Korean shows were more appealing. Yet, as one respondent noted,

> *I like to watch American programs. Actors and actresses are glamorous and the pictures are sleek. But the ideas are still American. How many Korean women are that independent? And how many men commit incest? I think American programs are about American people. They are not the same as watching the Korean programs. But I watch them for fun. And I learn the American way of living by watching them. (p. 43)*

Here, both consumption of and resistance to U.S. television are evident. This woman uses U.S. television to learn about the U.S. American "way of living," but she prefers to watch Korean shows because they relate to her cultural identity. As she says, "I like the Korean programs because I get the sense of what's going on in my country" (p. 43).

The use of popular culture to learn about other cultures should not be surprising. After all, many teachers encourage their students to use popular culture in this manner, not only to improve their language skills but also to learn many of the nuances of another culture. When Tom was first studying French, his French professor told the students that *Le dernier métro (The Last Metro)*, a film by director François Truffaut, was playing downtown. The point, of course, was to hear French spoken by natives. But Tom remembers being amazed at the subtle references to anti-Semitism, the treatment of lesbianism, and the film's style, which contrasted sharply with that of Hollywood films.

Popular Culture and Stereotyping

In what ways does reliance on popular culture create and reinforce stereotypes of different cultures? As we noted at the outset of this chapter, neither author has had the opportunity to travel all over the world. Our knowledge about other places, even places we have been, is largely influenced by popular culture. For people who do not travel and who interact in relatively homogeneous social circles, the impact of popular culture may be even greater.

Film studies scholar Richard Dyer (1993) tells us that

> the effectiveness of stereotypes resides in the way they invoke a concensus. . . . The stereotype is taken to express a general agreement about a social group, as if that agreement arose before, and independently of, the stereotype. Yet for the most part it is from stereotypes that we get our ideas about social groups. (p. 14)

Dyer makes an important observation that stereotypes are connected to social values and social judgments about other groups of people. These stereotypes are powerful because they function to tell us how "we" value and judge these other groups.

Many familiar stereotypes of ethnic groups are represented in the media. Scholar Lisa Flores (2000) describes the portrayal of a diverse group of high school students in the television show *Matt Waters*. Flores focuses her analysis on Angela, a Puerto Rican student. According to Flores, there is a strong theme of assimilation at work in this show. She notes,

> to follow the seeming logic of this assimilationist politics requires an initial belief in the goal of a single, unified American culture expressed in a harmonious community such as that found within the Matt Waters community. The assimilationist perspective also mandates an assumption that ethnic minorities cannot maintain cultural difference except in rejection of all of dominant or mainstream society. (pp. 37–38)

She turns to Chicana feminism to show how we can resist these popular culture representations.

African American women also traditionally have been portrayed stereotypically on TV, especially in the 1950s and 1960s, when the roles they held were secondary (e.g., as domestics). Scholar Bishetta Merritt (2000) also reminds us of the African American female characters who often appear as background scenery: the person buying drugs, the homeless person on the sidewalk, the hotel lobby prostitute. Merritt points out that these women still project images, even if they aren't the focus:

> If the majority of black women the television audience is exposed to are homeless, drug-addicted, or maids, and if viewers have no contact with African American women other than through television, what choice do they have but to believe that all women of this ethnic background reflect this television image? ... It is, therefore, important, as the twenty-first century approaches and the population of this country includes more and more people of color, that the television industry broaden the images of African American women to include their nuances and diversity. (p. 53)

In her more recent study of local news coverage of Freaknik, an annual African American spring break event in Atlanta that ended in 2000, communication scholar Marian Meyers (2004) studied the ways that the violence perpetrated by African American men on African American women was represented. She found that the media coverage brought together issues of race, class, and gender and therefore tended to identify the perpetrators as nonstudent local troublemakers rather than as students. The news coverage also "minimizes the seriousness of the violence and portrays its victims primarily as stereotypic Jezebels who provoke male violence through their own behavior" (p. 96). The continued use of this sexualized stereotype for African American women displaces responsibility for what happened from the male perpetrators to the women who were attacked.

POINT OF VIEW

This essay points out the problem of stereotypes perpetuated by the media.

WHAT'S AMERICAN?

Say the words "quintessentially American kid" to most anyone, and the image that comes to mind is one of a white American—blond-haired, blue-eyed, etc.

Why is it that an African-American kid is never referred to as a quintessentially American kid? Why not a Hispanic child, an Asian child or an Indian child? Are they not just as American? Part of the reason for the slight is that stereotyping is ages old, as compelling as it is devastating.

In the wake of the recent school shootings that have rocked America, the hypocrisy of stereotyping people reached another insulting crescendo. . . .

Kip Kinkel, the 15-year-old boy who allegedly killed his parents and two classmates in Oregon last month, was described in Newsweek *magazine as having "an innocent look that is part Huck Finn and part Alfred E. Newman—boyish and quintessentially American."*

You knew he was white. . . .

The New York Times *and* Newsweek *also described Kinkel with words such as "skinny," "slight," "diminutive," "freckle-faced," with an "innocent look." Luke Woodham, convicted recently in Mississippi of killing two students, was the "chubby, poor kid at Pearl High School who always seemed to get picked on." Mitchel Johnson and Andrew Golden, who allegedly killed four girls and a teacher in Jonesboro, Arkansas, were "little boys." Andrew Wurst, who allegedly killed a teacher in Edinboro, Pennsylvania, was a "shy and quirky eighth grader with an offbeat sense of humor." . . .*

When's the last time a black child who allegedly committed a comparable crime was described in such wholesome detail, instead of as cold or adultlike?

The danger in such description is that black children are demonized in people's minds, making it easier to dismiss their humanity and easier to mete out more harsh and unfair judgments and punishment than whites receive.

Source: From "What's American? When Is the Last Time You Heard a Young Black Suspect Described as 'Innocent-Looking' or 'Shy'?" *The Post Standard*, July 3, 1998, p. A6.

What about those ethnic groups that simply don't appear except as infrequent stereotypes—for example, Native Americans and Asian Americans? How do these stereotypes influence intercultural interaction? Do people behave any differently if they don't hold stereotypes about people with whom they are interacting? Two communication researchers, Valerie Manusov and Radha Hegde (1993), investigated these questions in a study in which they identified two groups of college students: those who had some preconceived ideas about India (which were fairly positive) and those who didn't. Manusov and Hegde asked all of the students to interact, one at a time, with an international student from India who was part of the study.

When the students with preconceptions talked with the Indian student, they interacted differently from those who had no expectations. Specifically, students from the former group relied less on small talk, covered more topics, and asked fewer questions within each topic. Overall, their conversations were more like those between people who know each other. The students with the preconceptions also were more positive about the conversation.

What can we learn from this study? Having some information and positive expectations may lead to more in-depth conversations and positive outcomes than having no information. But what happens when negative stereotypes are present? It is possible that expectations are fulfilled in this case too.

For example, in several studies at Princeton University, whites interviewed both white and black "job applicants" who were actually part of the study and were trained to behave consistently, no matter how interviewers acted toward them. The interviews were videotaped. The interviewers clearly behaved differently toward blacks: Their speech deteriorated, they made more grammatical errors, they spent less time, and they showed fewer "immediacy" behaviors—that is, they were less friendly and less outgoing. In a second study, interviewers were trained to be either "immediate" or "nonimmediate" as they interviewed white job applicants. A panel of judges watched the videotapes and agreed that those applicants interviewed by the "nonimmediate" interviewer performed less well and were more nervous. This suggests that the African American applicants in the first study never had a chance: They were only reacting to the nonimmediate behavior of the interviewers. Mark Snyder (1998) summarizes: "Considered together, the two investigations suggest that in interracial encounters, racial stereotypes may constrain behavior in ways to cause both blacks and whites to behave in accordance with those stereotypes" (p. 455).

POINT OF VIEW

Popular culture—and movies, in particular—is an important place to begin to understand our society and our own identities. This excerpt discusses how movies can both help and hurt individuals' understanding of their own identities and those of others.

Over the years, Hollywood's given me great and terrible things—a culture as tangible as the mix of race and ethnicity I grew up around—and somewhere between my "reel" and "real" lives lie my deepest beliefs and my greatest fears, my nightmares and my dreams. As a kid and now an adult with a perpetual identity crisis, Hollywood has been a constant mirror for me, and what I've screened has resulted in validation and self-loathing, vindication and betrayal (I of it, and it of me). I was raised in a swirl of cultures that at times melded seamlessly and at others clashed violently—a contradiction that exists at the very heart of Hollywood, the tension between its most noble and most debased instincts.

For starters, I think I'd hate white people if it wasn't for Hollywood. This is not to say that I haven't hated some white people, and sure, the entire race, on occasion. But how can you hate someone you're on such intimate terms with—on screen and off?

Source: From Rubén Martínez, "Technicolor." In C. C. O'Hearn (Ed.), *Half and Half: Writers on Growing Up Biracial and Bicultural* (New York: Pantheon Books, 1998), p. 248.

U.S. POPULAR CULTURE AND POWER

One of the dynamics of intercultural communication that we have highlighted throughout this text is power. In considering popular culture, we need to think about not only how people interpret and consume popular culture but also how these popular culture texts represent particular groups in specific ways. If people largely view other cultural groups through the lens of popular culture, then we need to think about the power relations that are embedded in these popular culture dynamics.

Global Circulation of Images and Commodities

As noted previously, much of the internationally circulated popular culture is U.S. popular culture. U.S.-made films, for example, are widely distributed by an industry that is backed by considerable financial resources. Some media scholars have noted that the U.S. film industry earns far more money outside the United States than from domestic box office receipts (Guback, 1969; Guback & Varis, 1982). This situation ensures that Hollywood will continue to seek overseas markets and that it will have the financial resources to do so. The film *Spider-Man* exemplifies this economic position of Hollywood. Although the producers and distributors certainly made a considerable amount of money from the domestic screenings, they earned significant amounts of money from non-U.S. showings as well.

Many other U.S. media are widely available outside the United States, including television and newspapers. For example, MTV and CNN are broadcast internationally. And the *International Herald Tribune*, published jointly by the *New York Times* and the *Washington Post*, is widely available in some parts of the world. The implications of the dominance by U.S. media and popular culture have yet to be determined, although you might imagine the consequences. India produces more films than the United States but makes less money in box office receipts. (See "Point of View" box.)

Not all popular culture comes from the United States. For example, James Bond is a British phenomenon, but the famous character has been exported to the United States. In their study of the popularity of the Bond series, scholars Tony Bennett and Janet Woollacott (1987) note that in the Bond film *A License to Kill* "the threat to the dominance of white American male culture is removed not by a representative of that culture, and certainly not by a somewhat foppish English spy, but by the self-destruction of the forces ranged against it" (pp. 293–294). Here, a British character becomes a hero for U.S. and international audiences through the U.S. film industry. It is not always easy to know what is and what is not U.S. popular culture.

Much popular culture that is expressed in non-English languages has a difficult time on the global scene. Although Céline Dion, who sings in English, has been able to reach a worldwide audience, a fellow French Canadian, Garou, who sings in French, has not reached the same level of notoriety. Still, Garou (Pierre Garand) is extremely popular in the francophone world. His album *Seul* was the top-selling album in France in 2001, and he sold "1.5 million copies in Europe (France, Belgium, Switzerland) (*1.5 million d'exemplaires en Europe [France, Belgique, Suisse]*)" (Arseneault, 2001, p. 76). He is so popular in France that he "cannot have a private life, nor walk alone. There's no question that if he goes to restaurants or bars, he will be harassed, if not to say attacked" (*En Europe, Garou ne peut pas avoir une vie privée, ni se promener seul. Pas question pour lui de sortir dans les restos ou dans les bars sans se faire harceler, pour ne pas dire agresser*) (p. 76). Have you ever heard of Garou? To reach a worldwide audience, must he sing in English? Garou released his next CD, Reviens, in 2003 and decided that because of "the generosity of his French-speaking public . . . [the album] would be written and sung in French" (http://www.garouland. com/Reviens/english/bio_08.html). What does this tell us about popular culture? What does it tell us about the unequal power relations that are evident in popular culture? How does it influence how we think about the world?

Cultural Imperialism

It is difficult to measure the impact of the U.S. and Western media and popular culture on the rest of the world, but we do know that we cannot ignore this dynamic. The U.S. government in the 1920s believed that having U.S. movies on foreign screens would boost the sales of U.S. products because the productions would be furnished with U.S. goods. The government thus worked closely with the Hays Office (officially, the Motion Picture Producers and Distributors of America) to break into foreign markets, most notably in the United Kingdom (Nakayama & Vachon, 1991).

Discussions about **media imperialism, electronic colonialism,** and **cultural imperialism,** which began in the 1920s, continue today. The interrelationships among economics, nationalism, and culture make it difficult to determine with much certainty how significant cultural imperialism might be. The issue of cultural imperialism is complex because the definition is complex. In his survey of the cultural imperialism debates, scholar John Tomlinson (1991) identifies five ways of thinking about cultural imperialism: (1) as cultural domination, (2) as media imperialism, (3) as nationalist discourse, (4) as a critique of global capitalism, and (5) as a critique of modernity (pp. 19–23). Tomlinson's analysis underscores the interrelatedness of issues of ethnicity, culture, and nationalism in the context of economics, technology, and capitalism—resources that are distributed unevenly throughout the world. To understand the concerns about cultural imperialism, therefore, it is necessary to consider the complexity of the impact of U.S. popular culture. There is no easy way to measure the impact of popular culture, but we should be sensitive to its influences on intercultural communication. Let's look at some examples.

Some governments have become concerned about the amount of popular culture coming into their countries. The French government,

media imperialism Domination or control through media.
electronic colonialism Domination or exploitation utilizing technological forms.
cultural imperialism Domination through the spread of cultural products.

THE REEL WORLD

Nigerians don't go to the movies; the movies come to them. With few operating cinemas in Nigeria's largest city of Lagos, screenings often occur in local restaurants and private homes; videos are sold at market stands and sometimes hawked to motorists caught in traffic. This distribution of films from "Nollywood," as the country's ultralow-budget industry is known, may seem unusual, but it still satisfies the demand for movies—an obsession shared by people around the world.

In 2003, according to film industry source *Screen Digest*, some seven billion movie tickets were sold worldwide, earning an estimated 22 billion dollars. The greatest share of these global box-office receipts—more than 43 percent—came from U.S. theaters. Japanese theaters charged the most for tickets: Reserved seats can cost up to $25. Though India made more films than Hollywood, it made less money from them; the price of admission to an Indian theater averaged just 20 cents.

Many American blockbusters rake in more money internationally than at home. *Titanic*, the highest grossing film of all time, made two-thirds of its 1.8-billion-dollar take overseas. American movies have long been retooled for foreign sale. In the 1930s stars such as the comedy team Laurel and Hardy reshot their films in German and other languages—coached with phonetically spelled cue cards. Now native speakers are recorded over original actors' voices with varying success. In the French version of *Star Wars*, the villain's voice is considerably less menacing, and his name's been changed to Dark Vador.

American movies may be popular abroad, but foreign concession stands still cater to local tastes. Some European audiences wash their popcorn down with beer. In China the popcorn's sweetened. Other film snack favorites there—spicy cabbage, salted plums, dried squid shreds—have a flavor all their own.

Source: From Scott Elder, "The Reel World," Geographica, *National Geographic*, March 2005.

for example, has expressed dismay about the domination of the English-language broadcasting of CNN because it feels it projects a view of the world it does not share. In order to challenge this view, the French are launching their own international broadcasting network to present their views on the world. Although informally referred to as "CNN à la française," this new "channel would promote a vision of a 'multipolar' world that is not dominated by one superpower, such as the United States" (Louet, 2005). This new channel will not initially be available in the United States, but it hopes to expand from Europe, Africa, and the Middle East to Asia, South America, and the United States later. This will allow the French to compete with CNN, the BBC, and Al Jazeera as international broadcasting networks.

In a study on this tension between global networks and local networks, Jonathan Cohen (2005) examined the situation in Israel. He looked at Israel's 99 channels and identified six different ways that these channels function in the global and local environment. He then noted, "Foreign television is often thought to be harmful because it separates people from their national communities" (p. 451), but he warned that we should not so easily view foreign television in this way. He doesn't think it is yet clear that watching U.S. television shows "like *Sex and the City* or *The Apprentice* weakens viewers' connections to Israeli culture or strengthens them by providing a stark contrast to viewers' lives" (p. 451). Think back to Stuart Hall's encoding and decoding model. Cohen is emphasizing that we cannot assume people who watch certain shows will decode them in any particular way. The influence of media is more complex than a simple imposition of meaning from abroad.

Sometimes the Western images are imported and welcomed by the ruling interests in other countries. For example, the government of the Ivory Coast in West Africa has used foreign (mostly French) media to promote its image of a "new" Ivoirien cultural identity. The government purchased a satellite dish that permits 1,400 hours of French programming annually, which represents 77% of all programming. But it has been criticized by many for borrowing heavily from the Western media—for inviting cultural imperialism:

> *While television, as mirror, sometimes reflects multiple Ivoirien cultures, the latter are expected to acquiesce to a singular national culture in the image of the Party, which is also synonymous with a Western cultural image. . . . The cultural priority is openness for the sake of modernization in the quest of the Ivoirien national identity. (Land, 1992, p. 25)*

In another take on globalization, communication scholar Radhika Parameswaran (2004) undertook a textual analysis of Indian newspaper and magazine coverage of India's six Miss Universe and Miss World titleholders. In the context of a global economy, these women are upheld as role models who are ordinary women who worked hard to become a beauty queen while maintaining their national identities. Noting that "the therapeutic vocabulary of the beauty queen as role model, a recent construct of liberal individualism in South Asia, induces amnesia and insulates middle class citizens from the contradictions that such individualized discourses of empowerment can conceal.... [G]lobalization's ideologies of prosperity in India offer no recourse for the vast majority of poor citizens to attain even the humble ordinariness of the middle class consumer who desires the status of the global beauty queen" (p. 367). By asking what social functions these narratives serve, this critical study argues that they serve the more elite segments of society in India.

In all of these examples, popular culture plays an enormous role in explaining relations around the globe. It is through popular culture that we try to understand the dynamics of other cultures and nations. Although these representations are problematic, we also rely on popular culture to understand many kinds of issues: the conflict in Kashmir between India and Pakistan, the sex abuse scandals in the Catholic Church, the conflict in the West Bank between Israelis and Palestinians, and global warming. For many of us, the world exists through popular culture.

DISCUSSION QUESTIONS

1. Why do people select some popular culture forms over others?
2. How do the choices you make about what forms of popular culture to consume influence the formation of your cultural identity?
3. What factors influence culture industries to portray cultural groups as they do?
4. How does the portrayal of different cultural groups by the media influence intercultural interactions with those groups?
5. What stereotypes are perpetuated by U.S. popular culture and exported to other countries?
6. How do our social roles affect our consumption of popular culture?
7. What strategies can people apply to resist popular culture?

ACTIVITIES

1. *Popular Culture.* Meet with other students in small groups and answer the following questions:

    a. Which popular culture texts (magazines, TV shows, and so on) do you watch or buy? Why?

    b. Which popular culture texts do you choose not to buy or watch? Which do you *not* like? Why?

    c. Think about and discuss why people like some products compared to others. (For example, do they support our worldview and assumptions?)

2. *Ethnic Representation in Popular Culture.* For a week, keep a log of the TV shows you watch. Record the following information for each show and discuss in small groups:

    a. How many different ethnic groups were portrayed in this show?

    b. What roles did these ethnic groups have in the show?

    c. What ethnic groups were represented in the major roles?

    d. What ethnic groups were represented in the minor roles?

    e. What ethnic groups were represented in the good-guy roles?

    f. What ethnic groups were represented in the bad-guy roles?

    g. What types of roles did women have in the show?

    h. What intercultural interaction occurred in the show?

    i. What was the outcome of the interaction?

    j. How do the roles and interactions support or refute common stereotypes of the ethnic groups involved?

REFERENCES

Arseneault, M. (2001, December 15). Il chante avec les loups. *L'actualité,* pp. 76–82.

Bennett, T., & Woollacott, J. (1987). *Bond and beyond: The political career of a popular culture hero.* New York: Methuen.

Boone, J. A. (1995). Rubbing Aladdin's lamp. In M. Dorenkamp & R. Henke (Eds.), *Negotiating lesbian and gay subjects* (pp. 149–177). New York: Routledge.

Borzi, P. (2005, November 26). A dispute of great spirit rages on: North Dakota fights to keep a logo, Indians consider its use profane. *New York Times,* pp. B15–B16.

Brummett, B. (1994). *Rhetoric in popular culture.* New York: St. Martin's Press.

Buescher, D. T., & Ono, K. A. (1996). Civilized colonialism: *Pocahontas* as neocolonial rhetoric. *Women's Studies in Communication, 19,* 127–153.

Butterworth, M. (2005). Ritual in the 'church of baseball': Suppressing the discourse of democracy after 9/11. *Communication & Critical/Cultural Studies, 2,* 107–129.

Cohen, J. (2005). Global and local viewing experiences in the age of multichannel television: The Israeli experience. *Communication Theory, 15,* 437–455.

Dyer, R. (1993). *The matter of images:*

Essays on representations. New York: Routledge.

Fiske, J. (1989). *Understanding popular culture.* New York: Routledge.

Flores, L. (2000). Challenging the myth of assimilation: A Chicana feminist perspective. In Mary Jane Collier (Ed.), *Constituting cultural difference through discourse* (pp. 26–46). International and Intercultural Communication Annual 12. Thousand Oaks, CA: Sage.

Glascock, J. (2004). The Jasper dragging death: Crisis communication and the community newspaper. *Communication Studies, 55,* 29–47.

Guback, T. (1969). *The international film industry: Western Europe and America since 1945.* Bloomington: Indiana University Press.

Guback, T., & Varis, T. (1982). *Transnational communication and cultural industries.* Paris: Unesco.

Gunn, J., & Brummett, B. (2004). Popular culture after globalization. *Journal of Communication, 54,* 705–721.

Hall, S. (1980). Encoding/decoding. In S. Hall, D. Hobson, A. Lowe, & P. Willis (Eds.), *Culture, media, language.* London: Hutchinson.

Jojola, T. (1998). Absurd reality II: Hollywood goes to the Indians. In P. C. Rollins & J. E. O'Connor (Eds.), *Hollywood's Indian: The portrayal of the Native American in film* (pp. 12–26). Lexington: University Press of Kentucky.

Katz, E., & Liebes, T. (1987). Decoding *Dallas:* Notes from a cross-cultural study. In H. Newcomb (Ed.), *Television: The critical view* (4th ed., pp. 419–432). New York: Oxford University Press.

La Pastina, A. C. (2004). Telenovela reception in rural Brazil: Gendered readings and sexual mores. *Critical Studies in Media Communication, 21,* 162–181.

Land, M. (1992). Ivoirien television, willing vector of cultural imperialism. *The Howard Journal of Communications, 4,* 10–27.

Lee, M., & Cho, C. H. (1990, January). Women watching together: An ethnographic study of Korean soap opera fans in the U.S. *Cultural Studies, 4*(1), 30–44.

Lipsitz, G. (1990). *Time passages: Collective memory and American popular culture.* Minneapolis: University of Minnesota Press.

Louet, S. (2005, November 30). "French CNN" seen operational by end of 2006. Reuters Business Channel. Retrieved from December 3, 2005. http://today.reuters.com/business/newsArticle.aspx?type=media&storyID=nL30762703

Manusov, V., & Hegde, R. (1993). Communicative outcomes of stereotype-based expectancies: An observational study of cross-cultural dyads. *Communication Quarterly, 41,* 338–354.

Merritt, B. D. (2000). Illusive reflections: African American women on primetime television. In A. González, M. Houston, & V. Chen (Eds.), *Our voices* (3rd ed., pp. 47–53). Los Angeles: Roxbury.

Meyers, M. (2004). African American women and violence: Gender, race, and class in the news. *Critical Studies in Media Communication, 21,* 95–118.

Moon, D. G., & Nakayama, T. K. (2005). Strategic social identities and judgments: A murder in Appalachia. *Howard Journal of Communications, 16,* 1–22.

Nakayama, T. K., & Vachon, L. A. (1991). Imperialist victory in peacetime: State functions and the British cinema industry. *Current Research in Film, 5,* 161–174.

Newcomb, H., & Hirsch, P. M. (1987). Television as a cultural forum. In H. Newcomb (Ed.), *Television: The critical view* (4th ed., pp. 455–470). New York: Oxford University Press.

Oliver, M. B., Jackson, R. L., Moses, N. N., & Dangerfield, C. L. (2004). The face of crime: Viewers' memory of race-related facial features of individuals pictured in the news. *Journal of Communications, 54*, 88–104.

Parameswaran, R. (2004). Global queens, national celebrities: Tales of feminine triumph in postliberalization India. *Critical Studies in Media Communication, 21*, 346–370.

Snyder, M. (1998). Self-fulfilling stereotypes. In P. Rothenburg (Ed.), *Race, class and gender in the United States* (4th ed., pp. 452–457). New York: St. Martin's Press.

Tan, A., Fujioka, F., & Tan, G. (2000). Television use, stereotypes of African Americans and opinions on affirmative action: An affective model of policy reasoning.

Communication Monographs, 67(4), 362–371.

Tomlinson, J. (1991). *Cultural imperialism.* Baltimore: Johns Hopkins University Press.

Tovares, R. (2002). Mascot matters: Race, history, and the University of North Dakota's "Fighting Sioux" logo. *Journal of Communication Inquiry, 26*(2), 76–94.

CULTURE, COMMUNICATION, AND INTERCULTURAL RELATIONSHIPS

CHAPTER OBJECTIVES

After reading this chapter, you should be able to:

1. Describe six dialectics of intercultural relationships.

2. Identify three benefits and three challenges to intercultural relationships.

3. Identify three approaches to understanding intercultural relationships.

4. Describe some cultural differences in the notion of friendship.

5. Describe cultural differences in relational development.

6. Describe "turning points" in intercultural friendships.

7. Explain the frequency of intercultural dating today.

8. Identify challenges of intercultural marriages.

9. Identify four interaction styles in intercultural marriages.

10. Identify and describe characteristics of gay and lesbian friendships.

11. Describe how institutional, historical, or political contexts can facilitate or hinder intercultural relationships.

How do we develop relationships with people who differ from us in terms of age, ethnicity, religion, class, or sexual orientation? Think about friends who differ from you in any of these ways. How did you get to know them? Are these relationships any different from those that are characterized by similarity? Why do we develop relationships with some people and not with others?

There may be almost as many reasons for relationships as there are relationships themselves. Some relationships develop because of circumstances (e.g., working on a course project with another student). Some develop because of proximity or repeated contact (e.g., with neighbors in dorms or apartments). Others develop because of a strong physical attraction or a strong similarity (e.g., same interests, attitudes, or personality traits). Sometimes relationships develop between dissimilar people, simply because they are different. There seems to be some truth to *both* adages "Birds of a feather flock together" and "Opposites attract."

What is the role of communication in intercultural relationships? And how do contexts (social, historical, political) influence our relationships? In this chapter, we explore the benefits and challenges of intercultural relationships, examine how relationships develop over time, and identify some cultural differences in relational development and maintenance. Throughout the chapter, we emphasize a dialectical perspective on intercultural relationships—both friendship and romantic. Contextual issues exist along with individual relational issues, so for each of these topics we'll examine contextual issues.

There are increasing opportunities to meet people from other cultures through the Internet and increasing cultural diversity in many schools and workplaces, yet a recent survey shows that today's first-year college students have less interest in meeting people who are different from them (Farrell, 2005). In surveys, young people repeatedly say they are open to intercultural romantic relationships, yet for some groups, the rate of intercultural dating is exactly the same as it was 20 years ago (Clark-Ibanez & Felmlee, 2004).

Why do some people get involved in intercultural relationships and others not? Why do some intercultural relationships seem to flourish and others not? We think the answer lies in a dialectic: Although individual style and preference may play a large role, the contexts in which people meet and interact have much to contribute to the viability of intercultural friendships and romantic relationships. That is, social, religious, and educational contexts may promote *or* discourage intercultural relationships. Historical and political contexts also play a big role. For example, it was only 50 years ago that it was illegal for whites and African Americans to marry (Root, 2001). This, no doubt, is part of the reason that rates of interracial dating and marriage are the lowest among these two groups when compared to rates for other ethnic and racial groups (Martin, Bradford, Drzewiecka & Chitgopekar, 2003). Who we choose to befriend is determined both by our individual preferences *and* by social, religious, and political contexts.

In this chapter we first describe six dialectics and the benefit and challenges of intercultural relationships. Then we present the contributions of three communication perspectives on intercultural relationships—starting with the social science approach that emphasizes cross-cultural comparisons of relational notions. We then move to the interpretive perspective that has contributed in depth information about various types of intercultural relationships, and finally we discuss the critical approach that emphasizes the role of context in determining who we form relationships with and how these relationships develop.

THINKING DIALECTICALLY ABOUT INTERCULTURAL RELATIONSHIPS

Researcher Leslie A. Baxter (1993) suggests that a dialectical model explains the dynamics of relationships. She and her colleagues have identified several basic dialectical tensions in relationship: novelty–predictability, autonomy–connection, and openness–closedness (Baxter & Montgomery, 1996). That is, we can simultaneously feel the need to be both connected and autonomous in relationships with our parents, friends, and romantic partners. We may also feel the need simultaneously for novelty and predictability and the need to be open and yet private in our relationships. According to one study, Taiwanese students in close relationships experience these same dialectical tensions (Chen, Drzewiecka, & Sias, 2001). We can extend the notion of dialectical tensions to encompass the entire relational sphere (Chen, 2002; Martin, Nakayama, & Flores, 2002). Let's see how each of these dialectics work.

Personal-Contextual Dialectic

Intercultural relationships are both personal and contextual. There are aspects of the relationship that are personal—consistent from situation to situation—but context also plays a huge role in how intercultural relationships are developed and maintained. For example, are there contexts where you would be more or less comfortable in an intercultural relationship? How do your family, your church, your religious friends react to intercultural relationships? Studies have shown that the number-one predictor of whether individuals engage in intercultural dating is the diversity of their social networks—that is, if you are in contexts where there is diversity, it is more likely you will meet and go out with people from other ethnic/racial backgrounds (Clark-Ibanez & Felmlee, 2004).

Even who we are attracted to is largely determined by cultural contexts. Notions of attractiveness are defined for us and reinforced by what we see on TV and film and in other media. The standard of beauty for American women seems to be white and blond, and at least one study states that 90% of models in U.S. women's magazines are white (Frith, Shaw, & Cheng, 2005). This trend was noticed by one of our students:

> *I stopped by an airport newsstand and was struck by the similarity of the covers on the popular magazines displayed there (e.g.,* Vanity Fair, Cosmopolitan, Self). *Out of the 24 magazines, 19 had a white model with long blond hair on their covers! Two magazines had Caucasian brunettes, and two covers featured nonwhite women (one was Jennifer Lopez, the other Oprah Winfrey—on the cover of her* O *magazine).*

At the same time, Asian and Asian American women are often portrayed in popular culture texts and discourses as erotic, exotic, and submissive and thus highly attractive to white men (Root, 2001). One young man, Shane, described his attraction to Asian women:

> *I think they're so exotic. Really, what concerns me about the girl is the eyes, and Asian women have beautiful eyes, the form and the shape of them. It's a plus for me. I had another Asian girlfriend before. And I like their skin color, tannish, not just white, white, white. A girl with color. It's just different; it's more sexual, it's not just like plain Jane. ("Talking About Race," 2000, p. 59)*

This kind of attraction has spawned an entire business of mail-order Asian brides. Communication scholar Rona Halualani (1995) analyzed how these businesses perpetuate and market stereotypes of Asian women as idealized wives—submissive, sexual, and eager to please men. In contrast, Asian men are often stereotyped in ways that downplay their masculinity (Eng, 2001).

Of course, we all want to believe we choose our relational partners outside of the influences of these social discourses. We all want to believe we fell in love with this man or this woman because he or she is "special." Yet if we want to understand the problems and dynamics of intercultural communication, we must be attentive to these large contextual discourses about racial and sexual identities and realize there is the tension of both personal and contextual forces in any intercultural relationship.

Differences-Similarities Dialectic

According to the **similarity principle**, we tend to be attracted to people who we perceive to be similar to ourselves, and evidence indicates that this principle works for many cultural groups (Osbeck & Moghaddam, 1997; Tan & Singh, 1995). Finding people who agree with our beliefs confirms our own beliefs and provides us with **cognitive consistency** (if we like ourselves, we'll probably like others who share our views). In fact, we may explicitly seek partners who hold the same beliefs and values because of deep spiritual, moral, or religious conviction. In intercultural relationships, in contrast, we may be attracted to persons who are somewhat different from ourselves. The differences that form the basis of attraction may involve personality traits and may contribute to complementarity or balance in the relationship. An introverted individual may seek a more outgoing partner, or a spendthrift may be attracted to an individual who is more careful with money. Some individuals are attracted to people simply because they have a different cultural background. Intercultural relationships present intriguing opportunities to experience new ways of living in and looking at the world.

Most of us seek a balance between novelty and predictability in our relationships. Research shows that the most successful relationships have a balance of differences and similarities (Luo & Klohnen, 2005). In intercultural relationships especially, it is important to consider differences and similarities at the same time. Tamie, a student from Japan, explains how this dialectic works in her relationship with her roommate/friend Hong-Ju, a Korean graduate student:

We are both women and about the same age—30. Both of us are pursuing a Ph.D. degree and aspire to become successful professional scholars and educators. When we cook in our apartment, there are several common foods (e.g., rice, dried seaweed) while our eating styles may be different (e.g., Hong-Ju's cooking tends to include more spicy food than mine).

---

similarity principle A principle of relational attraction suggesting that individuals tend to be attracted to people they perceive to be similar to themselves.
cognitive consistency Having a logical connection between existing knowledge and a new stimulus.

We also share some common cultural values (e.g., importance of respect for elders). Yet Hong-Ju is married (a long-distance marriage), and I am single. Finally, we both consider ourselves as "not so typical" Korean or Japanese women. Hong-Ju's long-distance marriage and my staying single even in my 30s are usually considered as nontraditional in our respective countries. Eventually, this "nontraditionalness" creates in both of us a shared and proud sense of identity and bond.

Cultural-Individual Dialectic

Communication in intercultural relationships is both cultural and individual, that is, idiosyncratic. We have described various cultural differences that exist in value orientations, in both nonverbal and verbal communication. Although we have provided some generalizations about how various cultural groups differ, it is important to remember that communication is both cultural and individual. Tamie describes how she deals with this cultural-individual dialectic in her classroom teaching:

I have become very aware of cultural differences between U.S. classrooms and Japanese classrooms. In terms of my teaching style, I have noticed myself delivering the course content in a more linear, straightforward, fast-paced manner than I would in Japan. Therefore, there is definitely a certain cultural expectation that I am aware of as I teach in the U.S. However, I am also aware that there are unique individual styles and preferences among U.S. students—some students are outspoken and comfortable in speaking up; others take more time before speaking up, as they reflect and think more holistically. So this cultural–individual dialectic is always at work in my intercultural teaching experience here in the U.S.

Privilege-Disadvantage Dialectic

We have stressed the importance of (and the difficulty of understanding) power and power differentials in intercultural relationships. People may be simultaneously privileged and disadvantaged, or privileged in some contexts and disadvantaged in others. For example, Laura, a bilingual university student, feels at a greater advantage in settings in which conversations take place in Spanish and English than she does in all-English settings. Her friends who speak only English probably feel the opposite. People in more powerful positions in particular need to be sensitive to power differentials, which may be less obvious to them.

Static-Dynamic Dialectic

This dialectic suggests that people and relationships are constantly in flux, responding to various personal and contextual dynamics. Intercultural relationships are no different in this regard. When Judith first met her friend Patricia (a third-generation, Mexican American, older student), Patricia was single and had just transferred to Arizona State University from a community college. At that time, both were living alone (Judith was in a commuter marriage), but both were close to their families. Patricia is now married, has a daughter, and has almost completed her graduate education. In this context, Judith and Patricia cannot respond to each other as the people they were five years ago but must respond to each other as they are now. Changes occur very slowly sometimes, but we need to remind ourselves that relationships are both static and dynamic.

History/Past–Present/Future Dialectic

Rather than trying to understand relationships by examining the relational partners alone, it is helpful to consider the contexts in which relationships occur. Often, this means the historical context. As noted in Chapter 4, cultural groups have different relationships with each other; some of these relationships are more positive and others more negative. For example, the historical and continuing hostility between the United States and Cuba means that each cultural group has fewer opportunities to meet people from the other nation and thus fewer opportunities to develop relationships. One student, John, gives his views on the past–present dialectic:

> *I don't feel as if people should feel guilty about what their family, ethnic group, or country did in the past, but they should definitely empathize with those their ancestors have hurt, understand what they did, understand the implications of what they did, and understand how the past (whether we have ties to it or not) greatly affects the present.*

BENEFITS AND CHALLENGES OF INTERCULTURAL RELATIONSHIPS

Benefits

Most people have a variety of **intercultural relationships** that may

intercultural relationships Relationships that are formed between individuals from different cultures.

feature differences in age, physical ability, gender, ethnicity, class, religion, race, or nationality. The potential rewards and opportunities in these relationships are tremendous. The key to these relationships often involves maintaining a balance between differences and similarities. One example is the relationship between Judith and a Chicana colleague. When they first met, they thought they had little in common, coming as they did from very different ethnic and cultural backgrounds. But once they found commonality in their academic work, they discovered that they actually had a great deal in common. For instance, both come from large religious families, both have parents who contributed a great deal to their communities, and both are close to their older sisters and their nieces. Through the relationship, they also have learned a lot about each other's different worlds.

The benefits of such relationships include (1) acquiring knowledge about the world, (2) breaking stereotypes, and (3) acquiring new skills. You can probably think of a lot more. In intercultural relationships, we often learn specific information about unfamiliar cultural patterns and languages. Nancy, an undergraduate student, describes how she learned about culture and religion through her relationship with her boyfriend:

> *My family and I are Buddhists; however, we are not very religious. We still celebrate the holidays and traditions, but we do not attend the temple often. Anyway, my boyfriend, being Catholic, asked me to go to his church for an Easter celebration one year. I decided to go because I am an open person and not restricted to believing in just one religion. Anyhow, I went to his church, and I must say it was a good learning experience and a fun one, too. I was glad that I went to see what "Catholics" do to celebrate Easter.*

A romance or a close intercultural friendship may be the vehicle through which we learn something about history. Jennifer, a student in one of our classes, told us how she learned more about the Holocaust from her Jewish friends and about the Middle Passage from her African American friends. These are examples of **relational learning** — learning that comes from a particular relationship but generalizes to other contexts. Relational learning is often much more compelling than knowledge gained from books, classes, and so on. And once we develop one close intercultural relationship, it becomes much easier to form others.

Intercultural relationships also can help break stereotypes. Andy, a

---

relational learning Learning that comes from a particular relationship but generalizes to other contexts.

Young people often encounter disapproval for interethnic relationships, sometimes from both sides. Thomas Matthew Pilgrim and Robert Brown, from Athens, Georgia, are good friends. They describe how they got together and how they each get some static from their respective friends and family.

Matthew: *Ask anybody in Athens about me and Robert, they'll say that we are always together. I'm 15. He's 17. We think just alike, act just alike and dress just alike. If he wasn't black and if I wasn't white, people could think that we were brothers. A brother in every sense of the word.*

I'm part Mexican. I'm probably the only white person in Athens with their hair braided. I just did it because it's long; it's hard to keep up with. Most of the people I know are black or Mexican. As far as I know they don't have a problem with me. But there's always got to be an odd person that has to say something. One woman said, "Look, white boy, why you got your hair braided?" I just stopped caring what people think about me. [My] family are just really big———. All they like are people with the same skin as them. But race doesn't matter to me and my sister. And Robert and the other people I hang with don't care that I'm white. They were who I stuck with when I first moved here two and a half years ago. They took to me and really helped me. He's my best friend.

Robert: *I was going to fight him at first. I'm not going to lie. The homeboys I used to hang around with were like, "Hey man, look at that white boy." But my friend Jason knew Matt, so it was cool. I asked him his name. I told him mine. We started chilling from there. All my friends are black except for Matthew. It'd be about 30 of us and Matt. . . . He fits right in with me. He acts like everybody else that I hang around with. I don't care that he's white. If you want to find me, you look for Matt. Every day, all day, we hang out. We play basketball, beat each other up, listen to rap. We have fun. . . .*

Source: From "'Hometown Homeboys,' What They Were Thinking About Race," *New York Times Magazine*, special issue (How Race Is Lived in America), July 16, 2000, p. 26.

student at Arizona State University, told us about how he used to view Mexicans as lazy. This opinion was formed from media images, discussions with friends, and political speeches about immigration in the Southwest. However, when he met and made friends with emigrants from rural Mexico, his opinion changed. He saw that in everyday life his friends were anything but indolent. They had family responsibilities and sometimes worked two jobs to make ends meet. Later, we'll discuss how breaking stereotypes actually works in relationships.

We often learn how to do new things in intercultural relationships. Through her friendships with students in the United States and abroad, Judith has learned to make paella (a Spanish dish) and *nopalitos con puerca* (a cactus-and-pork stew), to play bridge in French, and to downhill ski. Through intercultural relationships, newcomers to a society can acquire important skills. Andy's immigrant friends often ask him for help with new tasks and activities, such as buying car insurance or shopping for food. When Tom first moved to France, his new French friends helped him navigate the university cafeteria. All of these potential benefits can lead to a sense of interconnectedness with others and can establish a lifelong pattern of communication across differences. We also hope that it helps us become better intercultural communicators.

Challenges

Intercultural relationships are unique in several ways, and as such present particular challenges. By definition, they are characterized by cultural differences in communication style, values, and perceptions. The dissimilarities probably are most prominent in the early stages of relational development when people tend to exchange less personal information. However, if some commonality is established and the relationship develops beyond the initial stages, these cultural differences may have less of an impact because all relationships become more idiosyncratic as they move to more intimate stages. There seems to be an interplay of both differences and similarities in intercultural relationships. The differences are a given, and the challenge can be to discover and build on the similarities—common interests, activities, beliefs, or goals.

Negative stereotyping often comes into play in intercultural relationships. As we discussed in Chapter 5, stereotypes are a way of categorizing and processing information but are detrimental when they are negative and are held rigidly. Sometimes people must work to get information that can counteract the stereotype. Navita Cummings James (2000), a communication scholar, describes the beliefs and stereotypes about white people passed along to her from her family:

- Whites can be violent and treacherous.
- Whites have an inferiority complex that compels them to "put down" blacks and other minorities.

- White men are arrogant, and white women are lazy.
- "Good" whites are the exception.

More importantly, James goes on to describe how she did not let these stereotypes become "an intellectual prison of my self identity or beliefs about Whites" (p. 45). Through intercultural relationships and effort, her beliefs evolved and the stereotypes diminished. She learned that race is not a predictor of intelligence but that income and opportunities are. She learned that all people, regardless of color, deserve to be treated with dignity and respect. And she made definite choices about how to relate to others and to cultivate a variety of friends, and not merely African Americans.

Another challenge in intercultural relationships involves the anxiety that people often experience initially. Some anxiety is present in the early stages of any relationship, but the anxiety is greater in intercultural relationships. Anxiety arises from concern about possible negative consequences. We may be afraid that we'll look stupid or that we'll offend someone because we're unfamiliar with that person's language or culture. Differences in age do not usually evoke such anxiety, but differences in physical ability, class, or race are likely to—at least initially. For example, a student describes his experience of being on a soccer team with players from Kenya, Jamaica, Egypt, and Mexico:

In our first meeting, we were to get acquainted with everyone and introduce ourselves. At the end of the meeting, we all stood around talking— reducing anxiety. Eventually, our conversations were directed toward self-disclosure and relating our experiences. I believe this helped me prepare for more experiences along this line.

The level of anxiety may be higher if one or both parties have negative expectations based on a previous interaction or on stereotypes (Stephan & Stephan, 1992). In contrast, intercultural interactions in which one or both parties have few negative expectations and no negative prior contact probably have less anxiety. For example, one student tells of traveling to New Zealand as an 18-year-old on a sports team:

I remember quite vividly experiencing uncertainty and anxiety and being forced to deal with it. Eighteen years old in a foreign land, and forced to deal with factors I did not know existed. . . . As I look back, I see that I was merely experiencing what I would later come to know as uncertainty and anxiety management.

The student goes on to describe how, with few negative preconceptions and no real language barrier, he quickly found similarity with people he met and had "truly an unforgettable experience."

Writer Letty Cottin Pogrebin (1987) emphasizes that intercultural relationships take more "care and feeding" than do those relationships between people who are very similar. Intercultural relationships are often more work than ingroup relationships. A lot of the work has to do with explaining—explaining to themselves, to each other, and to their respective communities.

First, in some way, conscious or unconscious, we ask ourselves, What is the meaning of being friends with someone who is not like me? Am I making this friend out of necessity, for my job, or because everyone I'm around is different from me in some way? Am I making this friend because I want to gain entry into this group for personal benefit? Because I feel guilty?

Second, we explain to each other. This is the process of ongoing mutual clarification, one of the healthiest characteristics of intercultural relationships. It is the process of learning to see from the other's perspective. For example, Judith discovered that, even when she thought she was being very indirect with her Japanese students, they still thought she was being rather direct. In this way, Judith came to understand that others can interpret events and conversation in very different ways.

Third, people who cross boundaries often have to explain this to their respective communities. Thus, your friends may question your close relationship with someone who is much older or is of a different ethnicity. This may be especially true for those who date someone from a different culture. For example, one of our students recounted how his friend terminated an intercultural relationship because of his parents' attitudes:

My Jewish friend was dating a Christian girl he met during his freshman year in college. He proposed marriage when they both graduated last year. But throughout their relationship, the parents of my friend let it be known that they were not happy with the fact that they were dating. My friend and his girlfriend are no longer seeing one another. My friend has told me he believes the parents' disapproval of the relationship was one of the reasons for their eventual split.

Historically, the biggest obstacles to boundary-crossing friendships have come not from minority communities but from majority communities (McCullough, 1998). Those in the majority (e.g., whites) have the most to gain by maintaining social inequality and are less likely to initiate boundary-crossing friendships. In contrast, minority groups have more to gain. Developing intercultural relationships can help them survive—economically, professionally, and personally.

Finally, in intercultural relationships, individuals recognize and respect the differences. In these relationships, we often have to remind ourselves that we can never know exactly what it's like to walk in another person's shoes. Furthermore, those in the majority group tend to know less about those in minority groups than vice versa. As Pogrebin (1992) stated, "Mutual respect, acceptance, tolerance for the faux pas and the occasional closed door, open discussion and patient mutual education, all this gives crossing friendships—when they work at all—a special kind of depth" (p. 318). Perhaps this is especially true of interracial relationships in the United States. Pat, an African American woman, describes the importance of honesty and openness in her relationship with her friend Rose, who is white:

> *"Rose is one of the few White women that I have an honest, direct relationship with. . . . She is very aware that I am a Black woman and she is a White woman. . . . I care about her very deeply. . . . And I am committed to our friendship and I respect her a whole lot. . . . I like her values. I like how she thinks about people, about nature, her integrity and her principles. . . . It is her willingness to make race her issue." (quoted in McCullough, 1998, p. 193)*

INTERCULTURAL RELATIONSHIPS

As with other topics, there are three communication approaches to studying intercultural relationships, and each makes a unique contribution to our understanding of how we develop and maintain relationships across differences. The social science approach identifies cross-cultural differences in how relationships are defined, initiated, and developed. The interpretive approach explores in depth the nature of these relationships and the role communication plays. The critical approach emphasizes the influence of various contexts—institutional, political, and historical—in facilitating and/or discouraging the development and maintenance of intercultural relationships.

Social Science Approach: Cross-Cultural Differences

The social science approach identifies various cross-cultural differences in relationships—including notions of friendships and the initiation and development of relationships.

Differences in Notions of Friendship   What are the characteristics of a friend? How do notions of friendship vary across cultures? To some people, a friend is someone to see or talk with occasionally, someone to do things with—go to a movie, discuss interests, maybe share some problems. This person might be one of many friends. If the friend moves away, the two people might eventually lose contact, and both might make new friends. Other people, however, view friendship much more seriously. For them, a friendship takes a long time to develop, includes many obligations (perhaps lending money or doing favors), and is a lifelong proposition.

Friendships are seen in very different ways around the world. For example, in most Western cultures, these relationships are seen as mostly voluntary and spontaneous, in contrast to family or work relationships. Although our friendships may be more constrained than we think (we do form relationships with people who are often very similar to ourselves), nonetheless, we enter into them voluntarily (Bell & Coleman, 1999).

Cultural differences in notions about friendships are related to ideas discussed earlier—ideas about identity and values. In societies that stress values like individualism and independence, as is the case in most Western cultures, it makes sense to view friendship and romance as voluntary relationships. However, people who view the self always in relation to others—that is, collectivists—hold a notion of friendship that is also less individual oriented and less spontaneous (Carrier, 1999). For example, in China, where the value of collectivism is very strong, friendships are long term and involve obligations:

> *The meaning of friendship itself differs from the American version. Chinese make few casual, short-term acquaintanceships as Americans learn*

to do so readily in school, at work, or while out amusing themselves. Once made, however, Chinese friendships are expected to last and to give each party very strong claims on the other's resources, time and loyalty. (Gates, 1987, p. 6)

Friendship in China cannot be understood without attention to an important related concept, **guanxi**—"relationships of social connection built on shared identities such as native place, kinship or attending the same school" (Smart, 1999, p. 120). It is through *guanxi* that things get done (e.g., jobs acquired or bureaucratic snafus resolved), often "through the back door." Although "connections" are important in the United States, they are not viewed in so positive a light. Here, one should not have to resort to connections to get something done. In China, in contrast, being able to get something done through connections, or *guanxi*, is seen as very positive, and so these relationships are purposefully cultivated. *Guanxi* is not the same thing as friendship, but friendship provides an acceptable base on which *guanxi* can be built (Smart, 1999).

This emphasis in China on cultivating close relationships, filled with obligations (and always open to *guanxi*), can be a bit overwhelming to people from Western cultures, but it can also be rewarding. A prominent journalist, Fox Butterfield (1982), who spent many years in China, describes these rewards:

Friendship in China offered assurances and an intimacy that we have abandoned in America; it gave the Chinese psychic as well as material rewards that we have lost. We ourselves did feel close to the Wangs [their Chinese friends], but as Westerners, the constant gift giving and obligations left us uneasy. (p. 47)

Differences in Relational Development Cultural differences often come into play in the very beginning stages of relational development, in initial interactions. Different cultural rules govern how to regard strangers. In some cultural communities, all strangers are viewed as sources of potential relationships; in others, relationships can develop only after long and careful scrutiny. For example, in traditional German Mennonite society, strangers, especially those outside the religious group, are regarded with suspicion and not as potential friends. In contrast, many U.S. Americans are known to disclose personal information in very public contexts. One international student observes,

---

guanxi A Chinese term for relational network.

POINT OF VIEW

In collectivist cultures, like Taiwan Province of China, relationships are very important and often involve a positive sense of interdependence and involvement with others.

The Taiwanese view of relationships is grounded in the concept of family. In Taiwanese culture, family is considered the most important environment shaping appropriate communication. Maintaining good relationships provides the foundation of social harmony. Taiwanese are guided by several principles in maintaining relationships with others: gan qing, ren qing, bao, lian, *and* mian.

GAN QING

Taiwanese relationship partners expect to provide mutual aid and care to one another. Gan qing *refers to this sense of interdependency.*

REN QING AND BAO

Ren qing *is somewhat equivalent to Western notions of "favor," but functions more as a mechanism regulating personal relationships. If one asks* ren qing *from someone, he or she has to return it eventually or be considered "heartless." This reciprocating behavior is* bao. Ren qing *and* bao *are often used interchangeably. A person understands* ren qing *if he or she knows how to reciprocate* (bao).

LIAN AND MIAN

[O]ne would not risk harming his/her relationship by not paying back the ren qing. *Such behavior may affect their* lian *and* mian. *Taiwanese conceptualize "face" in two ways:* lian *(face) and* mian *(image).* Lian *represents a person's personal integrity and moral character, and* mian *is a person's public image. These concepts reflect Taiwanese collectivist notions of face. One's behavior not only affects one's own* lian *and* mian, *but also their family and friends'* lian *and* mian.

Source: From T. C.-C. Chen, J. A. Drzewiecka, and P. M. Sias, "Dialectical Tensions in Taiwanese International Student Friendship," *Communication Quarterly, 49* (2001): 57.

One thing that was very different from what I was used to in Iceland was that people, even people that I didn't know at all, were telling me their whole life stories, or so it felt like. Even some women at the checkout line at the supermarket were talking about how many times they had been

POINT OF VIEW

In some societies, the development of relationships is intricately related to issues of status and formality. Communication scholar Wintilo Garcia explains how these issues are expressed in Mexican Spanish.

The Mexican use of the Spanish words tu *and* usted *signals the immediacy and status of the relational partners.* Tu *is the informal application of the pronoun* you. *It is common that individuals refer to their friends, family members, or children by this form of the word. The word* usted *is the formal form of the pronoun* you. *Cultural norms and rules require individuals to use this form when addressing new acquaintances, older people, professional (white-collar) people, and people who possess some sort of power. . . . In Mexico, as relationships become more intimate, the form of address changes. This often occurs over time where people who were once referred to by* usted *will later be referred to by* tu. *. . . Usually this transformation is initiated by the person who holds a perceived higher class. This is reasonable because high class individuals are perceived to possess more power in the relationship. In Mexico, the usual request phrase from the high class player is* tuteame *(interpreted as* you "tu" me*), which implies a desire for relational equality. In order for this request to be fulfilled, relational players must negotiate the pattern of communication. . . . For example, if a student normally addresses professors by the title* Doctor G *and* Doctor T, *it implies a status and class difference. In general, to change this form of address, the professor must initiate the request.*

Source: From "Respeto: A Mexican Base for Interpersonal Relationships," by Wintilo Garcia, in *Communication in Personal Relationships Across Cultures,* edited by W. B. Gudykunst, S. Ting-Toomey, and T. Nishida, 1996, pp. 137–155.

married or divorced or about the money they had, which, in my culture, we are not used to just telling anyone about.

The renowned communication scholar Dean Barnlund (1989), along with his colleagues, found many differences in relational development in their students in Japanese and U.S. colleges. Students in both countries were asked about their interactions with strangers and friends and about their views on friendship and more intimate relationships. The U.S. American students were more open and receptive to strangers; they talked to strangers in many different contexts—perhaps at a bus stop, in line at the grocery store, or in classes. In contrast, the

Japanese students talked to significantly fewer strangers than did U.S. Americans over the same period.

Barnlund suggests that these differences may be related to different cultural patterns, such as a preference for high- or low-context communication. In a high-context culture, relationships will not develop as easily without background or contextual information. For example, Yuichi, a Japanese student, had just begun his graduate work at a university in the midwestern United States. The department held its annual get-acquainted potluck, at which students and faculty chatted informally. Yuichi was panic stricken in this situation because he couldn't tell who was a member of the faculty and who was a student. Because he had no prior information about the individuals present (and couldn't determine their status from the way they dressed), he was uncertain about how to act and communicate. He was worried that he would address someone too informally or formally. The difficulty he experienced was not shared by others at the potluck, to whom status and position were less important in communication. Similar cultural differences affect communication at other stages of relational development.

Friendships   As relationships develop in **intimacy,** friends share more personal and private information.

Over a half century ago, Kurt Lewin (1948), a renowned psychologist, conducted a classic cross-cultural study in self-disclosure whose findings still hold true today. Lewin proposed that the personal/private self can be modeled as three concentric circles representing three areas of information we share with others. The first circle is an outer boundary that includes superficial information about ourselves and our lives—our general interests, our daily life, and so on. The middle circle includes more personal information—perhaps our life history, our family background, and so on. Then there is the inner core, which includes very personal and private information, some of which we share with no one. These spheres of information may correspond with the phases in relational development. Thus, in the exploratory stage, people exchange some personal information, and in the stability phase, they may disclose more intimate information.

According to Lewin, there is the most variation in the extent to which the outer area is more or less permeable. For example, for many European Americans, the outer boundary is highly permeable; they may disclose a wide range of relatively superficial information with many people, even those they don't know well, in many contexts. The

---

intimacy The extent of emotional closeness.

middle, or second, area is less permeable; this information is shared with fewer people and in fewer contexts. And information in the inner area is shared with very few. In contrast, for many other cultural and ethnic groups, the outer boundary is much more closed. International students in the United States often remark that U.S. students seem superficial. That is, U.S. students welcome interaction with strangers and share information of a superficial nature—for example, before class or at a party. When some international students experience this, they assume they are moving into the exploratory "friend" phase (the middle circle), only to discover that the U.S. student considers the international student to be merely an acquaintance. A student from Singapore explains,

I learned in the first couple months that people are warm yet cold. For example, I would find people saying "Hi" to me when I'm walking on campus or asking me how I am doing. It used to make me feel slighted that even as I made my greeting back to them, they were already a mile away. Then when real interaction occurs—for example, in class—somehow I sense that people tend to be very superficial and false. Yet they disclose a lot of information—for example, talking about personal relationships, which I wasn't comfortable with. I used to think that because of such self-disclosure you would share a special relationship with the other person, but it's not so because the same person who was telling you about her personal relationship yesterday has no idea who you are today. Now I have learned to not be offended or feel slighted by such incidences.

It's probably more accurate to say that what most people in the world consider simply a "friend" is what a U.S. American would consider a "close friend." A German student explains that in Germany people are hardly able to call somebody a friend, even if they have known that person for more than a year. Only if they have a "special emotional relationship" can they call the person a friend (Gareis, 1995, p. 128). For most U.S. Americans, the "special emotional relationship" is reserved for a so-called good or close friend.

Mary Jane Collier conducted a study with these three groups and Asian Americans in which she investigated conversational rules in close friendships (Collier, 1996). Again, she found many similarities in how these groups thought about close friendship. However, she also found some differences. For instance, Latino/a, Asian American, and African American students said that it took, on average, about a year to develop a close friendship; European Americans felt that it took only a few months. She also found differences in what each group thought was important in close friendships: "Latinos emphasized relational support, Asian Americans emphasized a caring, positive exchange of ideas, African Americans emphasized respect and acceptance and Anglo [European] Americans emphasized recognizing the needs of individuals" (p. 315). Clearly, such distinctions affect how people of different cultural groups develop friendships.

There also are cultural differences in how much nonverbal expression is encouraged. Again, according to Barnlund's and other studies, U.S. Americans expressed much more intimacy nonverbally than did the Japanese respondents (Nishida, 1996).

Romantic Relationships Some intimate relationships develop into **romantic relationships**. Several studies have compared the development of these types of intimate relationships across cultures. For example, communication researcher Gao Ge (1991) compared romantic heterosexual relationships among Chinese and U.S. American young people. Based on interviews with students about their romantic relationships, she identified common themes of openness, involvement, shared nonverbal meanings, and relationship assessment. However, there were some variations between the two groups. The U.S. American students emphasized the importance of physical attraction, passion, and love, which Gao interprets as a reflection of a more individualistic orientation. In contrast, the Chinese students stressed the importance of their partners' connectedness to their families and other relational connections, reflecting a more collectivistic orientation.

In another study, Gao (2001) compared intimacy, passion, and commitment in Chinese and U.S. American heterosexual romantic relationships. Based on her previous research and on cultural values, she predicted that intimacy and passion would be higher for U.S. couples, given that passion and intimacy are more individually centered relationship goals. She also predicted that commitment—a more collectivistic relational value—would be higher for Chinese couples. She found that passion *was* significantly higher in U.S. American couples than in Chinese couples but that the amount of intimacy and commitment did not vary cross-culturally. This may mean that intimacy is a universal dimension of romantic relationships, but the finding about commitment is more puzzling. Gao speculates that this finding may be related to the fact that all the couples in her study were in advanced stages of serious relationship, at which time commitment is more universally expected. Her hypothesis about commitment may have applied to couples in earlier stages in their relationships.

This was confirmed in a similar study comparing North American,

---

romantic relationships Intimate relationships that comprise love, involvement, sharing, openness, connectedness, and so on.

Japanese, and Russian beliefs about romantic love. In this study, North Americans emphasized romantic love, passionate love, and love based on friendship more than did the Japanese or Russians. Other, more collectivistic cultural groups emphasized the acceptance of the potential mate by family members and commitment over romantic or passionate love (Sprecher et al., 1994).

Research on the development of romantic relationships in the United States has focused on the importance of the individual's autonomy. Togetherness is important as long as it doesn't interfere too much with a person's freedom. Being open, talking things out, and retaining a strong sense of self are seen as specific strategies for maintaining a healthy intimate relationship. This emphasis on autonomy—trying to balance the needs of two "separate" individuals—in relationships can be difficult. Also, extreme individualism makes it challenging for either partner to justify sacrificing or giving more than she or he is receiving. All of this leads to fundamental conflicts in trying to reconcile personal freedom with relational obligations (Dion & Dion, 1988). In fact, one study found that people who held extremely individualistic orientations experienced less sense of love, care, trust, and physical attraction toward their partners in romantic relationships (Dion & Dion, 1991). These problems are less common in collectivistic societies.

Interpretive Approach: Communicating in Intercultural Relationships

Now that we have considered the contributions of the social science research, let's turn our attention to more in-depth examination of how we communicate across cultural differences. As we've noted, intercultural relationships may be very similar to intracultural relationships. However, there may be some unique characteristics that can guide our thinking about communicating in these relationships.

Based on interviews with U.S. and Japanese students who were friends, researcher Sandra Sudweeks and colleagues (1990) identified competence, similarity, involvement, and turning points as characterizing important aspects of intercultural relationships. For example, the students talked about the importance of linguistic and cultural competence. At first, language was a common issue. Even when people speak the same language, they sometimes have language difficulties that can prevent relationships from flourishing. The same holds true for cultural information. Dissimilarity may account for the initial attraction, but these students mentioned the importance of finding some *similarity* in their relationships that transcended the cultural differences. For example, they looked for a shared interest in sports or other activities.

Or they were attracted by similar physical appearance, lifestyle, or attitude. Sometimes shared religious beliefs can help establish common bonds (Graham, Moeai, & Shizuru, 1985).

Relationships take time to develop; students interviewed by Sudweeks and colleagues mentioned how important it was that the other person make time for the relationship. This is one aspect of involvement. Intimacy of interaction is another element, as are shared friendship networks. According to the study, sharing the same friends is more important for Japanese students than for U.S. American students because the Japanese students had left their friendships behind.

Finally, the students mentioned significant occurrences that were related to perceived changes in the relationship—turning points that moved the relationship forward or backward. For example, asking a friend to do a favor or to share an activity might be a turning point. The students remarked that if the other person refused, the relationship often didn't develop beyond that point. However, a turning point of understanding—**self-disclosure**—may move the relationship to a new level.

Another communication scholar, Brenda J. Allen (2000), gives us an example of a turning point. She describes her relationship across sexual orientation lines with a colleague in her department:

> *We found that we had similar ideas about issues, activities and improvement on our own critical thinking skills in the classroom. . . . [We] were both baby boomers from the Midwest, only months apart in age. We also came from lower-class families, and religion played a strong role in our childhood. (p. 179)*

Allen describes the turning point in their relationship when her friend revealed that she was gay: "As a heterosexual I had never before given much thought to sexual orientation or gays 'coming out of the closet.' Thanks to Anna, I have become far more sensitive and enlightened" (p. 180).

The process of dealing with differences, finding similarities, and moving beyond stereotypes and prejudice is summed up by a U.S. American student talking about her relationship with a Singaporean friend:

> *"We just had different expectations, different attitudes in the beginning, but at the end we were so close that we didn't have to talk about it. . . . After we erased all prejudices, that we thought the other person has to be*

---

self-disclosure Revealing information about oneself.

different, after we erased that by talking, we just understood each other."
(quoted in Gareis, 1995, p. 136)

Intercultural Work Relationships For many people, work is the place where they encounter the most diversity—working with people from different religions, generations, language backgrounds, ethnicity, races, and nationality. These encounters may be face-to-face or mediated—through telephone or computer. Understanding this diversity is especially important as organizations move from an assimilationist perspective ("Hire the quota and let them assimilate to us") to a more integrative perspective. One leading diversity expert refers to the latter as "foxhole diversity," the view that if the enemy is all around, you need people in the foxhole with you to support you; you need to cut through the superfluous and think about what skills and expertise your foxhole colleagues really need to possess as job requirements, not just what you'd prefer. We may prefer that our co-workers look like us and have the same language and religious background, but these preferences are not the same as the requirements for the job (Chozick, 2005). And more and more organizations are seeing the bottom-line payoff for a truly diverse workforce in a global economy—moving beyond concerns of women and minorities to concerns of generational differences, the pressures on gays and lesbians who have to hide part of their lives, and challenges in incorporating disabled workers (Hymowitz, 2005).

So the challenge in the workplace is to get along with people who may be very different, and some of the work relationships may turn into friendships, as one of our students reported:

> *At my job in the Memorial Union, I work with students of all ethnicities, races, and nationalities. At first I was kind of intimidated, but I've found that I've got to know some of them, since work issues always provide an easy topic to discuss and some of the discussions have led to more socializing. While I can't say these are among my closest friends, I probably wouldn't have had the chance to meet so many different people if I weren' t working at this job.*

Power, of course, often comes into play because most work relationships are within a hierarchy. There are subordinate–superior relationships and peer relationships, and the nature of the relationship constrains the interaction. If your boss tells you your hairstyle violates company policy, that's one thing. If your office mate, your company peer, tells you the photos on your desk offend her, that's something else. There is more room for negotiation and discussion.

It is difficult when race, ethnicity, and class are all part of the hierarchy—as is common in the tourist and restaurant business. The experience of one of our students is quite common:

> *In the restaurant where I work, all the servers (like me) are female and white, and all the busboys and kitchen help are Latino, who mostly speak Spanish, and the two bosses are white males—who makes everyone speak English when they're around. I kind of like to practice my Spanish a little in talking with the Latino workers, and I have a pretty good relationship with them. Some of the other servers really refuse to speak Spanish.*

Because there is a hierarchy, the busboys and kitchen help must speak English—even if the server can speak Spanish whenever she feels like practicing her Spanish.

Intercultural Relationships Online As we noted in Chapter 1, more and more people are using the Internet to communicate—for fun and for work, so much so that computer-mediated communication (CMC) has become an ordinary part of our daily life (Herring, 2004). The Internet presents us with enormous opportunities to form relationships across cultures and leads us to speculate how online relationships differ from RL (real-life) relationships and whether it is easier or more difficult to communicate across cultures online. The answers to these questions seem to be dialectical. Online communication is both similar to *and* different from RL relationships, and it both facilitates and inhibits the development of intercultural relationships.

Some scholars suggest that online communication can facilitate the development of intercultural relationships because of the filtering of nonverbal cues and the lack of so-called gating. That is, there is no **line of sight** data (information about gender, age, race, or nationality) in online communication. So online relationships are less likely to be "anchored" in these social/cultural conventions, prejudices, or stereotypes (Postmes, Spears, & Lea, 1998). And the reasoning goes, if one can develop a solid online relationship, not based on physical attributes or attractiveness, by the time online friends meet in person, these line of sight data don't matter so much (McKenna, Green, & Gleason, 2002). Of course this doesn't really address the problem of prejudices based on physical appearance. As scholar Radhika Gajjala points out,

---

line of sight Information about other people's identity based upon visible physical characteristics.

Why should it be wonderful for women and colored people to be able to hide who they are and to be able to disguise their gender, race, and culture in favor of passing as Caucasian? Why must we be ashamed of being women or colored or both? What's wrong with being colored? What's wrong with being a woman? (p. 84)

A number of studies show that online relationships are very similar to RL relationships. For example, Denise Carter (2004) studied CMC in "Cybertown"—a virtual "city" where people from all over the world "live" in virtual houses, spend city "cash," visit and socialize in various places around town—the plaza, beach, and café. She visited Cybertown several times a day for several years—and interviewed many of the hundreds of residents. She found that about half the residents transferred their relationship offline. She concludes that these friendships are very much like RL friendships, characterized by freedom, commitment, intimacy and trust, and very much a part of everyday life.

She found that, because there was no gating based on line of sight data, cultural differences played a very small role in Cybertown relationships. People from all over the globe interacted; formed friendships based on similar interests, values, and beliefs; and by the time many transferred their relationships offline, there was a solid basis of trust. Other scholars support Carter's conclusions—that the lack of physical cues in CMC helps facilitate cohesion dynamics in international settings, which might not occur in video or face-to-face (FTF) encounters (Gasner, 1999; Henderson & Gilding, 2004; Walther, 1996; Walther & Parho, 2005).

It needs to be pointed out that Cybertown residents, although from different countries, all spoke English, so misunderstandings related to language differences were minimized. Also, many experts point out that language and other cultural differences hold significant challenges for online relationships, particularly in initial stages of relational development. However, very few studies document particular difficulties. You might speculate on some communication challenges in online relationships: language challenges and communication-style challenges.

Language differences can make online communication and relationship development difficult, although the asynchronicity of CMC does allow non-native speakers more time to compose a message and to decode and respond than is true in FTF interaction. In addition to possible misunderstandings of specific words and phrases, language conventions such as humor can often be misunderstood. Understanding humor in a language often requires a sophisticated understanding of subtle nuances; irony, sarcasm, and cynicism in online communication across cultures should be approached with great caution (St. Amant, 2002). And when humor is misunderstood, it often takes complicated explanations to clarify, as one communication professor discovered:

> *One of the classmates in my online course made a remark, meant to be slightly sarcastic and humorous, about one of the group projects he was involved in for our course. However, the remark was perceived by some of the international members of his group to be in poor taste. Some thought it very rude and insulting. Others just found it childish. It took almost half the semester to figure out what had gone wrong, why the remark was misunderstood and to get things back on a good footing. I can't imagine it would have taken even half that long if the interaction had been face-to-face instead of on the Internet.*

Sometimes problems caused by language differences are exacerbated because one or both interactants may not be aware of the problem, because confusion or misunderstanding is general shown nonverbally—by a quizzical look or a raised eyebrow. Online communicators may have to work a little harder to make sure they understand each other and to give the other some leeway in expressing different cultural values and communication styles.

What happens when low-context and high-context communicators interact online? Because the Internet filters out almost all contextual cues (tone of voice, eye gaze, facial expression, etc.), scholars speculate that conversations between low- and high-context communicators might be difficult online (Olaniran, 2001). The low-context communicator might be very comfortable being direct about feelings and opinions, whereas the high-context communicator might feel rather constrained by CMC. When misunderstandings occur, it might be especially difficult to identify the source of misunderstanding and resolve it (Snyder, 2003).

For example, a Korean colleague who teaches at an American university reported that she often feels constrained in e-mail conversations with her U. S. colleagues. Having a preference for high-context communication, she finds the direct, low-context style of her colleagues a bit off-putting. This is especially true when they discuss sensitive issues over e-mail, and her colleagues ask her to give an explicit opinion that might conflict with others' opinions. She reports that she sometimes doesn't respond to these e-mail messages or tries to carry on the discussion with them face-to-face where contextual, nonverbal cues are available to her.

Another possible issue for high-and low-context communication differences concerns identity information. For many high-context cultures, background information of the speaker is part of the contextual information needed to understand and respond to a message, and as St. Amant (2002) explains,

> *However, in CMC, cues essential for determining identity are absent; therefore, it lacks context information that people from certain cultures need to determine how to interact in a given communication situation. As a result, participants from such cultures may feel uncomfortable, frustrated or reserved, because without these identity-based context cues, they cannot determine what is acceptable and what is unacceptable behavior in a given discourse situation. (p. 201)*

Of course, being reserved or quiet in a CMC environment can have implications for how one is perceived—particularly by those with context communication preferences.

Similarly, what are the challenges when someone from a high-power distance culture communicates from a low-power distance culture? The high-power person might be uncomfortable with the informality and relative disregard for hierarchy expressed by the low-power distance person. And depending on preference for face-saving strategies, it might be difficult to discuss communication differences, with interactants choosing different ways to protect or save theirs or the other person's face. For example, one study found that in Japan and Korea using a fax machine was much more popular in corporate communications than e-mail (Lee, 2002). This may be because people from East Asian countries such as Japan, Korea, and China, unlike people in Western countries, share the tradition of Confucianism, which emphasizes the social order in everyday living and showing respect for elders or seniors in the workplace and other contexts.

These beliefs influence their use of communication technologies, as illustrated in this report from a Korean marketing specialist, who is a virtual team member:

> *Whenever I want to report something and try to send the document via email, upon turning on a computer email facility, I hesitate and somehow give up and decide to go to see him [boss] in person or make a telephone call or send him a fax or an express surface mail. . . . The thing is that I have this feeling of being rude to him if I send the document via email. . . . In our Confucius culture, one has to show respect to seniors. . . . I think that email cannot convey signs of respect in an effective manner. . . . [S]ending via fax or surface mail at least shows some pains*

taken in order to give respect to the boss, and that matters. I feel that email might look too easy and casual to the degree that I might look like I don't show enough respect for my boss. (Lee, 2002, pp. 231–231)

Intercultural Dating   Why do people date others from different cultural backgrounds? Probably for the same reasons we form any intercultural relationship. We are attracted to them, and the relationship offers benefits—increased knowledge about the world and the breaking of stereotypes. This has been the experience of Peiting, a Tawainese American dating Paul, a Danish exchange student: "Dating Paul offers me this whole new perspective of life as a Caucasian and a Dane." Also, she encounters ideas that differ from those of most of her U.S. American friends: "We'll talk for hours about American films, about Danish government, even about variations in our countries attitudes toward drinking" (quoted in Russo, 2001).

Several decades ago, researcher Phillip E. Lampe (1982) investigated interethnic dating among students attending a college in Texas. He discovered that the reasons students gave for dating within and outside their own ethnic group were very similar: They were attracted to the other person, physically and/or sexually. In contrast, the reasons students gave for not dating someone within or outside their own ethnic group were very different. The main reason for not dating *within* the ethnic group was lack of attraction. However, the reasons for not dating *outside* the ethnic group were not having an opportunity to do so and not having thought about it. Lampe interpreted this distinction in responses as reflecting the social and political structure of U.S. American society. That is, most individuals, by the time they reach adolescence, have been taught that it is better to date within one's ethnic and racial group and probably have had very little opportunity to date interethnically.

Have things changed since Lampe's study? Many people assume that they have, that U.S. Americans today are much more open to intercultural relationships. We decided to conduct a study similar to Lampe's to find out. What we found was somewhat surprising and confirms how individual dating experiences and societal contexts are still closely related (Martin, Bradford, Chitgopekar, & Drzewiecka, 2003). Like Lampe's respondents, about 60% of our respondents said they had dated interculturally, with Mexican Americans doing so more frequently than African Americans or whites. Many of the remaining 40% gave the same reasons as respondents in Lampe's study for not dating interculturally: They had no desire or no opportunity. So, even though Lampe's study was conducted in the early 1980s, the same conditions seem to hold, at least in some parts of the United States, particularly for African Americans and whites. The reality remains that most Americans live, go to school, and worship in segregated groups (Stephan, 1999). And this was certainly true in our study, as 80% of the white students said they grew up in all-white neighborhoods.

We also found that the social context and past experiences were a strong influence on whether young people dated interculturally. Not surprisingly, those who did date interculturally were more likely to have grown up in ethnically diverse neighborhoods and to have more ethnically diverse acquaintances and friends. In addition, they came from families in which other family members had dated interculturally. This suggests that family attitudes play a big role. Indeed, other studies confirm that families often instill negative attitudes regarding interracial friendships or romantic relationships (Harris & Kalbfleisch, 2000; Kouri & Lasswell, 1993; Mills, Daly, Longmore, & Kilbride, 1995). And these attitudes are learned at a very young age. As Derryck, a young black child said, when asked about his relationship with his white friend, "Black and white kids can be friends with each other, if you're in the same class. But they can't get married, because they don't match. They can't have a kid together" ("Talking About Race," 2000, p. 47). Interracial friendships may be more accepted in elementary school, but they are less accepted in teenage years (Graham & Cohen, 1997).

Finally, whether individuals date interculturally may also depend on the region of the country in which they grow up. A study conducted in California, for example, showed a slightly higher incidence of intercultural dating there than we found in our study (Tucker & Mitchell-Kernan, 1995). As the 2000 census shows, there is more diversity in the West and Southwest. Given what we know about the influence of context on interpersonal relationships, we would expect more diverse schools and neighborhoods, and thus more opportunity for intercultural contact in these areas.

Permanent Relationships In spite of substantial resistance to intercultural (especially interracial) romantic relationships, increasing numbers of people are marrying across racial and ethnic lines, so much so that scholar Maria P. P. Root (2001) says we are in the midst of a "quiet revolution." Who is most likely to intermarry in the United States? According to Root, women (except for black women) intermarry more than men. Also, older rather than younger people tend to intermarry, except where similar-size groups live in proximity to one another. For example, in Hawaii, California, and Arizona, younger persons are more

Diana, a native of Singapore, is ethnically Chinese, and Rogan is a white American; both are students at Georgetown University. The couple met early during the fall semester and have been dating since. This newspaper article describes how people react to them as an intercultural couple.

While both Rogan and Diana's parents accept their current relationship, Diana's family is somewhat more apprehensive toward the situation. "They don't mind if I date Rogan now, in college, but they see it as temporary," she said. "Their ideal, for something long term, would be a Chinese boy."

The couple feels they haven't experienced negative reactions from the Georgetown community. They have, however, encountered some awkward moments because of other students' stereotypes. During the early months of their relationship, the two often headed out for the night with Rogan's close friend, Larry. Larry is also of Chinese descent. "When I met Rogan's friends, they often thought I was dating Larry," Diana recalled. While the problem faded with time, Diana did feel annoyed at the assumptions others automatically made based on appearances.

Despite the problems encountered the couple see many advantages to dating outside their cultural groups. . . . [Rogan] feels especially struck with the new viewpoint Diana's culture brings to the relationship. "We have to think differently, but it keeps it interesting," he stated. It's also really cool to be with someone who doesn't always want to go down to the Tombs for a burger. Instead Diana will cook some great meal I've never even heard of."

While intercultural relationships may present difficulties, Rogan and Diana still have the typical ebb and flow of a traditional couple. "We do have our arguments," Diana said. "Rogan's still upset that I didn't know who was playing in the Super Bowl. But I guess that would probably happen with any boy."

Source: From R. Russo, "Intercultural Relationships Flourish Despite Differences," *The Hoya* (Georgetown University student newspaper), February 9, 2001.

likely to intermarry. In addition, later generations of immigrants have higher rates of intermarriage than earlier ones.

Why are the rates of intermarriage so low for certain groups? The answer has to do with various contextual issues related to gender and social status. For example, there are fewer objections to Asian American–white than to black–white marriages. Gender stereotypes come into play in that Asian women are, even now, viewed as traditionally feminine, subservient, and obedient, as well as petite—making them attractive as partners for white men. This has led to increasing numbers of Asian American women intermarrying. The same is true for Latinas and Native American women, but not black women. As Root observes, blackness for them still has caste connotations, which means they are partnered in intermarriages less than any other group. White women, in contrast, intermarry more frequently.

The larger social discourses on interracial relationships should not be ignored. Columnist Hoyt Sze (1992) notes,

> *Naturally, people outmarry [marry outside their racial group] for love. But we must ask ourselves how much of this love is racist, unequal love. Unfortunately, interracial love is still inextricably linked to colonialism. How else does one explain the disproportional rates at which Asian American women and African American men marry out? Is it just a coincidence that the mainstream media objectify the same groups as "exotic-erotic" playthings? I know that Asian American men and African American women aren't fundamentally lacking in attractiveness or desirability. (p. 10)*

If we try to understand romantic love only on the interpersonal level, how might we explain the high rates of outmarriage by some groups and not others?

In any case, the current trend to intermarry may change things. As the rates of intermarriage continue to increase, these families will produce more children who challenge the current race and gender stereotypes, and the structural barriers to intermarriage will be eroded (Lee & Edmonston, 2005). As Root (2001) observes, "Intermarriage has ripple effects that touch many people's lives. It is a symbolic vehicle through which we can talk about race and gender and reexamine our ideas about race" (p. 12). And the fact is that younger people do have more tolerant attitudes about intermarriage. Although intermarriage will not solve all intercultural problems, the increasing numbers of multicultural people will have a positive impact.

What are the major concerns of couples who marry interculturally? One study compared experiences of inter- and intracultural couples. Their concerns, like those of dating couples, often involved dealing with pressures from their families and from society in general. An additional issue involved raising children. Sometimes these concerns are intertwined. Although many couples are concerned with raising children and dealing with family pressures, those in intercultural

Most people describe their reasons for intermarriage in terms of romantic love. Mariel, a 24-year-old Chicana raised in a suburb of Los Angeles, reflected on what influenced her decision to marry her black husband and how fortunate she was that her family approved.

I was really active in La Raza *and feel committed to my people, so I always thought I would marry a Chicano guy. I love my older brothers and even thought I might marry one of their friends. When I went away to college. . . . I was just exposed to so many people. My political ideals didn't change. But I met my husband in my second year. He was very supportive of my commitments. We just started doing things together, studying, talking, going to parties. He fit in well with my friends and I liked his friends. It was like we would go to parties and there were all sorts of people there and I'd find I always had more in common with him than just about anyone in a room. We had really good talks. And music. We both loved music and movies. So one thing led to another. I tried to talk myself out my feelings for him, thinking I should just keep it as good friends, but then I thought, "Shouldn't the man I marry be my best friend?" My family liked him. I mean, like, if my brothers didn't like him, this would have been real hard. They have a lot of influence on me even though I make up my own mind. We talked a lot about what it meant to marry someone different than your own cultural background. But I realized I didn't have to give up my commitment to my people. We believed in the same issues. Now it might have been different if he was white. I'm not sure how that would have gone over.*

Source: From M. P. P. Root, *Love's Revolution: Interracial Marriage*, (Philadelphia: Temple University Press, 2001), pp. 7–8.

marriages deal with these issues to a greater extent. They are more likely to disagree about how to raise the children and are more likely to encounter opposition and resistance from their families about the marriage (Graham, Moeai, & Shizuru, 1985).

Writer Dugan Romano (1997) interviewed couples in which one spouse came from another country to identify challenges of these international marriages. Some are common problems faced by most couples, including friends, politics, finances, sex, in-laws, illness and suffering, and children. But some issues are exacerbated in these intercultural marriages; these involve values, eating and drinking habits, gender roles, attitudes regarding time, religion, place of residence, stress, and ethnocentrism.

Of course, every husband and wife develop their own idiosyncratic way of relating to each other, but intercultural marriage poses consistent challenges. Romano also points out that most couples have their own systems for working out the power balance in their relationships, for deciding who gives and who takes. She identifies four styles of interaction: submission, compromise, obliteration, and consensus. Couples may adopt different styles depending on the context.

The **submission style** is the most common. In this style, one partner submits to the culture of the other partner, abandoning or denying his or her own. The submission may occur in public, whereas in private life the relationship may be more balanced. Romano points out that this model rarely works in the long run. People cannot erase their core cultural background, no matter how hard they try.

In the **compromise style**, each partner gives up some of his or her culturally bound habits and beliefs to accommodate the other person. Although this may seem fair, it really means that both people sacrifice things that are important to them. For example, the Christian who gives up having a Christmas tree and celebrating Christmas for the sake of a Jewish spouse may eventually come to resent the sacrifice.

In the **obliteration style**, both partners deal with differences by attempting to erase their individual cultures. They may form a new culture, with new beliefs and habits, especially if they live in a country that is home to neither of them. This may seem to be the only way for people whose backgrounds are completely irreconcilable to survive. However, because it's difficult for people to completely cut themselves off from their own cultural backgrounds, obliteration is not a viable long-term solution.

The style that is the most desirable, not surprisingly, is the **consensus style**, which is based on agreement and negotiation. It is related to compromise in that both partners give and take, but it is not

---

submission style A style of interaction for an intercultural couple in which one partner yields to the other partner's cultural patterns, abandoning or denying his or her own culture. (Compare with **compromise style**, **consensus style**, and **obliteration style**.)

compromise style A style of interaction for an intercultural couple in which both partners give up some part of their own cultural habits and beliefs to minimize cross-cultural differences. (Compare with **consensus style**, **obliteration style**, and **submission style**.)

obliteration style A style of interaction for an intercultural couple in which both partners attempt to erase their individual cultures in dealing with cultural differences. (Compare with **compromise style**, **consensus style**, and **submission style**.)

consensus style A style of interaction for an intercultural couple in which partners deal with cross-cultural differences by negotiating their relationship. (Compare with **compromise style**, **obliteration style**, and **submission style**.)

a tradeoff; rather, it is a win-win proposition. Consensus may incorporate elements of the other models. On occasion, one spouse might temporarily "submit" to the other's culture or temporarily give up something to accommodate the other. For example, while visiting her husband's Muslim family, a Swiss wife might substantially change her demeanor, dressing more modestly and acting less assertive. Consensus requires flexibility and negotiation. Romano stresses that couples who are considering permanent international relationships should prepare for the commitment by living together, spending extended time with the other's family, learning the partner's language, studying the religion, and learning the cuisine. The couple should also consider legal issues like their own and their children's citizenship, finances and taxation, ownership of property, women's rights, and divorce.

Gay and Lesbian Relationships Most of the discussion so far was derived from research on heterosexual friendships and romantic relationships. Much less information is available about gay and lesbian relationships. What we do know is that these relationships are a fact of society: homosexuality has existed in every society and in every era (Chesebro, 1981, 1997).

What we know about gay and lesbian relationships is often in contrast to the "model" of heterosexual relationships. Gay and lesbian relationships may be intracultural or intercultural. Although there are many similarities between gay/lesbian and straight relationships, they may differ in several areas, including the roles of same-sex friendships and cross-sex friendships and the relative importance of friendships.

Same-sex friendship relationships may have different roles for gay and straight males in the United States. Typically, U.S. males are socialized toward less self-expression and emotional intimacy. Most heterosexual men turn to women for emotional support; often, a wife or female romantic partner, rather than a same-sex friend, is the major source of emotional support.

This was not always the case in the United States, and it is not the case today in many countries, where male friendship often closely parallels romantic love. In India, for example, "men are as free as women to form intimate friendships with revelations of deep feelings, failures, and worries and to show their affection physically by holding hands" (Gareis, 1995, p. 36). Same-sex friendships and romantic relationships both may involve expectations of undying loyalty, deep devotion, and intense emotional gratification (Hammond & Jablow, 1987). This seems to be true as well for gay men, who tend to seek emotional support from same-sex friendships (Sherrod & Nardi, 1988). However this differentiation doesn't seem to hold for straight women and lesbians, who more often seek intimacy through same-sex friendships. That is, they seek intimate friendships with women more than with men.

The role of sexuality also may be different in heterosexual relationships than in gay and lesbian relationships. In heterosexual relationships, friendship and sexual involvement sometimes seem mutually exclusive. As the character Harry said to Sally in the film *When Harry Met Sally*, "Men can never be friends with women. The sex thing always gets in the way." Cross-sex friendships always seem ambiguous because of the "sex thing."

This ambiguity does not seem to hold in gay and lesbian relationships. Friendships can start with sexual attraction and involvement but endure after sexual involvement is terminated. There is frequently a clear distinction between "lover" and "friend" for both gays and lesbians similar to the "incest taboo" among a family of friends (Nardi, 1992, p. 114). Close friendships may play a more important role for gays than for straights. Gays and lesbians often suffer discrimination and hostility from the straight world (Nakayama, 1998), and they often have strained relationships with their families. For these reasons, the social support from friends in the gay community can play a crucial role. Sometimes friends act as family, as one young man explains,

"Friends become part of my extended family. A lot of us are estranged from our families because we're gay and our parents don't understand or don't want to understand. That's a separation there. I can't talk to them about my relationships. I don't go to them; I've finally learned my lesson: family is out. Now I've got a close circle of good friends that I can sit and talk to about anything. I learned to do without the family." (quoted in Nardi, 1992, p. 110)

Many of the issues in heterosexual romantic relationships apply to gay/lesbian couples as well. However, some relational issues, especially those pertaining to permanence and relational dissolution, are unique to gay partners.

In the United States, there is little legal recognition of permanent gay and lesbian relationships. At the time of this writing, only three states—Vermont, Massachusetts, and Connecticut—recognize same-sex civil unions (Fahrenthold, 2005). In fact, many states have passed laws stating that only marriages between a man and a woman will be recognized (Neil, 2005). The federal government also has passed the Defense of Marriage Act, which allows states to not recognize same-sex marriages registered in other states. These political and legal actions have implications for the development and maintenance, as well as the termination, of gay and lesbian relationships in the United States.

Some countries, however, formally recognize same-sex relationships and thereby create different social conditions for gay and lesbian relationships (Fish, 2005). Same-sex relationships, like heterosexual relationships, are profoundly influenced by the cultural contexts in which they occur. For example, Vietnam does not stipulate that marriage must be between members of the opposite sex ("Mariage Vietnamien Lesbien," 1998), and King Sihanouk has supported gay marriages in Thailand ("Cambodian King Backs Gay Marriage," 2004). In the Netherlands, Belgium, Spain, and Canada, gay and lesbian couples are allowed to marry with all the same legal rights and responsibilities as heterosexual spouses (Knox, 2005). In many European countries (and also Australia and New Zealand), gay relationships are recognized as legal "partnerships"; in some of these countries (e.g., Denmark, Finland, Iceland, Norway, and Sweden), same-sex couples are provided rights similar to those enjoyed by married couples. In other countries (Czech Republic, France, Germany, Luxembourg, Norway, Sweden, and Switzerland) the rights of these partnerships pertaining to health and medical benefits and financial rights (such as tax status and inheritance) are more restricted (ABC Newsonline, 1999; Cole, 2001; Fish, 2005; see also http://www.ilga-europe.org/europe/issues/marriage_and_partnership). However, in many places in the world, the social contexts are much more problematic for gay partners in permanent relationships.

Regardless of one's position on the desirability of gay and lesbian marriage, it is important to understand the implications for same-sex relationships, which include issues of dissolution. The dissolution of heterosexual relationships often is delayed because of family and societal pressures, religious beliefs, child custody battles, and so on. However, some gay relationships probably terminate much earlier because they are not subject to these pressures. This also may mean that, even though they are shorter lived, gay and lesbian relationships are happier and more mutually productive (Bell & Weinberg, 1978).

Critical Approach: Contextual Influences

It is important to consider intercultural relationships in the contexts in which they emerge—whether the contexts are supportive or whether they discourage intercultural relationships. Let's examine several of these contextual influences: family and neighborhood, educational and religious institutions, and historical and political contexts.

Family and Neighborhood Contexts   According to Dodd and Baldwin (2002), the first place we learn about communication adaptability and receptivity—how to respond to those who are different and how to respond to new situations—is in the family. Did your family encourage you to seek our intercultural relationships? Did your parents have a culturally diverse set of friends? And some types of relationships are more accepted than others. For example, parents may encourage children to develop friendships across religious, racial, and class lines but discourage romantic relationships with members of these same groups. Parents often play an important role in who their children date—particularly for daughters. In a recent study, it was found that women were much more likely than men to mention pressure from family members as a reason that interethnic dating would be difficult. As one Latina said,

> *It would be hard . . . because my parents wouldn't agree with it and neither would my Hispanic friends. They've all told me not to mix blood. Stay with your own. (Clark-Ibanez & Felmlee, 2004, p. 300)*

Even more important than what parents say is what they do. In this same study, it was the diversity of parents' friendship network, not the parents' attitudes, that determined the likelihood of the child's dating interethnically. Those whose parents had diverse friends were more likely to date interethnically than those whose parents had less diverse friends.

The diversity of one's neighborhood also has a great influence on whether one forms intercultural friendships. Here, the proximity principle comes into play. That is, we are more likely to be attracted to and form relationships with those we see often. How diverse was your childhood neighborhood?

Religious and Educational Contexts   Institutions like schools and churches/synagogues can play a huge part in promoting or discouraging intercultural friendships. It was not that long ago that some colleges banned interracial dating, and an often quoted statistic is that the most segregated hour of the week is Sunday morning—when Christians are in church. At the same time, religious institutions can provide much-needed support. One interracial couple found support by participating in a series of workshops for interracial families sponsored by their church:

> *I think that being in this community helps us a lot . . . being in interracial family workshops, those kind of things; . . . it's an injection for us*

and that we value. And being able to expose ourselves to different types of interracial families. . . . I feel very interested and involved and somewhat knowledgeable and interested in the various adoption controversies that are going on and noticing again in this community the various levels of interracial activity. (Rosenblatt, Karis, & Powell, 1995, p. 271)

It is important to note, however, that even more critical than the diversity of the context is the diversity of one's social network. Having ethnically varied friends has more of an influence on the propensity to engage in an interethnic romance than does being in a diverse social environment in general. "The role of friends is particularly important, perhaps because an individual is most likely to be introduced to a partner by a common friend, and because social approval from one's friends is a potent predictor of relationship stability" (Clark-Ibanez & Felmlee, 2004, p. 301).

Historical and Political Contexts As noted in Chapter 4, history is an important context for understanding intercultural interactions and relationships. Many U.S. men in military service during various wars have returned to the United States with wives whom they met and married while stationed abroad. And many of the servicemen who experienced such intercultural relationships argued successfully against miscegenation laws, or laws that prohibited interracial marriages.

An example of the role that history and politics can play in intercultural communication can be seen in the experiences of William Kelly (2001), a communication scholar who lived in Japan for many years. He recounts his experiences when he first went to Japan to teach English 25 years ago. There were few U.S. Americans in Japan, and they were treated with great deference. In retrospect, he realizes that he was quite arrogant in his view of the Japanese:

I expected Japanese to assimilate to my culture. I also felt superior to them. Due to their culture, I believed that Japanese would never reach the goals of individual freedom, rational thought in daily life and speaking English like a U.S. American. Therefore they would always remain aspiring U.S. Americans, not capable of achieving equality. (p. 7)

His relationship with the Japanese can best be understood in the context of the history of U.S.-Japanese relations. As we learned in Chapter 1, Asians in the United States were treated very badly in the late 18th and early 19th centuries. (Remember the Oriental Exclusion Act of 1882 as well as the Johnson-Read Act of 1924, which severely restricted Japanese immigration to the United States.) Then came

World War II and the internment of Japanese Americans, followed by the U.S. occupation of Japan. As a result, in the 1960s, 1970s, and 1980s, although the Japanese deferred to U.S. economic and political superiority, there was restrained resentment, and sometimes outright racism, toward U.S. Americans living in Japan. For example, in the 1980s, U.S. Americans in Japan could not enter certain establishments, obtain loans, or have the same jobs as Japanese.

This example reveals the importance of the material and the symbolic realm in understanding culture. Kelly explains,

It was the material conditions of white U.S. power and privilege that led me to assume a stance of superiority in relation to the Japanese people I encountered. The communication grooves that I unthinkingly entered when I began living in Japan were the outcome of a colonial relationship between the United States and Japan. . . . Japanese racial discrimination against whites has often been a defensive measure to keep members of a powerful nation within well-defined spheres. The goal has been to maintain a private area of Japanese people where the overbearing Western presence was absent and where Japanese could be "themselves." (p. 9)

Over the years, Kelly developed a different way of relating to Japanese. This came about primarily as a result of his encounters with U.S. Americans in Japan who were truly respectful of the Japanese. They learned Japanese, had many Japanese friends, and tried to adapt to the Japanese way of life—thereby achieving a more equal power balance. Eventually, he says, he was able to reach a level of understanding that accepted both similarities and differences between Japan and the United States.

Kelly points out that his efforts to communicate with Japanese people in a truly respectful manner were assisted by the diminishing of the unequal power relations between the United States and Japan:

By the 1990s, there were many Japanese who had experienced the West that were no longer so positive about Westerners, and especially Americans. They expected white people to learn the Japanese language and communicate in a more Japanese way. . . . Many Japanese had gone overseas to work or study and there was less of an inferiority complex among Japanese towards white Americans. European Americans had been very gradually losing their place of privilege. (p. 11)

All this points to the effect of power on hierarchical relations of communication. Although power does not determine communication patterns in any simple causal sense, it does have an impact on the direction communication takes within intercultural relations. Although U.S.-Japanese communication is still affected in numerous ways by the legacy of the U.S. occupation of Japan, increased economic power has given the Japanese people a new sense of pride.

There are other examples of how colonial histories framed relationships. The British, for example, constructed myriad intercultural relationships, recognized or not, within the lands they colonized. Writer Anton Gill (1995), in his book *Ruling Passions*, discusses various ways in which the colonialists tried to engage in or to avoid intercultural relations, as well as the legacy of interracial children left in their wake. He was concerned with British social policies in the colonies, particularly as they related to offspring, who were often unwanted and abandoned.

The dialectical tension rests, on the one hand, in the social, political, and economic contexts that make some kinds of intercultural relationships possible and, on the other hand, in the desires and motives of the partners involved. There are no easy explanations for whom we meet, when we meet them, and under what conditions we might have a relationship. Different cultural groups have different demographics, histories, and social concerns. Scholar Harry Kitano and his colleagues (1984) discuss some of these issues for Asian Americans. Scholars Robert Anderson and Rogelis Saenz (1994) apply the demographics of Mexican American communities to argue for the importance of larger structural factors—such as proximity—in understanding interracial marriage.

DISCUSSION QUESTIONS

1. What are some of the benefits of intercultural relationships?
2. What factors contribute to our forming relationships with some people and not with others?
3. How is the development of intercultural relationships different from that of intracultural relationships?
4. What challenges do intercultural couples face when they decide to make their relationships permanent?
5. What are the advantages of taking a dialectical perspective on intercultural relationships?

ACTIVITIES

1. *Intercultural Relationships.* List all of your friends to whom you feel

close. Identify any friends on the list who are from other cultures. Answer the following questions, and discuss your answers with other class members.

a. Do people generally have more friends from their own culture or from other cultures? Why?

b. In what ways are intercultural friendships different from or similar to friendships with people from the same culture?

c. What are some reasons people might have for not forming intercultural friendships?

2. *Friendship Dialectics.* Choose one friend who is different from you. Describe a situation or situations in which you experienced the dialectics discussed in this chapter. (Hint: Think of the ways in which the two of you are both similar and different—age, gender, background, interests, personality, and so on. Think of the ways your relationship has both changed and stayed the same—attitudes, experiences, interests, and so on.)

REFERENCES

ABC News Online. (1999, October 14). France grants equal legal rights to gay couples. Australian Broadcasting Corporation.

Allen, B. J. (2000). Sapphire and Sappho: Allies in authenticity. In A. Gonzalez, M. Houston, & V. Chen (Eds.), *Our voices: Essays in culture, ethnicity and communication* (3rd ed., pp. 179–183). Los Angeles: Roxbury.

Anderson, R. N., & Saenz, R. (1994). Structural determinants of Mexican American intermarriage, 1975–1980. *Social Science Quarterly,* 75(2), 414–430.

Barnlund, D. S. (1989). *Communication styles of Japanese and Americans: Images and reality.* Belmont, CA: Wadsworth.

Baxter, L. A. (1993). The social side of personal relationships: A dialectical perspective. In S. Duck (Ed.), *Social context and relationships* (pp. 139–165). Newbury Park, CA: Sage.

Baxter, L. A., & Montgomery, B. (1996). *Relating: Dialogues and dialectics.* New York: Guilford Press.

Bell, A. P., & Weinberg, M. S. (1978). *Homosexualities: A study of diversity between men and women.* New York: Simon & Schuster.

Bell, S., & Coleman, S. (1999). The anthropology of friendship: Enduring themes and future possibilities. In S. Bell & S. Coleman (Eds.), *The anthropology of friendship* (pp. 1–20). New York: Berg.

Butterfield, F. (1982). *Alive in the bitter sea.* Toronto: Bantam Books.

Cambodian king backs gay marriage. (2004, February 20). BBC News. Accessed at http://news.bbc.co.uk/2/hi/asia-pacific/3505915.stm

Carrier, J. G. (1999). People who can be friends: Selves and social relationships. In S. Bell & S. Coleman (Eds.), *The anthropology of friendship* (pp. 21–28). New York: Berg.

Carter, D. M. (2004). Living in virtual communities: Making friends online. *Journal of Urban Technology, 11*, 109–136.

Chen, L. (2002). Communication in intercultural relationships. In W. B. Gudykunst & B. Mody (Eds.), *Handbook of international and intercultural communication* (pp. 241–258). Thousand Oaks, CA: Sage.

Chen, T. C.-C., Drzewiecka, J. A., & Sias, P. M. (2001). Dialectical tensions in Taiwanese international student friendships. *Communication Quarterly, 49*, 57–66.

Chesebro, J. W. (Ed.). (1981). *Gayspeak: Gay male and lesbian communication*. New York: Pilgrim Press.

Chesebro, J. W. (1997). Ethical communication and sexual orientation. In J. M. Makau & R. C. Arnett (Eds.), *Communication ethics in an age of diversity* (pp. 126–154). Bloomington: University of Illinois Press.

Chozick, A. (2005, November 14). Beyond the numbers. *Wall Street Journal*, p. R4.

Clark-Ibanez, M. K., & Felmlee, D. (2004). Interethnic relationships: The role of social network diversity. *Journal of Marriage and Family, 66*, 229–245.

Cole, D. (2001, July 31). Germany opens door to gay marriage. *Agence Presse*. www.gfn.com/archives/story.phtml?sid=9975

Collier M. J. (1996). Communication competence problematics in ethnic friendships. *Communication Monographs, 63*, 314–346.

Dion, K. K., & Dion, K. L. (1991). Psychological individualism and romantic love. *Journal of Social Behavior and Personality, 6*, 17–33.

Dion, K. L., & Dion, K. K. (1988). Romantic love: Individual and cultural perspectives. In R. Sternberg & M. Barnes (Eds.), *The psychology of love* (pp. 264–289). New Haven, CT: Yale University Press.

Dodd, C. H., & Baldwin, J. R. (2002). The role of family and macrocultures in intercultural relationships. In J. N. Martin, T. K. Nakayama, & L. A. Flores (Eds.), *Readings in intercultural communication* (2nd ed., pp. 279–289). Boston: McGraw-Hill.

Eng, D. L. (2001). *Racial castration: Managing masculinity in Asian America*. Durham, NC: Duke University Press.

Fahrenthold, D. A. (2005, October 2). Connecticut's first same-sex unions proceed civilly. *The Washington Post*, A3.

Farrell, E. (2005, February 4). More students plan to work to help pay for college. *Chronicle of Higher Education*, pp. A1, A34.

Fiebert, M. S., Nugent, D., Hershberger, S. L., & Kasdan, M. (2004). Dating and commitment choices as a function of ethnicity among American college students in California. *Psychological Reports, 94*, 1293–1300.

Fish, E. (2005). The road to recognition: A global perspective on gay marriage. *Harvard International Review, 27*, 32–35.

Frith, K., Shaw, P., & Cheng, H. (2005). The construction of beauty: A cross-cultural analysis of women's magazine advertising. *Journal of Communication, 55*, 56–70.

Gajjala, R. (2004). Negotiating cyberspace/negotiating RL. In A. Gonzalez, M. Houston, & V. Chen (Eds.), *Our voices: Essays in culture, ethnicity and communication* (4th ed., pp. 63–71). Los Angeles: Roxbury.

Gao, G. (1991). Stability of romantic relationships in China and the United States. In S. Ting-Toomey & F. Korzenny (Eds.), *Crosscultural interpersonal communication* (pp. 99–115). Newbury Park, CA: Sage.

Gao, G. (2001). Intimacy, passion, and commitment in Chinese and U.S. American romantic relationships. *International Journal of Intercultural Relations, 25,* 329–342.

Gareis, E. (1995). *Intercultural friendship: A qualitative study.* Lanham, MD: University Press of America.

Gasner, A. (1999). Globalization: The changing face of the workforce. *Business Today, 36,* 43–44.

Gates, H. (1987). *Chinese working-class lives.* Ithaca, NY: Cornell University Press.

Gill, A. (1995). *Ruling passions: Sex, race and empire.* London: BBC Books.

Graham, J. A., & Cohen, R. (1997). Race and sex factors in children's sociometric ratings and friendship choices. *Social Development, 6,* 355–372.

Graham, M. A., Moeai, J., & Shizuru, L. S. (1985). Intercultural marriages: An intrareligious perspective. *International Journal of Intercultural Relations, 9,* 427–434.

Gudykunst, W. B., & Matsumoto, Y. (1996). Cross-cultural variability of communication in personal relationships. In W. B. Gudykunst, S. Ting-Toomey, & T. Nishida (Eds.), *Communication in personal relationships across cultures* (pp. 19–56). Thousand Oaks, CA: Sage.

Halualani, R. T. (1995). The intersecting hegemonic discourses of an Asian mail-order bride catalog: Pilipina "oriental butterfly" dolls for sale. *Women's Studies in Communication, 18*(1), 45–64.

Hammond, D., & Jablow, A. (1987). Gilgamesh and the Sundance Kid: The myth of male friendship. In H. Brod (Ed.), *The making of masculinities: The new men's studies* (pp. 241–258). Boston: Allen & Unwin.

Harris, T. M., & Kalbfleisch, P. J. (2000). Interracial dating: The implications of race for initiating a romantic relationship. *The Howard Journal of Communications, 11,* 49–64.

Henderson, S., & Gilding, M. (2004). I've never clicked this much with anyone in my life: Trust and hyperpersonal communication in online friendships. *New Media & Society, 6,* 487–506.

Herring, S. C. (2004). Slouching toward the ordinary: Current trends in computer mediated communication. *New Media & Society, 6,* 26–31.

Hymowitz, C. (2005, November 14). The new diversity. *Wall Street Journal,* pp. R1, R3.

James, N. C. (2000). When Miss America was always white. In A. González, M. Houston, & V. Chen (Eds.), *Our voices: Essays in culture, ethnicity and communication* (3rd ed., pp. 42–46). Los Angeles: Roxbury.

Kelly, W. E. (2000). *A critical postmodern approach to U.S.-Japanese intercultural relations.* Unpublished doctoral dissertation, University of New Mexico, Albuquerque.

Kitano, H. H. L., Yeung, W.-T., Chai, L., & Hatanaka, H. (1984). Asian-American interracial marriage. *Journal of Marriage and the Family, 56,* 179–190.

Knox, N. (2005, August 11). Religion takes a back seat in Western Europe, *USA Today,* p. 01A.

Kouri, K. M., & Lasswell, M. (1993). *Black-white marriages.* New York: Haworth Press.

Lampe, P. (1982). Interethnic dating: Reasons for and against. *International Journal of Intercultural Relations, 6,* 115–126.

Lee, O. (2002). Cultural differences in E-mail use of virtual teams: A critical social theory perspective.

CyberPsychology & Behavior, 5, 227–232.

Lee, S. M., & Edmonston, B. (2005). New marriages, new families: U.S. racial and Hispanic intermarriage. *Population Bulletin, 60*(2), 3–36.

Lewin, K. (1948). Some social psychological differences between the United States and Germany. In G. Lewin (Ed.), *Resolving social conflicts.* New York: Harper.

Luo, S., & Klohnen, E. C. (2005). Assortative mating and marital quality in newlyweds: A couple-centered approach. *Journal of Personality and Social Psychology, 88,* 301–326.

Mariage vietnamien lesbien. (1998, May). *Illico,* 32–33.

Martin, J. N., Bradford, L. J., Drzewiecka, J. A., & Chitgopekar, A. S. (2003). Intercultural dating patterns among young white U.S. Americans: Have they changed in the past 20 years? *Howard Journal of Communications, 14,* 53–73.

Martin, J. N., Nakayama, T. K., & Flores, L. A. (2002). A dialectical approach to intercultural communication. In J. N. Martin, T. K. Nakayama, & L. A. Flores (Eds.), *Readings in intercultural communication* (2nd ed., pp. 3–13). Boston: McGraw-Hill.

McCullough, M. W. (1998). *Black and White women as friends: Building cross-race friendships.* Cresskill, NJ: Hampton Press.

McKenna, K. Y. A., Green, A. S., & Gleason, M. E. J. (2002). Relationship formation on the Internet: What's the big attraction? *Journal of Social Issues, 58,* 9–31.

Mercer, K. (1994). *Welcome to the jungle.* New York: Routledge.

Mills, J. K., Daly, J., Longmore, A., & Kilbride, G. (1995). A note on family acceptance involving interracial friendships and romantic relationships. *The Journal of*

Psychology, 129(3), 349–351.

Nakayama, T. K. (1998). Communication of heterosexism. In M. L. Hecht (Ed.), *Communication of prejudice* (pp. 112–121). Thousand Oaks, CA: Sage.

Nardi, P. M. (1992). That's what friends are for: Friends as family in the gay and lesbian community. In K. Plummer (Ed.), *Modern homosexualities: Fragments of lesbian and gay experience* (pp. 108–120). New York: Routledge.

Neil, M. (2005). Same-sex benefits bind. *ABA Journal, 91,* 22–24.

Nishida, T. (1996). Communication in personal relationships in Japan. In W. B. Gudykunst, S. Ting-Toomey, & T. Nishida (Eds.), *Communication in personal relationships across cultures* (pp. 102–121). Thousand Oaks, CA: Sage.

Olaniran, B. A. (2001). The effects of computer-mediated communication on transculturalism. In V. H. Milhouse, M. K. Asante, & P. O. Nwosu (Eds.), *Transcultural realities: Interdisciplinary perspectives on cross-cultural relations* (pp. 83–105). Thousand Oaks, CA: Sage.

Osbeck, L. M., & Moghaddam, F. M. (1997). Similarity and attraction among majority and minority groups in a multicultural context. *International Journal of Intercultural Relations, 21,* 113–123.

Pogrebin, L. C. (1987). *Among friends.* New York: McGraw-Hill.

Pogrebin, L. C. (1992). The same and different: Crossing boundaries of color, culture, sexual preference, disability, and age. In W. B. Gudykunst & Y. Y. Kim (Eds.), *Readings on communicating with strangers* (pp. 318–336). New York: McGraw-Hill.

Postmes, T., Spears, R., & Lea, M. (1998). Breaching or building the social boundaries? SIDE-effects of computer-mediated communication. *Communication Research, 25,* 689–715.

Romano, D. (1997). *Intercultural marriage: Promises and pitfalls* (2nd ed.). Yarmouth, ME: Intercultural Press.

Root, M. P. P. (2001). *Love's revolution: Interracial marriage.* Philadelphia: Temple University Press.

Rosenblatt, P. C., Karis, T. A., & Powell, R. D. (1995). *Multiracial couples: Black and white voices.* Thousand Oaks, CA: Sage.

Russo, R. (2001, February 9). Intercultural relationships flourish despite differences. *The (Georgetown) Hoya.*

Sherrod, D., & Nardi, P. M. (1988). *The nature and function of friendship in the lives of gay men and lesbians.* Paper presented at the annual meeting of the American Sociological Association, Atlanta.

Shibazaki, K., & Brennan, K. (1998). When birds of a different feathers flock together: A preliminary comparison of intra-ethnic and inter-ethnic dating relationships. *Journal of Social & Personal Relationships, 15,* 248–256.

Smart, A. (1999). Expression of interest: Friendship and *quanxi* in Chinese societies. In S. Bell & S. Coleman (Eds.), *The anthropology of friendship* (pp. 119–136). New York: Berg.

Snyder, G. (2003, May). Teams that span time zones face new work rules. Stanford Business. Web site of Stanford Graduate School of Business. Accessed at http://www.gsb.stanford.edu/news/bmag/sbsm0305/feature_virtual_teams.shtml

Sprecher, S., Aron, A., Hatfield, E., Cortese, A., Potapova, E., & Levitskaya, A. (1994). Love: American style, Russian style, and Japa-nese style. *Personal Relationships, 1,* 349–369.

St. Amant, K. (2002). When cultures and computers collide: Rethinking computer-mediated communication according to international and intercultural communication expectations. *Journal of Business and Technical Communication, 16,* 196–214.

Stephan, W. G. (1999). *Reducing prejudice and stereotyping in schools.* New York: Teachers College Press.

Stephan, W., & Stephan, C. (1992). Reducing intercultural anxiety through intercultural contact. *International Journal of Intercultural Relations, 16,* 89–106.

Sudweeks, S., Gudykunst, W. B., Ting-Toomey, S., & Nishida, T. (1990). Developmental themes in Japanese–North American relationships. *International Journal of Intercultural Relations, 14,* 207–233.

Sze, H. (1992, July 24). Racist love. Asian Week, pp. 10, 24.

Talking about race. (2000, July 16). *New York Times Magazine,* special issue (How Race Is Lived in America).

Tan, D., & Singh, R. (1995). Attitudes and attraction. *Personality and Social Psychology Bulletin, 21,* 975–986.

Tucker, M. B., & Mitchell-Kernan, C. (1995). Social structure and psychological correlates of interethnic dating. *Journal of Social and Personal Relationships, 12,* 341–361.

Walther, J. B. (1996). Computer-mediated communication: Impersonal, interpersonal, and hyperpersonal interaction. *Communication Research, 23,* 3–43.

Walther, J. B., & Parks, M. R. (2002). Cues filtered out, cues filtered in: Computer-mediated communication and relationships. In M. L. Knapp & J. A. Daly (Eds.), *Handbook of interpersonal communication* (pp. 529–563). Thousand Oaks, CA: Sage.

Yancy, G. (2002). Who interracially dates: An examination of the characteristics of those who have interracially dated. *Journal of Comparative Family Studies, 33,* 177–190.

CHAPTER 10

CULTURE, COMMUNICATION, AND CONFLICT

CHAPTER OBJECTIVES

After reading this chapter, you should be able to:

1. Identify two orientations to conflict.
2. Understand a dialectical approach to these orientations.
3. Be able to discuss three approaches— social science, interpretive, and critical—to studying conflict.
4. Be able to identify five types of interpersonal conflict.
5. Explain the role of gender, ethnicity, values, and conflict styles in interpersonal conflict.
6. Be able to discuss some of the contexts that contribute to social conflict.
7. Explain some strategies for dealing with conflict.
8. Be able to distinguish productive from destructive conflict.

The need to understand intercultural conflict seems more important now than ever. One thing we can be sure of is that conflict is inevitable. Conflicts are happening all around the world, as they always have, and at many different levels: interpersonal, social, national, and international. For example, at the interpersonal level, friends or romantic partners may disagree about their relationship among themselves or with friends and family. At the social level, cultural differences of opinion regarding the importance of preserving the environment compared with the importance of developing industry may fuel conflict between environmentalists and business interests.

An example of cultural conflict at the international level is the ongoing disagreement between the United States and a number of countries concerning capital punishment. France, in particular, has been very critical of the U.S. policy on the death penalty. French officials refused to extradite the man accused of murdering a New York doctor who performed abortions—doing so only when the U.S. prosecutor agreed to not seek the death penalty. Similarly, France criticized the decision by the Justice Department to seek the death penalty in the trial of Zacarias Moussaoui, a French citizen of Moroccan origin suspected of being the 20th hijacker in the 9/11 terrorist attacks. This disagreement has severely strained Franco-U.S. relations (Blocker, 2002).

Conflict also may arise from mediated communication. U.S. television, film, and other media have dominated the world market for many years. People in many other countries feel that this cultural dominance stunts their economic growth and imposes U.S. cultural values. This domination has led to resentment and conflict (Delgado, 2002).

There are three significant approaches to understanding conflict. One is the social science approach, which focuses on how cultural differences cause conflict and influence the management of the conflict on the interpersonal level. The other two approaches—the interpretive and the critical—focus more on intergroup relationships and on cultural, historical, and structural elements as the primary sources of conflict. These three approaches emphasize different aspects of the individual–contextual dialectic.

Understanding intercultural conflict is especially important because of the relationship between culture and conflict. That is, cultural differences can cause conflict, and once conflict occurs, cultural backgrounds and experiences influence how individuals deal with it. Culture shapes what people consider valuable and worth fighting over; it influences official positions taken and interpretations of others' actions (Ross, 1993a). We should say up front that little is known about how to deal effectively with intercultural conflict. Most research to date in the United States applies almost exclusively to majority culture members.

Our challenge is to review this body of research, take what can be applied in intercultural contexts, and perhaps suggest some new ways to think about conflict.

In this chapter, then, we identify characteristics of intercultural conflict, extending our dialectical perspective, and outline two broad orientations to conflict. We examine intercultural conflict in interpersonal contexts, incorporating more interpretive and critical theories into our understanding of conflict. We also examine how cultural background can influence conflict management. Finally, we discuss guidelines for viewing and engaging in conflict across cultural borders.

CHARACTERISTICS OF INTERCULTURAL CONFLICT

One way to think about **intercultural conflict** is from a dialectical perspective, applying many of the same dialectics discussed in Chapter 9. Let's see how this works in an actual dispute that arose in France. In late October and into November 2005, riots that began in a suburb of Paris—Clichy-sous-Bois—began to spread throughout the nation to over 300 cities, and, as seen around the world: "A blaze without precedent which stupefies the world, ruins the image of France abroad and becomes more and more dangerous for its inhabitants" (Mandonnet, Pelletier, Portrait, & Rosso, 2005, p. 22 [*Un embrasement sans précédent, qui stupéfie le monde, ruine l'image de la France à l'étranger et devient de plus en plus dangereux pour ses habitants.*]). As images of cars burning were broadcast, commentators rushed to offer reasons for this social upheaval and social conflict. Many offered comparisons to their own societies. Yet the rioting in France by those marginalized in French society—primarily the children and grandchildren of North African immigrants—underscores the point that disputes are often more complicated than they first appear. We can invoke the various dialectics to illuminate the complexity of this conflict. For example, the dispute has been described as rooted in Islamic discontent with the West. The cover of *U.S. News and World Report's* November 21, 2005, issue asked, "Is it religion or culture?" *The Economist* also noted that "[m]uch of the world's attention over these two weeks has been the role played by Islam" ("France's Failure," p. 11). Yet *The Economist* goes on to suggest that "[a] much greater contributor than Islam to the malaise in the suburbs is the lack of jobs" (p. 11).

Other commentators attempted to explain this upheaval in terms

intercultural conflict Conflict between two or more cultural groups.

of their own national experiences. A writer for the *Washington Post* noted, "The deeper difference is that however ignored or mistreated America's black underclass may be, most Americans do think of its members as Americans. By contrast, I doubt whether most Frenchmen even contemplate the possibility that the African and Arab immigrants and their offspring who make up their underclass, and who are both perpetrators and victims of these riots, could ever be truly French, even if they hold French passports (and millions do)" (Applebaum, 2005, p. A31). The focus on identity and belonging is repeated in a Canadian writer's view of the French riots. In a Toronto newspaper, *The Globe and Mail*, Timothy B. Smith (2005) suggests that

> [t]he French believe that multiculturalism would only privilege individuals by association with their ethnic, religious or racial roots. There is no such concept as Algerian French. By contrast, one can be Chinese Canadian and still be considered a full citizen. Before immigrants to Canada become equal in the economic sense, their culture is already considered equal in the theoretical sense. The one helps lead to the other. Canada is no bed of roses for thousands of recent immigrants toiling at minimum-wage jobs, but history suggests that, in the long run, many of them will enter the lower middle class. And, as the French riots suggest, no jobs are worse than bad jobs. Multiculturalism embodies a message of hope and puts a high ideal in our sights. France tells newcomers that their past belongs in another country. Most Canadians see immigrants in a positive light—they add diversity to the cultural scene, they spice up our cuisine, they make important economic contributions, they will help pay for the boomers' pensions. In the context of chronic high unemployment, a large chunk of the French-born majority sees immigrants as threats to its share of a limited system of spoils.

In a sense, then, the economic contexts, the cultural identities and belongingness, and the political and religious contexts all work together to shape this conflict. Some people do not believe that riots and violence are an appropriate way to change the social problems in French society or any society. Others believe this kind of violence is one of the few ways that society can be provoked into interrogating social inequities and begin the long process of changing any society. As one writer noted, connecting the United States to France, "America's lesson for the French is that they have a long, hard road ahead" (Ignatius, 2005, p. A31).

The point here is that there is no reason to seek a single source for conflict. The riots in France, for example, probably have multiple causes, and, by taking a dialectical approach to thinking about these riots, you can see how these various forces—economic, social, political, religious—may all play different roles at different times. Yet when confronted with such conflicts, how should society respond? How should you respond?

Intercultural conflict may be characterized by ambiguity, which causes us to resort quickly to our default style—the style that we learned growing up—in handling it. If your preferred way of handling conflict is to deal with it immediately, and you are in a conflict situation with someone who prefers to avoid it, the conflict may become exacerbated as you both retreat to your preferred style. As the confronting person becomes increasingly confrontational, the avoider simply retreats further.

Issues surrounding language may be important to intercultural conflict. One student, Stephanie, described a situation that occurred when she was studying in Spain. She went to an indoor swimming pool with her host family sisters. Being from Arizona, she was unaccustomed to swimming in such cold water, so she went outside to sunbathe. Her "sisters" asked her why she didn't swim with them. Stephanie explains,

> *At that point I realized they thought I should really be with them. . . . I didn't know how to express myself well enough to explain to them. . . . I tried, but I don't think it worked very well. So I just apologized. . . . I did basically ignore the conflict. I would have dealt with it, but I felt I did not have the language skills to explain myself effectively, so I did not even try. . . . That is why I had such a problem, because I could not even express what I would have liked to.*

When individuals don't know the language well, it is very difficult to handle conflict effectively. At the same time, silence is not always a bad thing. Sometimes it provides a "cooling off" period, allowing things to settle down. Depending on the cultural context, silence can be very appropriate.

Intercultural conflict also may be characterized by a combination of orientations to conflict and conflict management styles. Communication scholar Sheryl Lindsley (1999) interviewed managers in *maquiladoras*—sorting or assembly plants along the Mexican-U.S. border—and found many examples of conflict. For example, Mexican managers thought that U.S. managers were often rude and impolite in their dealings with each other and the workers. The biggest difference between U.S. Americans and Mexicans was in the way that U.S. Americans expressed disagreement at management meetings. One Mexican manager explained,

Although forgiveness is often a key element in conflict resolution, it is not always easy to forgive. Sometimes those who are hurt in conflict still live with everyday pain from the conflict, and they do not always find it easy to forgive. In Northern Ireland, the British government is asking many people to forgive the IRA to help build peace there.

Thirty-three years after Sam Malcolmson was shot by an Irish Republican Army gunman, the wound in his side is still open and leaking fluid. He has to change the dressing constantly. He takes morphine four times a day for blinding pain caused by bullet shards lodged in his spine. . . .

"People tell me I should forgive and forget so we can all move on," said Malcolmson, who was a 22-year-old police recruit when the IRA ambushed him in 1972. "They are asking an awful lot."

The British government is asking for such forgiveness on the grounds that it will help seal the peace in Northern Ireland after more than three decades of sectarian violence. . . .

Prime Minister Tony Blair told Parliament that the bill was "a very difficult" but essential part of peacemaking. The measure would follow the IRA's announcement in July that it had laid down its weapons for good.

"I don't minimize the anger there will be in some quarters, or the anguish if you are the relative of a policeman in Northern Ireland who was killed," Blair told legislators. "But I also genuinely believe we need to get this out of the way and dealt with so we can get on with the really tough" task of rebuilding the province's government and institutions.

Northern Ireland Secretary Peter Hain, Blair's top official for the province, said in an interview that the fugitives bill was "painful but necessary to bring closure on the past."

"The history of conflict resolution and this world is that sometimes you have to do things you ideally wouldn't want to, to bring closure," Hain said. Asked what he would tell victims' families, he said he would say that he understands the "appalling horror" of their experience but that "at least you can have the comfort of knowing that there won't be more victims like you in the future."

The measure has met ferocious opposition from people who say Blair is asking too much in the name of peace.

Source: From K. Sullivan, "In Northern Ireland, Forgiveness Is a Bitter Pill," *Washington Post*, December 7, 2005, p. A19.

When we are in a meeting together, the U.S. American will tell another manager, "I don't like what you did." . . . Mexicans interpret this as a personal insult. They have a difficult time understanding that U.S. Americans can insult each other in this way and then go off and play golf together . . . Mexicans would be polite, perhaps tell the person in private, or make a suggestion, rather than confronting. (quoted in Lindsley, 1999, p. 158)

As Lindsley points out, the conflict between the Mexican and U.S. American managers in their business meetings needs to be understood as a dialectical and "layered" process in which individual, dyadic, societal, and historical forces are recognized.

TWO ORIENTATIONS TO CONFLICT

Is conflict good or bad? Should conflict be welcomed because it provides opportunities to strengthen relationships? Or should it be avoided because it can only lead to problems for individuals and groups? What is the best way to handle conflict when it arises? Should people talk about it directly, deal with it indirectly, or avoid it?

It's not always easy to figure out the best way to deal with conflict. And what does culture have to do with it? To answer some of these questions, we first describe two very different ways of thinking about conflict. Then we outline some of the ways in which culture and conflict are related. As you read about these two orientations, try to keep in mind the importance of thinking dialectically. Neither orientation is always the best approach, nor does any culture only utilize one approach to conflict.

Conflict as Opportunity

The "opportunity" orientation to conflict is the one most commonly represented in U.S. interpersonal communication texts. **Conflict** is usually defined as involving a perceived or real *incompatibility* of goals, values, expectations, processes, or outcomes between two or more *interdependent* individuals or groups (Cupach & Canary, 1997; Wilmot & Hocker, 2001). According to theologian and mediatior David Augsburger (1992), this approach to conflict is based on four assumptions:

1. Conflict is a normal, useful process.

---

conflict The interference between two or more interdependent individuals or groups of people who perceive incompatible goals, values, or expectations in attaining those ends.

2. All issues are subject to change through negotiation.

3. Direct **confrontation** and conciliation are valued.

4. Conflict is a necessary renegotiation of an implied contract—a redistribution of opportunity, release of tensions, and renewal of relationships.

Let's examine these assumptions more fully.

Conflict may be a difficult process, but it ultimately offers an opportunity for strengthening relationships. Although this orientation to conflict recognizes that many people don't enjoy conflict, it emphasizes the potentially positive aspects. The main idea is that working through conflict constructively results in stronger, healthier, and more satisfying relationships (Canary, Cupach, & Messman, 1995). From this perspective, there are additional benefits for groups working through conflict: they can gain new information about other people or groups, diffuse more serious conflict, and increase cohesiveness (Filley, 1975).

Consider the second and third assumptions. Individuals should be encouraged to think of creative, and even far-reaching, solutions to conflict. Furthermore, the most desirable response to conflict is to recognize it and work through it in an open, productive way. In fact, many people consider conflict-free relationships to be unhealthy. In relationships without conflict, they suggest, partners are ignoring issues that need to be dealt with (Canary, Cupach, & Messman, 1995). Finally, because conflict represents a renegotiation of a contract, it is worthy of celebration.

This Western-based approach to conflict suggests a neutral-to-positive orientation, but it is not shared by all cultural groups. Let's look at another orientation.

Conflict as Destructive

Many cultural groups view conflict as ultimately unproductive for relationships, a perspective that may be rooted in spiritual or cultural values. Although we must be cautious about generalizing, this viewpoint is generally shared by many Asian cultures (reflecting the influence of Confucianism and Taoism) and in the United States by some religious groups, such as Quakers and the Amish. According to Augsburger (1992), four assumptions underlie this perspective:

1. Conflict is a destructive disturbance of the peace.

2. The social system should not be adjusted to meet the needs of members; rather, members should adapt to established values.

---

confrontation Direct resistance, often to the dominant forces.

3. Confrontations are destructive and ineffective.

4. Disputants should be disciplined.

Again, let's examine these assumptions. Consider the first one: Most Amish, for example, think of conflict not as an opportunity to promote personal growth but as almost certain to destroy the fabric of interpersonal and community harmony. When conflict does arise, the strong spiritual value of **pacifism** dictates a nonresistant response, such as avoidance or silence. Consider the second assumption, that members of society should adapt to existing values. Among the Amish, the nonresistant stance of *Gelassenheit*, or "yieldedness," forbids the use of force in human relations. Thus, the Amish avoid legal and personal confrontation whenever possible (Kraybill, 1989). This avoidance of conflict extends to a refusal to participate in military activities. For instance, during World War II, the federal government granted alternatives to military service for young Amish men. As a result, most Amish conscientious objectors received agricultural deferments, allowing them to work on their farms or on other agricultural projects. Amish children are instructed to turn the other cheek in any conflict situation, even if it means getting beaten up by the neighborhood bully. This emphasis extends to personal and business relationships; that is, the Amish would prefer to lose face or money than to escalate conflict. Similarly, cultural groups influenced by Buddhist, Taoist, Confucian, and Shinto traditions share a common tendency toward avoidance of confrontation and verbal aggression and absence of direct expression of feelings (Toupin, 1980).

Cultural groups that see conflict as destructive often avoid low-level conflict. However, another appropriate response is to seek intervention from a third party, or **intermediary.** On an informal level, a friend or colleague may be asked to intervene. Intermediaries are also used by those who think that interpersonal conflict provides opportunities, mainly in formal settings. For example, people hire lawyers to mediate disputes or negotiate commercial transactions, or they engage counselors or therapists to resolve or manage relational conflicts. Whereas confronting conflict is ultimately desirable, intervention is a less desirable option.

Finally, consider the fourth assumption, that disputants should be disciplined. Discipline is a means of censuring conflict. After all, communities celebrate their success in regaining harmony; they do not celebrate members' contribution to community change and growth

---

pacifism Opposition to the use of force under any circumstances.
intermediary In a formal setting, a professional third party, such as a lawyer, real estate agent, or counselor, who intervenes when two parties are in conflict. Informal intermediaries may be friends or colleagues who intervene.

through conflict. An example of how a community censures rather than facilitates conflict involves a Maori who was addressing other Maori from New Zealand. His speech turned nasty; he was using swear words and making scathing comments:

> *A woman went up to him, laying her hand on his arm and speaking softly. He shook her off and continued. The crowd now moved back from him as far as possible, and as if by general agreement, the listeners dropped their gaze to their toes until all he could see was the tops of their heads. The speaker slowed, faltered, was reduced to silence, and then sat down. (Augsburger, 1992, p. 80)*

This emphasis on nonviolence and pacifism may contrast with mainstream U.S. values, but as noted previously, many cultural groups practice a nonviolent approach to human and group relations. What are the basic principles of nonviolence applied to interpersonal relations? As Hocker and Wilmot (1991) point out, our language makes it difficult even to talk about this approach. Words and phrases like *passive resistance* and *pacifism* sound lofty and self-righteous. Actually, nonviolence is not the absence of conflict, and it is not a simple refusal to fight. Rather, it is a difficult (and sometimes risky) orientation to interpersonal relationships. The "peacemaking" approach (1) strongly values other people and encourages their growth, (2) attempts to de-escalate conflicts or keep them from escalating once they start, and (3) favors creative negotiations to resolve conflicts when they arise. We'll discuss this approach in detail later.

Researcher Stella Ting-Toomey (1997) describes how these two orientations—conflict as opportunity and conflict as destructive— are based on different underlying cultural values involving identity and face-saving. In the more individualistic approach, espoused by most interpersonal communication textbooks, the concern is how individuals can save their own dignity. The more communal approach espoused by both Amish and Japanese cultures and by other collectivistic groups is more concerned with maintaining interpersonal harmony and saving the dignity of others. For example, in classic Chinese thought, social harmony is the goal of human society—in personal virtue, marriage, family, village, and nation. Writer John C. Wu (1967) explains,

> *If one is entangled in conflict, the only salvation lies in being so clear-headed and inwardly strong that he is always ready to come to terms by meeting the opponent halfway. To carry the conflict to the bitter end has evil effects even when one is in the right, because the enmity is then perpetuated. (p. 227)*

Cultural Differences in Conflict Views: A Dialectical Perspective

Anthropologists have long been interested in how various cultures differ in the amount of conflict tolerated and the strategies for dealing with conflict. By taking a dialectical perspective, we can see no one approach to conflict is appropriate in all situations. It is important to recognize that these approaches are in dialectical tension with each other, and the best solution is not always one or the other but may lie somewhere in between. So although cultures may be predisposed to one orientation or another to conflict, this does not mean any culture only uses one approach.

Why are some cultures more prone to conflicts, whereas others have a low incidence of conflict? Anthropologist Marc Howard Ross (1993a, 1993b) spent many years investigating this question, studying views and norms regarding conflicts in small preindustrial cultures and in modern industrialized nations. According to Ross, in some cultures, conflict tends to be minimized and dealt with constructively; in other cultures, conflicts abound.

The reasons for this variation seem to lie in both structural and individual and interpersonal characteristics. Take two examples, Northern Ireland and Norway. Northern Ireland has been the scene of conflict for many years between two divided religious groups, Catholic and Protestant, with incompatible interests. These groups live in segregated communities, and members hold powerful stereotypes. In addition to a powerful class and socioeconomic hierarchy, there is a history of discrimination against Catholics in housing and jobs. Reasons for this conflict may also originate from a more personal level, such as male gender identity conflict, the absence of affection and warmth, a lack of social trust, and emotional distance between fathers and children—none of the predispositions useful in dealing with political differences in a democratic society.

In contrast, Norway traditionally has a low incidence of internal conflict, although Norwegians have fought with outsiders in the past. Certainly, social homogeneity is a structural plus (although there are some strong regional differences). There are also extensive "moralnets"—people who provide support to individuals in times of need, such as extended family, friends, and neighbors. Involvement in voluntary associations (characterized by attachments that are more instrumental than emotional) and overlapping social networks make it difficult for communities to divide into permanent factions. A strong collective sense of responsibility is expressed in a variety of ways, including an emphasis on equality and status leveling, attentiveness to community norms, and conformity and participation, with or without personal commitment.

On a more personal level, Norwegians are socialized to avoid conflict. There are high levels of maternal nurturance and supervision, as well as high levels of paternal involvement, and little is demanded of young children. Norwegians learn early in life that overt aggression or even indirect confrontation of others is unacceptable. Emotional self-control over negative feelings is important. And there are few aggressive models in the popular culture—newspapers do not sensationalize crime, television features little violence and no boxing, and films are controlled. For example, *E.T.* was considered too violent for children under age 12 (Ross, 1993b).

Low-conflict societies share several characteristics (Ross, 1993b). These include interpersonal practices that build security and trust; a strong linkage between individual and community interests, and high identification with the community so that individuals and groups in conflict trust that its interests are their own; a preference for joint problem solving, which leaves ultimate control over decisions in the hands of the disputants; available third parties, sometimes in the form of the entire community, to facilitate conflict management; an emphasis on the restoration of social harmony that is often at least as strong as the concern with the substantive issues in a dispute; the possibility of exit as a viable option; and strategies of conflict avoidance.

THE SOCIAL SCIENCE APPROACH TO CONFLICT

Perhaps if everyone agreed on the best way to view conflict, there would be less of it. But the reality is that different orientations to conflict may result in more conflict. In this section, which takes a social science approach, we identify five different types of conflict and some strategies for responding to conflict.

Types of Conflict

There are many different types of conflict, and we may manage these types in different ways. Communication scholar Mark Cole (1996) conducted interviews with Japanese students about their views on conflict and found most of the same general categories as those identified in the United States. These categories include the following:

- Affective conflict
- Conflict of interest

- Value conflict
- Cognitive conflict
- Goal conflict

Affective conflict occurs when individuals become aware that their feelings and emotions are incompatible. For example, suppose someone finds that his or her romantic love for a close friend is not reciprocated. The disagreement over their different levels of affection causes conflict.

A conflict of interest describes a situation in which people have incompatible preferences for a course of action or plan to pursue. For example, one student described an ongoing conflict with an ex-girlfriend: "The conflicts always seem to be a jealousy issue or a controlling issue, where even though we are not going out anymore, both of us still try to control the other's life to some degree. You could probably see that this is a conflict of interest." Another example of a conflict of interest is when parents disagree on the appropriate curfew time for their children.

Value conflict, a more serious type, occurs when people differ in ideologies on specific issues. For example, suppose Mario and Melinda have been dating for several months and are starting to argue frequently about their religious views, particularly as related to abortion. Melinda is pro-choice and has volunteered to do counseling in an abortion clinic. Mario, a devout Catholic, is opposed to abortion under any circumstances and is very unhappy about Melinda's volunteer work. This situation illustrates value conflict.

Cognitive conflict describes a situation in which two or more people become aware that their thought processes or perceptions are incongruent. For example, suppose Marissa and Derek argue frequently about whether Marissa's friend Jamal is paying too much attention to her; Derek suspects that Jamal wants to have a sexual encounter with Marissa. Their different perceptions of the situation constitute cognitive conflict.

Goal conflict occurs when people disagree about a preferred outcome or end state. For example, suppose Bob and Ray, who have been in a relationship for 10 years, have just bought a house. Bob wants to furnish the house slowly, making sure that money goes into the savings account for retirement, whereas Ray wants to furnish the house immediately, using money from their savings. Bob's and Ray's individual goals are in conflict with each other.

Strategies and Tactics for Dealing With Conflict

The ways in which people respond to conflict may be influenced by their cultural backgrounds. Most people deal with conflict the way they learned to while growing up and watching those around them deal with contentious situations. Conflict strategies usually reflect how people manage themselves in relational settings. For example, they may prefer to deal with conflicts directly.

Although individuals have a general predisposition to deal with conflict in particular ways, they may choose different tactics in different situations. People are not necessarily locked into a particular strategy. There are at least five specific styles of managing conflicts (Rahim, 1986; Rahim & Magner, 1995; Thomas & Kilmann, 1974):

- Dominating
- Integrating
- Compromising
- Obliging
- Avoiding

The **dominating style** reflects high concern for the self and low concern for the other person. It has been identified with having a win-lose orientation and with forcing behavior to win one's position. The behaviors associated with this style include loud and forceful verbalization, which may be counterproductive to conflict resolution. However, this view may indicate a Eurocentric bias because members of some cultural groups (including African Americans) see these behaviors as appropriate in many contexts (Speicher, 1994).

The **integrating style** reflects high concern for both the self and the other person and involves an open and direct exchange of information in an attempt to reach a solution acceptable to both parties. This style is seen as effective in most conflicts because it attempts to be fair and equitable. It assumes collaboration, empathy, objectivity, creativity, and recognition of feelings. However, it requires a lot of time and energy (Folger, Poole, & Stutman, 1993).

The **compromising style** reflects a moderate degree of concern for both the self and the other person. This style involves sharing and exchanging information in such a way that both individuals give up something to find a mutually acceptable solution. Sometimes this style is less effective than the integrating approach because people feel

dominating style A conflict management strategy whereby an individual achieves his or her goal at the expense of others' needs.
integrating style A conflict management strategy characterized by the open and direct exchange of information in an attempt to reach a solution acceptable to both parties.
compromising style A conflict management strategy that involves sharing and exchanging information to the extent that both individuals give up something to find a mutually acceptable decision.

forced to give up something they value and so have less commitment to the solution.

The **obliging style** describes a situation in which one person in the conflict plays down the differences and incompatibilities and emphasizes commonalities that satisfy the concerns of the other person. Obliging may be most appropriate when one individual is more concerned with the relationship itself than with specific issues. This is often true of hierarchical relationships in which one person has more status or power than the other. However, a pattern of obliging can result in pseudosolutions, especially if one person or the other resents the constant accommodation, so the strategy can eventually backfire.

Finally, the **avoiding style** reflects, supposedly, a low concern for both the self and the other person. In the dominant U.S. cultural contexts, a person who uses this style is often viewed negatively, as attempting to withdraw, sidestep, deny, or bypass the conflict. However, in some cultural contexts, this is an appropriate strategy that, if used by both parties, may result in more harmonious relationships. For example, avoidance can allow individuals to think of some other response, especially if they have trouble "thinking on their feet." Avoidance may also be appropriate if the issue is trivial, if the relationship itself is unimportant to one person, or if others can better manage the conflict (Wilmot & Hocker, 2001).

There are many reasons why we tend to favor a particular conflict style in our interactions. A primary influence is family background; some families prefer a certain conflict style, and children come to accept this style as normal. For instance, the family may have settled conflict in a dominating way, with the person having the strongest argument (or muscle) getting his or her way.

Sometimes people try to reject the conflict styles they saw their parents using. Consider the following examples. One student, Bill, remembers hearing his parents argue long and loud, and his father often used a dominating style of conflict management. He vowed that he would never deal with conflict this way in his own family, and he has tried very hard to keep his vow. Another student, Stephanie, describes how she has changed her style of dealing with conflict as she has grown older:

I think as a child I was taught to ignore conflict and especially to not cause conflict. When I was growing up, I saw my mom act this way to-

---

obliging style A conflict management strategy characterized by playing down differences and incompatibilities while emphasizing commonalities.
avoiding style A conflict management strategy characterized in U.S. cultural contexts by a low concern for the self and others. In some other cultural contexts, however, this strategy may be seen as tactical in maintaining harmonious relationships.

ward my father and probably learned that women were supposed to act this way toward men. As a teenager, I figured out that this just wasn't how I wanted to be. Now I like conflict, not too much of it, but I definitely cannot ignore conflict. I have to deal with it or else I will worry about it. So I deal with it and get it over with.

It is important to recognize that people deal with conflict in a variety of ways, for a variety of reasons. A word of caution is in order about conflict management styles. Conflict specialists William Wilmot and Joyce Hocker (2001) warn that we should not think of preferred styles as static and set in stone. Rather, they suggest that purely individual styles really do not exist because we are each influenced by others in interaction. Therefore, our conflict management styles are not static across settings and relationships. For example, people may use dominating styles at work and avoid conflict at home, or they may use avoiding styles at work and compromise at home. And they may use different styles with different partners. For instance, with co-workers, individuals may tend to collaborate and work through conflict issues; with the boss, they may tend to employ more avoiding strategies. In addition, our styles often change over the course of a conflict and over the life span. For example, individuals who tend to avoid conflict may learn the benefits of engaging and working through conflicts.

Gender, Ethnicity, and Conflict

The relationship between gender and conflict management styles is not clear. Some studies show some gender differences, and others do not. For example, in some studies investigating gender differences among U.S. young people, women report that they are more collaborative in their styles than do men, who report themselves as being more competitive. However, in studies of older adults investigating conflict management styles in the workplace, these gender differences disappear (Wilmot & Hocker, 2001, p. 166).

The relationship between ethnicity, gender, and conflict management is even more complex. Do males and females of different ethnic backgrounds prefer different ways of dealing with conflict? Researcher Mary Jane Collier (1991) investigated this issue in a study in which she asked African American, white American, and Mexican American students to describe conflicts they had had with close friends and the ways they dealt with the conflicts. She also asked them what they should (and should not) have said and whether they thought that males and females handle conflict differently.

Collier found that male and female ethnic friends differed in their ideas about the best ways to deal with conflict. African American males and females offered generally similar descriptions of a problem-solving approach (integration style) as appropriate behavior in conflict management. (One friend said, "I told him to stay in school and that I would help him study." Another explained, "We decided together how to solve the problem" [p. 147].) The males tended to emphasize that appropriate arguments should be given, information should be offered, and opinions should be credible, whereas the females generally emphasized appropriate assertiveness without criticism. (One man complained, "She pushed her own way and opinion and totally disregarded mine" [p. 147].) Some of these findings seem to contradict earlier studies comparing African American and white communication styles. These contradictions might be related to differences among the groups studied (e.g., comparing working-class African Americans and middle-class whites). Furthermore, because these studies are based on very small samples, we should interpret their findings tentatively.

White males and females generally seemed to focus on the importance of accepting responsibility for their behavior. Males in particular mentioned the importance of being direct. (They used expressions like "getting things in the open" and "say right up front" [p. 145].) Females talked about the importance of concern for the other person and the relationship, and for situational flexibility. (One woman explained, "She showed respect for my position and I showed respect for hers" [p. 146].)

Mexican American males and females tended to differ in that males described the importance of talking to reach a mutual understanding. (One man wanted to "make a better effort to explain." Another said that he and his partner "stuck to the problem until we solved it together" [p. 147].) Females described several kinds of appropriate reinforcement of the relationship. In general, males and females in all groups described females as more compassionate and concerned with feelings, and males as more concerned with winning the conflict and being "right."

It is important to remember that, whereas ethnicity and gender may be related to ways of dealing with conflict, it is inappropriate (and inaccurate) to assume that any one person will behave in a particular way because of his or her ethnicity or gender.

Value Differences and Conflict Styles

Another way to understand cultural variations in intercultural conflict resolution is to look at how cultural values influence conflict management. Cultural values in individualistic societies differ from those in collectivistic societies. Individualistic societies place greater importance on the individual than on groups like the family or the work group. Individualism is often cited as the most important of European American values, as reflected in the autonomy and independence encouraged in children. For example, children in the United States are often encouraged to leave home after age 18, and older parents generally prefer to live on their own rather than with their children. In contrast, collectivistic societies often place greater importance on extended families and loyalty to groups.

Yoko, a Japanese student, recounted a conflict she had with a U.S. American student, Linda, with whom she was working on a class project. Linda seemed to take a very competitive, individualistic approach to the project, saying things like "I did this on the project" or referring to it as "my project." Yoko became increasingly irritated and less motivated to work on the project. She finally said to Linda, "Is this your project or our project?" Linda seemed surprised and didn't apologize; she only defended herself. The two women continued to work on the project but with a strained relationship.

Although these values have been related to national differences, they also may be true for other groups. For example, European Americans may value individualism more than do Latinos/as, and women may value collectivism more than do men.

These contrasting values may influence communication patterns. One theory, face negotiation, links cultural values to facework and conflict styles (Ting-Toomey, 2005). **Facework** refers to specific communication strategies we use to "save" our own or another person's face and is a universal concept; how we "do" facework varies from culture to culture and influences conflict styles. Communication scholar Ting-Toomey and her colleagues have conducted a number of studies showing that people from individualistic societies tend to be more concerned with saving their own face than another person's, and so they tend to use more controlling, confrontational, and solution-oriented conflict management styles (Ting-Toomey & Oetzel, 2002; Ting-Toomey, Yee-Jung, Shapiro, Garcia, Wright, & Oetzel, 2000).

In contrast, people from collectivistic societies tend to be more concerned with preserving group harmony and with saving the other person's face (and dignity) during conflict. They may use a less direct conversational style; protecting the other person's face and making him or her look good is considered a skillful facework style. These face concerns lead them to use more avoiding, obliging, and integrating conflict styles (Ting-Toomey & Oetzel, 2002). However, some evi-

---

facework Communication strategies used to "save" our own or someone else's "face," or public image.

dence indicates that not all collectivistic societies prefer indirect ways of dealing with conflict. How someone chooses to deal with conflict in any situation depends on the type of conflict and the relationship she or he has with the other person (Cai & Fink, 2002; Ting-Toomey, 2005; Ting-Toomey & Oetzel, 2002).

One study found that Japanese college students tended to use the avoiding style more often with acquaintances than with best friends in some types of conflicts (conflicts of values and opinions). In contrast, they used the integrating style more with best friends than with acquaintances. In interest conflicts, they used a dominating style more with acquaintances than with best friends (Cole, 1996). This suggests that with out-group members, as with acquaintances, for whom harmony is not as important, the Japanese use dominating or avoiding styles (depending on the conflict type). However, with in-group members like best friends, the way to maintain harmony is to work through the conflict with an integrating style.

INTERPRETIVE AND CRITICAL APPROACHES TO SOCIAL CONFLICT

Both the interpretive and the critical approaches tend to emphasize the social and cultural aspects of conflict. In these perspectives, conflict is far more complex than the ways that interpersonal conflict is enacted. It is deeply rooted in cultural differences in the social, economic, and historical contexts.

Social conflict arises from unequal or unjust social relationships between groups. Consider, for example, the social conflict in northern Wisconsin between many whites and Native Americans over fishing rights. Communication theorist Brad Hall (1994) concludes, in part, that "actual intercultural interactions which display the conflict (and generally receive the bulk of attention) are but the tip of the iceberg in understanding the complexities of such conflicts" (p. 82). Let's look more closely at the social, economic, and historical contexts of this contemporary conflict. This area of Wisconsin depends heavily on tourism and fishing. However, supposed overfishing by the Anishinabe (Chippewa) is being blamed for economic downturns in the area, leading to uneasy social relationships. A treaty was signed in 1837 giving the Anishinabe year-round fishing rights in exchange for the northern

---

social conflict Conflict that arises from unequal or unjust social relationships between groups.

third of Wisconsin. Awareness of these factors is necessary to understanding the complexities of the current conflict.

These complexities are embedded in cultural differences. In addition, the conflict may be motivated by a desire to bring about social change. In **social movements,** individuals work together to bring about social change. They often use confrontation as a strategy to highlight the injustices of the present system. So, for example, when African American students in Greensboro, North Carolina, sat down at white-only lunch counters in the 1960s, they were pointing out the injustices of segregation. Although the students were nonviolent, their actions drew a violent reaction that, for many people, legitimized the claims of injustice.

Historical and political contexts also are sources of conflict. Many **international conflicts** have arisen over border disputes. For example, Argentina and the United Kingdom both claimed the Islas Malvinas (or Falkland Islands) in the south Atlantic, which led to a short war in 1982. Disputes between France and Germany over the Alsace-Lorraine region lasted much longer—from about 1871 to 1945. Similar disputes have arisen between Japan and Russia over islands north of Japan. The historical reasons for such conflicts help us understand the claims of both sides. Contextualizing intercultural conflict can help us understand why the conflict occurs and identify ways to resolve those conflicts.

Social Contexts

How we manage conflict may depend on the particular context or situation. For example, we may choose to use an avoiding style if we are arguing with a close friend about serious relational issues in a movie theater. In contrast, we may feel freer to use a more confrontational style at a social movement rally.

Nikki, a student working part time at a restaurant, recalls an incident involving a large group of German tourists. The tourists thought she had added a 15% tip to the bill because they were tourists; they hadn't realized it was the company policy when serving large groups. Nikki explains that she was much more conciliatory when dealing with this group in the restaurant than she would have been in a more social context. She thought the tourists were rude, but she practiced good listening skills and took more of a problem-solving approach than she would have otherwise.

---

social movements Organized activities in which individuals work together to bring about social change.
international conflicts Conflicts between two or more nations.

Jacqueline, from Singapore, is annoyed by U.S. Americans who comment on how well she speaks English because English is her first language even though she is ethnically Chinese. She used to say nothing in response; now sometimes she retorts, "So is yours," reflecting her struggle against the stereotype that Asians cannot speak English. In this context, the social movement against racism gives meaning to the conflict that arises for Jacqueline.

Many conflicts arise and must be understood against the backdrop of large-scale social movements designed to change contemporary society. For example, the women's suffrage movement of the early 20th century was not an individual effort but a mass effort to win women the right to vote in the United States. Many similar contemporary social movements give meaning to conflicts. These include movements against racism, sexism, and homophobia and movements in support of animal rights, the environment, free speech, and civil rights. College campuses are likely locations for much activism. Journalist Tony Vellela (1988) comments, "It may have subsided, and it certainly changed, reflecting changing times and circumstances, but progressive student political activism never really stopped after the much-heralded anti-Vietnam War era" (p. 5).

There is, of course, no comprehensive list of existing social movements. They arise and dissipate, depending on the opposition they provoke, the attention they attract, and the strategies they use. As part of social change, social movements need confrontation to highlight the perceived injustice.

Confrontation, then, can be seen as an opportunity for social change. In arguing for a change, Dr. Martin Luther King, Jr. (1984) emphasized the importance of nonviolent confrontation:

Nonviolent resistance is not a method for cowards; it does resist. . . . [It] does not seek to defeat or humiliate the opponent, but to win his friendship and understanding. The nonviolent resister must often express his protest through noncooperation or boycotts, but he realizes that these are not ends themselves; they are merely means to awaken a sense of moral shame in the opponent. (pp. 108–109)

This type of confrontation exposes the injustices of society and opens the way for social change. Although nonviolence is not the only form of confrontation employed by social movements, its use has a long history—from Mahatma Gandhi's struggle for India's independence from Britain, to the civil rights struggle in the United States, to the struggle against apartheid in South Africa. In each case, images of violent responses to nonviolent protesters tended to legitimize the social movements and delegitimize the existing social system. For example, in the 1950s and 1960s, the televised images of police dogs attacking schoolchildren and riot squads turning fire hoses on peaceful protesters in Birmingham, Alabama, swung public sentiment in favor of the civil rights movement.

Some social movements have also used violent forms of confrontation. Groups such as Action Directe in France, the Irish Republican Army, Earth First, and independence movements in Corsica, Algeria, Kosovo, and Chechnya have all been accused of using violence. As a result, they tend to be labeled as terrorists rather than mere protesters. Even the suggestion of violence can be threatening to the public. For example, in 1964, Malcolm X (1984) spoke in favor of civil rights: "The question tonight, as I understand it, is 'The Negro Revolt and Where Do We Go From Here?' or 'What Next?' In my little humble way of understanding it, it points toward either the ballot or the bullet" (p. 126). Malcolm X's rhetoric terrified many U.S. Americans, who then refused to give legitimacy to his movement. To understand communication practices such as these, it is important to study their social contexts. Social movements highlight many issues relevant to intercultural interaction.

Economic Contexts

Many conflicts are fueled by economic problems, which may be expressed in cultural differences. Many people find it easier to explain economic troubles by pointing to cultural differences or by assigning blame. For example, in the United States, we have heard many arguments about limiting immigration, with attention focusing largely on non-European immigrants. Concerns about illegal immigrants from Mexico far overshadow concerns about illegal immigrants from, say, Ireland. And discussions about the contributions to society made by different immigrant groups tend to favor European immigrants. Writer Andrew Hacker (1997) compares the median household income of U.S. Americans of various backgrounds, pointing out the lack of attention given to less successful U.S. Americans of some European heritages:

> *We rarely hear media pundits pondering aloud why the Irish lag so far behind the Greeks in median income, and why all four Scandinavian nationalities fall in the bottom half of the European roster. But it has been deemed best not to accentuate distinctions, and rather to reserve remarks of that sort for members of another race. (p. 158)*

Indeed, U.S. Americans of French ancestry and Dutch ancestry earn less (and therefore contribute less?) than U.S. Americans who trace their ancestry to the Philippines, India, Lebanon, China, Thailand, Greece, Italy, Poland, and many other countries. And yet we do not hear calls for halting immigration from France or the Netherlands. In what ways is the economic argument really hiding a racist argument?

We might also ask who benefits from this finger-pointing. Paul Kivel (1996) suggests that blaming immigrants, people of color, and Jews for economic problems diverts attention from the decision makers who are responsible for the problem.

As the economic contexts change, we see more cultural conflict taking place. The former East Germany, for example, now has many more racially motivated attacks as the region attempts to rebuild its economy. Prejudice and stereotyping that lead to conflict are often related to perceived economic threats and competition. In this sense, economics fuels scapegoating and intercultural conflict and is an important context for understanding intercultural conflict.

Historical and Political Contexts

Most of us recall the childhood saying "Sticks and stones may break my bones, but words will never hurt me." In fact, we know that derogatory words can be a powerful source of conflict. The force that many derogatory words carry comes from their historical usage and the history of oppression to which they refer. As we noted in Chapter 4, much of our identity comes from history. It is only through understanding the past that we can understand what it means to be members of particular cultural groups. For example, understanding the history of Ireland helps give meaning to Irish American identity.

Sometimes identities are constructed in opposition to or in conflict with other identities. When people are not seen as members of a culture, they may develop other identities that are seen in opposition to the mainstream culture. In December 2005, during the Australian summer, nearly 5,000 white Australian men "attacked anyone they believed was of Arab descent" (Sallis, 2005, p. A23) on Cronulla Beach near Sydney. Waving Australian flags and wrapping themselves in nationalist rhetoric, these racial conflicts spread to other parts of Sydney. To understand some of the contexts for this social conflict, we should acknowledge the history of Australia's "white Australia" policy. We might also want to point to the economic disparities between Arab Australians and white Australians, as well as the different places they live in the Sydney area. Although one Australian writer feels that today, the "notion of an all-white Australia is a fantasy and an anachronism," she also notes that "I have Muslim friends who used to feel that they were Australians, but now cannot identify themselves in the negative space created for them in our community" (Sallis, 2005, p. A23). Again, we have to recognize that this violence did not arise from an interpersonal conflict but is deeply rooted in the historical policies of Australia, the terrorist bombings in Bali, Indonesia—the most populous Muslim nation—that killed many Australians, and the history of immigration in Australia. The contemporary participants are caught in a web of historical and contemporary events that has drawn lines around cultural identities that exclude others.

These dynamics are at work all around the world. Historical antagonisms become part of cultural identities and practices that place people in positions of conflict. Whether in the Middle East, Northern Ireland, Rwanda, Uganda, Nigeria, Sri Lanka, East Timor, Kosovo, or Chechnya, these historical antagonisms lead to various forms of conflict.

When people witness conflict, they often assume that it is caused by personal issues between individuals. By reducing conflict to the level of interpersonal interaction, we lose sight of the larger social and political forces that contextualize these conflicts. People are in conflict for reasons that extend far beyond personal communication styles.

MANAGING INTERCULTURAL CONFLICT

Productive Versus Destructive Conflict

One way to think about conflict across cultures is in terms of what is more or less successful conflict management or resolution. Given all of the variations in how people deal with conflict, what happens when there is conflict in intercultural relationships?

Scholar David Augsburger (1992) suggests that productive intercultural conflict is different from destructive conflict in four ways. First, in productive conflict, individuals or groups narrow the conflict in terms of definition, focus, and issues. In destructive conflict, they escalate the issues or negative attitudes. For example, if a partner says, "You never do the dishes" or "You always put me down in front of my friends," the conflict is likely to escalate. Instead, the partner could focus on a specific instance of being put down.

Second, in productive conflict, individuals or groups limit conflict to the original issue. In destructive conflict, they escalate the conflict from the original issues, with any aspect of the relationship open for reexamination. For example, guests on talk shows about extramarital affairs might initially refer to a specific affair and then expand the conflict to include numerous prior arguments.

Third, in productive conflict, individuals or groups direct the conflict toward cooperative problem solving. For example, a partner may ask, "How can we work this out?" In contrast, in destructive conflict, strategies involve the use of power, threats, coercion, and deception. For example, an individual might threaten his or her partner: "Either you do what I want, or else." Finally, in productive conflict, individuals or groups trust leadership that stresses mutually satisfactory outcomes. In destructive conflict, they polarize behind single-minded and militant leadership.

Competition Versus Cooperation

As you can see, the general theme in destructive conflict is competitive escalation, often into long-term negativity. The conflicting parties have set up a self-perpetuating, mutually confirming expectation. "Each is treating the other badly because it feels that the other deserves to be treated badly because the other treats it badly and so on" (Deutsch, 1987, p. 41).

How can individuals and groups promote cooperative processes in conflict situations? The general atmosphere of a relationship will promote specific processes and acts (Deutsch, 1973). For instance, a *competitive* atmosphere will promote coercion, deception, suspicion, and rigidity, and lead to poor communication. In contrast, a *cooperative* atmosphere will promote perceived similarity, trust, and flexibility, and lead to open communication. The key is to establish a positive, cooperative atmosphere in the beginning stages of the relationship or group interaction. It is much more difficult to turn a competitive relationship into a cooperative one once the conflict has started to escalate.

Essential to setting a cooperative atmosphere is exploration. Whereas competition often relies on argumentation, cooperation relies on exploration. Exploration may be done in various ways in different cultures, but it has several basic steps. The parties must first put the issue of conflict on hold and then explore other options or delegate the problem to a third party. Blaming is suspended, so it's possible to generate new ideas or positions. "If all conflicting parties are committed to the process, there is a sense of joint ownership of the recommended solution. . . . [M]oving toward enemies as if they were friends exerts a paradoxical force on them and can bring transcendence" (Hocker & Wilmot, 1991, p. 191).

However, exploration does not have to be logically consistent or rational. As Augsburger (1992) points out, "Exploration can be pro-

vocative, speculative, and emotional" (p. 61). It should encourage individuals to think of innovative and interesting solutions to the conflict
at hand. For example, Bill and David were having an ongoing disagreement about a project they were working on, and their relationship
was becoming more and more strained. One day, Bill spontaneously
suggested that they go out to eat together and really talk about the
problem. David was surprised because they did not normally socialize—their relationship revolved around work. They talked about the
problem, spent some time getting to know each other, and found they
had some things in common. Although the problem didn't magically
go away, it became easier to manage. Bill's spontaneous invitation to
talk helped facilitate the resolution of the conflict.

Dealing With Conflict

There are no easy answers in dealing with intercultural conflict. Sometimes, we can apply the principles of dialectics; other times, we may
need to step back and show self-restraint. Occasionally, though, it may
be more appropriate to assert ourselves and not be afraid of strong
emotion. Here, we offer seven suggestions for dealing with conflict:

1. Stay centered and do not polarize.
2. Maintain contact.
3. Recognize the existence of different styles.
4. Identify your preferred style.
5. Be creative and expand your style repertoire.
6. Recognize the importance of conflict context.
7. Be willing to forgive.

Let's look at these guidelines in more detail.

Stay Centered and Do Not Polarize It's important to move beyond
traditional stereotypes and either-or thinking. David Augsburger (1992)
elaborates on this approach to dealing with conflict:

> *Immediately challenge the intrusion of either-or thinking, traditional
> stereotypes, and reductionistic explanations of the other's motives as
> simple while seeing your own as complex. Sustain the conflicting images
> of reality, one from the antagonist and one of your own, in parallel co-
> existence within your mind. Be open to a third, centered perspective that
> may bring a new synthesis into view. (p. 66)*

The parties involved must practice self-restraint. It's okay to get angry,

ANTI-AMERICANISM

Anti-Americanism has a very long history and is complicated by the economic, military, and political differences between the United States and other nations around the world. Anti-Americanism can operate on many levels—from the interpersonal to the social—and you may want to reflect on this aspect of intercultural interaction and the potential for conflict that may arise. How well do you understand anti-Americanism, and what is the best way to deal with it? Here are some voices that help explain anti-Americanism.

There are hardly any universals left in our postmodern times, but loathing for America is about as close as we can get to a universal sentiment: it is the one dynamic that unites fundamentalists and liberals, Arabs and Latin Americans, Asians and Europeans, and even the overshadowed Canadians, with the rest of the world. (Sardar & Davies, 2002, p. 195)

Today, however, when I talk with friends and relatives in London, when I visit Europe, the anti-Americanism is more than just sardonic asides, rueful Monty Python–style jibes, and haughty intimations of superiority. Today something much more visceral is in the air. I go to my old home and I get the distinct impression that . . . people really loathe America somewhere deep, deep in their gut. (Abramsky, 2004, p. B9)

America has the power and resources to refuse self-reflection. More pointedly, it is a nation that has developed a tradition of being oblivious to self-reflection. Yet, America is also a nation that produces strident self-criticism and many strands of dissenting opinion from writers, artists, academics, professionals and even politicians. (Sardar & Davies, 2002, p. 13)

To fully understand anti-Americanism, we have to step back and question what it means to be an "American." For President George W. Bush, it is a fanciful morality story of all-good versus all-evil. . . . In the words he has repeated time and again: "I had made it clear to the world that either you're with us or you're with the enemy, and that doctrine still stands." What does this history of empire-building mean for Americans today? And who truly counts as an American? (Tchen, 2004, pp. 301–302)

Sources: From S. Abramsky, "Waking Up from the American Dream," *Chronicle of Higher Education*, July 23, 2004, p. B9; Z. Sardar and M. Davies, *Why Do People Hate America?* (New York: The Disinformation Company, 2002); and J. K. W. Tchen, "Vigilante Americanism." In A. Ross and K. Ross (Eds.), *Anti-Americanism* (New York: New York University Press, 2004), pp. 301–314.

but it's important to move past the anger and to refrain from acting out feelings. For example, Jenni and her co-worker both practiced self-restraint and stayed centered in a recent disagreement about religion. Jenni explains,

> *My friend is a devout Catholic, and I am a devout Mormon. She asked me about where we get some of our doctrine and how it relates to the Bible. We never really solved our differences, but compromised and "agreed to disagree." This was necessary to keep our friendship and respect as co-workers. I felt bad that she couldn't see the points I was coming from. I do think it turned out for the best, though, because we don't feel tension around each other.*

Maintain Contact This does not mean that the parties have to stay in the conflict situation—sometimes it's necessary to step away for a while. However, the parties should not cut off the relationship. Rather, they should attempt a dialogue rather than isolate themselves from each other or engage in fighting. **Dialogue** differs from normal conversation in that it is

> *slow, careful, full of feeling, respectful and attentive. This movement toward an apparently opposing viewpoint must be learned; few develop this approach to others without a deep sense of the importance of each human being, and a belief in collaboratively searching for new solutions that honor each person. (Wilmot & Hocker, 2001, p. 257)*

Dialogue is possible only between two persons or two groups whose power relationship is more or less in balance. Dialogue offers an important opportunity to come to a richer understanding of intercultural conflicts and experiences.

Our student John experienced an intercultural conflict in an accounting class in which his maintaining contact paid off. He was placed in a group with three Japanese students who were all friends. He recalls:

> *Right from the beginning things were quite awkward; their mathematics abilities far exceeded mine. After only two days, they had met twice without me and completed part of the assignment. I had been left out of the decision-making process.*

Rather than avoiding the problem, however, he decided to invite them

---

dialogue Conversation that is "slow, careful, full of feeling, respectful and attentive" (Wilmot & Hocker, 2001, p. 257).

In dealing with intercultural conflicts, this author suggests, people should start with a different assumption about the reasons behind the conflict. Is it possible to approach and resolve intercultural conflicts without such an attitude, without giving the benefit of the doubt?

I'm challenged by Gandhian principles to understand—indeed, to know—that the proper response to institutional injustice is action. But it must be wrapped in love. Therein is the power. And the difficulty. Loving one's enemy is to bury deep one's egoistic tendencies. It requires "a supraconsciousness," the Trappist monk and Gandhian scholar Thomas Merton said, advocating: ". . . the strength of heart which is capable of liberating the oppressed and the oppressor together. . . . In any event, without that capacity for pity, neither of them will be able to recognize the truth of their situation: a common relationship in a common complex of sin."

This coming together—this reconciliation, which often seems so impossible to achieve in racial matters but which must never be given up as an impossibility—can often start, indeed, one by one—giving the other person the benefit of the doubt, assuming somebody just misspoke or misunderstood.

Source: From Patricia Raybon, *My First White Friend: Confessions on Race, Love, and Forgiveness* (New York: Penguin, 1996), p. 158.

all over to his house to talk about the project. Everyone was able to loosen up and discuss what had gone wrong, and the conflict was handled productively: "Although I was unhappy with the way things went during the earlier parts of the project, the end result was three new acquaintances and an A in accounting."

Recognize the Existence of Different Styles Conflict is often exacerbated because of the unwillingness of partners to recognize management style differences. Communication scholar Barbara L. Speicher (1994) analyzes a conflict that occurred between two student leaders on the same committee: the chair, Peter, an African American male, and Kathy, a European American female who was president of the organization. The two had a history of interpersonal antagonism. They disagreed on how meetings should be run and on how data should be collected in a particular project they were working on. They interviewed the other participants afterward and learned that most thought the conflict was related mainly to the interpersonal history of the two and to the issue at hand, but not to either race or gender.

Speicher then describes how her analysis of videotapes of the conflict showed that both Kathy and Peter adhered to cultural norms for communication between blacks and whites in the United States:

> *Peter was assertive, took the floor when he had an important point to make and became loud and emphatic as the conflict accelerated. . . . The Eurocentric discomfort with and disapproval of his adamancy led to either silence (avoidance) or attempts to calm him down and diminish rather than resolve the conflict. (p. 204)*

Speicher notes that part of the problem was related to differences in perceptions of rationalism—"the sacred cow of Western thought"—and emotionalism. In Western thought, these two behaviors often are seen as mutually exclusive. But this is not so in Afrocentric thinking. Peter believed that he was being rational, giving solid evidence for each of his claims, and also being emotional. To his Eurocentric colleagues, his high affect seemed to communicate that he was taking something personally, that his vehemence precluded rationality or resolution. Speicher suggests that perhaps we need to rethink the way we define conflict competence. From an Afrocentric point of view, one can be emotional and rational and still be deemed competent.

Speicher also points out the danger of attributing individual behavior to group differences: "While such work can help us understand one another, it can also encourage viewing an interlocutor as a representative of a group (stereotyping) rather than as an individual" (p. 206). However, she goes on to say that in this particular case

> *failure to recognize cultural differences led to a negative evaluation of an individual. The problems that emerged in this exchange were attributed almost exclusively to Peter's behavior. The evaluation was compounded by the certainty on the part of the European Americans, as expressed in the interviews, that their interpretation was the correct one, a notion reinforced by the Eurocentric literature on conflict. (p. 206)*

This particular combination of differing but complementary styles often results in damaged relationships and frozen agendas—the rational/avoiding–emotional/confronting "dance." Other combinations may be problematic but less overtly damaging. For example, two people with assertive emotional styles may understand each other and know how to work through the conflict. Likewise, things can work if both people avoid open conflict, particularly in long-term committed relationships (Pike & Sillars, 1985). Jointly avoiding conflict does not necessarily mean that it goes away, but it may give people time to think about how to deal with the conflict and talk about it.

Identify Your Preferred Style   Although people may change their way of dealing with conflict based on the situation and the type of conflict, most tend to use the same style in most situations. For example, Tom and Judith both prefer an avoiding style. If we are pushed into conflict or feel strongly that we need to resolve a particular issue, we can speak up for ourselves. However, we both prefer more indirect means of dealing with current and potential conflicts. We often choose to work things out on a more personal, indirect level.

It is also important to recognize which conflict styles "push your conflict button." Some styles are more or less compatible; it's important to know which styles are congruent with your own. If you prefer a more confronting style and you have a disagreement with someone like Tom or Judith, it may drive you crazy.

Be Creative and Expand Your Style Repertoire   If a particular way of dealing with conflict is not working, be willing to try a different style. Of course, this is easier said than done. As conflict specialists William Wilmot and Joyce Hocker (2001) explain, people often seem to get "frozen" into a conflict style. For example, some people consistently deny any problems in a relationship, whereas others consistently escalate small conflicts into large ones.

There are many reasons for getting stuck in a conflict management style, according to Wilmot and Hocker. The style may have developed during a time when the person felt good about himself or herself—when the particular conflict management style worked well. Consider, for example, the high school athlete who develops an aggressive style on and off the playing field, a style that people seem to respect. A limited repertoire may be related to gender differences. Some women get stuck in an avoiding style, whereas some men get stuck in a confronting style. A limited repertoire also may come from cultural background—a culture that encourages confronting conflict or a culture (like Judith's and Tom's) that rewards avoiding conflict. A combination of these reasons is the likely cause of getting stuck in the use of one conflict management style. For example, even though Tom and Judith prefer an avoiding style, we have occasionally found it effective to be more assertive and direct in intercultural conflicts in which the dominant communication style was more confrontational.

In most aspects of intercultural communication, adaptability and flexibility serve us well—and conflict communication is no exception. This means that there is no so-called objective way to deal with conflict. Many times, as in other aspects of relationships, it's best simply to listen and not say anything. One strategy that mediators use is to allow one person to talk for an extended time while the other person listens.

Recognize the Importance of Conflict Context As noted earlier in this chapter, it is important to understand the larger social, economic, political, and historical contexts that give meaning to many types of conflict. Conflict arises for many reasons, and it is misleading to think that all conflict can be understood within the interpersonal context alone. For example, when one student, George, went home for a family reunion, everyone seemed to be talking about their romantic relationships, spouses, children, and so on. When George, who is gay, talked about his own partner, George's uncle asked why gay people had to flaunt their lifestyle. George reacted angrily. The conflict was not simply between George and his uncle; it rests in the social context that accepts straight people talking frequently and openly about their relationships but that does not validate the same discussion of romantic relationships from gay people. The same talk is interpreted differently because of the social context.

People often act in ways that cause conflict. However, it is important to let the context explain the behavior as much as possible. Otherwise, the behavior may not make sense. Once you understand the contexts that frame the conflict, whether cultural, social, historical, or political, you will be in a better position to understand and conceive of the possibilities for resolution. For example, Savina, who is white, was shopping with her friend Lashieki. The employee at the cash register referred to someone as "that black girl," and Lashieki, who is African American, demanded, "Why did they have to refer to her as that black girl?" Lashieki's response can only be understood by knowing something about the context of majority–minority relations in the United States. That is, whites are rarely referred to by color, whereas people of color are often defined solely on the basis of race.

Be Willing to Forgive A final suggestion for facilitating conflict, particularly in long-term relationships, is to consider forgiveness. This means letting go of—not forgetting—feelings of revenge (Lulofs, 1994). This may be particularly useful in intercultural conflict (Augsburger, 1992).

Teaching forgiveness between estranged individuals is as old as recorded history; it is present in every culture and is part of the human condition (Arendt, 1954). Forgiveness can be a healthy reaction. Psychologists point out that blaming others and feeling resentment lead to a victim mentality. And a lack of forgiveness may actually lead to stress, burnout, and physical problems (Lulofs, 1994).

There are several models of forgiveness. Most include an acknowledgment of feelings of hurt and anger and a need for healing. In a forgiveness loop, forgiveness is seen as socially constructed and based in communication. If someone is in a stressed relationship, he or she can create actions and behaviors that make forgiveness seem real; then he or she can communicate this to the other person, enabling the relationship to move forward. An example of forgiveness on a national level involves the National Sorry Day and the Journey of Healing, which serve to acknowledge and apologize for the wretched treatment of Aboriginals by non-Aboriginal Australians. Another example is the Truth and Reconciliation Commission in South Africa, formed to investigate and facilitate the healing of racial wounds as a result of apartheid. The committee hears stories of the atrocities that were committed, but the ultimate goal is forgiveness, not revenge (Henderson, 1999).

Forgiveness may take a long time. It is important to distinguish between what is forgiveness and what is not, because false forgiveness can be self-righteous and obtrusive; it almost nurtures past transgression. As writer Roxane Lulofs (1994) explains, forgiveness is not

simply forgetting that something happened. It does not deny anger. It does not put us in a position of superiority. It is not a declaration of the end of all conflict, of ever risking again with the other person (or anybody else). It is not one way. . . . We do not forgive in order to be martyrs to the relationship. We forgive because it is better for us and better for the other person. We forgive because we want to act freely again, not react out of past pain. . . . [It] is the final stage of conflict and is the one thing that is most likely to prevent repetitive, destructive cycles of conflict. (pp. 283–284, 289)

Mediation

Sometimes two individuals or groups cannot work through conflict on their own. They may request an intermediary, or one may be assigned to intervene. In some societies, these third parties may be rather informal. In Western societies, though, they tend to be built into the legal and judicial system. For example, lawyers or counselors may act as mediators to settle community or family disputes.

Contemporary Western **mediation** models often ignore cul-

---

mediation The act of resolving conflict by having someone intervene between two parties.

POINT OF VIEW

Conflict specialist David Augsburger identifies six key Western assumptions—conflict myths—and notes their inadequacies in intercultural settings.

1. **People and problems can be separated cleanly; interests and positions can be distinguished sharply.** . . . In most cultures of the world, equal attention must be given to both person and problem, to relationship and goals and to private interests as well as public positions if a creative resolution is to be reached.

2. **Open self-disclosure is a positive value in negotiations. An open process of public data shared in candid style is assumed necessary for trust.** . . . "Open covenants, openly arrived at," Woodrow Wilson insisted, as did Harry Truman, were the basis for setting up the United Nations. However, when constituents can hear what is being sacrificed in reaching an agreement, then compromise becomes improbable and often impossible precisely because of that openness. The real negotiation is done in corridors or behind closed doors, and is announced publicly when agreements have been reached. Virtually nothing of any substance is agreed on in the official public UN debates.

3. **Immediacy, directness, decisiveness, and haste are preferred strategies in timing.** The Western valuation that time is money can press the negotiator to come to terms prematurely. Many different cultures find that the best way to reach an agreement is to give the matter sufficient time to allow adjustments to be made, accommodations to emerge, and acceptance to evolve and emerge. Believing that "time is people," they are in less haste to reach closure.

tural variations in conflict processes. Fortunately, more scholars and mediators are looking at other cultural models that may work better in intercultural conflicts. Augsburger (1992) suggests that the culturally sensitive mediator engages in conflict transformation (not conflict resolution or conflict management). The conflict transformer assists disputants to think in new ways about the conflict—for example, to transform attitudes by redirecting negative perceptions. This requires a commitment by both parties to treat each other with goodwill and mutual respect. Of course, this is often much easier said than done.

4. **Language employed should be reasonable, rational, and responsible.** In some cultures, deprecative language, extreme accusations and vitriolic expressions are used as a negotiating power tactic. Admiral Joy, the senior UN delegate to the armistice talks at the end of the Korean War, has told of a note that was exchanged between North Korean delegates. In Korean characters large enough to be read by the noncommunist representatives, the note proclaimed, "These imperialist errand boys are lower than dogs in a morgue." Joy states that this was "the ultimate Korean insult."

5. **No is no and yes is yes (an affirmation is absolute, a negation final).** In some cultures, one does not say no to an offer; requests are not phrased to elicit negations; when an offer is affirmed, the real meanings are weighed and assessed carefully. Many negotiators have left a meeting with a perceived agreement only to find that the real position was more subtle, more concealed, and the reverse of their public expectations. A Mexican proverb advises, "There are a hundred ways of saying no, without saying it."

6. **When an agreement is reached, implementation will take care of itself as a logical consequence.** The agreements negotiated may mean different things to parties in a reconciliation. Built-in processes, ongoing negotiations, open channels for resolving problems as they arise in ongoing interpretation, and circumstances that would warrant renegotiation are all useful elements for ensuring ongoing success.

Source: From D. Augsburger, *Conflict Mediation Across Cultures* (Louisville, KY: Westminster/John Knox Press, 1992), pp. 206–208.

Behavior can be transformed by limiting all action to collaborative behavior; this can break the negative cycle but requires a commitment to seek a noncoercive process of negotiation even when there has been intense provocation. For example, in the recent Northern Ireland agreement, mediation resulted in commitment by most people to change the vision of Northern Ireland, in spite of horrendous provocation on the part of some extremists.

Traditional societies often use mediation models based on nondirect means. The models vary but share many characteristics. Whereas

North American mediation tends to be more formal and structured, involving direct confrontation and communication, most traditional cultural models are more communally based, with involvement by trusted leaders. Indirect communication is preferred in order to permit individuals to save face. In addition, the process is more dynamic, directed toward resolving tension in the community—the responsibility of the disputants to their larger community is central (Augsburger, 1992, p. 204).

Augsburger provides the example of mediation in the Gitksan Nation, in northwest British Columbia, where mediation of disputes begins with placement of the problem "in the middle of the table." Everyone involved—including those in authority and the witnesses—must make suggestions in a peaceful manner until they come to a decision all can live with. Even conflicts ending in murder are resolved in this consensus-oriented fashion. For instance, "land would be transferred as compensation to help deal with the pain of the loss. The murderer might be required to give up his or her name and go nameless for a period to show respect for the life taken" (p. 213). Eventually, however, the land or anything else that was given up would be returned, "when the pain has passed and time has taken care of the grief" (p. 213). Augsburger points out that this traditional communal approach to mediation is based on collectivistic beliefs that make individualistic solutions to conflicts unacceptable.

Contemporary mediators have learned some lessons from the traditional non-Western models, and mediation is used increasingly in the United States and other countries to resolve conflicts. Mediation is advantageous because it relies on the disputing parties' active involvement in and commitment to the resolution. Also, it represents the work of all involved, so it's likely to be more creative and integrative. Finally, mediation is often cheaper than adversarial legal resolution (Wilmot & Hocker, 2001, p. 276).

DISCUSSION QUESTIONS

1. How does the "conflict as opportunity" orientation differ from the "conflict as destructive" orientation?

2. Why is it important to understand the context in which intercultural conflict occurs?

3. How are conflict strategies used in social movements?

4. How does an attitude of forgiveness facilitate conflict resolution?

5. What are some general suggestions for dealing with intercultural conflict?

ACTIVITIES

Cultures in Conflict. For this assignment, work in groups of four. As a group, select two countries or cultural groups that are currently in conflict or that have historically been in conflict. In your group, form two pairs. One pair will research the conflict from the perspective of one of the two cultural groups or countries; the other pair will research the conflict from the perspective of the other group or country. Use library and community resources (including interviews with members of the culture if possible). Outline the major issues and arguments. Explore the role of cultural values, and political, economic, and historical contexts that may contribute to the conflict. Be prepared to present an oral or written report of your research.

REFERENCES

Applebaum, A. (2005, November 9). "But, what country is this?" *Washington Post*, p. A31.

Arendt, H. (1954). *The human condition.* Chicago: University of Chicago Press.

Augsburger, D. (1992). *Conflict mediation across cultures.* Louisville, KY: Westminster/John Knox Press.

Blocker, J. (2002, April 1). France/U.S.: Criticism tempered on decision to seek death penalty for Moussaoui. Radio Free Europe/Radio Liberty. www.rferl.org/nca/features/2002/04/01042002055307.asp

Cai, D. A., & Fink, E. L. (2002). Conflict style differences between individualists and collectivists. *Communication Monographs, 69,* 67–87.

Canary, D. J., Cupach, W. R., & Messman, S. J. (1995). *Relationship conflict.* Thousand Oaks, CA: Sage.

Cole, M. (1996). *Interpersonal conflict communication in Japanese cultural contexts.* Unpublished dissertation, Arizona State University, Tempe.

Collier, M. J. (1991). Conflict competence within African, Mexican,

and Anglo American friendships. In S. Ting-Toomey & F. Korzenny (Eds.), *Cross-cultural interpersonal communication* (pp. 132–154). Newbury Park, CA: Sage.

Cupach, W. R., & Canary, D. J. (1997). *Competence in interpersonal conflict.* New York: McGraw-Hill.

Delgado, F. (2002). Mass-mediated communication and intercultural conflict. In J. N. Martin, T. K. Nakayama, & L. A. Flores (Eds.), *Readings in intercultural communication: Experiences and contexts* (2nd ed., pp. 351–359). New York: McGraw-Hill.

Deutsch, M. (1973). *The resolution of conflict: Constructive and destructive processes.* New Haven, CT: Yale University Press.

Deutsch, M. (1987). A theoretical perspective on conflict and conflict resolution. In D. Sandole & I. Sandole-Staroste (Eds.), *Conflict management and problem solving* (pp. 38–49). New York: New York University Press.

Filley, A. C. (1975). *Interpersonal con-*

flict resolution. Glenview, IL: Scott, Foresman.

Folger, J. P., Poole, M. S., & Stutman, R. K. (1993). *Working through conflict: Strategies for relationships, groups, and organizations* (2nd ed.). New York: HarperCollins.

France's failure. (2005, November 12). *The Economist,* pp. 11–12.

Hacker, A. (1997). *Money: Who has how much and why.* New York: Scribner.

Hall, B. "J." (1994). Understanding intercultural conflict through kernel images and rhetorical visions. *The International Journal of Conflict Management, 5*(1), 62–86.

Henderson, M. (1999). *Forgiveness: Breaking the chain of hate.* Wilsonville, OR: Book-Partners.

Hocker, J. L., & Wilmot, W. W. (1991). *Interpersonal conflict* (3rd ed.). Dubuque, IA: Brown.

Ignatius, D. (2005, November 9). Why France is burning. *Washington Post,* p. A31.

King, M. L., Jr. (1984). Pilgrimage in nonviolence. In J. C. Albert & S. E. Albert (Eds.), *The sixties papers: Documents of a rebellious decade* (pp. 108–112). New York: Praeger. (Original work published 1965)

Kivel, P. (1996). *Uprooting racism: How white people can work for racial justice.* Gabriola Islands, BC: New Society.

Kraybill, D. (1989). *The riddle of Amish culture.* Baltimore: Johns Hopkins University Press.

Lindsley, S. L. (1999). A layered model of problematic intercultural communication in U.S.-owned *maquiladoras* in Mexico. *Communication Monographs, 66,* 145–167.

Lulofs, R. S. (1994). *Conflict: From theory to action.* Scottsdale, AZ: Gorsuch Scarisbrick.

Malcolm X. (1984). The ballot or the bullet. In J. C. Albert & S. E. Albert (Eds.), *The sixties papers: Documents of a rebellious decade*

(pp. 126–132). New York: Praeger. (Original work published 1965)

Mandonnet, E., Pelletier, E., Pontaut, J.-M., & Rosso, R. (2005, November 10–16). Pourquoi la France brûle. *L'Express International,* pp. 22–28.

Pike, G. R., & Sillars, A. L. (1985). Reciprocity of marital communication. *Journal of Social and Personal Relationships, 2,* 303–324.

Rahim, M. A. (1986). *Managing conflict in organizations.* New York: Praeger.

Rahim, M. A., & Magner, N. R. (1995). Confirmatory factor analysis of the styles of handling interpersonal conflict: First-order factor model and its invariance across groups. *Journal of Applied Psychology, 80,* 122–132.

Ross, M. H. (1993a). *The culture of conflict: Interpretations and interests in comparative perspective.* New Haven, CT: Yale University Press.

Ross, M. H. (1993b). *The management of conflict: Interpretations and interests in comparative perspective.* New Haven, CT: Yale University Press.

Sallis, E. (2005, December 17). Australia's dangerous fantasy. *New York Times,* p. A23.

Smith, P. B, Dugan, S., Peterson, M. F., & Leung, K. (1998). Individualism/collectivism and the handling of disagreement: A 23-country study. *International Journal of Intercultural Relations, 22,* 351–367.

Smith, T. B. (2005, November 8). France could learn from Canada. *The Globe and Mail* (Toronto). Accessed December 18, 2005, from http://www.theglobeandmail.com/servlet/story/RTGAM.20051107.wcomment1108/BNStory/International/

Speicher, B. L. (1994). Interethnic conflict: Attribution and cultural ignorance. *Howard Journal of Communications, 5,* 195–213.

Thomas, K., & Kilmann, R. H. (1974).

Thomas-Kilmann conflict MODE instrument. Tuxedo, NY: Xicom.

Ting-Toomey, S. (1997). Intercultural conflict competence. In W. R. Cupach & D. J. Canary (Eds.), *Competence in interpersonal con flict* (pp. 120–147). New York: McGraw-Hill.

Ting-Toomey, S. (2005). The matrix of face: an updated face-negotiation theory. In W. B. Gudykunst (Ed.), *Theorizing about intercultural communication* (pp. 71–92). Thousand Oaks, CA: Sage.

Ting-Toomey, S., & Oetzel, J. G. (2002). Cross-cultural face concerns and conflict styles: Current status and future directions. In W. B. Gudykunst & B. Mody (Eds.), *Handbook of international and intercultural communication* (2nd ed., pp. 141–163). Thousand Oaks, CA: Sage.

Ting-Toomey, S., Yee-Jung, K. K., Shapiro, R., Garcia, W, Wright, T. J., & Oetzel, J. G. (2000). Ethnic/cultural identity salience and conflict styles in four U.S. ethnic groups. *International Journal of Intercultural Relations, 24*, 47–81.

Toupin, A. (1980). Counseling Asians: Psychotherapy in the context of racism and Asian-American history. *American Journal of Orthopsychiatry, 50*, 76–86.

Vellela, T. (1988). *New voices: Student political activism in the '80s and '90s.* Boston: South End Press.

Wilmot, W. W., & Hocker, J. L. (2001). *Interpersonal conflict* (6th ed.). New York: McGraw-Hill.

Wu, J. C. H. (1967). Chinese legal and political philosophy. In C. Moore (Ed.), *The Chinese mind* (pp. 213–237). Honolulu: East-West Center, University of Hawaii.

11

THE OUTLOOK FOR INTERCULTURAL COMMUNICATION

CHAPTER OBJECTIVES

After reading this chapter, you should be able to:

1. Identify and describe four individual components of competence.

2. Explain how various contexts influence individual intercultural competence.

3. Describe the importance of applying knowledge about intercultural communication.

4. Describe the various ways one can enter into intercultural dialogue.

5. Identify strategies for building coalitions across cultures.

6. Understand the relationship between social justice and intercultural competence.

7. Identify and describe specific strategies for working for social justice.

8. Explain the role of forgiveness in intercultural communication.

9. Identify several challenges for future intercultural communication.

Now that we are nearing the end of our journey through this textbook, you might ask, How do you really know whether you are a good intercultural communicator? We have covered a lot of topics and discussed some ideas that will help you be a better communicator. But you can't learn how to be a good communicator merely by reading books. Just as in learning to be a good public speaker or a good relational partner, it takes experience. In this chapter, we want to leave you with some specific ideas and suggestions for improving your skills in communicating across cultures.

We can approach intercultural competence in several ways. We begin this chapter with the social science approach, identifying specific components of competence: motivation, knowledge, attitudes, behaviors, and skills. We then turn to interpretive and critical approaches, emphasizing the contextual issues in competence. Finally, we continue our dialectical perspective, combining individual and contextual elements to offer specific suggestions for improving intercultural relations by building alliances and coalitions across cultures.

THE COMPONENTS OF COMPETENCE

What are the things we have to know, the attitudes and behaviors, to make us competent communicators? Do we have to be motivated to be good at intercultural communication? Intercultural communication scholars have been investigating these questions for many years (Chen & Starosta, 1996). Scholars taking a social science perspective have identified four basic components, or building blocks, of intercultural competence: motivation, knowledge, attitudes, and behaviors (Wiseman, 2002). We present these components here because we think they serve as a useful starting point. However, interpretive and critical scholars remind us that we need to contextualize these components (Collier, 1998, 2005). We need to ask ourselves, Who came up with these components? Are they applicable to everyone? For example, if a group of Native American scholars came up with guidelines for what it takes to be interculturally competent, would these guidelines apply to other cultural groups? Do the same competencies work in every context? Again, it is useful to remember our dialectical perspective. Intercultural communication competence may rely on individual competence, but context is also important. Let's look first at the individual components.

Individual Components

Motivation   Perhaps the most important dimension of communication competence is **motivation.** If we aren't motivated to communicate with others, it probably doesn't matter what other skills we possess. We can't assume that people always want to communicate. This is a difficult idea to wrestle with, especially for those of us who have dedicated our lives to studying and understanding intercultural communication. And yet, motivation is an important aspect of developing intercultural competence.

Why might people not be motivated to engage in intercultural communication? One reason is that members of large powerful groups often think they don't need to know much about other cultures; there is simply no incentive. In contrast, people from less powerful groups have a strong incentive to learn about and interact with more powerful groups. For example, female managers in corporations are motivated to learn about and adjust to the dominant male norms, Latinos/as are motivated to learn European American norms, and visitors overseas are motivated to learn about and adjust to the norms of foreign cultures. The survival of these less powerful groups often depends on members' motivation to succeed at intercultural interaction (Johnson, 2001).

Sometimes people can *become* motivated to learn about other cultures and to communicate interculturally. For example, the events of 9/11 motivated many U.S. Americans to become more aware of how U.S. worldviews and behavior, on both a personal and a political level, are intertwined with those in other cultures and countries. As an essay in the *Christian Science Monitor* reported, educators scrambled to incorporate more material about Islam and the Middle East in their curricula, to help students make some sense out of the historical and political reasons for the terrorist attacks.

> *For educators, the rush for knowledge has been gratifying. But to some, it dramatically underscores the fact that an inward-looking America routinely fails to ground its citizens in the complexities of world history. Most schools serve up little or no material related to the Middle East or a basic understanding of Islam. "Maybe there are courses about the Middle East in some of the more affluent school districts," says Bill Schechter, a history teacher at Lincoln-Sudbury Regional High School in Sudbury, Mass. "But in most schools there's just a bit about the crusades in world history, and*

---

motivation As an individual component of intercultural communication competence, the desire to make a commitment in relationships, to learn about the self and others, and to remain flexible.

then 30 minutes at some point during the school year to talk about the current crisis." (Coeyman, 2001, n.p.)

A second reason that people aren't motivated is because intercultural communication can be uncomfortable. As discussed previously, anxiety, uncertainty, and fear are common aspects of intercultural interactions. And yet, moving out of our "communication comfort zone" often leads to insights into other individuals, groups, and cultures. One of our students, Kati, explains,

If you keep your eyes open and your mind aware, you can learn something new about intercultural communication every day. . . . I think that you learn the most by traveling and/or making a conscious effort to interact with those in another culture or nation or race. Especially being thrust outside of your "comfort zone" (most Americans never get out of their comfort zone) will force you to see the diverse beauty and differences in other cultures.

Sometimes people do not address delicate intercultural issues out of fear—fear of being isolated from friends and family members who may be prejudiced and not motivated themselves. In one study, college students said they censored their communication in class discussions about race because they were afraid their comments would be taken as offensive, racist, or ignorant; they were afraid of being attacked or yelled at, and they didn't want to be perceived as "trying to prove" they weren't racist (Harris, Miller, & Trego, 2004). Tatum (1997) points out that this fear, and the resulting silences, have huge costs to us as individuals and for our society. Individually, when we are not motivated to reach out across cultural divides, we suffer from distorted perception (we don't really know how individuals from other cultures may view us or a particular situation) and a lack of personal growth. On the societal level, when we are not motivated to embrace other cultures and other ways of thinking and behavior, our organizations suffer from a loss of productivity and human potential (not everyone gets the opportunity to contribute ideas).

Third, motivation is lacking in contexts in which historical events or political circumstances have resulted in communication breakdowns. For example, it is understandable, given the history of animosity in the Middle East, that Israeli and Arab students would not be motivated to communicate with each other. It is also understandable why a Serbian student would not want to room with a Croatian student, or why a Greek Cypriot would not want to forge a friendship with a Turkish

Cypriot, given that these two ethnic communities have been engaged in one of the most protracted international disputes of all time.

To use an example closer to home, many blacks and whites in the United States are not motivated to forge friendships with each other. This may be partly due to social pressure. One study investigated why so few whites have black friends and why the interracial marriage rate is so low between whites and blacks. The researchers analyzed data from three separate ethnographic interview studies of whites and blacks and concluded that lack of interracial friendships is not because of lack of interracial contact. They found that 90% of the whites interviewed grew up in white-only neighborhoods, but even those who grew up in racially mixed neighborhoods and went to racially mixed schools and had the opportunity to form close relationships with African Americans failed to do so. Those who did have black friends as adolescents tended to not maintain these friendships as adults. The researchers conclude that it is not only the social isolation from blacks that prevents whites from forming close friendship. Rather, the limited interaction is a result of "white habitus"—shared negative attitudes about blacks or blaming blacks for not trying harder to make friends with them, and an "oblivion about the racial components of their own socialization" (Bonilla-Silva, Embrick, Ketchum, & Saenz, 2004).

The point here is that it doesn't matter how good a communicator you are if you are not motivated to use those communication skills. For some people, the first step in developing intercultural communication competence may be to examine their motivation to reach out to others who are culturally different.

Knowledge   The **knowledge** component comprises various cognitive aspects of communication competence; it involves what we know about ourselves and others, and about various aspects of communication. Perhaps most important is **self-knowledge**—knowing how you may be perceived as a communicator and what your strengths and weaknesses are. How can you know what these are? Sometimes you can learn by listening to what others say and by observing how they perceive you. One student describes her attempts to become a better intercultural communicator:

---

knowledge As an individual component of intercultural communication competence, the quality of knowing about oneself (that is, one's strengths and weaknesses), others, and various aspects of communication.
self-knowledge Related to intercultural communication competence, the quality of knowing how one is perceived as a communicator, as well as one's strengths and weaknesses.

Honestly, I feel it begins within yourself. I feel that if each person in our class opens his or her eyes just a little more than what they were before coming into class it will make a difference. This class has really opened my eyes to other people's opinions and feelings.

Acquiring self-knowledge is a long and sometimes complicated process. It involves being open to information coming in many different ways. A white student describes her growing awareness of what it means to be white in the United States after listening to Chicano and African American guest speakers:

They each spoke about their experiences that they have had [with others prejudging them]. . . . We discover our white identity by listening to others. We hear these hardships that they have had to endure and we realize that we never have had to experience that. You learn a lot about yourself that way. . . . By listening to our guests speak today, I realized that sometimes other ethnicities might not view my culture very highly.

We often don't know how we're perceived because we don't search for this information or because there is not sufficient trust in a relationship for people to reveal such things. Of course, knowledge about how other people think and behave will help you be a more effective communicator. However, learning about others in only abstract terms can lead to stereotyping. It is often better to learn through relational experience, as this student did:

I know that four or five years ago being gay did not have the same effect on me that it does now. My friend Jack told me a couple of years ago that he was gay, and we have had many discussions on the topic. I have a new understanding of what it means to be gay. A few years ago I didn't take a stance on whether it was right or wrong to be gay, and if anyone made a joke I would laugh. Now that I gained experience from Jack, I respect his way of life and would always support him. This point is valid because the more one experiences things with other people from different backgrounds, the more one will be able to respect and understand other people.

Of course, we can't know everything about all cultures or develop relationships with people from all cultural groups, so it's important to develop some general knowledge about cultural differences. For example, in this book, we have described cultural variations in both verbal and nonverbal communication. To avoid stereotyping, perhaps it is better simply to be aware of the range in thought and behavior across cultures, and not to assume that, because someone belongs to a particular group, he or she will behave in a particular way.

Linguistic knowledge is another important aspect of intercultural competence. Awareness of the difficulty of learning a second language helps us appreciate the extent of the challenges that sojourners and immigrants face in their new cultural contexts. Also, knowing a second or third language expands our communication repertoire and increases our empathy for culturally different individuals. For example, as Judith struggles through her conversational Spanish class, she is reminded again of how difficult it is to accomplish ordinary things in a second language. And when she sits in class and worries that the instructor might call on her, she is reminded of the anxiety of many international students and immigrants trying to navigate a new country and language.

Attitudes   Many **attitudes** contribute to intercultural communication competence, including tolerance for ambiguity, empathy, and nonjudgmentalism.

Tolerance for ambiguity refers to the ease in dealing with situations in which much is unknown. Whether we are abroad or at home, interacting with people who look different from us and who behave in ways that are strange to us requires a tolerance for ambiguity. When Judith was studying Spanish in Mexico recently, she was struck by the range of attitudes of her fellow students from the United States. Some seemed very tolerant of the classroom procedures in Mexico, but others seemed to want the classes to be run as they would be in the States.

Tolerance for ambiguity is one of the most difficult things to attain. As mentioned previously, people have a natural preference for predictability; uncertainty can be disquieting. Nick, an exchange student in Mexico, discusses how tolerance and language ability are particularly important—and problematic—in stressful situations:

> *I had lost my wallet in the marketplace and asked my wife to wire money to me. I couldn't figure out which Western Union location (there are many) I was supposed to go to to pick up my money. I finally went to the central post office, only to be told that my money had been delivered somewhere else—and I couldn't understand where. I was frustrated, tired*

---

linguistic knowledge Knowledge of other languages besides one's native language or of the difficulty of learning a second or third language.

attitudes An individual's dispositions or mental sets. As a component of intercultural communication competence, attitudes include tolerance for ambiguity, empathy, and nonjudgmentalism.

tolerance for ambiguity The ease with which an individual copes with situations in which a great deal is unknown.

POINT OF VIEW

In his book *Last Watch of the Night*, Paul Monette points out that it is important to recognize the many forms of intolerance most of us experience as we grow up. This excerpt is from a speech he gave at the Library of Congress during National Book Week. The writer he refers to, Urvashi Vaid, is a lesbian who has written about issues of tolerance. Think about how the intolerance around you may affect you and how difficult it is sometimes to be tolerant of the many diversities you encounter.

> *Most of our families do the very best they can to bring us up whole and make us worthy citizens. But it's a very rare person who manages to arrive at adulthood without being saddled by some form of racism or sexism or homophobia. It is our task as grownups to face those prejudices in ourselves and rethink them. The absolute minimum we can get out of such a self-examination is tolerance, one for another. We gay and lesbian people believe we should be allowed to celebrate ourselves and give back to the larger culture, make our unique contributions—but if all we get is tolerance, we'll take it and build on it.*
>
> *We don't know what history is going to say even about this week, or where the gay and lesbian revolution is going to go. But we are a revolution that has come to be based very, very strongly on diversity. We have to fight like everyone else to be open in that diversity; but I love Urvashi Vaid's idea that it's not a matter of there being one of each on every board and every faculty and every organization. It's a matter of being each in one. You'll pardon my French, but it's not so hard to be politically correct. All you have to do is not be an ———.*

Source: From Paul Monette, *Last Watch of the Night* (New York: Harcourt Brace, 1994), pp. 122–123.

and worried—and my language skills were deteriorating rapidly! Fortunately, I pulled myself together, tried to be patient, and joked with the postal workers. It took six hours to get my money, but by the end of the day, I had my money and had made some new friends at the post office!

Empathy refers to the ability to know what it's like to "walk in another person's shoes." Empathic skills are culture bound. We cannot really view the world through another person's eyes without knowing something about his or her experiences and life. To illustrate, suppose

empathy The capacity to "walk in another person's shoes."

a U.S. American and a Japanese have been introduced and are conversing. The Japanese responds to the U.S. American's first remark with a giggle. The U.S. American feels pleasurable empathic sensations and makes an impulsive comment, indicating a congenial, accepting reaction. However, the Japanese observer now feels intensely uncomfortable. What the U.S American doesn't realize is that the giggle may not mean that the Japanese is feeling pleasure. Japanese often giggle to indicate embarrassment and unease. In this case, the U.S. American's "empathy" is missing the mark. In this sense, empathy is the capacity to imagine oneself in another role, within the context of one's cultural identity.

Intercultural communication scholars have attempted to come up with a more culturally sensitive view of empathy. For example, Ben Broome (1991, 1993) stresses that to achieve empathy across cultural boundaries, people must forge strong relationships and strive for the creation of shared meaning in their interpersonal encounters. However, because this is difficult to achieve when people come from very different cultural backgrounds, Broome suggests that this shared meaning must be seen as both provisional and dynamic, that understanding is not an all-or-nothing proposition. In addition, cross-cultural empathy must integrate both thinking and feeling—we must try to understand not only what others *say* (content) but also how they *feel* (empathy). Finally, he reminds us that to achieve cross-cultural empathy, we must seek to understand the context of both others' lived experiences and the specific encounters.

Magoroh Maruyama (1970), an anthropologist-philosopher, agrees that achieving cross-cultural empathy and trying to see the world exactly as the other person sees is very difficult. She describes the process as **transpection**, a postmodern phenomenon that often involves trying to learn foreign beliefs, assumptions, perspectives, and feelings in a foreign context. Transpection, then, can be achieved only with practice and requires structured experience and self-reflection.

Communication scholar Milton Bennett (1998) suggests a "Platinum Rule" ("Do unto others as *they themselves* would have done unto them") instead of the Golden Rule ("Do unto others as *you* would have done unto you") (p. 213). This, of course, requires movement beyond a culture-bound sympathy or empathy for others.

Achieving **nonjudgmentalism** is much easier said than done. We might like to think that we do not judge others according to our own cultural frames of reference, but it is very difficult. One of our

---

transpection Cross-cultural empathy.
nonjudgmentalism Free from evaluating according to one's own cultural frame of reference.

colleagues recalls being at a university meeting at which a group of Icelandic administrators and a group of U.S. American faculty were discussing implementing a study-abroad exchange program. The Icelandic faculty were particularly taciturn, and our colleague wanted to lighten up the meeting a little. Eventually, however, she realized that the taciturnity probably reflected different norms of behavior. She had unknowingly judged the tenor of the meeting based on her own style of communication.

The **D.I.E. exercise** is helpful in developing a nonjudgmental attitude (Wendt, 1984). It involves making a distinction between description (D), interpretation (I), and evaluation (E) in the processing of information. Descriptive statements convey factual information that can be verified through the senses (e.g., "There are 25 chairs in the room" and "I am 5 feet tall"). Interpretive statements attach meaning to the description (e.g., "You must be tired"). Evaluative statements clarify how we feel about something (e.g., "When you're always tired, we can't have any fun together"). Only descriptive statements are nonjudgmental.

This exercise can help us recognize whether we are processing information on a descriptive, interpretive, or evaluative level. Confusing the different levels can lead to misunderstanding and ineffective communication. For example, if I think a student is standing too close to me, I may interpret the behavior as "This student is pushy," or I may evaluate it as "This student is pushy, and I don't like pushy students." However, if I force myself to describe the student's behavior, I may say to myself, "This student is standing 8 inches away from me, whereas most students stand farther away." This observation enables me to search for other (perhaps cultural) reasons for the behavior. The student may be worried about a grade and may be anxious to get some questions answered. Perhaps the student is used to standing closer to people than I am. Or perhaps the student really is pushy.

It is impossible to always stay at the descriptive level. But it is important to know when we are describing and when we are interpreting. Most communication is at the interpretive level. For example, have you ever been set up for a blind date and asked for a description of the person? The descriptions you might get (e.g., tall, dark, handsome, nice, kind, generous) are not really descriptions; rather, they are interpretations that reflect individual and cultural viewpoints (Wendt, 1984).

Behaviors and Skills   Behaviors and skills are another component of intercultural competence. What are the most competent behaviors?

D.I.E. exercise A device that helps us determine if we are communicating at a descriptive, interpretive, or evaluative level. Only descriptive statements are nonjudgmental.

Are there any universal behaviors that work well in all cultural contexts? At one level, there probably are. Communication scholar Brent D. Ruben devised a list of universal behaviors that actually includes some attitudes. These behaviors are a display of respect, interaction management, ambiguity tolerance, empathy, relational rather than task behavior, and interaction posture (Ruben, 1976, 1977; Ruben & Kealey, 1979).

Some general behaviors seem applicable to many cultural groups and contexts (Koester & Olebe, 1988; Olebe & Koester, 1989). However, these skills become problematic when we try to apply them in specific ways. For example, being respectful works well in all intercultural interactions, and many scholars identify this particular skill as important (Collier, 1988; Martin & Hammer, 1989). However, how one expresses respect behaviorally may vary from culture to culture and from context to context. For example, European Americans show respect by making direct eye contact, whereas some Native Americans show respect by avoiding eye contact.

In one research project, we asked European American and Chicano students to identify nonverbal behaviors that they thought would be seen as competent. They identified some of the same behaviors (smiling, direct eye contact, nice appearance, and so on), but they assigned different levels of importance to various behaviors depending on the context (Martin, Hammer, & Bradford, 1994). There seem to be two levels of behavioral competence. The macro level includes many culture-general behaviors, such as be respectful, show interest, act friendly, and be polite. Then there is the micro level, at which these general behaviors are implemented in culture-specific ways.

It is important to be aware of these different levels of behaviors and be able to adapt to them. Let's see how this works. In one study, Mitch Hammer and his colleagues evaluated the effectiveness of a cross-cultural training program for Japanese and U.S. American managers in a joint venture (a steel company) in Ohio. One goal was to determine if the managers' intercultural communication skills had improved significantly. The research team used a general behavioral framework of communication competence that included the following dimensions: immediacy, involvement, other orientation, interaction management, and social relaxation (Hammer, Martin, Otani, & Koyama, 1990). The two groups (Japanese managers and U.S. American managers) rated these dimensions differently. The U.S. Americans said that the most important dimension was involvement (how expressive one is in conversation), whereas the Japanese managers said that the other orientation (being tuned in to the other person) was most important. The researchers also judged how well each group of managers adapted to the other group's communication style. They videotaped the interaction and asked Japanese raters to judge the U.S. American managers on how well they adapted to the Japanese style, and vice versa. For example, good interaction management for the Japanese meant initiating and terminating interaction, and making sure everyone had a chance to talk; for U.S. Americans, it meant asking opinions of the Japanese, being patient with silence, and avoiding strong disagreement and assertive statements. As this example shows, intercultural communication competence means being able to exhibit or adapt to different kinds of behaviors, depending on the other person's or group's cultural background.

William Howell (1982), a renowned intercultural scholar, investigated how top CEOs made decisions. He found, to his surprise, that they did not follow the analytic process prescribed in business school courses—analysis of cost, benefits, and so on. Rather, they made decisions in a very holistic way. That is, they reflected on the problem and talked about it with their friends and counterparts in other companies; then they would ignore the problem for a while, coming back to it when their minds were fresh to frame the answer. Howell emphasized that intercultural communication is similar, that only so much can be gained by conscious analysis, and that the highest level of communication competence requires a combination of holistic and analytic thinking. He identified four levels of intercultural communication competence: (1) unconscious incompetence, (2) conscious incompetence, (3) conscious competence, and (4) unconscious competence.

Unconscious incompetence is the "be yourself" approach, in which we are not conscious of differences and do not need to act in any particular way. Sometimes this works. However, being ourselves works best in interactions with individuals who are very similar to us. In intercultural contexts, being ourselves often means that we're not very effective and don't realize our ineptness.

At the level of **conscious incompetence**, people realize that things may not be going very well in the interaction, but they are not sure why. Most of us have experienced intercultural interactions in which we felt that something wasn't quite right but couldn't quite figure out what it was. This describes the feeling of conscious incompetence.

As instructors of intercultural communication, we teach at a conscious, intentional level. Our instruction focuses on analytic thinking

---

unconscious incompetence One of four levels of intercultural communication competence: the "be yourself" level at which there is no consciousness of differences or need to act in any particular way.

conscious incompetence One of four levels of intercultural communication competence: the awareness that one is not having success but the inability to figure out why.

In this essay, S. L. Rosen discusses the powerful stereotyping (or essentializing) of Asian people—referred to as Orientalism. By way of illustration, he analyzes a description of Japanese taken from a travelers' guidebook.

> *Orientalism is a total misseeing of the other through a veil of interpretations of reality which are relatively impenetrable and resistant to change. . . . Orientalism as cultural myth has been articulated through metaphors which characterize the East in ways which emphasize its strangeness and otherness . . . the Oriental person is a single image, a sweeping generalization; an essentialized image which carries with it the taint of inferiority.*
>
> *To give one powerful example of this essentializing process of image formation which is entailed by Orientalism, we quote from a book entitled* When Cultures Collide *by Richard D. Lewis (1982), a kind of manual for people traveling and doing business around the world to help them understand the various cultures they come in contact with. By no means the worst of its kind, Lewis' book expresses very well the way we use metaphors to trivialize another culture in a totalistic way, so as to make it easier to capture it in the network of our own understandings.*
>
> ▪ *Japanese children are encouraged to be completely dependent and keep a sense of interdependence throughout their lives.*
>
> ▪ *Everything must be placed in context in Japan.*
>
> ▪ *Japanese are constrained by their thought processes in a language very different from any other.*

and learning. This describes the level of **conscious competence**. Reaching this level is a necessary part of the process of becoming a competent communicator. Howell would say that reaching this level is necessary but not sufficient.

Unconscious competence is the level at which communication goes smoothly but is not a conscious process. You've probably heard of marathon runners "hitting the wall," or reaching the limits of their endurance. Usually, inexplicably, they continue running past this point. Communication at the unconscious competent level is like this. This

---

conscious competence One of four levels of intercultural communication competence: the practice of intentional, analytic thinking and learning.
unconscious competence One of four levels of intercultural communication competence: the level at which an individual is attitudinally and cognitively prepared but lets go of conscious thought and relies on holistic cognitive processing.

- *They do not like meeting newcomers.*
- *They represent their group and cannot therefore pronounce on any matters without consultation and cannot initiate an exchange of views.*
- *Westerners are individuals, but the Japanese represent a company which represents Japan.*
- *As we all know, Japanese do not like to lose face.*
- *The Japanese go to incredible lengths to be polite. . . .*

This kind of Orientalism [essentializing] carries with it the implication that Asian people are much more conformist than we are, and less respecting of the dignity of individual rights, i.e., inferior. Social and cognitive psychology tells us that stereotyping is a kind of mental schema making designed to help us grasp reality—to make things more understandable and less threatening; these mental schema such as stereotypes provide us with the illusion of understanding by dividing up and categorizing the flux of experience into easily manageable cognitive maps. Orientalism has been the prevalent mode by which this cognitive need to schematize has manifested itself in apprehending Asian people.

Source: From S. L. Rosen, "Japan as Other: Orientalism and Cultural Conflict," *Intercultural Communication*, 4, 2000; www.immi.se/intercultural

level of competence is not something we can acquire by consciously trying to. It occurs when the analytic and holistic parts are functioning together. When we concentrate too hard or get too analytic, things don't always go easier.

Have you ever prepared for an interview by trying to anticipate every question and forming every answer, and then not done very well? This silent rehearsing—worrying and thinking too hard—is called the "internal monologue." According to Howell, people should avoid this extraneous and obstructive activity, which *prevents* them from being successful communicators (Howell, 1979). You've also probably had the experience of trying unsuccessfully to recall something, letting go of it, and then remembering it as soon as you're thinking about something else. This is what unconscious competence is—being well prepared cognitively and attitudinally, but knowing when to "let go" and rely on your holistic cognitive processing.

Contextual Components

As we have stressed throughout this book, an important aspect of being a competent communicator is understanding the context in which communication occurs. Intercultural communication happens in many contexts. An interpretive perspective reminds us that a good communicator is sensitive to these contexts.

We have emphasized that *many* contexts can influence intercultural communication. For instance, by focusing only on the historical context, you may overlook the relational context; by emphasizing the cultural context, you may be ignoring the gender or racial contexts of the intercultural interaction; and so on. It may seem difficult to keep all of these shifting contexts in mind. However, by analyzing your own intercultural successes and failures, you will come to a better understanding of intercultural communication.

Another aspect of context is the communicator's position within a speech community. Reflect on your own social position in relation to various speech communities and contexts. For example, if you are the only woman in a largely male environment or the only person of color in an otherwise white community, you may face particular expectations or have people project motivations onto your messages. Recognizing your own relation to the speech community and the context will help you better understand intercultural communication.

A critical perspective reminds us that individuals' competence may be constrained by the political, economic, and historical contexts. Intercultural communication scholar Mary Jane Collier (1998) reflects,

> *I have come to see that competence, a central issue in my early work, is a construct that is based on implicit privilege. . . . Relevant questions from postcolonial critics include, "Competence and acceptance from whom? Who decides the criteria? Who doesn't? Competent or acceptable on the basis of what social and historical context?" (p. 142)*

For example, characteristics of effective communication for women in the United States have changed dramatically in the last 50 years. In the 1960s, an "effective" female communicator was expected to be rather passive (both verbally and nonverbally), indirect, and nurturing. Assertive women met with disapproval and sanctions. Today, the "effective" female is expected to behave rather differently from this. As the 21st century unfolds, there is a broader range of acceptable behaviors that define competence for females. They may be unassertive in some contexts, but they are also free, and even expected, to be more assertive in many contexts. Similarly, effective black communicators in the 1960s were expected to be nonassertive in verbal and nonverbal style. Blacks like Muhammad Ali who went against these expectations were severely sanctioned. In short, we need to understand that notions of communication competence depend on specific social, political, and historical contexts. And we need to question who is setting these standards.

These are important questions raised by the critical perspective that force us to rethink intercultural communication competence. Indeed, you now have the skills to push your own thinking about intercultural communication—both strengths and weaknesses—as it helps and hinders your ability to communicate.

APPLYING KNOWLEDGE ABOUT INTERCULTURAL COMMUNICATION

Now that we have taken you down the path of intercultural communication, we would like to conclude with specific suggestions for becoming better intercultural communicators. Our dialectical approach recognizes the important role of individual skills *and* contextual constraints in improving intercultural relations. The dialectical perspective also emphasizes the relational aspects of intercultural communication. Perhaps the first step in applying our knowledge to intercultural communication is to recognize the connectedness of humans and the importance of dialogue.

Entering Into Dialogue

To recognize and embrace our connectedness even to people who are different from us, we have to engage in true dialogue. A central notion of dialogue is sharing and reciprocity. Communication scholars Starosta and Chen (2005) suggest that a focus on mutual *listening*, instead of talking, forms the core of successful intercultural dialogue. How to do this? A "sharing of narratives" is one metaphor:

> *We come to the world with a master narrative that explains what things are, which ones count for what, what is good or bad about them, and we*

"braid" these accounts of fact and value into a somewhat coherent personal web of meaning. (p. 277)

Starosta and Chen go on to suggest that a good intercultural listener exchanges narrative accounts to expand his or her repertoire of possibilities in explaining the world—and this interest and skill is built on a foundation of openness, curiosity, and empathy.

An Eastern model of listening is also useful here. Japanese scholar Ishii (1984) models intercultural communication as listening. In this model, the effective intercultural communicator, sensitive to the other, thinks *carefully* before speaking and delivers a message that is never threatening or condemnatory and one that appears open to multiple possible interpretations. The listener hears the message, considers it, reconsiders it, trying on different possible interpretations—trying to understand the speaker's possible intent. When the listener believes she has understood the point being made, she frames a response, again in a nonthreatening manner. You can see that ambiguity is a feature of such listening, which may seem contradictory to other guidelines for competent communication that extol being clear and concise. Perhaps this points to a dialectical view. Intercultural dialogue may have to be clear *and* somewhat ambiguous.

But how can we *really* hear the voices of those who come from cultures very different from our own—and especially those who have not been heard from? As you think about all the messages you hear every day, the most obvious voices and images are often the most privileged. To resist the tendency to focus only on the loudest, most obvious voices, we should strive for "harmonic discourse." This is discourse in which all voices "retain their individual integrity, yet combine to form a whole discourse that is orderly and congruous" (Stewart, 1997, p. 119).

Any conciliation between cultures must reclaim the notion of a voice for *all* interactants. In intercultural contexts, there are two options for those who feel left out—exit or expression. When people feel excluded, they often simply shut down, physically or mentally abandoning the conversation. When this happens, their potential contributions—to some decision, activity, or change—are lost. Obviously, the preferred alternative is to give voice to them. People's silence is broken when they feel that they can contribute, that their views are valued. And those who have historically been silenced sometimes need an invitation. Or those who have a more reserved conversation style may need prompting, as was the case with this traveler from Finland:

·

I was on a business trip in England with some colleagues. We visited universities, where we were shown different departments and their activities. The presenters spoke volubly, and we, in accordance with Finnish speaking rules, waited for our turn in order to make comments and ask questions. However, we never got a turn; neither had we time to react to the situations.

In sum, one way to become a more competent communicator is to work on "dialogue" skills by trying to engage in true dialogue. It's important to work on speaking and listening skills. A second step is to become interpersonal allies with people from other cultures.

Becoming Interpersonal Allies

The dialectical approach involves becoming allies with others, in working for better intergroup relations. But we need a new way to think about multiculturalism and cultural diversity—one that recognizes the complexities of communicating across cultures and that addresses power issues. Otherwise, we can get stuck within a competitive framework: If we win something, the other person or group loses, and we can *only* win if others lose. This kind of thinking can make us feel frustrated and guilty.

The goal is to find a way in which we can achieve equitable unity despite holding many different and contradictory truths, a unity based on conscious coalition, a unity of affinity and political kinship, in which we all win.

How can we do this? We first identify what **intercultural alliances** might look like. Communication scholar Mary Jane Collier (1998) interviewed many people in intercultural friendships and identified three issues that characterize intercultural alliances. The first has to do with power and privilege: Intercultural friends recognize and try to understand how ethnic, gender, and class differences lead to power and try to manage these power issues.

In their study of college students, Chesler, Peet, and Sevig (2003) described how difficult it is to understand power issues in interracial relationships. Their findings are based on interviews with white college students. They found that most students came to college with little experience in interracial relations and were generally unaware or held negative attitudes toward racial issues, or even saw themselves as victims, as described by one young man:

---

intercultural alliances Bonds between individuals or groups across cultures characterized by a shared recognition of power and the impact of history and by an orientation of affirmation.

In outlining specific ways in which white people can fight racism, Paul Kivel lists questions they can ask to better understand specific contexts in which they live and work.

WORKPLACE

1. What is the gender, race and class composition in your workplace? Which groups hold which positions?

2. Who, by race, gender and class, has the power to make decisions about hiring, firing, wages and working conditions in your workplace? Who gets promoted and who doesn't?

3. Is hiring non-discriminatory? Are job openings posted and distributed? Do they attract a wide variety of applicants? Are certain groups excluded? Does the diversity of your workplace reflect the diversity of the wider community?

4. Are there "invisible" workers, people who cook, clean or do maintenance, for example, who are not generally noticed or paid well?

5. What is the racial composition of the people who actually own your workplace? Who makes money from the profits of your work?

RELIGION

1. What is your religious upbringing?

2. What did you learn about people of color in Sunday school or sermons? About Jewish people?

3. Was your religious community all white? Was the leadership of your religious organization all white?

I think white males have a hard time because we are constantly blamed for being power-holding oppressors, yet we are not given many concrete ways to change. Then we just feel guilty or rebel. (p. 227)

Through educational and personal experiences, some did come to understand privilege, but it is often a difficult process. As we discussed in Chapter 5, it involves a phase of feeling guilty and paralyzed. As one student described it, "I was horribly liberal-guilt ridden, paralyzed, I was totally blowing every little minor interaction that I had with peo-

4. *What attitudes were expressed about people of color through discussion of missionary work, charity or social problems?*

5. *What do you know about the history of resistance to racism in your religious denomination?*

HOME AND FAMILY

1. *Were people of color and racism talked about in your childhood home? Think about particular incidents when it was. Was there tension around it? What was the general tone? Who initiated discussions and who resisted them?*

2. *Was there silence in your home on issues of racism or anti-Semitism? What did you learn from the silence?*

3. *As a child, what stories, TV shows or books influenced you the most in your attitudes about people of color? What do you carry with you from that exposure?*

4. *Talk with your partner, housemates and friends about [racial] issues. Notice the whiteness of your surroundings out loud to family and friends. This needn't be done aggressively or with great anger. You don't need to attack other people. Ask questions, notice things out loud, express your concerns and give other people room to think about and respond to what you say.*

5. *If you did a room-by-room assessment of your home today, would you find a diversity of images and items? If the answer is no, what do you and other family members lose because of that lack? How does it contribute to racial prejudice and discrimination?*

Source: From Paul Kivel, *Uprooting Racism: How White People Can Work for Racial Justice*, (Gabriola Island, BC: New Society Publishers, 1996), pp. 182–183, 199, 222.

ple of color way out of proportion. . . . I saw how hard it was for me to stop doing that and start being more productive" (p. 227).

Understanding and acknowledging one's privilege, as Collier notes, is often necessary in intercultural friendships. This student describes this acknowledgment:

I learned that being white, [there are] so many privileges that I didn't even know of . . . like loans from the bank, not being stopped by the police and other things me and white kids can get away with. I had not noticed the extent to which white privilege has affected and continues to affect many aspects of my everyday life. I thought "I" had accomplished so much, but how much of where I am is due to my accumulated privilege, my family, economic status, school advantages? (Chesler et al., 2003, p. 227)

Being on two different sides of the power issue can challenge individuals in intercultural relationships. For example, Eleanor, an African American woman, and her friend Mairead, who is white, describe how they negotiate this issue in their own relationship. Often the only African American participating in discussions of race, Eleanor says she gets tired of "educating white girls" about racism. Mairead recognizes the problem of unwittingly saying or doing racist things and "hurting my friend." This is not merely a matter of benign faux pas, but is an ongoing source of oppression for black women, something with far deeper implications than simply saying the right thing in a social situation involving equals (McCullough, 1998, p. 83). Eleanor sometimes needs to withdraw from her white friends to restore herself. For her part, Mairead recognizes that she needs to educate herself about issues of racism. And the two women realize that negotiating time-out from a friendship or time to work on personal issues alone is one aspect of intercultural friendship in a racially segregated society.

Collier's (1998) second component of intercultural alliances has to do with the impact of history: Intercultural friends recognize that people from historically powerful groups view history differently than do those who belong to less powerful groups. As we learned in Chapter 4, history often plays an important part in intercultural interactions. One of our colleagues describes how she and her friend Michael had very different views on history:

I was always amazed at how often my friend Michael talked about his relatives' experience during the Holocaust—even though his family wasn't directly involved. He was constantly told as he was growing up that prejudice against Jews could easily lead to another holocaust—and that he always had to be vigilant against anti-Semitism. For me, not being Jewish, I used to get impatient with him, but after learning more about the history and getting to know Michael better, I realize that this is an important part of who he is, and I've actually learned a lot from him about the experiences of a group of people that I knew little about. And I appreciate that side of him better.

History also plays a part in black–white relationships. We're often struck by how, in discussions about race in our classes, white students go to great lengths to affirm that they aren't racist, often telling stories about friends and family members—who, unlike them, are racist. They seem to want to be absolved of past or present responsibilities where race was concerned. And whites expect persons of color to communicate in ways that are friendly, comfortable, and absolving. In this case, true dialogue for whites involves a genuine commitment to listening, to not being defensive, and to recognizing the historical contexts that impact us all. True intercultural friends accept rather than question others' experiences, particularly when historical inequities and power issues are involved. They recognize the importance of historical power differentials and affirm others' cultural experiences even when this calls into question their own worldviews.

Collier's (1998) third component of intercultural alliances has to do with orientations of affirmation. Intercultural friends value and appreciate differences and are committed to the relationship even when they encounter difficulties and misunderstandings. For example, our student Shara comes from a cultural background that emphasizes commitment to family and family obligations. Her friend Kati has very little contact with her parents and siblings. They aren't estranged; they just aren't close. Kati would like to spend time with Shara on holidays, but Shara always spends holidays with her family, who live in another state. This issue has caused tension between the two over the years. But they each realize that these different values are important aspects of their identities. And in complex and dialectical ways, they learn from each other. Shara sometimes envies Kati for her relative freedom and lack of family obligations. But she also feels sorry for Kati that she doesn't have the kind of family support to back her up when she needs help. Similarly, Kati envies Shara's relationships with her large extended family and all the activities and help they provide. But she also sometimes feels sorry for Shara that she never seems to have any time for herself.

Building Coalitions

As we have emphasized throughout this book, many identities and contexts give meaning to who you really are. That is, your identities of gender, sexual orientation, race, region, religion, age, social class, and so on, gain specific meaning and force in different contexts. Coalitions can arise from these multiple identities. There are many good examples, such as the Seeds of Peace project, which brings together Jewish and Palestinian young people to work toward peace and harmony. Other local coalitions work to promote dialogue between blacks and whites, and between gays and straights. Another example is the post-9/11 book club coalition of Christian, Jewish, and Muslim women (see "Point of View" box).

Some contexts that arise in the future may cause you to rethink many of your identities. The rhetoric that people use to mobilize co-alitions may speak to you in various ways. As you strive to build better intercultural relations, you may need to transcend some of your identities, as the workers in Hawaii did, or you may reinforce other identities. These shifting identities allow you to build coalitions among seemingly different peoples, to foster positive intercultural relationships for a better world.

Coalitions, which are built of multiple identities, are never easy to build. In the process, you may find that some of your own identities feel neglected or injured. Part of the process is the commitment to work through these emotional blows, rather than simply withdrawing to the safety of older identities. Work your way to a richer, more meaningful life by navigating between safety and stability, and change.

Social Justice and Transformation

As we near the end our journey, we would like to refer back to our ethical challenge in the first chapter—the responsibility that comes with the acquisition of intercultural knowledge and insights. As we noted then, this educational experience is not just transformative for you, the individual, but should also benefit the larger society and other cultural groups in the increasingly interdependent world.

The first step in working for social justice is acknowledging that oppression and inequities exist—as we have tried to point out, cultural differences are not just interesting and fascinating, they exist within a hierarchy in which some are privileged and set the rules for others (Allen, 2004).

Starosta and Chen (2005) point out that intercultural listening should be followed by application. Dialogue should ultimately set things right that have been wrong. Good listening "promotes intercultural and interracial harmony, the amelioration of poverty, the introduction of justice, and mutual respect and harmony" (p. 282).

Johnson (2001) gives the following very concrete suggestions for working toward social justice and personal transformation.

1. Acknowledge that trouble exists. There are many obstacles to doing this. Many involved in oppression—those at the top—deny it, trivialize, call it something else, or blame those who are oppressed.

2. Pay attention. We have given you many suggestions for how to "pay attention," including intercultural listening. Johnson points out that there is a great deal of literature available representing many mar-

ginalized "voices," but these are rarely heard. For this reason, he suggests it is a good idea not to rely on the media for meaningful analysis of social oppression and inequalities—there is little money to be made from the stories of the powerless. While the media often give play to people of color who criticize affirmative action, or women who criticize feminism, there is little attention given to serious discussions of gender and violence, or class and race issues.

3. Do something. The more you pay attention to privilege and oppression, the more you'll see opportunities to do something.

Make noise, be seen. Stand up, volunteer, speak out, write letters, sign petitions, show up. Every oppressive system feeds on silence.

Find little ways to withdraw supports from paths of least resistance. You can start with yourself—by not laughing at racist or heterosexist jokes, by or objecting to others' jokes.

I remember the first time I met my sister's boyfriend and he made a disparaging reference to gay people, I knew I had to say something. I objected in a nice way, and we ended up talking for hours. I think he had just never thought about it very much and we're good friends to this day, although we disagree on almost every political and social issue!

Dare to make people feel uncomfortable, beginning with yourself. Ask your professors how many people of color are on the college's communication faculty. Ask why administrators at your children's schools are white men, and why the teachers and secretaries are women. You might think this doesn't make much difference, but it can. . . . And discomfort is unavoidable. One student describes her discomfort: "I love movies, and now I point out all the instances of racist and homophobic humor in movies. My friends think I'm nuts, but they humored me, and now they're starting to point them out to me."

Actively promote change in how systems are organized around privilege. (See the "Point of View" box earlier in this chapter with Kivel's lists of questions to ask in workplace, houses of worship, home and family.)

Don't keep it to yourself. Work with other people—build interpersonal alliances and build coalitions, as discussed earlier. Join organizations dedicated to change the systems that produce privilege and oppression. Most college and university campuses have student organizations that work on issues of gender, race, and sexual orientation. A list of such organization follows.

National Association for the Advancement of Colored People (NAACP)

National Organization for Women (NOW)

POINT OF VIEW

This essay gives an example of an intercultural coalition—how a post-9/11 book club brought Christian, Jewish, and Muslim women together to become interpersonal allies.

> *Laughter rings out in the salmon-colored living room of the parsonage at First Church in Cambridge, Mass. More than a dozen women— Christian, Jewish, and Muslim—are sharing insights garnered from "Gilead," a 2004 novel about the faith and struggles of a Christian minister in Iowa.*
>
> *The easy camaraderie as they discuss their distinctive approaches to prayer reflects three years of monthly meetings of the Daughters of Abraham, as they call themselves. The book club has explored the realms of the three monotheistic faiths—and blossomed into comfortable relationships that reach into each other's daily lives. . . .*
>
> *The club's origin, however, lies in the immediate anguish of Sept. 11, 2001. That night, an interfaith service hastily called by the minister at First Church (United Church of Christ) packed the sanctuary.*
>
> *"The service was powerful and people were crying; there were women in head scarves sitting next to me," recalls club founder Edie Howe. "I had this strong thought of how we were all the children of Abraham, and how unnecessary and tragic it was. I thought, 'What can I do about this?'"*
>
> *Her answer was to start the women's book club as a first step toward improving understanding. To ensure a joint commitment, she sought out Jews and Muslims who might share her interest and held planning discussions. A group of 18 met for the first time in September 2002 and has been meeting ever since. Though expectations vary, all share an interest in how other faiths are expressed in individual lives . . . .*
>
> *Keeping a booklist, they vote on priorities and read a book a month, alternating among the three religions. Tastes range across novels, history, poetry, memoirs, and religious philosophy. During*

National Conference for Community and Justice

National Gay and Lesbian Task Force

The Southern Poverty Law Center

The National Organization of Men against Sexism

National Urban League

There are also many opportunities on the Internet. Conhaim (2004) *their summer hiatus in 2004—after the group had developed a level of trust—they read books on the history and politics of the Middle East.*

"The Crusades Through Arab Eyes" was particularly informative, says Ms. Fischman, because of its non-Western vantage point.

"One book that really struck me was 'The Rock,' a historical novel by Iraqi author Kanan Makiya about the building of the Dome of the Rock in Jerusalem," says Ms. Minton. "The book quotes extensively from Jewish, Christian, and Muslim sacred texts but doesn't give you the footnote on the page. The quotes are so similar you can't tell where they come from without looking them up in the back."

From Islamic poetry, to a mystery involving the ritual baths of Jewish tradition, to C. S. Lewis's exploration of good and evil in "The Screwtape Letters," the varied choices spur conversation on the commonalities and differences in beliefs and practices. And sometimes they reveal surprising similarities. . . .

Most club members are heartened by the way it has spilled into their lives.

"People meet for lunch, help out when members are not well, suggest a good movie—like Jewish or Iranian film festivals—and [have] dinner ahead of time," says Ms. Howe. "And they attend weddings, bar mitzvahs, celebrations at the end of Ramadan."

Wherever the book club discussions roam, they clearly have come to be meaningful for those participating. It's still going strong, Minton says, because of the quality of the relationships, the fun and laughter, and the intellectual stimulation.

"We always come out of the meeting feeling better than when we went in."

Source: From J. Lampman, "How a Post-9/11 Book Club Brought Christian, Jewish, and Muslim Women Together," *Christian Science Monitor*, November 30, 2005, pp. 14–16.

points out the many Web-based projects through which Internet users can participate in online dialogues, gain insights into many different global cultures, and work for social justice. See the box "Internet Resources for Intercultural Interaction."

Forgiveness

Sometimes the cultural divide simply seems too huge. Sometimes there are grievances perpetrated by one cultural group upon another or by one individual on another that are so brutal as to make the suggestions listed above sound hollow and idealistic. What can we say to the widow of Daniel Pearl, the *Wall Street Journal* writer who was brutally murdered in Pakistan? He and his wife were known for promoting intercultural understanding in their personal and professional lives. Or to Pauline Mitchell, the mother of Fred Martinez, a Native American who was brutally murdered because he was *nadleeh* (a Native American term meaning "two spirited—with spirit of both male and female"). His mother described the horror of his death: "He'd been chased, beaten with a rock. He had been left to bleed, with a fractured skull, alone in the dark in a little canyon. . . ."

We would like to return to the notion of forgiveness we introduced in Chapter 10. Although limited and problematic, forgiveness is an option for promoting intercultural understanding and reconciliation. As we noted, forgiveness is more than a simple rite of religious correctness; it requires a deep intellectual and emotional commitment during moments of great pain. It also requires a letting go, a moving on, a true transformation of spirit. Dean Murphy (2002), writing in the *New York Times*, reports how scholars, leaders, and other individuals live out the concept of forgiveness. One example is Archbishop Desmond Tutu, the Nobel Laureate and chairman of South Africa's Truth and Reconciliation Commission and an advocate of forgiveness. He puts it in the context of the African concept of *ubuntu*—that a person is only a person through other people. Again, the importance of human connection and relationships emerges. Tutu says that forgiveness can be seen as an act of self-interest because forgivers are released from the bonds that hold them captive to the forgiven.

And many have stressed this aspect—that people can't be consumed by the wrongs that others have done to them because then their oppressors have won. According to civil rights advocate Roy Wilkins, "If you are consumed by rage, even at a terrible wrong, you have been reduced" (quoted in Murphy, 2002, p. 1). Religious and medical professionals also advocate the healing benefits of forgiveness.

Forgiveness has been likened to a train. People get on the train but must make various stops before forgiveness becomes a way off. The trick is not to miss your stop. And perhaps we might remember these cautionary words from Philip Yancy, an award-winning Christian author who writes about grace and forgiveness in the face of atrocities and brutality: "The only thing harder than forgiveness is the alternative" (quoted in Henderson, 1999, p. 176).

http://friendshipthrougheducation.org/ptpi/htm

This Web site, People to People International, which started after September 11, provides many resources for cyber dialogue and educational collaboration, primarily for elementary and high school children. Students can get pen pals and work on collaborative projects.

http://www.ciee.org

The Council on International Educational Exchange (CIEE) offers information about overseas study and work programs (including volunteering and teaching) for young people on its Web site, with resources for individuals, employers, communities, and educational institutions.

http://www.laetusinpraesens.org/links/webdial.php

This Web site links to different kinds of dialogue groups (intercultural, interfaith, etc.); resources on how to start such groups; and articles, books, and frameworks for understanding and implementing dialogue groups.

http://www.globalexchange.org/

The Web site of Global Exchange, a membership-based international human rights organization "dedicated to promoting social, economic, and environmental justice around the world," provides news on current global issues, organizes "reality tours" that take participants on education tours to various regions of the world, and offers opportunities to get involved in efforts to build international partnerships and affect change.

http://www.culturelink.org/dbase/links.html

Culturelink lists worldwide cultural "E-resources" on its site. They include intergovernmental organizations, national institutions, research institutions, art organizations, and publications.

http://www.hri.ca/racism/Links/

This Web site provides information about UN and NGO programs to combat racism in many areas of the world. There are links to various programs in the Americas, Europe, and Africa.

http://www.eycb.coe.int/eycbwwwroot/index.asp?language
=eng&url=/eycbwwwroot/eng/LINKS_TO.ASP

This Web site provides a number of useful references to European educational Internet resources on key intercultural issues. Web sites are collected under the following themes: intercultural learning, nonformal learning, participation, minorities, conflict resolution, human rights, and human rights education.

In this essay, the writer addresses the complexities of the notion of forgiveness. He begins the essay talking about the delayed justice in the case of the 1958 bombing of the black church in Birmingham, Alabama, that killed four little girls. Roy Wilkins, a longtime civil rights advocate, has always been a firm believer in the merits of forgiveness.

But events like the bombing in Birmingham help Mr. Wilkins recognize the limitations of forgiveness. In some cases, people can free their hearts of hatred without forgiving. Birmingham, he said, might be one of those cases. "I really don't think it is necessary to forgive every act," he said. "Where forgiveness applies to the Birmingham situation is what has happened in that city, and this is that blacks, by and large, have entered in the life of the city and they don't hold Bull Connor against white people who live in the city." A more personal forgiveness is made difficult in Birmingham because the killers have not sought it; Mr. Cherry denied his guilt even after the verdict. "There has to be some show of respect or remorse," said Mr. Jones, the prosecutor. "For there to be true forgiveness, it has to come from both sides."

Yet that did not happen, at least at first, in the case of Amy Biehl, a Fulbright scholar from Southern California who was stoned and stabbed to death in South Africa in 1993. Her killing stunned that country, but more shocking for many people was the forgiving response of her parents, Peter J. and Linda Biehl.

The Biehls quit their jobs to work full time on racial reconciliation. They testified in favor of political amnesty for the killers. They even offered two of them jobs. "To us it is liberating to forgive," Mr. Biehl, who died on March 31, once said.

At the time, Biehl's crusade seemed preposterous, almost beyond human. But that view changed in the past decade as forgiveness

WHAT THE FUTURE HOLDS

We live in a rapidly changing environment with increasing diversity both domestically and internationally. We see these changes occurring on economic issues, political issues, historical issues, and ideological issues. For example, the rapid rise of the European Union, both as a political entity and in terms of its currency—the euro against a falling U.S. dollar—have the potential to change rapidly the way U.S. Americans live. If other nations begin to shift their investments from the *evolved into a more mainstream tool of holistic healing, conflict resolution and self-help. . . . The Rev. Michael Lapsley, who was an anti-apartheid activist, talked about Sept. 11 forgiveness on a recent visit to New York. He is familiar with the notion of the facelessness of some evildoers—when he was a chaplain for the African National Congress he lost an eye and both hands after he opened an anonymous letter bomb in 1990.*

Forgiveness, Father Lapsley says, is a matter of choice, and since the American government ultimately responded militarily to the terror attacks, many Americans never examined any alternative. Yet because so many worldwide shared in America's horror and grief over Sept. 11, he explained, "Your pain has been acknowledged. That gives you freedom to take a position away from war and hatred and revenge."

But what about hunting down the perpetrators? What about justice?

In June, the Rev. Myrna Bethke, a member of the September Eleventh Families for Peaceful Tomorrows, will travel to Kabul with an interfaith delegation. Ms. Bethke, a Methodist minister in Freehold, N.J., had a brother who was killed at the World Trade Center.

She says she has forgiven his killers, but makes a distinction between retaliation, which she is against, and consequences, which she is for. She is going to Kabul in part to help remind herself that the people there have names and faces—making it harder to want to retaliate against them.

Forgiving her brother's killing, she says, released her from a tremendous burden. "You are free to live again," Ms. Bethke said.

Source: From Dean Murphy, "Beyond Justice: The Eternal Struggle to Forgive," *New York Times*, May 26, 2002, Section 4, p. 1.

United States to other nations, the "dollar could lose much more value on international markets; foreign investors could pull out of American markets, sending stock market indexes steeply downward; the U.S. government could be forced to raise taxes to make up for the bonds it can no longer sell around the world. If all that happened, Americans would wake up to the revolution in Europe in the most painful way" (Reid, 2004, p. 243).

Not only foreign investors, but U.S. Americans are also beginning to look overseas for their investments. Largely because "foreign funds more than doubled the returns of their domestic counterparts last year, American investors poured more new money into foreign stock funds in 2005—an estimated $149 billion—than in the previous four years combined. In fact, they put more new money to work in foreign funds than they did in domestic stock portfolios, which usually garner the bulk of investor dollars" (Lim, 2006, p. 23). These economic changes point to a more global economy, but they also point to the decreasing ability of U.S. Americans to continue to live in an isolated, monolingual world. The increasing demands of the new world order necessitate understanding cultures around the world, along with very different ways of understanding this new world.

In military terms, the United States is embarking on more and more overseas operations. Although not the primary reason for their assignments overseas, U.S. soldiers can play important roles in foreign relations as cultural ambassadors. Culturally insensitive soldiers can also wreak havoc on the image of the United States abroad, as happened in Afghanistan when U.S. soldiers used burnt corpses as propaganda, leading to an extremely negative reaction from the Islamic world. As part of this effort in enhancing intercultural contact, "American forces receive some cultural sensitivity training before arriving here, but with new troops rotating through every 7 to 12 months, the instruction can be spotty and inconsistent" (Schmitt, 2006, p. 7). Thus, the military has distributed laminated wallet-sized cultural guides to help the soldiers avoid negative encounters (see "Point of View" box).

In political terms, the rise of anti-Americanism is an increasing challenge for U.S. Americans. Although many U.S. Americans became aware of the French anti-Americanism in the wake of their disagreement over the invasion of Iraq, anti-Americanism is a worldwide phenomenon and certainly not a recent perspective (Ross & Ross, 2004). U.S. Americans may focus on the French, but rising anti-Americanism in Latin America, particularly Venezuela, and other areas around the world should not be overlooked. Whether or not you agree with the reasons for anti-Americanism—and these reasons are not the same around the world—you should know the reasons that people may feel this way. Without understanding the reasons for anti-American feelings, it is difficult to engage in meaningful intercultural dialogue.

The lack of understanding of other cultures is often felt by those who think that U.S. Americans should be more sympathetic to their situation. The 2005 riots in France, for example, mirror the riots in Los Angeles in 1992. Both were sparked by groups who felt disenfranchised from the larger society, although many more people were killed in the Los Angeles riots. One French writer notes, "We French expected a little more empathy considering the 1992 Los Angeles riots, when the authorities responded in force, and the city experienced curfews, 8,000 arrests, and scores of deaths" (Maier, 2006, p. 15).

Similarly, in the context of this new global world, with its emerging national security concerns, anti-Americanism, global economic relations, and political challenges, U.S. Americans may need to rethink their easy isolation in a monolingual society. "The disinclination of Americans to learn foreign languages is a running joke in Europe. But it's a serious matter for federal officials who cited both security needs and the quest for global competitiveness in announcing the $114 million National Security Language Initiative. The plan calls for students to begin studying 'critical need' foreign languages, including Arabic, Farsi and Chinese, as early as kindergarten" (Kingsbury, 2006, p. 35). This emphasis on learning foreign languages may benefit the United States as a whole in many ways, aside from national security and global economics, including intercultural understanding. But what will happen to those U.S. Americans who do not learn other languages? What will their economic futures look like? Will they be left behind in this new competitive environment?

Finally, we should also note that many communities are looking to their past to begin the long process of reconciliation by recognizing the reasons for the inequalities that persist. Wilmington, North Carolina, is one such place where a race riot occurred that had far-reaching consequences, and the state of North Carolina has commissioned a study of this history. "On the heels of Florida's investigation into the 1923 Rosewood Massacre, Oklahoma's inquiry into the 1921 Tulsa Race Riot, and the centennial of the Port City's tragic event in 1898, the General Assembly in 2000 enacted legislation calling for the creation of a commission to examine the riot and to develop a historical record" (Wilmington Race Riot Commission, 2005, p. 5). The Wilmington race riot was an "uprising engineered by white supremacists who unseated a government that had been elected by an alliance that included black citizens and white progressives. Scores of black citizens were killed during the uprising—no one yet knows how many—and prominent blacks and whites were banished from the city under threat of death. White supremacists hijacked the state government, stripped black citizens of the right to vote and brought black political participation to a close" (Staples, 2006, p. 13). Although called a riot, it might also be thought of as a coup d'état or an armed insurrection that led to the overthrow of a democratically elected government (with no response from the state or federal government). The economic development of the black community threatened many whites who wreaked havoc and destroyed some of these communities in the United States. In Wilmington, when "the full scope of what the plotters had in mind

POINT OF VIEW

INTERCULTURAL TRAINING FOR U.S. AMERICAN SOLDIERS IN IRAQ

This writer lists suggestions U.S. soldiers are given to help them avoid negative encounters with Iraqi citizens.

- *Do not walk in front of someone at prayer.*

- *Do not ask a Muslim if he is a Sunni or Shiite.*

- *Identify, show respect to and communicate with elders. Work with elders to accomplish your mission.*

- *Do not unnecessarily humiliate men by forcing them onto the ground in front of their families.*

- *Males may never ask a man about his wife, daughters or sisters. Females can.*

- *Do not yell or use profanity. It is a sign of weakness, poor upbringing and lack of discipline.*

- *When a guest, do not focus complimentary comments on your host's possessions, as he/she will feel culturally obligated to give them to you.*

- *Do not stare at women, touch them or try to shake a woman's hand (unless she extends her hand first).*

- *Do not react negatively if Afghan men kiss, embrace or hold hands. This is polite behavior in Afghan society.*

- *Speak about your families. Afghans like to know you have them.*

- *If you are eating something, offer to share.*

- *Dress modestly. Do not wear shorts. Men should not go shirtless.*

Source: E. Schmitt, "A Man Does Not Ask a Man About His Wife," *New York Times*, January 8, 2006, Section 4, p. 7.

became clear, black people by the hundreds left the city, taking their ideas and commercial energies elsewhere. The city has yet to recover from the exodus" (p. 13).

How we face these past events, how they help us understand the ways that history has changed us, and what we can do to face these past injustices are an important part of rebuilding intercultural relations and intercultural understanding. What other states are willing to examine their pasts? How might this historical honesty be helpful in intercultural communication?

There are no easy answers to what the future holds. But it is important to think dialectically about these issues, to see the dialectical tensions at work throughout the world. For example, a fractured, fragmented Europe is in dialectical tension with a unified Europe. We can see the history/past–present/future dialectic at work here. The fragmented Europe returns to its historical roots, but the unified Europe represents a forward-looking attempt to deal with the global economy. As a unifying force, a global economy also creates fragmentation.

The task of this book has been to help you begin to think dialectically, to begin to see the many contradictions and tensions at work in the world. Understanding these contradictions and tensions is key to understanding the events themselves. We acknowledge that there are no easy answers to the challenge of intercultural communication, but we hope we have given you the groundwork to begin your own intercultural journeys.

Continue to push yourself to see the complexities of life, and you will have taken an important step toward successful intercultural communication. Have the confidence to engage in intercultural communication, but be aware that there is always more to learn.

DISCUSSION QUESTIONS

1. In what ways is the notion of intercultural competence helpful? In what ways is it limiting?

2. How can you be an interpersonal ally? How do you know if you are being an ally?

3. How might you better assess your unconscious competence and unconscious incompetence?

4. How might the European Union affect the United States?

5. How does your own social position (gender, class, age, and so on) influence your intercultural communication competence? Does this competence change from one context to another?

ACTIVITIES

1. *Global Trends and Intercultural Communication.* Identify and list global trends that are likely to influence intercultural communication in the future. Reflect on the contexts and dialectics that might help you better understand these trends.

2. *Roadblocks to Communication.* Identify and list some of the biggest roadblocks to successful intercultural communication in the

future. In what ways will the increasingly global economy be a positive or negative factor in intercultural communication?

3. *Strategies for Becoming Allies.* In a dialogue with someone who is culturally different from you, generate a list of ways that each of you might become an ally of the other. Note the specific communication strategies that will help you become each other's allies.

REFERENCES

Allen, B. J. (2004). *Difference matters: Communicating social identity.* Long Grove, IL: Waveland Press.

Arnett, R. C. (1997). Communication and community in an age of diversity. In J. M. Makau & R. C. Arnett (Eds.), *Communication ethics in an age of diversity* (pp. 27–47). Chicago: University of Illinois Press.

Bennett, M. J. (1998). Overcoming the Golden Rule: Sympathy and empathy. In M. J. Bennett (Ed.), *Basic concepts in intercultural communication: Selected readings* (pp. 191–214). Yarmouth, ME: Intercultural Press.

Bonilla-Silva, E., Embreck, D. G., Ketchum, P. R., & Saenz, R. (2004). Where is the love?: Why whites have limited interaction with blacks. *Journal of Intergroup Relations, 1,* 24–38.

Broome, B. J. (1991). Building shared meaning: Implications of a relational approach to empathy for teaching intercultural communication. *Communication Education, 40,* 235–249.

Broome, B. J. (1993). Managing differences in conflict resolution: The role of relational empathy. In D. J. D. Sandole & H. van der Merwe (Eds.), *Conflict resolution theory and practice: Integration and application* (pp. 97–111). Manchester, England: Manchester University Press.

Chen, G. M., & Starosta, W. J. (1996). Intercultural communication competence: A synthesis. In B. R. Burleson (Ed.), *Communication yearbook, 19* (pp. 353–383). Thousand Oaks, CA: Sage.

Chesler, M. A., Peet, M., & Sevig, T. (2003). Blinded by whiteness: The development of white college students' racial awareness. In A. W. Doane & E. Bonilla-Silva (Eds.), *White out: The continuing significance of racism* (pp. 215–230). New York: Routledge.

Coeyman, M. (2001, October 16). The rush to rewrite history. *Christian Science Monitor.* http://www.csmonitor.com/2001/1016/p13s1-lekt.html

Collier, M. J. (1988). A comparison of conversations among and between domestic culture groups: How intra- and intercultural competencies vary. *Communication Quarterly, 36,* 122–144.

Collier, M. J. (1998). Researching cultural identity: Reconciling interpretive and postcolonial perspectives. In D. V. Tanno & A. González (Eds.), *Communication and identity across cultures* (pp. 122–147). Thousand Oaks, CA: Sage.

Collier, M. J. (2002). Intercultural friendships as interpersonal alliances. In J. N. Martin, T. K. Nakayama, & L. A. Flores (Eds.), *Readings in intercultural communication: Experiences and contexts* (pp. 301–310). Boston: McGraw-Hill.

Collier, M. J. (2005). Theorizing cultural identification: Critical updates and continuing evolution. In W. B. Gudykunst (Ed.), *Theorizing about intercultural communication* (pp. 235–256). Thousand Oaks, CA: Sage.

Conhaim, W. W. (2004, November). The Global Net: Part II. *Information Today*, 21(10), 41–42.

Cose, E. (1993). *The rage of a privileged class.* New York: HarperCollins.

Deetz, S., Cohen, D., & Edley, P. P. (1997). Toward a dialogic ethic in the context of international business organization. In F. L. Casmir (Ed.), *Ethics in intercultural communication* (pp. 183–223). Mahwah, NJ: Lawrence Erlbaum.

Hammer, M. R., Martin, J. N., Otani, M., & Koyama, M. (1990, March). *Analyzing intercultural competence: Evaluating communication skills of Japanese and American managers.* Paper presented at the First Annual Intercultural and International Communication Conference, California State University, Fullerton.

Harris, T. M, Miller, A. N., & Trego, A. (2004). A co-cultural examination of community building in the interracial communication classroom. *Journal of Intergroup Relations, 31,* 39–63.

Henderson, H. (1999). *Forgiveness: Breaking the chain of hate.* Wilsonville, OR: Book-Partners.

Howell, W. (1979). Theoretical directions in intercultural communication. In M. Asante, E. Newmark, & C. Blake (Eds.), *Handbook of intercultural communication.* Beverly Hills, CA: Sage.

Howell, W. S. (1982). *The empathic communicator.* Belmont, CA: Wadsworth.

Imahori, T., & Lanigan, M. L. (1989). Relational model of intercultural communication competence. *International Journal of Intercultural Relations, 13,* 269–286.

Ishii, S. (1984). *Enryo-sasshi* communication: A key to understanding Japanese interpersonal relations. *Cross Currents, 11,* 49–58.

Johnson, A. G. (2001). *Privilege, power, and difference.* New York: McGraw-Hill.

Kingsbury, A. (2006, January 16). Untying U.S. tongues. *U.S. News & World Report,* p. 35.

Koester, J., & Olebe, M. (1988). The behavioral assessment scale for intercultural communication effectiveness. *International Journal of Intercultural Relations, 12,* 233–246.

Lim, P. J. (2006, January 8). Looking ahead means looking abroad. *New York Times,* Business section, pp. 23, 30.

Maier, C. (2006, January 8). The French disconnection. *New York Times,* Section 4, p. 15.

Martin, J. N., & Hammer, M. R. (1989). Behavioral categories of intercultural communication competence: Everyday communicators' perceptions. *International Journal of Intercultural Relations, 13,* 303–332.

Martin, J. N., Hammer, M. R., & Bradford, L. (1994). The influence of cultural and situational contexts on Hispanic and non-Hispanic communication competence behaviors. *Communication Quarterly, 42,* 160–179.

Maruyama, M. (1970). *Toward a cultural futurology.* Paper presented at the annual meeting of the American Anthropological Association, published by the Training Center for Community Programs, University of Minnesota, Minneapolis.

McCullough, M. W. (1998). *Black and White women as friends: Building cross-race friendships.* Cresskill, NJ: Hampton Press.

Murphy, D. E. (2002, May 26). Beyond justice: The eternal struggle to forgive. *New York Times,* Section 4, p. 1.

Olebe, M., & Koester, J. (1989). Exploring the cross-cultural equivalence of the behavioral assessment scale for intercultural communication. *International Journal of Intercultural Relations, 13,* 333–347.

Reid, T. R. (2004). *The United States of Europe: The new superpower and the end of American supremacy*. New York: Penguin.

Ross, A., & Ross, K. (Eds.). (2004). *Anti-Americanism*. New York: New York University Press.

Ruben, B. D. (1976). Assessing communication competency for intercultural adaptation. *Group and Organization Studies, 1,* 334–354.

Ruben, B. D. (1977). Guidelines for cross cultural communication effectiveness. *Group and Organization Studies, 2,* 470–479.

Ruben, B. D., & Kealey, D. J. (1979). Behavioral assessment of communication competence and the prediction of cross-cultural adaptation. *International Journal of Intercultural Relations, 3,* 15–47.

Schmitt, E. (2006, January 8). A man does not ask a man about his wife. *New York Times,* Section 4, p. 7.

Staples, B. (2006, January 8). When democracy died in Wilmington, N.C. *New York Times,* Section 4, p. 13.

Starosta, W. J., & Chen, G.-M. (2005). Intercultural listening: Collected reflections, collated refractions. In W. J. Starosta & G.-M. Chen (Eds.), *Taking stock in intercultural communication: Where to now?* (pp. 274–285). Washington, DC: National Communication Association.

Stewart, L. P. (1997). Facilitating connections: Issues of gender, culture, and diversity. In J. M. Makau & R. C. Arnett (Eds.), *Communication ethics in an age of diversity* (pp. 111–125). Chicago: University of Illinois Press.

Tatum, B. (1997). *Why are all the Black kids sitting together in the cafeteria?* (pp. 193–206). New York: Basic Books.

Touraine, A., Dubet, F., Hegedus, Z., & Wieviorka, M. (1981). *Le pays contre l'Etat: Luttes occitanes*. Paris: Editions du Seuil.

Wendt, J. (1984). D.I.E.: A way to improve communication. *Communication Education, 33,* 397–401.

Wilmington Race Riot Commission. (2005, December 15). 1898 Wilmington Race Riot Report—Draft. Raleigh: North Carolina Department of Cultural Resources. Available at http://www.ah.dcr.state.ne.us/1898-wrrc/report/report.htm

Wiseman, R. L. (2002). Intercultural communication competence. In W. B. Gudykunst & B. Mody (Eds.), *Handbook of international and intercultural communication* (2nd ed., pp. 207–224). Thousand Oaks, CA: Sage.

Wood, J. T. (1997). Diversity in dialogue: Commonalities and differences between friends. In J. M. Makau & R. C. Arnett (Eds.), *Communication ethics in an age of diversity* (pp. 5–26). Chicago: University of Illinois Press.

Credits

TEXT

Chapter 1 Page 10, from L. Aaronson, "Beyond 'Please Fondle My Buttocks.'" Retrieved March 31, 2005, from http://www.salon.com; Page 24, from C. Ray, "The Potential of Immigrants," *Nation's Business*, August 1998. Reprinted by permission of U.S. Chamber of Commerce; Page 32, from Jonathan Watts, "China Chops Nike Ad; Multinational Apologizes After Outcry," *The Guardian* (London), December 8, 2004, p. 15. Copyright Guardian Newspapers Limited 2004. Reprinted by permission; Page 36, from Benjamin Feinberg, "What Students Don't Learn Abroad," *The Chronicle Review*, May 2, 2000, p. B20. Reprinted by permission of the author; **Chapter 2** Page 62, from Matt Sedensky, "Humor Helps Hurricane Katrina Victims Cope," from AP, October 22, 2005; Page 81, from Robin Marantz Henig, "Genetic Misunderstandings: The Linking of Jews with Cancer Is an Accident of Science and How Ethnic Groups Are Studied," as appeared in *The Washington Post* October 13, 1997. Used with permission. Copyright Robin Marantz Henig; **Chapter 3** Page 92, from Wen Shu Lee, "Dialogue on the Edges: Ferment in Communication and Culture." In M. J. Collier et al. (Eds.), *Transforming Communication About Culture* (Thousand Oaks, CA: Sage, 2002), pp. 219–280. Reprinted by permission of Sage Publications, Inc.; Page 97, from Tiger Woods Statement on Race/Ethnicity; Page 93, from L. A. Erbert et al., "Turning Points and Dialectical Interpretations of Immigrant Experiences in the United States," *Western Journal of Communication*, 67 (2003): 113–137; Page 105, from T.-S. Lim and S.-H. Choi, "Interpersonal Relationships in Korea." In W. B. Gudykunst, S. Ting-Toomey, and T. Nishida (Eds.), *Communication in Personal Relationships Across Cultures* (Thousand Oaks, CA: Sage, 1996), pp. 122–136. Reprinted by permission of Sage Publications, Inc.; Page 102, "Hofstede Value Orientations" table adapted from G. Hofstede and G. J. Hofstede, *Cultures and Organizations: Software of the Mind* (2nd ed.). Copyright © 2004 Geert Hofstede BV. Reprinted with permission; Page 118, from Rose Weitz, *What Women's Hair Tells Us About Women's Lives*. New York: Farrar, Straus and Giroux, 2004; **Chapter 4** Page 139, from Beata Pasek, "Auschwitz Haunts Town," *The Arizona Republic*, June 9, 2002, p. A24; Page 142, from Simon Romero, "Hispanics Uncovering Roots as Inquisition's 'Hidden' Jews," *New York Times*, October 29, 2005, p. A17. Copyright © 2005 The New York Times Co. Reprinted by permission; Page 154, from Mark Shaffer, "Navajos Protest National Status for Old Spanish Trail," *The Arizona Republic*, June 9, 2002, pp. B1, B8. Reprinted by permission; **Chapter 5** Page 169, from Ge Gao, "Self and Other: A Chinese Perspective on Interpersonal Relationships." In W. G. Gudykunst, S. Ting-Toomey, and T. Nishida (Eds.), *Communication in Personal Relationships Across Cultures* (Thousand Oaks, CA: Sage, 1996), pp. 83–84. Reprinted by permission of Sage Publications, Inc.; Page 184, from Associated